Gardening by Mail

Gardening by Mail

✤ A SOURCE BOOK ✤

Barbara J. Barton

GINNY HUNT, ASSOCIATE EDITOR

Everything for the Garden and Gardener

A directory of mail-order resources for
gardeners in the United States and Canada,
including seed companies, nurseries,
suppliers of all garden necessaries and
ornaments, horticultural and plant societies,
magazines, libraries, and a list of useful
books on plants and gardening

Fifth Edition ✽ *Updated and Revised*
A Tusker Press Book

A MARINER BOOK

HOUGHTON MIFFLIN COMPANY • BOSTON • NEW YORK

Dedicated to my parents, Hildor and Marguerite Barton,
and to my aunt, Margit Barton McNulty;
they thought I could do anything, made it possible,
and it worked!

Copyright © 1997 by Barbara J. Barton

For information about permission to reproduce selections from this book,
write to Permissions, Houghton Mifflin Company, 215 Park Avenue South,
New York, New York 10003.

Library of Congress Cataloging-in-Publication Data

Barton, Barbara J.
Gardening by mail : a source book : everything for the garden and
gardener / Barbara J. Barton. — 5th ed.
p. cm.
"A directory of mail-order resources for gardeners in the United States and Canada, including
seed companies, nurseries, suppliers of all garden necessaries and ornaments, horticultural and
plant societies, magazines, libraries, and a list of useful books on plants and gardening"
"A Tusker Press book."
Includes bibliographical references and index.
ISBN 0-395-87770-9
1. Gardening — United States — Directories. 2. Gardening equipment industry — United
States — Directories. 3. Gardening — Canada — Directories. 4. Gardening equipment
industry — Canada — Directories. 5. Mail-order business — United States — Directories.
6. Mail-order business — Canada — Directories. I. Title.
SB450.943.U6B37 1994 93-33278
635'.029'47 — dc20 CIP

Printed in the United States of America

BP 10 9 8 7 6 5 4 3 2

Originated and composed by Tusker Press
P.O. Box 1338
Sebastopol, California 95473-1338
Phone (707) 829-9189, Fax (707) 829-2409
E-mail: tusker@ap.net
World Wide Web: http://vg.com/gbm

TABLE OF CONTENTS

Introduction

Listings

Indexes

Practical Matters

A table of the symbols and abbreviations used in this book
appears inside the front and back covers.

Dear Gardener:

I don't know how you fell in love with growing things, but I came home from work one day to find a Wayside Gardens catalog in the mail. It was as fatal and irresistible as Cupid's dart -- soon I was carrying seed catalogs to read on the bus, rushing to secondhand book stores during my lunch hour, always trying to learn more.

As this insatiable habit was developing, one of my greatest frustrations was that there seemed to be no easy way to find out everything I wanted to know. If I saw a lovely plant, where could I get one to try to grow myself? Surely there must be wonderful gardening magazines, but there were very few on newsstands -- what did *real* gardeners do? Were there plant and horticultural societies? Would they allow *me* to join? Where might I find a horticultural library to browse in? Even though I'm a long time reference librarian myself, it all seemed so difficult! Only *old* gardeners knew -- and it took them years to find out.

When suddenly I had the time and the opportunity, I decided to "whip together" the ideal reference book for people like me -- full of sources of seeds, plants and garden supplies, societies to join, libraries to haunt, magazines to curl up with, and a list of good books on plants and practical gardening, "good reads" and books with inspiring pictures to feast the imagination.

My mind began to spin with grandiose ideas. I'd index everyone listed in many ways to make the book even more useful. I'd describe their catalogs, whether you could visit them and when, and whether they had display gardens to visit, and I'd list them by location so I could plan trips to include horticultural high spots! I'd mention their shipping seasons, whether they sold wholesale to the trade, what their minimum order was, whether they shipped to buyers overseas, and whether they listed their plants by botanical name. Every day I thought of some new and indispensable tidbit of information that the gardeners of North America just *had* to be told. This first "whipping together" took me three years!

Fourteen years after I first started collecting information, I'm much wiser and know that putting together the ideal reference book is nearly impossible. It's very difficult to get thousands of people to send back information promptly and in a standard format, and it's only current on the day they mail it! Most people are very helpful, some are very uncooperative, and a few will reply long after the book has gone to press, with a note saying "I just found this on my desk..."

Readers of the four earlier editions, the first two of which I published myself as Tusker Press, know the stirring saga of the plucky librarian who forged ahead, undeterred by rejection slips, with money cascading out of her pockets and double chins set at a determined angle. Seven years ago I was lucky enough to get Houghton Mifflin as my publisher and Frances Tenenbaum as my editor; they've made everything much easier for me.

I can't help feeling as I write this introduction that I'm writing to many friends out there in the world of plants and gardening; many of you have written to me and I've talked to others on the telephone. Through my chats and contacts with people listed in this book and with my readers, I feel connected from my little spot in the country to the wide world of those who love plants. You can imagine my delight when one of "my people" writes a book or an article, or is the subject of a story in a magazine. I love hearing from you and encourage you to share information and your opinions and suggestions with me.

What's new? There are always companies going out of business, and new ones starting up, so there are many new sources. We've moved into the electronic age by including eMail and World Wide Web addresses, and we've greatly increased the plant indexing to make it easier to find specific plants. In order to make room for more plant indexing, we've eliminated the magazine title index, and changed the product and geographical indexes to the same format as the plant index. Sorry, but we've also gone to a slightly smaller type size.

i

Things here at Lafalot keep lurching along, in the four years since I revised this book for the 4th edition I've been doing various things in addition to my regular part time job in a law library. I have been volunteering as a docent at Quarryhill Botanical Garden in Sonoma County, a very exciting new collection of plants grown from seed collected in China. I have been helping to get the California Garden & Landscape History Society up and running, and continue to organize the meetings of our local horticultural society. I now have ten little grand-nieces and nephews, and they are all truly a joy. On the pet front, there have been terrible losses. Alice, my dog and best friend of nearly fourteen years, had to be put to sleep -- she lies under a tree in my garden, and there isn't a day that I don't miss her. Kelpie succumbed to old age, and Trout made a fatal mistake in crossing my busy road, and they also lie in the garden. Sandy, the Australian shepherd, and Phoebe the cat have been joined by Ruffy, a lively and adorable tabby kitten, so we're keeping the numbers up in spite of the grim reaper.

Revising this book is always a flat out effort; in order for it to be current it has to be revised pretty much at the last minute, and then it needs more than one old librarian to get it all pulled together quickly. Shortly after starting this revision, with less time than before to get it done, I suddenly had to have two operations. I am fine now, but it has been a reminder of the preciousness of loving friends and family. I was lucky enough to get the help of two fellow plant loving friends and garden writers: Janet Sanchez came in over several months to update the societies, magazines and libraries, and Rosemary McCreary was able to come in and help out during the crucial weeks while I recovered from surgery. To them, and to my brother Bob Barton and sister Bay Alexander who took care of me when I came home, I owe a speedy and almost care-free recovery. To the beloved friends who visited, brought me food and flowers, baked "health cookies," gave me rides, called to chat and sent me books and eMails, I will be forever grateful!

As before, Ginny Hunt was indispensable; her helpfulness and generosity with time which she really couldn't spare but gave anyway make her the virtual co-author of this book. Her knowledge of plants has vastly improved the indexing of the nursery catalogs, her careful annotations in the nursery and seed sources section are so close to the ones I write myself that we joke that we can't remember who wrote which one. This book couldn't have been revised without her. Robert Kourik came in at the last minute to test World Wide Web sites, so that we would be sure they worked, and computer problems and panics have been smoothed by the dear and patient Rick Ryall, who completely updated the original program written years ago by Nancy Jacobsen, and made it easier than ever to use.

Many thanks to the people who helped us track down current information on elusive societies and other vital facts. And, as always, I'm very grateful to the businesses that let me use line drawings from their catalogs to decorate this book -- I think the drawings are just about the nicest part.

IMPORTANT INFORMATION FOR USING THIS SOURCE BOOK

This is an annotated directory of sources for everything that a gardener might want or need to purchase through the mail. My purpose is to provide you with information that will help you find what you want: this is not a "buyer's guide" which rates or recommends companies. I make every effort to describe the contents of catalogs or other sales material as fairly and accurately as I can.

This book is written primarily for gardeners in the US and Canada. You can imagine my excitement when people from all over the world began to call and write to find out how they could buy it. Because most of the readers are in North America, the information is still presented in a way which will be most useful to them, but we do give information on which companies will ship overseas, and how much gardeners overseas should send for a catalog. To reduce the confusion of foreign telephone numbers, we've tried to standardize them a bit.

WHO'S LISTED -- All of the retail mail-order garden businesses and organizations which met my criteria, and that I could locate and contact for information by my deadline. Some previous listees have been dropped for a variety of reasons; a few because of reader complaints, but most because they had gone out of business, their forwarding orders had expired, or they did not respond to many requests for information. Everyone listed has been sent a questionnaire and letter asking for detailed information and their catalog or literature. For those who didn't reply fully, the notes give you all the information I received; I'm sorry that it isn't always complete. It's always hard to make the final choice: we strive to bring you the widest selection of plants and products with a good geographical spread. I have always asked companies to let me know if they don't want to be listed; some companies I would love to include have asked not to be listed, or even more frustrating, have resisted all attempts to get them to reply to questionnaires and phone calls.

ADDRESSES -- When I know them, I have given both the mailing address and the sales location of the business (these are frequently the same). <u>Please always use the first or top address given for inquiries by mail</u>. When the nursery or shop is in a different town from the post office address, this is given in parentheses after the street address.

ABBREVIATIONS -- There's a list of the abbreviations used in the listings inside the front and back covers of the book. There is a list of state, provincial and country name abbreviations at the end of this introductory section.

CALL AHEAD or BY APPOINTMENT ONLY -- Many of the smaller businesses are run by one person who sometimes has a full-time job elsewhere and almost always has to run the mundane errands of us ordinary folk. Please honor their requests that you contact them before coming to visit, and please don't try to visit those companies that don't welcome visitors; if they don't give a sales location or give days open or other information on how to visit, they sell only by mail order.

RETAIL & WHOLESALE -- It is common for businesses to sell multiple items at a declining cost per item; many also sell "wholesale to the trade" (those who buy the merchandise for resale or other business uses). Unless I indicate that they will sell wholesale to anyone who will buy the minimum amount, do not ask to buy from a wholesale catalog unless you qualify. It's best to send your inquiry on your business letterhead.

TELEPHONE & FAX NUMBERS -- Many people have used this book as a sort of horticultural telephone directory; this time I have included many more Fax numbers. Communicating by Fax is often easier and cheaper than using the phone. It lets you ask a simple question without having to call at the proper time, which is especially useful for overseas inquiries. Where the Fax number is the same as the telephone number, you'll have to listen for special instructions on how to connect with the Fax machine. This usually precludes Faxing from a computer or by autodial. In the last few years there have been **many changes in area codes**, and there will be many more as the phone companies add capacity for new communications devices; we give you the phone numbers we have been given. In foreign telephone numbers, we have given country codes; you don't dial the (0) from outside that country.

TELEPHONE & FAX ORDERS -- Many companies will accept telephone or Fax orders with a credit card, which is especially convenient where foreign exchange is a problem. If you order by Fax, remember to include your credit card number, expiration date, your name and signature as they appear on the card, and your telephone number and/or Fax number. You could photocopy the blank order form from the catalog, fill it in and Fax that.

eMAIL AND WORLD WIDE WEB ADDRESSES -- I have included many of these, which are becoming increasingly common to all businesses; they let you reach around the world for the price of a local phone call. I give them with real reservations, as I know that this is an endeavor in violent flux!! You should write changes into your book as you learn about them. **Please note that all World Wide Web addresses start with <http://>**, to save space we had to leave that prefix off.

PAYMENT TO OTHER COUNTRIES -- I have tried to indicate where you may pay with international reply coupons, available at most post offices, or international money orders, available at larger post offices. Some overseas businesses and societies ask for US Bills, as the bank charges for changing foreign checks are sometimes more than the check is worth; wrap them well. Others will accept US personal checks, and will inform you of the amount to send. You can often charge purchases to your credit card, which automatically takes care of foreign exchange.

Listed in the Product Sources Index is a foreign exchange service which will issue and collect checks in foreign currencies for a modest charge, and information on buying international money orders at your Post Office. Canadians can write checks in US dollars, and a check to Canada in US dollars is usually acceptable; you shouldn't worry about the different value of Canadian dollars for small amounts. Except as noted, all prices not in US or Canadian dollars are in the currency of the country where the business or organization is located. Orders to US or Canadian companies from overseas are usually paid by international money orders, checks in US dollars on a US bank, or by credit card which is the easiest of all.

SELF-ADDRESSED STAMPED ENVELOPES -- Always send a business size envelope (10 inches or 27 cm. long) as your SASE -- most of the lists will not fit into anything smaller. Also note if the business has requested more than the usual first-class postage; the list may well be too heavy for one stamp. Foreign companies that request a SASE should be sent a self-addressed long envelope and one or two international reply coupons.

PLANT AND AGRICULTURAL REGULATIONS -- You should check with local offices of your state or provincial agricultural authorities, the US Department of Agriculture or Agriculture Canada to see whether seeds, bulbs or plants from other states or countries may be imported and what permits are needed. You will notice that some companies will not ship to certain states because of agricultural regulations, and many companies will not ship to other countries for the same reason; I have tried to indicate where companies say they cannot ship. Because of regulations, companies are justified in charging a fee for the time-consuming preparation of export papers. Please do not ask companies to send you catalogs if they do not ship to your state or country.

ENDANGERED AND WILD-COLLECTED PLANTS -- In most cases, endangered plants are protected by state or federal laws or by international treaty. In addition to endangered and protected plants, many plants have been collected from the wild by "nurseries" specializing in "native plants." Some of these plants collected in the wild are slow to regenerate; their populations will gradually diminish because of collecting. Ethical companies indicate the sources of their rare and endangered seeds, bulbs and plants, and propagate native plants from seeds or cuttings; some rescue plants from sites about to be developed or collect from private land with permission. Look for companies that sell *nursery-propagated* native plants and bulbs -- if in doubt, ask; please don't encourage the collecting of endangered wild growing species by buying suspect plants.

BOTANICAL AND COMMON NAMES -- After I've studied the catalog, I indicate whether botanical names are used, but I have not checked on the correctness or currency of the names. Some catalogs are maddeningly inconsistent, using botanical names for some plants and not for others, or making up their own fanciful common names. It is common for herbs, fruits and vegetables to be listed by common and cultivar names, and many popular garden plants are listed by their cultivar names, frequently without botanical names. I have used the term "collectors' list" to indicate plant lists that assume knowledgeable buyers, usually listing plants only by botanical/cultivar name and having brief or no plant descriptions.

TRADE NAMES -- In the Product Sources Index I have identified trade names as either registered trademarks (R) or trademarks (TM), if the company has included that information in their reply to me.

NOTES ON CATALOGS -- The notes are based on a study of the catalog; if I have not received the most current one, the notes are necessarily very brief. I have used the expressions "nice," "good," "wide," "broad" or "huge selection" to indicate the breadth of selection offered, not as a quality judgment on what's offered. I try to get as much information as I can into limited space. Many of these annotations don't change very much from one edition to the next -- it's so hard to cram so much information into a few lines that sometimes there's just no other way to say it. I think of myself as a master of annotation Haiku! I also hate to eliminate good jokes, no matter how old.

LISTINGS -- Being in *Gardening By Mail* costs nothing to those listed; these listings are **not** advertisements, and all the descriptions are mine or Ginny's, based on a study of catalogs or literature. I do ask every company that wants to be listed to fill out a detailed questionnaire every few years and to put me on their mailing list to receive a catalog every year; the choice of listings is mine alone. Companies that would like to be listed in future editions or the updates to this edition will find a form in the Practical Matters section at the back of the book. Please contact me and don't wait for me to hunt you down!

REQUESTING CATALOGS or LITERATURE -- One thing businesses like to know is where their customers heard about them. To let people know that you found them in *Gardening By Mail*, I have included a form for ordering or requesting catalogs and information in Practical Matters. It is very helpful to me if you use this form, as it lets the businesses know that *Gardening by Mail* is bringing them inquiries. If you don't use the form, please tell them you read about them in *Gardening By Mail*.

Please keep in mind that catalogs and postage are expensive and request only catalogs for merchandise that is truly of interest to you, or from companies that will ship to your state or province. An avalanche of requests can be considered more disaster than benefit to a small business; please be patient and considerate of the effort that goes into offering something special and working without much help. One company asked not to be listed again because my readers "never" sent the SASE requested for a list; if you don't send the company what they ask for their catalog, they are perfectly justified in not replying to your request.

READER FEEDBACK -- Hearing from readers has been the greatest pleasure of working on this book -- you've given me both pats on the back and well aimed kicks when deserved, and a lot of good suggestions. One complaint I really don't deserve is that I enticed you into requesting more catalogs or ordering more plants than you really needed to have -- self-control is *your* problem! There's a Reader Feedback/Update Order Form form in the Practical Matters section, so that you can tell me what you think.

UPDATES -- For past editions we have issued several Updates a year, giving changes of address and the names of companies that have gone out of business. For this 5th edition, we will issue only one printed Update each year.

GARDEN WRITERS -- Many editors and writers use this book to find sources for articles and books they are working on. I suggest that you *always* check every source to be sure that it is still current, and that they want you to list them. One small seed supplier was driven nearly over the edge because after the last *Gardening by Mail* came out his name suddenly appeared everywhere, in articles and on the Internet, and he couldn't keep up with the demand or all the letters: he went out of business. He told me that I was the *only* person who ever asked if he *wanted* to be listed. And, while we love making your research easier, we also appreciate credit when you publish.

REQUESTS FOR ADDITIONAL INFORMATION FROM TUSKER PRESS -- Between revisions, Tusker Press is only me, Barbara Barton, and not a huge enterprise with many researchers! I've tried to point you in the right direction with quite detailed plant and product indexing and a list of good plant finding books in the Books section. I'm flattered that you think I know where to find *everything*, but with this book in hand you know almost as much as I do. Please don't write or call to ask me where to find a specific plant or product: I just don't have time to search them out or to answer personal requests.

A FEW WORDS ABOUT ORDERING PLANTS, SEEDS AND BULBS BY MAIL

WHY ORDER BY MAIL? -- Why do people order plants and seeds by mail? Many of us have local sources for ordinary or even unusual plants; but some of us live where few nurseries exist, others are so besotted by rarities that only specialist nurseries have what we want, and still others grow orchids or tropical fruit in greenhouses and need to order from other climates. Some of us order for reasons of perceived economy, and some for greater selection or just to have something exotic from a faraway source. Whatever the reason, there's a season of the year when only a good seed or nursery catalog can warm the gardener's heart.

I've been working with plant and seed catalogs for fourteen years now and have inadvertently become something of an expert on catalogs and what they convey to their readers. I'd like to share some thoughts and warnings so that you'll be happy with your purchases and avoid unpleasant experiences as much as possible.

TIPS ON READING A CATALOG -- There is a science to reading a catalog which will almost always repay you in good results. When you receive a catalog, don't go first to the plants and their prices; search first for information on the company. I always look to see if the catalog gives the name of the proprietor or someone to contact if need be; if there is no name and no telephone number, read on with increased caution. After all, these people are in business and should be willing to communicate with their customers. Some companies asked me not to put their phone numbers in this book, but most do put it on their catalogs.

Does the company list plants by correct botanical names and/or specific cultivar names? Does it guarantee that plants are true to name? Does it offer to replace plants that arrive in bad condition, and how long do you have to request a replacement? Does it tell you frankly what size the plants or bulbs you receive will be? If the plants are endangered or "native," does the company specify that their plants are nursery grown and propagated? When will it ship your plants? Place your orders so that your plants will travel in comfort; harsh winters or hot summers can quickly ruin even healthy plants in transit, and you shouldn't blame predictable weather problems on the nursery or the carrier. Discuss the conditions for shipping when you place your order, and do what the nursery recommends.

PLANT DESCRIPTIONS -- When you feel some confidence in the company, then you can study the plant lists. You will quickly notice that there are catalogs aimed at all levels of plant expertise, starting with those that list plants only by common name and topping off with catalogs that list plants only by botanical name. Each is meant for a particular audience. Catalogs aimed at unsophisticated gardeners have an obligation to give good descriptions of the plants and how to grow them; they can also educate their customers when they include the correct botanical names. Catalogs that make up fanciful common names such as "dainty little dancing alpine fairy bells" or are deliberately vague, using "Viburnum sp." for common plants they should easily be able to identify, should go to the bottom of your catalog pile.

I particularly like a catalog that gives good and honest plant descriptions. Some catalogs would have you believe that every plant they sell is perfect; the plain truth is that some varieties are much better behaved than others, some need special coddling, some reseed all over the garden, some smell not so sweet! The descriptions should offer the pros *and* the cons in addition to height and color of flower; they should also tell you something about growing the plant -- soil, exposure, hardiness, need for water, fertilizer, division and pruning; it simply isn't true that most plants will grow happily anywhere you live or under all conditions. Catalogs meant for sophisticated plant collectors do not go into such detail but can rely on the advanced knowledge of their readers.

FINALLY, THE PRICES! Which do you think is cheapest, the $8 plant from a reputable nursery that will replace it within a reasonable period, or the $3.95 runt that arrives half dead from a company that won't answer your letters of complaint or sends a credit or a plant in the same condition to replace it? This is an extreme example, and I hope I have eliminated companies like the latter, but we all know there's no free lunch. It's expensive to grow good plants, especially those that take years to reach shipping size.

How difficult or expensive is it to grow a plant? Daylilies or hostas are obviously easier to propagate than specially grafted dwarf conifers or Japaneses maples and are priced not by difficulty of propagation but by the newness and rarity of the cultivar. Plants are also priced by age and size, and if you are willing to take them small and grow them on yourself, you can save money.

There are fads in plants as in all things. People who enter flower shows or are hybridizers want only the newest and rarest and are willing to pay steep prices; there are usually older varieties on the same list that are just as lovely and cost a fraction of the price. If you're just starting out, or want to try a number of varieties to see what you like best, many nurseries offer special plant collections, which are usually bargains.

PLACING AN ORDER -- When ordering plants, first try to pick a company you feel comfortable with, then place a small trial order. It's a good idea when ordering plants to be shipped at another season to include a self-addressed postcard with your order, already written for the company to fill in the blanks, stating when it received your order and confirming the amount of your payment, and when it expects to ship your order -- be sure to include the company's name and address so you won't confuse your orders.

One reader complained because I did not describe the condition and size of plants received from each nursery. How could I possibly order a wide selection of plants from many hundreds of plant catalogs, then evaluate and grow them on to see how healthy they are? To be fair I would somehow have to order without giving my name, I'd have to have enormous test gardens and greenhouses, unlimited water and expert help; and I would have to be rich beyond my wildest dreams!

HOW TO COMPLAIN -- Finally, if you do have reason to complain, write to the company at once and detail your complaint. Be sure to mention the date of your order, when it was received, and what was wrong with the plant(s); keep a copy of your order and all correspondence for your records. If you do not receive a reply within several weeks, telephone, or photocopy your original letter and order and send them again with another letter. Before you do more, give the company a fair chance to make things right. One seedsman told me that he's received demands for refunds or replacements for seeds he's never carried, so be sure you're corresponding with the company who caused the problem.

If you still receive no reply, or have ordered and paid for merchandise that did not arrive at the proper shipping season, write to the postal inspector in care of the post office where the business is located (check with the country's consulate or embassy in the case of foreign companies). I cannot straighten out consumer disputes, but I do drop companies about which I have received several complaints; please let me know of such instances. I would never knowingly list a company I suspect of being shady; such businesses don't belong in this book.

I'd love to see a day when all nursery catalogs are botanically correct, honest and forthcoming, informative, well illustrated and fun to read; in this book you'll find a good many that meet all or most of those criteria. When I'm doing the last minute scramble to pull all the last facts and details together and have a few momentary dark thoughts, I remind myself of all the dear people who answer my questionnaires and send their catalogs promptly, and of all the charming notes I've received from readers.

In the end, this book is written for just two people: I include everything I'd want to find for *my own* use and pleasure, and that I'd want to pass on to *you*, my like-minded gardening friend. Enjoy this book -- you have my enthusiastic permission to mark it up and add your own notes to your heart's content! What's meant to be beautiful isn't always satisfying -- what's truly useful is always beautiful *and* satisfying!

State, Provincial and Country Abbreviations
Used in the Listings and Indexes

U.S. and Canada

AB	Alberta, Canada
AK	Alaska
AL	Alabama
AR	Arkansas
AZ	Arizona
BC	British Columbia, Canada
CA	California
CO	Colorado
CT	Connecticut
DC	District of Columbia
DE	Delaware
FL	Florida
GA	Georgia
HI	Hawaii
IA	Iowa
ID	Idaho
IL	Illinois
IN	Indiana
KS	Kansas
KY	Kentucky
LA	Louisiana
MA	Massachusetts
MB	Manitoba, Canada
MD	Maryland
ME	Maine
MI	Michigan
MN	Minnesota
MO	Missouri
MS	Mississippi
MT	Montana
NB	New Brunswick, Canada
NC	North Carolina
ND	North Dakota
NE	Nebraska
NF	Newfoundland, Canada
NH	New Hampshire
NJ	New Jersey
NM	New Mexico
NS	Nova Scotia, Canada
NV	Nevada
NY	New York

U.S. and Canada (continued)

OH	Ohio
OK	Oklahoma
ON	Ontario, Canada
OR	Oregon
PA	Pennsylvania
PE	Prince Edward Island, Canada
PQ	Province of Quebec, Canada
PR	Puerto Rico
RI	Rhode Island
SC	South Carolina
SD	South Dakota
SK	Saskatchewan, Canada
TN	Tennessee
TX	Texas
UT	Utah
VA	Virginia
VT	Vermont
WA	Washington
WI	Wisconsin
WV	West Virginia
WY	Wyoming

Overseas

Au	Australia
Co	Costa Rica
Cz	Czech Republic
En	England
Ge	Germany
In	India
Ne	New Zealand
No	Northern Ireland
Sc	Scotland
So	South Africa
Wa	Wales

SAMPLE ENTRY FROM GARDENING BY MAIL

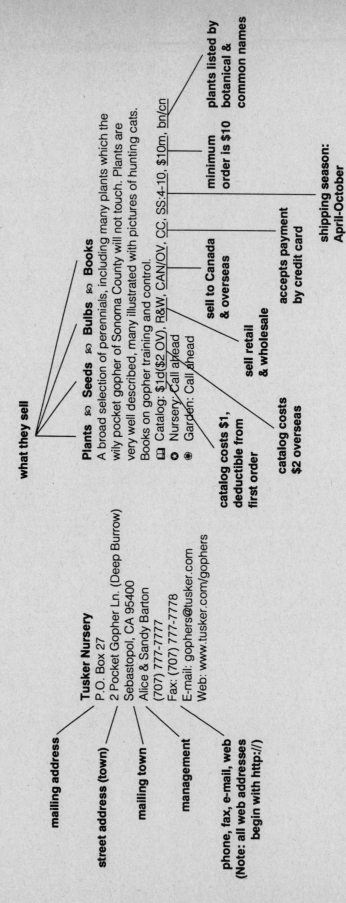

what they sell

mailing address

street address (town)

mailing town

management

phone, fax, e-mail, web
(Note: all web addresses
begin with http://)

Tusker Nursery
P.O. Box 27
2 Pocket Gopher Ln. (Deep Burrow)
Sebastopol, CA 95400
Alice & Sandy Barton
(707) 777-7777
Fax: (707) 777-7778
E-mail: gophers@tusker.com
Web: www.tusker.com/gophers

Plants ∾ **Seeds** ∾ **Bulbs** ∾ **Books**
A broad selection of perennials, including many plants which the
wily pocket gopher of Sonoma County will not touch. Plants are
very well described, many illustrated with pictures of hunting cats.
Books on gopher training and control.
Catalog: $1d ($2 OV), R&W, CAN/OV, CC, SS:4-10, $10m, bn/cn
Nursery: Call ahead
Garden: Call ahead

catalog costs $1,
deductible from
first order

catalog costs
$2 overseas

sell retail
& wholesale

sell to Canada
& overseas

accepts payment
by credit card

minimum
order is $10

plants listed by
botanical &
common names

shipping season:
April-October

viii

PLANT AND SEED SOURCES

Plant and seed sources are listed alphabetically. Former company names and alternative names used in advertising are cross-referenced to the main listing. Specialties (plants, seeds, supplies, books, bulbs) are indicated on the top line of the notes on catalogs. If no shipping season information is given, the company will ship at any time during the year.

For display gardens, greenhouses, orchards and other plant displays, the months given are the best months to visit. Check to see whether you can visit at other times; if the nursery has regular hours, you can probably visit anytime it is open.

See the Index section for:

H. Plant Sources Index: an index of plant and seed sources by plant specialties. A two-letter code tells you which state/province/country the source is located in, so that you can order from the nearest source or a source in a similar climate zone if you like.

J. Geographical Index: an index of plant and seed sources by location. Sources in the U.S. and Canada are listed by state or province and then by city or post office; other sources are listed by country only. Always check the main listing to see if you should call ahead or make an appointment to visit.

OTHER SOURCES OF SEEDS AND PLANTS

In addition to using the sources listed, you can sometimes locate harder-to-find plants in the seed exchanges and plant sales of horticultural societies or botanical gardens. You can also place an advertisement in the "plants wanted" section of many society magazines. These are usually free, but the plant must be rare in commerce.

Many societies provide their members with lists of specialist nurseries, and there is a list of plant-finding source books in the Books section.

Finally, many gardeners are very generous with seeds and cuttings of their plants when they are properly asked — be you likewise!

A table of the symbols and abbreviations used in this book appears inside the front and back covers.

A & D Nursery
6808 180th S.E.
Snohomish, WA 98290-8340
Don Smetana & Keith Abel
(360) 668-9690
Fax: (360) 668-6031
E-mail: bbbloom@ix.netcom.com

Plants
A & D Nursery is very popular with their customers in the spring when the **peonies** are in bloom -- they grow about 700 cultivars, plus another 600 **hostas** and over 1200 **daylilies** in their display garden; every year they list some of the many plants that they grow, a good selection, with very good plant descriptions. Sell other perennials at the nursery. (1969)
- Catalog: $2d, CC, SS:4-11, $30m
- Nursery: March-November, daily
- Garden: April-October, daily

Abbey Gardens
P.O. Box 2249
La Habra, CA 90632-2249
Lem & Pat Higgs
Fax: (562) 905-3522

Plants ᐳ Books
Catalog offers a very broad selection of **cacti and succulents** to hobbyists and collectors; some b&w photos, plants briefly described. I don't know why, but I can't look at a cactus catalog without wanting one of everything -- they are very fascinating plants! The nursery also sells some books. (1968)
- Catalog: $2d, CC, $20m, bn

Abundant Life Seed Foundation
P.O. Box 772
930 Lawrence Street
Port Townsend, WA 98368-0772
Aleta Anderson, Mgr.
(360) 385-5660 or 7192
Fax: (360) 385-7455
Web: csf.Colorado.edu/perma/abundant

Seeds ᐳ Books
"A non-profit educational foundation...raising and collecting open-pollinated cultivars without chemicals." Offers a wide choice of seeds: **vegetables, Northwestern native plants, Native American grains, garden flowers** and books on many garden subjects. Bulk seed prices available. (1975)
- Catalog: $2($5 OV), CAN/OV, CC, cn/bn
- Nursery: All year, M-F
- Garden: June-September, call ahead

Adamgrove
Route 1, Box 1472
California, MO 65018
Eric & Bob Tankesley-Clarke

Plants
Catalog offers a huge selection of bearded, beardless, spuria, Louisiana and species **iris**, all well described, with some cultural information, many illustrated in color photographs. Also offers a somewhat smaller selection of **daylilies**, both diploid and tetraploid. (1983)
- Catalog: $3d($6 OV), R&W, CAN/OV, SS:5,7-10, $15m

Adams County Nursery, Inc.
P.O. Box 108
26 Nursery Lane
Aspers, PA 17304
Baugher Family
(717) 677-8105
Fax: (717) 677-4124

Plants
Offers a broad variety of **fruit** -- apples, pears, peaches and nectarines, sweet and sour cherries, plums and apricots, on a variety of rootstocks for various growing conditions, for both home gardeners and large commercial growers. Informative catalog. (1905)
- Catalog: Free, R&W, CC, SS:11-5, $45m
- Nursery: November-May, M-Sa, call ahead

Stacy Adams Nursery
1033 Jarrell Hogg Road
West Point, GA 31833
Marshall & Stacy Adams
(706) 882-0447
E-mail: plants@atl.mindspring.com
Web: www.mindspring.com/~plants/adams.catalogue.html

Plants
Offers a good selection of **native Southeastern trees and shrubs**: maples, hickories, gordonia, halesia, magnolias, many species of oaks, and others. Plants are well but briefly described. No shipping to AZ, CA or HI. (1984)
- Catalog: $1, R&W, SS:11-3, $25m, bn/cn
- Nursery: All year, by appointment only

Adrian's Flowers of Fashion Nursery
855 Parkway Boulevard
Alliance, OH 44601
William W. Zumbar
(330) 823-1964

Plants
Bill Zumbar is a hybridizer of **dwarf, miniature and small hostas**; most of the plants listed are his own hybrids, each very well described. (1964)
📖 Catalog: Long SASE w/2 FCS, R&W, CAN/OV, SS:6-9
☼ Nursery: May-October, daily
✿ Garden: May-October, by appointment only

Agroforestry Research Trust
46 Hunters Moon, Dartington
Totnes, Devon, England TQ9 6JT
Charitable Trust

Seeds ∽ **Books**
This one's a bit of a mystery: they list seeds of a variety of **trees, shrubs, and** some **edible fruiting trees and shrubs**, all of which have some economic or medicinal use; all are well described. They also sell a number of books on trees and shrubs; nowhere in the catalog is the work of the Trust described. Some interesting stuff, nonetheless! (1971)
📖 Catalog: $2, OV, bn

Agua Viva Seed Ranch
Route 1, Box 8
Taos, NM 87571
Steve Rosenblath
(505) 758-4520, (800) 248-9080
Fax: (505) 758-1745
E-mail: aguaviva@taos.newmex.com
Web: taosnet.com/aguaviva/

Plants ∽ **Seeds** ∽ **Bulbs**
Offers seeds and plants of **perennials for dry gardens** (by this we mean gardens which grow with only occasional watering during the summer). They offer wildflower seed mixes too, some "good doer" daylilies, tall bearded iris, and hollyhocks in lovely individual colors. (1994)
📖 Catalog: Free, CAN/OV, CC
☼ Nursery: January-November, M-F
✿ Garden: June-October, M-F

Aimers Seeds
81 Temperance Street
Aurora, ON, Canada L4G 2R1
W. R. Aimers
(905) 841-6226
Fax: (905) 727-7333

Seeds
Offering a very good selection of **annual and perennial garden flowers**, with many choices of sweet peas, delphiniums, pansies, primulas and much more. Also offer **vegetable seed**, imported from a European seed grower.
📖 Catalog: $4, R&W, US/OV, CC, bn/cn
☼ Nursery: All year, M-Sa

Air Expose
4703 Leffingwell Street
Houston, TX 77026-3434
George Haynes III
(713) 672-7017

Plants
Offers a wide selection of **hibiscus**, both subtropical and hardy, and **bougainvillea**, plants described only by size and color of flowers. (1981)
📖 Catalog: $2d, R&W, CAN, SS:4-10, $15m
☼ Nursery: April-October, daily, call ahead
✿ Garden: May-October, daily, call ahead

Aitken's Salmon Creek Garden
608 N.W. 119th Street
Vancouver, WA 98685
Terry & Barbara Aitken
(360) 573-4472
Fax: (360) 576-7012
E-mail: aitken@e-z.net
Web: www.e-z.net/~aitken

Plants
"Hybridize and sell all varieties of **bearded iris** in addition to a selection of Japanese, Siberians, Pacific Coast Natives, Louisianas, spurias and a few species iris." A wide selection with plants very briefly described, some shown in color photos. Also offering some orchids; send FCS for list. (1978)
📖 Catalog: $2($3 OV), R&W, CAN/OV, CC, SS:7-9, $15m
☼ Nursery: April-October, daily
✿ Garden: April-October, daily, by appointment only

Albright Seed Company
487 Dawson Drive #5S
Camarillo, CA 93012-8009
Paul J. Albright, Jr.
(805) 484-0551
Fax: (805) 987-9021
E-mail: paulseed@msn.com

Seeds
Offer seed of **grass, turf and pasture mixes**, as well as **wildflowers**. They list mixes for many uses -- lush lawns, lawn substitues, xeriscapes, erosion control, and pastures. Also sell wildflower mixes for various uses, as well as by single species; seed sold by the pound.
📖 Catalog: Free, R&W, CAN/OV, CC, $25m
☼ Nursery: All year, M-Sa

Allen Plant Company
P.O. Box 310
Fruitland, MD 21826-0310
Nancy Allen, Pres.
(410) 742-7123, 742-7122
Fax: (410) 742-7120

Plants
Color catalog of **strawberries**, 'Jersey Knight' **asparagus** (99.5% male), **raspberries, blueberries** and **thornless blackberries**; plants are well described with growing suggestions. (1885)
📖 Catalog: Free, CC, SS:11-7, $11m

Allen, Sterling & Lothrop
191 US Route 1
Falmouth, ME 04105-1385
Shawn Brannigan, Mgr.
(207) 781-4142
Fax: (207) 781-4143

Seeds
Catalog offers a good selection of **short-season vegetables**, annual and perennial flowers, all well described with cultural suggestions. No shipping to OR, HI or AK. (1911)
- 📖 Catalog: $1d, CC, cn
- ○ Nursery: All year, M-Sa
- ✱ Garden: Spring-Summer, M-Sa

Aloha Tropicals
1247 Browning Court
2210 Bautista Road
Vista, CA 92083-4759
Andy Zuckowich
(760) 941-0920
Fax: (760) 941-0920
E-mail: alohatrop@aol.com
Web: www.alohatropicals.com

Plants
All kinds of **gingers, bananas** and other tropical plants are offered: costus, heliconias, globbas, hedychiums, alpinias, as well as some **tropical fruits**. All plants well described, some illustrated in color.
- 📖 Catalog: $3d, R&W, CC, SS:3-11, $20m
- ○ Nursery: All year, by appointment only
- ✱ Garden: April-September, by appointment only

Alpen Gardens
173 Lawrence Lane
Kalispell, MT 59901-4633
Bill & Lois McClaren
(406) 257-2540
E-mail: mccl@cyberport.net

Plants
"Specializing in early varieties, new introductions and cream-of-the-crop **dahlias**." A collectors' list that gives brief descriptions of each variety and stars their top choices; plants listed by size and type of flower. (1979)
- 📖 Catalog: Free, CAN/OV, CC, SS:11-5
- ○ Nursery: Daily, call ahead

Alpine Gardens
12446 County F
Stitzer, WI 53825
Charlotte Nelson
(608) 822-6382

Plants
A nice selection of **sedums, sempervivums and jovibarbas** and other alpine plants, listed only by botanical name with no plant descriptions. All are grown outside all year in Wisconsin, so they're very hardy. Cannot ship to AZ, CA, OR, TX or WA. (1976)
- 📖 Catalog: $2, R&W, SS:4-5,8, $15m
- ○ Nursery: April-October, daily, call ahead
- ✱ Garden: April-October, daily, call ahead

Alpine Valley Gardens

See Amador Flower Farm.

Alplains
P.O. Box 489
Kiowa, CO 80117-0489
Alan D. Bradshaw
(303) 621-2247
Fax: (303) 621-2864

Seeds
A very good selection of hard-to-find **Rocky Mountain natives, alpine** and **rock garden plants** and unusual **perennials**, each very well described. Source location given for many of the habitat collected seeds, many are tough natives of the plains. (1989)
- 📖 Catalog: $2d(2 IRC OV), CAN/OV, bn
- ✱ Garden: May-August, by appointment only

Amador Flower Farm
22001 Shenandoah School Road
Plymouth, CA 95669-9511
Jeanne Deaver
(209) 245-6660
Fax: (209) 245-6661
E-mail: daylilies@daylilyfarm.com
Web: www.daylilyfarm.com

Plants
Formerly Alpine Valley Gardens, where I used to follow Dot Sloat around, picking **daylilies** out of the field (my favorite is 'Corky'). They sold their stock to Amador Flower Farm which is too far to rush on a whim, but they offer a very good selection; plants described in table format. (1990)
- 📖 Catalog: $1d, R&W, CAN, CC, $25m
- ○ Nursery: All year, daily, call ahead
- ✱ Garden: May-November, call ahead

Jacques Amand, Bulb Specialists
P.O. Box 59001
Potomac, MD 20859
Elaine M. Wiggers
(800) 452-5414
Fax: (800) 452-5414
E-mail: JAmand@bulbjam.com
Web: www.bulbjam.com

Bulbs
Now with an order department in the US, Amand is a well-known British supplier of **spring- and summer-blooming bulbs** offering a broad selection of alliums, colchicums, crocus, cyclamen, fritillaries, hybrid and species lilies, daffodils, tulips and others. Each plant is briefly described, some shown in color. Orders shipped from England at no extra charge. (1930)
📖 Catalog: $2d, R&W, CC, SS:9-12, bn

Amaryllis, Inc.
P.O. Box 318
1452 Glenmore Avenue
Baton Rouge, LA 70821
Ed Beckham
(504) 924-5560 or 4521

Bulbs
Offers a broad variety of named hybrid and species **amaryllis** from Holland and India; some shown in color photos, very brief plant descriptions. (1942)
📖 Catalog: $1, R&W, CAN/OV, SS:11-2, $20m
○ Nursery: All year, call ahead
❀ Garden: May-January, by appointment only

Ambergate Gardens
8730 County Road 43
Chaska, MN 55318-9358
Michael & Jean Heger
(612) 443-2248
Fax: (612) 443-2248

Plants
Small nursery specializing in **Martagon lilies** and other hardy **perennials, native plants and ornamental grasses,** some of them unusual, as well as a good selection of **hostas**; all plants are well described. They also supply durable custom-engraved plastic plant labels. (1985)
📖 Catalog: $2, CAN, CC, SS:4-5,8-10, $25m, bn/cn
○ Nursery: May-October, Tu-Su
❀ Garden: May-September, Tu-Su

Amberway Gardens
5803 Amberway Drive
St. Louis, MO 63128
Sue & Ken Kremer
(314) 842-6103
Fax: (314) 842-6103

Plants
Offers a broad selection of **iris of all types**: tall, median and dwarf bearded, Japanese, Siberian, and Louisiana, horned, and some species. Reblooming iris are abundant here. There is only room for the briefest descriptions. (1988)
📖 Catalog: $1.25d, CC, SS:7-9, $15m
○ Nursery: Daily, February-November, call ahead
❀ Garden: April-June, September-October, call ahead

Ames' Orchard & Nursery
18292 Wildlife Road
Fayetteville, AR 72701
Guy & Carolyn Ames
(501) 443-0282, (800) 443-0283

Plants ℘ Tools
Offers a variety of **fruit trees, grapes and berries** with emphasis on disease resistance and tolerance in less than ideal growing conditions. Customers are usually home gardeners or small orchardists trying to reduce spraying. Very informative catalog: apples, Asian and European pears, peaches, plums and more. Also sells pruning tools and orchard supplies. (1983)
📖 Catalog: Free, R&W, CC, SS:11-4
○ Nursery: All year, by appointment only

Anderson Iris Gardens
22179 Keather Avenue North
Forest Lake, MN 55025
Sharol Longaker
(612) 433-5268

Plants
Offers a broad selection of hardy **tall bearded iris and herbaceous peonies;** all plants are briefly described. Some iris are their own introductions, many are recent award winners; they have added some daylilies. (1978)
📖 Catalog: $1, SS:7-10
○ Nursery: June-October, daily, call ahead
❀ Garden: June-July, daily, call ahead

Antique Rose Emporium
9300 Lueckemeyer Road
Brenham, TX 77833
Mike Shoup
(409) 836-9051
Fax: (409) 836-0928
E-mail: mshoup@phoenix.net

Plants ℘ Books
Color catalog offers a broad selection of **old garden roses**, each well described, with a good deal of historical and cultural information. Roses are grown on their own roots, selected for fragrance and long bloom in Zones 6 and above. They also offer a selection of rose books. (1983)
📖 Catalog: $5, R&W, CC, SS:10-5
○ Nursery: All year, daily
❀ Garden: Spring & Fall, daily

Antonelli Brothers Begonia Gardens
2545 Capitola Road
Santa Cruz, CA 95062
E.B. Antonelli & D.K. Bobbitt
(408) 475-5222, (888) 423-46642
Fax: (408) 475-7066
Web: www.infopoint.com/sc/market/antnelli

Plants ∞ Seeds ∞ Supplies ∞ Bulbs
Well known for their **tuberous begonias**, their lath houses are a glorious sight in the summer. They offer a good selection as tubers or seedlings, including hanging-basket begonias and a number of collections. They also offer over 400 **fuchsias**, and tigridias, tuberoses, gladiolus, dahlias, ranunculus and anemones. Ship bulbs to Canada, only seed overseas. 1935)
📖 Catalog: $1($2 OV), R&W, CAN/OV, CC, SS:2-6, $15m
○ Nursery: All year, daily
✾ Garden: June-October, daily

Appalachian Gardens
P.O. Box 87
410 Westview Avenue
Waynesboro, PA 17268-0087
Tom & Fern McCloud & Ezra Grubb
(717) 762-4312, (888) 327-5483
Fax: (717) 762-7532

Plants
Good list of **hardy ornamental trees** and **shrubs**: azaleas, holly, conifers, dogwoods, box, berberis, viburnums, kalmias, rhododendrons; all plants very well described, some harder to find. Charge $1 per plant to bare root plants to AL, AR, AZ, CA, FL, ID, KS, MN, NV, OR, SC, TN, UT and WA. (1986)
📖 Catalog: Free, R&W, CC, bn/cn
○ Nursery: All year, M-F, call ahead
✾ Garden: Call ahead

Appalachian Wildflower Nursery
723 Honey Creek Road
Reedsville, PA 17084
Don Hackenberry

Plants ∞ Books
Small nursery specializes in **rock garden plants and garden perennials**, with emphasis on local native plants. Lists species iris, gentians, phlox, primula, gaultheria, hellebores and others. Also offers books on perennials. (1973)
📖 Catalog: $2d, SS:3-5,9-11, bn
○ Nursery: Spring-Fall, Th-Sa, call ahead
✾ Garden: Spring-Fall, Sa, call ahead

Applesource
1716 Apples Road
Chapin, IL 62628
Tom & Jill Vorbeck
(800) 588-3854
Fax: (217) 245-7844
E-mail: vorbeck@csj.net

Applesource is not a source of plants, but a service that will send you unusual varieties of both **new and antique apples** during harvest season so that you can taste before you decide which cultivars to plant. Good holiday gift for yourself or a friend. Catalog is mailed in September. (1983)
📖 Catalog: Free, CAN, CC, SS:10-3, $20m
○ Nursery: August-December, daily

Arborvillage Nursery
P.O. Box 227
15604 County Road "CC"
Holt, MO 64048
Lanny & Derrick Rawdon
(816) 264-3911

Plants
Offers a good selection of **ornamental trees and shrubs**, including some hard to find elsewhere: species and Japanese maples, horse chestnuts, birches, hickories, real chestnuts, dogwoods, magnolias, flowering crabapples, oaks, lilacs, viburnums and conifers among others. Plants are well and lovingly described. A must for tree mavens! (1978)
📖 Catalog: $1($5 OV), CAN/OV, CC, bn/cn
○ Nursery: All year, M-F, by appointment only
✾ Garden: June-September, by appointment only

Jim & Jenny Archibald
Bryn Collen, Ffostrasol
Llandysul, Dyfed, Wales SA44 5SB
Jim & Jenny Archibald

Seeds
The Archibalds have been **roving seed collectors** for years, now spending more of their time at "Bryn Collen." Their lists vary each year depending on where they've been, and what other collectors have been able to supply, but their list is always terrific, with good plant descriptions. Because they collect very carefully, seed is frequently in quite limited supply.
📖 Catalog: $3(US Bills), OV, bn

Arena Rose Company
P.O. Box 3096
Paso Robles, CA 93447
Sylvester Arena
(805) 227-4094
Fax: (805) 227-4095
E-mail: arenarose@aol.com

Plants
Offers a nice selection of **old roses** suited to the hot climate of the Southwest; the roses are tested and then grafted onto Dr. Huey rootstocks. More varieties being tested for future catalogs. (1991)
📖 Catalog: $5, R&W, CAN, CC, SS:12-4, $12m

Arrowhead Alpines
P.O. Box 857
1310 N. Gregory Road
Fowlerville, MI 48836
Bob & Brigitta Stewart
(517) 223-3581
Fax: (517) 223-8750
E-mail: stewart@livingonline.com

Plants ∞ Seeds
This small nursery specializes in seeds and plants of **perennial and alpine plants**, and the list is very broad and impressive. Some seed is imported from plant breeders in Britain, Europe and some former Soviet bloc countries. They issue a plant and a seed catalog; very brief plant descriptions. (1982)
- Catalog: $2 each, R&W, SS:3-5,9-11, bn
- Nursery: May-October, W-Su, or by appointment
- Garden: May-October, W-Su, or by appointment

Artistic Plants
608 Holly Drive
Burleson, TX 76028
Estella Flather
(817) 295-0802

Plants ∞ Books ∞ Supplies ∞ Tools
A **bonsai** nursery, offering starter plants for bonsai, and some finished plants, all briefly described. Also sells bonsai tools, pots and books. No plants to HI or CA. (1985)
- Catalog: $2d, CC, $20m, bn
- Nursery: All year, Th-Su, call ahead
- Garden: March-November, Th-Su, call ahead

Ashwood Nurseries
Greensforge
Kingswinford, W.Mid., England DY6 0AE
John Massey
44 (0) 1384 401-996

Seeds
Seeds of **lewisia** species and hybrids; they have hybridized a number of colors not found in the species. Their catalog shows the plants in color and gives good cultural information. Also seeds of **cyclamen, hellebores** and **auricula primulas**. Seed list available in September. (1967)
- Catalog: $4(US Bills or 6 IRC), R&W, OV, CC, bn
- Nursery: Daily except December 25-26
- Garden: Daily except December 25-26

Avant Gardens
710 High Hill Road
Dartmouth, MA 02747
Chris & Katherine Tracey
Fax: (508) 998-8819*51

Plants
"Offering over 175 selections of uncommon **annuals** and **tender perennials** for your containers and gardens." Included are coleus, fancy-leaved pelargoniums, many salvias, and more. Brief descriptions.
- Catalog: $3, CC, SS:4-10, $20m, bn
- Nursery: April-September, Tu-Sa
- Garden: August-September, Tu-Sa

Avon Bulbs
Burnt House Farm, Mid-Lambrook
South Petherton, Somerset, England TA13 5HE
Chris Ireland-Jones

Bulbs
Source for many **spring and summer and fall-blooming bulbs**: alliums, crocosmia, galanthus, lilies, hardy cyclamen, arums, colchicums, crocus, fritillaries, erythronium, species gladiolus, iris, tulips, narcissus and trilliums. Plants well described, some shown in color; an import permit is needed for some, a CITES certificate needed for others. (1979)
- Catalog: $5(US Bills), OV, CC, SS:3,10, $50m, bn
- Nursery: March, October, by appointment only

Aztekakti
11306 Gateway East
El Paso, TX 799267
David & Lupina Guerra
(915) 858-1130
Fax: (915) 858-1130
E-mail: smg915@aol.com

Plants ∞ Seeds
Specializes in rare and hard-to-find **Mexican and South American cactus** and some **succulents, desert and subtropical trees** -- plants and seeds, some habitat-collected. Only seeds can be shipped overseas. (1976)
- Catalog: $1(3 IRC OV), R&W, CAN/OV, CC, $20m, bn
- Nursery: All year, daily, call ahead
- Garden: Spring-Summer, daily, call ahead

B & D Lilies
P.O. Box 2007
330 P Street
Port Townsend, WA 98368
Bob & Dianna Gibson
(360) 385-1738
Fax: (360) 385-9996

Plants ∞ Bulbs
Offers a broad selection of **hybrid and species lilies** and several special collections of lilies; each is well described, many are shown in color. Offer "heirlooms," tried and true hybrids which perform well in home gardens. Also sells **daylilies** through their Snow Creek Daylily Gardens catalog($2). (1977)
- Catalog: $3d, R&W, CC, SS:4,10-11, $20m, bn
- Nursery: January-November, M-F, call ahead

B & T World Seeds
Rue des Marchandes
Paguignan, Olonzac, France 34210
Sleigh-Wheatley Family
33 (0) 4-68-91-29-63
Fax: 33 (0) 4-68-91-30-39
E-mail: 100600.2351@compuserve.com

Seeds
Seed for thousands of species of **tropical and subtropical plants**: fruit, cactus, palms, proteas, bromeliads, carnivorous plants, flowering trees and shrubs. They publish seed lists in 180 categories; for two International Reply Coupons they'll send a list of seed lists. The master list with 34,000 entries sells for $23; also available on computer disk, and some lists can be downloaded from their Web Site. Many seeds are collected to order and sent when viable; tell them what you're looking for. Web address is: <ourworld/compuserve.com/homepages/B_and_T_World_Seeds/>. (1985)
📖 Catalog: List order form: 2 IRC, R&W, OV, $10m, bn

Balash Gardens
26595 H Drive North
Albion, MI 49224
Nicholas Balash
(517) 629-5997

Plants
Nick Balash is a hybridizer and grower of "new and expensive" cultivars of **daylilies**, but don't be put off, he offers a number of daylilies at quite reasonable prices. too. Good brief plant descriptions. (1984)
📖 Catalog: $1d, R&W, SS:4-5,8-9, $35m
○ Nursery: April-October, by appointment only
❀ Garden: June-September, by appointment only

A Bamboo Shoot Nursery
P.O. Box 121
12001 Eel River Road
Potter Valley, CA 95469
Dave & Harriette Lowrie
(707) 743-1710

Plants
Offers a broad selection of **bamboo**, including some rare varieties (there is even a waiting list); plants are briefly but well described in a table format. Larger specimens may be available at the nursery.
📖 Catalog: Free, R&W, CAN, SS:9-7, $50m, bn/cn
○ Nursery: All year, Tu-F, call ahead
❀ Garden: Spring-Fall, call ahead

Bamboo Sourcery
666 Wagnon Road
Sebastopol, CA 95472
Gerald Bol Family Trust
(707) 823-5866
Fax: (707) 829-8106

Plants
Collectors' list of **bamboos** -- over 100 varieties, listed by botanical and cultivar name with good descriptions and cultural information -- available in one-gallon or larger containers. Some are quite rare, some are non-invasive and make handsome garden ornamentals, others make good indoor plants. Quarterly availability lists. (1985)
📖 Catalog: $2($3 OV), CAN/OV, CC, bn
○ Nursery: By appointment only
❀ Garden: By appointment only

The Banana Tree
715 Northampton Street
Easton, PA 18042
Fred Saleet
(610) 253-9589
Fax: (610) 253-4864

Seeds ☙ Books
Seeds of a wide selection of **tropical plants** for collectors and "astute growers of tropicals;" offers tropical fruits, ferns and bromeliads, palms, gingers, proteas, cashews, carambola and much more; all plants are well described. Also rhizomes of **heliconia** and the "tuber-like bulbs" of **bananas**. (1960)
📖 Catalog: $3($4 OV or 6 IRC), R&W, CAN/OV, CC, $8m, bn
○ Nursery: All year, daily, by appointment only
❀ Garden: By appointment only

Barber Nursery
Route 3, Box 205
Willis, TX 77378
William Barber
(409) 856-8074

Plants
Nice selection of **seedling trees and shrubs** -- conifers, maples, oaks and ornamental southern species -- listed by botanical and common name only. Small plants at reasonable prices, most grown from seed collected in Texas, Louisiana and Arkansas; Bill says most are fairly hardy. (1978)
📖 Catalog: Free, R&W, CAN/OV, SS:11-4, $25m, bn/cn
○ Nursery: All year, daily, call ahead
❀ Garden: All year, daily, call ahead

Barnhaven Primroses
Langerhouad
Plouzelambre, France 22420
Angela Bradford
33 (0) 2-96-35-54
Fax: 33 (0) 2-96-35-55
E-mail: bradford@wanadoo.fr

Seeds
Florence Bellis' Oregon **primroses** have moved on to Normandy, but are still in good hands. Angela Bradford is still producing seed by hand-pollination, some from pure strains selected and bred over 50 years ago. The selection and plant descriptions are very good. Orders can be paid in pounds, francs or by credit card. Ask for catalog in English or French. (1990)
- Catalog: $3d(US Bills) or 4 IRC, OV, CC
- Nursery: By appointment only
- Garden: March-May, call ahead

Bay Laurel Nursery
2500 El Camino Real
Atascadero, CA 93422
Jim Patterson & Kristie Wells
(805) 466-3406
Fax: (805) 466-6455

Plants ✍ **Tools**
Offers a broad selection of **fruit trees**, including many new varieties from Zaiger Genetics -- including their inter-specific hybrids: fruit trees available on a variety of rootstocks. Also lists **berries, wine and table grapes**, and some ornamental trees and shrubs. Good plant descriptions.
- Catalog: Free, CC, SS:1-3
- Nursery: All year, daily

Bay View Gardens
1201 Bay Street
Santa Cruz, CA 95060
Joseph Ghio
(408) 423-3656

Plants
A broad selection of **iris**: tall bearded, Louisiana, spuria and very special Pacific Coast natives; plants are well described. Joe Ghio is a well-known hybridizer, and winner of many AIS awards. Also sells collections and even "surprise packages" at season's end. (1965)
- Catalog: $2($3 OV), CAN/OV, SS:7-10

Bear Creek Nursery
P.O. Box 411
Northport, WA 99157-0411
Donna & Hunter Carleton
Fax: (509) 732-4417
E-mail: BearCreekin@plix.com

Plants ✍ **Tools**
"Hardy fruits, nuts, shrubs and rootstocks for the home gardener and orchardist." Large selection of antique apples, berries and hardy nut trees; good plant descriptions and cultural information. Specializes in cold-hardy and drought-resistant stock -- trees and shrubs for windbreaks, wildlife and hardwood; also sells pruning tools. (1979)
- Catalog: Free, R&W, CC, SS:1-6, cn/bn

Beaver Creek Nursery
7526 Pelleaux Road
Knoxville, TN 37938
Mike Stansberry
(423) 922-3961

Plants
Specializes in collectors' **trees and shrubs**: species maples, stewartias, viburnums, magnolias, hollies, mildew-resistant crape myrtles and other ornamental plants, including Southern natives. A good selection; each plant well described. Some of the plants are quite recent introductions. Cannot ship to CA, OR or WA. (1986)
- Catalog: $1, CC, SS:10-11,3-5, $20m, bn/cn
- Nursery: March-November, Th-Sa
- Garden: March-November, Th-Sa

Becker's Seed Potatoes
RR 1
Trout Creek, ON, Canada P0H 2L0
Murray & Sharon Becker
(705) 724-2305
Fax: (705) 724-1392

Plants ✍ **Books**
Offers 38 varieties of **seed potatoes**, listed by maturity date and well described by flavor and use. Also offers "garden packs" -- ten eyes each of four varieties that will mature over a long period, and a few books on potatoes. Ships within Canada only. (1985)
- Catalog: Free, R&W, CC, SS:4

Bedford Dahlias
65 Leyton Road
Bedford, OH 44146
Eugene A. Woznicki
(216) 232-2852

Plants
Offers a good selection of **dahlias**, many of them newer introductions and show varieties, some imported from England and Japan. Most varieties are well described; they are shipped at the time you specify. (1980)
- Catalog: 2 FCS, CAN/OV, SS:1-5

Belisle's Violet House
4041 N. Metnik Road
Ojibwa, WI 54862-4132
Marcia Belisle
E-mail: Belislesvh@aol.com

Plants
Offers leaves and cuttings of a broad selection of **African violets** and other **gesneriads**, all of which are given brief one-line descriptions. Listed are aeschynanthus, codonanthe, columnea, drymonia, eucodonia, episcia, kohleria, nautilocalyx, nematanthus, paradrymonia, petrocosmea, many **sinningias**, streptocarpus, and some **hoyas** and other houseplants.
📖 Catalog: $2, SS:5-9, $15m

Bell Family Nursery

See Hydrangeas Plus.

Berton Seeds Company, Ltd.
4260 Weston Road
Weston, ON, Canada M9L 1W9
A. Berton
(416) 745-5655
Fax: (416) 745-5655

Seeds
A nice selection of **vegetable seed from Italy**, ask for their packet list, which is free. Packets are $1.19 each, with a $2 handling charge for orders less than $10. Wholesale buyers should order their color catalog for $10. (1977)
📖 Catalog: See notes, R&W, US/OV, $10m

Big Tree Daylily Garden
777 General Hutchison Parkway
Longwood, FL 32750-3705
Kathleen Chenet
(407) 831-5430

Plants
Offers a large selection of **daylilies**, mostly recent introductions judging from the prices. They also offer a number of older varieties if you're not the sort who wants the newest for hybridizing. Plants are briefly described. (1964)
📖 Catalog: $1d, CC, SS:3-10, $25m
✪ Nursery: April-August, daily, call ahead
❀ Garden: May-August, call ahead

Bio-Quest International

See Jim Duggan Flower Nursery.

Bird Rock Tropicals
6523 El Camino Real
Carlsbad, CA 92009
Pamela Koide
(760) 438-9393
Fax: (760) 438-1316
E-mail: 70544.3146@compuserve.com

Plants
A collectors' list of species and hybrid **tillandsias**, and some **vrieseas**, as well as other **bromeliads**. A broad selection, adding more all the time; no plant descriptions. (1981)
📖 Catalog: Long SASE, R&W, CAN/OV, CC, $50m, bn
✪ Nursery: All year, M-Sa
❀ Garden: All year, M-Sa

Bisnaga Cactus Nursery

See New Mexico Cactus Research.

© Santa Barbara Heirloom Nursery
Artist: Chris Provinzano

Black Copper Kits
111 Ringwood Avenue
Pompton Lakes, NJ 07442
Harold Welsh

Plants ∾ Supplies
Offers some **carnivorous plants**, terrarium supplies, leaflets and growing supplies; plants not described. (1978)
📖 Catalog: 1 FCS/$.50, SS:2-11, $5m, cn/bn

Bloomingfields Farm
P.O. Box 5
9 Route 55 (Sherman)
Gaylordsville, CT 06755-0005
Lee & Diana Bristol
(860) 354-6951

Plants
Daylilies listed by color with good descriptions, season of bloom and cultural hints given. Many are of blooming size. Nice selection. (1969)
📖 Catalog: Free, CAN/OV, CC, SS:4-11
✪ Nursery: June-August, F-Su pm
❀ Garden: July-August, F-Su pm

Bluebird Greenhouse
4821 Jessie Road
Apex, NC 27502
Libbie Glembocki
(919) 362-0530
Fax: (919) 362-5822
E-mail: Libbie@IBM.net
Web: RTPnet.org/~avsa/bbhome.htm

Plants
Offers a nice selection of **African violets**, available as leaves or plants, from a number of prominent hybridizers; some are very recent introductions. Each plant is well described. (1983)
📖 Catalog: $1, R&W, SS:5-10, $10m
✪ Nursery: All year, M-F am, or by appointment

Bluebird Haven Iris Garden
6940 Fairplay Road
Somerset, CA 95684
John & Mary Hess
(916) 620-5017

Plants
Small nursery in the California Mother Lode offers many types of **iris**, from dwarf to tall bearded, reblooming and horned, all briefly described. If you're interested in "antique iris" (pre-1964) they offer many of these, too. (1980)
📖 Catalog: $1, R&W, SS:7-9, $15m
✪ Nursery: April-May, daily
❀ Garden: April-May, Tu-Su

Bluebird Nursery
8320 Freeman Road
Boonville, NY 13309
Sandra Murphy

Plants
Small nursery offers a selection of **"species roses and their hybrids** grown on their own roots," as well as some woodland and meadow **wildflowers**. All plants briefly but well described. No shipping to HI.
📖 Catalog: Free, SS:10, cn/bn

Bluebird Orchard & Nursery
4711 3 Mile Road NE
Grand Rapids, MI 49505
Timothy Strickler
(616) 361-0919

Plants
Tim Strickler has moved, and will be offering only **apple scionwood** from his collection of about 200 old and choice apple varieties. He will issue an availability list each October; send a postcard to request the list. (1982)
📖 Catalog: See notes, SS:3-4, $10m

Kurt Bluemel, Inc.
2740 Greene Lane
Baldwin, MD 21013-9523
Kurt Bluemel
(410) 557-7229
Fax: (410) 557-9785
E-mail: kbi@bluemel.com
Web: www.bluemel.com/kbi/

Plants
A very extensive list of **ornamental grasses, sedges and rushes**, as well as **perennials, bamboos, and ferns**, and some new imports. All very briefly described, with hardiness zones. There are also useful tables listing grasses by desirable traits and for specific purposes. (1964)
📖 Catalog: $3, R&W, CAN/OV, CC, SS:3-5,9-11, $50m, bn/cn
✪ Nursery: All year, call ahead
❀ Garden: Summer-Fall, by appointment only

Bluestem Nursery
1949 Fife Road
Christina Lake, BC, Canada V0H 1E3
Jim Brockmeyer
(250) 447-6363

Plants
Specializing in **ornamental grasses** and **willows**, they offer a good selection of both these groups. Plants are very well described, with information on culture and uses.
📖 Catalog: $2, R&W, US/OV, SS:3-7, bn/cn

Bluestem Prairie Nursery
13197 E. 13th Road
Hillsboro, IL 62049
Ken Schaal
(217) 532-6344

Plants &0 **Seeds**

Specializes in **prairie plants** of the Midwest, especially Illinois; a good selection of plants, and a larger selection of seeds of prairie plants and grasses. No plant descriptions except for color of flower, height and preferred habitat. Seeds shipped November-February because most need stratification; only seeds shipped overseas. Plants shipped bare root. (1985)
- 📖 Catalog: Free, CAN/OV, SS:3-4, cn/bn
- ✿ Garden: May-October, by appointment only

Bluestone Perennials
7211 Middle Ridge Road
Madison, OH 44057
William Boonstra
(800) 852-5243
Fax: (216) 428-7198
E-mail: bluestone@harborcom.net
Web: www.bluestoneperennials.com

Plants

A broad selection of **hardy perennials**. They offer many plants for the perennial border, with specialties in chrysanthemums and ground covers. Also offer some shrubs; good plant descriptions with cultural information and color photos. Small plants at moderate prices. (1972)
- 📖 Catalog: Free, R&W, CC, SS:3-6,8-10, bn/cn
- ✪ Nursery: March-June, August-October, M-F

Bois d'Arc Gardens
1831 Bull Run Road
Schriever, LA 70395
Ed & Rusty Ostheimer
(504) 446-2329
Fax: (504) 446-2329
E-mail: BDG@cajun.net

Plants

These specialists in **Louisiana iris** grow over 600 varieties, but only list about 200 a year in their catalog. They feature Kirk Strawn introductions - he is selecting for more flowers on each plant. Also offer tetraploids and many other cultivars, plus a few species iris.
- 📖 Catalog: $2($5 OV), R&W, CAN/OV, SS:8-11, $25m
- ✪ Nursery: April, M-F, 4-6pm; Sa-Su, all day, call ahead
- ✿ Garden: April, call ahead

Robert Bolton & Son
Birdbrook
Halstead, Essex, England CO9 4BQ
44 (0) 1440 785-246
Fax: 44 (0) 1440 788-000

Seeds

Bolton's are **sweet pea** specialists and hybridizers; they offer a good selection of cultivars, each well described. They also offer a number of collections of favorite cultivars and mixed color packets. Orders must be paid in pounds sterling; see Foreign Exchange Services in Products Sources Index. (1901)
- 📖 Catalog: Free, R&W, OV, CC
- ✿ Garden: June-July, call ahead

Bonnie Brae Gardens
P.O. Box 342
Corbett, OR 97019
Frank & Jean Driver
(503) 695-5190

Bulbs

A nice selection of show quality **novelty daffodils**; varieties described by name, class and hybridizer with very brief personal comments and descriptions of growth habit and season of bloom. Many of the varieties are good naturalizers. (1984)
- 📖 Catalog: Long SASE, CAN/OV, SS:9-10, $10m
- ✿ Garden: March-April, call ahead

Bonsai Boy of New York
7 Format Lane
Smithtown, NY 11787
Eugene Neiro
(516) 265-2763, (800) 790-2763
Fax: (516) 265-4850
E-mail: bonsai@emapnet.com
Web: branch.com/bonsai

Plants

Offers young finished **bonsai** plants, each type shown in a small black and white photograph, and include a number of bonsai suitable for indoor growing. Plants can be shipped to PR. (1979)
- 📖 Catalog: Free, R&W, CAN, CC, bn
- ✪ Nursery: All year, Sa-Su, by appointment only
- ✿ Garden: April-September, by appointment only

Bonsai Farm
13827 Highway 87 South, #3
Adkins, TX 78101
Jerry A. Sorge
(210) 649-2109

Plants &0 **Books** &0 **Supplies** &0 **Tools**

List offers a number of plants to use for **bonsai**, both indoor and outdoor, as well as a large selection of bonsai supplies -- pots, tools, planting supplies, soil amendments, and books. Plants very well described. Only books and supplies to Canada and overseas. (1971)
- 📖 Catalog: $1d($2 OV), CC, $10m, cn/bn
- ✪ Nursery: All year, M-Sa

Borbeleta Gardens
15980 Canby Avenue
Faribault, MN 55021-7652
Dave Campbell
(507) 334-2807
Fax: (507) 334-0365

Plants ❧ Bulbs
"We grow four specialty perennials: **lilies, daylilies, bearded iris** and **Siberian iris**." Many of these are from internationally known hybridizers. Also develop and introduce their own cultivars. Plants are well described. (1971)
📖 Catalog: $3, R&W, CAN/OV, SS:4-10
✪ Nursery: May-September, M-Sa
❀ Garden: May-August, M-Sa

The Borneo Collection
"Treefarm"
El Arish, North QLD, Australia 4855
David K. Chandlee
61 (0) 70 4068-5263

Seeds
David Chandlee is a plant explorer in Borneo, and the author of a chapter in Glenn Tankard's book "Tropical Fruit." He offers a nice selection of **tropical fruit** seeds, most of which are shipped when fresh. No plant descriptions, so do your homework! He also sells the Tankard book, ask for information on price and postage. (1985)
📖 Catalog: $3(US Bills), OV, $15m, cn/bn

Boulder Wall Gardens
McLean Road
Walpole, NH 03608-0165
Charles F. Andros
(603) 756-9056
E-mail: lindena@cheshire.net

Plants
"Offering the rare, sterile, full-flowered form of **bloodroot** (Sanguinaria canadensis) discovered in Dayton, Ohio, in 1916." Plants available as rhizomes shipped in late August or September. Sells **dwarf bearded iris** also.
📖 Catalog: Free, R&W, CAN/OV, SS:8-9

Bountiful Gardens
18001 Shafer Ranch Road
Willits, CA 95490-9626
Bill & Betsy Bruneau, Mgrs.
(707) 459-6410
Fax: (707) 459-6410
E-mail: bountiful@zapcom.net
Web: trine.com/GardenNet/

Seeds ❧ Books ❧ Supplies ❧ Tools
Catalog offers a broad selection of **open-pollinated vegetable seeds** from Chase Seeds and the Henry Doubleday Foundation in England and other sources around the world, as well as seeds of herbs, flowers, green manure crops and grains; all well described in an informative catalog. Also sells a wide selection of gardening books, tools and organic supplies. Send $2 for their "Rare Seed Catalog." (1983)
📖 Catalog: Free($2 or 3 IRC OV), R&W, CAN/OV, CC, cn/bn
✪ Nursery: Common Ground Garden Supply, Palo Alto, CA

The Bovees Nursery
1737 S.W. Coronado
Portland, OR 97219
Lucie Sorensen-Smith & George Watson
(503) 244-9341, (800) 435-9250
Fax: (503) 246-0415

Plants
A collector's catalog of **species and hybrid rhododendrons**, with an extensive listing of **vireya rhododendrons**, and **deciduous azaleas**. Also listed are companion perennials and shrubs. (1953)
📖 Catalog: $2d, CAN/OV, CC, SS:W, $25m, bn/cn
✪ Nursery: All year except January & August, Th-Su
❀ Garden: April-June, Th-Su

S & N Brackley
117 Winslow Road, Wingrave
Aylesbury, Bucks., England HP22 4QB
S. & N. Brackley
44 (0) 1296 681-384
Fax: 44 (0) 1296 682-395

Seeds
Specializes in **sweet peas**: offers many cultivars, including many old-fashioned sweet-smelling varieties. Sold by individual cultivar, each briefly described, or in several special mixes. Airmail postage on all orders is £2; all orders must be paid in pounds sterling. (1890)
📖 Catalog: 2 IRC, R&W, OV, $10m
✪ Nursery: All year, M-F, by appointment only

Brawner Geraniums

See Deerwood Geraniums.

Breck's
6523 N. Galena Road
Peoria, IL 61632
Foster & Gallagher, Inc.
(800) 722-9069
Fax: (800) 996-2852

Bulbs
Color catalog offers a large selection of **spring-blooming bulbs** -- tulips, daffodils, alliums, iris and more; each plant glowingly described, some given rather fanciful names. No shipping to AK or HI. (1818)
📖 Catalog: Free, CAN, SS:8-11, $5m, cn

Bridgewood Gardens
P.O. Box 800
Crownsville, MD 21032
Crownsville Nursery
(410) 849-3916
Fax: (410) 849-3427

Plants
Offer a nice selection of **hostas**, including their own introductions. As well as the general listing, you can choose from "best of the blues," "upscale favorites," and "plain old green" hostas. Plants are well described. No shipping to AK, AZ, CA, HI, OR and WA.
- Catalog: Free, CC, SS:3-11
- Nursery: April-October, daily
- Garden: April-October, daily

Brittingham Plant Farms
P.O. Box 2538
Salisbury, MD 21802-2538
Wayne & Sylvia Robertson
(410) 749-5153
Fax: (800) 749-5148

Plants
Specializes in virus-free **strawberry** plants, as well as **asparagus** roots, **raspberries, blackberries, blueberries, rhubarb and grapes**; all very well described, with cultural and hardiness information. (1945)
- Catalog: Free, R&W, CC, $4m

Broken Arrow Nursery
13 Broken Arrow Road
Hamden, CT 06518
Richard & Sarah Jaynes
(203) 288-1026
Fax: (203) 287-1035

Plants
Specializes in **kalmias, species and hybrid rhododendrons** and a number of other choice **woodland trees and shrubs** -- fothergilla, pieris, Japanese lilac, enkianthus, deciduous azaleas, dawn redwood and others. Mr. Jaynes is the author of "Kalmia: The Laurel Book," (3rd ed. 1997, Timber Pr.). Many of the kalmia are his own selections. Cannot ship to CA, HI or AZ. (1984)
- Catalog: $2, R&W, SS:3-4,9-11, $15m, bn/cn
- Nursery: April-October, daily, call ahead
- Garden: May-June, call ahead

Brothers Herbs & Peonies
27015 S.W. Ladd Hill Road
Sherwood, OR 97140
Richard W. Rogers & Gordon Barron
(503) 625-7548
Fax: (503) 625-1667

Plants
Tree peonies -- recent domestic hybrids and varieties imported from China, with those delicious names, 'Sweet Green Ball,' 'Honeydew from Heaven' and 'Snowy Lotus'. Plants are well described; herbs will be added in coming years. Also sells his father's (Al Rogers) book on Peonies. (1996)
- Catalog: $2, CAN, CC, SS:9-12, $50m
- Nursery: March-December, M-Sa
- Garden: April-May, M-Sa

Brown's Edgewood Gardens
2611 Corrine Drive
Orlando, FL 32803
Brandon Brown
(407) 896-3203
Fax: (407) 898-0889
E-mail: brownherb@aol.com

Plants ∞ Books ∞ Supplies
Offers a nice selection of **herbs**, organic gardening supplies, books on herbs and herb growing, herbal flea collars and other herbal items. The nursery is closed at Christmas for two weeks. (1987)
- Catalog: $3, CC, SS:W, $10m, cn/bn
- Nursery: All year, daily, July-September, W-Su

Brown's Kalmia Nursery
8527 Semiahmoo Drive
Blaine, WA 98230
Ed & Barbara Brown
(360) 371-2489 or 5551
Fax: (360) 371-3516

Plants
Specialize in **kalmias**, offering a nice selection of hybrids from liners to blooming sizes with good descriptions. Have added a few old garden and modern shrub roses. Sell other garden plants at the nursery. (1983)
- Catalog: $1, R&W, CAN, CC, SS:4-6, $20m
- Nursery: April-December, Sa-Tu, call ahead
- Garden: May-June, Sa-Tu, call ahead

Buena Creek Gardens
P.O. Box 2033
San Marcos, CA 92079-2033
Steve Brigham
(760) 744-2810, 744-8367
Fax: (760) 744-0510

Plants
Offering a good selection of **shrubs, vines and perennials**, most of them suited to Mediterranean climates. Many choices of brugmansias, abutilons, salvias and more. Plants listed by botanical name only.
- Catalog: $2, CAN/OV, CC, bn
- Nursery: All year, W-Sa
- Garden: All year, daily

The Bulb Crate
2560 Deerfield Road
Riverwoods, IL 60015-3807
Alice Hosford
(847) 317-1414
Fax: (847) 317-1417
E-mail: abulb@aol.com

Plants   **Bulbs**
Small company sells **hybrid lilies, herbaceous and tree peonies, and tulips**; all are briefly described. Also offered are several collections for long seasons of bloom. (1987)
📖   Catalog: $1d, R&W, CAN, CC, $10m
✪   Nursery: All year, M-Sa, call ahead
❀   Garden: May-October, by appointment only

Bundles of Bulbs

See Charles H. Mueller Co.

Burk's Nursery
P.O. Box 1207
11020 Avilla West (Alexander)
Benton, AR 72018-1207
Lois Burks
(501) 794-3266
Fax: (501) 794-3266

Plants
Former owners of California Epi Center have a new nursery specializing in **haworthias and gasterias**; a very broad selection with good brief plant descriptions and habitat information; all plants seed-grown or nursery-propagated. Serious collectors will crow! (1988)
📖   Catalog: $1d(3 IRC OV), CAN/OV, CC, SS:4-11, $15m, bn

Burnt Ridge Nursery
432 Burnt Ridge Road
Onalaska, WA 98570
Michael & Carolyn Dolan
(360) 985-2873
Fax: (360) 985-2873

Plants
Small nursery specializes in **perennial crops** -- hardy and regular kiwis, as well as beeches, Asian pears, berries, dawn redwood, bald cypress, fig trees, hybrid chestnuts, walnuts and filberts and other **fruiting trees**; all plants well described. (1980)
📖   Catalog: 1 FCS, CC, SS:W, cn/bn
✪   Nursery: All year, call ahead
❀   Garden: By appointment only

W. Atlee Burpee & Company
300 Park Avenue
Warminster, PA 18974
Geo. J. Ball, Inc.
(215) 674-4900, (800) 888-1447
Fax: (215) 674-4170
Web: burpee.garden.com

Plants   **Seeds**   **Books**   **Supplies**   **Tools**   **Bulbs**
A **gardening fixture** for many years, they offer flowers, vegetables, perennial plants, berries and fruit trees in a fat color catalog; each plant well described. Offer spring bulbs in a separate summer catalog. Also carry many tools, supplies, some canning equipment and beekeeping supplies. (1876)
📖   Catalog: Free, R&W, CC, cn/bn
✪   Nursery: September-June, daily

D. V. Burrell Seed Growers Co.
P.O. Box 150
405 N. Main Street
Rocky Ford, CO 81067-0150
William & Richard Burrell
(719) 254-3318
Fax: (719) 254-3319

Seeds   **Supplies**   **Tools**
A good selection of **vegetable seed**, especially watermelons, cantaloupes, hot peppers, corn and popcorn, tomatoes and onions, as well as **annual flowers**. Also offers some growing supplies and a good deal of growing information for their commercial grower customers. (1898)
📖   Catalog: Free($5 OV), R&W, CAN/OV, CC, $8m
✪   Nursery: All year, M-F

Burt Associates Bamboo
P.O. Box 719
3 Landmark Road
Westford, MA 01886
Albert Adelman
(508) 692-3240
E-mail: bamboo@tiac.net
Web: www.tiac.net/users/bamboo

Plants
Offers a nice selection of **bamboos**, many of which are hardy, but specialize in varieties which make dramatic indoor plants. Some rare varieties are in short supply, but sound lovely. Also a few "bamboo accessories" from Japan. No shipping to HI. (1990)
📖   Catalog: $2d, CAN, CC, bn
✪   Nursery: May-September, W-Su
❀   Garden: June-September, W-Su

Bushland Flora
17 Trotman Crescent
Yanchep, WA, Australia 6035
Brian Hargett
61 (0) 9561-1636

Seeds   **Books**
Collectors' list with seeds of 750 species of **Australian plants**, each briefly described; also offers some color-illustrated books on these plants. Many acacias, banksias, eucalyptus, melaleucas, callistemons, helichrysums and helipterums (everlastings) and others; planting guides with orders. Send your "wish list" for species not listed; they're sometimes available. (1972)
📖   Catalog: ($2 or 3 IRC OV), OV, A$10m, bn/cn

Busse Gardens
5873 Oliver Avenue S.W.
Cokato, MN 55321-4229
Ainie & Norman Busse
(320) 286-2654, (800) 544-3192
Fax: (320) 286-6601

Plants
An extensive catalog of **hardy perennials** of all types; offers an especially large selection of hostas, Siberian iris, daylilies, ferns, astilbes, phlox, hardy geraniums, heucheras, herbaceous peonies and wildflowers for rock gardens and woodland, well to briefly described. No shipping to CA. (1973)
📖 Catalog: $2d, R&W, CC, SS:4-10, $25m, bn/cn
✪ Nursery: May-September, M-Sa
✺ Garden: June-August, M-Sa

The Butchart Gardens
P.O. Box 4010
Victoria, BC, Canada V8X 3X4
Butchart Family
(250) 652-4422
Fax: (250) 652-1475
E-mail: email@butchartgardens.bc.ca
Web: butchartgardens.bc.ca/butchart/

Seeds
Butchart Gardens in Victoria sells seed of many of the **annual and perennial flowers** grown in their famous gardens; plants are well described, and prices are very reasonable. They also sell a number of collections: cottage garden, window box, rock garden, children's and hanging baskets. (1904)
📖 Catalog: $1d, US/OV, CC, cn/bn
✪ Nursery: Gift shop, daily
✺ Garden: All year, daily, admission charge

Butterbrooke Farm Seed
78 Barry Road
Oxford, CT 06478-1529
Thomas Butterworth
(203) 888-2000

Seeds
Offers seed of **open-pollinated, short-season vegetables** for Northern climates, not treated chemically; priced at $.65 a packet. Sells booklets and a video on organic vegetable growing; customers may join their seed co-op. (1979)
📖 Catalog: Long SASE(1 IRC OV), R&W, CAN/OV
✪ Nursery: Daily, call ahead
✺ Garden: May-October, call ahead

F. W. Byles Nursery
P.O. Box 7705
Olympia, WA 98507-7705
Gudrun & Frank Byles
(360) 352-4725
Fax: (360) 352-1921
E-mail: byles@juno.com
Web: trine.com/GardenNet

Plants
Formerly Hughes Nursery, they offer a collectors' list of **Japanese maples**, mostly listed by Japanese cultivar names, and a few other species maples; well described with cultural suggestions. A good selection of hard-to-find trees, listed by shape and leaf color/character; rarities will be grafted to order. Ship to Canada and Europe. (1964)
📖 Catalog: $1.50d, CAN/OV, bn/cn
✪ Nursery: All year, by appointment only

C K S
P.O. Box 74
Ostrava-Poruba, Czech Republic 708 00
Milan Sembol, Mgr.
42 (0) 69 447-525
Fax: 42 (0) 69 691-2066

Seeds ∾ Bulbs
Specializes in **alpine and bulbous plants**, available from a seed or bulb list. Specify which list you're interested in. Seed list contains wild-collected seed of plants for rock gardens from southern and eastern Europe. No plant descriptions in bulb catalog. $50 minimum for bulb orders. (1980)
📖 Catalog: $2(US Bills), R&W, OV, SS:11-2, bn
✪ Nursery: September-June, by appointment only
✺ Garden: April-June, by appointment only

CRM Ecosystems

See Prairie Ridge Nursery.

CTDA
174 Cambridge Street
London, England SW1V 4QE
Dr. Basil Smith
44 (0) 1719 765-115

Seeds
Dr. Smith collects and ships fresh seed from 12 species and many strains of hardy **cyclamen**, each well described on his list. He has many selections of C. hederifolium and C. coum, and also offers fresh seed of **hellebores**, 4 species and many color selections of H. orientalis. He's added seeds of several cultivars of snowdrops (Galanthus). (1989)
📖 Catalog: 2 IRC, OV, $20m, bn
✪ Nursery: By appointment only
✺ Garden: January-March, by appointment only

Caladium World
P.O. Box 629
121 Caladium Row
Sebring, FL 33871-0629
L. E. Selph
(941) 385-7661
Fax: (941) 385-5836

Bulbs
Specialize in **caladium bulbs**, those brilliantly colored fancy leaved plants that survive so well through the Southern summers. Several are illustrated in their color leaflet. (1979)
📖 Catalog: Free, R&W, SS:2-9, $11m
○ Nursery: All year, M-Sa, call ahead

California Carnivores
7020 Trenton-Healdsburg Road
Forestville, CA 95436
Peter D'Amato & Marilee Maertz
(707) 838-1630
Web: spiderweb.com/carnivore/

Plants
Offers a good selection of **carnivorous plants**: droseras, sarracenias, utricularias, pinguiculas and nepenthes, all very well described in the catalog, which also gives a lot of growing information. Their greenhouse is located at a winery, where they have over 400 varieties on display; their growing guide is $3, the price list is free with SASE. (1989)
📖 Catalog: See notes, CC, SS:3-11, $25m, bn
○ Nursery: All year, daily
✿ Garden: April-October, daily

Callahan Seeds
6045 Foley Lane
Central Point, OR 97502
Frank T. Callahan II
(541) 855-1164

Seeds
An extensive list of seeds of **native Northwestern trees and shrubs** as well as some from most other continents, about 400 species listed by botanical and common names only. They will also custom-collect seeds from "wish lists" -- seeds available in packets and in bulk. Good list.
📖 Catalog: $1($2 OV), R&W, CAN/OV, bn/cn

Camellia Forest Nursery
125 Carolina Forest Road
Chapel Hill, NC 27516
Kai-Mei & David Parks
(919) 967-5529
Fax: (919) 967-5529
E-mail: camforest@aol.com
Web: home.aol.com/camforest

Plants
Camellias selected for hardiness and disease resistance, both species and unusual hybrids just being introduced; also species maples and viburnums, unusual **ornamental trees and shrubs**, dwarf conifers and holly. Wide selection of collectors' plants; some are recent introductions from China and Japan. Plants are briefly described. (1978)
📖 Catalog: 4 FCS(4 IRC OV), R&W, CAN, SS:3-4,10-11, $25m
○ Nursery: All year, by appointment only
✿ Garden: Spring, Fall, by appointment only

Campanula Connoisseur
702 Traver Trail
Glenwood Springs, CO 81601
Janna Belau

Plants
Here's an amazing small nursery, specializing in **campanulas**, and offering over 40 varieties and adding more all the time. Each is very well described, and some come in several color forms. Isn't it great what people do? No shipping to HI. (1990)
📖 Catalog: $1, SS:4-6,9-10, bn

Campberry Farms
R.R.1
Niagara-on-the-Lake, ON, Canada L0S 1J0
R.D. Campbell
(905) 262-4927

Plants ∾ **Seeds**
Specializing in extra hardy **nut trees, fruit trees, berries** and native trees; offers seeds of hardy trees in the fall. Also does consulting on commercial nut growing in the north, and sells several leaflets of cultural suggestions. Cannot ship to CA, FL, HI, or OR. (1972)
📖 Catalog: $2, R&W, US, SS:4-5,9-12, $20m
○ Nursery: March-May, by appointment only
✿ Garden: July-October, by appointment only

Canyon Creek Nursery
3527 Dry Creek Road
Oroville, CA 95965
John & Susan Whittlesey
(530) 533-2166

Plants
A very good selection of **perennials**, including many violas and violets, hardy geraniums, the "chocolate" cosmos, euphorbias, salvias, campanulas, hardy fuchsias and many more; all very well described with cultural suggestions. Surely the chief attraction of the Oroville area! (1985)
📖 Catalog: $2, CC, SS:2-5,9-11, bn
○ Nursery: All year, call ahead

Cape Cod Vireyas
405 Jones Road
Falmouth, MA 02540
Dr. Richard W. Chaikin
(508) 548-1613
Fax: (508) 540-5899
E-mail: vireya@aol.com
Web: members.aol.com/rchaikin/vireya.html

Plants
Offers a good selection of named cultivars of **vireya rhododendrons**, including cultivars from England, Australia and New Zealand. In all but the mildest areas, these are greenhouse plants, where they can grow in containers or hanging baskets; they come in many colors, and are well described. (1988)
- Catalog: $3d($4 OV), CAN/OV, SS:4-11, $8m
- Nursery: April-November, by appointment only
- Garden: April-November, by appointment only

Cape Flora
P.O. Box 10556, Linton Grange
Port Elizabeth, South Africa 6015
Welland Cowley
27 (0) 41 732-096
Fax: 27 (0) 41 733-188

Seeds ℘ **Bulbs**
A specialist in **South African bulbs** and seed of **species pelargoniums** and **succulents**; plants are listed by botanical name with only color of flower given. Prices are in dollars, and you should specify that you are interested in seed, unless you want to pay the higher costs of phytosanitary certificates and airmail delivery for bulbs. (1981)
- Catalog: $5(US Bills), R&W, OV, CC, $100m, bn
- Nursery: By appointment only
- Garden: By appointment only

Cape Iris Gardens
822 Rodney Vista Blvd.
Cape Girardeau, MO 63701
O. David Niswonger
(573) 334-3383

Plants
Dave hybridizes **tall bearded, spuria, Siberian and median iris**, and offers a very good selection of all types, including his own introductions. Many varieties are in demand by other hybridizers. He also offers a few of his own daylily and daffodil introductions. (1963)
- Catalog: $1d, R&W, CAN/OV, SS:7-10
- Garden: May-June, call ahead

Caprice Farm Nursery
15425 S.W. Pleasant Hill Road
Sherwood, OR 97140
Cyndi & Charlie Turnbow, Robin Blue
(503) 625-7241
Fax: (503) 625-5588

Plants ℘ **Books**
A good selection of **hostas, Siberian iris, daylilies** and **herbaceous peonies**, some quite rare. All plants are very well described, and some are illustrated in color; much here to gladden the heart! Also sell Al Rogers' book on Peonies. (1978)
- Catalog: $2d, R&W, CAN, CC, SS:3-11
- Nursery: April-November, M-Sa, call ahead
- Garden: April-October, M-Sa, call ahead

Carino Nurseries
P.O. Box 538
Indiana, PA 15701
James L. Carino
(412) 463-3350, (800) 223-7075
Fax: (412) 463-3050

Plants
Specializes in **seedling trees** and **deciduous trees and shrubs** for windbreaks, wildlife food, Christmas trees and garden use. Trees available as seedlings and as larger transplants. Minimum order varies. (1947)
- Catalog: $1, R&W, CC, SS:3-5,9-11, $25m, cn
- Nursery: Call ahead
- Garden: Call ahead

Carlson's Gardens
P.O. Box 305
South Salem, NY 10590
Bob Carlson
(914) 763-5958
E-mail: bigazaleas@aol.com

Plants
A broad selection of **azaleas and rhododendrons** for collectors: native and hybrid azaleas such as Knaphill-Exbury, Robin Hill, Gable, North Tisbury, Glenn Dale and their own "Face 'em Down" evergreens. Also large and small leafed hybrid rhododendrons (Dexter, Leach, Gable) and **kalmias**. No shipping to AK, CA or HI. (1970)
- Catalog: $3, CC, SS:4-11, bn/cn
- Nursery: April-November, daily, by appointment only
- Garden: April-July, by appointment only

Carmel Valley Seed Company
P.O. Box 582
Carmel Valley, CA 93924-0582
Joel R. Panzer
Fax: (408) 659-8028

Seeds
Offers **wildflower seed** by individual flower and in mixes; their minimum order is one pound of seed. No plant descriptions, but they send along a pamphlet on how to establish your wildflowers; they also list good books on wildflower gardening. (1986)
- Catalog: $2d, R&W, CAN/OV, $10m, bn/cn

Carncairn Daffodils, Ltd.
Carncairn Grange, Broughshane
Ballymena, Co. Antrim, No. Ireland BT43 7HF
Mrs. Kate Reade
44 (0) 1266 861-216
Fax: 44 (0) 1266 861-216

Bulbs
Collectors' list of **daffodils**: a broad selection of types with division and color class given for each, along with a good description; many are their own introductions. Bulbs are shipped airmail.
📖 Catalog: Free, OV, SS:8-9
✪ Nursery: August-September, call ahead
❀ Garden: March-May, call ahead

Carroll Gardens
444 E. Main Street
Westminster, MD 21157
Alan L. Summers
(410) 848-5422, (800) 638-6334
Fax: (410) 857-4112

Plants ☙ Books
Informative catalog lists a huge selection of **perennials, herbs, roses, vines conifers, trees and shrubs and spring and summer bulbs,** all very well described with cultural information. Many dianthus, campanulas, clematis, tradescantias, hydrangeas, lilies, box, viburnums, clematis, and much more; many fine woody plants suitable for small gardens.
📖 Catalog: $3d, CAN, CC, SS:2-11, bn/cn
✪ Nursery: All year, daily

Carter & Holmes, Inc.
P.O. Box 668
629 Mendenhall Road
Newberry, SC 29108
Owen Holmes & Mary Carter
(803) 276-0579
Fax: (803) 276-0588
E-mail: orchids@carterandholmes.com
Web: www.carterandholmes.com

Plants ☙ Books ☙ Supplies
A broad selection of **orchids**; they are especially well known for their cattleya and phalaenopsis hybrids, many of which are shown in color and are irresistible. Plants are listed by color, with good descriptions. Also sells orchid growing supplies. (1948)
📖 Catalog: $2d($5 OV), R&W, CAN/OV, CC, SS:W
✪ Nursery: All year, M-Sa
❀ Garden: September-March, M-Sa

Cascade Bulb & Seed
P.O. Box 271
Scotts Mills, OR 97375-0271
Dr. Joseph C. Halinar
E-mail: halinar@open.org
Web: www.open.org/halinar/cbs.htm

Seeds ☙ Bulbs
Small grower specializing in seed of **species and hybrid lilies, daylilies, alliums, and hostas** for hybridizers and collectors; brief plant notes include information on hybridizing qualities. Supplies limited; you'll have to choose substitutes, but they all sound desirable. Some plants available; list distributed in November. Send eMail address for eMail catalog. (1980)
📖 Catalog: 1 FCS(1 IRC OV), R&W, CAN/OV, SS:3-10

© California Carnivores
Artist: Judith Finn

Cascade Daffodils
P.O. Box 10626
White Bear Lake, MN 55110-0626
David Karnstedt
(612) 426-9616
E-mail: davekarn@aol.com

Bulbs
A very broad selection of **novelty daffodils**, both standard and miniature categories. Each plant is described by name of hybridizer, class and brief comments; collectors will know and want them. They sound delicious! (1986)
📖 Catalog: $2($3 OV), CAN/OV, SS:9-10, $15m
✪ Nursery: April-August, Sa-Su, by appointment only
✿ Garden: April-May, by appointment only

Cascade Forestry Nursery
22033 Fillmore Road
Cascade, IA 52033
Employee owned
(319) 852-3042
Fax: (319) 852-5004
E-mail: cascade@netins.net

Plants ∞ Supplies
Offers **hardy nut trees, conifers and other trees and shrubs** primarily for reforestation, woodlots and windbreaks; plants not described. Plants offered from seedling size to several feet tall, depending on variety. They help customers find buyers for veneer quality hardwoods, offer forestry consulting and planting services. (1973)
📖 Catalog: Free, R&W, CAN/OV, $35m, cn/bn
✪ Nursery: All year, M-Sa
✿ Garden: All year, M-Sa

Cattail Meadows, Ltd.
P.O. Box 39391
Solon, OH 44139
Edward Tuhela, Laura & Steve Tuhela-Reuning

Plants ∞ Seeds
A nice listing of **native plants** of the midwestern US, many of them suited to shade gardens. Most plants are perennials; all are well described. Shade, wetland and wildlife garden "collections" are offered, as well as a meadow seed mix. (1991)
📖 Catalog: $1d, SS:4-6,9-11, bn/cn
✪ Nursery: By appointment only

Cedar Valley Nursery
3833 McElfresh Road S.W.
Centralia, WA 98531
Charles C. Boyd
(360) 736-7490
Fax: (360) 736-6600

Plants
A tissue-culture laboatory which offers a good selection of red and black **raspberries**, and also a variety of **blackberry** cultivars. The advantage of tissue culture is the rapid propagation of new introductions, and disease free plants. They will also do custom propagation of your plants. (1978)
📖 Catalog: Free, R&W, CAN/OV, $25m

Chadwell Himalayan Seed
81 Parlaunt Road
Slough, Berks., England SL3 8BE
Christopher Chadwell
44 (0) 1753 542-823
Fax: 44 (0) 1753 542-823

Seeds
Specializes in the **flora of the northwest Himalaya and the Orient**, seed available from expeditions and local collectors. List has section of easy seeds for beginners and good plant descriptions for most of the plants offered. Japanese and Mexican plants are a recent addition. (1984)
📖 Catalog: $3(US Bills), R&W, OV, bn
✿ Garden: May-July, by appointment only

Chappell Nursery
1114 Trumbull Highway
Lebanon, CT 06249
Laura Chappell
(860) 642-6896
E-mail: rhodchap@neca.com

Plants
A small nursery offering **hybrid rhododendrons, deciduous azaleas**, and **kalmias**, with hardiness and eventual height given in very brief tables. Also offers a few other trees and shrubs for similar growing conditions: no shipping to OR or WA. (1988)
📖 Catalog: Long SASE, R&W, SS:W, $50m
✪ Nursery: All year, by appointment only
✿ Garden: March-October, by appointment only

Chehalem Creek Nursery
31677 N. Lake Creek Dr.
Tangent, OR 97389
Theresa Wagner

Plants
Offers **red and black currants, gooseberries, jostaberries**, ornamental **ribes**, hybrid **chestnuts** and, of all things, **aquilegias**. No plant descriptions. (1977)
📖 Catalog: $2d, R&W, CAN/OV, SS:12-3, $10m

Chehalem Gardens
P.O. Box 693
Newberg, OR 97132
Tom & Ellen Abrego
(503) 538-8920
E-mail: bhuz@teleport.com

Plants
A list for lovers of **Siberian and spuria iris**. They have "regular" and tetraploid Siberian iris; the latter are sturdier and richer in color with larger blooms. Each plant briefly but well described. A small nursery; stock may be limited on some plants. Can't ship to FL or HI. (1982)
📖 Catalog: Free, SS:8-9, $15m
✪ Nursery: May-June, Sa-Su, by appointment only
✿ Garden: May-June, Sa-Su, by appointment only

Chehalis Rare Plant Nursery
19081 Julie Road
Lebanon, MO 65536
Herbert Dickson

Seeds
Small specialty seed company offers only **primula** seed by mail: single, double, show and exhibition alpine auricula, the results of forty years of selection and breeding. (1968)
📖 Catalog: SASE, CAN/OV, $6m

Chestnut Hill Nursery
15105 N.W. 94th Avenue
Alachua, FL 32615
R.D. Wallace
(904) 462-2820, (800) 669-2067
Fax: (904) 462-4330

Plants ✍ **Books**
Specialize in blight-resistant Dunstan hybrid **chestnuts**. They also offer **Oriental persimmons and figs**, and books on chestnut and persimmon orch-arding. Other low-chill fruits available at the nursery. Cannot ship to CA. (1980)
📖 Catalog: Free, R&W, CC, SS:1-3, $30m
✪ Nursery: All year, Tu-F, by appointment only
✿ Garden: September-October, orchard, by appointment only

Chiltern Seeds
Bortree Stile
Ulverston, Cumbria, England LA12 7PB
44 (0) 1229 581-137
Fax: 44 (0) 1229 584-549
E-mail: 101344.1340@compuserve.com

Seeds
Catalog is a sure delight; offers seed of about 4,000 plants for every purpose, each very well described. The catalog is a useful reference book containing **ornamental plants** from all over the world. Also sells seed of Oriental, unus-ual and common vegetables, herbs and British wildflowers.
📖 Catalog: $5(US Bills), OV, CC, bn/cn

Paul Christian -- Rare Plants
P.O. Box 468
Wrexham, Clwyd, Wales LL13 9XR
Dr. P.J. Christian
44 (0) 1978 366-399
Fax: 44 (0) 1978 366-399
E-mail: paul@rareplants.co.uk
Web: rareplants.co.uk

Bulbs
Source of rare **bulbs, corms and tubers**: alliums, anemones, arums, colchi-cum, corydalis, crocus, erythroniums, fritillaria, species iris, trillium, species tulips and more, from all over the world. Plants briefly described. There is a fee for inspections and health certificates, as well as air mail postage charged at cost. Two catalogs a year, bulbs for outdoors, or tender bulbs for green-houses, $5 for both catalogs, or $3 each.
📖 Catalog: $3(US Bills), US, CC, SS:9-11,2-4, $50m, bn

Cloud Mountain Nursery
6906 Goodwin Road
Everson, WA 98247
Tom & Cheryl Thornton
(360) 966-5859
Fax: (360) 966-0921
E-mail: cloud-mt@pacificrim.net

Plants
Offers a nice selection of **fruit trees and berries**: apples, European and Asian pears, plums, cherries, kiwis, peaches, table grapes and currants, blueberries, raspberries and strawberries. They also offer some flowering trees and shrubs, Japanese maples and hardy bamboos. Informative catalog. (1978)
📖 Catalog: $1, CC, SS:2-4, $10m
✪ Nursery: February-December, daily
✿ Garden: February-December, daily

Coastal Gardens & Nursery
4611 Socastee Boulevard
Myrtle Beach, SC 29575
Rudy & Ursula Herz
(803) 293-2000
Fax: (803) 293-4448

Plants
A large selection of **hostas**, as well as an interesting assortment of perennials, woodland, bog and aquatic plants. Also some **trees and shrubs**. Plants are well described, and sure to thrive in the Southeast. (1974)
📖 Catalog: $2($5 OV), CAN/OV, $35m, bn/cn
✪ Nursery: All year, call ahead
✿ Garden: April-June, call ahead

Coburg Planting Fields
573 East 600 North
Valparaiso, IN 46383
Philipp Brockington & Howard H. Reeve, Jr.
(219) 462-4288
E-mail: pbrockin@wesemann.valpo.edu

Plants
Offers **daylilies** -- a nice selection of both old and new varieties, grown in the rich farm soil of Indiana; all are shipped with double fans. Some varieties may be limited, so they suggest calling to check on availability; each plant is briefly described by color, season of bloom and name of hybridizer. (1984)
- Catalog: $2d, CAN, SS:5-9
- Nursery: June-August, daily
- Garden: July, early August, call ahead

Coenosium Gardens
4412 354th Street East
Eatonville, WA 98328
Robert & Dianne Fincham
(360) 832-8655
Fax: (360) 832-8655

Plants 🙟 Supplies
A collector of conifers who offers a very broad selection of **conifers, dwarf conifers, oaks, beeches** and other plants for bonsai. Each plant well described; some rarer items propagated to order. Send your "wish list." (1979)
- Catalog: $3d, CAN/OV, $35m, bn
- Garden: By appointment only

Cold Stream Farm
2030 Free Soil Road
Free Soil, MI 49411-9752
Mike Hradel
(616) 464-5809

Plants
Specializes in hybrid poplars for woodlots, wildlife habitat and erosion control, other native **trees and shrubs** useful for woodland planting and wildlife cover plantings, in seedling size; no descriptions. (1978)
- Catalog: Free, R&W, SS:3-5,9-12, $5m, cn
- Nursery: March-May, September-Dec., by appointment only

Collector's Nursery
16804 N.E. 102nd Avenue
Battle Ground, WA 98604
Bill Janssen & Diana Reeck
(360) 574-3832
Fax: (360) 571-8540
E-mail: dianar@teleport.com

Plants
Plant collectors know this nursery as a source of interesting **perennials**, offering **corydalis, epimediums, hostas**, and more. They also grow many choice trees and shrubs. Good selection, all plants well described. (1989)
- Catalog: $2, CC, SS:4-6,9-11, bn
- Nursery: All year, by appointment only
- Garden: All year, by appointment only

Color Farm Growers
2710 Thornhill Road
Auburndale, FL 33823
Vern Ogren
(941) 967-9895

Plants
Specializes in **old-fashioned heirloom types of coleus**, which they consider superior garden plants -- some are even sun-tolerant. They have also hybridized these plants and offer a large selection; each plant well described in all its glowing colors. New introductions yearly, and mixed collections. (1985)
- Catalog: $1, CAN, SS:3-10, $10m

Colvos Creek Nursery
P.O. Box 1512
Vashon Island, WA 98070
Michael Lee
(206) 749-9508
Fax: (206) 463-3917
E-mail: colvoscreek@juno.com

Plants
A broad selection of unusual **trees and shrubs**: acacias, species maples, eucalyptus, conifers, flowering shrubs, oaks, redwoods, and yuccas, among others. They are testing new introductions and send out catalog supplements as new items are ready for sale. No shipping to HI. (1972)
- Catalog: $3, R&W, CAN/OV, $15m, bn/cn
- Nursery: All year, F-Sa
- Garden: By appointment only

Comanche Acres Iris Gardens
Route 1, Box 258
Gower, MO 64454
Jim & Lamoyne Hedgecock
(816) 424-6436, (800) 382-4747

Plants 🙟 Bulbs
Specializes in **tall bearded iris** and offers a selection that includes a number of award winners, all well described in a color catalog. Also offers a few border bearded iris. (1981)
- Catalog: $3d($6 OV), CAN/OV, CC, SS:7-9, $10m
- Nursery: May, daily
- Garden: May, daily

Companion Plants
7247 N. Coolville Ridge Road
Athens, OH 45701
Peter Borchard
(614) 592-4643
Fax: (614) 593-3092
E-mail: complants@frognet.net
Web: www.frognet.net/companion_plants/

Plants ∞ Seeds
Over 400 **herb** plants for sale and about 120 varieties of seed -- all very
well described in an informative catalog. Selection includes **scented
geraniums, everlastings** and **woodland plants**. Will ship only seeds to
Canada and overseas. (1982)
- 📖 Catalog: $3, R&W, CAN/OV, CC, SS:W, bn/cn
- ☉ Nursery: March-November, Th-Su
- ❀ Garden: April-October, Th-Su

Compass Seeds

See The Seed Guild.

The Compleat Garden

See Completely Clematis.

Completely Clematis
217 Argilla Road
Ipswich, MA 01938-2617
Susan G. Austin
(508) 356-3197
Fax: (508) 356-3197

Plants
Offers nothing but **clematis**; a good selection of large flowered hybrids, and
small flowered species and varieties, all well described, complete with that
important pruning information. (1985)
- 📖 Catalog: $3, CAN, CC, SS:4-6, $30m, bn
- ☉ Nursery: May-October, M-F or by appointment
- ❀ Garden: May-October, M-F or by appointment

Concord Nurseries, Inc.
10175 Mile Block Road
North Collins, NY 14111-9770
David M. Taylor
(800) 223-2211
Fax: (800) 448-1267

Plants
A wholesale nursery which offers a broad selection of **table and wine
grapes**; they are categorized as American Grape varieties, French hybrid
varieties, American premium seeded and seedless varieties and grafted
Vinifera varieties; no descriptions. Minimum retail order is 25 vines or $50.
No shipping to CA, FL, OR or WA. (1894)
- 📖 Catalog: $1, SS:10-4, $50m

Connell's Dahlias
10616 Waller Road East
Tacoma, WA 98446
Connell Family
(206) 531-0292, (800) 673-5139
Fax: (206) 536-7725

Plants
Offers a broad selection of **dahlias** (their own hybrids and selections from
around the world), grouped by type; each briefly but well described, some
illustrated in color. Several collections are available for those who want
to start with only a few! Also offers **gladiolus** and the wonderful annual
publication "Dahlias of Today." (1973)
- 📖 Catalog: $2, CAN/OV, CC, SS:4
- ☉ Nursery: March-June, M-Sa, call ahead
- ❀ Garden: August-September, M-Sa

The Conservancy
51563 Range Road 212A
10820 Whyte Avenue (Edmonton)
Sherwood Park, AB, Canada T8G 1B1
James Bowick
(403) 434-7401
Fax: (403) 434-7401

Seeds
Specializes in "seed of **trees, shrubs, perennials, wildflowers** and **grasses**
native to, or adapted to, climate zones 1 to 4." This includes conifers, deciduous trees and shrubs, vines and herbaceous perennials for natural landscaping; all from a private preserve and all well described. (1991)
- 📖 Catalog: $2, US/OV, CC, $10m, bn

The Cook's Garden
P.O. Box 535
Londonderry, VT 05148
Shepherd & Ellen Ogden, Mgrs.
(800) 457-9703
Fax: (800) 457-9705
Web: www.cooksgarden.com

Seeds ∞ Books ∞ Supplies
Specializes in **vegetables and salad greens, edible flowers** and
ornamental vegetables for home gardeners/cooks and specialty market
gardeners. A very broad selection with good plant descriptions and growing
hints; also some seed starting supplies and books, including their "The
Cook's Garden." They have moved their trial and display garden to Intervale
Road, Burlington, VT next to Gardener's Supply Company. (1977)
- 📖 Catalog: Free, R&W, CAN/OV, CC
- ❀ Garden: See notes

Cooks Nursery/Eagle Bay Hosta Garden
10749 Bennett Road
Dunkirk, NY 14048
Ransom B. Lydell
(716) 366-8844, 792-7581
E-mail: ranbl@reg.net

Plants
Small nursery offers **hostas**, and they must be pretty hardy from a nursery on the shore of Lake Erie. Each plant is well described, there are "golden oldies" at very reasonable prices, as well as recent introductions. (1928)
- Catalog: $1, R&W, CAN, CC, SS:5-11
- Nursery: May-November, M-F
- Garden: June-October, by appointment only

Cooley's Gardens
P.O. Box 126
11553 Silverton Road N.E.
Silverton, OR 97381-0126
Richard C. Ernst
(503) 873-5463, (800) 225-5391
Fax: (503) 873-5812

Plants
Color catalog offers large selection of **tall bearded iris**; most are shown in photographs, all are well described. They also offer a number of iris which can be selected as a your-choice collection at a good savings. (1928)
- Catalog: $5d($15 OV), R&W, CAN/OV, CC, SS:7-9, $15m
- Nursery: All year, M-F; daily during bloomtime
- Garden: May-June, daily, call ahead

Coombland Gardens & Nursery
Coneyhurst, Billingshurst
West Sussex, England RH14 9DY
David & Joanna Browne
44 (0) 1403 741-727
Fax: 44 (0) 1403 741-079

Seeds
An impressive list of **perennials** and **shrubs**. Many campanulas, gentians, hardy geraniums, primulas, also some trees and bulbs. No plant descriptions, and listings are by plant family, not alphabetical by botanical name. (1981)
- Catalog: $3(5 IRC), OV, SS:11-2, $15m, bn
- Nursery: March-October, M-F, call ahead
- Garden: June, by appointment only

Cooper's Garden

See Terra Nova Gardening.

Coopers Nut House
1378 Willow Glen Road
Fallbrook, CA 92028-6407
Thompson Cooper
(760) 728-6407
Fax: (760) 728-4690
E-mail: tcooper@tfb.com
Web: www.tfb.com/~tcooper/

Plants
Specialize in **macadamia nuts** (the only edible protea!); grafted trees are available. They also consult with growers. Macadamias are hardy to 27F. (1970)
- Catalog: 1 FCS, CAN/OV
- Nursery: All year, daily, call ahead
- Garden: All year, daily, call ahead

Cordon Bleu Farms
P.O. Box 2033
418 Buena Creek Road
San Marcos, CA 92079-2033
Steve Brigham
(760) 744-8367
Fax: (760) 744-0510

Plants
Offers a broad selection of **daylilies** of all types -- large and spider flowered, miniatures and doubles; plants well described, some illustrated in color. See also Buena Creek Gardens. (1970)
- Catalog: $2d, CAN/OV
- Nursery: All year, W-Sa
- Garden: June-July, W-Sa

Corn Hill Nursery
R.R. 5
Petitcodiac, NB, Canada E0A 2H0
Robert & Kathleen Osborne
(506) 756-3635
Fax: (506) 756-1087

Plants
A nursery selling **fruit trees and ornamental trees and shrubs** within Canada, they specialize in own-root, hardy modern shrub and old garden **roses**, which they will ship to the US and overseas. The rose descriptions are very good; for more information you should see Robert Osborne's book "Hardy Roses" (Garden Way) on growing roses in the north. (1982)
- Catalog: $2, R&W, US/OV, CC, SS:3-5,10-11
- Nursery: April-November, daily
- Garden: June-July, daily

Covered Bridge Gardens
1821 Honey Run Road
Chico, CA 95928-8850
Betty & Harry Harwood
(916) 342-6661

Plants
A **daylily** specialist, with plants of all types: large flowered, spiders, variants and exotics, doubles, and small and miniatures, each very briefly described. Their garden is an official A.H.S. Display Garden, with recent introductions from prominent breeders. (1986)
- 📖 Catalog: $1d, CAN, CC, SS:4-10, $25m
- ○ Nursery: June 1-July 15, daily, other times by appointment
- ❀ Garden: May-September, by appointment only

Craven's Nursery
1 Foulds Terrace
Bingley, W. Yorkshire, England BD16 4LZ
Stephen & Marlene Craven
44 (0) 1274 561-412
Fax: 44 (0) 1274 561-412

Seeds
A specialist in **primula** seed, and offering a very good selection: auriculas, wandas, many species primulas, and mixes and selections of special show varieties. All plants are well described, some shown in charming drawings.
- 📖 Catalog: $2(US Bills), OV, $50m, bn
- ○ Nursery: All year, Th-Su, by appointment only
- ❀ Garden: May-August, Th-Su, by appointment only

Cricket Hill Garden
670 Walnut Hill Road
Thomaston, CT 06787
Kasha & David Furman
(860) 283-1042
Fax: (860) 283-1042
E-mail: crickethill@treepeony.com
Web: www.treepeony.com

Plants ☜ Books
Cricket Hill imports and sells **tree peonies** from China; all are three years old or three branched. They have wonderful names: 'Intoxicated Celestial Peach,' 'Coiled Dragon in the Mist Grasping a Purple Pearl,' 'Heaven Scented and Wet with Dew!' Expensive, but think of the bragging rights! Color photos. (1988)
- 📖 Catalog: $3($5 OV), CAN/OV, SS: 9-11, $60m
- ○ Nursery: May-June, Oct.-Nov., Th-Su, call ahead
- ❀ Garden: May-June, call ahead

Cricklewood Nursery
11907 Nevers Road
Snohomish, WA 98290-6804
Evie Douglas
(360) 568-2829
E-mail: cricklewod@aol.com

Plants
Small nursery specializes in old-fashioned **"English cottage border perennials"** and **rock garden plants** -- a very nice selection listed only by botanical name. Offers hardy geraniums, species primulas and many others. Some plants available in quantities too small to list -- ask. (1982)
- 📖 Catalog: $1d, SS:3-6,9-10, bn
- ○ Nursery: April-May, F-Sa, by appointment only
- ❀ Garden: May-June, by appointment only

Crintonic Gardens
County Line Road
Gates Mills, OH 44040
Curt Hanson
(216) 423-3349

Plants
A **daylily** hybridizer who offers his own new and recent introductions, and recent tetraploid and diploid introductions of other prominent hybridizers. These are much sought after by other daylily hybridizers, but are too expensive for the ordinary gardener. New varieties well described. (1982)
- 📖 Catalog: $2d($4 OV), R&W, CAN/OV, SS:5-9, $50m
- ○ Nursery: June-July, daily, call ahead
- ❀ Garden: July, call ahead

The Croft Wild Bulb Nursery
P.O. Box 61
off Kologha Road
Stutterheim, Eastern Cape, South Africa 4930
Cameron & Rhoda McMaster
27 (0) 436 32796
Fax: 27 (0) 436 31931

Seeds ☜ Bulbs
A collectors' list of **South African bulbs**, available as seed or bulbs. Included are bulbines, nerines, cyrtanthus, species gladiolus and more. No descriptions; plants are listed by family.
- 📖 Catalog: Free, OV, SS:1,6-8, bn
- ○ Nursery: All year, daily, call ahead
- ❀ Garden: November-May, call ahead

Crosman Seed Corp.
P.O. Box 110
W. Commercial Street & Crosman Terrace
East Rochester, NY 14445
William Mapstone Family
(716) 586-1928
Fax: (716) 586-6093

Seeds
Calling themselves "America's oldest packet seed house," they offer a good selection of **vegetable, herb and annual flower** seeds on a combined seed list/order form; no descriptions of plants, prices very reasonable. (1838)
- 📖 Catalog: Free, R&W, $5m
- ○ Nursery: All year, M-F

The Crownsville Nursery
P.O. Box 797
Crownsville, MD 21032
Chick & Jennifer Wasitis, David Bowman
(410) 849-3143
Fax: (410) 849-3427

Plants
Catalog offers a nice selection of **perennials and ornamental grasses, ferns, and flowering shrubs** -- each very well described with cultural information. Includes daylilies, campanulas, hardy geraniums, phlox, rudbeckias and hostas. No shipping to AZ, AK, CA, HI, OR or WA.
📖 Catalog: $2, CC, SS:3-6,8-11, $25m, bn/cn
✪ Nursery: All year, M-F, call ahead

Crystal Palace Perennials, Ltd.
P.O. Box 154
12029 Wicker Ave. (Cedar Lake)
St. John, IN 46373
Greg & Sue Speichert
(219) 374-9419
Fax: (219) 374-9052
E-mail: GSpeichert@aol.com
Web: www.crystalpalaceperennial.com

Plants ∾ Books ∾ Supplies
Aquatic plants, water lilies and lotus, both hardy and tropical, and very well described -- all the plants you'd need for pond or bog. Also sell water garden supplies, and give a good deal of practical advice in the catalog. (1989)
📖 Catalog: $3d($5 OV), R&W, CAN/OV, CC, SS:3-9, $25m, bn/cn
✪ Nursery: April-September, M-Sa
✿ Garden: May-August, M-Sa

The Cummins Garden
22 Robertsville Road
Marlboro, NJ 07746
Elizabeth K. Cummins
(732) 536-2591

Plants
Specialize in **dwarf and small leaved rhododendrons, azaleas and dwarf conifers** for the rock garden and bonsai, also kalmias, pieris, and other acid-loving plants; all well described. Can't ship to AZ, CA, OR or WA. (1972)
📖 Catalog: $2d, R&W, CC, SS:4-6,9-11, $25m, bn/cn
✪ Nursery: All year, daily, call ahead
✿ Garden: April-June, September-October, call ahead

Cummins Nursery
18 Glass Factory Bay
Geneva, NY 14456
Cummins Family
(315) 789-7083

Plants
Specializing in **disease-resistant apples**, they also offer pears, cherries, peaches, plums and apricots, as well as rootstocks, including the Geneva apple rootstock, which Dr. James Cummins helped develop. Trees are very well described. They will happily custom-graft whatever you like.
📖 Catalog: Free, R&W, SS:11,3-5, $50m

Cycad Gardens
4524 Toland Way
Los Angeles, CA 90041
Loran & Eva Whitelock
(213) 255-6651
Fax: (213) 344-0858

Plants
Specializes in **cycad seedlings** -- bowenia, ceratozamia, cycas, dioon, encephalartos, lepidozamia, macrozamia, stangeria and zamia -- with notes on origins. Some plants also available in gallon sizes; you can send a "wish list" for other rare items that may be available from time to time. (1978)
📖 Catalog: Long SASE, $30m, bn
✪ Nursery: By appointment only
✿ Garden: Spring-Summer, call ahead

Dabney Herbs
P.O. Box 22061
Louisville, KY 40252
Davy Dabney
(502) 893-5198
Fax: (502) 893-5198
E-mail: davydabney@aye.net
Web: www.dabneyherbs.com

Plants ∾ Books ∾ Supplies
Offers a good selection of **herbs, scented geraniums, ginseng, perennials and wildflowers**, all well described, as well as books, potpourri supplies and cooking extracts in an informative catalog. (1986)
📖 Catalog: $2, R&W, CC, SS:3-6,10-12, cn/bn

Dacha Barinka
46232 Strathcona Road
Chilliwack, BC, Canada V2P 3T2
David Schmierbach
(604) 792-0957

Plants ∾ Seeds
Offers seeds for **everlasting flowers, vegetables, herbs** and Chinese vegetables, as well as seeds and starts of onions, garlic and chives. Also some table and wine grapes, nut trees and miscellaneous ornamental plants. (1982)
📖 Catalog: $1d, US/OV, SS:3-5,8-10

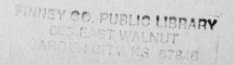

The Daffodil Mart
85 Broad Street
Torrington, CT 06790-6668
Eliot Wadsworth II
(800) 255-2852
Fax: (800) 420-2852

Books ⁊ **Supplies** ⁊ **Tools** ⁊ **Bulbs**
A very extensive catalog of **bulbs** -- many hundreds of species and varieties in addition to a large selection of novelty, miniature and species daffodils. Also some growing supplies and books. Prices drop as quantity rises. (1935)
📖 Catalog: Free, R&W, CAN, CC, SS:4,11, $50m, bn

Daisy Farm, Inc.

See Palm Hammock Orchid Estate, Inc.

William Dam Seeds
P.O. Box 8400
279 Highway 8 (Flamborough)
Dundas, ON, Canada L9H 6M1
Rene W. Dam
(905) 628-6641
Fax: (905) 627-1729

Plants ⁊ **Seeds** ⁊ **Books** ⁊ **Supplies**
Color catalog of short season **vegetables, herbs, annuals and perennials**. Plants are well described, and Canadian gardeners can order bulbs, seed potatoes and berries as well. Also carries organic growing supplies, and gardening books. (1949)
📖 Catalog: $2, R&W, US/OV, CC, $10m
✪ Nursery: All year, M-Sa
✿ Garden: July-August, M-Sa

Dan's Dahlias
994 South Bank Road
Oakville, WA 98568
Dan Pearson
(360) 482-2607

Plants
Offers a nice selection of both "exhibition type" **dahlias** and varieties best for the cut flower market; brief descriptions. (1983)
📖 Catalog: Free, CAN/OV, CC, SS:4-5
✪ Nursery: August-October, daily, call ahead

Dan's Garden Shop
5821 Woodwinds Circle
Frederick, MD 21703-7579
Dan Youngberg
(301) 695-5966
E-mail: dan@fred.net
Web: www.fred.net/alv/home.html

Seeds ⁊ **Books** ⁊ **Supplies**
A mini-garden emporium, they offer seeds of **herbs, vegetables and flowers** for the home garden, and growing and propagating supplies. Each variety is well described. They also sell some books on gardening; mostly useful to beginning gardeners. (1977)
📖 Catalog: Free, CAN, CC, cn
✪ Nursery: All year, M-Sa

Davidson-Wilson Greenhouses
RR 2, Box 168
Crawfordsville, IN 47933-9426
Barbara Wilson & Marilyn Davidson
(765) 364-0556
Fax: (800) 276-3691
E-mail: barb@link2000.net
Web: www.gardenscape.com

Plants
Specializes in **ivy and scented geraniums, begonias,** and **impatiens**, some **houseplants, herbs** and **succulents**; b&w photos illustrate many plants, each briefly to well described. They will sell wholesale to the public with a minimum of 25 plants ordered. (1980)
📖 Catalog: $3.50, R&W, CAN/OV, CC, SS:W, $45m
✪ Nursery: All year, M-Sa
✿ Garden: June-September, M-Sa

Corwin Davis Nursery

See Toll Gate Gardens and Nursery.

Daylily Discounters
1 Daylily Plaza
Alachua, FL 32615
Tom Allin, Mgr.
(904) 462-1539
Fax: (904) 462-5111
E-mail: catalog@daylily-discounters.com
Web: www.daylily-discounters.com

Plants
A **daylily** nursery which offers varieties with a proven track record nationally, most hardy to Zone 5; all are very well described, and many are illustrated in color photographs. They are now the distributor of the hybrids of William Munson of Wimberlyway. Also offer a few companion perennials. (1988)
📖 Catalog: $2, R&W, CAN/OV, CC, $25m
✪ Nursery: All year, M-F
✿ Garden: Open House in May

Daylily World
P.O. Box 1612
260 N. White Cedar Road
Sanford, FL 32772-1612
David Kirchhoff
(407) 322-4034
Fax: (407) 322-4026

Plants
A very broad selection of **daylilies** in a catalog with many color photos; new introductions well described, older varieties briefly described. They have many diploids and tetraploids, and many seem to be double. Both David Kirchhoff and Mort Morss are award winners for hybridizing. (1971)
📖 Catalog: $5d($5 US Bills OV) CAN/OV, CC, $30m
✪ Nursery: April-June, W-Su, call ahead, or by appointment
❀ Garden: April-June, W-Su, call ahead, or by appointment

Daystar
1270 Hallowell-Litchfield Road
West Gardiner, ME 04345-3571
Marjorie Walsh

Plants
A good selection of **heathers** and **dwarf conifers** with many unusual shrubs, trees and perennials, including daphnes, climbing hydrangea, and some rhododendrons. Plants are very briefly described. (1969)
📖 Catalog: $1, R&W, CC, SS:4-6,9-11, $20m, bn
✪ Nursery: April-November, by appointment only
❀ Garden: May-October, by appointment only

Deep Diversity
P.O. Box 15700
Santa Fe, NM 87506-5700
Seeds of Change

Seeds
This is a fascinating catalog, offering a broad selection of plants, primarily **open-pollinated vegetables**, many of them heirloom varieties, but it also lists a number of conifers, flowering trees and other plants from all parts of the world. All plants are listed by family, with an alphabetical index of common and botanical names at the back. (1993)
📖 Catalog: $5, CAN/OV, CC, $5m

Deerwood Geraniums
Route 4, Box 525 A
Buckhannon, WV 26201
Faye Brawner
(304) 472-4203

Plants
Faye Brawner is a **geranium** hybridizer and collector of rare **pelargoniums**; she offers a very broad selection of all types of geraniums and pelargoniums, grouped by type and very briefly described. (1970)
📖 Catalog: $3($5 OV), OV, SS:4-10, $20m
✪ Nursery: By appointment only

DeGiorgi Seed Company
6011 'N' Street
Omaha, NE 68117-1634
Greg & Robin Allen
(402) 731-3901, (800) 858-2580
Fax: (402) 731-8475

Seeds 🙰 Books 🙰 Supplies
A good old-fashioned catalog, offering a broad selection of garden **annuals, perennials, wildflowers, ornamental grasses** and **vegetables** for home and commercial growers. All varieties are well described, with cultural suggestions; also offers a few books and some supplies. (1905)
📖 Catalog: Free, R&W, CAN/OV, CC, $10m, cn/bn
✪ Nursery: All year, daily
❀ Garden: June-September, daily

© Freshwater Farms
Artist: Fiona Burgess

DeGrandchamp's Farms
15575 - 77th Street
South Haven, MI 49090
DeGrandchamp Family
(616) 637-3915
Fax: (616) 637-2531
E-mail: dechamp@cybersol.com

Plants
Specialize in **blueberries** -- and list 26 varieties by season of ripening, with charts to describe their other qualities. They also list 7 cultivars of **lingon-berry** and 10 kinds of **cranberry**. No shipping to AZ, CA, HI, OR or WA.
- Catalog: Free, R&W, CC, SS:3-12, $30m
- Nursery: March-December, M-F, call ahead

Delta Farm & Nursery
3925 N. Delta Highway
Eugene, OR 97408-7100
Ronald D. & Faye Spidell
(541) 485-2992
Fax: (541) 485-1985
E-mail: deltafarm@nu-world.com

Plants
A very broad list of **fuchsias**, with many **species fuchsias** -- available as small plants or cuttings. The plants are well but briefly described, with information on origin or date of introduction. Great list!
- Catalog: $1d, CC, SS:4-5, $10m, bn
- Nursery: March-July, daily or by appointment
- Garden: May-July, daily

Desert Citizens
P.O. Box 409
Kiowa, CO 74553
Richard & Dessa Cole

Seeds
A good selection of **desert trees, shrubs and perennials**, mostly native to the American Southwest. Includes desert grasses, as well as agaves, penstemons; plants briefly but well described.
- Catalog: $1, bn/cn

Desert Moon Nursery
P.O. Box 600
30 Luna del Desierto
Veguita, NM 87062
Theodore & Candace Hodoba
(505) 864-0614

Plants   Seeds
Offers a fine listing of nursery propagated **Southwestern native plants**; cactus and succulents, yuccas, agaves, and wildflowers, grown for their interesting shapes, lovely flowers, or utility (shade and windbreaks). All plants are well described, they also list seed of many species. Only seeds can be sent to overseas customers. (1987)
- Catalog: $1, CAN/OV, SS:4-10, $15m, bn/cn
- Nursery: April-October, by appointment only
- Garden: May, August-September, by appointment only

Desert Theatre
17 Behler Road
Watsonville, CA 95076
Kate Jackson
(408) 728-5513
Fax: (408) 728-4091

Plants
A broad selection of **cactus and succulents** from South America and Africa, including aloes, lithops, notocactus, haworthias, echeverias, euphorbias, gymnocalyciums, mammillarias, rebutias and sulcorebutias, listed by botanical name; catalog gives brief descriptions. (1979)
- Catalog: $2, R&W, SS:2-10, $20m, bn
- Nursery: All year, Tu-Su
- Garden: April-June, Tu-Sa

Marca Dickie Nursery
P.O. Box 1270
Boyes Hot Springs, CA 95416-1270
Marca & Robert Dickie
(707) 996-0364, (800) 990-0364 (CA)

Plants
A small nursery near Tusker Press World Headquarters, offering a nice selection of **Japanese maples** on a collectors' list (no plant descriptions). No shipping to FL & HI. (1979)
- Catalog: Free, R&W, SS:12-3, $25m
- Nursery: All year, by appointment only
- Garden: April-November, by appointment only

Digger's Club
105 Latrobe Parade
Dromana, VIC, Australia 3936
Clive & Penny Blazey
61 (0) 35 987-1877
E-mail: diggers@pac.com.au

Seeds   Books   Supplies
Offering seeds of **heirloom vegetables**, and some **annuals and ever-lastings, and Australian wildflowers**, well described in a color catalog. You can join their "Digger's Club" for special discounts, but anyone can order from their catalog. Books and growing supplies offered also.
- Catalog: Free, CAN/OV, CC, cn/bn
- Nursery: All year, M-F
- Garden: September-April, M-F

Digging Dog Nursery
P.O. Box 471
Albion, CA 95410
Deborah Whigham & Gary Ratway
(707) 937-1130, 937-1235
Fax: (707) 937-2480

Plants
Offers a nice selection of "good doers," **perennials, shrubs and trees** which they have grown for years on the northern California coast, many are cultivars I haven't seen listed elsewhere: artemisias, asters, campanulas, dianthus, eupatorium, hardy geraniums, penstemons, ornamental grasses and a number of flowering shrubs and a few trees. Good plant descriptions. (1980)
- Catalog: $3, CC, SS:2-6,9-11, $30m, bn/cn
- Nursery: All year, Tu-Sa, by appointment only
- Garden: Spring-Fall, by appointment only

Dilworth Nursery
1200 Election Road
Oxford, PA 19363
Rick & Jackie Dilworth
(610) 932-0347
Fax: (610) 932-9057

Plants
Specialists in "dwarf and unusual nursery stock," they have a nice selection of **dwarf conifers** and **flowering shrubs**. Their list has no plant descriptions, but aficionados will know what these choice plants do. No shipping to AK, AZ, CA, FL, HI, OR or WA. (1976)
- Catalog: Free, R&W, SS:2-5,9-11, bn
- Nursery: March-November, M-Sa
- Garden: March-November, M-Sa, call ahead

Dixondale Farms
P.O. Box 127
Carrizo Springs, TX 78834-6127
Wallace & Bill Martin, Bruce & Jeanie Frasier
(210) 876-2430
Fax: (210) 876-9640

Plants
Offers a nice selection of **onion plants** for home gardeners: Texas Supersweet, Granex (yellow Granex also called Vidalia, Maui or Noonday), White Bermuda, Walla Walla, Spanish, Cimarron and Sweet Red. (1913)
- Catalog: Free, R&W, CC, SS:12-5, $25m
- Nursery: January-May, M-F

Donaroma's Nursery
P.O. Box 2189
Upper Main Street
Edgartown, MA 02539-2189
Michael Donaroma
(508) 627-8366
Fax: (508) 627-7855

Plants
Nursery on Martha's Vineyard that specializes in **perennials** and **wildflowers**; a very good selection, well described. Send out availability lists in spring and fall. Broad choice of aquilegia, astilbe, campanula, delphinium, dianthus, lupine, meconopsis, papaver, silene and veronica and many others.
- Catalog: Free, R&W, CC, SS:3-5,9-12, $10m, bn/cn
- Nursery: All year, M-Sa
- Garden: Summer, M-Sa

Donovan's Roses
P.O. Box 37800
Shreveport, LA 71133-7800
Thomas & Kathy Schimschock
(318) 861-6693

Plants
Offers a nice selection of recently introduced **roses**, hybrid teas, floribundas, shrubs, and climbers, many of which were All America Rose Selections or World Class Roses -- many of these are the roses in demand by rose show people. Good plant descriptions. (1982)
- Catalog: Long SASE, SS:1-4

Down on the Farm Seeds
P.O. Box 184
Hiram, OH 44234
Rose A. Guth

Seeds
Run by an Ohio farm family, specializing in open-pollinated and heirloom varieties; all seeds are untreated. A good selection of **vegetables, including 52 tomatoes** as well as herbs and old fashioned garden flowers. All are briefly described. Also sells ashwood baskets and wooden pot labels. (1990)
- Catalog: $1d($3 OV), CAN/OV, $1m, cn

Doyle Farm Nursery
158 Norris Road
Delta, PA 17314
Jacquelin Doyle
(717) 862-3134

Plants
Offers a nice selection of **perennials**, each plant very briefly described, with symbols for culture. No shipping to AZ, CA, OR and WA.
- Catalog: $1, R&W, SS:4-6,9-10, bn/cn
- Nursery: By appointment only
- Garden: June, September, call ahead

Draycott Gardens
16185 Falls Road
Upperco, MD 21155
Carol S. Warner
(410) 374-4778

Plants
Specializing in **Siberian and Japanese iris**, they have taken over the collection of Clarence Mahan of the Iris Pond. Also offer their own hybrids and new introductions from local hybridizers, and a few **species iris**. Plants are well described.

  📖 Catalog: $1d, CAN/OV, SS:8-9, $15m
  ❀ Garden: May-June, by appointment only

Jim Duggan Flower Nursery
1452 Santa Fe Drive
Encinitas, CA 92024
Jim Duggan
(760) 943-1658
E-mail: jimsflowers@abac.com

Bulbs
A good selection of **South African bulbs** for containers, rock gardens, or naturalizing in dry summer areas; these bulbs need a Mediterranean climate. Brief descriptions; growing 200 species. Bought the stock of Bio-Quest International; choice will increase as he builds up stock. List mailed in June. (1991)

  📖 Catalog: $2, CAN/OV, SS:6-9, $15m, bn
  ✪ Nursery: All year, W-Sa
  ❀ Garden: January-April, W-Sa

Dunford Farms
P.O. Box 238
Sumner, WA 98390
Donald Duncan & Warren Gifford

Plants ∽ **Bulbs**
Sells **agapanthus** `Headbourne Hybrids' and **alstroemerias**; aurantiaca, pelegrina, eight selections of their own hybrid Inca(R) lilies, and two showy older hybrids, `Kay Davis' and `Walter Fleming.' They have added **cyclamen** coum and hederifolium and some other perennials. (1973)

  📖 Catalog: $1, SS:2-5, $9m

Dunlap Enterprises

See Pat's Pets.

Dutch Gardens
P.O. Box 200
Adelphia, NJ 07710-0200
John & Nick Langeveld
(800) 818-3861
Fax: (908) 780-7720
E-mail: cs@dutchgardens.nl
Web: www.dutchgardens.nl

Plants ∽ **Bulbs**
Color catalog of spring-flowering **Dutch bulbs** offers all of the most popular varieties. They have another catalog of **summer-blooming bulbs** -- lilies, gladiolus, dahlias, cannas, amaryllis and some perennials. Brief cultural hints, bulk order plans. No shipping to AK, HI, PR. (1960)

  📖 Catalog: Free, R&W, CC, SS:3-5,8-11, cn/bn

E & R Seed
1356 E 200 S
Monroe, IN 46772
Ervin & Ruth Ann Hilty

Seeds ∽ **Supplies** ∽ **Tools**
Offers a broad variety of "garden seed," i.e. **vegetables and flowers** for the home garden, as well as growing supplies, tools, canning supplies, bird houses, humane traps, even a rabbit hutch kit. Every variety is briefly described. (1983)

  📖 Catalog: Free, R&W, SS:3-5, cn/bn
  ✪ Nursery: All year, M-Sa

Early's Farm & Garden Centre, Inc.
2615 Lorne Avenue
Saskatoon, SK, Canada S7J 0S5
J. C. Bloski, Mgr.
(306) 931-1982
Fax: (306) 931-7110

Seeds ∽ **Supplies** ∽ **Tools** ∽ **Bulbs**
This old firm re-entered the mail order business in 1985 with a color catalog offering **garden flower and vegetable seeds, gladiolus bulbs** and a huge selection of supplies and tools -- everything for Northern gardening. I love the name Saskatoon, Saskatchewan -- say it slowly, with feeling. (1907)

  📖 Catalog: $2d, R&W, US, CC, $25m
  ✪ Nursery: All year, M-Sa
  ❀ Garden: Greenhouse, April-September

Earth's Rising Trees
P.O. Box 334
Monroe, OR 97456-0334
Delbert McCombs
(541) 847-5950
Fax: (541) 847-5950

Plants
A small nursery offering organically grown **fruit trees**, including antique apples, European and Asian pears, figs, plums and peaches. (And their locally favorite peach called 'Gum's Mango!') Varieties and their rootstocks well described.

  📖 Catalog: Free, R&W, CAN, SS:1-5
  ✪ Nursery: December-April, by appointment only

Earthly Goods, Ltd.
P.O. Box 614
New Albany, IN 47151-0614
Stephen Brown & Ann Streckfus
(812) 944-2903
Fax: (812) 944-2903
E-mail: earthlyg@aye.net
Web: www.earthlygoods.com

Seeds   Supplies
Offers a good selection of **wildflower seeds**, both single species and many mixes for various regions and situations. Also sell **prairie grasses** by the pound to use with your flower mixes. Nice selection, brief descriptions. (1992)
📖 Catalog: Free, CAN/OV, CC, $15m, cn/bn

Eastern Plant Specialties
P.O. Box 226
Georgetown, ME 04548
Mark Stavish
(207) 371-2888 (Summer)

Plants
A good selection of hardy **rhododendrons and azaleas**, unusual and dwarf conifers, kalmias, pieris, holly, ornamental trees, dwarf shrubs and ground cover plants; all well described, some illustrated. Catalog full of rare and hardy collectors' plants; lists of plants for special uses. In winter, phone number is (908) 382-2508. No shipping to AZ or CA.
📖 Catalog: $3d, R&W, CC, SS:2-6,9-12, $15m, cn/bn
✪ Nursery: June-October, by appointment only
❀ Garden: June-September, by appointment only

Eastwoods Nurseries
604 Long Mountain Road
Washington, VA 22747
Henry Eastwood & Frances Schroeder
(540) 675-1234

Plants
Small nursery offers a nice selection of **Japanese maples**, each lovingly described. They also offer a special gift seedling maple especially for children, which is a very nice idea for a special occasion. (1991)
📖 Catalog: $2d($3 OV), R&W, CAN/OV
✪ Nursery: March-October, Sa, by appointment only
❀ Garden: May, October, Sa, by appointment only

Eco-Gardens
P.O. Box 1227
Decatur, GA 30031
Don L. Jacobs
(404) 294-6468

Plants   Books
Eco-Gardens is a private collection of **native and exotic plants** hardy in the Piedmont region; they sell surplus plants, some of their own breeding, to raise operating funds. Nice selection of **perennials, hellebores, trilliums, sedums**, and **asarums**; brief descriptions. Don is the co-author of a recent book on trilliums; it is available for $30ppd. (1976)
📖 Catalog: $2, OV, SS:W, $25m, bn/cn
✪ Nursery: All year, by appointment only
❀ Garden: March-April, by appointment only

Ecoscape
424 National St.
Santa Cruz, CA 95060
Alan C. Beverly
(408) 459-8106
Fax: (408) 459-8106
E-mail: ecoscape@scruznet.com
Web: www.scruz.net/~ecoscape

Plants
Here's a specialist! He sells one plant, **Aloe polyphylla**, "the gem of the Drakensberg." A beautiful plant with a precise spiral of leaves, endangered in its native habitat. These plants are seed grown and two years old. Flyer shows them in color. (1991)
📖 Catalog: Free, R&W, CC, $20m
✪ Nursery: By appointment only
❀ Garden: May-October, by appointment only

Edge of the Rockies
P.O. Box 1218
Bayfield, CO 81122
Lisa L. Landis

Seeds
A small company sells **native seeds from the southern Rocky Mountains** to the desert of the Colorado Plateau; from subalpine to the edge of the foothills. A nice selection, each plant very well described.
📖 Catalog: $2.50, CAN/OV

Edgewood Farm & Nursery
1186 Middle River Road
Stanardsville, VA 22973-9405
Norman Schwartz
(804) 985-3782
Fax: (804) 985-6904

Plants
Offers a huge selection of **herbs and perennials**, including many catmints, origanums, germanders, thymes, salvias and about 30 old cultivars of dianthus. They grow 700 varieties of herbs and 1,500 perennials and a good number of **species iris**; send your "wish list." No shipping to AZ, CA, OR or WA. Run a Bed & Breakfast at same location in a 1790 Colonial house. (1987)
📖 Catalog: $3d, CC, SS:3-5,9-10, $15m, bn
✪ Nursery: March-October, Th-Sa, Su pm
❀ Garden: April-June, Th-Sa, Su pm

Edible Landscaping
P.O. Box 77
361 Spirit Ridge Lane
Afton, VA 22920
Michael McConkey
(804) 361-9134, (800) 524-4156
Fax: (804) 361-1916
E-mail: el@cstone.net
Web: www.eat-it.com

Plants
A selection of **fruit for Mid-Atlantic gardens**, including Actinidia arguta (hardy kiwi), figs, black currants, several gooseberries, Oriental persimmons, mulberries, jujube, pawpaw, citrus, bush cherries, plums, pears and more; most plants are well described, many shown in color photographs. (1980)
📖 Catalog: $2, CAN/OV, CC, $10m, cn/bn
✪ Nursery: All year, daily
✿ Garden: Orchard, daily

Edmunds' Roses
6235 S.W. Kahle Road
Wilsonville, OR 97070-9799
Philip & Kathy Edmunds
(503) 682-1476, (888) 481-7673
Fax: (503) 682-1275
E-mail: edmdsroses@aol.com
Web: www.edmundsroses.com

Plants ∽ Supplies
An informative color catalog offers a broad selection of modern hybrid tea, floribunda, grandiflora and climbing **roses**, all well described with cultural suggestions. They also offer goatskin gloves and Felco pruning shears. (1950)
📖 Catalog: Free, CAN, CC, SS:11-5
✪ Nursery: All year, M-F
✿ Garden: September, M-F, call ahead

Elixir Farm Botanicals, LLC
General Delivery
Brixey, MO 65618
Lavinia McKinney
(417) 261-2393
Fax: (417) 261-2355
E-mail: efb@aristotle.net
Web: http://trine.com/GardenNet/ElixirFarm/efb.htm

Plants ∽ Seeds ∽ Books
Offers seeds of **herbs** used in traditional Oriental herbal medicine: most are shown in color photographs, with the Chinese characters given for many names as well. Each plant well described. They sell plants of a few herbs, as well as books on medicinal herbs. (1989)
📖 Catalog: $2d, CAN/OV, CC, SS:4-5,9-10, $10m, bn/cn

Elk Mountain Nursery
142 Webb Cove Road
Asheville, NC 28804
Craig Mailloux
(704) 251-9622
E-mail: elkmountain@circle.net
Web: www.circle.net/elkmountain

Plants ∽ Books
An up-and-coming new nursery offering **shade, groundcover and woodland** plants of the Southeast; a good selection, each plant very well described, with some information on best planting location. Also offer some books on wildflowers and native plants. No shipping to AK, AZ, CA, OR, WA or HI. (1991)
📖 Catalog: $2, CC, SS:4-10, $15m

Ellison Horticultural Pty., Ltd.
P.O. Box 365
300 Greenwell Point Road (Worrigee)
Nowra, NSW, Australia 2541
R. & D. Lebrocque, Don Ellison
61 (0) 4421-4255, 4421-6670
Fax: 61 (0) 4423-0859

Seeds
Bulk suppliers of **Australian tree, shrub and palm seed**, a very broad selection, including some plants from other parts of the world, with very brief plant descriptions; many are shown in color. Good selection of **passion flowers**, among other plants. Smallest packet seems to be 25 grams. (1983)
📖 Catalog: $5(US Bills), R&W, OV, CC, $30m, bn/cn
✪ Nursery: All year, M-F
✿ Garden: By appointment only

Englearth Gardens
2461 - 22nd Street
Hopkins, MI 49328
Ken & Mary Englearth Herrema
(616) 793-7196

Plants
Specializes in **daylilies and hostas** -- and offers a good selection. Also sells collections of hostas and daylilies, and iris for naturalizing. Each plant is briefly described. (1931)
📖 Catalog: $1d, R&W, CAN, CC, SS:4-10, $20m
✪ Nursery: April-October, Tu-Sa
✿ Garden: July, M-Sa

Ensata Gardens
9823 E. Michigan Avenue
Galesburg, MI 49053
John Coble & Bob Bauer
(616) 665-7500
Fax: (616) 665-7500
E-mail: ensata@aol.com

Plants
Small nursery specializing in **Japanese and Siberian iris**. They have a very broad selection of Japanese iris, smaller selection of Siberian iris; all plants are well described, and some shown in color. Also have a Japanese garden display area, for those lucky enough to be close by. (1985)
📖 Catalog: $2($3 OV), R&W, CAN/OV, CC, SS:5-10, $10m
✿ Garden: June-July, daily, call ahead

Epi World
10607 Glenview Avenue
Cupertino, CA 95014-4514
Jim Pence
(408) 865-0566
Fax: (408) 996-7454
E-mail: epijim@aol.com

Plants
Offers a nice selection of **epiphyllums, schlumbergera,** known respectively as orchid cactus and christmas cactus; each plant well described. Also offers some starter collections. (1989)
- Catalog: $2, R&W, CC, SS:4-11, $15m
- Nursery: All year, by appointment only
- Garden: April-May, by appointment only

Ericaceae
P.O. Box 293
Deep River, CT 06417-0293
Mathias C. Zack
(860) 526-5100

Plants
A small nursery which specializes in the hardy **rhododendron** hybrids of David Leach; offers about twenty cultivars, all well described, and several cultivars of **heather** and **kalmia** which like the same growing conditions.
- Catalog: Free, SS:9-6
- Nursery: By appointment only
- Garden: Spring, by appointment only

Erikson's Daylily Gardens
24642- 51 Avenue
Langley, BC, Canada V2Z 1H9
Pam Erikson
(604) 856-5758, 856-0716
Fax: (604) 530-5786
E-mail: pam_erikson@mindlink.bc.ca

Plants
Offers a broad selection of **daylilies,** including their own introductions; plants briefly but well described, with mention of the awards they have won.
- Catalog: $2($4 OV), R&W, CAN/OV, SS:4-9
- Nursery: March-August, by appointment only
- Garden: July, by appointment only

Euroseeds
P.O. Box 95
Novy Jicin, Czech Republic 741 01
Mojmir Pavelka

Seeds
The opening of Eastern Europe has brought us new seed sources; Euroseeds specializes in rare **alpine and rock garden plants** from Romania, Bulgaria, Turkey, Slovenia and other parts of Europe. Campanulas, daphnes, gentians, flax, primulas on a list with brief plant descriptions. (1991)
- Catalog: $2(US Bills), R&W, OV, bn
- Nursery: October-June, daily, by appointment only

Murray Evans Daffodils

See Oregon Trail Daffodils.

Evergreen Gardenworks
P.O. Box 1357
430 North Oak Street
Ukiah, CA 95482
Susan Meier
(707) 462-8909
E-mail: bonsai@pacific.net
Web: www.pacific.net/~bonsai

Plants
A small nursery which specializes in **bonsai, dwarf shrubs** and **alpines,** A good selection: species and Japanese maples, hornbeams, many flowering quinces and crabs, cotoneaster, conifers, flowering cherries and elms. No shipping to HI or AK, some restrictions to Southern states. (1989)
- Catalog: $3, CC, bn/cn
- Nursery: March-November, Th-Su, call ahead
- Garden: April-September, call ahead

Evergreen Y. H. Enterprises
P.O. Box 17538
Anaheim, CA 92817-7538
Wen Hwang
(714) 637-5769
Fax: (714) 637-5769
E-mail: wshwang@aol.com

Seeds ✍ **Books** ✍ **Supplies**
Offers a broad selection of **Oriental vegetables,** even that cute "baby corn!" Varieties listed in English and Chinese and well described. Sells Oriental gardening and cookbooks and seasonings. (1978)
- Catalog: $2d($3 OV or 6 IRC), R&W, CAN/OV, $10m

Exotica Rare Fruit Nursery
P.O. Box 160
2508-B East Vista Way
Vista, CA 92085
Steve Spangler
(760) 724-9093, 724-9393
Fax: (760) 724-7724

Plants
Offers **tropical fruits and flowering trees and nuts,** Hawaiian ornamentals, palms and Mexican and South American fruit -- all for southern climates. Listed are bananas, figs, sapotes, cherimoyas, low-chill apples and palms. They also do consultation on edible landscaping. (1975)
- Catalog: Long SASE($2 OV), R&W, OV, $25, cn/bn
- Nursery: All year, daily, call ahead
- Garden: March-November, call ahead

Fairweather Gardens
P. O. Box 330
Greenwich, NJ 08323
Robert Popham & Robert Hoffman
(609) 451-6261
Fax: (609) 451-0303

Plants
I have grown to love **viburnums**, and this nursery has a very good selection. They offer a fine selection of **ornamental trees and shrubs**, many are new or recent introductions, including camellias, hollies, magnolias and oaks. The catalog is very informative. No shipping west of the Rockies. (1989)
📖 Catalog: $3, CC, SS:9-11,3-4, bn/cn

Fancy Fronds
P.O. Box 1090
Gold Bar, WA 98251-1090
Judith I. Jones
(360) 793-1472

Plants
A good selection of **hardy ferns**, including ferns from England, China, Japan and New Zealand and other temperate areas, all very well described and some illustrated with line drawings -- special requests invited. (1976)
📖 Catalog: $2d, SS:3-6,9-10, $20m, bn/cn
☀ Nursery: By appointment only
❀ Garden: May-October, by appointment only

Fantastic Plants
5865 Steeplechase Drive
Bartlett, TN 38134-5509
Mark D. Pitts
(901) 377-1912, (800) 967-1912
Fax: (901) 372-6818

Plants
Offering **Japanese maples** and many unusual **trees and shrubs**, including dogwoods, magnolias, witch hazels, weeping kadsura and contorted hazelnut. Also a few perennials, ornamental grasses and hardy ferns. Plants are well described. (1992)
📖 Catalog: $3d, CAN, CC, bn/cn
❀ Garden: By appointment only

Far West Bulb Farm
P.O. Box 515
Oregon House, CA 95962
Ames & Nancy Gilbert
(916) 692-2565
Fax: (916) 692-2565

Seeds ∽ Bulbs
Offering seeds and bulbs of nursery-grown **California native bulbs**, this small nursery has a selection of **calochortus, fritillarias, some lilies** and more. Plants are well described, and location of the original seed parent is given.
📖 Catalog: Long SASE, CAN/OV, SS:9, $25m, bn/cn

Feathers Wild Flower Seeds
P.O. Box 13
Constantia, Western Cape, South Africa 7848
Rene & Alan Jeftha
27 (0) 21 794-6432
Fax: 27 (0) 21 21-7207
E-mail: alan@mallinicks.co.za

Seeds
Offering a good selection of **proteas, leucospermums, leucodendrons** and seeds of a few other South African shrubs; very brief descriptions. (1958)
📖 Catalog: $3, OV, $30m, bn
☀ Nursery: All year, M-F, call ahead
❀ Garden: August-November, by appointment only

Fedco Seeds & Moose Tubers
P.O. Box 520
Waterville, ME 04903-0520
Cooperative

Plants ∽ Seeds ∽ Books ∽ Supplies ∽ Bulbs
Seeds of **short-season vegetables, potatoes and other tubers, herbs, annual and perennial flowers.** An extensive list with each variety well described; they keep costs down by encouraging group orders. They also sell **hardy fruit and nut trees, berries and fruiting shrubs** in the "Fedco Trees" list -- and some supplies and books on gardening. No shipping to CA, AZ or HI. (1978)
📖 Catalog: $2, R&W, SS:4,10

Fern Hill Farm
P.O. Box 185
Clarksboro, NJ 08020-0185
John F. Gyer

Seeds
Sells only **'Dr. Martin' Pole Lima Bean** seed; there's no description of this particular variety, but it must be heavy bearing and something special. (1971)
📖 Catalog: Long SASE, CAN, $5m

Ferncliff Gardens
8394 McTaggart St.
Mission, BC, Canada V2V 6S6
David Jack
(604) 826-2447
Fax: (604) 826-4316

Plants
David Jack hybridizes "giant" **dahlias**, and introduces new varieties each year; in addition, he offers **herbaceous peonies, daylilies, gladiolus** and **tall and dwarf bearded iris**, each briefly described. Ships only dahlias to the US. (1920)
📖 Catalog: $2d, US, CC, SS:3-10, $25m
☀ Nursery: March-September, M-Sa; October-Feb., M-F
❀ Garden: August-September, daily

Ferry-Morse Seeds
P.O. Box 488
Fulton, KY 42041-0488
Jack Simpson, Pres.
(800) 283-3400
Fax: (800) 283-2700
E-mail: advasee@apex.net
Web: www.trine.com/GardenNet/FerryMorse

Plants   Seeds   Supplies   Bulbs
One of America's oldest seed companies, Ferry-Morse has recently started selling seeds by mail. A color catalog shows many of their offerings of garden **flowers and vegetables**; another catalog offers **spring bulbs**. Both catalogs offer gift items featuring old seed packet designs. (1856)
- Catalog: Free, R&W, CAN, CC, cn

Field & Forest Products, Inc.
N3296 Kuzuzek Road
Peshtigo, WI 54157
Joseph H. Krawczyk & Mary Ellen Kozak
(715) 582-4997, (800) 792-6220
Fax: (715) 582-0181
E-mail: ffp@mrnet.com

Seeds   Books   Supplies   Tools
Small company selling **shiitake mushroom spawn** (eleven strains for growing under various temperatures and conditions), **oyster mushroom spawn** and complete growing supplies, books and tools. Informative catalog; they also sell their own books on mushroom growing and some cookbooks. (1983)
- Catalog: $2d, R&W, CAN/OV, CC
- Garden: By appointment only

Field House Alpines
Leake Road, Gotham
Nottingham, England NG11 0JN
Doug Lochhead & Val Woolley
44 (0) 1159 830-278

Seeds
Field House Alpines is a well-known British nursery specializing in seed of **alpine and rock garden plants** and **show auriculas and primulas**; a good selection with brief plant descriptions. Includes many color forms of **lewisia** and some **native plants of Iceland**. (1940)
- Catalog: 5 IRC, OV, CC, $32m, bn
- Nursery: All year, F-W, call ahead
- Garden: April-May, by appointment only

Henry Field Seed & Nursery Co.
415 North Burnett
Shenandoah, IA 51602
Don Kruml
(605) 665-9391
Fax: (605) 665-2601

Plants   Seeds   Supplies   Tools
A true **garden emporium**: vegetable and flower seeds, fruit and nut trees, grapes, berries, roses, ornamental flowering trees, shrubs and vines and growing supplies and tools. Field has been purchased by Gurney's, but still publishes a separate catalog; orders taken and shipped by Gurney's. (1892)
- Catalog: Free, CC, SS:2-6,9-11

Fieldstone Gardens, Inc.
620 Quaker Lane
Vassalboro, ME 04989-9713
Steven D. Jones
(207) 923-3836
Fax: (207) 923-3836
E-mail: fsgarden@pivot.net
Web: FieldstoneGardens.com

Plants
Extensive list of **perennials and rock garden plants**: Siberian iris, asters, astilbe, campanulas, clematis, delphiniums, epimediums, hardy geraniums, herbaceous peonies, phlox and much more. Plants are well described, with cultural suggestions. Beautiful old farm and garden. (1981)
- Catalog: $2($3 OV), CAN/OV, CC, SS:4-6,9-11, bn/cn
- Nursery: April-November, Tu-Su
- Garden: May-October, Tu-Su

The Fig Tree Nursery
P.O. Box 124
Gulf Hammock, FL 32639
Gertrude Watson
(904) 486-2930

Plants   Books
Offers a variety of **fig trees**, as well as **pears, muscadine grapes, mulberries and pomegranates**, each well but briefly described. Also sells her own book on "Growing Fruit Trees and Vines," ($2.80 ppd). Can't ship plants to AZ or CA.
- Catalog: $1d, SS:10-3, $10m
- Nursery: M-Sa, call ahead

Filaree Farm
182 Conconully Highway
Okanogan, WA 98840
Watershine Engeland
(509) 422-6940

Plants   Seeds   Supplies
Offers a huge selection of **garlic** varieties, organically grown and fondly described, as well as green manure crops, growing supplies for garlic growers, garlic tee shirts and gifts, and Ron Engeland's book "Growing Great Garlic: the Definitive Guide for Organic Gardeners and Small Farmers." (1977)
- Catalog: $2, R&W, CC, SS:9-11,2-3, $8m
- Nursery: By appointment only
- Garden: By appointment only

Finch Blueberry Nursery
P.O. Box 699
Bailey, NC 27807
Daniel Finch
(919) 235-4664, (800) 245-4662
Fax: (919) 235-2411

Plants
Offers a nice selection of northern highbush, southern highbush and rabbit-eye **blueberries**, each variety well described. Flyer gives good information on blueberry culture; they sell mixed selections for cross-pollination and long bearing season. Prices are "wholesale to the public."
📖 Catalog: Free, CAN/OV, CC, SS:10-5
✪ Nursery: All year, M-F

A Fleur D'Eau
140 Route 202
Stanbridge-East, PQ, Canada J0J 2H0
Danielle Bilodeau & Robert Lapalme
(514) 248-7008
Fax: (514) 248-4623
E-mail: fleurdo@acces-cible.net
Web: jardins.versicolores.ca/fleurdo

Plants 🔊 Books 🔊 Supplies
Offers **water plants** and supplies for your pond or container water garden, fish, and books in English and French. Catalog is very informative, with plants and products well described. Catalog available in English or French. (1987)
📖 Catalog: $4, R&W, US, CC, SS:5-9, $50m, bn/cn
✪ Nursery: April-October, call ahead
❀ Garden: June-September, call ahead

Flickingers' Nursery
P.O. Box 245
Sagamore, PA 16250-0245
Richard Flickinger
(800) 368-7381
Fax: (412) 783-6528

Plants
A wholesaler of **seedling trees** -- the same price to everyone, but a minimum of fifty trees of one variety. A nice selection of spruces, pines and firs, also Carolina hemlocks, birch and dogwood. Also sells Vinca minor. No shipping to AK, CA, or HI. (1947)
📖 Catalog: Free, R&W, CAN, CC, SS:3-4, $50m
✪ Nursery: All year, M-Sa

Florabunda Seeds
641 Rainbow Road
Salt Spring Island, BC, Canada V8K 2M7
Wendy Montana

Seeds
Offers seeds of "**cottage garden, historic, and wild flowers,**" plants are listed by their traditional common names, but botanical names are given; each plant is very well described. A nice selection, with symbols to show which plants are for cutting, or attract hummingbirds or butterflies. (1994)
📖 Catalog: $2d(4 IRC), US/OV, cn/bn

Florida Colors Nursery
23740 S.W. 147th Avenue
Homestead, FL 33032
Luc & Carol Vannoorbeeck
(305) 258-1086
Fax: (305) 258-6317

Plants
Offers a good selection of grafted hybrid **hibiscus**; plants are listed by cultivar name with information on size and color of flower. They also sell 40 kinds of **plumeria** and 9 kind of **guavas**. No shipping to AZ or CA. (1977)
📖 Catalog: Free, CAN/OV, $8m
✪ Nursery: All year, M-F
❀ Garden: April-December, M-Sa

Earth's crammed with Heaven & every common bush aflame with God.

Florida Mycology Research Center
P.O. Box 8104
Pensacola, FL 32505
Stephen L. Peele, Curator
(904) 327-4378
E-mail: 72253.1553@compuserve.com

Seeds ฌ Supplies
Stephen Peele seems to be a true mushroom-wonk, he is interested in all phases of **mushroom** research and cultivation, edits "The Mushroom Culture," a periodic journal, and offers mushroom spore and growing supplies. He also writes and publishes treatises on mushrooms. You can arrange a special mushroom hunt by appointment: $100. (1972)
  📖 Catalog: $10d($13 OV), R&W, CAN/OV, bn
  ❀ Garden: Summer, by appointment only

Flower Scent Gardens
14820 Moine Road
Doylestown, OH 44230-9744
Glenn E. Varner
(330) 658-5946

Plants ฌ Seeds
Offers **fragrant plants**: carnations and pinks, phlox, daylilies, lavenders and rosemarys, some violets, the "chocolate" cosmos, scented geraniums, and various fragrant vines and shrubs such as philadelphus. Each plant is very well described. The seed list is separate and costs $1($2 OV). They only ship seeds to Canada and overseas. (1994)
  📖 Catalog: $2d, CAN/OV, SS:4-10, cn/bn
  ❍ Nursery: May-October, M-Sa, call ahead

Flowers & Greens
P.O. Box 1802
Davis, CA 95617
Roy M. Sachs
(916) 756-9238
Fax: (916) 756-9238
E-mail: rmsachs@ucdavis.edu

Plants ฌ Bulbs
Flowers & Greens has set itself the task of developing improved **alstroemerias**; available by color or in mixes, some species as well; cultural information sent with the order. Great cut flowers. (1990)
  📖 Catalog: $2d($2.50 OV), R&W, CAN/OV, $15m
  ❍ Nursery: M-F, by appointment only
  ❀ Garden: June-July, by appointment only

Flowery Branch Seed Company
P.O. Box 1330
Flowery Branch, GA 30542
Dean Pailler
(770) 536-8380
Fax: (770) 532-7825
E-mail: seedsman@hotmail.com
Web: www.flowerybranch.com

Seeds
They call the catalog "A Garden of Delights," and it offers just that --a very broad selection of **herbs, perennials, annuals and everlastings** (some available by individual colors). Plants well described in a plump catalog. Many hollyhocks, strawflowers, basils, salvias, as well as some unusual ornamental grasses and foxgloves.
  📖 Catalog: $4($6 OV), R&W, CAN/OV, CC, bn/cn

Floyd Cove Nursery
1050 Enterprise-Osteen Road
Enterprise, FL 32725-9355
Patrick M. Stamile
Fax: (407) 860-0086

Plants
A very broad selection of **daylilies**, many of them the newest, most wanted cultivars, many diploids and tetraploids, as well as their recent introductions and classics. Plants very briefly described, a few are shown in color. (1978)
  📖 Catalog: $2d($4 OV), CAN/OV, CC
  ❍ Nursery: May, W-Su, by appointment only
  ❀ Garden: By appointment only

Foliage Gardens
2003 - 128th Avenue S.E.
Bellevue, WA 98005
Sue & Harry Olsen
(206) 747-2998
E-mail: FoliageG@juno.com

Plants
A very good selection of **ferns, both hardy and for greenhouses**, listed by botanical name with good plant descriptions. All plants grown from spore; new varieties added all the time. Harry is grafting Japanese maples, and offers a nice selection, along with a few other ornamental flowering trees. (1976)
  📖 Catalog: $2, CAN, SS:5-6,9-11, $15m, bn
  ❍ Nursery: All year, by appointment only
  ❀ Garden: May-October, by appointment only

Foothill Cottage Gardens
13925 Sontag Road
Grass Valley, CA 95945
Carolyn Singer
(916) 272-4362

Plants
Located in the Sierra foothills, this nursery offers tough **perennials** which can tolerate drought and the informative catalog notes which plants the deer (there, anyway) won't touch. A nice selection, including dianthus, achilleas, thymes, asters, herbs and daylilies. Gardening classes at the nursery. (1980)
  📖 Catalog: $3, SS:3-6,9-11, $4m, bn
  ❍ Nursery: Feb.-Nov., Tu,Th,Sa or by appointment
  ❀ Garden: April-October, Tu,Th,Sa

Forest Seeds of California
1100 Indian Hill Road
Placerville, CA 95667
Bob Graton
(916) 621-1551
Fax: (916) 621-1040

Seeds
A California Registered Professional Forester who collects and sells seed of various **western conifers**; the geographical source of his seed is given for each selection: firs, incense cedar, cypress, sequoias, pines and spruce, as well as some native hardwood trees and shrubs including oaks. Bob collects seed of a few non-native trees also. (1988)
📖 Catalog: $1, R&W, CAN/OV, $10m, bn/cn

Forestfarm
990 Tetherow Road
Williams, OR 97544-9599
Ray & Peg Prag
(541) 846-7269
Fax: (541) 846-6963
E-mail: forestfarm@a1pro.net

Plants
A collectors' list of many interesting **Western natives, garden perennials** and **trees and shrubs**. 2,000+ small plants at reasonable prices, some quite unusual; each plant well described. Also sells hardy eucalyptus, bee plants, conifers, species roses, woodland plants and much more -- a curl-up-with catalog! Starting to offer larger plants by popular request. This nursery has a model catalog and a fantastic selection. No shipping to HI. (1974)
📖 Catalog: $4, CAN, CC, SS:W, bn/cn
✪ Nursery: All year, Th,F, Su, call ahead

Four Winds Growers
P.O. Box 3538
Fremont, CA 94539
Donald F. Dillon
(510) 656-2591
Fax: (510) 656-1360
Web: www.mother.com/fourwinds

Plants
Specializes in **dwarf citrus**: oranges, tangerines, mandarin oranges, limes, grapefruit, lemons, tangelos and kumquats -- 30 varieties in all. These are true dwarf trees, growing to only eight feet; informative leaflet tells how to grow them. Cannot ship to AZ, FL or TX. (1954)
📖 Catalog: Long SASE, R&W, CC, SS:3-10
✪ Nursery: All year, M-F

Fox Hill Nursery
347 Lunt Road
Freeport, ME 04032
Eric & Jennifer Welzel
(207) 729-1511
Fax: (207) 729-6108
E-mail: foxhilnrsy@aol.com
Web: javanet.com/~foxhill/

Plants ✺ Supplies
Offering a good selection of hardy **lilacs** grown on their own roots, each variety very well described with general cultural suggestions. They have added some deciduous azaleas, shrub roses and a few hydrangeas. Also sells seaweed fertilizers. No shipping to HI. (1986)
📖 Catalog: Free, R&W, CC, SS:4-5,9-10, $20m, bn
✪ Nursery: April-November, daily, call ahead
❀ Garden: May-June, daily, call ahead

Fox Hollow Seed Company
P.O. Box 588
Kittanning, PA 16201
Charles Glendening & John Van Sicklin
(412) 548-7333
Fax: (412) 548-7333

Seeds
Small seed company offers open-pollinated varieties of **herbs** and **vegetables**, as well as some old-fashioned garden flowers. All plants are well described. (1987)
📖 Catalog: Free, CAN, CC, cn/bn

The Fragrant Path
P.O. Box 328
Ft. Calhoun, NE 68023
E. R. Rasmussen

Seeds
Catalog is devoted to seeds of **fragrant, rare and old-fashioned plants** of all kinds, with irresistible descriptions, literary quotations and charming sketches. A wide selection of annuals, perennials, herbs and even vines and shrubs; can you live without trying "Kiss-me-over-the-garden-gate?" Cottage gardeners beware! (1982)
📖 Catalog: $2, CAN, $5m, bn/cn

Fraser's Thimble Farm
175 Arbutus Road
Salt Spring Island, BC, Canada V8K 1A3
Richard & Nancy Fraser
(250) 537-5788
Fax: (250) 537-5788
E-mail: thimble@saltspring.com

Plants ✺ Bulbs
A broad selection of **native plants of the Pacific Northwest**, including trees, shrubs, perennials and bulbs, as well as many plants from other places. An especially good listing of **ferns, terrestrial orchids, trilliums and arisaemas**. All plants well described. They also issue a bulb list in the fall and a "collector's" list in winter ($2 each for a three year subscription). For US customers there is a $100 minimum order, but with the selection, that should be easy! (1987)
📖 Catalog: $2d, R&W, CAN/OV, CC, SS:9-4, $25m, bn/cn
✪ Nursery: All year, daily

Fred's Plant Farm
4589 Ralston Road
Martin, TN 38237
Katie McMinn
(800) 550-2575

Plants
Sells only **sweet potato plants**, but eight different kinds, offered in quantities from 50 to 10,00 plants. Cannot ship to CA. (1947)
- Catalog: Free, R&W, CC, SS:4-7, $15m
- Nursery: April-July, September-November, M-Sa, call ahead
- Garden: Spring, Fall, call ahead

French's Bulb Importer
P.O. Box 565
Pittsfield, VT 05762-0565
Howard French
(802) 746-8148, (800) 286-8198
Fax: (802) 746-7940

Bulbs
Offer a good selection of **spring-blooming bulbs** - hyacinths, freesias, tulips, narcissus, anemones, ranunculus and more. Also offers "pre-cooled bulbs for indoor forcing," for those who want extra early flowers, as well as some annual seeds for greenhouse growing and a few autumn blooming **crocus**. (1943)
- Catalog: Free, CC, SS:8-12, $10m
- Nursery: All year, M-Sa

Freshops
36180 Kings Valley Highway
Philomath, OR 97370
Dave Wills
(541) 929-2736
Fax: (541) 929-2702
Web: www.freshops.com

Plants
Here's a specialist! Dave sells fourteen varieties of female **hop rhizomes**: why female -- because only female plants produce the flowers used in brewing. Each variety is described for growth habit and bitterness. No shipping to WA, New Zealand or Mexico. (1982)
- Catalog: Free($1 OV), R&W, CAN/OV, CC, SS:3-5, $6m

Freshwater Farms
5851 Myrtle Avenue
Eureka, CA 95503
Rick Storre
(707) 444-8261, (800) 200-8969
Fax: (707) 442-2490
E-mail: rstorre@worldnet.att.net
Web: www.freshwaterfarms.com

Plants 🙵 Seeds
This nursery collects a very broad range of seeds of **wetland plants** for revegetation, and offers plants of many of these. All are **California natives** -- included are many grasses and sedges, shrubs, trees and perennials. Many of the plants are available in small sizes; seeds are available by the ounce or pound. No plant descriptions.
- Catalog: Free, R&W, CAN/OV, CC, bn/cn
- Nursery: All year, M-Sa
- Garden: Call ahead

Frey's Dahlias
12054 Brick Road
Turner, OR 97392
Sharon Frey
(503) 743-3910
Web: www.gardeners-advantage.com

Plants
The Freys offer a nice selection of older varieties of **dahlia** and some dahlia collections by type. All cultivars are very briefly described. (1993)
- Catalog: Free, R&W, CAN/OV, CC, SS:3-5
- Nursery: March-October, M-Sa, call ahead
- Garden: August-October, call ahead

Friendship Gardens
341 Schwartz Road
Gettysburg, PA 17325
Joan & Ken Roberts

Plants
This nursery specializes in **reblooming iris**, and offers tall bearded, dwarf bearded, miniature tall bearded, and median bearded iris. Each plant is very well described, most are fairly recent introductions. (1991)
- Catalog: $2($4 OV), CAN/OV, SS:7-9, $10
- Garden: By appointment only

Frosty Hollow Ecological Restoration
P.O. Box 53
Langley, WA 98260
Marianne Edain & Steve Erickson
(360) 579-2332
Fax: (360) 579-6456
E-mail: hed@whidbey.com

Seeds
Small company does habitat collection of pre-ordered seeds; they offer a wide variety of **Northwestern native plants** for which they collect seed -- wildflowers, ornamental trees and shrubs and conifers. Will collect to order; also consult on landscape restoration and permaculture design. (1982)
- Catalog: Long SASE($1 OV), R&W, CAN/OV, $20m, bn/cn

Fruit Spirit Botanical Gardens
Dunoon Road
Dorroughby, NSW, Australia 2480
Paul Recher
61 (0) 66 895-192

Seeds
Here's something different: seeds of **exotic fruits and nuts**, more than 160 species, some collected fresh at a botanical garden which specializes in tropical plants. Also **Australian native plants, palms and ornamentals**. Seeds available in "home packs" and larger quantities; will also trade seed.
- Catalog: $2(US Bills), R&W, OV, A$20m, bn
- Nursery: All year, by appointment only
- Garden: All year, by appointment only

Fun Guy Farm
R.R. #1
Goodwood, ON, Canada L0C 1A0
Bruno Pretto & Paula Vopni
(416) 963-5520
Fax: (905) 642-3016
E-mail: bpretto@io.org
Web: www.io.org/~bpretto

Plants ∞ **Books** ∞ **Supplies** ∞ **Tools**
Supplies **mushroom spawn** for shiitake, oysters and kombucha, along with home growing kits for other species. Also offers equipment for mushroom cultivation, and a great list of books on cultivation, cooking and identification of fungi (fun guy!). (1994)
- Catalog: Free, R&W, US/OV, CC, C$5m
- Nursery: All year, M-F, by appointment only
- Garden: Summer & Fall, by appointment only

Fungi Perfecti
P.O. Box 7634
Olympia, WA 98507-7634
Paul Stamets
(360) 426-9292, (800) 780-9126
Fax: (360) 426-9377
E-mail: mycomedia@aol.com
Web: www.fungi.com

Seeds ∞ **Books** ∞ **Supplies**
Catalog offers **mushroom spawn**, growing kits, supplies and books for the amateur and commercial grower. Varieties include shiitake, oyster, Coprinus comatus and Stropharia rugoso-annulata, and many more. Paul is co-author of "The Mushroom Cultivator," and teaches mushroom seminars. They will send a free brochure if you don't want the full catalog. (1980)
- Catalog: $4.50d($7 OV), R&W, CAN/OV, CC, $26m, bn/cn

G & B Orchid Laboratory, Inc.
2426 Cherimoya Drive
Vista, CA 92084
Barry L. Cohen
(760) 727-2611
Fax: (760) 727-0017
E-mail: cessnapilt@aol.com
Web: www.orchidsource.com

Plants ∞ **Supplies**
Specializes in **phalaenopsis, cymbidium, dendrobium and species orchids** in great variety, each briefly described. Also sells several types of flasking media, laboratory glassware, plastic pots, and a variety of fertilizers and chemicals for orchid hobbyists and hybridizers. (1970)
- Catalog: $1($2 OV), R&W, CAN/OV, CC, $25m
- Nursery: All year, M-Sa
- Garden: February-June, glasshouse, M-Sa

Garden City Seeds
778 Highway 93 North
Hamilton, MT 59840
John Schneeburger & Karen Coombs
(406) 961-4837
Fax: (406) 961-4877
E-mail: gardencity@juno.com

Plants ∞ **Seeds** ∞ **Books** ∞ **Supplies**
Offers heirloom and open-pollinated seeds for short growing seasons: **vegetables, flowers and herbs** and **seed potatoes, garlic, onion sets** and **strawberries**, as well as books, organic pest controls and fertilizers. Catalog is informative, with good information on growing and seed saving.
- Catalog: Free($4 OV), R&W, CAN/OV, CC
- Nursery: All year, M-Sa
- Garden: July-August, by appointment only

Garden of Delights
14560 S.W. 14th Street
Davie, FL 33325-4217
Murray Corman
(954) 370-9004
Fax: (954) 236-4588
E-mail: godelights@aol.com

Plants
Here's a list of **tropical fruits and nuts** so unusual that I've never heard of many of them -- collectors will swoon! A source of plants of sapotes, cherimoyas, cashews, maya breadnut, jelly palm, star apple, governor's plum, ice cream bean and yam bean. Super stuff! (1975)
- Catalog: $2d, R&W, CAN/OV, $60m, bn/cn
- Nursery: All year, daily, by appointment only
- Garden: All year, daily, by appointment only

Garden Perennials
Route 1, Box 164
Wayne, NE 68787-9801
Gail Korn
(402) 375-3615
E-mail: gkorn@bloomnet.com

Plants
Sells a broad selection of **perennials**, including many daylilies; all plants are very well described with cultural symbols and information. Plants are field-grown clumps, most well-suited to thrive in dry conditions. (1981)
- Catalog: $1d, CC, SS:4-10, bn/cn
- Nursery: April-October, daily
- Garden: July, September, daily

Garden Place
P.O. Box 388
6776 Heisley Road
Mentor, OH 44061-0388
John A. Schultz III
Fax: (216) 255-9535

Plants
A very large selection of **perennials**, each well but briefly described. The catalog gives growing tips and has informative tables of plants by color, height, use, exposure, etc. Plants sold singly or in groups of 3 or 12 and shipped bare-root. Selection too broad to describe! (1972)
📖 Catalog: $1, CAN, CC, SS:9-5, $15m, bn/cn

Garden Valley Dahlias
406 Lower Garden Valley Road
Roseburg, OR 97470
Leon V. Olson
(541) 673-8521
Web: server.wizzard.net/bcruger/DAHLIACO.HTM

Plants
A collectors' list of **dahlias**, briefly described as to color and form; some are Leon's hybrids. List changes frequently; many varieties in short supply. (1969)
📖 Catalog: 1 FCS, CAN/OV, SS:4, $2m
✪ Nursery: August-October, daily, call ahead
✸ Garden: August-October, call ahead

Garden Valley Ranch Nursery
498 Pepper Road
Petaluma, CA 94952
Rayford Reddell
(707) 795-0919
Fax: (707) 792-0349
E-mail: bareroot@gardenvalley.com
Web: www.gardenvalley.com

Plants ❧ Books
Offers a very nice selection of **roses**: hybrid teas, floribundas, grandifloras, climbers, and some old fashioned and shrub roses. All plants well described; they also offer rose books, including those by Rayford Reddell and "French garden arches." No shipping to HI. (1989)
📖 Catalog: Free, R&W, CC, SS:1-2, $42m
✪ Nursery: All year, W-Su
✸ Garden: May-November, W-Su

Garden Vision
63 Williamsville Road
Hubbardston, MA 01452-1315
Darrell R. Probst
(508) 928-4808

Plants
Delight in the shade garden! This new nursery offers only **epimediums**, over 40 species and varieties, many only recently collected by botanical expeditions. New kinds being added all the time. No shipping to HI.
📖 Catalog: Long SASE, CAN, SS:8-9

Gardenimport, Inc.
P.O. Box 760
Thornhill, ON, Canada L3T 4A5
Dugald Cameron, Pres.
(905) 731-1950
Fax: (905) 881-3499
E-mail: flower@gardenimport.com
Web: www.gardenimport.com

Plants ❧ Seeds ❧ Bulbs
Issue two catalogs a year: the spring catalog lists **plants, summer flowering bulbs**, and **flower and vegetable seeds** from Suttons in England. The fall catalog lists **spring flowering bulbs**. Most plants and bulbs are illustrated in color, and are well described. (1982)
📖 Catalog: $5d, R&W, US, CC, SS:5-10, bn/cn
✪ Nursery: All year, M-Sa

Gardens North
5984 Third Line Road North
North Gower, ON, Canada K0A 2T0
Kristl Walek
(613) 489-0065
Fax: (613) 489-0065
E-mail: garnorth@istar.ca

Seeds ❧ Books
A Canadian seed company offering a very good selection of **perennials** and **ornamental grasses**, primarily species and stable hybrids and varieties; most are hardy to USDA zone 4. Good plant descriptions and growing information. Also offers a nice selection of books on perennials. (1991)
📖 Catalog: $4($5 OV), R&W, US/OV, CC, bn
✪ Nursery: May-July, Th-Su, call ahead
✸ Garden: May-July, Th-Su, call ahead

Gardens of the Blue Ridge
P.O. Box 10
9056 Pittman Gap Road
Pineola, NC 28662
Fletcher Family
(704) 733-2417
Fax: (704) 733-8894

Plants ❧ Books
Catalog lists a good selection of **wildflowers, ferns, native orchids** and **native trees and shrubs**, all well described and some illustrated in color photos. Many are hard-to-find Southeastern native plants; all are nursery-propagated. Great-grandsons of the founder have taken over. (1892)
📖 Catalog: $3d, CAN/OV, CC, SS:3-10, $25m, bn/cn
✪ Nursery: All year, M-Sa am, call ahead
✸ Garden: May-June, M-Sa am, call ahead

Geraniaceae
122 Hillcrest Avenue
Kentfield, CA 94904
Robin Parer
(415) 461-4168
Fax: (415) 461-7209

Plants
Specializing in **hardy geraniums**, and their close relatives, this small nursery has an extensive list of geraniums for the border and rock garden, as well as scented geraniums, species pelargoniums, and "angel" and "pansy face" pelargoniums. Plants are well described, quantities may be limited.
- 📖 Catalog: $4, R&W, SS:4-10, bn
- ✪ Nursery: By appointment only
- ✸ Garden: April-June, by appointment only

Girard Nurseries
P.O. Box 428
6839 North Ridge East, Route 20
Geneva, OH 44041-0428
Peter Girard, Jr.
(216) 466-2881
Fax: (216) 466-3999

Plants ✣ **Seeds**
Color catalog offers a selection of **rhododendrons and azaleas**: their own Girard Evergreen and Deciduous azaleas as well as some native species azaleas. Also offered are their own rhododendron hybrids and some other selected varieties. They carry a good selection of **conifers, flowering trees and shrubs, holly**, six cultivars of **ginkgo** and seeds of trees, shrubs and conifers. Cannot ship to CA or HI. (1946)
- 📖 Catalog: Free, R&W, CC, SS:3-6,9-11, $20m
- ✪ Nursery: March-May, July-December, daily
- ✸ Garden: May-October, daily

Glasshouse Works
P.O. Box 97, Church Street
Stewart, OH 45778-0097
Tom Winn & Ken Frieling
(614) 662-2142, (800) 837-2142
Fax: (614) 662-2120
E-mail: plants@glasshouseworks.com
Web: www.glasshouseworks.com

Plants ✣ **Books**
A very extensive list of **exotic and tropical plants**, and more -- a list to thrill the collector with a greenhouse or tropical climate. Among the many: ferns, gingers, bromeliads, succulents, aroids, jasmines, passion flowers and ivies, all briefly described. Specialty is **variegated plants** of all kinds and plants for tropical indoor bonsai. Nice selection of books, also. (1973)
- 📖 Catalog: $2($5 OV), CAN/OV, CC, SS:4-12, $10m, bn/cn
- ✪ Nursery: All year, F-Sa
- ✸ Garden: Spring-Fall, F-Sa

Going Bananas
24401 S.W. 197 Avenue
Homestead, FL 33031
Don & Katie Chafin
(305) 247-0397
Fax: (305) 247-7877

Plants
Catalog lists over 40 varieties of **bananas** -- even more sold at the nursery. Some available as corms or plants, each variety is very well described. They all sound delicious! No shipping to CA. (1978)
- 📖 Catalog: Long SASE w/$1($2 OV), OV
- ✪ Nursery: All year, M-Sa, call ahead
- ✸ Garden: April-October, M-Sa, call ahead

Golden Lake Greenhouses
10782 Citrus Drive
Moorpark, CA 93021-3735
Paula & Gregg Lake

Plants ✣ **Books**
Specializes in **bromeliads**, offering a nice selection of tillandsias, aechmeas, billbergias, neoregelias and vrieseas; most with very brief descriptions. Also sells some **hoyas, ceropegias, rhipsalis and epiphyllums**. (1968)
- 📖 Catalog: $2($3 OV), CAN/OV, bn

Good Scents
1308 N. Meridian Road
Meridian, ID 83642
Lisa Doll
(208) 887-1784

Plants
Offers a good selection of **herbs**, including some not found in every herb list. Plants are briefly to well described. (1992)
- 📖 Catalog: $1, R&W, CAN, CC, SS:3-9, cn/bn
- ✪ Nursery: All year, M-Sa
- ✸ Garden: April-September, M-Sa

Goodness Grows
P.O. Box 311
Highway 77 North
Lexington, GA 30648
Marc Richardson & Richard Berry
(706) 743-5055
Fax: (706) 743-5112

Plants
Specializes in **perennials and Southeastern native plants**, offering a very good selection for all sorts of garden conditions; all plants are well described with cultural suggestions. All orders by credit card; they close on December 22nd, and reopen in March. (1977)
- 📖 Catalog: Free, CC, SS:3-5,9-11, bn/cn
- ✪ Nursery: March-December, M-Sa
- ✸ Garden: March-November, M-Sa

Goodwin Creek Gardens
P.O. Box 83
Williams, OR 97544
Jim & Dotti Becker
(541) 846-7357
Fax: (541) 846-7357

Plants 🔊 Seeds 🔊 Books
Sells plants and seeds of **everlasting annual and perennial flowers, herbs and wildflowers**. A good selection; plants are well but briefly described. Also sell their book, "An Everlasting Garden" with illustrations and instructions on growing and drying many plants. Will ship seeds to Canada. (1978)
📖 Catalog: $1($2 OV), CAN, CC, SS:W, bn/cn

Gossler Farms Nursery
1200 Weaver Road
Springfield, OR 97478-9691
Marjory, Roger & Eric Gossler
(541) 746-3922
Fax: (541) 744-7924

Plants 🔊 Books
A very large selection of **magnolias**, each well described. Also a number of **daphnes, stewartias, franklinia, hamamelis, kalmias, beeches, viburnums** and other unusual trees and shrubs, even some **perennials** have crept in. All plants well described with cultural suggestions. Collectors of very special trees and shrubs will be delighted! (1968)
📖 Catalog: $2, R&W, CAN, CC, SS:10-12,2-4, bn/cn
⊙ Nursery: All year, by appointment only
❀ Garden: All year, by appointment only

The Gourmet Gardener
8650 College Boulevard
Overland Park, KS 66210
Chris Combest
(913) 345-0490
Fax: (913) 451-2443
Web: www.gourmetgardener.com

Seeds 🔊 Books
The Gourmet gardener specializes in **vegetables from France**, as well as edible flowers, annuals and everlastings, and a selection of books on gardening and cooking. (1989)
📖 Catalog: $2d, CAN/OV, CC, cn/bn

Gourmet Mushrooms
P.O. Box 515
Graton, CA 95444-0515
Jim Peters, Mgr.
(707) 829-7301
Fax: (707) 823-1507
E-mail: gourmet@pon.net
Web: www.arrowweb.com/MUSHROOM

Plants
Another neighbor of Tusker Press, offering **mushroom spawn** for morels, shiitake, hericium and pleurotus mushroom -- several come in already planted pots, the morels are grown in "habitats" which they tell you how to create in your city or country garden. Starting to sell orchids too. No shipping to HI. (1970)
📖 Catalog: Long SASE, CAN, CC, $9m

Graceful Gardens
Box 100
Mecklenburg, NY 14863
Amanda & Mark Shenstone
(607) 387-5529
E-mail: grace@clarityconnect.com
Web: www.gracefulgardens.com

Plants
Perennials, with a good selection of **delphiniums** and **lupines** are offered by this small nursery, along with some annuals for the cottage garden. They also offer some collections, if you want to try a variety of perennials. No shipping to CA or HI.
📖 Catalog: Free, CC, SS:4-9, $20m
⊙ Nursery: By appointment only
❀ Garden: Call ahead

Russell Graham, Purveyor of Plants
4030 Eagle Crest Road N.W.
Salem, OR 97304
Russell & Yvonne Graham
(503) 362-1135

Plants 🔊 Bulbs
A collectors' catalog, offering **species bulbs** like lilies, iris, and hardy cyclamen, as well as hardy ferns, trillium and ornamental grasses; plants well described and sure to tempt plant fanatics. Small nursery, good selection. (1980)
📖 Catalog: $2, R&W, SS:2-4,9-11, $35m, bn/cn
⊙ Nursery: By appointment only
❀ Garden: By appointment only

Gray/Davis Epiphyllums
P.O. Box 710443
Santee, CA 92072-0443
Jean Gray & Michele Davis
(619) 448-2540
Fax: (619) 561-0485

Plants
Jean and Michele started out to preserve old varieties of **epiphyllums**, but found they couldn't resist the new varieties too. They grow over 2,000 hybrids at the nursery (make a "wish list"), and offer a good selection of cuttings, and some rooted cuttings, all well described with some color pictures. (1988)
📖 Catalog: $3($5 OV), R&W, CAN/OV, SS:4-10, $15m
⊙ Nursery: All year, M-Sa, by appointment only
❀ Garden: April-June, by appointment only

Peter Grayson - Sweet Peas
34 Glenthorne Close, Brampton
Chesterfield, Derbyshire, England S40 3AR
Peter Grayson
44 (0) 1246 278-503
Fax: 44 (0) 1246 566-918
E-mail: matthewfry@cableinet.co.uk
Web: www.internetgarden.co.uk

Seeds
List divided into "old-fashioned" and "modern" **sweet peas**, and lathyrus species. Offers mixed packets, and introduces the first of the Grayson "Heritage Type," a peach sweetpea! Also offers hollyhock, oriental poppy, and morning glory seed. I love the strong, delicate perfume of sweet peas.
- 📖 Catalog: $2d, R&W, OV, $10m
- ✪ Nursery: All year, M-Sa, call ahead
- ✺ Garden: July, by appointment only

Great Basin Natives
P.O. Box 114
75 West 300 South
Holden, UT 84636
Johnson Family
(801) 795-2236
E-mail: gbn@sisna.com
Web: www.millardvv.com/nativeplants/

Plants ∞ Books
A native plant nursery offering seed grown **plants of the Great Basin**: trees and shrubs, perennials, and some grasses, including many penstemons, and artemisias, lupines and ephedras. A nice selection, well described. (1994)
- 📖 Catalog: Free, R&W, SS:5-10, $10m, bn/cn
- ✪ Nursery: All year, Tu-Sa
- ✺ Garden: June-September, call ahead

Green & Hagstrom, Inc.
P.O. Box 658
7767 Fernvale Road
Nashville, TN 37062
Jack & Cathy Green, Mgrs.
(615) 799-0708
Fax: (615) 799-9515
E-mail: JGreen@datatek
Web: www.greenandhagstrom.com

Plants ∞ Books ∞ Supplies
Offering **water lilies**, both hardy and tropical, as well as **water iris, cannas, lotus** and other water loving plants. Also a wide range of supplies for the water garden, including statuary, fish supplies and ceramic containers.
- 📖 Catalog: $2, R&W, CAN, CC, SS:4-9, cn/bn
- ✪ Nursery: March-November, daily
- ✺ Garden: May-September, daily

The Green Escape
P.O. Box 1417
1212 Ohio Avenue
Palm Harbor, FL 34682
Joan & Marshall Weintraub
(813) 784-1991
Fax: (813) 787-0193

Plants ∞ Books ∞ Supplies
Offers close to 500 species of rare and uncommon **palms**: indoor and cold hardy species, many that do well in low light. List arecas, arenga, calamus, chamaedorea, gaussia, howea, licuala, pinanga, johannesteijsmannia (yes!), livistona, sabal, thrinax and veitchia; all well described. Each comes with specific cultural information; no shipping to HI. (1988)
- 📖 Catalog: $6d, CAN/OV, $40m, bn/cn
- ✪ Nursery: All year, F-M
- ✺ Garden: All year, F-M

Green Hill Farm
5715 Hideaway Drive
Green Hill Drive
Chapel Hill, NC 27516
Bob Solberg
(919) 309-0649
Fax: (919) 383-4533

Plants
Someday they'll invent an effective snail killer, and I'll try growing some **hostas** -- they're wildly popular where snails can't overwinter. Offered are their own and the new introductions of other hybridizers, very exciting plants judging by the descriptions. (1990)
- 📖 Catalog: Free, R&W, CC, SS:3-5,8-10, $20m
- ✪ Nursery: May-June, F-Sa, by appointment only
- ✺ Garden: May-June, F-Sa, by appointment only

Green Mountain Transplants
R.R. 1, Box 6C
East Montpelier, VT 05651
Dexter & Susan Merritt
(802) 454-1533
Fax: (802) 454-1204
E-mail: gmtranspl@aol.com

Plants ∞ Supplies
Offer **vegetable and flower transplants** in 40 or 98 cell flats; you can mix the varieties any way you want. A good selection of vegetables and some annual and perennial flowers, well described; also offer wooden harvest baskets and growing supplies. (1991)
- 📖 Catalog: Free, R&W, CC, SS:4-6
- ✪ Nursery: June, daily

Green Plant Research
P.O. Box 597
51-404 Maumauluukaa Street
Kaaawa, HI 96730
Ted Green
(808) 237-8672
Fax: (808) 237-8672

Plants
A broad selection of **hoyas, dischidias and other asclepiads,** offered as cuttings, and well described, as well as a few species and hybrid **orchids.** These plants come from private collections and collecting trips in Samoa, Australia, New Guinea, the Solomon Islands, New Hebrides, Java, Singapore, Malaysia and the Philippines. No shipping to Germany. (1975)
- 📖 Catalog: Free, CAN/OV, $25m, bn/cn
- ✪ Nursery: By appointment only
- ❀ Garden: By appointment only

Greenmantle Nursery
3010 Ettersburg Road
Garberville, CA 95542
Ram & Marissa Fishman
(707) 986-7504

Plants
Catalog packed with cultural information, offers **antique apples,** many collected from old homesteads in Humboldt County. Also pears, cherries, plums, quince and disease-resistant chestnuts. On another list, about 200 old garden **roses,** many rare varieties and species imported from England. (1983)
- 📖 Catalog: $3, (rose list, long SASE), SS:1-4
- ✪ Nursery: Late May-June, by appointment only
- ❀ Garden: Late May-June, by appointment only

greenseeds(TM) from Underwood Gardens
4N381 Maple Avenue
Bensenville, IL 60106-2738
Maryann Underwood & Maren Oslac
Fax: (630) 616-0232
Web: www.seedman.com/greenseed.html

Seeds
Offers a very good selection of **heirloom vegetables,** each variety very well described. Also listed are **herbs, gourds, melons,** and some garden flowers. Buyers may join their members group and receive discounts and special offers of unusual varieties. (1993)
- 📖 Catalog: $1($2.50 OV), CAN/OV, CC, cn/bn

Greer Gardens
1280 Goodpasture Island Road
Eugene, OR 97401-1794
Harold Greer
(541) 686-8266
Fax: (541) 686-0910
E-mail: greergard@aol.com

Plants ☙ Books ☙ Supplies
Color catalog offers a very large selection of **rhododendrons and azaleas, vireyas,** and an ever-growing list of **ornamental trees,** maples (many palmatum cultivars), dwarf conifers, acid-loving shrubs and vines, perennials and bonsai materials; all well described in a very informative catalog (famous for its enthusiasm!). Also many books on trees and plants, and videos. (1955)
- 📖 Catalog: $3($5 OV), CAN/OV, CC, bn
- ✪ Nursery: All year, daily
- ❀ Garden: All year, March-June, daily

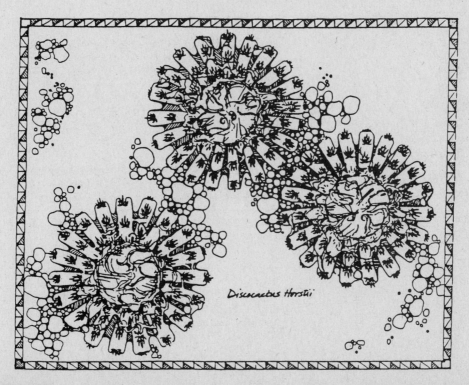

Discocactus Horstii

© Miles' to Go
Artist: Susan Montgomery

Griffin Gardens
6618 Upper 28th Street
Oakdale, MN 55128
Lori Griffin
(612) 770-4449

Plants ∽ Seeds
Lori Griffin specializes in **brugmansia** (7 varieties) and **datura** (4 varieties), those luscious trumpet flowers that smell so sweet at night. She will sell cuttings or plants after danger of frost. Also offers seed of some daturas. (1995)
📖 Catalog: Long SASE, SS:5-9, bn
☉ Nursery: May-September, by appointment only
❀ Garden: July-August, by appointment only

Grigsby Cactus Gardens
2534 Bella Vista Drive
Vista, CA 92084-7836
Madelyn Lee
(760) 727-1323
Fax: (760) 727-1578
Web: trine.com/GardenNet/

Plants
Catalog a real collectors' list of unusual **cacti & succulents**, all well described. They specialize in euphorbias, sansevierias, aloes, haworthias, mammillarias and other specimen plants and rare succulents. Send four or five "wish letters" to regular customers each year, offering new, rare and unusual plants. (1965)
📖 Catalog: $2d, R&W, CC, SS:3-11, $20m, bn
☉ Nursery: By appointment only
❀ Garden: May-June, by appointment only

Grimo Nut Nursery
979 Lakeshore Road, R.R.3
Niagara-on-the-Lake, ON, Canada L0S 1J0
Ernie Grimo
(905) 934-6887
Fax: (905) 934-6887

Plants ∽ Supplies
A selection of **hardy nuts** for Northern climates, seedlings and grafted trees: persian walnuts, black walnuts, heartnuts, butternuts, Chinese chestnuts, apricots (sweet kernels), filberts, hickory and more -- well described in an informative list. Sells nut harvesting supplies. No shipping to CA, Mexico, South America or Asia. (1974)
📖 Catalog: $1d($3 OV), R&W, US/OV, SS:4, $20m
☉ Nursery: April-June, M-Sa, call ahead
❀ Garden: July-September, by appointment only

Grootendorst Nurseries

See Southmeadow Fruit Gardens.

Gurney's Seed & Nursery Co.
110 Capital Street
Yankton, SD 57078
Don Kruml, Pres.
(605) 665-4451, 665-1930
Fax: (605) 665-9718
Web: www.vgmarketplace.com

Plants ∽ Seeds ∽ Supplies
Color tabloid catalog offers a very **broad selection of plants and seeds** for the home gardener -- fruit trees, roses, flowering trees and shrubs, nuts, berries, grapes and vegetable and flower seeds, all well described. Also gardening and canning supplies and advice in an informative catalog. (1866)
📖 Catalog: Free, CC, SS:2-6,9-11, cn
☉ Nursery: All year, daily

Hammond's Acres of Rhodys
25911 - 70th Avenue N.E.
Arlington, WA 98223
David & Joan Hammond
(360) 435-9206
Fax: (360) 403-9177

Plants
Offer a broad selection of **rhododendrons and azaleas**, both hybrids and species, listed only by name, hardiness, season and color of bloom. They grow 6,000 hybrids and species, and list about 600, if you don't find what you want, send them your "wish list." (1976)
📖 Catalog: $2, R&W, CC, SS:W, $7m
☉ Nursery: All year, daily
❀ Garden: April-May, daily

Hansen Nursery
P.O. Box 1228
North Bend, OR 97459
Robin L. Hansen
(541) 756-1156

Plants
A small nursery which specializes in seed grown species **cyclamen**; at present offers eleven species and describes each very well, with notes on cultivation and hardiness. Offers some **native plants** from the Pacific Northwest also. Will ship to Canada, but there's a $100 minimum. (1985)
📖 Catalog: Long SASE, R&W, CAN, SS:3-11, $15m, bn
☉ Nursery: By appointment only
❀ Garden: June, September-October, by appointment only

Harborcrest Gardens
Box 5430, Station B
Victoria, BC, Canada V8R 6S4
James C. Yates, Mgr.
Fax: (250) 592-6217

Plants
Offer a very good selection of **African violets, hoyas, bougainvilleas** and many other plants for the house and greenhouse for Canadians. Plants are briefly but well described.
📖 Catalog: Free, CC, SS:4-10, bn/cn

Hardscrabble Enterprises
P. O. Box 1124
Franklin, WV 26807
Paul & Nan Goland
(304) 358-2921

Seeds ఠ **Books** ఠ **Supplies**
Sell spawn of shiitake, lion's mane, maitake (Hen-of-the-Woods) **mushrooms** and all of the equipment necessary to grow them in your own woodlot. Price of the catalog includes growing instructions and their newsletter; they will buy dried shiitake mushrooms from organic growers. (1985)
📖 Catalog: $3, R&W
✪ Nursery: By appointment only

Hardy Roses for the North
P.O. Box 2048
5680 Hughes Road (Grand Forks)
Grand Forks, BC, Canada V0H 1H0
Barry Poppenheim
(250) 442-8442
Fax: (250) 442-2766
E-mail: roses@hardyroses.com
Web: www.hardyroses.com

Plants ఠ **Books**
Offer the hardy Canadian Explorer and Parkland **roses**, bred in Canada for extreme hardiness, as well as some English roses, hybrid rugosas, miniatures and old garden roses: all are well described. Orders to the US are sent with a phytosanitary certificate by USPO Priority Mail or UPS. Americans should request catalog from P.O. Box 273, Danville, WA 99121-0273. (1990)
📖 Catalog: $5($11 OV), US/OV, CC, SS:4-10
✪ Nursery: April-September, Tu-Su
❀ Garden: June-September, Tu-Su

Harris Seeds
P.O. Box 22960
60 Saginaw Drive
Rochester, NY 14692-2960
Richard Chamberlain, Pres.
(716) 442-0410, (800) 514-4441
Fax: (716) 442-9386

Plants ఠ **Seeds** ఠ **Supplies** ఠ **Tools** ఠ **Bulbs**
Color catalog offers a broad selection of **flower and vegetable seeds,** many developed by their own research staff and all well described. They list "special merit" vegetables which they feel perform best -- and have those cute baby pumpkins. They also sell some tools and growing supplies. (1879)
📖 Catalog: Free, CC

Hartle-Gilman Gardens
4708 E. Rose Street
Owatonna, MN 55060-9416
Dr. Robert Gilman, Dean & Marsha Hartle
(507) 451-3191
Fax: (507) 455-0087

Bulbs
Hartle-Gilman Gardens introduces their own hybrid **lilies,** and those of several other hybridizers in Minnesota, Wisconsin and Connecticut, and they also offer some older favorites. All lilies are well described. Canadians need an import permit to order, and must pay extra for a phytosanitary certificate. (1980)
📖 Catalog: Free($1 OV), CAN/OV, SS:9-11, $5m
✪ Nursery: June-August, call ahead
❀ Garden: June-July, by appointment only

Hartmann's Plantation, Inc.
P.O. Box E
310 - 60th Street
Grand Junction, MI 49056
Daniel Hartmann
(616) 253-4281
Fax: (616) 253-4457

Plants
Selection of **Northern and Southern blueberries,** as well as "Arctic" kiwis, pawpaw, wintergreen, lemongrass and three varieties of bush cherries. Also offer a few miniature roses. (1942)
📖 Catalog: Free, R&W, CAN/OV, CC, SS:9-6, $5m
✪ Nursery: All year, M-F, by appointment only
❀ Garden: April-September, M-F, by appointment only

Hauser's Superior View Farm
Route 1, Box 199
Bayfield, WI 54814
James & Marilyn Hauser
(715) 779-5404

Plants
Offers a nice selection of hardy field-grown **perennials** -- sold by 3's, a dozen or a hundred; only name and flower color given. A good choice of lupines, delphiniums and others; also asparagus and rhubarb. Also offers homemade jams, jellies and apple butter. (1908)
📖 Catalog: $1, R&W, SS:4-6,9-10, $25m
❀ Garden: Summer-Fall, call ahead

Heard Gardens, Ltd.
5355 Merle Hay Road
Johnston, IA 50131-1207
Bob Rennebohm
(515) 276-4533
Fax: (515) 276-8322

Plants
Specialize in **lilacs** propagated on their own roots; some 50 varieties, each briefly described. Also offered are several species lilacs, and three low-chill varieties which bloom well in southern climates. (1959)
📖 Catalog: $2, CAN/OV, CC, SS:3-4,10-11
✪ Nursery: April-October, daily, call for hours
❀ Garden: May-October, daily

The Heather Garden
6 Roland Kimball Road
Freeport, ME 04032
Greta Waterman
(207) 865-0407

Plants
"Specializes in hardy **heathers** that are salt-spray tolerant." This small nursery offers 28 varieties of calluna, briefly but well described.
- Catalog: Free, SS:4-9, $10m
- Nursery: April-October, daily, by appointment only
- Garden: May-October, daily, by appointment only

Heather Heaven
P.O. Box 71
3342 School Street
Fortuna, CA 95540
Norma Spencer

Plants
A very nice selection of **heathers**, including **callunas, daboecias** and **ericas**, described in table format, with good cultural information.
- Catalog: Free, R&W, CAN, $15m
- Nursery: All year, by appointment only
- Garden: By appointment only

Heaths & Heathers
E. 502 Haskell Hill Road
Shelton, WA 98584-8429
Karla Lortz
(360) 427-5318, (800) 294-3284
Fax: (360) 427-5318
E-mail: heaths@gte.net

Plants
The indefatigable Alice Knight and family have retired, and Karla Lortz has taken on the **heather** collection, including many **callunas, daboecias and ericas**. The plant list is very extensive, with information on flower and foliage color, bloom time and size in compact tables.
- Catalog: Long SASE w\2 FCS, R&W, CC, SS:9-6, $15m, bn

Hedera etc.
P.O. Box 461
Manatawny Road (Pine Forge)
Lionville, PA 19353-0461
Russell A. Windle & Johanna M. Milne
(610) 970-9175

Plants
Offers over 300 "true to name" **ivy** cultivars, including a number of recent introductions. All plants are very well described. (1994)
- Catalog: $2d, R&W, CAN/OV, bn
- Nursery: M-F, by appointment only
- Garden: By appointment only

Heirloom Old Garden Roses
24062 NE Riverside Drive
St. Paul, OR 97137
Louise & John Clements
(503) 538-1576
Fax: (503) 538-5902
E-mail: louise@heirloomroses.com
Web: www.heirloomroses.com

Plants & Books
Specializes in old garden and modern shrub **roses**, and offers a huge selection; all are very well described and some are shown in color in a very informative catalog. They have over 1,000 roses in their display gardens. Also offer many books on roses and rose culture.
- Catalog: $5, CC, SS:W
- Nursery: All year, daily
- Garden: May-October, daily

Heirloom Seed Project
2451 Kissel Hill Road
Lancaster, PA 17601-4899
Maggie Posselius, Coordinator
Fax: (717) 560-2147

Seeds
Landis Valley Museum is a living history museum recreating 18th and 19th century rural Pennsylvania German life. They have a seed preservation program to preserve **vegetables** with a history in their area, and also offer some antique apple scionwood. Catalog is informative and interesting. (1986)
- Catalog: $4d($5 OV), CAN/OV, CC
- Garden: Historical Gardens at Museum

Heirloom Seeds
P.O. Box 245
West Elizabeth, PA 15088-0245
Tom & Barb Hauch
(412) 384-0852
Fax: (412) 384-0852
E-mail: heirloom@usaor.net
Web: www.usaor.net/heirloom

Seeds
Small family business specializing in seeds of open-pollinated **heirloom tomatoes and vegetables** "that taste good," and a few herb seeds. Catalog has good descriptions of each variety and some cultural information. They also offer some "old-fashioned" annual flowers, and books. (1988)
- Catalog: $1d, CAN, CC

The Herb Garden
P.O. Box 773
Route 3, Carson Road
Pilot Mountain, NC 27041-0773
Ann B. Beall

Plants & Books & Supplies
Offers a very good selection of **herbs**, especially artemisias, basils, bee balms, lavenders, rosemarys, mints and thymes; all well described with some cultural information. Also sells dried herbs, teas and seasonings, potpourri supplies, and natural pest controls for your pets. Can't ship plants to CA, AZ, OR, WA or HI; will ship dried products and supplies to these states. (1983)
📖 Catalog: $4, SS:4-6,9-10, $15m, cn/bn

Herbs-Liscious
1702 S. Sixth Street
Marshalltown, IA 50158
Carol Lacko-Beem
(515) 752-4976
Fax: (515) 753-5193
E-mail: herbs@marshallnet.com

Plants & Seeds & Books & Supplies
Offers a good selection of **herb plants**, with no plant descriptions; in a catalog along with dried herbs for flavorings, herb baths, essential oils, herb books, etc. They will search for and fill requests for more unusual herbs if asked. Seed list available for SASE. (1987)
📖 Catalog: $2d, R&W, CAN, CC, SS:4-11, $10m, cn
⊙ Nursery: All year, Th-Sa, or by appointment
❀ Garden: May-September, Th-Sa, or by appointment

Heritage Rosarium
211 Haviland Mill Road
Brookville, MD 20833
Nicholas Weber
(301) 774-2806 (eves. and weekends)

Plants
Offers a large selection of old garden, modern shrub and species **roses**, available on a custom-root basis. About 400 varieties are listed only by cultivar or species name, with symbols for type, color and date of introduction; get out your "old rose" books. They will also root or bud your own roses to increase old favorites, and help with rose identification. (1985)
📖 Catalog: $1, CAN, SS:2-11
⊙ Nursery: March-October, Sa-Su, by appointment only
❀ Garden: May-June, Sa-Su, by appointment only

Heritage Roses of Tanglewood Farms
16831 Mitchell Creek Drive
Ft. Bragg, CA 95437-8727
Joyce Demits
(707) 964-3748

Plants & Bulbs
Joyce and her sister have split their Heritage Rose Gardens into two new nurseries. Joyce offers a nice selection of **species and old garden roses**, all briefly described. (1996)
📖 Catalog: $1, CAN/OV, SS:1-3, bn
⊙ Nursery: All year, by appointment only
❀ Garden: May-October, by appointment only

Heritage Rose Gardens

See Heritage Roses of Tanglewood Farm and/or Ros-Equus.

Heronswood Nursery
7530 NE 288th Street
Kingston, WA 98346-9502
Daniel J. Hinkley & Robert L. Jones
(360) 297-4172
Fax: (360) 297-8321

Plants
Offers a broad selection of **ornamental woody plants**: maples, berberis, box, callicarpa, cercidiphyllum, cotoneaster, daphne, eucryphia, hydrangea, holly, mahonia, pernettya, pieris, rubus, sarcococca, viburnum, willows and conifers. Also many choice **perennials**. Plants are very well described; catalog and selection grow every year. (1987)
📖 Catalog: $4($5 OV), CAN/OV, CC, SS:3-5,9-10, $30m, bn
⊙ Nursery: May-February, by appointment only
❀ Garden: May-September, by appointment only

Hickory Hill Gardens
169 Ice Plant Road
Loretto, PA 15940
Clayton Burkey
(814) 886-2823
E-mail: eburkey126@aol.com

Plants
A very broad selection of **daylilies**, each plant briefly but well described; many are their own introductions. Also advertises as Burkey Gardens. (1981)
📖 Catalog: $2.75($5 OV), CAN/OV, SS:5-6,8-10, $20m
⊙ Nursery: July-September, by appointment only
❀ Garden: July-August, by appointment only

Hidden Springs Nursery -- Edible Landscaping
170 Hidden Springs Lane
Cookeville, TN 38501
Hector Black

Plants
Offers plants for **edible landscaping** and low maintenance fruits for sustainable agriculture, with emphasis on disease and pest resistance. Antique apples, apricots, grapes, mayhaws, hardy kiwis, medlars and quinces, pears, plums, goumi and several nitrogen-fixing shrubs for reclamation. (1978)
- Catalog: $1, SS:11-4, $20m
- Nursery: By appointment only
- Garden: Spring-Fall, by appointment only

High Altitude Gardens
P.O. Box 1048
4150 B Black Oak Drive
Hailey, ID 83333-1048
Bill McDorman
(208) 788-4363
Fax: (208) 788-3452
E-mail: higarden@micron.net

Seeds   Books   Supplies   Tools
Seed of open-pollinated **gourmet and heirloom vegetables, herbs, wildflowers** and **native grasses**, adapted to the cold, short-season, high-altitude climate of the mountain West. Informative catalog with cultural suggestions; also sells some growing supplies and books. Also called Seeds Trust - High Altitude Gardens. (1984)
- Catalog: Free($5 OV), CAN/OV, CC, cn/bn
- Nursery: All year, M-F, by appointment only

High Country Gardens
2902 Rufina Street
Santa Fe, NM 87505-2929
David M. Salman, Pres.
(535) 438-3031, (800) 925-9387
Fax: (800) 925-0097
E-mail: plants@highcountrygardens.com

Plants   Books   Supplies
Specializes in **perennials** for Southwestern growing conditions, plants are generally drought tolerant and hardy; a good selection, including many native plants, shown and well described in a color catalog. Good selections of penstemons, artemisias, and agastaches; some books, too. They even sell "plugs" of thymes and xeric grasses to make "water wise turf." (1984)
- Catalog: Free, CC, SS:2-6,9-11, $24m, bn/cn
- Nursery: All year, daily
- Garden: May-October, daily

High Country Roses
P.O. Box 148
9122 East Highway 40
Jensen, UT 84035
Heather Campbell & Day DeLaHunt
(801) 789-5512
Fax: (801) 789-5517
E-mail: roses@easilink.com
Web: easilink.com/~smf/

Plants
Very hardy old garden **roses** grown in the Rockies -- a good selection of species, old garden varieties and shrub roses, all grown on their own roots and well described. (1971)
- Catalog: $2, R&W, CC, SS:3-11, $10m, bn/cn
- Nursery: March-October, M-Sa
- Garden: April-October, call ahead

High Mowing Organic Seed Farm
R.D. 1, Box 95
Derby Line, VT 05830
Thomas M.L. Stearns
(802) 895-4696

Seeds
Specializing in **heirloom vegetables** for New England, Tom Stearns grows all he sells on a farm "where winters are long and summers short." Offered is a good selection, briefly described, with some cultural information.
- Catalog: Free, R&W, CAN
- Nursery: Call ahead

Highfield Garden
4704 N.E. Cedar Creek Road
Woodland, WA 98674
Gil & Irene Moss
(360) 225-6525

Plants
Offers a very good selection of **hardy geraniums** and other border **perennials** and ornamental grasses. All plants are well but briefly described, drawing special attention to their individual beauties. (1990)
- Catalog: $1, SS:4-5,9-10, bn
- Nursery: By appointment only
- Garden: June, by appointment only

Highlander Nursery
P.O. Box 177
Pettigrew, AR 72752
Lee & Louise McCoy
(501) 677-2300

Plants   Supplies
Specializes in hardy and low-chill **blueberries**, a dozen varieties which bear from early to late in the season. Also offers two dwarf varieties: one makes a nice container, bonsai or border plant, and the other a ground cover. (1986)
- Catalog: Free, R&W, SS:10-6
- Nursery: All year, daily, call ahead
- Garden: All year, daily, call ahead

Hill 'n dale
6427 N. Fruit Avenue
Fresno, CA 93711
Dale Kloppenburg
(209) 439-8249
Fax: (209) 439-8249
E-mail: cembra@juno.com

Plants ஐ **Books**
A very extensive list of **hoyas**, both species and named cultivars, with a number of **dischidias** and some **aeschynanthus**. Dale has added to his collection on trips to Australia, Guadalcanal, the Solomon Islands and the Philippines, so there are more to come. Cuttings only; three books. (1957)
📖 Catalog: $1(2 IRC OV), R&W, CAN/OV, SS:5-10, $35m, bn
✪ Nursery: All year, by appointment only
❀ Garden: May-October, by appointment only

Hobbs and Hopkins Ltd.
1712 SE Ankeny Street
Portland, OR 97214
Keith & Christy Hopkins
(503) 239-7518, (800) 345-3295
Fax: (503) 230-0391
E-mail: lawn@teleport.com
Web: www.teleport.com/~lawn

Seeds
Offers seed mix for "Fleur de Lawn," a low-growing **flowering lawn mixture**. Also offers other lawn grass seed. (1979)
📖 Catalog: Free, R&W, CAN, CC
✪ Nursery: All year, M-F
❀ Garden: March-October. M-F

Holladay Jungle
P.O. Box 5727
1602 E. Fountain Way
Fresno, CA 93755
Barbara Holladay
(209) 229-9858
E-mail: tillandsia@earthlink.net
Web: home.earthlink.net/~tillandsia/

Plants
A broad selection of **tillandsias** available bare-root; there are no plant descriptions, but you should be able to find them in a good book. They "grow on trees and rocks without soil and all flower." (1984)
📖 Catalog: Free, R&W, CAN/OV, $15m, bn
✪ Nursery: All year, by appointment only
❀ Garden: All year, by appointment only

Holland Gardens
29106 Meridian East
Graham, WA 98338-9032
Martin S. Holland
(206) 847-5425

Plants
Talk about specialized! Offers only one old **iris**, which his mother grew since 1917; it is registered as 'Sweet Lena' with the American Iris Society after her. Pale blue with white trim, it has a very strong, sweet fragrance and 5 to 7 blooms on a stalk; it's thought to be **Iris pallida androfertila**.
📖 Catalog: $1d, R&W, CAN/OV, SS:7-9, $10m
✪ Nursery: Daily, call ahead
❀ Garden: May-June, call ahead

Holland Wildflower Farm
P. O. Box 328
Elkins, AR 72727
Robert & Julie Holland
(501) 643-2622, (800) 684-3734
Fax: (501) 643-2622
E-mail: info@hwildflower.com
Web: www.hwildflower.com

Plants ஐ **Seeds**
Small nursery sells plants and seeds of **prairie wildflowers** ideal for harsh winters and hot summers. Send long SASE with 2 FCS for seed and plant price list; they also sell a booklet on growing wildflowers in which each plant is well described with cultural suggestions for $3.25. (1985)
📖 Catalog: See notes, R&W, CAN/OV, CC, $15m, bn/cn
✪ Nursery: By appointment only
❀ Garden: May-June, September-October, by appointment only

Holly Lane Iris Gardens
10930 Holly Lane
Osseo, MN 55369
Jack J. Worel
(612) 420-4876
E-mail: wqmp29a@prodigy.com

Plants
Offers a broad selection of **bearded iris**: tall, border and dwarf bearded (some are "historical"), as well as Siberians and some species. Also daylilies, and hostas; each plant briefly described. (1983)
📖 Catalog: 2 FCS, CAN, SS:5-9, $10m
✪ Nursery: May-September, Tu-Su
❀ Garden: June, August, Tu-Su

Holly Ridge Nursery
5925 South Ridge Road West
Geneva, OH 44041
Paul Hanslik & Lucinda Little
(216) 466-0134, (800) 465-5901
Fax: (216) 466-0134

Plants
A source of **hollies**; a good selection, and they are adding plants from their collection of more than 60 varieties of American hollies. These are very hardy, and have red, yellow or orange berries. Plants well described; no shipping to AZ, CA, OR or WA. (1991)
📖 Catalog: Free, R&W, CAN, $25m
✪ Nursery: All year, M-Sa

Homan Brothers Seed
P.O. Box 337
7141 N. 51st Avenue, Suite 1 (Phoenix)
Glendale, AZ 85311-0337
Jeff Homan, Pres.
(602) 244-1650
Fax: (602) 435-8777

Seeds
Specializes in habitat collected seed of **native plants of the Sonoran and Mojave Deserts**; they offer native grasses, wildflowers and shrubs; described in brief tables. (1991)
📖 Catalog: Long SASE w/2 FCS, R&W, CAN/OV, CC, $20m, bn/cn

Homestead Division of Sunnybrook Farms
9448 Mayfield Road
Chesterland, OH 44026
Peter & Jean Ruh
(216) 729-9838

Plants ⬥ **Seeds** ⬥ **Tools**
A huge selection of **hostas** (and hosta seeds), also a number of **epimediums**, and a Japanese fern. Plants briefly to well described. They also offer a few of their favorite hand tools and plant labels. Send SASE for seed list. (1980)
📖 Catalog: $2($3 OV), CAN/OV, SS:4-10, $25m
✿ Nursery: April-October, daily, by appointment only
❀ Garden: May-July, by appointment only

Homestead Farms
Route 2, Box 31A
Owensville, MO 65066
Ronald & Brett Vitoux
(573) 437-4277
Fax: (573) 437-4277

Plants ⬥ **Books**
Offers a nice selection of **daylilies, hostas, clematis, peonies**, with some Siberian iris and hardy ferns. While the choice is not large, the plants are well described and many are award winners, both old and new. They also have a few books on their specialties. (1983)
📖 Catalog: Free, CC, SS:4-10
✿ Nursery: April-October, W-Sa, call ahead
❀ Garden: May-September, W-Sa, call ahead

Homestead Gardens
125 Homestead Road
Kalispell, MT 59901
Ray & Iris Jones
(406) 756-6631

Plants
Offers a very nice list of **dahlias**, grouped by size or type, and very briefly described. Many are described as winners, so they must have many dahlia exhibitors as customers. (1989)
📖 Catalog: Free, CAN, CC, SS:1-5
❀ Garden: July-September, daily, call ahead

Honeywood Lilies
P.O. Box 68
Parkside, SK, Canada S0J 2A0
Allan B. Daku
(306) 747-3296
Fax: (306) 747-3395

Plants ⬥ **Bulbs**
Specializes in **lilies**, offering a nice variety of all types and some collections. Also offers herbaceous peonies, alliums, a few hardy daylilies and "minor bulbs." Canadian gardeners can write for their iris and perennial catalog($2d), they only ship these within Canada.
📖 Catalog: $2d, R&W, US, SS:4-10, $10m, cn/bn
✿ Nursery: April-October, daily
❀ Garden: June-August, call ahead

Hoosier Orchid Company
8440 West 82nd Street
Indianapolis, IN 46278-1062
William & Megan Rhodehamel
(317) 291-6269
Fax: (317) 291-8949

Plants
Specializes in seed grown **orchid species**, a very good selection with excellent plant descriptions; they also offer their own inter-specific hybrids. They have a orchid species seed propagation program, and will grow yours from seed and share the plants with you. (1988)
📖 Catalog: Free, R&W, CAN/OV, CC, SS:3-11, bn
✿ Nursery: All year, Tu-Sa
❀ Garden: All year, Tu-Sa

Horizon Herbs
P.O. Box 69
Williams, OR 97544
Mayche Cech
(541) 846-6704
Fax: (541) 846-6233
E-mail: herbseed@chatlink.com
Web: www.chatlink.com/~herbseed

Plants ⬥ **Seeds**
Specializes in "Strictly Medicinal"(R) **herbs**; offered as seeds, with some kinds available as live roots, grown organically. Plants are well described, with notes on cultivation. Also offer a series of pamphlets on specific herbs and herb topics.
📖 Catalog: $1($1 or 3 IRC OV), R&W, CAN/OV, CC, cn/bn

Jerry Horne Rare Plants
10195 S.W. 70th Street
Miami, FL 33173
Jerry Horne
(305) 270-1235

Plants
A collectors' list of rare and exotic **tropical plants**. Platyceriums, ferns, palms, cycads, aroids and others, all briefly described. (1975)
- Catalog: Long SASE($1 OV), CAN/OV, $15m, bn
- Nursery: All year, by appointment only
- Garden: All year, by appointment only

Hortico, Inc.
723 Robson Road, RR 1
Waterdown, ON, Canada L0R 2H1
William Vanderkruk
(905) 689-6984, 689-6002
Fax: (905) 689-6566

Plants
A very broad selection of garden **perennials**, hardy ornamental **trees** and **shrubs, roses, ferns, wildflowers and conifers** briefly described. Essentially a wholesale nursery, but will sell in small quantities to home gardeners at retail prices. Ask for rose, shrub or perennials list, $3 each.
- Catalog: $3, R&W, US/OV, $15m, bn/cn
- Nursery: All year, M-Sa
- Garden: August-September, M-Sa

Horus Botanicals, Ethnobotanical Seeds
HCR 82, Box 29
Salem, AR 72576
Blane Bourgeois & Kelly McClure

Plants ∞ Seeds
A small seed company offering a good selection of **open-pollinated vegetables and herbs** from many cultures around the world. Each is very well described, but get out your glasses, the print is tiny! They also offer a limited number of unusual plants that are shipped in the fall, US only. (1988)
- Catalog: $3($4 OV), CAN/OV, bn/cn

Hoyas by Michael Miyashiro
3852 Claudine Street
Honolulu, HI 96816
Michael Miyashiro
Fax: (808) 949-1550

Plants ∞ Seeds
Growers and shippers of **hoyas**; list has good plant descriptions of rare species and hybrid varieties -- they can also provide seeds. Request hoya list or catalog of available miscellaneous tropical plants. (1985)
- Catalog: Long SASE w/2 FCS(2 IRC OV), R&W, CAN/OV, $30m, bn

Hsu's Ginseng Enterprises, Inc.
P.O. Box 509
T6819 County Highway W
Wausau, WI 54402
Paul Hsu
(715) 675-2325, (800) 826-1577
Fax: (715) 675-3175
E-mail: info@hsuginseng.com
Web: www.hsuginseng.com

Plants ∞ Seeds ∞ Books
This company sells stratified seed and "rootlets" of **ginseng**; varieties from America, Canada and Korea. Some customers grow ginseng commercially and sell it back to Hsu's for marketing. Also sell books on ginseng and rent a video on growing it. It's actually a very pretty woodland plant if you want to try growing your own tea. Do not ship to AZ, FL, HI, LA, or TX. (1974)
- Catalog: Free, CAN/OV, CC, SS:4,9, $10m
- Nursery: All year, M-F
- Garden: May-September, by appointment only

J. L. Hudson, Seedsman
Star Route 2, Box 337
La Honda, CA 94020
J. L. Hudson & Sheri Calkins

Seeds ∞ Books
"Specialize in **rare seeds** from all over the world -- except Antarctica." Now called the "Ethnobotanical Catalog of Seeds," it's informative, with a broad selection, historic, cultural and literary references and current scientific information, illustrated with old prints. More than a catalog, it's an education. Also offers some books. (1911)
- Catalog: $1($4 OV or 7 IRC), R&W, CAN/OV, bn/cn

Huff's Garden Mums
710 Juniatta Street
Burlington, KS 66839
Charles Huff
(800) 279-4675

Plants
A huge selection of **chrysanthemums** -- each very briefly described and organized by type. Still carries old favorites, and offers a number of collections by type or use for those who are bewildered by the choice. (1955)
- Catalog: Free, R&W, CC, SS:3-6, $10m
- Nursery: By appointment only
- Garden: September-October, call ahead

Huggins Farm Irises

See Mary's Garden.

Hughes Nursery

See F. W. Byles Nursery.

Huronview Nurseries & Garden Centre
6429 Brigden Road
Bright's Grove, ON, Canada N0N 1C0
John Cook
Fax: (519) 869-8518
E-mail: jonathanc@wwdc.com

Plants ∞ Supplies
This grower of **species orchids** has a nice selection, and includes a few **hybrid orchids**. Descriptions are very brief, but interested customers are encouraged to ask more about the plants. Ships only in Canada.
  📖 Catalog: Free, CC, SS:4-10, $50m, bn
  ✪ Nursery: All year, M-Sa, call ahead
  ❀ Garden: All year, M-Sa, call ahead

Hydrangeas Plus
P.O. Box 389
Aurora, OR 97002
T. L. Bell
(503) 651-2887
Fax: (503) 651-2648
E-mail: bellfam@canby.com

Plants
Hydrangeas have become wildly popular, and with good reason. Here's a source of some species and many cultivars, many shown in color photographs, and all very well described.
  📖 Catalog: $3.50d, R&W, CAN/OV, CC

Indigo Marsh
2513 West Lucas St., B-6
Florence, SC 29501
The Locklairs
(803) 679-0999
Fax: (803) 679-0965
E-mail: indigo@southtech.net
Web: www.indigomarsh.com

Plants
Offers a good selection of **flowering shrubs and perennials**, including many cultivars of clematis, clerodendron, phlox, ginger, and many other interesting plants such as Petunia integrifolia which should put those annual monsters right out of business. Sells beneficial insects and biological controls, too. (1990)
  📖 Catalog: $2, R&W, CC, SS:3-5, bn/cn
  ✪ Nursery: All year, M-Sa
  ❀ Garden: April-May, October-November, M-Sa

Ingraham's Cottage Roses
P.O. Box 126
Scotts Mills, OR 97375
Jill Ingraham

Plants
Offers a nice selection of **old garden and modern roses**, on their own roots. Plants are propagated to order, take 18 to 24 months to delivery. (1989)
  📖 Catalog: $1, CAN/OV, SS:2-3, $11m
  ✪ Nursery: By appointment only

W. E. Th. Ingwersen, Ltd.
Birch Farm Nursery, Gravetye
East Grinstead, W. Sussex, England RH19 4LE
M. P. Ingwersen
44 (0) 1342 810-236

Seeds
One of the best-known nurseries in England, specializing in **alpine and rock garden** plants. They publish a seed list, on which you will surely find desirable plants. Seed list is 4 IRC to the US. Payment for orders must be in pounds sterling. See Foreign Exchange Services in Products Sources Index. (1926)
  📖 Catalog: See notes, OV, bn
  ✪ Nursery: March-September, daily
  ❀ Garden: Spring-Summer, daily

© Bear Creek Nursery
  Artist: Takao Butterfield

Inner Coast Nursery
Box 115, Mansons Landing
Cortes Island, BC, Canada V0P 1K0
Elena & Bill Wheeler
(250) 935-6384
Fax: (250) 935-6384
E-mail: innersea@oberon.ark.com
Web: oberon.ark.com/~innersea

Plants
"Organic growers of over 300 varieties of rare, heritage and exceptional **fruit trees**, including many apples, plums, peaches, cherries, pears and nuts. Plants are very well described; but only Canadian gardeners can taste the fruit, as they only ship trees within Canada. Will do custom propagation also.
📖 Catalog: $5, R&W, SS:11-4, $25m
☼ Nursery: By appointment only
❀ Garden: By appointment only

Intermountain Cactus
1478 North 750 East
Kaysville, UT 84037
Robert A. Johnson
(801) 546-2006

Plants
Offers a selection of **very hardy cactus** (some to -20 to -50F), most of which are profuse bloomers, including about 77 selections of opuntia, pediocactus, echinocereus, and coryphantha. Opuntias sold by pad or by clump. Very brief descriptions. (1976)
📖 Catalog: $1, SS:4-11, $20m, bn
☼ Nursery: April-November, daily, call ahead
❀ Garden: May-June, call ahead

Ion Exchange
1878 Old Mission Drive
Harpers Ferry, IA 52146-7533
Donna & Howard Bright
(319) 535-7231, (800) 291-2143
Fax: (319) 535-7362
E-mail: hbright@means.net
Web: www.ionxchange.com

Plants ⁊ **Seeds** ⁊ **Books**
Offer a good selection of seed of **prairie wildflowers**: seeds sold by the packet, ounce or pound. Also offer mixes for meadows, marshes, dry sites and to attract butterflies and hummingbirds. Small plants sold in mixed packages. Great selection of books on Midwestern and prairie plants. (1988)
📖 Catalog: Free, CAN/OV, bn/cn
☼ Nursery: All year, by appointment only
❀ Garden: By appointment only

Iris & Plus
P.O. Box 903
1269 Route 139
Sutton, PQ, Canada J0E 2K0
Danielle Paquette
(514) 538-2048
Fax: (514) 538-7353

Plants
Offers a nice selection of **daylilies, hostas, iris and astilbes**: bearded iris of all types, Japanese and Siberian iris. Catalog is in both English and French, plants are briefly described. (1990)
📖 Catalog: $2d, R&W, US, SS:5-10
☼ Nursery: May-September, daily
❀ Garden: June-August, call ahead

Iris Acres
Route 4, Box 189
Winamac, IN 46996
Thurlow & Jean Sanders
(219) 946-4197

Plants
A very extensive list of "winter tested" **bearded iris in all sizes**, including reblooming and "space age" types; all plants briefly described. List offers general information on planting and care of iris. (1959)
📖 Catalog: $1d, CAN/OV, SS:7-9
☼ Nursery: May-August, call ahead
❀ Garden: May-June, call ahead

Iris Country
6219 Topaz Street N.E.
Brooks, OR 97305
Roger R. Nelson
(503) 393-4739

Plants
Roger's specialty is **tall and border bearded iris** selected for maximum vigor and hardiness, he tests them all over the country. Also listed are some older favorites, beardless, historical bearded iris, and some Siberian and spuria iris. All are well described. (1968)
📖 Catalog: $1.50d, CAN, SS:6-10, $15m
☼ Nursery: May-October, call ahead
❀ Garden: Call ahead

The Iris Gallery
33450 Little Valley Road
Fort Bragg, CA 95437
Jay & Terri Hudson
(707) 964-3907
Fax: (707) 964-3907
E-mail: irishud@mcn.org

Plants
A nice selection of **bearded iris** from tall bearded to dwarf, as well as **Pacific Coast, Siberian, Japanese, Louisiana, spurias** and species and water iris. Plants are briefly described. Jay took on the Pacific Coast iris of Colin Rigby of Portable Acres when he retired to Washington state. (1991)
📖 Catalog: $1d($2 OV), CAN/OV, SS:8-11, $15m
☼ Nursery: May-June, daily
❀ Garden: May-June, daily

Iris Pond

See Draycott Gardens.

Island Seed Company
P.O. Box 4278 Depot #3
Victoria, BC, Canada V8X 3X8
Elizabeth & John Beatty
Fax: (604) 479-0221

Seeds
Offers seed of heirloom and open-pollinated **vegetables, herbs** and a few annual and perennial **flowers**. Varieties are well described, with some information on history, culture and uses. (1960)
📖 Catalog: $2, R&W, US, CC, $10m

It's About Thyme
11726 Manchaca Road
Austin, TX 78748
Diane Winslow
(512) 280-1192
Fax: (512) 280-6356
E-mail: itsthyme@bga.com
Web: mvpimages.net/itsthyme

Plants
Offers a good selection of **herbs**, including Southwestern herbs and peppers, and scented geraniums, all briefly described. They will be adding old garden roses to coming lists; these are limited in quantity at present. (1979)
📖 Catalog: $1d, CC, SS:3-6, $25m, cn/bn
⊙ Nursery: All year, daily
❀ Garden: All year, daily

Ivies of the World
P.O. Box 408
Weirsdale, FL 32195-0408
Tim & Judy Rankin
(352) 821-2201
Fax: (352) 821-2201
E-mail: rookh@aol.com

Plants
Offers more than 250 cultivars of **ivy**, mainly rooted cuttings; plants are grouped by type and well described. This nursery was formerly Tropexotic Growers, and before that The Alestake of Elkwood, VA (for those of you who haven't been keeping track). They're adding new varieties all the time. (1986)
📖 Catalog: $2, R&W, CAN, $20m
⊙ Nursery: By appointment only

Ivy Garth Perennials
P.O. Box 606
Gates Mills, OH 44040-0606
Barbara Bletcher
(216) 423-0567
Fax: (216) 423-0410
E-mail: ivygarth@aol.com

Plants
Specializing in mature, well established **perennials**, plants are listed by time of bloom, and sun or shade needs. "Plants have overwintered in northeast Ohio, whipped by Lake Erie gales," so they must be truly hardy! Good descriptions. No shipping to AZ, CA, CO, OR, WA or UT. (1993)
📖 Catalog: Free, SS:4-6, bn/cn
❀ Garden: By appointment only

J & L Orchids
20 Sherwood Road
Easton, CT 06612
C. Head, M. Webb & L. Winn
(203) 261-3772
Fax: (203) 261-8730
E-mail: jlorchid@snet.net
Web: www.netins.net/showcase/novacon/orchids/jl.htm

Plants
A broad selection of **species orchids** from all over the world, as well as hybrids, all very well described with many lovely drawings. Specializes in rare and unusual species and miniatures which can be grown in the home under lights or on a windowsill; also offers "beginners' samplers." (1960)
📖 Catalog: $1($4 OV), CAN/OV, SS:3-11, bn
⊙ Nursery: All year, M-Sa
❀ Garden: December-April, M-Sa

J. E. M. Orchids
6595 Morikami Park Road
Delray Beach, FL 33446-2308
Gene & Jean Monnier
(561) 498-4308
Fax: (561) 498-4308
E-mail: orchids@magg.net
Web: www.magg.net/~orchids

Plants
Offers **hybrid orchids and new world species**: oncidium intergenerics, mini-cattleyas, paphiopedilums, phalaenopsis, dendrobiums, catasetum, zygopetinae and others, each very briefly described with information on crosses. (1974)
📖 Catalog: $2d($5 OV), R&W, CAN/OV, CC, SS:4-10, $25m
⊙ Nursery: All year, M-Sa
❀ Garden: All year, M-Sa

Jackson & Perkins Co.
2518 S. Pacific Highway
Medford, OR 97501
Bear Creek Corporation
(800) 292-4769, 872-7673
Fax: (800) 242-0329
Web: www.jacksonandperkins.com

Plants ∽ Bulbs
Color catalogs offer a wide selection of modern hybrid tea, grandiflora, floribunda and climbing **roses**, mostly of their own breeding, as well as perennials, hybrid lilies and other summer-blooming bulbs. Another catalog offers spring bulbs, and another offers garden ornaments and gifts. (1872)
📖 Catalog: Free, CAN, CC
❀ Garden: May-August, Rose Test Garden

Japonica Water Gardens
36484 Camp Creek Road
Springfield, OR 97478
Ron & William Howes
(541) 746-5378

Plants
Offers a nice selection of **water plants**, including hardy water lilies, cannas, grasses and Japanese iris. Plants are briefly described. Also offers hardy **bamboos**, and **carnivorous plants**. Limited shipping to CA. (1991)
📖 Catalog: 2 FCS, R&W, SS:W, $15m, bn/cn
🔾 Nursery: By appointment only

Jasperson's Hersey Nursery
2915 - 74th Avenue
Wilson, WI 54027
Lu Jasperson
(715) 772-4749

Plants
Small nursery specializes in tall bearded **iris, gladioli and daylilies**, listed only by color and cultivar name. Some of the daylilies are new introductions from a local hybridizer. (1987)
📖 Catalog: $.75, R&W, SS:4-10, $15m
🔾 Nursery: April-October, M-Sa, call ahead
❀ Garden: April-October, M-Sa, call ahead

The Thomas Jefferson Center
Monticello
P.O. Box 316
Charlottesville, VA 22902-0316
Peggy C. Newcomb, Dir.
Fax: (804) 977-6140
Web: www.monticello.org

Seeds
Seeds from the **historic flowers and vegetables** grown at Monticello and at Tufton Farm. The center is a force in the preservation of garden plants grown in the 18th century. They also offer books on historic or old-fashioned flowers, including reprints of early books, and books by and about Jefferson as a gardener. Other historic plants are sold at Monticello. (1987)
📖 Catalog: $1, CAN, CC, SS:3-5,10, $2m, cn/bn
🔾 Nursery: April-October, daily
❀ Garden: Spring-Fall, by appointment only

Jelitto Perennial Seeds, USA Office
125 Chenoweth Lane
Louisville, KY 40207
Allen W. Bush, Mgr.
(502) 895-0807
Fax: (502) 895-3934

Seeds
Seed of a very broad selection of **perennials**, including many new varieties, **rock garden and alpine plants and ornamental grasses** listed by botanical name. This German company sells mostly wholesale, but will accept orders as small as $50. Catalog is in English, with cultural instructions for germinating seeds, symbols for use and some color photographs. (1957)
📖 Catalog: $5, R&W, CAN/OV, CC, $50m, bn

Jernigan Gardens
840 Maple Grove Church Road
Dunn, NC 28334
Winifred Williams
(910) 567-2135, 677-0101

Plants
A collectors' list of **daylilies**, very briefly described, with concise tables of information. Also offers a good selection of **hostas** and some Siberian iris in mixed colors. (1955)
📖 Catalog: $1d, R&W, SS:4-11, $25m
🔾 Nursery: April-July, call ahead
❀ Garden: April-July, call ahead

Jersey Asparagus Farms
105 Porchtown Road
Pittsgrove, NJ 08318-4519
Scott Walker
(609) 358-2548, (800) 499-0013
Fax: (609) 358-6127
E-mail: 74724.3444@compuserve.com
Web: www.jerseyasparagus.com

Plants
Specialize in the Jersey male hybrid **asparagus**, which are very tolerant to fusarium diseases, resistant to rust, and are much higher yielding than the older varieties. Also offer two kinds of **strawberries** for farm markets. (1985)
📖 Catalog: Free, R&W, CAN, SS:11-5, $13m
🔾 Nursery: All year, M-F

Joe Pye Weed's Garden
337 Acton Street
Carlisle, MA 01741-1432
Marty Schafer & Jan Sacks

Plants
Specialists in **Siberian, iris versicolor, and species iris**, many of the Siberians are of their own breeding. They also list "apogons" -- they are beardless iris, but I know no more than that! Collectors will know. (1984)
📖 Catalog: Long SASE, CAN/OV, SS:8-9, $10m, bn

Joe's Nursery
P.O. Box 1867
Vista, CA 92085-1867
Joseph W. Kraatz
(760) 758-7042
Fax: (760) 758-4712
E-mail: exoticlvs@aol.com
Web: members.aol.com/exoticlvs

Plants
A collector's list of **palms, cycads, aloes, agaves, euphorbias, bromeliads, yuccas, nolinas, pachypodiums, species ficus, sansevierias,** and various succulents and other subtropicals; some plant descriptions, and a nice selection. (1986)
📖 Catalog: $1, CC, SS:W, $25m, bn

Johnny's Selected Seeds
Route 1, Box 2580
Foss Hill Road
Albion, ME 04910-9731
Robert L. Johnston, Jr.
(207) 437-9294
Fax: (800) 437-4290
E-mail: homegarden@johnnyseeds.com
Web: www.johnnyseeds.com

Seeds 🔊 Books 🔊 Supplies
Catalog lists a broad selection of **vegetables, herbs and garden annuals,** as well as specialty grains and seed for commercial crops; also a good selection of growing supplies and books. All plants are very well described, with cultural suggestions and germination guides; particularly suited to Northern growing. (1973)
📖 Catalog: Free, R&W, CAN/OV, CC
○ Nursery: All year, M-Sa
✸ Garden: July-August, call ahead

Johnson Nursery, Inc.
Route 5, Box 29-J
Highway 52 E.
Ellijay, GA 30540-9294
Bill & Elisa S. Ford
(706) 276-3187, (888) 276-3187
Fax: (706) 276-3186

Plants 🔊 Supplies 🔊 Tools
Catalog offers a good selection of **fruit trees** -- apples, old peach varieties, pears, plums, cherries, figs, berries and some grapes -- all well described. Also sells orchard supplies. (1981)
📖 Catalog: Free, R&W, CC, SS:12-4
○ Nursery: All year, M-Sa

Joy Creek Nursery
20300 N.W. Watson Road
Scappoose, OR 97056-9612
Mike Smith, Maurice Horn & Scott Christy
(503) 543-7474
Fax: (503) 543-6933

Plants
This nursery offers a very nice selection of **perennials,** and some **shrubs,** including unusual varieties of penstemons, euphorbias, eryngiums, hydrangeas and species clematis. All plants well described; new varieties being added all the time. (1992)
📖 Catalog: $2d($4 OV), CAN/OV, CC, SS:3-6,9-10, bn/cn
○ Nursery: March-October, daily
✸ Garden: March-October, daily

J. W. Jung Seed Co.
335 S. High Street
Randolph, WI 53957-0001
Richard Zondag
(920) 326-3121, (800) 247-5864
Fax: (800) 692-5864
E-mail: jungseed@peoples.net

Plants 🔊 Seeds 🔊 Supplies 🔊 Bulbs
Color catalog offers a broad selection of seeds for the flower and vegetable garden, as well as nursery stock -- **fruit trees, roses, perennials, ornamental trees, shrubs and vines.** Also issues a bulb catalog in the summer. Carries tools and supplies, too. No shipping to AK or HI. (1907)
📖 Catalog: Free, CC, SS:3-10
○ Nursery: All year, M-F
✸ Garden: July-September (Randolph trial garden)

Junglemania
301 National Street
Santa Cruz, CA 95060
Edward Hawkins

Plants
"Emphasis is on texture and color, and also, the use of exotic flora and foliage in unconventional flower arrangements." This small nursery specializes in **cannas,** and exotic **foliage perennials.** Plants are briefly described. No shipping to HI. (1994)
📖 Catalog: Long SASE, SS:5-9, $20m, bn/cn
✸ Garden: April-October, by appointment only

Just Enough Sinningias
P.O. Box 560493
Orlando, FL 32856
Patti Schwindt
E-mail: PattiSchwindt@compuserve.com

Plants
Patti specializes in **miniature sinningias,** offering a nice selection in an informative catalog with lots of information on ancestry. These little plants are great houseplants, and are frequently used in terrariums. (1990)
📖 Catalog: $2($3 OV), CAN/OV

Just Fruits
30 St. Francis Street
Crawfordville, FL 32327
Roxanne Cowley
(904) 926-5644

Plants
Fruits for the Southeast and fruits which thrive under "low chill" conditions:
figs, kiwi, bananas, peaches and nectarines, grapes, Asian and regular pears,
mayhaws, apples, plums, berries, hardy citrus and much more. All fruits well
described; can't ship to AZ, CA or citrus to some states. (1983)
📖 Catalog: $3d($5 OV), R&W, CAN/OV, $25m
○ Nursery: September-June, Th-Su
❀ Garden: All year, Th-Su, call ahead

Justice Miniature Roses
5947 S.W. Kahle Road
Wilsonville, OR 97070
Jerry and Tara Justice
(503) 682-2370
E-mail: justrose@gte.net

Plants
A broad selection of **miniature roses**, all very well described, with some
growing advice. In 1987 they started introducing varieties hybridized in Ireland
by Sean McCann, and they also hybridize roses themselves. (1982)
📖 Catalog: Free, R&W, OV, SS:3-10
○ Nursery: All year, daily, call ahead
❀ Garden: April-September, call ahead

K & L Cactus & Succulent Nursery
9500 Brook Ranch Road East
Ione, CA 95640-9417
Keith & Lorraine Thomas
(209) 274-0360
Fax: (209) 274-0360

Plants ⅏ **Seeds** ⅏ **Books** ⅏ **Supplies**
Color and b&w catalog offers extensive list of **flowering desert and jungle
cacti, succulents** and some seed; each well but briefly described. Also sells
some cactus books and a few supplies. (1971)
📖 Catalog: $3d($5 OV), CAN/OV, CC, $25m, bn

KSA Jojoba
19025 Parthenia Street
Northridge, CA 91324-4820
Kathie Aamodt
(818) 701-1534
Fax: (818) 933-0194

Plants ⅏ **Seeds** ⅏ **Supplies**
Sells only **jojoba** -- seeds, seedlings and rooted cuttings of Simmondsia
chinensis, and a variety of jojoba products such as soap, shampoos and
automotive products. No plant descriptions. (1979)
📖 Catalog: Long SASE w/2 FCS, R&W, CAN/OV, CC
○ Nursery: All year, M-F, by appointment only

Kapoho Palms
P.O. Box 3
Pahoa, HI 96778
Frank Streeter
(808) 936-2580, (617) 497-0008
Fax: (806) 965-7797
E-mail: streeter@orphic.com

Plants
Offers a good selection of **palms**, and some **cycads** on a collectors' list without plant descriptions. There is a contact in the Boston area to answer questions. Cycads cannot be shipped overseas. (1987)
📖 Catalog: $1 or SASE w/2 FCS, R&W, OV, $60m, bn

Karleen's Achimenes
1407 W. Magnolia Street
Valdosta, GA 31601-4235
Karleen Lane
(912) 242-1368

Plants ⅏ **Seeds**
A small hobby business, but offers a wide selection (over 500) of achimenes
and other **gesneriads** -- sinningias, gloxinias, smithiantha, eucodonias and
kohlerias. Most fairly briefly but well described. (1978)
📖 Catalog: $1.50($2 OV), CAN/OV, SS:W, $20m, bn
○ Nursery: May-October, M-Sa, call ahead
❀ Garden: May-October, call ahead

Kartuz Greenhouses
P.O. Box 790
1408 Sunset Drive
Vista, CA 92085-0790
Michael J. Kartuz
(760) 941-3613
Fax: (760) 941-1123
E-mail: mikekartuz@aol.com

Plants
The catalog, a collectors' dream, offers flowering plants for the home, green-
house and outside in warm areas -- **begonias and species gesneriads** and
many other rare flowering plants and vines -- all very well described. Even
more plants available at the nursery. (1960)
📖 Catalog: $2, CAN, CC, $20m, bn
○ Nursery: All year, W-Sa, by appointment only
❀ Garden: June-October, W-Sa, by appointment only

Kasch Nursery
2860 N.E. Kelly Place
Gresham, OR 97030-2793
Lorry & Tim Kasch
(503) 661-0357

Plants
Offers a good selection of rooted and grafted **conifers**, both "regular" big
ones and dwarfs; plants are briefly described by growth habit, hardiness, and
size at maturity. Limited overseas shipping. (1983)
📖 Catalog: Free, R&W, CAN/OV, bn

Kay's Greenhouses
207 W. Southcross
San Antonio, TX 78221-1155
Kay Tucker
Fax: (210) 927-4917

Plants
A broad selection of **rhizomatous and cane begonias**, both plants and cuttings. Each plant is briefly described by color of leaves and bloom. Ask if you're looking for something rare, she has more plants than she lists. No shipping to Australia. (1987)
- Catalog: $2, R&W, CAN/OV, SS:W, $10m
- Nursery: Daily, by appointment only
- Garden: By appointment only

Sam Kedem Greenhouse & Nursery
12414 - 191st Street E.
Hastings, MN 55033
Sam Kedem
(612) 437-7516
Fax: (612) 437-7195
E-mail: Thekedems@aol.com

Plants
Offers **hardy roses** for northern climates: roses of all types including old garden, climbers, modern shrubs, miniatures, ground covers and tree roses. Most are briefly described, with lists of roses by use. Also offered are some flowering shrubs and perennials to grow with the roses. (1988)
- Catalog: Free($2 OV), R&W, CAN, SS:4-10
- Nursery: May-September, daily
- Garden: June-August, daily

Kelleygreen Nursery
P.O. Box 62
Drain, OR 97435
Jan Kelley
(800) 477-5676, (541) 836-2990

Plants
Collectors' list -- a nice selection of **hybrid rhododendrons, deciduous and evergreen azaleas, Japanese maples, pieris and kalmias**. All varieties are well described, and there is good general cultural information. (1978)
- Catalog: Free, CC, SS:3-6,9-12, $15m, bn
- Nursery: All year, by appointment only
- Garden: May, by appointment only

Kelly's Color
P.O. Box 724
1838 Eastside Road
Etna, CA 96027
Marsha Hayden, Mgr.
Fax: (916) 467-5733

Plants
A broad selection of **sedums, sempervivums, jovibarba and heuffeliis**, well described in a tightly packed collectors' list, with good cultural information. Most of the plants are hardy to Zone 1 and come in many colors and leaf textures, even cobweb types. They also offer a few **lewisias**. (1956)
- Catalog: $2, R&W, CAN/OV, SS:4-9, $10m, bn
- Nursery: All year, M-F, by appointment only
- Garden: By appointment only

Kelly's Plant World
10266 E. Princeton
Sanger, CA 93657
Herbert Kelly, Jr.
(209) 294-7676

Plants ✎ Bulbs
"Specializes in **rare and unusual plants** from around the globe," including trees, shrubs, perennials, many varieties of **cannas, crinums, aspidistras, amaryllis,** and other **summer blooming bulbs**. He grows many more plants than he lists; you can call and ask him what's available. (1970)
- Catalog: $1, R&W, $50m
- Nursery: By appointment only

Kensington Orchids
3301 Plyers Mill Road
Kensington, MD 20895-2722
Merritt W. Huntington
(301) 933-0036
Fax: (301) 933-9441

Plants ✎ Books ✎ Supplies
List offers phalaenopsis, doritaenopsis and oncidium hybrids, cattleyas, dendrobium, vanda, ascocenda and paphiopedilum **orchids** in seedling and flowering sizes, very briefly described. Also sells books and orchid growing supplies. (1946)
- Catalog: $1d, R&W, CAN/OV, CC, SS:W, $25m
- Nursery: All year, daily
- Garden: All year, greenhouses, daily

Keith Keppel
P.O. Box 18154
Salem, OR 97305
Keith Keppel
(503) 391-9241

Plants
Keith has retired and moved to Oregon: he issues an extensive list of **tall bearded iris**, many his own introductions; plants very well described, with very good information on parentage. He caters to the "iris crowd," which means he has the latest and most desirable new iris. (1955)
- Catalog: $2d, SS:7-8, CAN, SS:7-8
- Nursery: May, daily, call ahead
- Garden: May, daily during daylight hours

Kester's Wild Game Food Nurseries
P.O. Box 516
4582 Highway 116 East
Omro, WI 54963-0516
David & Patricia Kester
(920) 685-2929, (800) 558-8815
Fax: (920) 685-6727
E-mail: pkester@vbe.com

Plants ℘ Seeds
A wide selection of **plants to feed wildlife: plants for ponds**, various grains and wild rice (including an edible variety). The catalog offers a lot of cultural and wildlife food management information, and lists seed and plants, including aquatic plants, for feeding pet birds. (1899)
- Catalog: $3, R&W, CC, SS:2-10, cn/bn
- Nursery: All year, M-Sa, call ahead

Kilgore Seed Company
1400 W. First Street
Sanford, FL 32771
J. H. Hunziker
(407) 323-6630

Seeds ℘ Supplies ℘ Tools
A regional seed company, offering **vegetables and flowers** for the Gulf Coast area of the US, but suited to any subtropical or tropical climate. A wide selection, each very well described, with cultural suggestions; they also sell gardening supplies and tools. (1918)
- Catalog: Free ($2 OV), CAN/OV
- Nursery: All year, M-F

Killdeer Farms
21606 NW 51st Avenue
Ridgefield, WA 98642
Steve & Jane Barton
(360) 887-1790

Plants
Specializing in **geraniums** of all types -- ivy, miniatures, cascading types, regal and scented leaf varieties as well as fancy leaf and a few species pelargoniums. Great selection, brief descriptions.
- Catalog: Free, R&W, CAN/OV, CC
- Nursery: April-June, W-Su, or by appointment
- Garden: By appointment only

King's Mums
P.O. Box 368
20303 E. Liberty Road
Clements, CA 95227
Ted & Lanna King

Plants ℘ Supplies
Color catalog offers wide choice of **chrysanthemums** -- a real collectors' list; all plants well described, with cultural information. Sells mum collections, growing supplies, and the handbooks of the National Chrysanthemum Society. (1964)
- Catalog: $2d, SS:2-6, $10m
- Nursery: October-November, daily, call ahead
- Garden: October-November, daily, call ahead

Kirkland Daylilies
P.O. Box 176
Newville, AL 36353
Marjorie C. Kirkland
(334) 889-3313

Plants
Specializes in large-flowered **daylilies**; almost all of them have flowers seven inches or more across. Plants are listed in an informative table. Also offers hybrid **amaryllis**, described by color; send SASE for list. (1990)
- Catalog: Free, SS:4-10, $30m
- Nursery: May-November, daily
- Garden: May-June, call ahead

Kitazawa Seed Co.
1111 Chapman Street
San Jose, CA 95126
Helen Komatsu
(408) 243-1330

Seeds
A good selection of seeds for **Oriental vegetables**; plants are well described. Eighteen varieties of daikon, the Japanese radish, and 14 kinds of mustard. Also squash, melons, greens, eggplants, beans and more. (1917)
- Catalog: Free, R&W, $3m

Klehm Growers
44 W 637 State Route 72
Hampshire, IL 60140-8268
Arnold J. Klehm
(847) 683-4761
Fax: (847) 683-4766
E-mail: klehmgro@aol.com

Plants
A nice selection of **orchids**, mostly hybrid seedlings of phalaenopsis, but also vandaceous, cattleya alliance, paphiopedilums, cymbidiums and species; some are their own "Meriklehms." All plants are briefly described, some special collections, too. (1980)
- Catalog: Free, R&W, CAN/OV, CC, SS:W, bn
- Nursery: All year, M-F, call ahead

Klehm Nursery
4210 N. Duncan Road
Champaign, IL 61821
Klehm Family
(800) 553-3715
Fax: (217) 373-8403
E-mail: klehm@soltec.net
Web: www.klehm.com

Plants ಬ Books
Offers a broad selection of **hosta, daylilies, iris** and herbaceous and tree **peonies, ferns, ornamental grasses and perennials**; all plants well described, with general cultural information, many are their own hybrids. They also offer a few books on the plants which are their specialty. (1852)
📖 Catalog: $4d, R&W, CAN, SS:4-11, bn

Gerhard Koehres Cactus & Succulent Nursery
Wingertstrasse 33
Erzhausen/Darmstadt, Germany D-64387
Gerhard Koehres
49 (0) 6150-7241
Fax: 49 (0) 6150-84168

Seeds
A very extensive list of **cactus and succulent** seeds, as well as some tillandsias and palms, listed by botanical name; no plant descriptions, but sure to please collectors. Offered are aylostera, copiapoa, frailea, gymnocalyciums, parodia, agaves, aloes, euphorbias, mesembs and many more!
📖 Catalog: $2(US Bills), R&W, OV, bn
✽ Garden: By appointment only

V. Kraus Nurseries, Ltd.

See Martin & Kraus.

Krohne Plant Farms
65295 CR 342
Hartford, MI 49057
William Krohne
(616) 424-5423

Plants
Fifteen varieties of **strawberries** which will produce in Northern climates; informative leaflet. Will sell in quantities as low as 25 per customer; quantity discounts for commercial growers. Also offers eight kinds of asparagus crowns (purple ones, too!). No shipping to AK, AZ, CA, FL, or HI. (1974)
📖 Catalog: Free, R&W, SS:2-5, $9m
❍ Nursery: February-May, call ahead
✽ Garden: June, M-Sa, call ahead

Kuk's Forest Nursery
10174 Barr Road
Brecksville, OH 44141-3302
Robert Kuk
(216) 546-2675
Fax: (216) 546-2675

Plants
Not a source of mighty trees, Robert Kuk is a **hosta** hybridizer who offers his own introductions as well as other new and old varieties. A good selection, each variety is well described. (1986)
📖 Catalog: $2($4 OV), R&W, CAN/OV, CC, SS:5-10, $30m
❍ Nursery: June-September, Sa-Su, by appointment only
✽ Garden: June-September, by appointment only

Kumar International
Ajitmal
Etawah (U.P.), India 206121
A. K. Agarwal

Seeds
Offers a good selection of seeds of **conifers, ornamental trees and shrubs, palms, bamboos, and tropical fruit trees**; no plant descriptions, only botanical names. Ask for price list, which is not included in catalog. (1976)
📖 Catalog: $1(US Bills), R&W, OV, $10m, bn
❍ Nursery: By appointment only

Kusa Seed Research Foundation
P.O. Box 761
Ojai, CA 93024
Lorenz Schaller

Seeds
Non-profit group devoted to seedcrops of folk origin, especially **cereal grains**. Sells seed of crops which can be grown by home gardeners and small-scale farmers: special strains of millet, hull-less barley, Einkorn wheat, lentils, sesame, oats and others; all well described. (1980)
📖 Catalog: $2.50 + Long SASE w/2 FCS($5 OV), CAN/OV

Lady Bug Beautiful Gardens
857 Leopard Trail
Winter Springs, FL 32708-4127
Ra Hansen
(407) 699-0172
Fax: (407) 699-9923
E-mail: ladybug@magicnet.net

Plants
Offers a wide selection of **daylilies**, some of which are their own introductions; cultivars are both new introductions and older varieties, all are well described in a friendly, chatty catalog with some color photographs. Garden is an official American Hemerocallis Display Garden. (1976)
📖 Catalog: $4d($6 OV), R&W, SS:2-10, $35m
❍ Nursery: All year, M-Th, by appointment only
✽ Garden: May-June, M-Th, by appointment only

Lamtree Farm
2323 Copeland Road
Warrensville, NC 28693
Lee A. Morrison
(910) 385-6144

Plants
Small nursery sells a limited but choice selection of **trees and shrubs**: frank-linia, leucothoe, native rhododendrons and azaleas, styrax, halesia, stewartias and more; good plant descriptions. Can't ship to CA, OR or WA. (1979)
📖 Catalog: $2, R&W, CC, SS:W, bn/cn
✪ Nursery: By appointment only

Landis Valley Museum

See Heirloom Seed Project, Landis Valley Museum.

D. Landreth Seed Company
P.O. Box 6426
Baltimore, MD 21230-0426
Stockholders
(410) 727-3922, (800) 654-2407
Fax: (410) 244-8633

Seeds
"America's oldest seed house" -- George Washington and Thomas Jefferson were early customers. Offers a broad selection of new and old varieties of **vegetables**, all well described with cultural information, as well as a smaller selection of **herbs** and **garden annuals**. (1784)
📖 Catalog: Free, R&W, CAN/OV, $20m

Landscape Alternatives, Inc.
1705 St. Albans Street
Roseville, MN 55113
(612) 488-3142
Fax: (612) 488-3860

Plants
Specializes in nursery-propagated native **Minnesota wildflowers** and prairie and other ornamental **grasses** for distinctive low-maintenance landscapes. A good selection, with very brief plant descriptions. They also offer a few garden perennials. Cannot ship to CA or HI. (1986)
📖 Catalog: $2, R&W, CC, SS:5-9, $25m, cn/bn
✪ Nursery: May-October, Tu-Su, call ahead
❀ Garden: June-August, Tu-Su, call ahead

Larner Seeds
P.O. Box 407
Bolinas, CA 94924-0407
Judith Larner Lowry
(415) 868-9407
Fax: (415) 868-9820

Seeds ɣ Books
Seed for the Western landscape -- a good selection of **native wildflowers**, annual and perennial, and **trees, shrubs, vines and grasses**. Catalog emphasizes use in natural landscaping and offers several mixes for various habitats. Also offers books on natural landscaping and their own series of pamphlets on growing native plants. (1978)
📖 Catalog: $2.50($3.50 OV), R&W, CAN/OV, CC, $15m, bn/cn
✪ Nursery: All year, Tu, Sa
❀ Garden: April-July, Tu, Sa, call ahead

© Canyon Creek Nursery
Artist: Susan M. Whittlesey

Las Pilitas Nursery
Star Route, Box 23 X
Las Pilitas Road
Santa Margarita, CA 93453
Bert & Celeste Wilson
(805) 438-5992
Fax: (805) 438-5993
E-mail: bawilson@slonet.org

Plants ⬥ Bulbs
A very extensive list of **California native plants** of all kinds. Price list is free; 240 page catalog is available for $8($15 overseas). Price list gives botanical and common name only, and quantities of plants available. The catalog has become a very useful and extensive treatise on growing our Western native plants -- a bargain at $8! (1979)
📖 Catalog: See notes, R&W, CAN/OV, CC, bn/cn
○ Nursery: All year, Sa
❀ Garden: All year, Sa

Lauray of Salisbury
432 Undermountain Road (Route 41)
Salisbury, CT 06068-1102
Judith Becker
(860) 435-2263

Plants
A very extensive collectors' list of **begonias, gesneriads, cacti, succulents, epiphyllums and hybrid and species orchids**, all well but briefly described, with some cultural notes on genera.
📖 Catalog: $2, CAN/OV, SS:4-10, $10m, bn
○ Nursery: All year, daily, call ahead
❀ Garden: All year, glasshouse, call ahead

Laurie's Landscape
2959 Hobson Road
Downers Grove, IL 60517-1513
Laurie Skrzenta
(630) 969-1270

Plants
A nice selection of **hostas, herbaceous peonies**, and a few **perennials** and ornamental trees and shrubs; plants are very briefly described. Cannot ship to AZ, CA, OR or WA. (1988)
📖 Catalog: Long SASE, SS:7-10, $50m
○ Nursery: May-June, Sept.-Oct., by appointment only
❀ Garden: May-June, August, by appointment only

Lawson's Nursery
2730 Yellow Creek Road
Ball Ground, GA 30107
Jim & Bernice Lawson
(770) 893-2141

Plants ⬥ Books
A good selection of **antique apple and pear trees**; all well described with historical background -- even a 14th century apple called 'Rambo!' They've added a few **blueberries, grapes, cherries, plums, peaches and nuts**. Sell the Potter Walnut Cracker, the "Granddaddy of the Walnut Crackers." (1968)
📖 Catalog: Free, R&W, CAN/OV, CC, SS:11-3, $25m
○ Nursery: September-May, M-Sa, call ahead
❀ Garden: By appointment only

Lazy K Nursery, Inc.
705 Wright Road
Pine Mountain, GA 31822
Ernest F. Koone III
(706) 663-4991
E-mail: EKooneIII@aol.com

Plants
Offers 13 species of Southeastern **deciduous azaleas**, and 10 hybrids and cultivars of these as well as some companion plants. Many of the species are intensely fragrant as well as very beautiful. No shipping to AZ, CA, OR or WA.
📖 Catalog: $1d, R&W, SS:10-3, $25m, bn/cn
○ Nursery: All year, Tu-Sa, call ahead
❀ Garden: Call ahead

Le Jardin du Gourmet
P.O. Box 75
St. Johnsbury Center, VT 05863
Paul Taylor
(802) 748-1446
Fax: (802) 748-9592
E-mail: Flowers.Herbs@KingCon.com

Plants ⬥ Seeds ⬥ Books
Offer a good selection of **herb and vegetable** seeds in both regular and $.25 sample packets. Ship herb plants only in the US, as well as garlic and shallots. Also sell books on herbs, and some imported spices, teas, and other gourmet supplies. (1954)
📖 Catalog: $.50, R&W, CAN/OV, CC, cn
○ Nursery: All year, M-Sa, call ahead

Ledden Brothers
P.O. Box 7
195 Centre Street
Sewell, NJ 08080-0007
Don & Dale Ledden
(609) 468-1002
Fax: (609) 464-0947
Web: www.leddens.com

Seeds ⬥ Supplies ⬥ Tools ⬥ Bulbs
Orol Ledden & Sons has gone out of business, but Ledden Brothers is carrying on the family tradition. Catalog offers over 600 varieties of **flowers, vegetables, grasses** and **cover crops** and some summer-blooming **bulbs**, all well described. Also sells growing supplies and tools, and fertilizers. (1904)
📖 Catalog: Free, R&W, CAN, $5m
○ Nursery: All year, daily
❀ Garden: April-September, daily

Lee Gardens
P.O. Box 5
25986 Sauder Road
Tremont, IL 61568
Janis Lee
(309) 925-5262
Fax: (309) 925-5010
E-mail: jiboshi@aol.com

Plants
Hostas, ligularias, daylilies, wildflowers and other sun and shade-loving
perennials, both common and rare; a good selection with very brief plant
descriptions. (1988)
📖 Catalog: $2d, CC, SS:4-9, $25m, bn
☉ Nursery: April-October, M-Sa
❀ Garden: May-September, M-Sa

Lee's Botanical Garden
P.O. Box 669
390 Davis Street
LaBelle, FL 33975
Bruce Lee Bednar
(941) 675-8728

Plants
Collectors' list of **carnivorous plants** -- sarracenia, nepenthes, dionaea,
drosera, pinguicula, utricularia, catopsis; no plant descriptions, but collectors
will know them -- some are his own hybrids. Also offers some **ferns** and
terrestrial orchids. No shipping to Mexico or countries that require CITES
certificate. (1980)
📖 Catalog: Free, R&W, OV, $10m, bn
☉ Nursery: By appointment only
❀ Garden: By appointment only

Legendary Ethnobotanical Resources
16245 S.W. 304 Street
Miami, FL 33033
Luis Eloy Riesgo
(305) 242-0877
E-mail: info@ethnobotany.com
Web: www.ethnobotany.com

Plants ᴔ **Seeds** ᴔ **Books** ᴔ **Supplies**
Specializing in "useful plants," including many **tropical fruits** and **tropical
trees, shrubs and perennials**. Listed are cherimoyas, coffee, erythrinas, and
quite a few species of morning glory. Plants are well described. Also sell herbs,
books and more.
📖 Catalog: $2, R&W, CAN/OV, CC, $10m, bn/cn
☉ Nursery: All year, M-W, call ahead
❀ Garden: All year, M-W, call ahead

Lenette Greenhouses
1440 Pom Orchid Lane
Kannapolis, NC 28081
K. G. Griffith
(704) 938-2042
Fax: (704) 938-7578

Plants ᴔ **Supplies**
Catalog offers cattleya and phalaenopsis **hybrid orchids**, in community pots,
flasks and blooming sizes, even "stud plants." Plants very briefly described.
Also offers miniature cymbidium crosses and a few oncidiums, vandas and
paphiopedilums and zygopetalum hybrids. Some are their own hybrids.
📖 Catalog: Free, R&W, SS:W, $30m
☉ Nursery: All year, M-Sa
❀ Garden: All year, greenhouses, M-Sa

Lessard Banana Farm

See Going Bananas.

Henry Leuthardt Nurseries, Inc.
P.O. Box 666
Montauk Highway
East Moriches, NY 11940-0666
Henry P. Leuthardt
(516) 878-1387
Fax: (516) 878-1387

Plants
A selection of **fruit trees, berries and grapes**, including some old varieties;
all briefly to well described. This nursery is also a source of espaliered apple
and pear trees in several styles. Their "handbook" is $2, gives more informa-
tion than the free catalog. Ship only apple and pear trees to CA.
📖 Catalog: Free, R&W, SS:10-12,3-5
☉ Nursery: All year, daily, call ahead

Lewis Mountain Herbs & Everlastings
2345 State Route 247
Manchester, OH 45144
Judy Lewis
(937) 549-2484
Fax: (937) 549-2886
E-mail: 102622.2116@compuserve.com

Plants ᴔ **Supplies**
Offers a nice selection of **herbs, scented geraniums and everlastings**,
listed by common and botanical name, but with no plant descriptions. List
of dried herbs and everlastings available on request. (1985)
📖 Catalog: $1, R&W, CC, SS:4-10, cn/bn
☉ Nursery: All year, M-Sa
❀ Garden: May-October, M-Sa

Lewis Strawberry Nursery
3500 NC Highway 133
Rocky Point, NC 28457
C. E. Lewis
(910) 675-2394, (800) 453-5346
Fax: (910) 602-3106

Plants
Over 20 "scientifically grown" varieties of **strawberries**, sold in quantities of 100 and up; no descriptions. Most of the plants are June-bearers; they also carry everbearing or day-neutral varieties; ship all over the East and Midwest. (1954)
📖 Catalog: Free, R&W, OV, SS:11-6, $18m

Liberty Seed Company
P.O. Box 806
461 Robinson Dr. S.E.
New Philadelphia, OH 44663
William & Connie Watson
(330) 364-1611
Fax: (330) 364-6415

Seeds 🔊 Books 🔊 Supplies
Color and b&w catalog offers a broad selection of garden **annuals** and **perennials**, **vegetables** (including heirloom and open-pollinated varieties), giant pumpkins and super sweet corn; all well described and adapted to the Midwest. Also offers a selection of propagation and growing supplies. (1981)
📖 Catalog: Free, R&W, CC, $20m
☀ Nursery: All year, M-F; April-July, Sa-Su
❀ Garden: July-September, M-F

The Lily Nook
P.O. Box 846
Hwy. 16, 1 mile W of Neepawa
Neepawa, MB, Canada R0J 1H0
Nigel Strohman
(204) 476-3225
Fax: (204) 476-5482
E-mail: lilynook@mail.techplus.com
Web: www.techplus.com/lily/lily.htm

Bulbs
Offers a very good selection of **Asiatic lilies**, including some pot or border Asiatics, tetrapolid and triploid lilies for use in breeding, some **martagon lilies** and some **Orientals, longiflorum-Asiatic hybrids, and species lilies.** All are very briefly described. Americans can order the catalog from P.O. Box 657, Rolla, ND 58367. (1995)
📖 Catalog: $2, R&W, US/OV, CC, SS:5,9-10, $5m
☀ Nursery: July-September, M-Sa, call ahead
❀ Garden: July-August, call ahead

The Lily Pad
3403 Steamboat Island Rd. NW, #374
Olympia, WA 98502
Jan Detwiler
(360) 866-0291
Fax: (360) 866-7128
E-mail: 73744.1571@compuserve.com

Bulbs
A family-run bulb company; they started out selling cut flowers and found that more people wanted their **lily** bulbs. Offer a good selection of newer hybrids, many are shown in color; as well as a few herbaceous **peonies** and **daylilies**. (1984)
📖 Catalog: $1d, R&W, CC, SS:10-4

Lilypons Water Gardens
P.O. Box 10
6800 Lilypons Road
Buckeystown, MD 21717-0010
Charles & Sally Thomas
(301) 874-5133, (800) 999-5459
Fax: (301) 874-2325

Plants 🔊 Books 🔊 Supplies
Color catalog offers a broad selection of **water lilies, lotus, bog plants**, garden ponds, fountains, fish and water gardening supplies. They also have a nursery in Brookshire, Texas. The photographs are really irresistible! (1917)
📖 Catalog: Free($5 CAN,$12 OV), R&W, CAN/OV, CC, cn/bn
☀ Nursery: March-October, daily; November-February, M-Sa
❀ Garden: May-September, daily

Limerock Ornamental Grasses
70 Sawmill Road
Port Matilda, PA 16870
Norm & Phyllis Hooven
(814) 692-2272
Fax: (814) 692-9848

Plants
Offers a broad selection of **ornamental grasses**, each well described, with a list of grasses for various growing conditions and uses. There is a nice introduction to grasses with comments on form, color, texture and motion. They've recently added some fall blooming perennials, native plants and shrubs (ask for Perennial Bulletin, $2). No shipping to CA.
📖 Catalog: $3, CC, SS:3-10, bn/cn
☀ Nursery: April-October, M-Sa
❀ Garden: April-October, M-Sa

Linton & Linton Bamboo
310 Woodbine Road
Savannah, GA 31410
Frank & Mindy Linton
(912) 897-5755
Fax: (912) 921-5890
E-mail: coastal@uga.cc.uga.edu
Web: www.atlgarden.com

Plants
Bamboo -- available as field divisions or in containers, from giant timber types to dwarf varieties, including some varieties that sound pretty rare. Plants are briefly but well described.
📖 Catalog: Free, CAN/OV, bn
☀ Nursery: All year, daily, call ahead

Living Stones Nursery
2936 N. Stone Avenue
Tucson, AZ 85705
Jane Evans & Gene Joseph
(520) 628-8773

Plants
Jane Evans & Gene Joseph took over the very large **lithops** collection of Ed Storms, and also offer other **cacti and succulents, aloes** and others. A good selection; some plants described. (1987)
- Catalog: $2d, R&W, CAN/OV, CC, $15m, bn
- Nursery: All year, W-Sa, call ahead
- Garden: October-May, W-Sa, call ahead

Loehman's Cacti & Succulents
P.O. Box 871
Paramount, CA 90723
Tom & Carol Loehman
(562) 428-4501

Plants
Offers a good selection of **cacti and succulents**: echinocereus, ferocactus, gymnocalyciums, mammillarias, notocactus, dorstenias, echeverias, euphorbias, haworthias and more. Plants listed only by botanical name. (1975)
- Catalog: $1d, SS:W, $10m, bn

Logee's Greenhouses
141 North Street
Danielson, CT 06239
Byron Martin
(860) 774-8038
Fax: (860) 774-9932
E-mail: logees@neca.com
Web: www@logeesplants.com

Plants & Books
A very extensive list of **begonias and other greenhouse and exotic plants** -- many are outdoor plants in warmer climates; all well described with some cultural suggestions, many illustrated in color. It's impossible to convey the variety -- a collector's dream, a houseplant lover's candy store. Catalog published every other year, with sales lists in spring and fall. (1892)
- Catalog: Free, R&W, CAN/OV, CC, SS:W, $20m, bn/cn
- Nursery: All year, daily
- Garden: All year, daily

Long's Gardens
P.O. Box 19
3240 Broadway
Boulder, CO 80306-0019
Everett C. Long
(303) 442-2353
Fax: (303) 413-1323

Plants
List offers broad selection of hardy **tall bearded iris**, some are introductions by Colorado hybridizers. During blooming time you can select your favorites and dig them up on the spot. Sells a few border, intermediate and dwarf bearded iris; brief plant descriptions. (1905)
- Catalog: Free, R&W, CC, SS:7-9
- Nursery: May-June, daily, call ahead
- Garden: May-June, daily, call ahead

Loon Designs
R.R. #1
477 Davis Drive
Uxbridge, ON, Canada L9P 1R1
Oksana Chmelyk
(905) 852-5455
Fax: (905) 852-5455
E-mail: expresssod@interhop.net

Plants
Offers **hardy perennials** for the garden -- they have wintered over outside in Ontario. A good selection, listed in table form, with cultural information included. Only ships within Canada at this time.
- Catalog: $3d, SS:4-5,9-10, $25m, bn/cn
- Nursery: Mid-April-October, M-F; Sa-Su, call ahead
- Garden: July, call ahead

Loucks Nursery

See West Coast Japanese Maples.

Lowe's Roses
6 Sheffield Road
Nashua, NH 03062-3028
Malcolm (Mike) Lowe
(603) 888-2214
Fax: (603) 888-6112
E-mail: LoweRoses@aol.com

Plants
A catalog of old **roses**; a huge selection of many types, including species roses and some of the modern shrub roses of contemporary hybridizers in Europe and the US. Most of the roses are custom propagated to order; these take 18 months to deliver. The whole collection is over 2,000 varieties, so you might want to send your "wish list." (1979)
- Catalog: $3($5 OV), R&W, CAN/OV, SS:10,4, $12m, bn/cn
- Nursery: May-October, call ahead
- Garden: June, call ahead

Lower Marlboro Nursery
P.O. Box 1013
7011 Flint Hill Road (Owings)
Dunkirk, MD 20754
Mary-Stuart Sierra
(301) 812-0808
Fax: (301) 812-0808

Plants
Offers a nice selection of **Northeastern native plants**, many suitable for woodland plantings. Each plant is very well described, with planting suggestions. No shipping to AK, AZ, CA, HI, OR or WA. (1989)
📖 Catalog: $2, SS:4-5,9-10, bn/cn
⊙ Nursery: April-October, call ahead
❀ Garden: April-October, call ahead

Lyndon Lyon Greenhouses, Inc.
P. O. Box 249
14 Mutchlet Street
Dolgeville, NY 13329-0249
Paul Sorano
(315) 429-8291
Fax: (315) 429-3820

Plants
This firm is the originator of many favorite **African violets** and also sells **streptocarpus, episcias, columneas, rex begonias** and other houseplants; many are illustrated in color photographs, with good brief plant descriptions and some cultural information. (1954)
📖 Catalog: $3($5 OV), R&W, CAN/OV, CC, SS:5-10, $12m
⊙ Nursery: All year, M-Sa
❀ Garden: April-June, M-Sa

MCM Orchids
P.O. Box 4626
Wheaton, IL 60189-4626
Michael C. Morgan
(630) 668-4588
Fax: (630) 668-4687
E-mail: mcmorchids@aol.com
Web: shell.idt.net/~michmo19

Plants
Specialists in "**orchid species** for the collector of unique and unusual plants," they offer an extensive listing, with very brief notes. Includes 144 genera, and many of these list quite a few species.
📖 Catalog: FCS(2 IRC OV), CAN/OV, CC, $25m, bn
⊙ Nursery: By appointment only

McAllister's Iris Gardens
P.O. Box 112
Fairacres, NM 88033
Sharon McAllister
Fax: (505) 522-6731
E-mail: 73372.1745@compuserve.com

Plants
Small nursery specializing in **aril iris**, listed as three-quarter breds, half-breds, quarter-breds, and "arilbredmedians." Quite a few are their own introductions. All are well described. Collections, arilbred seeds and some **species iris** are also offered. No shipping to CA. (1991)
📖 Catalog: $1d, CAN/OV, SS:7-9
❀ Garden: March-April, by appointment only

McClure & Zimmerman
P.O. Box 368
108 W. Winnebago
Friesland, WI 53935
Richard Zondag
(920) 326-4220
Fax: (800) 692-5864

Books ≋ **Bulbs**
A very large selection of **bulbs**, both the common spring Dutch bulbs and a wide selection of species bulbs not so easy to find -- species tulips, bulbous iris, hardy cyclamen, summer-blooming bulbs; all very well described, many charmingly illustrated. Books on bulbs, too. (1980)
📖 Catalog: Free, CC, SS:4-5,8-12, bn

L. J. McCreary & Co. Perennial Seeds
P.O. Box 8053
Grangerland, TX 77302
Sandra McCreary

Seeds
A very good selection of seeds of **annual and perennial garden flowers**, many of them uncommon, including aquilegias, bellis, species clematis, delphiniums, hellebores, species roses and violas. Brief descriptions.
📖 Catalog: $2($4 OV), CAN/OV, $5m, bn/cn

McKinney's Glassehouse
P.O. Box 782282
Wichita, KS 67278-2282
James McKinney & Charles Pickard
(316) 686-9438

Plants ≋ **Supplies**
"We are **gesneriad specialists**, with a large supply of African violets, episcias, other gesneriads and diminutive terrarium plants." Adding new plants from the tropical rain forests of South America. Also list growing supplies and terrariums in many styles. (1946)
📖 Catalog: $2.50d, R&W, CAN, CC, SS:4-10, bn/cn
⊙ Nursery: All year, daily, call ahead
❀ Garden: All year, daily, call ahed

McMillen's Iris Garden
RR 1
Norwich, ON, Canada N0J 1P0
Gloria McMillen
(519) 468-6508
Fax: (519) 468-3214
E-mail: iris@execulink.com
Web: www.execulink.com/~iris

Plants
Offers a very large selection of **iris** and some **daylilies**; they grow over 1,000 iris and 100 daylilies in their gardens. Tall, median and dwarf bearded, and Siberian iris; good plant descriptions. (1973)
- Catalog: $2, R&W, US/OV, SS:8-9, $30m
- Nursery: May-June, August-September, call ahead
- Garden: May-June, call ahead

Mail-Order Natives
P.O. Box 9366
Lee, FL 32059
Amy H. Webb
(904) 973-4688
Web: www.mindspring.com/~plants/natives.catalogue.html

Plants
A broad selection of **trees and shrubs native to the southeastern US**, including many species of pawpaws, hickories, oaks and tupelos. Plants are well described with notes on use by butterflies. No shipping to AZ and CA.
- Catalog: Free, CAN, SS:11-3, bn/cn

Ann Mann's Orchids
9045 Ron-Den Lane
Windermere, FL 34786-8328
Ann Mann
(407) 876-2625
Web: www.cfog.com

Plants ℘ Supplies
Very large selection of **orchids, bromeliads, hoyas, anthuriums, alocasias** and other exotic plants, with cultural notes. Also sells their Centrifugal Micro-Fogger, for the small hobby greenhouse, as well as charcoal and other growing supplies, including their own "Husky-Fiber," and New Zealand sphagnum moss; only supplies shipped overseas and to Canada. (1969)
- Catalog: $1, CAN/OV, SS:4-10, $40m, bn
- Nursery: By appointment only
- Garden: By appointment only

Maple Tree Garden
P.O. Box 547
208 First Street
Ponca, NE 68770-0547
Larry L. Harder
(402) 755-2615

Plants
Bearded iris: standard tall, miniature and standard dwarf, intermediate, miniature tall and border, as well as arilbred and Siberian iris and **daylilies**. A real collectors' list; a broad selection with brief plant descriptions. (1961)
- Catalog: $1, SS:7-9, $10m
- Nursery: By appointment only
- Garden: May, July, by appointment only

Mar-Low Epi House
31527 Oakridge Crescent
Abbotsford, BC, Canada V2T 6A6
Marie K. Lowen
(604) 850-9588

Plants
An **epiphyllum** collector who offers plants and cuttings from her collection; described only by color; there will be new offerings each year. Americans can request catalogs from P.O. Box 1940, Sumas, WA 98295. (1988)
- Catalog: $2d($3 OV), US/OV, SS:4-10, $15m
- Nursery: April-October, W-Sa, call ahead
- Garden: April-October, W-Sa, call ahead

Martin & Kraus
P.O. Box 12
1191 Centre Road
Carlisle, ON, Canada L0R 1H0
Linda Kraus-Martin
(905) 689-0230
Fax: (905) 689-1358

Plants
The retail mail order arm of V. Kraus Nurseries, they offer a broad selection of hardy flowering and ornamental **trees and shrubs**, including many **roses**: hybrid teas, grandifloras, floribundas, climbers, modern shrub and miniatures. Also sell **fruit trees**, including many apples and plums, grapes, berries, rhubarb and asparagus. No plant descriptions. (1953)
- Catalog: $1(US$1 US), US/OV, CC, SS:4-5,11, $8m
- Nursery: April, May, November, call ahead
- Garden: July, by appointment only

Mary's Garden
Route 1, Box 348
Hico, TX 76457
Pete & Mary Huggins
(254) 796-4041

Plants
Broad selection of **bearded iris**: tall bearded, reblooming, intermediate, border, dwarf, horned, "space age" and "antique" (before 1950). The "antiques" are often used for landscaping period homes. Formerly Huggins Farm Irises.
- Catalog: $2d, CAN, SS:7-10, $15m
- Nursery: March-October, call ahead
- Garden: March-May, call ahead

Mary's Plant Farm & Landscaping
2410 Lanes Mill Road
Hamilton, OH 45013
Mary E. Harrison
(513) 894-0022

Plants
Offer a wide selection of **perennials**, including hardy geraniums, iris, ornamental grasses, herbs and hostas. Also sell a number of **trees and shrubs**, many good for smaller gardens: berberis, hydrangeas, spireas, lilacs, viburnums, amelanchier, dogwood and crabapples, as well as some wildflowers and ferns. Plants very briefly described. (1976)
- Catalog: $1d, CC, SS:4-10, bn
- Nursery: April-October, Tu-Sa, or by appointment
- Garden: April-October, Tu-Sa, or by appointment

Maryland Aquatic Nurseries
3427 N. Furnace Road
Jarrettsville, MD 21084
Richard J. Schuck
(410) 557-7615
Fax: (410) 692-2837
E-mail: info@marylandaquatic.com
Web: www.marylandaquatic.com

Plants 🔊 **Supplies**
Good selection of **plants for ponds, pools and bogs**: water lilies, Japanese and Louisiana iris, taro, ornamental grasses. All plants are well but briefly described. Also sell fish, supplies and water garden ornaments. (1986)
- Catalog: $5d, R&W, CAN/OV, CC, bn/cn
- Nursery: April-October, Sa
- Garden: May-September, M-Sa

Maryott's Gardens
1073 Bird Avenue
1069 Bird Avenue
San Jose, CA 95125
William R. Maryott
(408) 971-0444
Fax: (408) 971-6072
E-mail: 103262.1512@compuserve.com

Plants
A good choice of tall, intermediate and standard dwarf bearded **iris** for collectors; most are new or recent introductions, all are briefly described in their garden list. They also offer several collections of special iris. (1978)
- Catalog: $1d, R&W, CC, SS:7-8, $15m
- Nursery: April-May, daily
- Garden: April-May, daily

Matsu-Momiji Nursery
Route 2, Box 147-D
Hurricane, WV 25526
Steve Pilacik
(304) 562-9666

Plants 🔊 **Supplies** 🔊 **Tools**
A collectors' list of many cultivars of Japanese black pine (Pinus thunbergii), spruces, Japanese maples and other **plants for bonsai**, each fairly briefly described. Also finished bonsai, pots and supplies. (1980)
- Catalog: $2, R&W, CAN/OV, CC, $50m
- Nursery: By appointment only
- Garden: By appointment only

Meadow View Farms
3360 North Pacific Highway
Medford, OR 97501
GayLynn & Larry Dunagan
(541) 772-2169
Fax: (541) 772-2169

Plants
Offers a very good selection of **perennials and herbs**, including many good shade and dry garden plants. Each plant is well but briefly described, they also encourage you to send your "wish list," as they grow some plants in quantities too small to list. (1994)
- Catalog: $3, R&W, CAN, CC, $20m, bn
- Nursery: All year, M-Sa, March-September, Su
- Garden: May-August, same hours as nursery

Meehan's Miniatures
220 Saint Paul Street
Boonsboro, MD 21713-1304
Hugh & Martha Meehan
Fax: (301) 432-4409

Plants 🔊 **Supplies**
Offers **starter plants for bonsai**, both indoor and outdoor, including ficus, bougainvillea, elms and dwarf conifers. Also offers some bonsai supplies, and materials to make a waterfall. Plants well described. No shipping to AK, AZ, CA, FL, HI, LA, OR, WA or TX.
- Catalog: $1d, R&W, CAN, CC, $20m
- Nursery: All year, M-F, by appointment only

Mellinger's, Inc.
2310 W. South Range Road
North Lima, OH 44452-9731
Philip Steiner
(330) 549-9861, (800) 321-7444
Fax: (330) 549-3716
E-mail: mellgarden@aol.com

Plants 🔊 **Seeds** 🔊 **Books** 🔊 **Supplies** 🔊 **Tools** 🔊 **Bulbs**
Catalog is a large general store of home and commercial gardening supplies, books, **seeds and plants of all kinds**. It's hard to believe that they can carry so many items -- 4,000 by their count! It's a jumble, with plants in no logical order and brief plant descriptions; you get used to it. (1927)
- Catalog: Free($2.50 OV), R&W, CAN/OV, CC, $10m, cn/bn
- Nursery: All year, M-Sa
- Garden: Spring-Fall, M-Sa

Mendocino Heirloom Roses
P.O. Box 670
720 Road 'N' (Redwood Valley)
Mendocino, CA 95460
Gail Daly
(707) 937-0963
Fax: (707) 937-3744
E-mail: gdaly@mcn.org

Plants
A nice selection of old garden **roses** propagated on their own roots; all varieties are well described. They will also propagate on request, so send along your "wish list." (1991)
  📖 Catalog: $2d, SS:1-2
  ✪ Nursery: By appointment only
  ❀ Garden: May-June, by appointment only

Mesa Garden
P.O. Box 72
Belen, NM 87002-0072
Steven Brack
(505) 864-3131
Fax: (505) 864-3124
E-mail: cactus@swcp.com
Web: www.demon.co.uk/mace/cacmall.html

Plants ☙ Seeds
A very extensive collectors' list of **cacti and succulents**, both seed and seed-grown plants, with very brief descriptions including habitat data on wild-collected seed. Seed list in January, plant list in spring; guaranteed to thrill collectors! (1976)
  📖 Catalog: 2 FCS($1 OV), R&W, CAN/OV, CC, SS:3-10, bn
  ✪ Nursery: All year, M-F, call ahead
  ❀ Garden: Call ahead

Michael's Bromeliads
1365 Canterbury Road North
St. Petersburg, FL 33710
Michael H. Kiehl
(813) 347-0349
Fax: (813) 347-4273

Plants
"Specialize in providing specific plants and new varieties for the **bromeliad** collector, but also provide starter collections and growing information for the beginner." Offer aechmeas, billbergias, guzmanias, vriesias, tillandsias, cryptanthus, neoregelias; no plant descriptions. (1987)
  📖 Catalog: Free, CAN/OV, CC, $20m, bn
  ✪ Nursery: Sa-Su, or evenings, by appointment only

Mid-America Garden
3409 N. Geraldine Avenue
Oklahoma City, OK 73112-2806
Paul W. Black
(405) 946-5743

Plants
Color catalog offers a very broad selection of **bearded and reblooming iris** in several sizes; each plant very briefly described, but new introductions and current favorites get lots of ink. Many of Paul's introductions have won national and international awards. He's added **Siberian iris, daylilies, hostas** and **Asiatic lilies** in recent years. (1978)
  📖 Catalog: $3($4 OV), CAN/OV, SS:5-10, $20m
  ✪ Nursery: April-October, Tu-Su
  ❀ Garden: April-July, Tu-Su

Midwest Cactus
P.O. Box 163
New Melle, MO 63365
Christopher M. Smith
(314) 828-5389
E-mail: csmith01@mail.win.org

Plants
Specializes in cold hardy **opuntia cacti** for year-round outdoor gardens; plants are shown in b&w photographs, briefly described with good growing information. Also offers some sedums and yuccas. (1984)
  📖 Catalog: $2, R&W, CAN/OV, SS:5-9, $10m, bn
  ✪ Nursery: By appointment only
  ❀ Garden: June-August, by appointment only

Mighty Minis
7318 Sahara Court
Sacramento, CA 95828-3905
Jeannie Stokes
(916) 421-7284

Plants
A small nursery selling miniature **African violets** (plants and leaves): a broad selection; each gets a miniature description. They also grow a few **begonias** and other **gesneriads**. (1982)
  📖 Catalog: $2d, OV, SS:4-10, $4m
  ✪ Nursery: All year, M-Sa, call ahead

Milaeger's Gardens
4838 Douglas Avenue
Racine, WI 53402-2498
Milaeger Family
(414) 639-2371, (800) 669-9956
Fax: (414) 639-1855
E-mail: milaeger@execpc.com

Plants ☙ Books
A broad selection of **perennials**, including a good selection of clematis, shade plants, prairie wildflowers and ornamental grasses; all very well described, many illustrated in color photographs. The catalog is accurately called "The Perennial Wishbook." (1960)
  📖 Catalog: $1, R&W, CC, SS:4-10, $25m, bn/cn
  ✪ Nursery: All year, daily
  ❀ Garden: May-September, daily

Miles' to Go
P.O. Box 6
Cortaro, AZ 85652
Miles Anderson
(520) 682-7272
Fax: (520) 682-0480
E-mail: miles2go@aol.com
Web: www.miles2go.com

Plants
Offers many kinds of **cactus**, including "crests, variegates, and other monstrosities," as well as some succulents and caudiciforms. Plants are briefly but well described. Also offers a seed kit for children or beginners, and a handsome tee shirt.
- 📖 Catalog: Free, CC, $15m, bn
- ✪ Nursery: All year, M-F, call ahead

J. E. Miller Nurseries, Inc.
5060 West Lake Road
Canandaigua, NY 14424
John & David Miller
(716) 396-2647, (800) 836-9630
Fax: (716) 396-2154
E-mail: jmiller@millernurseries.com
Web: www.millernurseries.com

Plants ✍ **Supplies**
Color catalog offers a broad selection of **fruit and nut trees, berries** of all kinds, **grapes, ornamental trees** and supplies; each plant well described, many illustrated. Cannot ship to CA or HI. (1936)
- 📖 Catalog: Free, CC, SS:3-6,10-12, cn
- ✪ Nursery: All year, M-F, March-May, daily
- ❀ Garden: By appointment only

Miller's Manor Gardens
11974 E. 191st Street
Noblesville, IN 46060
Lynda & Roger Miller

Plants
Offers **bearded iris** of all types: an extensive list featuring newer median and dwarf iris, each very briefly described. Also offers a number of **Siberian iris** cultivars, as well as **daylilies and hostas**. Have added some perennials, which can't be shipped to AZ, CA, OR or WA. (1976)
- 📖 Catalog: $1d, R&W, CAN/OV, CC, SS:4-5,7-9, $10m
- ✪ Nursery: April-October, M-Tu,Th-Sa
- ❀ Garden: May, M-Tu,Th-Sa

The Mini-Rose Garden
P.O. Box 203
Austin Street
Cross Hill, SC 29332-0203
Michael & Betty Williams
(864) 998-4331, (888) 998-2424
Fax: (864) 998-4947

Plants
List offers a selection of award-winning **miniature roses** chosen for best performance; each briefly but well described, a few illustrated in color, including their own introductions. (1983)
- 📖 Catalog: Free, R&W, CC, $5m
- ✪ Nursery: All year, M-Sa, call ahead
- ❀ Garden: September-October, M-Sa, call ahead

© The Fragrant Path
Artist: Christine Rasmussen

Miniature Plant Kingdom
4125 Harrison Grade Road
Sebastopol, CA 95472
Don & Becky Herzog
(707) 874-2233
Fax: (707) 874-3242
E-mail: bonsaistarters@neteze.com

Plants
Offers a good selection of **miniature roses**, including their own hybrids, as well as **conifers and plants for bonsai**. The bonsai list has grown to take over most of the catalog; these are desirable plants, many of which have attractive fruit and/or flowers. Also offer **alpine plants.** (1965)
📖 Catalog: $2.50, R&W, CAN/OV, CC, SS:W, $7m
☯ Nursery: All year, Th-Tu (Su pm only)
❀ Garden: Spring-Summer, Th-Tu (Su pm only)

Grant Mitsch Novelty Daffodils
P.O. Box 218
Hubbard, OR 97032
Richard & Elise Havens
(503) 651-2742 (eves)
Fax: (503) 651-2792
E-mail: havensr@canby.com

Bulbs
Specialize in rarer hybrids of **daffodils**, including those of Elise Havens' father Grant E. Mitsch, as well as many others; each plant is very well described, and many are illustrated in color in an informative catalog. Grant Mitsch was introducing new cultivars until the time of his death at 81; the Havens carry on the family tradition. (1927)
📖 Catalog: $3d($5 OV), CAN/OV, SS:9-10
❀ Garden: Spring, call ahead

Mohns Nursery
P.O. Box 2301
Atascadero, CA 93423
Jim DeWelt

Plants
Offer their own `Minicaps' strain of perennial **Oriental poppies**, bred especially for the warm winter climate of central and southern California. They come in a choice of shades of red, pink, white or intense magenta. No shipping to FL, HI, LA or OR. (1983)
📖 Catalog: Free, SS:3-5, $8m

Monocot Nursery
Jacklands, Jacklands Bridge, Tickenham
Clevedon, Avon, England BS21 6SG
Michael R. Salmon

Bulbs
Oh, what a wonderful list! **Species bulbs** from all over Europe and the Mediterranean world: narcissus, leucojum, sternbergia, arums, crocus, species iris, nerine, romulea, oxalis, alliums, colchicums, fritillaria, scilla, species tulips and cyclamen. Site of original seed collection given - read it with a good bulb book at your side! (1960)
📖 Catalog: $3(US Bills), OV, SS:3,8-9, bn
☯ Nursery: All year, M-F
❀ Garden: February, October, call ahead

Moon Mountain Wildflowers
P.O. Box 725
Carpinteria, CA 93014-0725
Becky Lynn Schaff
(805) 684-2565
Fax: (805) 684-2798
E-mail: ssseeds@silcom.com

Seeds
Informative catalog lists **annual and perennial wildflowers and grasses** of many areas, including mixes suitable for many habitats or uses, sold in packets and in bulk. Plants well described with cultural suggestions. Also sells the lovely wildflower posters of the California Native Plant Society. (1981)
📖 Catalog: $3, R&W, CAN/OV, CC, $5m, bn/cn
☯ Nursery: Call ahead

Moore Water Gardens
P.O. Box 70
Port Stanley, ON, Canada N5L 1J4
Sue See
(519) 782-4052
Fax: (800) 728-6324

Plants ℘ Books ℘ Supplies
A good selection of **water lilies, lotus, aquatic plants**, supplies and ponds for water gardens, all well described in an informative catalog, some illustrated in color. Also a number of books on water gardening. (1930)
📖 Catalog: $2, R&W, CC, SS:4-10, bn/cn
☯ Nursery: All year, call ahead
❀ Garden: May-August, call ahead

Moose Tubers

See Fedco Seeds.

Morgan County Wholesale
18761 Kelsay Road
Barnett, MO 65011
Norman & Vera Kilmer
(573) 378-2655

Seeds ℘ Books ℘ Supplies
Offers a wide assortment of hybrid and open-pollinated **vegetable seeds** in packets or by the pound at quite reasonable prices. Also offers a few annual flowers. Sells books, fertilizers, insecticides, fungicides, and seeders. (1982)
📖 Catalog: $1, R&W, CC, SS:3-6, cn
☯ Nursery: All year, M-Sa

Mt. Tahoma Nursery
28111 - 112th Avenue East
Graham, WA 98338
Rick Lupp
(206) 847-9827
Web: www.eskimo.com/~mcalpin/rick/order.html

Plants
Small nursery offers a very nice selection of **alpine plants** for collectors, as well as a number of **small shrubs** ideal for gardeners with limited space. Nice listing of campanulas, gentians and species primulas, as well as other "gems." All plants well described, with brief indications as to culture. Troughs for alpines available at the nursery. (1985)
- Catalog: $1, SS:3-6,9-11, bn
- Nursery: By appointment only
- Garden: March-June, Sept.-Oct., by appointment only

Mountain Maples
P.O. Box 1329
Laytonville, CA 95454-1329
Don & Nancy Fiers
(707) 984-6522
Fax: (707) 984-7433

Plants ∞ Books
Offer over two hundred **Japanese maple** cultivars, and some **species maples**, each very well described for either bonsai or landscape use. Many listed by their Japanese cultivar names -- it would be ideal to have Vertrees' book on hand as you read the catalog. They have started to import **tree peonies** and offer **beeches** as well. Also offer a few books. (1985)
- Catalog: $2, R&W, CC, SS:2-5,10-11, bn
- Nursery: By appointment only
- Garden: April-June, October-November, by appointment only

Mountain Valley Growers, Inc.
38325 Pepperweed Road
Squaw Valley, CA 93675
V. J. & Keith Billings
(209) 338-2775
Fax: (209) 338-0075
E-mail: 70471.3066@compuserve.com

Plants
A very good selection of **herbs**, and drought tolerant **perennials**, including some new cultivars and hard to find varieties; all plants are well described with information on height at maturity and garden or culinary uses. There are herb collections for various uses offered, too. World Wide Web address is: <ourworld.compuserve.com/homepages/mountainvalleygrowers>.
- Catalog: Free, R&W, CC, SS:W, $18m, bn/cn

Charles H. Mueller Co.
7091 N. River Road
New Hope, PA 18938
Charles Fritz III
(215) 862-2033
Fax: (215) 862-3696

Bulbs
Offers a good selection of spring and summer blooming **bulbs**: the fall planting catalog offers novelty daffodils, tulips, alliums, crocus and other "little" bulbs. The summer blooming list offers lilies, daylilies, dahlias, cannas, tuberous begonias, gladiolus, caladiums and autumn crocus. (1935)
- Catalog: $1, R&W, CC, SS:3-11, $20m
- Garden: April-May, daily

Mums by Paschke
12286 East Main Road
North East, PA 16428
Jack & Shirley Paschke
(814) 725-9860
Fax: (814) 725-9860

Plants
Offers a good variety of **chrysanthemums**, many of which are described on their list. You can order collections of their choice, or pick your own. (1933)
- Catalog: Free, R&W, CC, SS:4-6, $12m
- Nursery: May-mid November, M-Sa, Su pm
- Garden: September-October, daily

Mushroompeople
P.O. Box 220
560 Farm Road
Summertown, TN 38483
The Second Foundation
(615) 964-2200, (800) 692-6329
Fax: (615) 964-2200
E-mail: mushroom@thefarm.org
Web: www.thefarm.org/mushroom

Seeds ∞ Books ∞ Supplies ∞ Tools
Specializes in spawn of **shiitake mushrooms**, both cold and warm weather strains, for log or sawdust cultivation. They also offer spawn for maitake, reishi, lion's mane, morels, king stropharia, and oyster mushrooms. Offer complete growing supplies, books on mushroom growing, hunting and cooking, and video cassettes of mushroom conferences and on shiitake growing in Japan. (1976)
- Catalog: Free, CAN/OV, CC, cn/bn

Musser Forests Inc.
P.O. Box 340
Route 119 North
Indiana, PA 15701-0340
Fred & Nancy Musser
(412) 465-5685, (800) 643-8319
Fax: (412) 465-9893

Plants
Supplies a broad selection of ornamental trees and shrubs in transplant sizes: **conifers**, flowering **trees and shrubs**, hedging plants, a few perennials and ground covers for the home gardener and commercial grower. Good descriptions, some color photographs. (1928)
- Catalog: Free, R&W, CAN/OV, CC, SS:3-5,9-11, $10m, cn/bn
- Nursery: March-Christmas, daily
- Garden: April-May, daily

Mycelium Fruits
P.O. Box 551
Iron Station, NC 28080-0551
Allan Melby
Fax: (704) 732-8681
E-mail: mfruits@vnet.net

Plants ∞ Books ∞ Supplies
Here's everything you need to set up **mushroom** culture: in vitro cultures or grain spawn, growing media and instruments, books on mushroom culture and a mushroom tee shirt. They can't ship cultures or spawn to Canada or overseas, but can send growing supplies and equipment. (1993)
📖 Catalog: $2d(US$3 OV), CAN/OV, CC, bn

NWN Nursery
1365 Watford Circle
Chipley, FL 32428
Kathy & John Foster
(904) 638-7572
Fax: (904) 638-7572

Plants ∞ Seeds
Specialize in **plants for the Southeast**, including many **native plants**: many members of the mallow family, hollies, ipomoeas, liriopes, magnolias, oaks, and wisterias. Also sell a number of semi-tropical plants. Only ship seeds to Canada and OV, and to AK, AZ, HI, OR and WA. (1988)
📖 Catalog: Free, CAN/OV, bn/cn
☮ Nursery: All year, M-Sa, call ahead
❀ Garden: Spring, Fall, call ahead

NZ Alpine Seeds
P.O. Box 10075, Halfway Bush
Dunedin, New Zealand
Steve & Mandy Newall
64 (00) 64 3476-7165 eves
Fax: 64 (00) 64 3474-600

Seeds
Wild collected seed of **New Zealand plants**, for your alpine garden or rockery, will be shipped when fresh. List includes cushion and mat forming plants, grasses, scree plants, shrubs and climbers. Payment by credit card or personal check in US dollars.
📖 Catalog: Free, R&W, OV, CC, SS: 1-5, $15m, bn

Nancy's Daylilies & Perennials
R.D. 1, Box 19
New Alexandria, PA 15670
Nancy Boone & Nancy Patrick
(412) 459-8135

Plants
Specializing in **daylilies**, with a broad selection; list includes date of introduction and brief descriptions.
📖 Catalog: $2d, R&W, CC, SS:8-9, $20m
☮ Nursery: May-October, W-Su
❀ Garden: June-early August, W-Su, call ahead

National Collection of Passiflora
Lampley Road, Kingston Seymour
Clevedon, No. Somerset, England BS21 6XS
R.J.R. Vanderplank
44 (0) 1934 833-350
Fax: 44 (0) 1934 877-255
E-mail: passion@thneewa.co.uk

Seeds
An extensive list of **passion flowers**, mostly species, with information on flower color, origin and culture. Seeds are available for some species and hybrids. Also sell John Vanderplank's book on "Passion Flowers." (1960)
📖 Catalog: $2, R&W, OV, CC, $20m, bn
☮ Nursery: All year, M-Sa
❀ Garden: May-September, M-Sa

Native American Seed
610 Main Street
Junction, TX 76849-0185
Jan & Bill Neiman
(915) 446-3600, (800) 728-4043
Fax: (915) 446-4537
E-mail: seedsource@aol.com
Web: www.seedsource.com

Seeds ∞ Books
The Neiman's line of work is prairie restoration in Texas; they also harvest seeds of **Texas wildflowers and native grasses**. Seeds are offered in mixes for different purposes, or by single species. Also offer a good selection of books on Texas wildflowers. (1988)
📖 Catalog: $1, R&W, CC, $15m, cn/bn

Native Gardens
5737 Fisher Lane
Greenback, TN 37742
Meredith & Ed Clebsch
(423) 856-0220
Fax: (423) 856-0220
E-mail: rcopallina@aol.com

Plants ∞ Seeds
Nursery-propagated **native plants** (and seeds) for meadows and natural landscaping, as well as some **perennials**. Concise tables in the catalog give good information on growing conditions, season and color of flower, habitat and soil, followed by more expanded notes on the native plants. Ship only seeds to AZ, CA, KS, OR, WA, Canada and overseas. (1983)
📖 Catalog: $2($3 OV), R&W, bn/cn
☮ Nursery: By appointment only
❀ Garden: April, July-September, by appointment only

Native Seeds/SEARCH
2509 N. Campbell Avenue, #325
526 N. 4th Avenue
Tucson, AZ 85719
Non-Profit Foundation
(520) 327-9123
Fax: (520) 327-5821
E-mail: jhosofaz@aol.com
Web: desert.net/SEEDS/home.htm

Seeds ∞ Books ∞ Supplies
Non-profit group offers traditional **Southwestern native crops**, many by Spanish names, as well as **wild food plants**; all plants briefly described, with cultural suggestions. Offers a few related publications, occasional workshops and Indian seed-drying baskets and other crafts. A wide selection of open-pollinated corn, beans, amaranth, gourds, squash and hot peppers. They have a display garden at the Tucson Botanical Garden, and a museum at the same location, open Tuesdays and Thursdays. (1983)
📖 Catalog: $1, CAN/OV, CC
❇ Nursery: All year, Tu-Sa
❇ Garden: September-November, Tu-Sa

Nature's Curiosity Shop
1388 Sunset Drive
Vista, CA 92083
Rick Nowakowski
(760) 726-1488
E-mail: naturescuriosity@msn.com
Web: futuresystems.com/natures

Plants
Offers **variegated plants** of all types, especially **succulents**: aeoniums, agaves, aloes, crassulas, gasterias, haworthias, agapanthus, crinums and cannas, and a variety of others, each briefly described. (1970)
📖 Catalog: Free, CAN, $15m, bn/cn
❇ Nursery: By appointment only
❇ Garden: Spring-Fall, by appointment only

Nature's Garden
40611 Highway 226
Scio, OR 97374-9351
Frederick W. Held

Plants ∞ Bulbs
A good selection of plants for the woodland, shady or sunny garden, including some **sedums and sempervivums, hardy ferns, gentians, species primulas, violas** and other choice rock garden plants, each very briefly described. No shipping to TX. (1974)
📖 Catalog: Long SASE, R&W, CAN/OV, SS:2-6,9-12, $20m, bn

Nature's Nook
1578 Marion Russell Road
Meridian, MS 39301-8807
Karen Partlow
(601) 485-5161
Fax: (601) 485-5161
E-mail: natures@cybertron.com
Web: www.cybertron.com/naturesnook

Plants
Offers tough **perennials and small shrubs** for the harsh garden conditions of the deep South. A nice selection, each plant well described. Can't ship to AK, AZ, CA, HI, OR or WA. (1995)
📖 Catalog: $3, CC, SS:3-11, $15m, bn/cn
❇ Nursery: Call ahead
❇ Garden: April-October, call ahead

Naylor Creek Nursery
2610 West Valley Road
Chimacum, WA 98325
Jack Hirsch & Gary Lindheimer
(360) 732-4983
Fax: (360) 732-7171

Plants
Offers a large selection of **hostas**, and also many cultivars of **astilbes, pulmonarias and epimediums**, each of these useful shade plants very briefly described. (1991)
📖 Catalog: Free, R&W, CAN/OV, CC, SS:4-10, $35m
❇ Nursery: May-September, Th-Su, call ahead
❇ Garden: May-September, Th-Su, call ahead

Neglected Bulbs
P.O. Box 1128
Berkeley, CA 94701
Hugh P. McDonald
(510) 524-5149

Bulbs
A very small operation, offering a great rarity: **native California bulbs**, as well as some amaryllids, and a few other non-native bulbs. Nursery grown bulbs include brodiaeas and calochortus. Stock is limited. (1990)
📖 Catalog: Long SASE, R&W, CAN/OV, SS:9-10, bn

Neon Palm Nursery
3525 Stony Point Road
Santa Rosa, CA 95407
Dale Motiska
(707) 585-8100

Plants
A good selection of **hardy subtropical plants**: many palms, cycads, winter-hardy cactus, yuccas, agaves, ferns, bamboos, conifers and others. There are no plant descriptions, but there are notes as to hardiness. (1983)
📖 Catalog: $2, SS:4-10, $50m, bn
❇ Nursery: All year, Tu-Su
❇ Garden: All year, Tu-Su

New Gardens
P.O. Box 357
Greenwich, NJ 08323
Gretchen S. Niedermayer
(609) 935-7368

Plants
A new nursery with a limited but nice selection of **shrubs** for the garden; offered are viburnums, holly, box, yakushimanum hybrid rhododendrons, climbing hydrangeas, and others. No shipping to most Western states.
📖 Catalog: $2d, CAN, SS:4-5,9-10, $40m, bn
✱ Garden: By appointment only

New Leaf Nurseries
2456 Foothill Drive
Vista, CA 92084-5809
Gerald Stewart
(760) 726-9269
Fax: (760) 941-0616

Plants
A specialist in **geraniums**, offers regals, zonals, ivy-leaved, scented geraniums and a few species pelargoniums. Also offers pamphlets on ivy geraniums. Cannot ship to Canada, Australia or New Zealand. Send $1 for availability list; specify which type of geranium you want. (1977)
📖 Catalog: See notes, OV, SS:W
❂ Nursery: All year, F-Sa, call ahead
✱ Garden: Call ahead

The New Peony Farm
P.O. Box 18235
St. Paul, MN 55118
Kent Crossley
Fax: (612) 457-7635
E-mail: cross006@maroon.tc.umn.edu

Plants
Catalog lists about 100 of the 300 varieties of herbaceous **peonies** which they grow; each plant well described. They are particularly interested in offering fine older cultivars in danger of being lost in commerce; they also offer single and double fernleaf peonies, mixed assortments by color. (1980)
📖 Catalog: Free, R&W, CAN/OV, SS:9-11
❂ Nursery: By appointment only
✱ Garden: June, by appointment only

Niche Gardens
1111 Dawson Road
Chapel Hill, NC 27516
Kim Hawks
(919) 967-0078
Fax: (919) 967-4026
E-mail: nichegdn@ipass.net
Web: www.nichegdn.com

Plants
Small nursery specializing in **Southeastern wildflowers and native plants, perennials, ornamental grasses, herbs, trees and shrubs** for rock gardens, bogs and dry areas. Plants are well described, with notes on use and placement, and come in several sizes; all are nursery-propagated. Workshops held at the nursery during the year, call for dates. (1986)
📖 Catalog: $3, CC, SS:W, $15, bn/cn
❂ Nursery: All year, M-F, weekends, Spring, Fall
✱ Garden: All year, M-F, weekends, Spring, Fall

Nicholls Gardens
4724 Angus Drive
Gainesville, VA 20155
Diana Nicholls
(703) 754-9623
E-mail: nichollsgardens@usa.net
Web: www.inet-images.com/nichollsgardens/

Plants
Small nursery sells a good selection of **iris** -- Siberian, Japanese, Louisiana, species and bearded, dwarf to tall (many are reblooming) -- as well as **daylilies, peonies** and a few **hardy cyclamen**. All plants are briefly but well described -- and would provide something in bloom from early spring to late fall. They are an official display garden for the Society for Japanese Iris; it looks very beautiful. (1984)
📖 Catalog: $1d($3 OV), CAN/OV, SS:4-10, $20m
❂ Nursery: April-September, daily, call ahead
✱ Garden: April-September, daily, call ahead

Nichols Garden Nursery, Inc.
1190 North Pacific Highway N.E.
Albany, OR 97321-4580
Nichols Family
(541) 928-9280
Fax: (541) 967-8406

Plants ☙ **Seeds** ☙ **Books** ☙ **Supplies**
An extensive selection of **herbs, and vegetable and flower** seeds; many vegetables selected for coastal Northwestern conditions. Plants well described with cultural hints -- also garden, herbal and winemaking supplies and books. Also offer elephant garlic. No plants or bulbs to Canada or overseas. (1950)
📖 Catalog: Free($2), R&W, CAN/OV, SS:4-5,9-10
❂ Nursery: All year, M-Sa, 1190 Old Salem Road N.E.
✱ Garden: April-October, M-Sa

Nicholson's Woodland Iris Garden

See Woodland Iris Garden.

Nindethana Seed Service
P.O. Box 2121
Albany, WA, Australia 6330
Peter C. Luscombe
61 (0) 98 44-3533
Fax: 61 (0) 98 44-3573

Seeds
Nindethana is doing direct sales again, instead of using an agent. They offer a broad selection of seeds of **Australian native plants**; no descriptions, only local common names. Prices are quoted in US dollars, quantities are 25 grams or 1 kilogram.
- Catalog: AU$5, R&W, OV, CC, bn/cn
- Nursery: All year, M-F, by appointment only

Nolin River Nut Tree Nursery
797 Port Wooden Road
Upton, KY 42784-9218
John & Lisa Brittain
(502) 369-8551

Plants
Formerly the Leslie Wilmoth Nursery, specializing in grafted **nut trees** -- pecans, hicans, hickories, heartnuts, butternuts, black and Persian walnuts, chestnuts -- over 175 varieties; also grafted **persimmons**. Listed by variety name; very brief plant descriptions. No shipping to CA or AZ. (1985)
- Catalog: Free, SS:3-4, cn/bn
- Nursery: All year, M-Sa, by appointment only
- Garden: Summer, by appointment only

Nor'East Miniature Roses
P.O. Box 307
Rowley, MA 01969
John Saville
(508) 948-7964
Fax: (508) 948-5487
Web: www.shore.net/~nemr/

Plants
Color catalog of **miniature roses**, including "mini" tree roses, both single plants and collections. Nice selection, plants well described. Some gift items offered too. Another office at P.O. Box 473, Ontario, CA 91762. (1972)
- Catalog: Free, R&W, CC
- Nursery: Daily, call ahead
- Garden: June-September, AARS Display Garden, call ahead

North Green Seeds
16 Witton Lane, Little Plumstead
Norwich, Norfolk, England NR15 5DL
John Morley & Richard Hobbs
44 (0) 1603 714-461
Fax: 44 (0) 1603 714-661

Seeds
Offers a good selection of seeds of **bulbous plants, trees, annuals and perennials**. They list, for instance, over 15 kinds of annual and perennial species sweet peas, only one of which is the traditional garden variety. Also many fritillaries, hellebores, species iris, and many other wonderful plants. Each plant well described. (1984)
- Catalog: 4 IRC, OV, bn

North Pine Iris Gardens
P.O. Box 595
308 No. Pine Street
Norfolk, NE 68701
Chuck & Mary Ferguson
(402) 371-3895

Plants
Specializes in bearded **iris** of all sizes, a broad selection with brief plant descriptions. Also sells some Siberian, arilbred and species iris, and about 200 **daylilies** and a few hostas.
- Catalog: $1, CAN/OV, SS:4-9
- Nursery: May-September, Sa-Su, by appointment only
- Garden: May-September, call ahead

North Star Gardens

See Indiana Berry & Plant Company.

Northern Groves
23818 Henderson Road
Corvallis, OR 97333-0291
Rick Valley
(541) 929-7152
Web: www.teleport.com/~dbrooks/bamboo.html

Plants
A source of **hardy bamboos**, a good selection with good plant descriptions for each plant. Lists "medium size, timber, mountain, sasa and dwarf bamboos." The catalog also has extensive information on growing bamboos. No shipping to HI. (1981)
- Catalog: $2($3 OV), R&W, CAN/OV, $5m, bn
- Nursery: By appointment only
- Garden: By appointment only

Northern Grown Perennials
Route 1, Box 43
Ferryville, WI 54628
Rod Lysne
E-mail: ngp@mwt.net

Plants
Offers a broad selection of **hostas and daylilies**, including spider, double and miniature daylilies. Some of these are their own introductions. Each plant very briefly described. Also, a few **herbaceous peonies**.
- Catalog: $1, R&W, SS:5-10, $25m
- Nursery: May-October, by appointment only
- Garden: June-August, by appointment only

Northland Gardens
315-A West Mountain Road
Queensbury, NY 12804
Tracy Tabor
(518) 798-4277, (800) 426-6724
Fax: (518) 798-9004

Plants ஒ Books ஒ Supplies ஒ Tools
A one-stop "bonsai centre;" **pre-bonsai and finished plants**, books, tools, pots and growing supplies. Plants available for both temperate and tropical bonsai, and some unusual plants at the nursery; no plant descriptions. (1986)
📖 Catalog: $2, CAN, CC, $10m, cn
✪ Nursery: All year, daily
❀ Garden: Summer, daily

Northplan/Mountain Seed
P.O. Box 9107
Moscow, ID 83843-1607
Loring M. Jones
(208) 882-8040
Fax: (208) 882-7446

Seeds
Seeds of **native trees and shrubs** for disturbed land restoration, erosion control and highway landscaping; **wildflower** mixes for various habitats and **range and reclamation grasses**. (1975)
📖 Catalog: $1(US$1 OV), R&W, CAN/OV, bn/cn

Northridge Gardens
9821 White Oak Avenue
Northridge, CA 91325-1341
Arnie & Susan Mitchnick
(818) 349-9798
Fax: (818) 349-9798

Plants ஒ Books
Offering **caudiciforms**, unusual **succulents**, plants for bonsai, **brachychitons, euphorbias, monadeniums, pachypodiums and aloes**, all briefly described. They put out a quarterly list of plants available. (1991)
📖 Catalog: $1d, R&W, CC, $20m, bn
✪ Nursery: All year, Sa, or by appointment
❀ Garden: All year, Sa, or by appointment

Northwest Mycological Consultants
702 N.W. 4th Street
Corvallis, OR 97330
Bill Denison, Mgr.
(541) 753-8198
Fax: (541) 752-3401

Seeds ஒ Supplies ஒ Tools
Offer a good selection of **mushroom spawn**: many strains of shiitake, also enoki, reiski, morel and black morel, several types of oyster and several others such as "hen of the woods" and "shaggy mane." They also sell books and mushroom growing supplies and consult with growers. (1985)
📖 Catalog: $2($5 OV), R&W, CAN/OV, CC
✪ Nursery: All year, M-F, call ahead

Northwind Nursery & Orchards
7910 335th Avenue N.W.
Princeton, MN 55371-4915
Frank Foltz

Plants ஒ Supplies ஒ Tools
Small family nursery offers a nice selection of hardy, organically grown **fruit trees**: apples, plums, pears, cherries, crabapples, mulberries, as well as wine and table grapes, raspberries and miscellaneous fruiting trees and shrubs for **edible landscaping**, each well described. Also sells books, tools, and organic growing supplies; gives classes in fruit culture. (1983)
📖 Catalog: $1d, SS:4-5,9-10, cn/bn
✪ Nursery: April-May, September-October, call ahead
❀ Garden: August-October, call ahead

Northwoods Nursery
27635 S. Oglesby Road
Canby, OR 97013
Kathy Fives
(503) 266-5432
Fax: (503) 266-5431
E-mail: 102742.3327@compuserve.com

Plants ஒ Books ஒ Supplies ஒ Tools
Offers **hybrid chestnuts, berries, apples, figs, hardy kiwis, pawpaws** and **Asian pears**, grown by organic methods "as much as possible." Many kiwis, other fruits and nuts and ornamental shrubs and trees which do well in the Northwest and some are suited to the urban-sized lot. (1979)
📖 Catalog: $3, CAN/OV, CC, SS:1-5,10-11
✪ Nursery: January-May, Th-Su, by appointment only

Nourse Farms, Inc.
41 River Road
South Deerfield, MA 01373
Timothy M. Nourse
(413) 665-2658
Fax: (413) 665-7888
E-mail: nourse@crocker.com
Web: www.noursefarms.com

Plants
Growers of tissue-cultured **strawberries** as a means of producing "virus-free" plants -- 31 varieties. They also sell **blackberries, raspberries, rhubarb, horseradish** and the Rutgers University "all-male" **asparagus** hybrids -- more vigorous and they do not set seed. Informative catalog with cultural suggestions. (1933)
📖 Catalog: Free, R&W, CAN, CC, SS:12-6
✪ Nursery: April-May, M-Sa

Nuccio's Nurseries
P.O. Box 6160
3555 Chaney Trail
Altadena, CA 91003
Julius, Tom & Jim Nuccio
(818) 794-3383

Plants
Huge selection of **camellias and azaleas**; all well to briefly described. Camellias include japonica, sasanqua, reticulata, rusticana and higo hybrids and a number of species; some camellia scions are available. Azalea hybrids of many types, including their own and a huge selection of Japanese satsukis, and a few gardenias. No shipping to LA, no azaleas to OR. (1935)
- Catalog: Free, CAN/OV, SS:10-4
- Nursery: All year, F-Tu; June-December, closed Su
- Garden: January-May

Oak Hill Gardens
P.O. Box 25
37W 550 Binnie Road
Dundee, IL 60118-0025
H. & D. Pigors, G. & L. Butler
(847) 428-8500
Fax: (847) 428-8527
E-mail: oakhillgardens@sprintmail.com

Plants ✍ Books ✍ Supplies
Informative catalog offers a broad selection of **species and hybrid orchids**, as well as **bromeliads** and other flowering and foliage indoor plants; each plant briefly described in table format. Also offers growing supplies and books on orchids and houseplants. (1973)
- Catalog: Free, R&W, CAN/OV, CC, SS:W, bn
- Nursery: All year, M-Sa
- Garden: All year, M-Sa

Oakes Daylilies
8204 Monday Road
Corryton, TN 37721
Stewart Oakes
(423) 687-3770, (800) 532-9545
Fax: (423) 688-8186
Web: paradisegarden@oakes.htm

Plants ✍ Books
Just **daylilies**, a collectors' list with varieties from many noted hybridizers and AHS award winners. Color catalog offers most popular varieties, with concentration on award winners; plants are well described. They also issue a Collector's Catalog listing 700 cultivars for $1. (1979)
- Catalog: Free, R&W, CAN/OV, CC, SS:2-10
- Garden: AHS Display Garden, call for open dates

Oakridge Nurseries
P.O. Box 182
East Kingston, NH 03827
Mary Ellen Marcella
(603) 642-7339
Fax: (603) 642-6827

Plants
Small nursery offers nice selection of **ferns and wildflower plants**, mature and ready for planting. Plants are well but briefly described. Some plants are rescued from sites about to be developed or logged over; they say they're very careful in their collecting! No shipping to AZ, CA or HI. (1971)
- Catalog: Free, R&W, CAN/OV, SS:2-5,8-11, $15m, cn/bn

Oakwood Daffodils
2330 West Bertrand Road
Niles, MI 49120
Dr. John Reed
(616) 684-3327
E-mail: scr@sbt.infi.net

Bulbs
Offers "Midwestern bred, grown and acclimatized **daffodils** for both show and garden;" the descriptions are very complete, listing color, character and breeding. Also offer their own registered introductions.
- Catalog: $1d($2 OV), CAN/OV, CC, SS:9-10, $10m
- Nursery: By appointment only
- Garden: Late April-May, call ahead

Oikos Tree Crops
P.O. Box 19425
Kalamazoo, MI 49019-0425
Ken Asmus
(616) 624-6233
Fax: (616) 624-4019
E-mail: oak24@aol.com

Plants ✍ Supplies
Offers "native, naturalized and exotic species for human and wildlife use:" **nuts, fruits and berries**, including chestnuts, hickories, walnuts, many oaks, and some magnolias, lilacs and ornamentals. Offers drought hardy species oaks from the Southwest and hybrid oaks. Also sell "Supertubes." (1985)
- Catalog: $1, R&W, CAN/OV, CC, $20m, cn/bn
- Nursery: All year, M-F, call ahead
- Garden: By appointment only

Olallie Daylily Gardens
HCR 63, Box 1
Marlboro Branch Road
South Newfane, VT 05351
Christopher & Amelia Darrow
(802) 348-6614
E-mail: darrowcs@sover.net

Plants
Christopher inherited his **daylilies** and interest in hybridizing from his grandfather, Dr. George Darrow, who was a plant breeder with the USDA. He offers a good selection of their own introductions and other favorite daylilies, as well as some Siberian iris and a nice selection of seedling perennials. (1982)
- Catalog: Free, CC, SS:5-9, $30m
- Nursery: May-September, W-M
- Garden: June-September, W-M

Old House Gardens
536 Third Street
Ann Arbor, MI 48103-4957
Scott G. Kunst
(313) 995-1486
Fax: (313) 995-1486
E-mail: ohg@arrownet.com

Books ℘ Bulbs
Scott Kunst is a consultant on historic garden restoration, and has started to sell **historic bulbs**, many from the 19th and early 20th century. All the bulbs offered are well researched for date of introduction; the catalog is very informative and fun to read. Offered are tulips, narcissus, hyacinths and others. Also some books on bulbs, both new works and reprints of very old volumes. (1993)
📖 Catalog: $2, R&W, SS:4,10-11

Olympic Coast Garden
84 Eaton Lane
Sequim, WA 98382
Roger Pierce

Plants
Roger's the son of two librarians, so he's naturally a great guy! He offers a good selection of **perennials** for the border, including an unusually good selection of **kniphofias**, as well as eryngiums, Shasta daisies, asters, daylilies, species and Siberian iris. All plants well described. (1992)
📖 Catalog: $1d, SS:9-5, $30m, bn
✪ Nursery: May-October, by appointment only
✸ Garden: May-October, by appointment only

Orchard Lane Growers
5014 Orchard Lane
Gloucester, VA 23061
Rollin Woolley

Plants
Offering **antique apples**, and custom grafting services, Rollin has an extensive selection to choose from. Current list has no descriptions, but that may change soon. No shipping to AK, AZ, CA, FL, HI, or LA.
📖 Catalog: $1d, CC, SS:11-12,2-4, $15m
✪ Nursery: October-May, M-Sa, by appointment only
✸ Garden: Fall, by appointment only

Orchid Art
1433 Kew Avenue
Hewlett, NY 11557
Rita Cohen
(516) 374-6426
Fax: (516) 374-2168

Plants
List a very good selection of **species orchids**, with a few hybrids; listed only by botanical name with no plant descriptions. Among the species: bulbophyllum, cirrhopetalum, coelogyne, cymbidium, dendrobium, encyclia, epidendrum, laelia and maxillaria. (1986)
📖 Catalog: Free, CC, bn
✪ Nursery: By appointment only
✸ Garden: By appointment only

© The Primrose Path
Artist: Martha Oliver

Orchid Gardens
2232 - 139th Avenue N.W.
Andover, MN 55304
Carl Phillips
(612) 755-0205

Plants
Collectors' list of **Midwestern wildflowers and hardy ferns**; a good selection with good descriptions and concise cultural notes in an informative catalog. Most plants are native to northern Minnesota, including native orchids, violets, ferns, vines, club mosses and some trees and shrubs. (1945)
- Catalog: $1, SS:5,9-10, cn/bn
- Nursery: April-May, September-October, by appointment only

Orchid Thoroughbreds
731 W. Siddonsburg Road
Dillsburg, PA 17019
Diane & Jack Vickery
(717) 432-8100
Fax: (717) 432-1199

Plants
Offers a nice selection of **species and hybrid orchids** of all kinds, with emphasis on easy to grow orchids for beginners and those which make good houseplants. Most plants are briefly described. (1984)
- Catalog: $2d, R&W, CC, SS:3-11
- Nursery: March-November, by appointment only
- Garden: Spring-Fall, by appointment only

Oregon Exotics Rare Fruit Nursery
1065 Messinger Road
Grants Pass, OR 97527
Jerry Black
(541) 846-7578
Fax: (541) 846-9400

Plants ⬥ Seeds
"Specializes in rare fruits, with emphasis on **hardy subtropical fruits** and their culture in Northern climates." Offers hardy citrus (citranges), ichandarins, hardy grapefruit relatives, dwarf citrus, feijoas, hicans, jujubes, loquats, blueberries, hardy kiwis and many varieties of figs. All are very well described. Some seeds available also. (1983)
- Catalog: $3($4 OV), R&W, CAN/OV, CC, SS:10-6, $15m, cn/bn

Oregon Miniature Roses
8285 S.W. 185th Avenue
Beaverton, OR 97007-6712
Ray Spooner
Fax: (503) 649-3528

Plants
Color catalog offers a good selection of **miniature roses**, each well described and many illustrated. Sells a few of their own hybrids, miniature tree roses and roses for hanging baskets. (1978)
- Catalog: Free, R&W, CC
- Nursery: All year, daily
- Garden: May-October, daily

Oregon Trail Daffodils
41905 S.E. Louden Road
Corbett, OR 97019
Bill & Diane Tribe
(503) 695-5513
E-mail: daffodil@europa.com

Bulbs
Specializing in the **novelty daffodils** of the late Murray Evans and new cultivars of Bill Pannill, a broad selection of specialty daffodils. Each variety is well described by class, breeding and seedling number; the owners are the fourth generation of the Evans family in the daffodil trade. (1989)
- Catalog: Free, R&W, CAN/OV, SS:9-11
- Garden: April, call ahead

Oregon Trail Groundcovers
P.O. Box 601
Canby, OR 97013
James R. Galyean
(503) 263-4688
Fax: (503) 266-9832

Plants
Only **vinca** or periwinkle, that adaptable groundcover, but in ten varieties: variegated, with white, blue or red violet flowers, even a double one. Minimum order is 50 plants.
- Catalog: $3d, CAN, CC, $35m

Orgel's Orchids
18950 S.W. 136th Street
Miami, FL 33196-1942
Orgel C. Bramblett
(305) 233-7168

Plants
Collectors' list of **carnivorous plants** -- an especially large selection of nepenthes, droseras, sarracenias and pinguiculas -- and **species orchids** -- listed by botanical name. (1972)
- Catalog: Free, $15m, bn
- Nursery: All year, by appointment only
- Garden: All year, growing area, by appointment only

D. Orriell -- Seed Exporters
45 Frape Avenue, Mt. Yokine
Perth, WA, Australia 6060
Patricia B. Orriell
Fax: 61 (0) 9619 344-8982

Seeds ∞ **Supplies**
Very extensive list of **Australian native plants** for collectors or botanical gardens; each plant briefly described. Includes hardy eucalyptus, wildflowers, ferns, palms, proteas, banksias and cycads, acacias and many tropical/greenhouse plants. Also sells Kirstenbosch "Instant Smoke Plus" seed primer for seeds which need fire to germinate - it works very well! (1978)
📖 Catalog: $6(US Bills), R&W, OV, $25m, bn/cn
✪ Nursery: All year, M-Sa, by appointment only

Owen Farms
2951 Curve-Nankipoo Road
Ripley, TN 38063-6653
Edric Owen
(901) 635-1588 (6-9 pm CST)

Plants
Offers a good selection of collectors' **trees, shrubs and perennials**: birch, dogwood, hydrangea, crape myrtle (including mildew-resistant cultivars), and garden perennials. All plants are very well described. (1985)
📖 Catalog: $2(2 IRC OV), R&W, CAN/OV, SS:W, bn/cn
✪ Nursery: All year, W-Su, call ahead
✹ Garden: April-November, W-Su, call ahead

Owens Orchids
P.O. Box 365
18 Orchidheights Drive
Pisgah Forest, NC 28768-0365
William & Joyce Owens
(704) 877-3313
Fax: (704) 884-5216

Plants
Good selection of **orchids** -- phalaenopsis and cattleya hybrids, many meristems and some seedlings, briefly described. Also offers an orchid-a-month plan and starter collections for beginners. Several lists a year.
📖 Catalog: Free, R&W, CAN/OV, CC, SS:W
✪ Nursery: All year, M-Sa
✹ Garden: All year, greenhouse, M-Sa

P & P Seed Company
14050 Route 62
Collins, NY 14034-9704
Waterman's, Inc.
(716) 532-5995, (800) 449-5681
Fax: (716) 532-5690
E-mail: 1gourd@aol.com

Seeds
Specialize in **giant vegetable** seed: pumpkins, squash, watermelons, gourds, cabbage and others, used by people growing for competition. They are the sponsor of the World Pumpkin Confederation, which hopes for a 1,000 lb. (half ton!) pumpkin by the turn of the century. (1984)
📖 Catalog: Long SASE(4 IRC OV), R&W, CAN/OV, CC, $4m

Pacific Rim Native Plants
44305 Old Orchard Road
Sardis, BC, Canada V2R 1A9
Pat & Paige Woodward
(604) 792-9279
Fax: (604) 792-1891
E-mail: pacificrim@ntonline.com
Web: www.ntonline.com/biz/pacificrim

Plants
A very good selection of **native plants of the Pacific Northwest**, listed by botanical name only. Included are eriogonums, species iris, erythroniums, many penstemons, flowering currants and huckleberries.
📖 Catalog: $3d, R&W, US/OV, CC, SS:3-10, $20, bn
✪ Nursery: March-October, by appointment only
✹ Garden: May-August, by appointment only

Pacific Tree Farms
4301 Lynwood Drive
Chula Vista, CA 91910
William L. Nelson
(760) 422-2400
Fax: (760) 422-2400

Plants ∞ **Books** ∞ **Supplies** ∞ **Tools**
A broad selection of **fruit, nut and ornamental trees** (including 32 pines), California native trees and shrubs, and tender fruits like **banana, cherimoya, lychee, date palm, pistachio** and more: good selection, no plant descriptions. Also books, grafting supplies and fertilizers. (1970)
📖 Catalog: $2($3.50 OV) R&W, CAN/OV, CC, bn/cn
✪ Nursery: All year, W-M
✹ Garden: All year, W-M

Carl Pallek & Son Nurseries
P.O. Box 137
1567 Highway 55
Virgil, ON, Canada L0S 1T0
Otto Pallek
(905) 468-7262
Fax: (905) 468-5246

Plants
Offers an extensive list of hybrid tea **roses**, as well as floribunda, grandiflora, climbers and a selection of old garden roses, each briefly described. Ships in Canada only, but Americans may pick up orders at the nursery; order 2 weeks early to allow preparation of inspection papers. (1959)
📖 Catalog: Free, SS:3-4,11-12
✪ Nursery: All year, M-Sa
✹ Garden: July-September, M-Sa

Palm Hammock Orchid Estate
9995 S.W. 66th Street
Miami, FL 33173
Tim & Ann Anderson
(305) 274-9813
Fax: (305) 274-9538
E-mail: timothya7@aol.com

Plants
Offer an extensive selection of both rhizomatous and cane **begonias**, as well as some ferns, orchids, peperomias and other **greenhouse plants**. Also have a list of miniature plants for dishgardens and terrariums. Plants are very briefly described. (1973)
📖 Catalog: Long SASE w/2 FCS, R&W, CC, $25m, cn/bn
✪ Nursery: All year, M-Sa
✸ Garden: All year, M-Sa

Palms for Tropical Landscaping
6600 S.W. 45th Street
Miami, FL 33155
Carol Graff
(305) 666-1457

Plants
Small nursery offers a wide selection of **palms**; over 130 individual species and varieties listed only by botanical name. They can be shipped in three inch, one or three gallon pots. Plants not listed might be available. (1983)
📖 Catalog: Long SASE($2 OV), R&W, CAN/OV, $100m, bn
✪ Nursery: Daily, by appointment only
✸ Garden: Daily, by appointment only

Paradise Water Gardens
14 May Street
Whitman, MA 02382
Paul Stetson
(617) 447-4711
Fax: (617) 447-4591
E-mail: pstet82980@aol.com

Plants ∞ **Books** ∞ **Supplies**
Specializes in plants and supplies for **water gardens** -- water lilies, aquatic and bog plants, fish for garden ponds, books on water gardening and supplies for pools and ponds. (1950)
📖 Catalog: $3d, R&W, CAN, CC, SS:W, $16m, cn/bn
✪ Nursery: All year, daily
✸ Garden: May-October, daily

Park Seed Company
1 Parkton Avenue
Greenwood, SC 29647-0001
Leonard Park & Karen Park Jennings
(864) 223-8555, (800) 845-3369
Fax: (864) 941-4502
E-mail: info@parkseed.com
Web: www.parkseed.com

Plants ∞ **Seeds** ∞ **Books** ∞ **Supplies** ∞ **Tools** ∞ **Bulbs**
Park offers a huge selection of plants, seeds and bulbs for the home gardener, many illustrated in color. In addition to **flowers and vegetables**, also sells propagating supplies and some books. The catalog seems to arrive shortly after Christmas to help fight the post-holiday blues (it works!). (1868)
📖 Catalog: Free, R&W, CAN/OV, CC, cn/bn
✪ Nursery: All year, M-Sa
✸ Garden: June-July, call ahead

Parkland Perennials
Box 3683
Spruce Grove, AB, Canada T7X 3A9
Marvin L. Joslin & Lance Varnel
(403) 963-7307
Fax: (403) 963-7307

Plants ∞ **Bulbs**
Specialize in **lilies - Asiatic, longiflorum Asiatic, and martagon hybrids** and offer a nice selection of these. Also offer **daylilies, Siberian iris** and **herbaceous peonies**, as well as some bearded iris. Good plant descriptions.
📖 Catalog: Free, R&W, US/OV, CC, SS:4-9, $25m
✪ Nursery: April-October, M-Sa, call ahead
✸ Garden: July, August, call ahead

Passionflower Herb & Perennial Nursery
1367 Barringer Mountain Road
Christiansburg, VA 24073
Jennipher Lommen and Thom Nelson
(540) 382-2653

Plants
A good selection of **herbs**, including agastaches, basils, scented geraniums, and salvias. Plants are well described.
📖 Catalog: $3d, CC, SS:4-11, $6m, bn/cn
✪ Nursery: April-June, Sept.-October, weekends, call ahead
✸ Garden: April-November, weekends, call ahead

Pat's Pets
4189 Jarvis Road
Hillsboro, MO 63050
Gary N. Dunlap
(314) 789-3604
E-mail: patspets@jcn1.com
Web: www.jcn1.com/patspets

Plants ∞ **Supplies**
Offers many **African violets** from a variety of hybridizers, as well as some species African violets, streptocarpus, sinningias, episcias, aeschynanthus, chiritas, achimenes, codonanthes and other gesneriads. All are briefly described, and available as leaves, stolons or starter plants. (1992)
📖 Catalog: $1.50d, R&W, CAN, $20m, cn/bn
✪ Nursery: All year, by appointment only
✸ Garden: All year, by appointment only

Patio Garden Ponds
2500 N. Moore Avenue
Moore, OK 73160
Joe Villemarette, Jr.
(405) 634-7663, (800) 487-5459
Fax: (405) 793-9669
E-mail: patiojoe@aol.com

Plants ∞ Books ∞ Supplies
Offers a full line of **water garden plants and supplies**, including the various
water treatments and water filters that they manufacture themselves. Plants
and products briefly described. (1986)
- Catalog: Free($5 OV), R&W, CAN/OV, CC, SS:4-10, $30m
- Nursery: All year, daily
- Garden: May-September, daily

Theodore Payne Foundation
10459 Tuxford Street
Sun Valley, CA 91352
Non-profit Organization
(818) 768-1802
Fax: (818) 768-5215
Web: www.via.net/~rferber/thp/thphome.html

Seeds ∞ Books
This non-profit foundation honors the work of Theodore Payne, who made
California wildflowers and native plants admired the world over. They sell
seeds by mail and plants at their headquarters; no plant descriptions. They
also sell many books on native flora -- including Payne's original 1956 catalog
with good plant descriptions (ask for price). (1963)
- Catalog: $1($3 OV), CAN/OV, CC, bn/cn
- Nursery: All year, W-Su
- Garden: January-May, Tu-Sa

Peace Seeds

See Seeds of Change.

Peekskill Nurseries
P.O. Box 428
Old Yorktown Road
Shrub Oak, NY 10588
L. Gary Lundquist
(914) 245-5595

Plants
Specializes in **ground covers**: pachysandra, vinca minor, euonymus, Baltic
ivy and Bar Harbor juniper. Plants well described and sold in quantities from
ten to thousands. (1937)
- Catalog: $1, R&W, SS:4-10, $10m, cn/bn
- Nursery: April-October, M-F, by appointment only

Penn Valley Orchids
239 Old Gulph Road
Wynnewood, PA 19096
William W. Wilson
(610) 642-9822
Fax: (610) 649-4230

Plants
A very broad selection of **hybrid orchids**, some one of a kind, with some
species orchids as well; most well but briefly described. Offers a huge list
of paphiopedilums, also cattleya alliance and others. Sells antique orchid
prints; send SASE for special list of prints and old journals. (1946)
- Catalog: $1($2 OV), R&W, CAN/OV, SS:W, bn
- Nursery: All year, by appointment only

Pense Nursery
16518 Marie Lane
Mountainburg, AR 72946
Phillip D. Pense
(501) 369-2494
Fax: (501) 369-2494
E-mail: ppense@cei.net
Web: www.alcasoft.com/pense

Plants
Specializes in **berries, wine and table grapes** -- boysenberries, dewberries,
raspberries, blackberries, gooseberries, blueberries, strawberries, French
hybrid wine grapes, table grapes, asparagus and rhubarb. Berry plants
available in quantities of 12, 25, 50 + up; single grapevines and elderberries
available with orders of berry plants. No grapes to CA, OR or WA. (1981)
- Catalog: Free, R&W, CAN, CC, SS:10-5, $12m

The Pepper Gal
P.O. Box 23006
Fort Lauderdale, FL 33307-3006
Betty Payton
(954) 537-5540
Fax: (954) 566-2208

Seeds ∞ Books
There's a new "Pepper Gal." The new gal, Betty, still has an extensive list
of lively **ornamental, hot and sweet peppers**, 200 varieties by her count,
with brief plant descriptions. She also has a great selection of ethnic cookbooks to experiment with your harvest! (1978)
- Catalog: Free, R&W, CAN/OV

Pepper Joe's
1650 Pembrooke Road
Norristown, PA 19403
Joseph M. Arditi
(610) 539-4383
Fax: (410) 628-0507
E-mail: Joseph0007@aol.com
Web: all-mall.com

Seeds
Offers a fairly short but hot list of peppers (or is that short list of **hot peppers**?). Included are purple, brown, white and rainbow peppers, and a mushroom pepper. Also sells a few tomatoes, a tee shirt and a hot pepper recipe
book. (1989)
- Catalog: Long SASE, CAN
- Garden: July-October, by appointment only

Perennial Pleasures Nursery
P.O. Box 147
East Hardwick, VT 05836-0147
Rachel Kane
(802) 472-5104
Fax: (802) 472-6572

Plants ∞ Seeds ∞ Books
Specializes in plants for historical restoration, and offers a very good selection of **perennials and herbs**. Informative catalog; they sell "period" plant and specialty garden collections, and books on restoration, herbs and seed saving. No plants to HI, Canada or OV. To top it off, they serve English Cream Teas and have a Bed & Breakfast. (1980)
- Catalog: $3($4 OV), CAN/OV, CC, SS:4-5,9-10, cn/bn
- Nursery: May-September, Tu-Su
- Garden: June-August, Tu-Su

Petaluma Rose Company
P.O. Box 750953
581 Gossage Avenue
Petaluma, CA 94975
Rick Weeks
(707) 769-8862
Fax: (707) 769-0394
E-mail: proseco@aol.com

Plants
Offers a good selection of **roses**: hybrid teas and grandifloras, floribundas, climbers, old garden and modern shrub roses, and grafted tree roses, listed by type. All plants are very well described. (1989)
- Catalog: $1, CC, SS:12-3
- Nursery: All year, daily
- Garden: May-October, daily

Peter Pauls Nurseries
4665 Chapin Road
Canandaigua, NY 14424-8713
James Pietropaolo
(716) 394-7397
Fax: (716) 394-4122
E-mail: ppnurse@eznet.net
Web: www.peterpauls.com

Plants ∞ Seeds ∞ Books
A good selection of **carnivorous plants**, and seeds thereof, as well as growing supplies, terrarium kits, plant collections and their book, "Carnivorous Plants of the World," on how to identify and grow carnivorous plants from seed to maturity. Featured are Venus's-flytrap, sarracenias, droseras, darlingtonia and pinguiculas. (1955)
- Catalog: Free(2 IRC OV), R&W, CAN/OV, CC, SS:4-11, bn

Peters Seed & Research
P.O. Box 1472
Myrtle Creek, OR 97457
Tim Peters
(541) 863-7298
Fax: (541) 863-3693

Seeds
Tim is a hybridizer, plant explorer, inventor and scientist by his own description: he sells **open-pollinated vegetables, grains and annuals**, many of his own breeding or selection. Some packets are mixed varieties, so that you can have many flavors to try. Melons, many tomatoes, squashes, and lots more. (1993)
- Catalog: Free, R&W, CAN/OV

Petite Vines
766 Westside Road
Healdsburg, CA 95448
Dr. Steve Mandy
(707) 433-6255
Fax: (707) 433-1618
E-mail: dutch@sonic.net
Web: www.branch.com/dutch/dutch.htm

Plants
Here's a specialist for you! They offer **bonsai grapevines**, which are really beautiful. So far their business has been mostly to winery tasting rooms, but if you love wine, or bonsai, here's something different. They also have a list of varietal wine grapes available for your home vineyard. (1993)
- Catalog: Free, R&W, CC
- Nursery: Daily
- Garden: Daily, call ahead

Phedar Nursery
Bunkers Hill, Romiley
Stockport, England SK6 3DS
Will McLewin
44 (0) 1614 303-772
Fax: 44 (0) 1614 303-772

Seeds
Here's one of the world experts on **hellebores**, who offers fresh seed from more than 50 species and varieties, another 10 spotted types by background flower color, and 6 seed mixtures. Sowing instructions are sent with the seed; he also sells "Hellebore Notes," very interesting information, $5 ppd. A second list offers seed of **species and herbaceous peonies**. (1989)
- Catalog: $2(US Bills), OV, SS:8-9, bn
- Nursery: By appointment only
- Garden: Spring, by appointment only

Phoenix Seed
P.O. Box 207
Snug, TAS, Australia 7054
Michael J. Self
61 (0) 362 679-663
Fax: 61 (0) 362 679-592
E-mail: phnxseed@ozemail.com.au

Seeds ∞ Books
Specializes in seed of **open-pollinated vegetables** as well as shrubs and trees grown for fruits, shelter or for wildlife. Many of these are from Australia or subtropical areas. Good descriptions, with uses of the plants described.
- Catalog: Free, ($2 OV), OV, cn/bn
- Nursery: Daily, by appointment only

Pickering Nurseries, Inc.
670 Kingston Road
Pickering, ON, Canada L1V 1A6
Joseph & Joel Schraven
(905) 839-2111
Fax: (905) 839-4807

Plants
A very extensive list of **roses** -- hybrid tea, floribunda and many old garden roses, with tables of information for size, ARS rating, fragrance and color and a section on how to winterize roses in very cold climates. Many of the roses are shown in color photographs. (1956)
- Catalog: $4, R&W, US/OV, SS:1-4,10-11, $24m
- Nursery: All year, call ahead
- Garden: July, daily, call ahead

Picov Greenhouses
380 Kingston Road East
Ajax, ON, Canada L1S 4S7
Barry Picov
(905) 686-2151, (800) 663-0300
Fax: (905) 686-2183
E-mail: picovs@idirect.com
Web: www.picovs.com

Plants & **Books** & **Supplies**
Offers a broad selection of **aquatic and bog plants**, poolside perennials, ferns and grasses, water garden supplies and even crabs for your pond. At the nursery they sell garden ornaments and water garden supplies. (1985)
- Catalog: Free, R&W, US, CC, SS:5-10, bn/cn
- Nursery: March-October, daily
- Garden: May-October, daily

Piedmont Plant Company
P.O. Box 424
807 N. Washington Street
Albany, GA 31702
Logan, Jones & Parker
(912) 883-7029
Fax: (912) 432-2888
E-mail: piedmont@surfsouth.com

Plants
Offers 40 varieties of **vegetable plants** -- onions, cabbage, lettuce, broccoli, cauliflower, tomatoes, peppers and eggplant, some illustrated in color, all well described. Can't ship to Western and Gulf states, AK or HI. (1906)
- Catalog: Free, R&W, CAN, CC, SS:4-5
- Nursery: All year, M-F, April-May, M-Sa

Pine Heights Nursery
Pepper Street
Everton Hills, QLD, Australia 4053
Donald V. Rix
61 (0) 7 3353-2761

Bulbs
An Australian source of **spring and summer-blooming bulbs**: alliums, crinums, gingers, haemanthus, hymenocallis, moraea, sprekelia, watsonia, zephyranthes, and many more. Also specialize in species and hybrid **hippeastrum** (amaryllis), both bulbs and seeds. Brief plant descriptions.
- Catalog: $2d(US Bills), OV, CC, $20m, bn/cn
- Nursery: All year, call ahead
- Garden: August-November, call ahead

Pine Ridge Gardens
832 Sycamore Road
London, AR 72847-8767
Mary-Ann King
(501) 293-4359

Plants
A very good selection of **native plants** of the south central US, included are perennials and a few shrubs. Also listed are some garden perennials, hostas, and Japanese and Siberian iris. Plants are well described; notes on bird and butterfly attraction. No shipping to AZ, AK or HI. (1992)
- Catalog: $1, SS:3-6,9-11, $20m, bn/cn
- Nursery: All year, by appointment only
- Garden: April-October, by appointment only

Pineapple Place
3961 Markham Woods Road
Longwood, FL 32779-3047
Carol & Geoffrey Johnson
(407) 333-0445
Fax: (407) 829-6616

Plants
Offers a very broad selection of **bromeliads**: aechmeas, billbergias, nidulariums, neoregelias, dyckias, pitcairnia, tillandsias, guzmanias, vrieseas and others, listed only by botanical names, but collectors will know them. They are inspected to ship anywhere.
- Catalog: Long SASE, CAN/OV, CC, SS:W, $20m, bn
- Nursery: All year, M-Sa, call ahead
- Garden: All year, M-Sa, call ahead

Pinecliffe Daylily Gardens
6604 Scottsville Road
Floyds Knob, IN 47119-9202
Donald & Kathy Smith
(812) 923-8113
Fax: (812) 923-9618
E-mail: dcs923@aol.com

Plants
Huge selection of **daylily** cultivars; plants are very briefly described in informative tables, many are recent or brand new introductions. They have 250,000 seedlings in their trial beds, 2,000 cultivars on display. (1982)
- Catalog: $2d, R&W, CAN/OV, SS:4-11, $25m
- Nursery: May-September, daily, by appointment only
- Garden: June-July, daily, by appointment only

Pinetree Garden Seeds
Box 300
616 A Lewiston Road
New Gloucester, ME 04260
Richard Meiners
(207) 926-3400
Fax: (888) 527-3337
E-mail: superseeds@worldnet.att.net
Web: www.superseeds.com

Seeds & Books & Supplies & Tools & Bulbs
Catalog offers a very broad selection of **vegetable, flower, herb** and **ever-lasting** seed in smaller, less expensive packets. Offers a good selection of heirloom and ethnic vegetables; all well described in an informative catalog. Also sells organic gardening supplies, spring and fall bulbs, tools and many books on gardening and self-sufficiency. (1979)
- Catalog: Free($1.50 OV), CAN/OV, CC
- Nursery: All year, M-Th, call ahead

Plant Delights Nursery
9241 Sauls Road
Raleigh, NC 27603
Tony & Michelle Avent
(919) 772-4794
Fax: (919) 662-0370
E-mail: tony@plantdel.com
Web: www.plantdel.com

Plants
It's true what they say, opening this catalog is "highly addictive" -- they offer a broad selection of **perennials**, with particular strengths in hostas, ornamental grasses, asarums, heucheras and pulmonarias; also some dwarf conifers. Good plant descriptions. Catalog: 10 FCS or a box of chocolates. (1988)
- Catalog: See notes, CAN/OV, CC, SS:3-11, $25m, bn/cn
- Nursery: By appointment only
- Garden: April-October, by appointment only

The Plant Farm
177 Vesuvius Bay Road
Salt Spring Island, BC, Canada V8K 1K3
Jeff & Morgan Savin
(250) 537-5995

Plants
Small nursery offers a good selection of **flowering trees and shrubs, rhodo-dendrons, hostas, ferns and perennials**, particularly plants for shade. Each plant well described. Ships only within Canada. (1990)
- Catalog: C$2, R&W, CC, SS:3-6,9-10, $25m, bn/cn
- Nursery: February-October, Th-M
- Garden: April-August, Th-M

Plant Hideaway

See Green Hill Farm.

Plant World Seeds
St. Marychurch Road
Newton Abbot, Devon, England TQ12 4SE
Ray Brown

Seeds
Color catalog offers a very good selection of rock garden and perennial plants, including **hardy geraniums, aquilegias, campanulas, and hellebores**. Also have a nice selection of species **violas**. Worldwide web address is <www.netlink.co.uk./users/plants/vl.issue3text/plantworld.new.html>. (1985)
- Catalog: $3(US bills), R&W, OV, CC, $30m, bn
- Nursery: April-September, Th-Tu
- Garden: May-July

Plantasia Cactus Gardens
867 Filer Avenue W.
Twin Falls, ID 83301
LaMar N. Orton
(208) 734-7959
E-mail: lorton@computer-depot.com

Plants
A source of **winter hardy cactus**, grown outdoors in Idaho where it some-times goes down to -20F and over 100F in the summer. Listed are a very good selection of opuntias, some cylindropuntia and corynopuntias (chollas), three coryphanthas and an echinocereus. (1992)
- Catalog: Long SASE w/2 FCS, CAN/OV, SS:4-11, $10m, bn
- Nursery: April-October, by appointment only
- Garden: April-July, by appointment only

Plants of the Southwest
Route 6, Box 11A, Agua Fria
Santa Fe, NM 87501
(505) 471-2212, 438-8888
Fax: (505) 438-8888
E-mail: contact@plantsofthesouthwest.com
Web: www.plantsofthesouthwest.com

Plants & Seeds & Books
Catalog full of landscaping and cultural information, with the object of sug-gesting water-saving gardens. Offers seeds and some plants of **native trees and shrubs, wildflowers and grasses**, -- also some **vegetable** seeds. Inspiring color pictures of many of their flowers. (1977)
- Catalog: $3.50, R&W, CC, SS:5-10, bn/cn
- Nursery: April-October, daily; other months, M-F
- Garden: June-October, daily

Plants of the Wild
P.O. Box 866
Tekoa, WA 99033
Kathy Hutton, Mgr.
(509) 284-2848
Fax: (509) 284-6464

Plants
Nice selection of seedling **Western native trees and shrubs,** many not commonly offered, with brief descriptions. These plants are useful for natural landscaping, wildlife cover, erosion control and reclamation.
- Catalog: $1($3 OV), R&W, CAN/OV, CC, bn/cn
- Nursery: All year, M-F, by appointment only
- Garden: May-September, M-F, call ahead

Pleasant Valley Glads & Dahlias
P.O. Box 494
163 Senator Ave.
Agawam, MA 01001
Gary Adams
(413) 786-9146, 789-0307

Bulbs
Offers a wide selection of **gladiolus**; many are recent introductions and prize winners. Each plant is well described. In addition, a number of **dahlias** are offered, listed by size of bloom and very briefly described.
- Catalog: $1d($2 OV), R&W, CAN/OV, SS:3-6, $20m
- Nursery: Call for appointment & directions
- Garden: August-frost, by appointment only

Pleasant View Nursery
Two Mile Oak, nr Denbury
Newton Abbot, Devon, England TQ12 6DG
B.D. & Christine Yeo
44 (0) 1803 813-388
Fax: 44 (0) 1803 813-388
E-mail: christine-yeo@pview.demon.co.uk
Web: www.pview.demon.co.uk

Seeds
Small nursery in England selling seed of fifty-one species **salvias,** each very briefly described. Mrs.Yeo also offers two books, each describing 100 varieties of salvia, with color photos; they are each US$15 postpaid (airmail), send only US bills or an international money order, no $ checks. (1987)
- Catalog: $2(2 IRC), OV, $15m, bn
- Nursery: March-October, W-Sa
- Garden: June-September, Wed, Fri pm

The Plumeria People
910 Leander Drive
Leander, TX 78641
Harry Leuzinger, Mgr.
(512) 259-0807

Plants & Books & Supplies & Bulbs
Tropical plant specialists: plumerias, bougainvillea, gingers, hibiscus, tender bulbs, flowering vines and shrubs, heliconias and more; a good selection, all very well described. Also books on growing tropical plants, including their "Handbook on Plumeria Culture," and growing supplies. (1981)
- Catalog: $3d, CC, SS:4-10, $20m, bn
- Nursery: All year, call ahead
- Garden: Spring-Summer, M-F, call ahead

Plumtree Nursery
387 Springtown Road
New Paltz, NY 12561
Lee Reich
(914) 255-0417

Plants & Books
Small nursery offers **unusual fruits**: including musk and yellow alpine strawberries, 'Consort' European currants, and maypops. Varieties are well described. Can't ship to CA, HI or AK. (1984)
- Catalog: $1, SS:3-12

Portable Acres

See The Iris Gallery.

Porterhowse Farms
41370 S.E. Thomas Road
Sandy, OR 97055
Don Howse & Lloyd Porter
(503) 668-5834
Fax: (503) 668-5834
E-mail: phfarm@aol.com

Plants
A fine source of **dwarf conifers, trees and shrubs, sedums, sempervivums and jovibarbas,** saxifragas and other rock garden plants; a good selection, well described. Also offer "Collector's Cases," boxes of mixed plants by type for various uses. (1979)
- Catalog: $6d, CAN, SS:3-10, bn
- Nursery: All year, Tu-Su, call ahead
- Garden: All year, Tu-Su, call ahead

Potterton & Martin
The Cottage Nursery
Moortown Road, Nettleton
Nr. Caistor, Lincs., England LN7 6HX
Mr. & Mrs. R. Potterton, Alan Martin
44 (0) 1472 851-792
Fax: 44 (0) 1472 851-792

Books & Bulbs
A British bulb specialist offering **dwarf bulbs,** which we would call the "little bulbs" -- a good selection of alliums, anemones, corydalis, calochortus, crocus, cyclamen, erythronium, fritillaria, species iris, narcissus, oxalis and pleione, among others. Good plant descriptions; some books. (1971)
- Catalog: $3(US Bills or 4 IRC), OV, CC, SS:1-4,8-11, bn
- Nursery: Daily, call ahead
- Garden: Spring, call ahead

Powell's Gardens
9468 U.S. Highway 70 E.
Princeton, NC 27569-7869
S.E. & Loleta Powell
(919) 936-4421

Plants
A huge selection of **iris**, many **daylilies and hosta**, and a broad selection of **perennials, dwarf conifers and some ornamental trees and shrubs**; the pages are tightly packed, with only the briefest of descriptions -- a true collectors' list. After 1997, only availability lists will be published. (1953)
📖 Catalog: $5($8 OV), CAN/OV, SS:3-10, $10m, bn/cn
✪ Nursery: All year, M-Sa
❀ Garden: April-October, M-Sa

Poyntzfield Herb Nursery
Black Isle, Dingwall
Ross & Cromarty, Scotland IV7 8LX
Duncan Ross
44 (0) 1381 610-352
Fax: 44 (0) 1381 610-352

Seeds
A Scottish herb nursery which will ship seeds of the **herbs** they grow, many are "native (and naturalized) in Scotland." Plants are well described. (1976)
📖 Catalog: $3(4 IRC), OV, SS:10-3, $10m, cn/bn
✪ Nursery: March-September, M-Sa, call ahead
❀ Garden: June-August, M-Sa, call ahead

Prairie Grown Garden Seeds
P.O. Box 118
Cochin, SK, Canada S0M 0L0
Jim Ternier
(306) 386-2737

Seeds
A regional seedsman, serving the Canadian prairie provinces and offering **vegetables for short-season growing** (100 frost free days) and a dry climate. All seeds are open-pollinated and grown without chemicals, and quite a few are older varieties. All well described. (1985)
📖 Catalog: $1, US/OV, bn/cn
❀ Garden: July-September, call ahead

Prairie Moon Nursery
Route 3, Box 163
Winona, MN 55987
Alan L. Wade
(507) 452-1362
Fax: (507) 454-5238

Plants ɞ Seeds ɞ Books
A very good selection of **grasses and wildflowers** for prairie restoration and wild gardens, both plants and seeds, listed by botanical and common name and habitat, with coded information on germination, size and color, and cultural needs. Also sells books on prairie plants and gardening. Ships only seeds to Canada and overseas. (1983)
📖 Catalog: $2($3 OV), R&W, CAN/OV, SS:4-5,9-10, bn/cn
✪ Nursery: All year, by appointment only
❀ Garden: July-August, restored prairie, by appointment only

© Larner Seers
  Artist: Terry Bell

Prairie Nursery
P.O. Box 306
Westfield, WI 53964
Neil Diboll
(608) 296-3679
Fax: (608) 296-2741

Plants ∞ **Seeds** ∞ **Books**
A small nursery specializing in **prairie plants and seed, grasses and forbs** (flowering herbaceous plants other than grasses); all plants well described, with many color pictures. They sell mixes for moist meadows, gardens on clay, and "prairie" gardens. Also books on prairie restoration and gardens. (1974)
📖 Catalog: Free, R&W, CAN/OV, CC, SS:4-6,8-11, $25m, cn/bn
☼ Nursery: All year, M-F, call ahead
❀ Garden: Dates of nursery tours in catalog

Prairie Oak Seeds
P.O. Box 382
Maryville, MO 64468-0382
Jeffrey Goettemoeller
(816) 562-3743

Seeds ∞ **Books**
Specializes in seeds for plants with **everlasting flowers**, many varieties available by individual colors or in mixes. They also sell books on growing and drying flowers, and a "Directory of Flower & Herb Buyers." ($7.50 ppd.) (1993)
📖 Catalog: $1, R&W, CAN, cn/bn

Prairie Ridge Nursery/CRM Ecosystems, Inc.
9738 Overland Road
Mt. Horeb, WI 53572-2832
Joyce Powers
(608) 437-5245
Fax: (608) 437-8982
E-mail: crmprairie@aol.com

Plants ∞ **Seeds**
Specializing in **prairie wildflowers, grasses and forbs**, both plants and seeds; plant information given in concise tables. They also sell plant and seed collections for various growing conditions and do consulting on the establishment of low-maintenance erosion-control plantings. (1974)
📖 Catalog: Free, R&W, CAN, CC, SS:4-5,10-11, $45m, bn/cn
☼ Nursery: May-October, M-Sa, by appointment only
❀ Garden: May-October, call ahead

Prairie Seed Source
P.O. Box 83
North Lake, WI 53064-0083
Robert Ahrenhoerster

Seeds
Another company striving to recreate prairie ecosystems and to encourage people to create their own. Offers seed of S.E. Wisconsin **prairie plants**, with very brief information in table form and outlines showing size and form of each plant. They also rent slide sets on prairie plants and restoration.
📖 Catalog: $1, CAN/OV, bn/cn
❀ Garden: Write for appointment

Prentiss Court Ground Covers
P.O. Box 8662
Greenville, SC 29604
Lesesne & Gene Dickson
(864) 277-4037
Fax: (864) 299-5015
E-mail: EMcND@aol.com

Plants
A small family enterprise offers **ground cover plants**: ajuga, cotoneaster, euonymous, ivy, hypericum, liriope, jasmine, daylilies, vincas and more. Plants offered bare-root (50 plant minimum) or in pots; brief plant descriptions. Can't ship to AK or HI. (1978)
📖 Catalog: $1, CC, $15m, bn

The Primrose Path
R.D. 2, Box 110
Scottdale, PA 15683
Charles & Martha Oliver
Fax: (412) 887-3077

Plants
A broad selection of **perennials**, including rock garden and woodland plants, all well described and with lists of plants for special uses. They have an active hybridization and selection program in phlox, heuchera, tiarella and primula; and offer a nice selection of these plants. No shipping to HI. (1985)
📖 Catalog: $2d, R&W, CC, SS:3-5,9-11, bn/cn
❀ Garden: April-October, by appointment only

Rainbow Acres
P.O. Box 1543
Sebring, FL 33871-1543
Robert A. Clarke
(941) 382-4449

Bulbs
Sells bulbs of **fancy leaf caladiums** by named variety or in mixes of reds, pinks or whites or mixed colors. No plant descriptions, about 20 varieties shown in color on their brochure. (1978)
📖 Catalog: Free, CC, SS:2-5, $19m
☼ Nursery: January-June, M-Sa

Rainbow Gardens Nursery & Bookshop
1444 E. Taylor Street
Vista, CA 92084-3308
Gerald Williams & Charles Everson
(760) 758-4290
Fax: (760) 945-8934
E-mail: rbgdns@aol.com

Plants 🔊 Books 🔊 Supplies
Specializes in **epiphyllums and other rainforest cacti, and hoyas**; a large selection. Plants well described, many shown in color photos. Bookshop has a separate catalog <www.demon.co.uk/rainbow/rbg.html> offering a huge selection of books on cacti, succulents, bromeliads, ferns and greenhouse propagation. (1977)
- 📖 Catalog: $2($5 OV), CAN/OV, CC, SS:4-11, $15m, bn/cn
- ✪ Nursery: All year, Tu-Sa, by appointment only
- ❀ Garden: April-May, Tu-Sa

Rainforest Gardens
13139 - 224th Street
Maple Ridge, BC, Canada V2X 7E7
Elke Knechtel
(604) 467-4218
Fax: (604) 467-3181
E-mail: info@rainforest-gardens.com
Web: www.dsoe.com/rainforest

Plants 🔊 Books
Specializes in **herbaceous perennials**, especially plants for the shade: this is British Columbia, don't forget! Offers a good selection of hardy geraniums for sun and shade, hostas, astilbes, ferns, primulas, hellebores, gentians, and many others, all very well described. Only ships within Canada. (1986)
- 📖 Catalog: $4d, CC, SS:3-6,9-10, $20m, bn/cn
- ✪ Nursery: March-October, W-Sa
- ❀ Garden: April-October, W-Sa

Rainforest Plantes et Fleurs

See Hoyas by Michael Miyashiro.

Rainforest Seed Company
P.O. Box 241
San Jose, Costa Rica 1017
Joe Azaria, Mgr.
Fax: (506) 232-9260

Seeds
A seed company which harvests seed from their own 1,500 acre protected rainforest: offers a nice selection of **trees and shrubs**, listed by common and botanical names. Each is very well described, though eventual size is not mentioned; I guess "majestic" = very large! Many would make fine greenhouse plants. You can send a personal check in US$ for the catalog. (1981)
- 📖 Catalog: $2, R&W, OV, cn/bn

Raintree Nursery
391 Butts Road
Morton, WA 98356
Sam Benowitz
(360) 496-6400
Fax: (360) 496-6465
E-mail: RaintreeNursery@juno.com

Plants 🔊 Books 🔊 Supplies
Offer edible plants, many **fruit and nut** varieties in a catalog full of orchard lore, edible landscaping and cultural suggestions. They also offer some ornamental trees and shrubs, grafting and pruning supplies and books on fruit growing and edible landscaping. (1974)
- 📖 Catalog: $1, R&W, CC, SS:1-5, $10m, cn/bn
- ✪ Nursery: W-Su, December-May

Randy's Nursery & Greenhouses
523 W. Crogan Street (Hwy 29)
Lawrenceville, GA 30245
Randy Kucera
(770) 822-0676
Fax: (770) 822-1259

Plants
Offers a very good selection of **perennials**, each well described with information on best planting conditions. They must be fun people, their catalog is laced with garden quotes and wisdom that makes you smile. No shipping to AK, AZ, CA, HI, OR and WA. (1988)
- 📖 Catalog: $2, CC, $25m, bn/cn
- ✪ Nursery: February-mid-December, daily
- ❀ Garden: April-May, daily

Rare Plant Research
13245 S.E. Harold
Portland, OR 97236
Burl L. Mostul, PhD.
(503) 762-0289
Fax: (503) 762-0289
E-mail: rareplantr@aol.com

Plants
Their "primary goal is to research **rare succulents** through botanical exploration...work has been done in Mexico, Costa Rica, Malaysia, Borneo and the US. The sale of propagated plants supports our botanical research and explorations." Adeniums, aloes, euphorbias, jatropas, monadeniums and many others, including a few hardy plants; notes as to source, very brief plant descriptions. Also a good selection of **lewisias**. (1988)
- 📖 Catalog: $2, R&W, CAN/OV, CC, $30m, bn
- ✪ Nursery: By appointment only

Rasland Farm
NC 82 at US 13
Godwin, NC 28344-9712
Sylvia Tippett
(910) 567-2705
Fax: (910) 567-2705
Web: www.alcasoft.com/rasland/

Plants 🔊 Supplies
A good selection of **herb** plants and **scented geraniums**; good but brief plant descriptions. Also a broad selection of herbal products: teas, potpourri supplies, cooking herbs, wreaths and more. No shipments to HI. (1981)
📖 Catalog: $3, CC, SS:4-6, $20m, cn/bn
✪ Nursery: All year, M-Sa
✿ Garden: May-September, M-Sa

Steve Ray's Bamboo Gardens
250 Cedar Cliff Road
Springville, AL 35146
Steve Ray
(205) 594-3438

Plants
Steve says that the age of bamboo is just beginning in the US -- he specializes in **hardy bamboos**, and lists 46 varieties in an informative catalog, many shown in b&w photographs. Larger plants can be dug at the grove. No shipping to CA or HI. (1980)
📖 Catalog: $3, SS:9-4, $20m, bn/cn
✪ Nursery: By appointment only
✿ Garden: All year, by appointment only

Reath's Nursery
County Road 577, N-195
Vulcan, MI 49892
Scott Reath
(906) 563-9777
Fax: (906) 563-9777

Plants
Offers herbaceous and tree **peonies**, including hybrids of Daphnis, Saunders and their own. Japanese tree peonies listed by Japanese cultivar name -- a true collectors' list; catalog has color photographs and good plant descriptions. Now sell **Siberian iris**, too.
📖 Catalog: $2, CAN/OV, SS:9-10

Red's Rhodies
15920 S.W. Oberst Lane
Sherwood, OR 97140-8436
Dick & Karen Cavender
(503) 625-6331
Fax: (503) 625-6331

Plants
In a change of direction, "Red" now specializes in **arisaemas** and **bletilla striata, calanthe, dactylorhiza and pleione orchids**; has a nice selection of species and hybrids, each well described. Offers a few **vireya rhododendrons** too. (1977)
📖 Catalog: $2, R&W, CAN/OV, SS:12-3, bn/cn
✪ Nursery: All year, by appointment only
✿ Garden: April-September, by appointment only

Redwood City Seed Co.
P.O. Box 361
Redwood City, CA 94064
Craig & Sue Dremann
(415) 325-7333
Web: www.batnet.com/rwc-seed/

Seeds 🔊 Books
Old-fashioned open-pollinated **vegetables and herbs**, mostly developed before 1906; unusual varieties, including Oriental types and Native American beans, corn, hot peppers and squash. These and other "useful" plants are well described, with growing hints. Books on plants and organic gardening. (1971)
📖 Catalog: $1($2 OV), R&W, CAN/OV, $3m, cn/bn

Reflective Gardens
24329 N.E. Snowhill Lane
Poulsbo, WA 98370-9101
Kelly Dodson & Sue Skelly
(360) 598-4649

Plants
Small nursery offers a good selection of unusual **perennials and rock garden plants**, many grown from seed collected in China and the Himalayas by botanical expeditions, others from collectors' gardens in the Northwest. Nice assortment of ranunculus, species peonies, and other choice items. (1991)
📖 Catalog: $2, CAN, SS:3-11, $20m, bn
✪ Nursery: By appointment only

Regan Nursery
4628 Decoto Road
Fremont, CA 94555
Larry Thompson & Marsha Hildebrand
(510) 797-3222
Fax: (510) 793-5408
Web: www.regannursery.com

Plants 🔊 Books
This **rose** nursery has it all -- a broad selection of hybrid teas, as well as some modern shrub roses, old garden roses, miniatures, species roses, and miniature and standard tree roses. Plants are listed in table format. (1958)
📖 Catalog: $3d, CC, SS:12-2, $10m
✪ Nursery: All year, daily
✿ Garden: March-October, daily

The Rhododendron Species Foundation
P.O. Box 3798
2525 S. 336th Street
Federal Way, WA 98063-3798
Non-Profit Foundation
(206) 838-4646
Fax: (206) 838-4686

Plants
A fund raising effort of The Rhododendron Species Foundation, here is a chance to get unusual species plants, including some rare companion plants. Members get priority, but anyone can order from their catalog. A very good selection, each plant well described. Payment must be in US$. (1970)
📖 Catalog: $3.50, R&W, CAN/OV, CC, bn
☼ Nursery: All year, F-W
❀ Garden: March-May, September-November, F-W

Richters Herbs
357 Highway 47
Goodwood, ON, Canada L0C 1A0
Otto Richter & Sons, Ltd.
(905) 640-6677
Fax: (905) 640-6641
E-mail: catalog@richters.com
Web: www.richters.com

Plants ∾ Seeds ∾ Books ∾ Supplies ∾ Tools
Catalog offers seed and plants of 600+ **herbs, wildflowers and everlasting flowers**, as well as dried herbs and essential oils, herbal gifts and books and videos on herbs; ships plants in Canada and by UPS to the US. Herbs are well described, with information on culture and traditional uses. (1971)
📖 Catalog: Free, R&W, US/OV, CC, SS:4-10, cn/bn
☼ Nursery: All year, daily
❀ Garden: All year, daily

River View Herbs
P.O. Box 92
Maitland, Hants Co., NS, Canada B0N 1T0
John Sipos & Jim Bruce
(902) 261-2109, 261-2274
Fax: (902) 261-2427

Plants ∾ Seeds
Offers a great selection of **herbs** and **scented geraniums** for Canadian gardeners. Included are lots of basils, lavenders, mints, thymes and salvias. Plants are well described. No shipping to US or overseas. (1988)
📖 Catalog: Free, R&W, CC, SS:5-10, cn/bn
☼ Nursery: Daily, May-September
❀ Garden: Daily, July-August

Riverdale Gardens
P.O. Box 524
Rockford, MN 55373
Tracy W. Jennings
(612) 477-4859

Plants
Specializes in dwarf and median **iris** and some aril-median crosses, and offers a very good selection. The plants are listed by type, and very well described. Offers tall bearded and Siberian iris, too. (1988)
📖 Catalog: $1d, R&W, CAN/OV, SS:7-9, $10m
☼ Nursery: May-June, W-Su, call ahead, or by appointment
❀ Garden: May-June, call ahead

Rob's Mini-o-lets
P.O. Box 9
7209 County Road 12
Naples, NY 14512
Ralph Robinson
(716) 374-8592
E-mail: robsviolet@aol.com

Plants
Rob is a hybridizer of miniature **African violets and streptocarpus**, and has won awards for "best new cultivar" three times. He lists his own introductions, and some favorites from others: a nice selection, well described. (1986)
📖 Catalog: $1, R&W, CAN/OV, CC, SS:W
☼ Nursery: All year, daily, afternoons
❀ Garden: All year, daily, afternoons

Robinett Bulb Farm
P.O. Box 1306
Sebastopol, CA 95473-1306
Jim Robinett
(707) 829-2729
Fax: (707) 823-1954
E-mail: jarobinett@worldnet.att.net

Bulbs
Bulbs of **West Coast natives**: alliums, brodiaea, calochortus, species lilies, fritillaries, erythroniums and others; also alstroemerias. Bulbs are nursery-grown and, because the business is small, may be in short supply; list sent in August. Retail orders only in years with even ending; wholesale only in alternate years. Minimum overseas retail order is $50. (1983)
📖 Catalog: Free, R&W, CAN/OV, SS:9-10, $30m, bn/cn

W. Robinson & Sons, Ltd.
Sunnybank, Forton
Nr. Preston, Lancs., England PR3 0BN
Robinson Family
44 (0) 524 791-210
Fax: 44 (0) 524 791-933

Seeds
A great source for seeds for those **giant vegetables** the Brits love to grow and show. They carry mammoth onions, pink or white celery, beets and cabbage, as well as other very fancy-sounding exhibition quality varieties. Some have even won the Royal Horticultural Society's Award of Merit! (1860)
📖 Catalog: Free, R&W, OV, CC

Robyn's Nest Nursery
7802 N.E. 63rd Street
Vancouver, WA 98662
Robyn Duback
(360) 256-7399

Plants
A small nursery offering a good selection of **perennials and rock garden plants**, particularly astilbes, ferns, hardy geraniums, epimediums, ornamental grasses, and many hostas; each plant well described, some of them hard to find. Charming animal illustrations, too! (1982)
📖 Catalog: $2($5 OV), CAN/OV, CC, SS:4-10, $20m, bn/cn
✪ Nursery: April-October, Th-Sa, call ahead
✤ Garden: April-October, Th-Sa, call ahead

Rock Spray Nursery
P.O. Box 693
Depot Road
Truro, MA 02666-0693
Kate Herrick
(508) 349-6769
Fax: (508) 349-2732
E-mail: kherrick@rockspray.com
Web: www.rockspray.com

Plants
Suppliers of **heaths and heathers**; they offer a good number of species and varieties of erica and calluna, briefly described by size, color and season of bloom, habit and color of foliage. They sell other seaside plants at the nursery. (1981)
📖 Catalog: $2, R&W, CAN, CC, SS:3-7,9-11, $5m, bn
✪ Nursery: April-October, daily
✤ Garden: April-October, daily

Rocky Ford Gourd
P.O. Box 222
178 Losee Street
Cygnet, OH 43413
Kern Ackerman, Mgr.
(419) 655-2152

Seeds
Offer a good selection of seeds for **gourds**, the names seem to describe the size and shape, there are no plant descriptions. Ohio is the home of the American Gourd Society -- we'll assume this group of growers are devotees. (1990)
📖 Catalog: Long SASE, CAN/OV, $2m, cn

Rocky Meadow Orchard & Nursery
360 Rocky Meadow Road N.W.
New Salisbury, IN 47161
Ed Fackler
(812) 347-2213

Plants ✍ Supplies
Specializes in apples, pears and Asian pears, plums and rootstocks for these **fruit trees**; scionwood list also available, send long SASE. Also does custom propagation, sells grafting supplies and does consultation on fruit culture. All fruit varieties are chosen with flavor as first priority. (1975)
📖 Catalog: $1, R&W, SS:11-5
✪ Nursery: November-May, M-Sa, by appointment only
✤ Garden: August-September, by appointment only

Rocky Mountain Rare Plants
1706 Deerpath Road
Franktown, CO 80116-9462
Rebecca Day-Skowron
E-mail: orders@rmrp.com
Web: www.rmrp.com

Seeds
Offers a great selection of seeds of **alpines** and **rock garden plants** grown in the strong sun of the Rocky Mountains. Good selection of species from around the world, with particular emphasis on regional natives. Plants are well described and germination advice is included. (1986)
📖 Catalog: $1($2 OV), R&W, CAN/OV, CC, bn

Rollingwood Garden
21234 Rollingwood Trail
37941 CR 439
Eustis, FL 32736
Elizabeth Salter
Fax: (352) 483-0515

Plants
Elizabeth & Jeff Salter are **daylily** royalty; she's the niece of Bill Munson and the daughter of Betty Hudson. The catalog shows a number of their own hybrids in color, and they have lovely crinkly edges -- not daylily tech talk, but you know what I mean. Elizabeth specializes in small flowers, Jeff in big.
📖 Catalog: $2($5 OV), CAN, CC, SS:3-11, $25m
✪ Nursery: May-June, F-Su
✤ Garden: May, call ahead

Lon J. Rombough
P.O. Box 365
Aurora, OR 97002-0365
Lon J. Rombough
(503) 678-1410
E-mail: lonrom@hevanet.com
Web: www.hevanet.com/lonrom

Plants
Lon is a fruit researcher who grows many old and new varieties of **wine and table grapes**, and will provide cuttings; you won't see many of these varieties on other lists. Canadian and overseas customers must handle the import paperwork, but he lists some great sounding varieties! Formerly listed as Lon's Oregon Grapes.
📖 Catalog: Long SASE, R&W, CAN/OV, SS:12-5, $5m

Ronniger's Seed Potatoes
P.O. Box 1838
18705 188th Street East
Orting, WA 98360
Greg A. Lutovsky
(360) 893-8782
Fax: (360) 893-3492

Plants ∾ **Seeds** ∾ **Books** ∾ **Supplies** ∾ **Tools**
Offer a broad selection of **seed potatoes**: early, mid and late-maturing varieties and several varieties of fingerlings. Each variety is well described by color, flavor, disease resistance and keeping qualities. They also offer sunchokes, onions, cover crop seed, garlic, books and growing supplies, as well as lots of information. (1988)
📖 Catalog: $1, R&W, CC, $10m
✪ Nursery: M-F, by appointment only

Ros-Equus
40350 Wilderness Road
Branscomb, CA 95417
Virginia Hopper
(707) 984-6959

Plants ∾ **Bulbs**
Virginia and her sister used to run Heritage Rose Gardens from two locations; now they each run their own rose nursery. Ros-Equus offers a very good selection of **old garden and species roses**, each very well described. (1996)
📖 Catalog: $1.50, SS:10-3
✪ Nursery: May-October, F-Sa
❀ Garden: June-October, F-Sa, call ahead

Rose Acres

See Roses, Wine & Evergreens.

Rose Hill Herbs and Perennials
1125 Roses Mill Road
Amherst, VA 24521
Joan & Neil Rothemich

Plants
A good selection of **herbs, perennials, scented geraniums and everlastings**; plants briefly to well described. Good selection of rosemarys, mints, basils, artemisias and thymes.
📖 Catalog: $2, SS:4-6,9-10, $20m

The Rose Ranch
P.O. Box 10087
240 Cooper Road
Salinas, CA 93912-7087
Alice & Anthony Hinton
(408) 758-6965

Plants
Alice Hinton and her son Anthony offer old garden and some modern **roses**; most of the older roses are own-root, some old roses and the modern roses are budded onto virus-free understock. They are also hybridizing and hope to introduce their own roses soon. A good selection, all well described. (1992)
📖 Catalog: $3(Plant list 1 FCS), R&W, $10m
✪ Nursery: All year, by appointment only
❀ Garden: April-June, by appointment only

The Roseraie at Bayfields
P.O. Box R
670 Bremen Road (Route 32)
Waldoboro, ME 04572-0919
Lloyd D. Brace
(207) 832-6330
Fax: (800) 933-4508
E-mail: roses@midcoast.com
Web: www.midcoast.com/roseraie

Plants ∾ **Supplies**
Catalog lists many **old garden roses**, each very well described. In addition to the catalog, they offer a 54-minute video showing many of their roses; $9 ppd. They also offer special rose fertilizers and a special system of rose supports and trellises. (1992)
📖 Catalog: Free, CC, SS:3-5,10-11
✪ Nursery: April-October, daily
❀ Garden: June-July, daily

Roses, Wine & Evergreens
3528 Montclair Road
8070 Fair Pines Lane (Garden Valley)
Cameron Park, CA 95682
Wayne & Barbara Procissi
(916) 677-9722

Plants
Barbara Procissi has taken over the shipping of **roses** for Muriel Humenick of Rose Acres in Diamond Springs; Rose Acres will still sell roses on site by appointment (916) 626-1722. They offer a good selection of old garden roses, as well as some miniatures and modern roses -- no descriptions. Muriel has a large number of stock plants, and will propagate desired plants to order.
📖 Catalog: Long SASE, CAN/OV, SS:1-2, $10m
✪ Nursery: All year, Sa-Su, by appointment only
❀ Garden: Spring, by appointment only

Roslyn Nursery
211 Burrs Lane
Dix Hills, NY 11746
Philip Waldman
(516) 643-9347
Fax: (516) 484-1555
E-mail: roslyn@concentric.net
Web: www.cris.com/~Roslyn/

Plants ঠ Books
Collectors' list of hybrid and species rhododendrons, evergreen and deciduous azaleas, dwarf conifers, ferns, hollies, pieris, kalmias, other **ornamental shrubs and trees and perennials**; each plant briefly described, with some color photographs. Large selection of choice landscape plants. (1980)
- 📖 Catalog: $3($5 OV), CAN/OV, CC, SS:3-6,8-11, bn
- ✪ Nursery: All year, M-Sa; April-May, Su
- ✸ Garden: May, growing area, daily

Roswell Seed Company
P.O. Box 725
115-117 South Main Street
Roswell, NM 88202-0725
Walter & Jim Gill
(505) 622-7701
Fax: (505) 623-2885

Seeds ঠ Supplies
Regional seed company sells **vegetables, grains and grasses** for New Mexico, Arizona, Oklahoma and Utah. Hybrid and open-pollinated crops well described; offers a good variety of grains, cover crops, native and pasture grasses, some annual flowers and growing supplies. (1900)
- 📖 Catalog: Free, R&W, CAN, CC, $5m
- ✪ Nursery: All year, M-Sa

Doug & Vivi Rowland
200 Spring Road, Kempston
Bedford, England MK42 8ND
Doug & Vivi Rowland
44 (0) 1234 358-970
Fax: 44 (0) 1234 358-970

Seeds
The ultimate collectors' list -- over a thousand **cactus, succulents** and other **desert plants**, densely typed in tiny print; no descriptions, enough to make your heart sing! They specialize in desert plant seed of all kinds; also offer seed of **carnivorous plants** and "exotic temperate plants." (1971)
- 📖 Catalog: Free, R&W, OV, bn

Royall River Roses
323 Pine Point Road
Scarborough, ME 04074
David King
(207) 829-5830, (800) 820-5830
Fax: (207) 885-0660

Plants ঠ Tools
Offers a good selection of old-fashioned, hardy and uncommon **roses**: old garden varieties and species roses, more modern shrub roses from Canada and the Midwest and some David Austin roses. Emphasis is on the hardy growers and roses which grow well organically and without "fussing." (1983)
- 📖 Catalog: $3($5 OV), R&W, CAN/OV, CC, SS:3-5
- ✪ Nursery: All year, M-Sa
- ✸ Garden: June, M-Sa

Rozell Rose Nursery & Violet Boutique
12206 Highway 31 West
Tyler, TX 75709
Billy & Carolyn Rozell
(903) 595-5137
Fax: (903) 593-7956

Plants ঠ Supplies
They may sell roses at the nursery, but the catalog lists only a good selection of **African violets**, including many new introductions, and some **episcias, sinningias and streptocarpus**, with good plant descriptions. They also offer some growing supplies.
- 📖 Catalog: $2.50($5 OV), R&W, CAN/OV, CC, SS:4-10, $20m
- ✪ Nursery: All year, by appointment only
- ✸ Garden: All year, by appointment only

Jim & Irene Russ - Quality Plants

See Kelly's Color.

Rust-En-Vrede Nursery
P.O. Box 753
Brackenfell, South Africa 7560
Alan Horstmann
27 (0) 21 981-4515
Fax: 27 (0) 21 981-0050

Seeds ঠ Books ঠ Bulbs
Offers seeds and bulbs of **South African bulbous plants** for serious collectors. Some of the seed is viable for only a short period; orders are held until seed is ripe and ready to plant. A nice selection with no plant descriptions. Also offer books on South African bulbs.
- 📖 Catalog: $2(US Bills), OV, $30m, bn

St. Lawrence Nurseries
325 State Highway 345
Potsdam, NY 13676
Diana & Bill MacKentley
(315) 265-6739
E-mail: trees@sln.potsdam.ny.us
Web: www.sln.potsdam.ny.us

Plants ঠ Books ঠ Tools
A broad selection of organically grown cold-hardy **fruit and nut trees**, other **edible fruits and berries**; plants very well described, with comparative tables on hardiness, fruit color and harvest season in an informative catalog. Books on fruit culture and pruning tools available.
- 📖 Catalog: $1, R&W, SS:4-5,10-11, cn/bn
- ✪ Nursery: All year, M-Sa
- ✸ Garden: May-October, call ahead

Salt Spring Seeds
P.O. Box 444, Ganges
Salt Spring Island, BC, Canada V8K 2WI
Dan Jason
(250) 537-5269

Seeds
Offers only their own organically grown and untreated **vegetable** seeds, they "feature high protein, good tasting and high-yielding crops...all adapted to northern climates." Each variety is well described, all open-pollinated, with a broad selection of beans.
📖 Catalog: $2, US/OV
❀ Garden: Summer, by appointment only

Sand Hill Preservation Center
1878 230th Street
Calamus, IA 52729
Glenn & Linda Drowns
(319) 246-2299

Seeds
"Dedicated to the preservation of heirloom seeds and poultry" -- offer a nice selection of **heirloom vegetables,** with an extensive listing of tomatoes (174 kinds). Also offer citron melons, sorghum and a few flowers. The poultry sound fascinating -- quail, bantams, chickens, duck, geese, turkeys. (1989)
📖 Catalog: Free, CAN/OV, SS:5-6

Sandy Mush Herb Nursery
316 Surrett Cove Road
Leicester, NC 28748-9622
Fairman & Kate Jayne
(704) 683-2014

Plants ဆ Seeds ဆ Books
A very broad selection of **herbs,** both seeds and plants, all very well described. Many scented geraniums, ornamental grasses, salvias, lavenders, thymes, other perennials, herbal gifts and books. (1978)
📖 Catalog: $4d, CC, $15m, bn/cn
❍ Nursery: All year, Th-Sa, call ahead
❀ Garden: May-October, Th-Sa, call ahead

A Sandy Rhododendron
41610 S.E. Coalman Road
Sandy, OR 97055
Chris Hoffman
(800) 688-4960
Fax: (503) 688-4860
E-mail: asr@teleport.com
Web: www.rhodo.com

Plants
Specializes in **hybrid and species rhododendrons,** many are introductions from hybridizers in a number of countries, and some from plant explorers. All are listed in tables with brief descriptions. You could also send your "wish list," as they grow many more varieties than they list. (1989)
📖 Catalog: Free, R&W, CAN/OV, CC, $50m
❍ Nursery: By appointment only

Santa Barbara Heirloom Nursery, Inc.
P.O. Box 4235
Santa Barbara, CA 93140-4235
JoAnna LaForce, Russ Waldrop, Michael Ommaha
(805) 968-5444
Fax: (805) 562-1248
E-mail: heirloom@heirloom.com
Web: www.heirloom.com/heirloom/

Plants ဆ Seeds ဆ Supplies
Shipped by Airborne Express, these **heirloom vegetable plants** arrive quickly and settle right into your garden. Offered are starts of hot and sweet peppers, many tomatoes, melons, okra, exotic greens as well as lettuces, herbs and more. Plants are very well described. Also sell some seeds, beneficial insects and some gifts for gardeners. No shipping to HI.
📖 Catalog: $2d, R&W, CC
❀ Garden: May-October, by appointment only

Santa Barbara Orchid Estate
1250 Orchid Drive
Santa Barbara, CA 93111
Parry & Alice Gripp
(805) 967-1284
Fax: (805) 683-3405

Plants ဆ Supplies
Offers many **cymbidium orchids** which do well outdoors in coastal California, as well as a good selection of **species orchids** -- too many to list! Each is very briefly described; get out your orchid reference books. (1957)
📖 Catalog: Free, CAN/OV, CC, SS:W
❍ Nursery: All year, daily
❀ Garden: March-May, daily

Saskaberia Nursery
P.O. Box 26
Prairie River, SK, Canada S0E 1J0
Stanley Zubrowski
(306) 889-4227

Plants
A small nursery specializing in **clematis,** and introducing their own hybrids; they say there will be more available all the time. Plants are well described.
📖 Catalog: $1 & Long SASE($2 OV), US/OV, SS:4,10, $20m

Savory's Gardens, Inc.
5300 Whiting Avenue
Edina, MN 55439-1249
Arlene & Dennis Savory
(612) 941-8755
Fax: (612) 941-3750

Plants
Around 200 varieties of **hosta** are listed. Plants are well described, some illustrated in color; many are their introductions. They grow over 800 varieties at the nursery, and sell ground covers and other perennials there. (1946)
📖 Catalog: $2($4 OV), R&W, CAN/OV, CC, SS:4-5,9-10, $25m, bn
✪ Nursery: May-October, M-Sa
✾ Garden: June, September, M-Sa

John Scheepers, Inc.
23 Tulip Drive
Bantam, CT 06750
Jan Ohms, Pres.
(860) 567-0838
Fax: (860) 567-5323

Bulbs
Issues catalog offering spring and summer-blooming **bulbs**, many illustrated in color, all well described: daffodils, tulips, crocus, species narcissus, alliums, and other spring bulbs, amaryllis and hybrid lilies. Now same ownership as Van Engelen, but sells in smaller quantities. (1910)
📖 Catalog: Free, R&W, CC, SS:9-12, $25m

S. Scherer & Sons
104 Waterside Road
Northport, NY 11768
Robert W. Scherer
(516) 261-7432
Fax: (516) 261-9325
Web: www.netstuff.com/scherer

Plants ℘ Supplies
Offers everything necessary for a garden pool or pond: **water lilies** and other **aquatic plants**, fiberglass pools, pool liners, fountain heads, pumps and low-voltage garden lights. Everything briefly but well described. (1907)
📖 Catalog: $1, R&W, CC, SS:4-9, $5m, cn/bn
✪ Nursery: All year, daily
✾ Garden: April-September, daily

Schipper & Co.
P.O. Box 7584
Greenwich, CT 06836-7584
Timothy P. Schipper
(888) 847-8637
Fax: (203) 862-8909
E-mail: schipper@colorblends.com
Web: www.colorblends.com

Bulbs
Offers a nice selection of spring flowering bulbs, but specializes in "Color-blends," **bulbs** chosen to complement each other when planted in groups. The pictures look quite smashing, so it works! No schipping to AK, HI. (1947)
📖 Catalog: $1, R&W, CC, SS: 9-12, $30m

Schmid Nursery & Garden
847 Westwood Boulevard
Jackson, MI 49203
Tom Schmid
(517) 787-5275

Plants
Herbaceous **peonies, daylilies, hostas** and some **ornamental grasses** are offered, including new hosta introductions. Very brief descriptions.
📖 Catalog: $3($5 OV), OV, CC, $30m
✪ Nursery: May-October, Sa-Su, by appointment only
✾ Garden: May-June, by appointment only

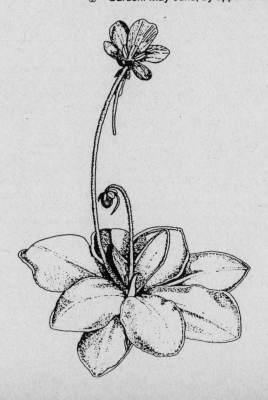

© California Carnivores
Artist: Judith Finn

Schreiner's Gardens
3625 Quinaby Road N.E.
Salem, OR 97303-9720
Schreiner Family
(503) 393-3232, (800) 525-2367
Fax: (503) 393-5590
Web: www.oregonlink.com/~salem/scva/iris

Plants
Color catalog describes tall bearded **iris**, "lilliputs" and intermediates, many their own introductions, and offers a number of collections; a very large selection. All plants very well described, with cultural advice. Can't ship to FL or HI. (1925)
📖 Catalog: $5($15 OV), R&W, CAN/OV, CC, SS:7-9, $15m
❀ Garden: Late May, daily

F. W. Schumacher Co., Inc.
36 Spring Hill Road
Sandwich, MA 02563-1023
Donald H. Allen
(508) 888-0659
Fax: (508) 833-0322

Seeds ᔓ Books
A very broad selection of seeds of **trees, shrubs, conifers, rhododendrons** and **azaleas** listed by botanical and common name, and with geographical source where important. Offers species maples, birches, dogwoods, cotoneasters, crabapples, hollies, species roses, viburnums and much more; they will also buy seed of rare plants. Some books on propagation, too. (1926)
📖 Catalog: Free, R&W, CAN/OV, bn

Scottsdale Fishponds
2617 N. 71st Place
Scottsdale, AZ 85257
Scott A. Butler
(602) 946-8025
Fax: (602) 675-9775

Plants ᔓ Supplies
Offers a good selection of **water lilies, lotus, and aquatic and bog plants** each well described. They also sell pond liners and fertilizers. (1986)
📖 Catalog: $3d, R&W, SS:3-10, $20m, cn/bn
✪ Nursery: March-November, Tu-Su, by appointment only
❀ Garden: April-August, by appointment only

Sea-Tac Dahlia Gardens
20020 Des Moines Memorial Drive
Seattle, WA 98198
Louis & Patti Eckhoff

Plants
Collectors' list of **dahlias**, with information given in a compact table; a good selection, especially for cut flowers. Louis's a dahlia hybridizer, his hybrids begin with `Sea' -- as in `Sea-Miss' -- a real winner. (1978)
📖 Catalog: Long SASE, SS:2-4, OV, $10m
✪ Nursery: March-October, daily, call ahead
❀ Garden: August-October, daily, call ahead

R. Seawright Daylilies & Hostas
P.O. Box 733
201 Bedford Road
Carlisle, MA 01741-0733
Robert D. Seawright
(508) 369-2172
Fax: (508) 369-2172
E-mail: seawrightr@aol.com
Web: members.aol.com/Seawrightr/home.html

Plants
A collectors' list of **daylilies** -- both diploids and tetraploids -- a wide selection; each very well described, with good general cultural advice. Also offers about 200 varieties of **hostas**.
📖 Catalog: $2d($3 OV), R&W, CAN/OV, CC, SS:5-9, $35m
✪ Nursery: May-August, daily
❀ Garden: June-July daily

Seca Scape of Utah
P.O. Box 2981
Salt Lake City, UT 84110
Dale Rose
(801) 461-9021

Plants
Specialize in trees and shrubs which thrive with little water and under extremes of climate: **native plants of the Rocky Mountains, Great Basin and Australia**: including conifers, eucalyptus and oaks; plants are well described.
📖 Catalog: Long SASE w/2 FCS, R&W, SS:3-5,9-11, $15m, cn/bn
✪ Nursery: By appointment only

The Seed Guild
The Coach House, Kersewell
Carnwath, Lanark, Scotland ML11 8LF
Duncan McDougall
44 (0) 1555 841-450
Fax: 44 (0) 1555 842-480
E-mail: seeds@btinternet.com
Web: www.gardenweb.com/seedgd

Seeds
Mr. McDougall has had a wonderful idea: he takes surplus seed from botanic gardens all over the world and makes it available to gardeners. His catalog is a densely printed list by botanical name of **trees, shrubs, perennials** (called "herbs") **alpines and bulbous plants.** Get out your reference books. There's a one-time fee of $10 to join, and annual fees at various rates, depending on how much seed you want, and if you want to pick a specific genus. (1996)
📖 Catalog: $3(3 IRC), R&W, OV, bn

Seedhunt
P.O. Box 96
200 Casserly Road (Watsonville)
Freedom, CA 95019-0096
Ginny Hunt
E-mail: seedhunt@aol.com

Seeds
I have to admit to special interest: Ginny's helped me to revise Gardening by Mail three times. She is a very knowledgeable plantsperson, and offers seeds of unusual **annual and perennial flowers**, particularly for Mediterranean climates and dry gardens. All are well described. (1995)
- Catalog: $1($2 OV), CAN/OV, bn
- Nursery: All year, by appointment only
- Garden: By appointment only

Seeds Blum
HC 33, Box 2057
Boise, ID 83706
Jan Blum & Karla Prabucki
(800) 742-1423
Fax: (208) 338-5658
E-mail: 103374.167@compuserve.com
Web: www.seedsblum.com

Seeds Books
Pronounced "Seeds Bloom" -- their catalog is informative, fun and helpful. They offer a number of **heirloom and open-pollinated vegetables**, as well as **annuals and perennials**. Included are sunchokes, herbs, potatoes, garlic, many grains, along with some unusual vegetables. They also sell books -- "fireside friends." (1982)
- Catalog: $3, CAN/OV, CC, cn/bn

Seeds of Change
P.O. Box 15700
Santa Fe, NM 87506-5700
Dave Smith, Mgr.
(888) 762-7333
Fax: (505) 438-7052
Web: www.seedsofchange.com

Seeds Books Supplies
Seeds of Change has merged with Peace Seeds, and offers a huge selection of **organically grown and open-pollinated vegetable** seed, including heirloom and Native American varieties. Over 500 varieties, including grains, herbs and garden flowers. All varieties are very well described for flavor, with growing suggestions. Also offer supplies and books. (1989)
- Catalog: Free, R&W, CAN/OV, CC, cn/bn

Seeds of Distinction
P.O. Box 86, Station A
Toronto (Etob), ON, Canada M9C 4V2
Raymond Sawdy
(416) 255-3060
Fax: (888) 327-9193
E-mail: sod@interlog.com
Web: www.interlog.com/~sod/

Seeds
They call them "rare originals," and there are many uncommon **annual and perennial garden flowers** listed here. Included are species lathyrus, many kinds of meconopsis, hollyhocks, primulas and much more. Plants are well described.
- Catalog: $3d, US, CC, $20m, bn/cn

Seeds Trust

See High Altitude Gardens.

Seeds West Garden Seeds
317 14th Street N.W.
Albuquerque, NM 87104
Leslie Campbell & Ronald Jacob
(505) 843-9713

Seeds
Specializes in **heirloom, hybrid and rare vegetable** varieties for difficult Western growing conditions: drought and poor soils. Some are native crops in the Southwest, such as blue and black corns. All varieties are well described, with growing suggestions. Also offers some flower seed. (1988)
- Catalog: $2, CAN/OV, CC

Seeds-by-Size
45 Crouchfield, Boxmoor
Hemel Hempstead, Herts., England HP1 1PA
John Robert Size
44 (0) 1442 251-458
Web: www.seeds-by-size.com.uk

Seeds
OK -- get out your strongest glasses and a glass of something relaxing! This list takes a lot of attention: it's a collection of mostly un-numbered sheets listing seeds of **garden flowers, vegetables and herbs** in tiny print, with only variety name and height indicated for flowers. However, there's lots here of interest to repay your frustration. Email address is <john-robert-size@seeds-by-size.prestel.co.uk>. (1979)
- Catalog: $2(USBills) or 3 IRC, R&W, OV, bn/cn

Select Plus International Nursery
1510 Pine
Mascouche, PQ, Canada J7L 2M4
Frank Moro
(514) 477-3797
Fax: (514) 477-3797
E-mail: lilacs@axess.com

Plants
Offers a very good selection of **lilacs**, including some species lilacs, and a number of varieties which bloom well in warmer winter areas. They also list a huge selection of varieties from which propagation can be done to order. Plants are well described, all are grown on their own roots. They carry a few old garden and shrub **roses** as well. (1991)
📖 Catalog: $2d($2 OV), R&W, US/OV, SS:4-5,9-11, $5m, bn
☉ Nursery: April-October, F-Su, by appointment only
❀ Garden: April-June, by appointment only

Select Seeds -- Antique Flowers
180 Stickney Hill Road
Union, CT 06076-4617
Marilyn Barlow
(860) 684-9310
Fax: (860) 684-9224
E-mail: select@neca.com
Web: trine.com/GardenNet/SelectSeeds/

Plants ∞ Seeds ∞ Books ∞ Supplies
This seed business grew out of an old garden restoration project; they specialize in **old-fashioned and heirloom perennials** found in cottage and period gardens, chosen for fragrance and flower cutting. Plants are well described. Also offers books on traditional flower gardening, and old-fashioned cedar garden markers. No plants to CA, OR, WA or Canada. (1987)
📖 Catalog: $1($3 OV), R&W, CAN/OV, CC, SS:4-5, cn/bn

Seneca Hill Perennials
3712 Co. Route 57
Oswego, NY 13126
Ellen Hornig
(315) 342-5915
E-mail: hornig@oswego.edu

Plants
Offering a nice selection of **perennials**, and some **flowering shrubs and trees**. Choices are limited, but there are some hard-to-find plants offered, including davidia, **arisaemas**, lysichitons and gentians. Brief descriptions.
📖 Catalog: $1, SS:4-5,8-10, bn/cn
☉ Nursery: May-August, call ahead
❀ Garden: May-August, call ahead

Sequoia Nursery -- Moore Miniature Roses
2519 E. Noble Avenue
Visalia, CA 93292
Ralph S. Moore
(209) 732-0309
Fax: (209) 732-0192

Plants
Specializes in the hybrids of Ralph Moore, a **miniature rose** pioneer who has patented over 150 cultivars. Color catalog introduces new varieties once a year and offers popular varieties for sale, including an increasing number of old garden roses and some new non-mini Moore hybrids. (1937)
📖 Catalog: Free, R&W, CC
☉ Nursery: All year, daily
❀ Garden: April-May, September-October, daily

Sevald Nursery
4937 3rd Avenue South
Minneapolis, MN 55409
Alvin & Judith Sevald
(218) 822-3279

Plants
Offers herbaceous **peonies** in a color catalog; they grow around 400 cultivars and list about 40 each year. Send your "wish list" to find out if they have varieties you're looking for. Phone early in the morning or in the evening. (1986)
📖 Catalog: $1d, R&W, CAN/OV, SS:9-10

Seymour's Selected Seeds
P.O. Box 1346
Sussex, VA 23884-0346
Shumway's
(803) 663-3084
Fax: (888) 739-6687

Seeds
Color catalog illustrates a broad variety of **annuals** and **perennials**, and some **hybrid vegetables**. Included are fancy forms of petunias, California poppies, hollyhocks and much more. Good descriptions.
📖 Catalog: Free, CAN, CC

Shady Oaks Nursery
112 10th Avenue S.E.
Waseca, MN 56093-3122
Gordon & Clayton Oslund
(507) 835-5033, (800) 504-8006
Fax: (507) 835-8772
E-mail: shadyoaks@shadyoaks.com
Web: www.shadyoaks.com

Plants ∞ Books
This nursery specializes in **plants which grow well in shade** and offers a good selection of perennials, ferns, wildflowers, ground covers, and hostas; each plant well described. Also offers several books on shade gardening and woodland plants. (1979)
📖 Catalog: Free, R&W, CC, SS:4-10, bn/cn
☉ Nursery: May-September, M-Sa
❀ Garden: May-September, M-Sa

Shanti Bithi Nursery
3047 High Ridge Road
Stamford, CT 06903
Jerome & Carole Rocherolle
(203) 329-0768
Fax: (203) 329-8872
E-mail: shanti@webcom.com
Web: www.webcom.com/shanti

Plants ∞ Books ∞ Supplies ∞ Tools
Importers of finished **bonsai**, some quite mature; and **starter plants for bonsai**; various plants are shown in color photos. Also sell bonsai tools, pots, supplies, books and stone lanterns, and hold bi-weekly workshop classes in the spring and fall. (1970)
- Catalog: $2, CC, $25m, bn
- Nursery: All year, M-Sa
- Garden: April, November, M-Sa

Sheffield's Seed Co., Inc.
273 Auburn Road (Route 34)
Locke, NY 13092
Richard Sheffield
(315) 497-1058
Fax: (315) 497-1059
E-mail: seed@sheffields.com
Web: www.sheffields.com

Seeds ∞ Books
Seed company specializing in seeds of woody plants: **conifers, ornamental trees and shrubs, and species roses**, over 1,000 species altogether, including some **perennials and herbs**. Plants are listed only by botanical name, with no descriptions. Minimum seed order is 2 grams per species, with a $2 handling charge per order. Also sells some books on seed propagation. (1978)
- Catalog: Free, R&W, CAN/OV, CC, bn

Shein's Cactus
3360 Drew Street
Marina, CA 93933
Rubin & Anne Shein
(408) 384-7765

Plants
A collectors' list of **cactus and succulents** by botanical name; no descriptions, but a large selection of rare and unusual plants. Offered are copiapoa, coryphanthas, echinocereus, lobivia, gymnocalycium, parodia, rebutia, sulcorebutia, weingartia, haworthias and many mammillarias; all plants seed-grown or nursery-propagated. (1977)
- Catalog: $1d, SS:3-10, $20m, bn
- Nursery: All year, M-F, by appointment only
- Garden: April-June, by appointment only

Shepard Iris Garden
3342 W. Orangewood Avenue
Phoenix, AZ 85051-1231
Don & Bobbie Shepard
(602) 841-1231
Fax: (602) 841-1231

Plants
A collectors' list offers a nice selection of tall bearded, arilbred, Louisiana, and spuria **iris**; each plant briefly described with useful cultural notes. Will ship to New Zealand. (1969)
- Catalog: $1, CAN, CC, SS:7-10
- Nursery: April; call ahead
- Garden: April, open daily

Shepherd Hill Farm
200 Peekskill Hollow Road
Putnam Valley, NY 10579-3217
Gerald Bleyer
(914) 528-5917
Fax: (914) 528-8343
E-mail: bleyer@ix.netcom.com

Plants
Gerry Bleyer fell in love with rhododendrons in our very own Golden Gate Park, so he's got to be a nice guy! He offers a good selection of cold hardy **rhododendrons and azaleas** for the East and Midwest, and some **dwarf conifers and Japanese maples**. No shipping to AZ, CA, OR or WA. (1985)
- Catalog: $2d, SS:3-6,9-11
- Nursery: All year, call ahead
- Garden: May, call ahead

Shepherd's Garden Seeds
30 Irene Street
Torrington, CT 06790
Eliot Wadsworth II
(860) 496-9624, 482-3638
Fax: (860) 482-0532
E-mail: garden@shepherdseeds.com
Web: www.shepherdseeds.com

Plants ∞ Seeds ∞ Books ∞ Supplies
European **vegetables, salad and herb varieties** for the cooking gardener and collections of herbs for various cuisines: Italian, French, Oriental and Mexican. Each vegetable is lovingly described, with cultural information and recipes. Also sells annual, everlasting and edible flowers, growing supplies and "fresh from the garden cookbooks." No shipping to AK or HI. (1983)
- Catalog: Free, R&W, CAN, CC, cn/bn

Sherry's Perennials
P.O. Box 39
R.R. 1 (Blenheim)
Cedar Springs, ON, Canada N0P 1E0
Sherry Godfrey
(519) 676-4541
Fax: (519) 676-7412

Plants
Offers a good selection of hardy **perennials and herbs**, with good plant descriptions and cultural information, and suggestions for plant combinations. Only ships within Canada. (1986)
- Catalog: $4d, CC, SS:4-6,9, $15m, bn/cn
- Nursery: April-October, W-M, call ahead
- Garden: April-October, W-M, call ahead

Sherwood's Greenhouses
P.O. Box 6
Sibley, LA 71073
J.S. Akin
(318) 377-3653

Plants
Small nursery sells a selection of **unusual fruits**: mayhaws (hawthorne), jujubes, pawpaw, keriberry, citrange and other citrus, and goumi. Among the more common fruits are hardy kiwis, figs, and blackberries; also some ornamental **flowering shrubs**. All plants very briefly described on one page. No shipping to AK or HI.
- 📖 Catalog: Long SASE, SS:12-2
- ○ Nursery: All year, M-Sa, call ahead
- ✽ Garden: Spring, M-Sa

John Shipton (Bulbs)
y Felin, Henllan Amgoed
Whitland, Dyfed, Wales SA34 0SL
John Shipton
44 (0) 1994 240-125
Fax: 44 (0) 1994 240-125
E-mail: bluebell@connect-wales.co.uk

Bulbs
"Native **bulbs** of the British Isles," and bulbs that will naturalize in similar climates: John Shipton does not collect his bulbs from the wild, but offers a nice selection, along with perennials that can be shipped as dormant rootstock. All plants well described.
- 📖 Catalog: 1 IRC, OV, SS:8-10, cn/bn
- ○ Nursery: All year, by appointment only

Shooting Star Nursery
444 Bates Road
Frankfort, KY 40601-9446
Sherri & Marc Evans
(502) 223-1679

Plants ∾ Seeds
Specializes in "nursery grown plants native to regions east of the Rocky Mountains, including **forest, prairie and wetland plants** and seeds." Each plant and its habitat are well described; they also offer a number of wildflower seed mixes, and do consulting on habitat restoration. No shipping to CA, OR or WA. (1989)
- 📖 Catalog: $2d, CC, SS:4-11, $10m, cn/bn
- ○ Nursery: By appointment only

Shoulder to Shoulder Farm

See Wild Garden Seed.

R. H. Shumway Seedsman
P.O. Box 1
Graniteville, SC 29829
J. Wayne Hilton
(803) 663-9771
Fax: (803) 663-9772

Seeds ∾ Supplies
Catalog offers a good selection of open-pollinated **vegetables, annual** and **perennial** flowers, green manure crops, and **berries**, illustrated with old-style line art. Also offers growing supplies. (1870)
- 📖 Catalog: Free, R&W, CAN, CC, SS:4-6, cn
- ○ Nursery: Spring, M-F, call ahead

Siegers Seed Co.
8265 Felch Street
Zeeland, MI 49464-9503
Richard L. Siegers
(616) 772-4999
Fax: (616) 772-0333

Seeds ∾ Supplies
Offers a wide selection of **vegetable** seed, both hybrid and open-pollinated, and herbs as well. All seeds sold in bulk; minimum seems to be based on size of seed. Also offers some growing supplies and seeders. (1957)
- 📖 Catalog: Free, R&W, CAN, CC
- ○ Nursery: All year, M-F, call ahead

Sierra Seed Supply
P.O. Box 42
Greenville, CA 95947
Greg Greger
(916) 284-7926
Fax: (916) 284-7926

Seeds
Offering wild-collected seed of **California native trees and shrubs**, as well as some **native bulbs and perennials**; seed must be pre-ordered, and will be sent while fresh.
- 📖 Catalog: Free, R&W, CAN/OV, SS:8-11, $10m, bn/cn

Silverhill Seeds
P.O. Box 53108
Kenilworth, Cape Town, South Africa 7745
Rachel & Rod Saunders
27 (21) 762-4245
Fax: 27 (21) 797-6609
E-mail: silseeds@iafrica.com

Seeds
Formerly Parsley's Cape Seeds, Silverhill specializes in seeds of **South African plants**: geraniaceae, ericaceae, proteaceae, carnivorous plants, succulents, bulbous plants, as well as annuals, perennials and ornamental shrubs and trees. Very large selection, brief plant descriptions. (1953)
- 📖 Catalog: $2(US Bills), R&W, OV, bn

Siskiyou Rare Plant Nursery
2825 Cummings Road
Medford, OR 97501
Baldassare Mineo
Fax: (541) 772-4917
Web: www.wavenet/upg/srpn

Plants ∽ **Books**
A collectors' catalog of **alpine and rock garden plants** offers about 1,500 plants, with rarer items available in small quantities; all very well described with cultural information. Fall supplement with plants for fall planting. Also sells books on alpine and rock garden plants. (1964)
- Catalog: $3($5 OV), CAN/OV, CC, SS:W, bn
- Nursery: March-November, by appointment only
- Garden: By appointment only

Sleepy Hollow Herb Farm
568 Jack Black Road
Lancaster, KY 40444-9306
Steve & Julie Marks
(606) 792-6183, (800) 726-1215

Plants
Offers a wide selection of organically grown **herb plants** and perennials, each briefly described; good choices of lavenders, scented geraniums, mints, rosemarys, salvias and thymes, among others. No shipping to HI. (1984)
- Catalog: $1, SS:3-10, $10m, cn/bn
- Nursery: March-October, by appointment only
- Garden: March-October, by appointment only

Slocum Water Gardens
1101 Cypress Gardens Boulevard
Winter Haven, FL 33884-1932
Peter D. Slocum
(941) 293-7151
Fax: (800) 322-1896

Plants ∽ **Books** ∽ **Supplies**
Color catalog offers a wide selection of **water lilies and lotus**, aquatic and bog plants and aquarium plants, all well described. Also offers growing supplies and books for water gardening. (1938)
- Catalog: $3d, R&W, CAN/OV, CC, $25m
- Nursery: All year, M-Sa
- Garden: April-November, M-Sa

Smith Nursery Co.
P.O. Box 515
203 9th Street
Charles City, IA 50616
Bill Smith
(515) 228-3239

Plants ∽ **Seeds**
A good selection of **ornamental shrubs and trees** in small sizes. The list I received had a jumble of common and botanical names -- dogwoods, linden, elderberries, lilacs, euonymus, sumacs, birch, locust, species maples, viburnums, poplars and willows, among others; no plant descriptions. Seed, too.
- Catalog: Free, R&W, CAN/OV, SS:1-6,9-12, cn
- Nursery: All year, M-Sa, call ahead

Snow Creek Daylily Gardens

See B & D Lilies.

Winn Soldani's Fancy Hibiscus(R)
1142 S.W. 1st Avenue
Pompano Beach, FL 33060-8706
Winn Soldani
(954) 782-0741, (800) 432-8332
Fax: (954) 782-7639
E-mail: winn@fancyhibiscus.com
Web: www.fancyhibiscus.com

Plants
Offers a good selection of **hibiscus**, the tropical kind, all grafted and some shown in a color brochure; all briefly described. Winn encourages you to send your "wish list," he grows more than he lists, and knows many other sources. No shipping to CA. (1986)
- Catalog: $2d($3.50 OV), CAN/OV, CC, $25m
- Nursery: All year, call ahead
- Garden: All year, call ahead

Sonoma Antique Apple Nursery
4395 Westside Road
Healdsburg, CA 95448
Carolyn & Terry Harrison
(707) 433-6420
Fax: (707) 433-6479
E-mail: tuyt20b@prodigy.com

Plants
Offer old English and American cider **apples**, and other varieties for cooking or eating, a good selection. Will select trees suitable for espalier. They have added more fruits: antique and Asian pears, figs, peaches and plums. In winter, they sell bare root trees at Vintage Gardens in Sebastopol.
- Catalog: $1, R&W, CAN, CC, SS:1-4, $14m

Sonoma Grapevines
1919 Dennis Lane
Santa Rosa, CA 95403
Rich Kunde
(707) 542-5510
Fax: (707) 542-4801
E-mail: sgi@sonomagrape.com
Web: www.sonomagrape.com

Plants
A source of **varietal wine, raisin and table grafted grapevines**, grafting scions and rootstocks; you have to start your vineyard on a scale of at least 25 plants of a variety or have like-minded neighbors. Chardonnay, semillon, cabernet sauvignon, merlot, pinot noir and chenin blanc from excellent sources. (1972)
- Catalog: Free, R&W, CAN/OV, SS:2-6, $25m
- Nursery: All year, M-Sa

Soules Garden
5809 Rahke Road
Indianapolis, IN 46217-3677
Clarence E. Soules
(317) 786-7839

Plants
Offers a good selection of new and recently introduced **daylilies**, including a nice listing of miniature and small flowered cultivars. They also have a good selection of **hostas**. All plants well to briefly described.
📖 Catalog: $1d, SS:4-10, $10m
○ Nursery: April-October, W-Sa, call ahead
❀ Garden: April-October, W-Sa, call ahead

Sourdough Iris Gardens
109 Sourdough Ridge Road
Bozeman, MT 59715-9264
Maurine K. Blackwell

Plants
Offers hardy older, often hard-to-find, varieties of tall bearded, intermediate and dwarf **iris**; plants briefly described, prices very reasonable.
📖 Catalog: Long SASE, SS:7-8, $6m
○ Nursery: July-August, M-F, call ahead
❀ Garden: June, by appointment only

South Bay Growers
12811 Highway 674
Lithia, FL 33547-1452
Eugene Coats
(813) 634-4727
E-mail: sobaygro@aol.com

Plants
Offering a nice selection of **succulents**, with many aloes, euphorbias and haworthias. Also some **cactus**. Collectors are urged to send their "wish list," as they grow many more plants than they list. Descriptions are very brief.
📖 Catalog: $1d, R&W, $20m, bn

South Cove Nursery
P.O. Box 615
Yarmouth, NS, Canada B5A 4B6
David & Carla Allen
(902) 742-3406
Fax: (902) 742-8260
E-mail: scove@klis.com
Web: www.at-data.ns.ca/GrassRoutes/scove

Plants
Offers a good selection of **herbs and perennials**; the owner is a garden columnist, so the plant descriptions are very informative. They'll ship all over Canada except to the Yukon and Northwest Territories. (1985)
📖 Catalog: $2, CC, SS:5-7, $12m, bn/cn
○ Nursery: April-October, daily, by appointment only
❀ Garden: April-October, daily, call ahead

Southern Exposure
35 Minor Street (at Rusk)
Beaumont, TX 77702-2414
Bob Whitman
(409) 835-0644
Fax: (409) 835-0644

Plants ❧ Supplies
Offers a huge selection of **cryptanthus**: 300 hybrids from Europe, Australia, the Orient and the US, as well as Brazilian species. Also sells aroids, bromeliads, platyceriums, rhipsalis, epiphyllums and philodendrons, and many variegated plants. Very brief plant descriptions. (1981)
📖 Catalog: $5($7 OV), CAN/OV, CC, SS:W, $15m, bn
○ Nursery: March-September, daily, by appointment only
❀ Garden: April-June, daily, by appointment only

Southern Exposure Seed Exchange(R)
P.O. Box 170
Earlysville, VA 22936
Jeff McCormack
(804) 973-4703
Fax: (804) 973-8717
Web: www.southernexposure.com

Seeds ❧ Books ❧ Supplies
Not a seed exchange in the swapping sense, this is a seed company offering many **heirloom and open-pollinated vegetables**, a broad selection in a very informative catalog, with good variety descriptions and cultural information. Also offered are herbs, grains, gourds, annual flowers and sunflowers, and books, growing and seed saving supplies. They have a new list, "Garden Medicinals" available on their website. (1982)
📖 Catalog: $2, R&W, CAN, CC, SS:9-10, cn/bn

Southern Perennials & Herbs
98 Bridges Road
Tylertown, MS 39667
Mike & Barbara Bridges
(601) 684-1769, (800) 774-0079
Fax: (601) 684-3729
E-mail: sph@neosoft.com
Web: www.s-p-h.com

Plants
Offers a very wide selection of **perennials, herbs, gingers, vines, grasses and flowering shrubs.** Each plant is concisely described with symbols for uses and planting locations; their plants are particularly suited for the deep South. No shipping to CA. (1987)
📖 Catalog: Free, R&W, CC, $25m, bn/cn
❀ Garden: Certain weekends in summer, call ahead

Southern Seeds
The Vicarage, Sheffield
Canterbury, New Zealand 8173
Malvern Anglican Parish
64 (0) 3318-3814
Fax: 64 (0) 3318-3814

Seeds
Specializes in **alpine and rock garden plants of New Zealand**, collected from the scree and tussock-grassland of the Waimakariri Catchment. Plants listed by botanical name only; list of reference books on New Zealand plants is included. Hebes, celmisias, coprosmas, fuchsias, brachyglottis, and more. Proceeds benefit the Malvern Anglican Parish. (1982)
- Catalog: $5(US Bills), OV, $25m, bn
- Nursery: By appointment only
- Garden: September-April, by appointment only

Southern Shade
2263 W. New Haven Avenue, #310
Melbourne, FL 32904-3805
Jerry R. Hooper
(407) 676-3458
Fax: (407) 676-3458

Plants
Offers **palms, cycads, aroids, gingers** and more on a list with brief to no plant descriptions, but to the aficionado of unusual plants, there might be much of interest. No shipping to AZ, TX or CA.
- Catalog: Long SASE, $25m, bn
- Garden: By appointment only

Southmeadow Fruit Gardens
P.O. Box 211
10603 Cleveland Avenue
Baroda, MI 49101
Peter T. Grootendorst, Mgr.
(616) 422-2411
Fax: (616) 422-1464
E-mail: smfruit@aol.com

Plants ☙ Books
Offers a huge selection of **fruit trees**, many of them antique varieties -- apples, pears, peaches, plums, cherries, grapes, gooseberries, even medlars; no descriptions. Sells a detailed reference guide to antique fruit varieties for $9 (the price list is free); offers "conservation fruits" for wildlife, and under the name Grootendorst Nurseries sells a wide variety of rootstocks for fruit trees. No shipping to HI.
- Catalog: See notes, OV, SS:10-5, $14m
- Nursery: All year, M-F, call ahead

Southwestern Exposure
10310 East Fennimore
Apache Junction, AZ 85220
Leonard & Bernice Bruens

Plants ☙ Seeds ☙ Supplies
Specialize in larger-sized arid land plants, and seeds of **Southwestern native plants**; they also offer special soil mixes for cactus, and will search among other Arizona nurseries for plants on your "wish list." A nice selection, all plants well described; some may be habitat collected. (1990)
- Catalog: Long SASE w/2 FCS, R&W, cn/bn

Southwestern Native Seeds
P.O. Box 50503
Tucson, AZ 85703
Sally & Tim Walker

Seeds
Collectors' list of about 385 species of **Western, Southwestern and Mexican natives** "for gardens, nurseries, rock gardens, landscaping, botanical gardens and for many other uses." Information on type, outstanding qualities, size, hardiness and rarity are given in concise tables; seeds are habitat-collected, listed by state of origin. (1975)
- Catalog: $2, CAN/OV, SS:11-2, $13m, bn

Spangle Creek Labs
W. 2802 Depot Springs Road
Spangle, WA 99031-9526
William & Carol Steele
(509) 245-3253
Web: www.ior.com/scl/

Plants
Talk about specialization: Spangle Creek Labs sells only laboratory grown seedlings of **cypripediums** -- eight species, each very well described and with detailed growing instructions. These are best for experienced wildflower growers and rock gardeners. (1990)
- Catalog: $2, R&W, CAN/OV, SS:4-5,10-11, $15m, bn

Spring Hill Nurseries Co.
6523 North Galena Road
Peoria, IL 61632
Foster & Gallagher, Inc.
(309) 689-3849, (800) 582-8527
Fax: (800) 991-2852
Web: www.springhillnursery.com

Plants ☙ Bulbs
Several catalogs a year: offers a broad selection of **perennials, flowering shrubs, ground covers and some roses**, summer-blooming bulbs and houseplants, all glowingly described. In 1997 they added a "Select Gardens" catalog offering some newer plant introductions. No shipping to AK or HI. (1849)
- Catalog: Free, SS:2-5,9-11, cn/bn

Spring Valley Roses
P.O. Box 7
N7637 330th Street
Spring Valley, WI 54767
Andrea & Mike Wieland
(715) 778-4481
Fax: (715) 778-4481
E-mail: svroses@win.bright.net
Web: www.springvalleyroses.com

Plants ഔ **Books** ഔ **Supplies**
The Wielands are selecting and propagating **very hardy roses** for the upper Midwest (down to zone 4), chosen for disease resistance and grown on their own roots. Offer many of the Canadian Explorer series, and also a good selection of rugosas, as well as rose books, rose arches, and plaques. (1992)
📖 Catalog: $1($3 OV), R&W, CAN/OV, CC, SS:4-5
✪ Nursery: May-August, Sa
✿ Garden: June-July, Sa

Springwood Pleiones
35, Heathfield
Leeds, West Yorkshire, England LS16 7AB
Ken Redshaw
44 (0) 1132 611-781

Bulbs
Small family business specializing in **pleione species and cultivars**; offers about thirty-eight species and varieties, each briefly described by color and growth habit. (1986)
📖 Catalog: $1 or 2 IRC, OV, SS:1, $100m, bn
✪ Nursery: January-May, by appointment only
✿ Garden: April, by appointment only

Spruce Gardens
2317 3rd Road
Wisner, NE 68791-3536
Calvin Reuter
(402) 529-6860

Plants
Offers a broad selection of **tall bearded iris**, about 1,200 cultivars, with about 300 median bearded iris as well, and some standard dwarf and miniature dwarf varieties, all very briefly described. (1987)
📖 Catalog: $1d, CAN/OV, CC, SS:7-8, $10m
✪ Nursery: May-June, daily
✿ Garden: May-June, daily

Squaw Mountain Gardens
P.O. Box 946
Estacada, OR 97023
Joyce Hoekstra, Janis & Arthur Noyes
(503) 630-5458
Fax: (503) 630-5849
E-mail: hennchicks@aol.com

Plants ഔ **Books**
A broad selection of **sedums, sempervivums** and some **arachnoideums, calcareums, ciliosums, jovibarbas, mamoreums and tectorums**; all briefly described with general cultural instructions. They have added some small perennials, ground covers, hardy ferns, dwarf evergreens and hardy ivy. Also sell books, ready-to-plant wreaths, and feather rock planters. (1983)
📖 Catalog: $3d, R&W, CAN/OV, SS:3-10, $15m, bn
✪ Nursery: March-October, by appointment only
✿ Garden: April-August, by appointment only

© Colvos Creek Nursery
Artist: Michael C. Lee

Starhill Forest Arboretum
Route 1, Box 272
Petersburg, IL 62675
Guy & Edie Sternberg

Seeds
Guy & Edie Sternberg are private collectors of **oaks** who offer seed acorns of species and hybrid oaks in their collection, as well as mixed packets of acorns from the oaks around Lincoln's tomb, a surprise packet and a sampler of oaks for your area. They also offer seed of some companion trees and shrubs, all of them interesting. No plant descriptions. (1976)
📖 Catalog: $1 or Long SASE, CAN/OV, SS:11, bn
❀ Garden: By appointment only

Stark Bro's Nurseries & Orchards Co.
P.O. Box 10
Louisiana, MO 63353-0010
Foster & Gallagher, Inc.
(573) 754-5511, (800) 325-4180
Fax: (573) 754-5290
E-mail: starkmo@louisiana.mo.us

Plants ℘ Supplies
This firm -- made famous by the `Delicious' apples they developed many years ago -- offers **fruit trees, grapes, ornamental trees and shrubs** in a color catalog, including good plant descriptions and some cultural hints. Lots of mouth-watering pictures of pies! No shipping to AK or HI. (1816)
📖 Catalog: Free, R&W, CC, SS:2-5,10-12, cn
✪ Nursery: February-December, M-Sa

Stark Gardens
631 G24 Highway
Norwalk, IA 50211-9431
Gunther Stark
(515) 981-4780

Plants
A small nursery offering a good selection of **hosta**, each plant well but briefly described. Also offer a few daylilies, some of which seem quite choice. (1960)
📖 Catalog: 2 FCS, R&W, SS:5-9, $10m
✪ Nursery: May-September, call ahead
❀ Garden: May-September, call ahead

Steele Plant Company
P.O. Box 191
212 Collins Street
Gleason, TN 38229
Ken Sanders
(901) 648-5476

Plants
They offer ten varieties of **sweet potato** plants, yam plants and other **vegetable plants** such as onions, cabbage, brussels sprouts, broccoli and cauliflower. Plants are available in quantities from a dozen to hundreds. Can't ship to CA. (1952)
📖 Catalog: 2 FCS, R&W, SS:4-6

Stigall Water Gardens
7306 Main Street
Kansas City, MO 64114-1410
Trent Stigall
(816) 822-1256
Fax: (816) 822-7226

Plants ℘ Supplies
Early in this century the Missouri Botanic Garden was the world center of water lily culture and hybridization, so it feels good to list an aquatic nursery in Missouri. Stigall Water Gardens offers a good selection of **water lilies** and other **aquatic plants** and all the supplies you'll need. (1990)
📖 Catalog: Free, R&W, CC, SS:4-9, cn/bn

Stock Seed Farms, Inc.
28008 Mill Road
Murdock, NE 68407-2350
Lyle & David Stock Family
(402) 867-3771
Fax: (402) 867-2442
E-mail: stockseed@navix.net
Web: www.stockseed.com

Seeds
Offers seed of **prairie wildflowers and grasses native to the Midwest**; all plants are well described in a pamphlet which contains good information on how to get started. They also sell wildflower mixes. (1958)
📖 Catalog: Free, R&W, CAN, $10m, cn/bn
✪ Nursery: All year, M-F

Stockton Iris Gardens
P.O. Box 55195
451 N. Lillian Avenue
Stockton, CA 95205
Abe Feuerstein
(209) 462-8106

Plants
A small nursery caters to the "iris crowd" with a broad selection of recent and new **tall bearded and median iris**. Quite a few are their own introductions, all are well described, many illustrated in color photos. Have added a few **Pacific Coast natives**. (1974)
📖 Catalog: $3d($6 OV), CAN/OV, SS:7-9, $20m
✪ Nursery: April, July-August, Sa-Su, by appointment only
❀ Garden: April, Sa-Su, by appointment only

Stokes Seed, Inc.
P.O. Box 548
183 E. Main Street (Fredonia)
Buffalo, NY 14240-0548
John F. Gale
(716) 695-6980
Fax: (888) 834-3334
E-mail: stokes@stokeseeds.com
Web: www.stokeseeds.com

Seeds ☙ Supplies
This large Canadian company publishes a very informative catalog aimed at
commercial farmers and growers, but also sells smaller packets to home
gardeners; each plant is well described, with a lot of cultural information.
They offer a huge selection of **vegetable and flower** seeds, some available
precision-sized or pelleted, and some supplies. Canadian customers should
write to Box 10, St. Catharines, ON, Canada L2R 6R6. (1881)
- 📖 Catalog: Free, R&W, CAN/OV, bn/cn
- ☉ Nursery: All year, M-F
- ❀ Garden: July-August, trial gardens, call ahead

Stokes Tropicals
P.O. Box 9868
4806 E. Old Spanish Trail
New Iberia, LA 70562
Glenn M. Stokes
(318) 365-6998, (800) 624-9706
Fax: (318) 365-6991
E-mail: gstokes@1stnet.com
Web: www.stokestropicals.com

Plants ☙ Books ☙ Supplies
Offers a nice selection of **tropical plants**: plumerias, gingers, bananas, and
others, each well described and many shown in color photographs. They also
sell their own tropical planting mix and fertilizer, and books on tropical plants.
(1995)
- 📖 Catalog: $4d($6 OV), R&W, CAN/OV, CC, $20m, bn/cn
- ☉ Nursery: All year, M-F
- ❀ Garden: April-October, M-F

Story House Herb Farm
587 Erwin Road
Murray, KY 42071
Cathleen Haley
(502) 753-5928

Plants
Offers nearly a hundred varieties of **herbs**, selected to perform well in the
kitchen garden. All are certified organically grown, and well described; there
is a concise cultural instructions chart. They also offer several collections for
specific culinary uses. No shipping to CA, HI or WA. (1990)
- 📖 Catalog: $2d, CC, SS:4-5, $16m, cn/bn
- ☉ Nursery: April-May, Sa
- ❀ Garden: April-May, Sa

Strong's Alpine Succulents
P.O. Box 50115
Parks, AZ 86018
Shirley Strong
(520) 635-1127
E-mail: sstrong@primenet.com

Plants ☙ Books
Shirley Strong lives at 7,000 feet in the mountains of Arizona, so her **sem-
pervivums, jovibarbas and sedums** are very hardy; she offers about a
hundred varieties with good, brief descriptions -- there's even a sheet of leaf
shapes and sizes for the selective. Visitors must request a map. (1989)
- 📖 Catalog: $2d, CAN/OV, CC, SS:6-9, bn/cn
- ☉ Nursery: June-September, by appointment only
- ❀ Garden: June-September, by appointment only

Succulenta
P.O. Box 480325
Los Angeles, CA 90048
Deborah Milne & Lykke Coleman
(213) 653-1552, 933-8676

Plants
Collectors' lists of **cactus and succulents**, including rare haworthias, euph-
orbias and caudiciforms; plants briefly described in their lists of new offerings.
No longer publish a catalog, but send periodic lists; you can always send a
"wish list." Plants are nursery-propagated. (1978)
- 📖 Catalog: $1, SS:3-10, bn

Summerville's Gladiolus World-Wide
436 Richwood Road
Glassboro, NJ 08028
Dana R. Summerville

Bulbs
Offers a broad selection of **gladiolus**; new varieties from well-known hybrid-
izers and many other favorites, including some miniatures and collections for
cutting and show; larger quantities at wholesale prices. (1965)
- 📖 Catalog: $1d, R&W, CAN/OV, SS:3-5
- ❀ Garden: Mid-July-August, call ahead

Sunburst Bulbs C.C.
P.O. Box 183
Howard Place, South Africa 7450
Waldo Van Essen
27 (0) 21 531-9829
Fax: 27 (0) 21 531-3181

Bulbs
Supplier of **South African bulbs**, as well as other **spring blooming bulbs**;
shown in color photographs with brief descriptions. Some bulbs available in
collections. No shipping to Australia or Canada. (1928)
- 📖 Catalog: Free, R&W, OV, CC, $25m, bn/cn

Sunlight Gardens
174 Golden Lane
Andersonville, TN 37705
Andrea Sessions & Marty Zenni
Fax: (423) 494-7086
E-mail: sungardens@aol.com

Plants
Specializes in nursery-propagated **wildflowers of southeastern and north-eastern North America**; a nice selection, very well described, and with the easy ones pointed out. Also offers collections for special conditions. No shipping to AZ, CA, HI, OR or WA. (1984)
- Catalog: $3(2 yrs.), R&W, CC, $15m, bn
- Nursery: All year, M-F

Sunny Land Seeds (Semillas Solanas)
P.O. Box 385
Paradox, CO 81429
Ruth Marie Moore
(970) 859-7248
Fax: (970) 859-7248

Seeds
Offers seeds of a variety of **Southwestern** and **South and Central American plants**: wildflowers, trees and shrubs, some hard-to-find. There are no plant descriptions, just botanical and common names, plant family, and abbreviations for type of plant and general germination instructions. (1986)
- Catalog: $1, R&W, CAN/OV, $10m, bn/cn
- Nursery: By appointment only

Sunnybrook Farms Nursery
P.O. Box 6
9448 Mayfield Road
Chesterland, OH 44026
Timothy Ruh
(440) 729-7232

Plants ∾ Books ∾ Supplies
Specializing in **herbs, perennials, scented geraniums, ivies**; a good selection in each category, each well described. Also offer special collections, dried herbs and essential oils. No shipping to AZ, CA, HI, TX, OR or WA. (1928)
- Catalog: $2d, CC, SS:3-10, $15m, cn/bn
- Nursery: All year, daily
- Garden: June-September, daily

Sunnyridge Gardens
1724 Drinnen Road
Knoxville, TN 37914
John B. Couturier
(423) 933-0723

Plants
The Couturiers grow 3,700 **daylilies** and 1,500 **iris**; their garden is both an official AHS and a Historical Iris Preservation Society display garden. They offer a broad selection of both daylilies and iris, including some Japanese and Siberian iris; plants are briefly described. (1983)
- Catalog: $1.50d, R&W, SS:4-10, $20m
- Nursery: April-October, daily, call ahead
- Garden: May-July, call ahead

Sunnyslope Gardens
8638 Huntington Drive
San Gabriel, CA 91775-1147
Philip K. Ishizu
(818) 287-4071
Fax: (818) 287-4120

Plants
Catalog offers a large selection of **chrysanthemums** of many types, including spiders, cascades, brush, spoon, anemones, cushion types and even mums for bonsai culture. Also sells a selection of giant everblooming **carnations**; brief descriptions with some cultural suggestions.
- Catalog: Free, R&W, CAN/OV, SS:2-7
- Nursery: All year, daily

Sunrise Nursery
13705 Pecan Hollow
Leander, TX 78641
Kathy Springer

Plants
Specializes in nursery-propagated **cactus and succulents** from all over the world, grown from seed or cuttings, and some hard-to-find: coryphanthus, echinocereus, escobaria, ferocactus, mammillarias, agaves, aloes, euphorbias, haworthias, lithops and pachypodiums, all briefly described. (1991)
- Catalog: $1d, $15m, bn
- Nursery: All year, Tu-Su, by appointment only
- Garden: March-November, by appointment only

Sunshine State Tropicals
6329 Alaska Avenue
New Port Richey, FL 34653
Greg Sytch
(813) 841-9618

Plants
Offers a very large selection of **cane, rex and rhizomatous begonias**, hundreds of plants with very brief descriptions. Also offer a few other **gesneriads** and tropical plants, inquire if you have a "wish list." (1990)
- Catalog: $1, R&W, CAN/OV, cn/bn
- Nursery: By appointment only
- Garden: March-November, by appointment only

Sunswept Laboratories
P.O. Box 1913
Studio City, CA 91614
Robert C. Hull
(818) 506-7271
Fax: (818) 506-4911

Plants
Broad selection of **species orchids**; list includes broughtonias, cymbidiums, catasetums, cattleyas, epidendrums, laelias, miltonias, oncidiums, zygopetalum and other rare and endangered orchids from seed or tissue culture, each briefly described. A good list of **hybrid orchids**, too, and a flask list. (1980)
📖 Catalog: $2, CAN/OV, CC, $50m, bn
✪ Nursery: All year, daily, by appointment only
✿ Garden: All year, daily, by appointment only

Superstition Iris Gardens
2536 Old Highway
Cathey's Valley, CA 95306
Richard A. Tasco
(209) 966-6277
E-mail: randrcv@sierratel.com

Plants
Specializes in **bearded iris** in various sizes, a good selection, each briefly described. They also offer **arilbred and historic iris**. They cannot ship to Australia or Russia. (1987)
📖 Catalog: $1.50($3 OV), R&W, CAN/OV, SS:7-8
✪ Nursery: Tu-Su, April 1-May 15
✿ Garden: Tu-Su, April 1-May 15

Surry Gardens
P.O. Box 145
Surry, ME 04684
James M. Dickinson
(207) 667-4493 or 5593
Fax: (207) 667-5532

Plants
Offers a good selection of **perennials and rock garden plants**, listed in compact tables with zone, bloom season, exposure, height, soil needs and a very brief description given; campanulas, primulas, asters, dianthus, platycodon, thyme and veronica. No shipping to states with Japanese beetle restrictions -- check with your state agriculture department. (1978)
📖 Catalog: Free, R&W, SS:4-7,9-10, $25m, bn
✪ Nursery: All year, daily
✿ Garden: May-September, daily

Sutton's Green Thumber
16592 Road 208
Porterville, CA 93257
George & Margaret Sutton
(209) 784-9011
Fax: (209) 784-6701

Plants
My parents lived near Porterville for many years, so I still look on this as a "local" nursery. They offer a very broad selection of **tall and median bearded iris**, very briefly described; included is a long list of "timeless ones" at very reasonable prices. Offer many rebloomers, too. (1984)
📖 Catalog: $1d($5 OV), R&W, CAN/OV, CC, SS:7-9, $15m
✪ Nursery: April, daily, or by appointment
✿ Garden: April, call ahead in other months

Swan Island Dahlias
P.O. Box 700
995 N.W. 22nd Avenue
Canby, OR 97013-0700
Nicholas & Ted Gitts
(503) 266-7711, (800) 410-6540
Fax: (503) 266-8768

Plants
Color catalog offers a broad selection of **dahlias**, many shown in photos and all well described. They offer several collections - "big bloomers, autumn, landscapers, Victorian" and others. Good cultural and historical information on dahlias. No shipping to Japan. (1930)
📖 Catalog: $3d($5 OV), R&W, CAN/OV, CC, SS:3-5, $15m
✪ Nursery: April-May, M-Sa
✿ Garden: August-October, call ahead

Swann's Daylily Garden
P.O. Box 7686
119 Mack Lane
Warner Robins, GA 31095-7686
Jean & Mark Swann
(912) 953-4778

Plants
Daylilies -- lots of them -- over 350 varieties listed in table form with very brief descriptions, and they have about 1000 more kinds in the garden, so ask if you are looking for something not listed.
📖 Catalog: FCS($1 OV), CAN/OV, SS:3-11
✪ Nursery: March-November, M-Sa, call ahead
✿ Garden: May-June, call ahead

Sweetbay Farm
4260 Enon Road
Coolidge, GA 31738
Dorothy & Brett Callaway
(912) 225-1688
Fax: (912) 227-0578

Plants & Books
Dorothy Callaway is the author of "The World of Magnolias," so you know that she knows her plants. They offer a nice selection of **magnolias**, as well as some **pawpaws**; plants are well described. They sell her book, tree shelters, and some magnolia gifts. (1994)
📖 Catalog: Free($2 OV), R&W, CAN/OV, CC, bn
✪ Nursery: All year, by appointment only

T & T Seeds, Ltd.
P.O. Box 1710
Winnipeg, MB, Canada R3C 3P6
Paddy, Kevin & Brian Twomey
(204) 895-9962, 895-9964
Fax: (204) 895-9967

Plants   **Seeds**   **Supplies**   **Bulbs**
Color catalog offers good selection of **vegetables, annuals and perennials**, summer-blooming bulbs, trees, shrubs, vines, fruit trees and berries, all well described. They also carry a broad selection of growing supplies. Ship only seeds to the US. (1946)
- Catalog: $2, US, CC, SS:W
- Nursery: All year, M-Sa

Tate Rose Nursery
10306 FM Road 2767
Tyler, TX 75708-9239
Otis Tate
(903) 593-1020
Fax: (903) 593-2250

Plants
A small family nursery offers a nice selection of modern hybrid **roses**: hybrid teas, floribundas, grandifloras and climbers. Can't ship to CA. (1942)
- Catalog: Free, R&W, CC, SS:1-4, $20m
- Nursery: November-April, M-F, call ahead

Teas Nursery Co., Inc.
P.O. Box 1603
4400 Bellaire Boulevard
Bellaire, TX 77402-1603
Teas Family
(713) 664-4400, (800) 446-7723
Fax: (713) 295-5170
E-mail: catalog@teasnursery.com
Web: www.teasnursery.com

Plants   **Books**   **Supplies**
This venerable business specializes in **tropical plants**: plants include hibiscus, plumerias, tillandsias and collections of orchids. Another catalog offers a very good selection of **roses** of all types. They also sell all sorts of growing supplies for orchids and houseplants, and books on growing them. (1843)
- Catalog: $2d, CAN/OV, CC, $5m, bn
- Nursery: All year, daily
- Garden: March-May, October-December, daily

Terra Edibles
R.R. 4
Stirling, ON, Canada K0K 3E0
Judy Gaunt
(613) 395-6271

Seeds
Offering **vegetables**, with a nice selection of heirloom tomatoes, beans, and other varieties from around the world. Also offer heirloom **sweet peas**, and a few other **flowers**.
- Catalog: $1, US/OV

Terra Nova Gardening
P.O. Box 19149, Diamond Lake Station
Minneapolis, MN 55419
Stephanie & Jon Nichols
(612) 825-7770
E-mail: info@terra-nova.org
Web: www.terra-nova.org

Plants
Formerly Cooper's Garden, they still specialize in species, Siberian and Louisiana **iris, daylilies, hostas** and some **perennials** for sun and shade. Offer a good selection, particularly of species iris; plants briefly to well described.
- Catalog: $2, CAN/OV, SS:4-5,8-9, bn/cn
- Nursery: By appointment only
- Garden: May-June, call ahead

Territorial Seed Company
P.O. Box 157
20 Palmer Avenue
Cottage Grove, OR 97424-0061
Tom & Julie Johns
(541) 942-9547
Fax: (541) 942-9881
E-mail: territorial@ordata.com
Web: www.territorial-seed.com

Plants   **Seeds**   **Books**   **Tools**
Informative catalog specializes in **vegetables** for the maritime climate areas of Oregon, Washington, British Columbia and northern California. Also offers sprinklers, drip irrigation supplies, tools, books, beneficial insects, and a list of local organic fertilizer suppliers. Also lists seeds of annuals, herbs and green manure crops, and ships vegetable plants. North of the border, write to 8475 Ontario Street, Vancouver, BC, Canada V5X 3E8. (1979)
- Catalog: Free, R&W, CC, cn/bn
- Nursery: All year, M-Sa; Summer, daily
- Garden: July-August, Sa

Theatrum Botanicum
P.O. Box 288
18300 Appian Way
Navarro, CA 95463
Rick Hepting
(707) 895-3886
E-mail: thebot@pacific.net
Web: www.hepting.com/thebot/

Plants   **Books**
Cold, snowy day? Reading this "Post-apocalyptic ethnobotanical guide to plant-human relativity" ought to perk you up! An **eclectic collection of plants**, listed by plant family, with good plant descriptions. Good selection of herbs, vines (including hops), salvias, ornamental grasses, and much more. There's an index from plant to plant family -- you'll learn a lot. (1989)
- Catalog: $2, CAN, SS:3-11, $20m, bn/cn
- Nursery: By appointment only
- Garden: March-October, by appointment only

Thompson & Morgan
P.O. Box 1308
22 Farraday Avenue
Jackson, NJ 08527-0308
Bruce J. Sangster, Pres.
(800) 274-7333
Fax: (908) 363-9356

Seeds
Color catalog with a huge selection of **plants of all types**. Good descriptions of plants and good germination and cultural information; the catalog and color photographs create yearnings on a grand scale. (1855)
- 📖 Catalog: Free, CAN/OV, bn/cn
- ✪ Nursery: All year, M-F

A Thousand Alliums
3915 S.W. Willow
Seattle, WA 98136
Jessie Attri
(206) 935-7506

Seeds ☙ Bulbs
Specializing in **alliums**, this small nursery offers seeds and bulbs of over 30 species and varieties. Some sound quite exotic and fun -- "softball sized flowers!" Plants are briefly but well described. Also sells Dilys Davies' book on these pungent flowers.
- 📖 Catalog: $2, CAN, SS:9-10, $25m, bn
- ✪ Nursery: February-October, by appointment only

The Thyme Garden
20546 Alsea Highway
Alsea, OR 97324
Rolfe & Janet Hagen
(541) 487-8671
E-mail: thymegarden@proaxis.com

Plants ☙ Seeds
Family run seed company offers **herbs and everlasting flowers**, many of them grown organically on their farm in the mountains of western Oregon. Good selection and plant descriptions; some plants also available. They sell dried herbs too. Seeds only to overseas customers. (1990)
- 📖 Catalog: $2($3 OV), CAN/OV, CC, cn/bn
- ✪ Nursery: April-August, F-M, call ahead
- ❀ Garden: April-August, F-M, call ahead

Tiki Nursery
P.O. Box 187
Fairview, NC 28730
Jack Pardo
(704) 628-2212

Plants
Offers a wide selection of **African violets**, sinningias, achimenes, streptocarpus and other **gesneriads** as well as begonias, **fuchsias** and a few other exotic houseplants. Each plant very briefly described. Plants must be shipped bare-root to CA and HI. (1977)
- 📖 Catalog: $2, CAN, CC, SS:4-10, $15m, bn

Tile Barn Nursery
Standen Street, Iden Green
Benenden, Kent, England TN17 4LB
Peter & Liz Moore
44 (0) 1580 240-221

Bulbs
Specialists in **hardy cyclamen**, offering many varieties, each very well described; their focus is on the rarer types. A mandatory CITES and Health Certificate Fee is added to the price of the tubers, as well as the postage cost. (1981)
- 📖 Catalog: $1(US Bills) or 2 IRC, OV, SS:5-7, $50m, bn
- ✪ Nursery: All year, W-Sa, call ahead
- ❀ Garden: September-April, W-Sa, call ahead

Tinari Greenhouses
2325 Valley Road, Box 190
Huntingdon Valley, PA 19006-0190
Frank & Anne Tinari
(215) 947-0144
Fax: (215) 947-2163

Plants ☙ Seeds ☙ Books ☙ Supplies
A nice selection of **African violets** -- many are their own hybrids; all briefly described. Offer "microminis," on a separate list, and seeds of regular, miniature, variegated and trailing violets. Also sell supplies and a few books. (1945)
- 📖 Catalog: $1, CC, SS:5-10
- ✪ Nursery: All year, daily; June-October, M-Sa

Tinmouth Channel Farm
RR 1, Box 428B
Tinmouth, VT 05773
Carolyn Fuhrer & Kathleen Duhnoski
(802) 446-2812
Fax: (800) 624-1718

Plants ☙ Seeds
Small nursery offers more than 200 varieties of annual and perennial **herbs**, garlic, **scented geraniums** and other hardy plants, all organically grown; each plant well described. Cultural hints are offered, including the formula of their own insecticide -- secret ingredients are red pepper and garlic -- don't see how it could fail! (1987)
- 📖 Catalog: $2, CAN, CC, SS:4-10, cn/bn
- ✪ Nursery: April-October, M-Sa, call ahead

Tiny Petals Nursery
489 Minot Avenue
Chula Vista, CA 91910
Susan O'Brien, Dick & Carol Sparks
(619) 498-4755
Fax: (619) 422-0385

Plants
A broad selection of **miniature roses**, featuring the hybrids of Dee Bennett: minis, micro-minis, trailers and climbers, all well described. Many color pictures in the catalog. (1973)
- Catalog: Free, CC, SS:1-11
- Nursery: January-November, F-M
- Garden: Late March-November, F-M

Toll Gate Gardens & Nursery
20803 Junction Road
Bellevue, MI 49021
Larry L. Sibley
(616) 781-5887
Fax: (616) 781-6535

Plants **Seeds**
Larry Sibley is the son-in-law of Corwin Davis, "the paw-paw man." He carries on selling plants and seeds of **pawpaw**; plants are either seedlings or grafts. Davis called pawpaw the "forgotten fruit: edible and beautiful trees for landscaping, nothing bothers them, insects or pests or diseases." Also seednuts or seedlings of Carpathian walnuts, Turkish tree hazels, butternuts, chestnuts and hardy pecans.
- Catalog: Free, CAN, SS:4-5
- Nursery: April-October, call ahead
- Garden: April-October, call ahead

Tomato Growers Supply Company
P.O. Box 2237
Fort Myers, FL 33902
Linda & Vince Sapp
(941) 768-1119
Fax: (941) 768-3476

Seeds **Books** **Supplies**
Over 200 varieties of **tomato** seed, growing supplies and books; all plants well described, with good general cultural instructions and days to maturity for each variety -- oh, the agony of choices, but they all sound so good it must be hard to go wrong! They offer hot and sweet **peppers**, too. (1984)
- Catalog: Free, CC

Totally Tomatoes
P.O. Box 1626
Augusta, GA 30903
Shumway's
(803) 663-0016
Fax: (888) 477-7333

Seeds
Seed company, offering 300 varieties of **tomatoes** and 50 varieties of **peppers**. You can buy from a 30-seed packet to a quarter ounce packet (2000-3000 seeds!). (1992)
- Catalog: Free, CAN, CC

Tower Perennial Gardens, Inc.
3412 E. 64th Court
E. 4010 Jamieson Road
Spokane, WA 99223
Alan Tower
(509) 448-6778
Fax: (509) 448-1661
E-mail: tower@spokane.net

Plants
Sells **hostas**, a good selection, each well described. They have added a retail nursery with trees, shrubs and other ornamentals, so call if you're in the area. No shipping to AK, AZ, FL, HI, LA or TX. (1989)
- Catalog: Free, CC, SS:5-10, bn
- Nursery: April-October, daily
- Garden: May-October, by appointment only

Town & Country Roses

See Sam Kedem Greenhouse & Nursery.

Tradewinds Bamboo Nursery
28446 Hunter Creek Loop
Gold Beach, OR 97444
Gib & Diane Cooper
(541) 247-0835
Fax: (541) 247-0835
E-mail: bambugib@harborside.com
Web: www.harborside.com/bamboo/

Plants **Books**
Offers a good selection of **bamboos** -- Phyllostachys pubescens (moso or giant timber bamboo) and several other genera -- arundinaria, chimonobambusa, pleioblastus, sasa, bambusa, chusquea and fargesia; briefly described. Also offers several books on bamboo and bamboo construction. (1986)
- Catalog: $2, CAN/OV, CC, bn
- Nursery: Call ahead
- Garden: Call ahead

Tranquil Lake Nursery
45 River Street
Rehoboth, MA 02769-1395
Warren P. Leach & Philip A. Boucher
(508) 252-4002, (800) 353-4344
Fax: (508) 252-4740

Plants
Catalog offers a good selection of **daylilies, Japanese and Siberian iris**; plants well described. Many more are available at the nursery; they grow older varieties, so send a "wish list." Sell other perennials at the nursery. Can only ship to certain countries overseas. (1958)
📖 Catalog: $1, R&W, CAN/OV, CC, SS:4-10, $10m
✪ Nursery: May-October, Tu-Su
✹ Garden: June-August, Tu-Su

Trans Pacific Nursery
16065 Oldsville Road
McMinnville, OR 97128
Jackson Muldoon
(503) 472-6215
Fax: (503) 434-1505
E-mail: gwroe@jack.macnet.com
Web: www.macnet.com/home/gwroe.home.html

Plants
A wide selection of **trees, shrubs, vines and perennials** from all over the world, many not easy to find; each plant well described. Among the plants are anigozanthos, banksia, carex, cotula, gunnera, huernia, hardenbergia, kennedia, erythrinas, metasequoia, parahebe, rhodohypoxis, violas, a few South African bulbs and Japanese maples. (1982)
📖 Catalog: $2($3 OV), CAN/OV, CC, SS:W, $10m, bn
✪ Nursery: All year, call ahead
✹ Garden: May-September, call ahead

Transplant Nursery
1586 Parkertown Road
Lavonia, GA 30553
Jeff & Lisa Beasley
(706) 356-8947
Fax: (706) 356-8842
E-mail: transplantnursery@hartcom.net

Plants
This nursery, which stopped shipping for a while, has come back to Gardening by Mail. I'm delighted to see them, because they have a very good selection of **azaleas and rhododendrons** from excellent hybridizers, as well as species azaleas and **camellias**, and ornamental trees and shrubs for similar growing conditions. Welcome back! No shipping to CA, OR and WA. World Wide Web address is <www.mindspring.com/%7Eplants/transplant.catalogue.html>. (1980)
📖 Catalog: $1, CC, SS:9-5, $25m, bn/cn
✪ Nursery: All year, M-F, Sa in Spring & Fall
✹ Garden: Mid-March to May, M-Sa

Travis' Violets
P.O. Box 42
Ochlocknee, GA 31773-0042
Travis Davis
(912) 574-5167 or 5236
Fax: (912) 574-5605
E-mail: tviolets@aol.com

Plants ∞ Supplies
Sell **African violets**, including their own hybrids and many others: Hortense's Honeys, Lyon's and Fredettes included. Sell both leaves and plants; all are well described. Also sell lighted plant stands. (1980)
📖 Catalog: $1d($3 OV), CAN/OV, CC, SS:4-11, $25m
✪ Nursery: All year, M-Sa, call ahead
✹ Garden: May-July, M-Sa, call ahead

Trennoll Nursery
3 West Page Avenue
Trenton, OH 45067-1614
James & Dorothy Parker
(513) 988-6121
Fax: (513) 988-7079

Plants ∞ Seeds
A very nice list of **alpine and rock garden plants**, including dianthus, hardy ferns, sempervivums, and many forms of iris cristata and dwarf phlox. Plants are well described. Also sells some seeds, with many **hosta seeds** offered.
📖 Catalog: $1d, CAN/OV, CC, SS:3-10, $25m, bn/cn
✪ Nursery: March-November, daily, by appointment only
✹ Garden: April-July, by appointment only

William Tricker, Inc.
7125 Tanglewood Drive
Independence, OH 44131
Richard Lee
(216) 524-3491, (800) 524-3492
Fax: (216) 524-6688

Plants ∞ Books ∞ Supplies
Color catalog of **water lilies and other aquatic and bog plants**, even a Victoria trickeri with leaves up to 6 feet across. In addition to a broad selection of plants, they sell books and videos on water gardening, fancy fish, pool supplies and remedies in an informative catalog. (1895)
📖 Catalog: $2($5 OV), R&W, CAN/OV, CC, cn/bn
✪ Nursery: All year, daily
✹ Garden: June-September, daily

Tripple Brook Farm
37 Middle Road
Southampton, MA 01073
Stephen Breyer
(413) 527-4626
Fax: (413) 527-9853

Plants
Small nursery with a good selection of **Northeastern native plants**, hardy bamboos, fruiting mulberries and hardy kiwi, iris, ornamental grasses, flowering shrubs and more -- catalog full of good cultural information, as well as small drawings of many plants -- a delight!
📖 Catalog: $1, CC, SS:3-12, bn/cn
✪ Nursery: All year, call ahead
❀ Garden: May-October, call ahead

Tropic to Tropic Plants
1170 53A Street
South Delta, BC, Canada V4M 3E3
Ray Mattei
(604) 943-6562
Fax: (604) 948-1996

Plants
Stressing the value of "micro-climates" in the garden, Ray grows **subtropical and tropical plants**, as well as **hardy citrus, bamboos**, a "cool hardy" **banana, gingers**, and assorted cactus, shrubs and perennials. US customers can write to P.O. Box 1136, Pt. Roberts WA 98281 for a catalog.
📖 Catalog: $3d($5.50 OV), R&W, US/OV, SS:4-10, bn/cn
✪ Nursery: March-November, daily, by appointment only
❀ Garden: May-September, by appointment only

Tropiflora
3530 Tallevast Road
Sarasota, FL 34243
Dennis & Linda Cathcart
(941) 351-2267, (800) 613-7520
Fax: (941) 351-6985
E-mail: tflora@gte.net
Web: home1.gte.net/tflora/

Plants ✍ **Books**
Tropiflora offers a nice selection of **bromeliads**, including **tillandsias**, aechmeas, guzmanias, vrieseas, and neoregelias and some species **orchids**. They publish the "Cargo Report" which describes new introductions bimonthly. Some plants are wild collected. Also offer books and growing supplies. (1976)
📖 Catalog: Free($10 OV), R&W, CAN/OV, CC, bn
✪ Nursery: All year, M-Sa

Underwood Shade Nursery
P.O. Box 1386
North Attleboro, MA 02763-0386
Russ Bragg & Connie Wick
(508) 222-2164
Fax: (508) 222-5152
E-mail: shadeplant@ici.net

Plants
Small nursery offers a nice selection of **shade tolerant plants**; wildflowers, species violas, aroids and more, each very well described with growing information. No shipping to AZ, NV or WY. (1993)
📖 Catalog: $2d, SS:4-5,9-10, bn/cn
✪ Nursery: April-October, by appointment only

© Siskiyou Rare Plant Nursery
Artist: Baldassare Mineo

Valente Gardens
123 Dillingham Road
No. Berwick, ME 03906
Ron & Cindy Valente
(207) 457-2076

Plants
"Specialize in hardy **daylilies** suitable for our very severe Maine climate." Included are their own introductions, as well as a good selection of newer cultivars. Plants are briefly but well described, many with notes on parentage.
📖 Catalog: 2 FCS, SS:5-8
✪ Nursery: Mid-July-mid-August, W-Su, call ahead
✺ Garden: Mid-July-mid-August, W-Su, call ahead

Valhalla Nursery
204 Nixon Place
Chula Vista, CA 91910-1123
R. Doug Roberts
E-mail: valnursery@aol.com

Plants
A **tropical plant** specialist, with a broad selection of tender plants for indoors and out, if you live in a warm climate: bamboos and grasses, flowering vines, gingers, hibiscus, palms and cycads, brugmansias, passion flowers, bananas, and much, much more. Good group descriptions, with brief descriptions of each variety. (1989)
📖 Catalog: $2($5 OV), R&W, CAN/OV, $15m, bn/cn

Valley Vista Kiwi
16531 Mt. Shelly Circle
Fountain Valley, CA 92708
Roger & Shirley Meyer
(714) 839-0796

Plants
Small nursery offers scionwood of more than thirty varieties of **kiwi** and **hardy kiwi**, 28 varieties of **jujube** (bare-root jujube trees available from January to March), and many other **unusual fruits** such as Surinam cherry, lychee, cherimoya and dwarf banana. No plant descriptions. (1975)
📖 Catalog: Long SASE($1 OV), CAN/OV, $10m, cn/bn
✪ Nursery: M-F, call ahead
✺ Garden: Call ahead

Van Bourgondien Bros.
P.O. Box 1000
245 Farmingdale Road, Route 109
Babylon, NY 11702-0598
Van Bourgondien Family
(516) 669-3500, (800) 622-9997
Fax: (516) 669-1228
E-mail: blooms@dutchbulbs.com
Web: dutchbulbs.com

Plants ✄ **Bulbs**
Color catalogs offer **spring and summer-blooming bulbs and perennials**; each plant briefly described, with cultural information given in symbols. Large selection, especially of bulbs, all shown in color; catalogs sent in fall and spring. No shipping to AK, HI, PR or Guam. (1919)
📖 Catalog: Free, CC, SS:2-6,9-12, cn/bn

Van Dyck's Flower Farms, Inc.
P.O. Box 430
Brightwaters, NY 11718-0430
Jan Van Dyck
(800) 248-2852
Fax: (516) 669-3518

Bulbs
Sell **spring blooming bulbs** -- offered are tulips, daffodils, hyacinths, Dutch iris, crocus and other "little" bulbs, and some hybrid lilies. Ships only to contiguous 48 states. (1992)
📖 Catalog: Free, CC, SS:9-12, $25m

Van Engelen, Inc.
23 Tulip Drive
Bantam, CT 06750
Jan S. Ohms
(860) 567-8734
Fax: (860) 567-5323

Bulbs
Sells **Dutch bulbs** in quantities of 50 and 100 per variety, but anyone who orders a minimum of $50 may take advantage of their bulk prices. Offers a broad selection; brief plant descriptions, cultural suggestions. (1946)
📖 Catalog: Free, R&W, CC, SS:9-12, $50m, cn/bn

Van Ness Water Gardens
2460 N. Euclid Avenue
Upland, CA 91784-1199
William C. Uber
(800) 205-2425
Fax: (909) 949-7217
Web: www.vnwg.com

Plants ✄ **Books** ✄ **Supplies**
Color catalog offers **everything for water gardens** -- water lilies and other aquatic plants, fish, ponds and supplies and books on water gardening, as well as a lot of information on how to do it. They also consult worldwide on fresh-water ecosystems and water gardens. (1932)
📖 Catalog: $2($8 OV), CAN/OV, CC, SS:W, $15m, cn/bn
✪ Nursery: All year, Tu-Sa, call ahead in December & January
✺ Garden: April-August, Tu-Sa

Vermont Bean Seed Co.
Garden Lane
Fair Haven, VT 05743
Shumway's
(802) 663-0217
Fax: (888) 500-7333

Seeds ∞ Supplies ∞ Tools
Specializes in **bean and vegetable seeds**; informative catalog with good
descriptions and growing instructions. Also a selection of growing supplies,
some annual, herb and perennial seeds. (1975)
📖 Catalog: Free($2 CAN), CAN, CC

Vermont Wildflower Farm
P.O. Box 5
Route 7
Charlotte, VT 05445-0005
Ray & Charlotte Allen
Fax: (573) 754-5290

Seeds
The garden is a tourist attraction in Vermont; they have seeded "thousands"
of wildflower species in their six-acre test garden. Offer **wildflower seeds
and seed mixes** for sun or shade, regionalized for the entire US. Color cat-
alog gives basic how-to information on getting started. (1981)
📖 Catalog: Free, CC, cn/bn
✪ Nursery: May-October, daily
❀ Garden: July-August, daily

Vesey's Seeds, Ltd.
York, PEI, Canada C0A 1P0
B. E. Simpson
(902) 368-7333, (800) 363-7333
Fax: (800) 686-0329
E-mail: catalog@veseys.com
Web: www.veseys.com

Seeds ∞ Books ∞ Supplies
A broad selection of **vegetables and flowers**, all well described with cul-
tural information. Specializes in short-season varieties for Canada and New
England. Also offers growing supplies, gardening books and hand-made white
ash baskets. Americans can request catalog from P.O. Box 9000, Calais, ME,
04619-6102. (1939)
📖 Catalog: Free, US, CC
✪ Nursery: All year, M-Sa
❀ Garden: July-September, M-Sa

Vicki's Exotic Plants
522 Vista Park Drive
Eagle Point, OR 97524
Vicki Graves
(541) 826-6318
Fax: (541) 826-7918

Plants
Offers a broad selection of **fibrous and rhizomatous begonias and hoyas**,
as well as some **gesneriads and dischidias**. All plants are lovingly described,
it's obviously collecting taken to the max.
📖 Catalog: Free($2 OV), CAN/OV, SS:3-11, $15m
✪ Nursery: By appointment only

Andre Viette Farm & Nursery
P.O. Box 1109
State Route 608
Fishersville, VA 22939
Andre Viette
(540) 943-2315, (800) 575-5538
Fax: (540) 943-0782
E-mail: viette@viette.com
Web: www.viette.com

Plants ∞ Tools
A very broad selection of **garden perennials**; very brief plant descriptions.
Plants are grouped by use or cultural conditions, shade or sun, or by type.
Many daylilies, iris, hostas, peonies, ornamental grasses, epimediums,
astilbes, liriopes, Oriental poppies and more. Cannot ship to CA. (1929)
📖 Catalog: $5, R&W, CC, SS:3-10, $60m, bn/cn
✪ Nursery: April-October, M-Sa, Su pm
❀ Garden: May-September, M-Sa, Su pm

Vintage Gardens
2833 Old Gravenstein Highway So.
Sebastopol, CA 95472
G. Lowery, D. Freid, L. Eisen, G. Phy
(707) 829-2035
Fax: (707) 829-9516
Web: www.spiderweb.com/vintage

Plants
Offers an extensive selection of "antique and extraordinary" **roses**, listed by
type and lovingly described; there are beautiful line drawings and color paint-
ings of some of the roses in the informative catalog. They seem to list some
roses I've never seen listed anywhere else. Availability list is free. (1992)
📖 Catalog: $5, CAN/OV, CC, SS:9-5, bn
✪ Nursery: All year, Tu-Su
❀ Garden: April-November, Tu-Su

Violets By Appointment
45 Third Street
West Sayville, NY 11796-1109
William H. Paauwe
(516) 589-2724

Plants ∞ Supplies
Offers a broad selection of **African violets**, shipped only as leaves. Plants are
listed alphabetically by hybridizer, with brief descriptions. Included are species
and trailers. (1987)
📖 Catalog: $1.50d, SS:4-7,9-10, $20m
✪ Nursery: M-Sa, by appointment only

Violets, Etc., Inc.
1011 Wood Avenue
1417 Cleveland Street
Clearwater, FL 34615
Bonnie Schmidlkofer

Plants ∞ Supplies
Offers a good selection of **African violet** leaves, including miniatures and trailers, and some **episcia and columnea** cuttings as well. Also sells growing supplies and small pots. (1995)
📖 Catalog: $2d
✪ Nursery: By appointment only

Volkmann Bros. Greenhouses
2714 Minert Street
Dallas, TX 75219
Henry & Walter Volkmann
(214) 526-3484

Plants ∞ Supplies
A nice selection of **African violets**, many of their own hybridizing, each briefly described and some shown in color. Also offer growing supplies, equipment and plant stands. (1949)
📖 Catalog: $1, R&W, CC, SS:W, $20m
✪ Nursery: All year, M-Sa, Su pm
❀ Garden: All year, M-Sa, Su pm

Walnut Hill Gardens
999 310th Street
Atalissa, IA 52720
Barrett & Lynn Stoll
(319) 946-3471

Plants
Offers **daylilies, hostas, species and Siberian iris** and some **ornamental grasses** that willl stand up to the harsh climate of the American Midwest. Plants are briefly but well described. More plants are available at the garden.
📖 Catalog: $2d, R&W, CAN/OV, SS:4-5,8-9, $25m
✪ Nursery: May-September, daily, by appointment only
❀ Garden: May-September, daily, by appointment only

Waterford Gardens
74 E. Allendale Road
Saddle River, NJ 07458
John A. Meeks
(201) 327-0721
Fax: (201) 327-0684
E-mail: splash@waterford-gardens.com
Web: waterford-gardens.com

Plants ∞ Books ∞ Supplies
Complete selection of **water lilies, lotus and other aquatic and bog plants**, as well as pools, supplies, fish, pumps, filters, remedies and books on water gardening. Many color photographs and good descriptions. They have greenhouses, ponds and display gardens to give you good ideas. (1985)
📖 Catalog: $5, R&W, CAN, CC, cn/bn
✪ Nursery: All year, M-Sa
❀ Garden: June-October, M-Sa

Watershed Garden Works
2039 44th Avenue
Longview, WA 98632
Scott & Dixie Edwards
E-mail: 76341.1145@compuserve.com

Plants ∞ Seeds
Specialize in **Northwestern native plants** for environmental restoration projects, seeds are collected from the wild. Nice selection, no plant descriptions. (1989)
📖 Catalog: Free, R&W, CAN/OV, CC, bn/cn
✪ Nursery: All year, M-F, by appointment only

The WaterWorks

See Tilley's Nursery.

The Waushara Gardens
N5491 5th Drive
Plainfield, WI 54966
George & Robert Melk
(715) 335-4462
Fax: (715) 335-4462

Books ∞ Bulbs
Color brochure offers a wide selection of **gladiolus** and pixiolas, hybrid lilies, dahlias, callas and other **summer-blooming bulbs**, well described. Sold in quantities suitable for the cut flower trade as well as for the home gardener. Also some books on glads and lilies. (1924)
📖 Catalog: Free, R&W, CAN/OV, CC, $18m, SS:1-6
❀ Garden: August-September, call ahead

Wavecrest Nursery & Landscaping Co.
2509 Lakeshore Drive
Fennville, MI 49408
Carol T. Hop
(616) 543-4175
Fax: (616) 543-4100

Plants ∞ Books
Offers a very nice selection of **ornamental trees and shrubs** -- berberis, dogwoods, hollies, various conifers -- with brief plant descriptions. They also carry books, and the shop at the nursery sells bonsai tools and statuary as well as bird watching and feeding supplies. (1955)
📖 Catalog: $1d, R&W, CC, SS:3-5, bn
✪ Nursery: Mid-March-November, daily
❀ Garden: May-October, daily

Wayside Gardens ✓
P.O. Box 1
Hodges, SC 29695-0001
William J. Park
(800) 845-1124
Fax: (800) 457-9712

Plants ∞ **Supplies**
Color catalog of **ornamental trees and shrubs, perennials and roses**, all well described and illustrated, with good cultural information and a cultural card with each plant purchased. A Wayside catalog that chanced my way started my passion for ornamental garden plants and was my first tutor. Wide selection; they introduce many new cultivars from the US, Europe and England.
📖 Catalog: $1d, CC, SS:1-5,9-11, bn/cn

We-Du Nurseries
Route 5, Box 724
Marion, NC 28752-9338
Dennis Niemeyer & Joani Lawarre
Fax: (704) 738-8131
E-mail: wedu@wnclink.com

Plants ∞ **Bulbs**
A collectors' catalog of **rock garden and woodland plants**, Southern natives, American, Japanese, Korean and Chinese wildflowers; some are very unusual. Each plant lovingly described; it's almost impossible to convey the pleasure of reading such a catalog and looking up the new plants. No shipping to HI. (1981)
📖 Catalog: $2d, CAN, CC, SS:3-12, $25m, bn
○ Nursery: All year, M-F, by appointment only
❀ Garden: April-October, by appointment only

Chris Weeks Peppers
P.O. Box 3207
Kill Devil Hills, NC 27948
Chris Weeks

Seeds
Small supplier of **hot pepper** seeds, he lists 40 varieties, some of which he claims are quite rare, and some hardier than usual. Calculating his profits at a dime an hour, he does it for the desire to distribute peppers to folks who appreciate the beauty, taste and pizzazz that hot peppers add to life. (1983)
📖 Catalog: $1($2 OV), CAN/OV, $2m

Weiss Brothers Nursery
11690 Colfax Highway
Grass Valley, CA 95945
Weiss Brothers
(916) 272-7657
Fax: (916) 272-3578

Plants ∞ **Books**
Offer a good selection of **perennials and herbs**, each briefly but well described, and some shown in color. Many achilleas, asters, coreopsis, delphiniums, monardas, and veronicas among others. No shipping to AK or HI.
📖 Catalog: Free, CC, SS:3-10, $25m, bn/cn
○ Nursery: Daily

Well-Sweep Herb Farm
317 Mt. Bethel Road
Port Murray, NJ 07865
Louise Hyde
(908) 852-5390

Plants ∞ **Seeds** ∞ **Books** ∞ **Supplies**
A very broad selection of **herb plants, perennials and scented geraniums**; brief plant descriptions. Also offers some herb seeds, dried flowers and other herb gifts, supplies and books. No plants to AZ, CA, OR or WA. (1971)
📖 Catalog: $2, CC, SS:4-11, cn/bn
○ Nursery: All year, M-Sa
❀ Garden: July-October, M-Sa

West Coast Japanese Maples
4650 Brickyard Road
Tillamook, OR 97141
Bob & Val Lichner
(503) 842-5498

Plants
Offer many varieties of **Japanese maples** - including dwarf and semi-dwarf cultivars as well as dissectums, variegated cultivars, and more. Many are called by their Japanese cultivar names. Formerly Loucks Nursery. (1995)
📖 Catalog: $1, CAN, SS:W
○ Nursery: All year, M-Sa, call ahead
❀ Garden: March-October, call ahead

Western Biologicals, Ltd.
P.O. Box 283
Aldergrove, BC, Canada V4W 2T8
William Chalmers
(604) 856-3339
Fax: (604) 856-3339

Seeds ∞ **Books** ∞ **Supplies**
Offer live cultures and granular spawn for a broad selection of **mushrooms**, with pages of cultural instructions. They also offer complete growing supplies and books for commercial or home growers. Hold workshops in tissue culture and mushroom growing. (1983)
📖 Catalog: $3, R&W, US/OV, bn
○ Nursery: Call ahead
❀ Garden: Spring-Fall, by appointment only

Western Native Seed
P.O. Box 1463
Salida, CO 81201
Alex Tonneson & Suzanne Folke
(719) 539-1071
Fax: (719) 539-6755

Seeds ∽ Books
Specialists in **trees, shrubs and Western native plants** as well as **wild-flowers and native grasses**; an extensive selection with no plant descriptions. Some of the seed is habitat collected, and they also offer several wild-flower mixes, and some books on regional plants. May be charges on foreign orders for a phytosanitary certificate. (1988)
📖 Catalog: Free, R&W, CAN/OV, CC, bn/cn

White Flower Farm
P.O. Box 50
Route 63
Litchfield, CT 06759-0050
Eliot Wadsworth II
(800) 411-6159, (800) 503-9624
Fax: (800) 496-1418
Web: www.whiteflowerfarm.com

Plants ∽ Supplies ∽ Tools ∽ Bulbs
Color catalog offers a broad selection of **shrubs and perennials** in the spring; very good plant descriptions and detailed cultural suggestions. They offer many **spring and summer-flowering bulbs** in their fall catalog. Also offer books, supplies and tools. (1950)
📖 Catalog: Free, CAN, CC, SS:3-11, bn/cn
☉ Nursery: All year, daily
❀ Garden: June-October, daily

Whitman Farms
3995 Gibson Road N.W.
Salem, OR 97304-9527
Lucile Whitman
(503) 585-8728
Fax: (503) 363-5020
E-mail: cilew@open.org

Plants
Offer grafted trees, including **species maples and magnolias, and nut trees**, also rooted cuttings of many varieties of edible **currants and gooseberries**, and a few **grapes** and **black walnuts**.
📖 Catalog: $1d, R&W, CAN, SS:8-6, $10m, bn
☉ Nursery: By appointment only

Gilbert H. Wild & Son, Inc.
P.O. Box 338
1112 Joplin Street
Sarcoxie, MO 64862-0338
Greg Jones
(417) 548-3514, (888) 449-4537
Fax: (417) 548-6831

Plants
Color catalog offers a large selection of **daylilies, iris and herbaceous peonies**; all plants very well described, many illustrated. Offers a number of collections and several your-choice collections at considerable savings. Many of the plants are their own hybrids. (1885)
📖 Catalog: $3d, R&W, CAN/OV, CC, SS:4-10
❀ Garden: May-July, M-F, call ahead

Wild Earth Native Plant Nursery
49 Mead Avenue
Wright DeBow Road (Jackson)
Freehold, NJ 07728
Richard L. Pillar
(732) 308-9777
Fax: (732) 308-9777
E-mail: 102644.1575@compuserve.com

Plants
Specializes in **native plants** of the mid-Atlantic region; the owner is a land-scape architect working in natural landscapes and restoration projects. Offers a good selection of **wildflowers, grasses, ferns and perennials**, well described with growing suggestions. No shipping to AZ, CA, FL, OR or WA. (1991)
📖 Catalog: $2d, R&W, SS:4-10, $15m, bn/cn
☉ Nursery: April-September, Tu-Su, call ahead

Wild Garden Seed
P.O. Box 1509
Philomath, OR 97370
Frank & Karen Morton
(541) 929-4068

Seeds
The Mortons run Shoulder to Shoulder Farm, a grower of gourmet salad vegetables for restaurants. As an off-shoot, they sell seeds of **salad vegetables**, **insectary plants** to attract beneficial insects, and **wildflowers** from their area of coastal Oregon. Every plant is very well described; seed supplies are limited, so place your order early. (1995)
📖 Catalog: $4d, R&W, $50m, bn/cn

Wild Ridge
17561 Vierra Canyon Road, Box 37
Prunedale, CA 93907
Michelle & Richard McCain, Patrick Worley
E-mail: wildridge@aol.com

Plants
Specializing in **passion flowers**, and offering over 60 species and hybrids, some of them Patrick's own introductions. They will be adding more vines, salvias, begonias and gesneriads to their list soon. Plants are well described.
📖 Catalog: $1, CAN/OV, $20m, bn

Wild Seed
P.O. Box 27751
Tempe, AZ 85285
Rita Jo Anthony
(602) 276-3536
Fax: (602) 276-3524

Seeds
Specializes in **Southwestern wildflowers and native plants**, and offers a very nice selection of desert and dryland wildflowers, annual and perennial. Also offer collections and mixes, including native grass mixes. No plant descriptions.
📖 Catalog: Free ($2 OV), R&W, CAN/OV, cn/bn

Wildflowers from Nature's Way
3162 Ray Street
Woodburn, IA 50275-8061
Dorothy Baringer

Plants ∞ **Seeds** ∞ **Books**
An extensive list of **prairie wildflowers and grasses**, available as small plants or seeds, available by the packet or pound. Seed mixes for specific sites and purposes are also available. Also offers some books on prairie planting. No plants to CA.
📖 Catalog: Long SASE, CAN/OV, SS:3-5, $10m, cn/bn
✪ Nursery: April-May, Sa-M, call ahead

Wildginger Woodlands
P.O. Box 1091
Webster, NY 14580-7791
Phyllis Farkas

Plants ∞ **Seeds**
A collectors' list of **rock garden and woodland plants**, including Northeastern native plants, shrubs, trees and ferns, offered as plants or seeds; no descriptions of plants, but many choice items such as trilliums and violas. She's had great success germinating fringed gentian: instructions with the seed. Cannot ship to IL. (1983)
📖 Catalog: $1d, SS:4-5,9-10, $10m, bn/cn

Wildman's African Violets
133 Rosemont Drive
Syracuse, NY 13205-3011
Jim Wildman
(315) 492-2562
E-mail: jimviolets@aol.com

Plants ∞ **Supplies**
Jim offers an extensive list of **African violet leaves** - plants are briefly but well described, with information on origin, flower color and shape, and appearance of leaves. Sells supplies as well. (1993)
📖 Catalog: $1, OV, SS:5-9, $10m
✪ Nursery: All year, by appointment only

Wildwood Farm
10300 Sonoma Highway
Kenwood, CA 95452
Sara & Ricardo Monte
(707) 833-1161

Plants
Offers a nice selection of **Japanese maples** as well as a few other ornamental trees and dwarf and large conifers. Each plant is well described. (1977)
📖 Catalog: $2d, SS:2-6,10-11, $25m, bn
✪ Nursery: All year, Tu-Su, call ahead in winter
❀ Garden: April-October, Tu-Su

Wilkerson Mill Gardens
9595 Wilkerson Mill Road
Palmetto, GA 30268
Elizabeth Dean & Gene Griffith
(770) 463-9717, 463-2200
Fax: (770) 463-9717

Plants ∞ **Books**
Specializes in **hydrangeas** - offering cultivars of paniculatas, quercifolias, arborescens, serratas and mopheads. Also a few climbers. Some varieties in short supply, but a great source for the hydrangea fancier! Great list! They also have a catalog of trees, shrubs, perennials and vines ($3d). Cannot ship to AK, AZ, CA, WA, OR, HI, ID, NM or NV. (1989)
📖 Catalog: $2d, SS:9-5, $25m, bn
✪ Nursery: March-June, Sept.-Nov., Tu-Su
❀ Garden: April, June, call ahead

Willhite Seed Co.
P.O. Box 23
Poolville, TX 76487-0023
Robyn Coffey
(817) 599-8656, (800) 828-1840
Fax: (817) 599-5843

Seeds ∞ **Supplies**
Color catalog features **watermelons, melons, pumpkins huge and small**, and a broad line of **garden vegetables** -- all very well described. Broad selection of corn, tomatoes, cowpeas, peppers, cucumbers, gourds and squash, including many favorite old varieties. Varieties especially suited to the South, with some from France and the Indian subcontinent. (1920)
📖 Catalog: Free, R&W, CAN/OV, CC

Nancy Wilson Speces & Miniature Narcissus
6525 Briceland-Thorn Road
Garberville, CA 95542
Nancy Wilson
(707) 923-2407
Fax: (707) 923-2407
E-mail: nwilson@asis.com

Bulbs
A very small nursery specializing in **species and miniature narcissus**. Each well described, but stock is limited; these are real collectors' items. She is looking for collectors willing to trade unusual items and wants to create a gene bank and recover old varieties. Delightful plants! (1980)
📖 Catalog: $1d, CAN/OV, SS:8-10, $10m, bn
❀ Garden: February-April, by appointment only

Wimberlyway Gardens

See Daylily Discounters.

Wind River Seed
3075 Lane 51-1/2
Manderson, WY 82432
Claire Gabriel & Richard A. Dunne
(307) 568-3361
Fax: (307) 568-3364
E-mail: wrs@trib.com
Web: www.mallwest.com/WRSEED

Seeds
Specializes in seed of reclamation plants: **grasses, legumes, shrubs** and **trees** for Western projects. Also offers a Wyoming Wildflower mix, and will custom mix for your situation. Do your studying first, there are no plant descriptions. Formerly known as Absaroka Seed. (1983)
📖 Catalog: Long SASE, R&W, CAN, CC, $50m, bn/cn

Windrose Ltd.
1093 Mill Road
Pen Argyl, PA 18072-9670
M. Nigel & Lisa Wright
(610) 588-1037
Fax: (610) 599-0968
E-mail: nigel1765@aol.com
Web: trine.com/GardenNet/Windrose/

Plants
Specializing in unusual **trees and shrubs** which are often hard to find because they don't transplant well; Windrose is growing them in deep treepots. Offers oaks, hickories, horse chestnuts, species maples, birches and some fine flowering trees and shrubs. Each is briefly described. (1992)
📖 Catalog: $3d, R&W, CC, SS:2-11, $20m, bn
❂ Nursery: All year, W-Su, by appointment only
❀ Garden: May-October, by appointment only

Windy Oaks Aquatics
W 377 S 10677 Betts Road
Eagle, WI 53119-0068
Marilyn Buscher
(414) 594-3033
Fax: (414) 594-3033
E-mail: windyoaks@pitnet.net

Plants ℘ Books ℘ Supplies
Small nursery specializing in **pond and bog plants**: hardy waterlilies and marginal plants, some tropical marginal plants, koi and water gardening supplies and books. Nice selection, no plant descriptions. (1982)
📖 Catalog: $1d($2 CAN), R&W, CAN, SS:W, bn
❂ Nursery: By appointment only
❀ Garden: April-September, call ahead

Wooden Shoe Bulb Company
33814 S. Meridian Road
Woodburn, OR 97071
Iverson Family
(503) 634-2243, (800) 711-2006
Fax: (503) 634-2710
Web: woodenshoe.com

Bulbs
Here's a source of **tulips, daffodils and other bulbs** which seems to grow their bulbs in Oregon; they have a local Tulip Festival in the spring, and sell cut tulips and other blooms by mail in the spring. Each variety is very briefly described. (1985)
📖 Catalog: Free, R&W, CAN, CC, SS:9-10, bn/cn
❂ Nursery: February-April, Sept.-October, daily, call ahead
❀ Garden: March-April, daily, call ahead

Woodland Iris Gardens
2405 Woodland Avenue
Modesto, CA 95358
Gordon & Lorraine Nicholson
(209) 578-4184

Plants
Offer mostly tall bearded **iris**, at quite reasonable prices; they also grow newer varieties from well-known hybridizers. They list a few historic iris as well as arilbreds, and miniature tall beardeds.
📖 Catalog: $1, CC, SS:7-9, $20m
❂ Nursery: April-May, daily
❀ Garden: April, daily

Woodlanders, Inc.
1128 Colleton Avenue
Aiken, SC 29801
Robt. & Julia Mackintosh, Robt. McCartney
(803) 648-7522
Fax: (803) 648-7522

Plants ∞ **Books**
A collectors' list of **Southeastern native trees, vines, shrubs, ferns, ground covers and perennials** and new or hard-to-find exotics; briefly described, with sources of further information. Looking up the plants is well worth the trouble, the list contains many treasures. Also sells books on plants and field guides. (1980)
- 📖 Catalog: $2($3 OV), CAN/OV, SS:10-3, $15m, bn
- ✪ Nursery: All year, M-F, by appointment only
- ✿ Garden: March-May, by appointment only

Woodside Gardens
1191 Egg & I Road
Chimacum, WA 98325
Pamela West
(360) 732-4754
Fax: (360) 732-4754
E-mail: woodside@olympus.net

Plants ∞ **Books**
Offers a very broad selection of **perennials**: asters, campanulas, dianthus, nepetas, salvias, violas, scented geraniums, many lavenders, oreganos, rosemarys, santolinas, thymes and much more. Each plant is well described. Also offers a number of books on plants and gardening. (1993)
- 📖 Catalog: $2, CC, SS:4-5,9-10, bn/cn
- ✪ Nursery: April-September, Tu-Su, by appointment only

Worcester County Horticultural Society
Tower Hill Botanic Garden
11 French Drive
Boylston, MA 01505-0598
(508) 869-6111
Fax: (508) 869-0314

Plants
Maintains a preservation orchard, from which they offer **scions of heirloom apple varieties**; over 100 pre-twentieth century varieties. Here's your chance to get 'Sops of Wine,' 'Crow Egg,' 'Utter,' 'Pomme Grise,' 'Esopus Spitzenburg' and other tasties.
- 📖 Catalog: Long SASE, SS:3-4, $10m
- ✿ Garden: Preservation orchard, April-October, daily

Wrenwood of Berkeley Springs
Route 4, Box 361
Berkeley Springs, WV 25411
Flora Hackimer
(304) 258-3071
Web: wvweb.com/www/wrenwood

Plants
Large selection of **herbs, perennials, scented geraniums, sedums and rock garden plants**, listed in an informative catalog. Many thymes, dianthus, salvias, oreganos, mints, basils and other temptations; many herbs are also wonderful garden perennials. No shipping to AZ, CA, HI, OR or WA. (1981)
- 📖 Catalog: $2.50, R&W, CC, SS:3-11, $36m, cn/bn
- ✪ Nursery: All year, call ahead
- ✿ Garden: June-September, call ahead

Wrightman Alpines
1503 Napperton Dr., R.R. 3
Kerwood, ON, Canada N0M 2B0
Harvey Wrightman
(519) 247-3751
Fax: (519) 247-3751

Plants
Small nursery which specializes in **alpine plants**, "especially new introductions from seed collections in the American West and Central Asia." A nice selection, with brief plant descriptions; Harvey says the list will change as new introductions become available. (1985)
- 📖 Catalog: $2, US, SS:4-5,9, $40m, bn
- ✪ Nursery: May-June, by appointment only
- ✿ Garden: May-June, by appointment only

Guy Wrinkle Exotic Plants
11610 Addison Street
North Hollywood, CA 91601
Guy Wrinkle
(310) 670-8637
Fax: (310) 670-1427
E-mail: wrinkle@idt.net

Plants ∞ **Bulbs**
Specializes in **collectors' plants** -- caudiciforms, euphorbias, species orchids and a large selection of cycads and rare succulents from trips to Africa and Mexico. Some are rare and in short supply; no plant descriptions. Guy has written "Cycads: Their Cultivation and Propagation." ($6ppd., $7 OV) (1980)
- 📖 Catalog: $1d($2 OV), R&W, CAN/OV, CC, SS:W, $15m, bn
- ✪ Nursery: All year, by appointment only

York Hill Farm
18 Warren Street
Georgetown, MA 01833
Darlyn C. Springer
(508) 352-6560
E-mail: yorkhillma@worldnet.att.net

Plants
A specialty nursery offering the "very newest" in **Japanese and Siberian iris**, and **hostas and daylilies**, with some other iris, companion perennials and ornamental grasses; most plants well described. Some of the Japanese iris and daylilies are their own introductions. (1990)
- 📖 Catalog: $1.50, SS:4-5,9-10, $25m, bn
- ✪ Nursery: June-September, Th-Sa, call ahead
- ✿ Garden: June-September, Th-Sa, call ahead

Roy Young, Seeds
23, Westland Chase, West Winch
King's Lynn, Norfolk, England PE33 0QH
Roy & Sheila Young

Seeds
"List of approximately 2,000 different **cactus and succulent** seeds obtained from either my own hand-pollinated plants or direct from habitat. Includes a guaranteed accurately named selection of every known **lithops**." CITES permits are required for some seeds, indicated on list. (1984)
📖 Catalog: $2(US Bills) or 3 IRC, R&W, OV, $10m, bn

Yucca Do Nursery
P.O. Box 104
Hempstead, TX 77445
Carl Schoenfeld
(409) 826-4580

Plants
Alas for Western gardeners! No more of those new, exciting Mexican plants to the Pacific Coast! Yucca Do will be issuing two catalogs; #1 will list **bulbous plants** that they will ship all over the world. Catalog #2 will list **plants from Texas and Mexico**; these will only be shipped to those Southeastern states that have no fire ant quarantine restrictions.
📖 Catalog: $2 each(see notes), $25m, bn

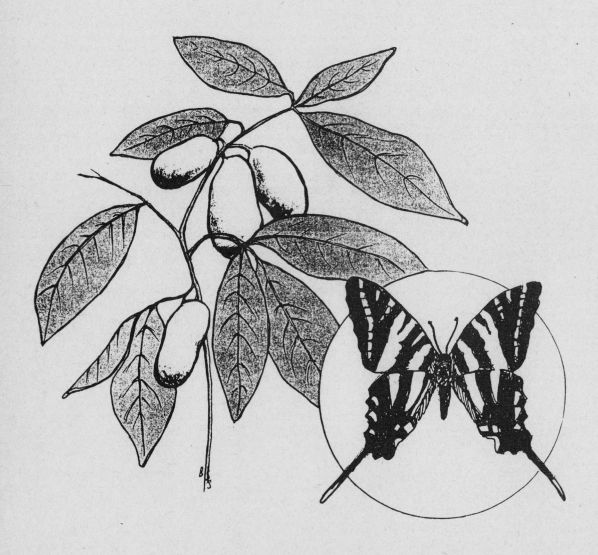

© Tripple Brook Farm
  Artist: Betty Still Schaffer

GARDEN SUPPLIERS AND SERVICES

Sources of garden supplies are listed alphabetically. Their specialties (furniture, ornaments, supplies, tools, books, and services) are indicated at the top of the notes on catalogs.

See the Index section for:

K. Product Sources Index: an index of suppliers and services listed by specialties. This index also includes nurseries and seed companies that offer products or services.

OTHER SOURCES OF GARDEN SUPPLIES AND SERVICES

For tools and garden ornaments, keep your eye on garage sales, salvage yards and dumps — and always be alert for old houses and gardens being demolished for "progress." These are good sources of old bricks and paving stones, gates, fences, trellises, benches and more. Sometimes you can strike a deal with the wreckers and haul it away yourself, as I did with a thousand bricks on the hottest day of the year!

For books, see the many sources of new and used books listed in this section. Also, it's wise to check used bookstores and the remainder tables of new bookstores routinely. Many of the societies listed in Section D sell books to their members, some of these are highly specialized books hard to find elsewhere.

For garden tours, also check the tour programs of horticultural and plant societies; many have excellent offerings. You might consider joining a tour of an overseas society to make new gardening friends. Several horticultural magazines, such as *Pacific Horticulture* and *Horticulture*, offer tours to their readers, and so do several specialist nurseries.

A table of the symbols and abbreviations used in this book
appears inside the front and back covers.

A & L Analytical Laboratories, Inc.
411 N. Third Street
Memphis, TN 38105-2723
Dr. Richard Large
(901) 527-2780, (800) 264-4522
Fax: (901) 526-1031
E-mail: allabs@baste.magibox.net
Web: www.al_labs.com

Services
A **testing laboratory** which will perform soil tests by mail; they also perform plant analysis, pesticide, fertilizer and feed analysis, water and wastewater analysis, as well as other tests. (1971)
📖 Catalog: $5($8 OV), R&W, CAN/OV, CC

A-1 Unique Insect Control
5504 Sperry Drive
Citrus Heights, CA 95621-7326
Jeanne Houston
(916) 961-7945
Fax: (916) 967-7082

Books 🔊 Supplies
Offers several types of **beneficial insects**: ladybugs, green lacewings, trichogramma wasps, praying mantis, fly parasites, whitefly parasites, predatory mites, mealybug predators and earthworms. Their flyer is helpful and offers some books. Formerly called Unique Insect Control. (1980)
📖 Catalog: Free, R&W, CAN/OV

Abracadata, Ltd.
P.O. Box 2440
Eugene, OR 97402-2440
Josephine Logan
(541) 342-3030, (800) 451-4871
Fax: (541) 683-1925
E-mail: abracadata@poboxes.com
Web: www.abracadata.com

Services
"Design your own home landscape," a **computer program** that draws landscape plans, positions trees, shrubs and hard features, allows you to view plans from different angles and plants at four different sizes. They also have a program for vegetable gardens, called Sprout!, and a railway design program in 8 different scales to help you design your garden railway.
📖 Catalog: Free, R&W, CAN/OV, CC

Adams & Adkins
104 South Early Street
Alexandria, VA 22304
Dorcas Adkins & Bob Adams
(703) 823-3404
Fax: (703) 823-5367

Ornaments
Offers the Water Flute(TM), a self-contained **Japanese style fountain** which comes in several sizes.They also make self-contained fountains in stone and verdigris -- all are charming, perfect for courtyard or patio. (1983)
📖 Catalog: Free, R&W, CAN/OV, CC
⊙ Shop: All year, M-F, call ahead

Adirondack Designs
350 Cypress Street
Fort Bragg, CA 95437
George Griffith, Mgr.
(707) 964-4940, (800) 222-0343
Fax: (707) 964-2701
E-mail: adirondack@webaxxess.com
Web: www.webaxxess.com/adirondack

Furniture
Sell the **Adirondack chair**, a garden classic, as well as a similar loveseat, sun lounge and swing, potting bench and side and coffee tables; made of California redwood for durability. All are beautifully made by developmentally disabled adults for a non-profit corporation. (1981)
📖 Catalog: Free, CAN/OV, CC
⊙ Shop: All year, M-F

AgAccess
P.O. Box 2008
Davis, CA 95617-2008
Karen Van Epen
(916) 756-7177
Fax: (916) 756-7188
E-mail: agaccess@davis.com
Web: www.mother.com/agaccess

Books
A bookstore in Davis, offers **books about agriculture and horticulture**. They no longer publish a big catalog, but you are encouraged to send your "wish list." They also publish some books, including "Healthy Harvest: A Global Directory of Sustainable Agriculture & Horticultural Organizations."
📖 Catalog: See notes, CAN/OV, CC
⊙ Shop: All year, M-Sa

Alternative Garden Supply, Inc.
P.O. Box 662
Cary, IL 60013-0662
David & Sondi Ittel
(847) 516-4776, (800) 444-2837
Fax: (847) 516-1655
E-mail: brewgrow@ma.net

Furniture ∾ **Supplies** ∾ **Tools**
The company has changed its focus to **hydroponic systems**; offers a good selection of plant lights, growing supplies, fertilizers and insect controls for the indoor grower. Have added home brewing supplies. Have five retail locations in the Midwest called Brew & Grow, call for locations.
📖 Catalog: $2d, CC
☼ Shop: All year, daily

Amaranth Stoneware
P.O. Box 266
52 Queen Street
Kingston, ON, Canada K7L 4V8
Paul & Marilyn King
(613) 541-1156, (800) 465-5444
Fax: (613) 541-0799

Ornaments ∾ **Supplies**
Stoneware and terra cotta **garden signs** for herb and vegetable gardens; available for a number of popular plants, as well as for "weeds," "cat crossing" and "thank you for not smoking." Other choices available. Accept only Visa credit cards. (1986)
📖 Catalog: Free, R&W, US/OV, CC
☼ Shop: All year, M-F

American Arborist Supplies
882 South Matlack Street, Unit A
West Chester, PA 19382
Alyce & Richard Miller
(610) 430-1214, (800) 441-8381
Fax: (610) 430-8560
E-mail: aas@inet.net
Web: www.arborist.com

Books ∾ **Supplies** ∾ **Tools**
Specializes in **tools and equipment for tree workers**: fat catalog with everything one could need: chainsaws, pruning tools, tree climbing gear and safety equipment, sprayers, and other tools, as well as books on arboriculture. They also offer a **rain barrel**. (1967)
📖 Catalog: $4d, CAN/OV, CC
☼ Shop: All year, M-F

The American Botanist, Booksellers
P.O. Box 532
1103 West Truitt
Chillicothe, IL 61523-0532
Keith Crotz
(309) 274-5254
Fax: (309) 274-6143
E-mail: agbook@mtco.com

Books ∾ **Services**
Specialize in **rare, used and out-of-print books** in all areas of agriculture, horticulture and botany. Also offer collection development and book search services and appraisals, and will buy book collections in their field. Have published fine replicas of historical 19th century books. (1983)
📖 Catalog: $2d, R&W, CAN/OV, CC
☼ Shop: All year, M,W,F, call ahead

American Standard Co.
P.O. Box 325
157 Water Street (Southington)
Plantsville, CT 06479-0325
Nathaniel & Stella Florian
(860) 628-9643, (800) 275-3618
Fax: (860) 628-6036
E-mail: sales@florianratchetcut.com
Web: www.florianratchetcut.com

Tools
Florian Ratchet-Cut(R) **pruning tools** with ratchet action have increased leverage and need less hand-power; they offer hand pruners, loppers and pole pruners. I have a pair of the hand pruners and love them -- they're sharp and lightweight, and really do all the work I ask of them.
📖 Catalog: Free, R&W, CAN/OV, CC, $30m
☼ Shop: All year, M-F

American Weather Enterprises
P.O. Box 1383
Media, PA 19063-1383
Ti Richard Sanders
(610) 565-1232, (800) 293-2555
Fax: (610) 892-0277
E-mail: trsbone@aol.com
Web: americanweather.com

Books ∾ **Supplies**
A nice selection of **weather instruments**: hygrometers, thermometers, barometers, anemometers, recording equipment, remote weather stations, sundials, weathervanes and home weather stations. Also offer books on weather and computer software for weather forecasting and hurricane tracking. (1980)
📖 Catalog: Free, CAN/OV, CC

Anderson Design
P.O. Box 4057
Bellingham, WA 98227-4057
Rick Anderson
(360) 650-1587, (800) 947-7697
Fax: (360) 650-0733
E-mail: andesign@pacificrim.net
Web: www.woodcraftnetwork.com/anderson.htm

Ornaments
Offer handsome Western red cedar **garden arches and trellises**, in a variety of styles and sizes, as well as fencing, lattice panels, and gates. During the winter they have special prices to keep the workers busy.
📖 Catalog: $2d, CAN/OV

Aquacide Company
1627 9th Street
White Bear Lake, MN 55110-0748
Francis P. Markoe
(612) 429-6742, (800) 328-9350
Fax: (612) 429-0563
E-mail: 76652.171@compuserve.com

Supplies
Offer a variety of **products to control algae and underwater weeds** in lakes and ponds; supposedly harmless to fish. Another product, Mosquito Beater, is a safe dry powder which keeps mosquitoes away for days. They also sell special tools for cutting and gathering weeds from ponds. (1956)
📖 Catalog: Free, CC

Aquamonitor
P.O. Box 327
Huntington, NY 11743-0327
Robert & Velma Whitener
(516) 427-5664

Supplies
Complete **mist irrigation systems** and/or automatic controls to monitor soil moisture for propagation in greenhouses; useful for any greenhouse plants, seedlings or cuttings which need constant moisture. Because the system monitors the soil, it waters when needed, not on an automatic timer. (1971)
📖 Catalog: Free, R&W, CAN/OV, $15m

Arbico, Inc.
P.O. Box 4247
18701 N. Lago del Oro Parkway
Tucson, AZ 85738-4247
Rick & Sheri Frey
(520) 825-9785, (800) 827-2847
Fax: (520) 825-2038
E-mail: ARBICO@aol.com
Web: www.usit.net/BICONET

Supplies
Specialize in **"sustainable environmental alternatives"** and offer **organic growing supplies**, beneficial insects, fertilizers, pest barriers and traps, and free consultation to customers. Informative catalog. (1979)
📖 Catalog: Free, R&W, CAN/OV, CC
✪ Shop: All year, M-F, Sa-Su by appointment only

Arborist Supply House, Inc.
P.O. Box 23607
4301 NE 13th Terrace
Fort Lauderdale, FL 33334
Geraldine Hoyt
(954) 561-9527, (800) 749-9528
Fax: (954) 561-9550

Books ☜ Supplies ☜ Tools
Offers specialized **equipment for arborists**, some of which is also useful to less specialized folk: pruning tools, safety equipment, deep-root barriers and a tree guard to protect from weed-whackers. Also sells books for tree workers, and books on tropical plants. (1984)
📖 Catalog: Free, R&W, CAN/OV, CC
✪ Shop: All year, M-Sa, call ahead

Archiva
944 Madison Avenue
New York, NY 10021
Joan Gers & Cynthia Conigliaro
(212) 439-9194
Fax: (212) 744-1626

Books
This bookstore calls itself "The Decorative Arts Bookshop," and they offer a broad selection of **new and used books** on architecture, interior design and gardening and garden design.
📖 Catalog: Free, CAN/OV, CC
✪ Shop: All year, daily

Avant Horticultural Products
5755 Balfrey Drive
West Palm Beach, FL 33413
C. Wyclif Head II
(561) 683-0171
Fax: (561) 683-0171

Supplies
Manufacturers of **reacted liquid plant foods**, which they claim are more immediately available to plants. There are several formulas -- for roses, blooming plants and agricultural crops, growth hormones, and a formula compatible with fungicides and insecticides. Avant Thermo-Chem offers winter protection to plants and is an antidesiccant. (1985)
📖 Catalog: Free, CAN, CC, $10m

Avian Aquatics(TM), Inc.
6 Point Circle
Lewes, DE 19958
William A. Fintel
(302) 645-8643, (800) 788-6478
Fax: (302) 645-5898

Ornaments
Sell a variety of **bird baths, misters, drippers and recirculating bird ponds**, all shown in a color catalog. They also sell videos on attracting birds to water. Ask for the retail price list with the catalog. (1990)
📖 Catalog: Free, CAN/OV, CC, $35m

David Bacon, Fine Handcrafted Furniture
16698 Fritillary Way
Grass Valley, CA 95945
David Bacon
(916) 273-8889
Fax: (916) 273-7928

Ornaments
A one-man woodworking shop that builds **window boxes and planters** of cedar, with liners to make them last longer. You can order an extra liner so that you can whip the tired one out and replace it with one that's fresh and ready to dazzle. (1977)
📖 Catalog: $1d, R&W, CAN, $45m

Baker's Lawn Ornaments
570 Berlin Plank Road
Somerset, PA 15501-2413
Valerie & Michael Baker
(814) 445-7028

Ornaments
Manufacture and sell **gazing globes**, a Victorian garden ornament popular in period garden restorations or used just for fun. They are either 10 or 12 inches in diameter, and come in red, green, blue, teal, gold, silver and purple.
▯ Catalog: Long SASE, R&W, CAN, $23m
☼ Shop: All year, M-Sa

Bamboo Gardens of Washington
5016 192nd Place N.E.
196th Ave. N.E. and S.R. 202
Redmond, WA 98053-4602
Jeannine Florance
(206) 868-5166
Fax: (206) 868-5360

Supplies
This bamboo nursery sells **bamboo fencing, fence supplies & poles** by mail, as well as **water basins and water pipes**. They also sell bamboo plants at the nursery. (1986)
▯ Catalog: Free, R&W, CAN, CC
☼ Shop: Spring-Fall, daily; call ahead in Winter

Carol Barnett, Books
3562 N.E. Liberty Street
Portland, OR 97211-7248
Carol Barnett
(503) 282-7036

Books ∞ **Services**
Specializes in **used, rare and out-of-print books** on gardens, horticulture and botany, with brief descriptions of contents as well as notes on condition. Occasionally reprints small books of historical horticultural interest, such as "Pearson on the Orchard House, 1867." She will also do book searches if you send her a "wish list." (1983)
▯ Catalog: Free, CAN/OV

The Basket Case
P.O. Box 7848
West Trenton, NJ 09628-7848
Barbara Strange
(609) 883-5347
Fax: (609) 883-5347
E-mail: TBCBarbara@aol.com

Supplies
A very small company which makes beautiful and affordable **baskets**, each handcrafted in maple, which is strong and durable. They come in a variety of sizes and styles, including harvest baskets, trugs, picnic baskets, even a lap desk and laundry baskets. (1992)
▯ Catalog: Free, R&W, CAN/OV, CC
☼ Shop: By appointment only

Beaver River Associates
P.O. Box 94
West Kingston, RI 02892-0094
Joshua Nelson
(401) 782-8747
Fax: (401) 782-8747
E-mail: riwiggler@aol.com
Web: www.MerchantsBay.com/BeaverRiver

Supplies
Offers **redworms** and **worm composting systems**; literature gives a good perspective on how and why to do it -- apparently kids love worm farms! They also offer PeatFree(TM) **coir fiber**, a substitute for peat moss in compressed bricks, and **worm castings**. (1989)
▯ Catalog: Free, R&W, CAN/OV, CC

Beckner & Beckner
15 Portola Avenue
San Rafael, CA 94903-4214
Joe & Ruth Beckner
(415) 472-4203, (800) 582-6676
E-mail: 105013.105@compuserve.com
Web: ourworld.compuserve.com/homepages/Ruth_Beckner

Tools
The Beckners have invented the "Compost Air(R)," a tool which fits onto a power drill and **turns compost** in a flash. (1995)
▯ Catalog: Long SASE, R&W, CAN/OV, CC, $20m
☼ Shop: M-F, by appointment only

Bell's Book Store
536 Emerson Street
Palo Alto, CA 94301
Mrs. Herbert Bell
(415) 323-7822

Books
Offer a good selection of **new, used and out-of-print books** on gardening. They have a good annotated book list on "Old Garden Roses" (call or write for price), but no regular catalog. Send a "wish list" to see if they have what you want. (1935)
▯ Catalog: See notes, CAN/OV, CC
☼ Shop: All year, M-Sa

Benner's Gardens, Inc.
P.O. Box 875
Bala Cynwyd, PA 19004-0875
Al & David Benner
(800) 753-4660
Fax: (215) 477-9429
E-mail: Benners@erols.com
Web: trine.com/GardenNet/DeerControl/

Supplies
Offer black plastic **mesh deer barrier**; strong yet almost invisible a few feet away, it comes in two weights. Also offer a mesh netting to protect individual plants, and "Deer Off" to spray on plants for temporary relief from browsing.
📖 Catalog: Free($2 OV), CAN/OV, CC

Berry Hill Limited
75 Burwell Road
St. Thomas, ON, Canada N5P 3R5
Ann Foster
(519) 631-0480, (800) 668-3072 (CAN only)
Fax: (519) 631-8935

Books ∞ **Supplies** ∞ **Tools**
Here's a wonderful old-time **farm equipment and country kitchen** catalog: full of canning supplies, equipment for dairy and poultry yards, garden bells, weathervanes, a cider press, wine making equipment and tools and equipment for the garden. They also sell many practical "how-to" books. (1948)
📖 Catalog: $2(C$7 OV), US/OV, CC, $10m
⊙ Shop: All year, M-Sa

Best Tag
8316 N. Lombard, Suite 303
Portland, OR 97203
Louise Hope & John Zey
(503) 621-3484
Fax: (503) 652-2366
E-mail: besttag@besttag.com
Web: www.besttag.com/besttag

Supplies
Offer **anodized aluminum plant labels**, the kind you can write on with pencil and which can be read for years. They come in two sizes, and either size costs $19 a hundred, $86 for five hundred. They liked them so well they started making them themselves when they were no longer available in this country.
📖 Catalog: Free, R&W, CAN/OV, $19m

Better Yield Insects
23163 Gladhill Lane
St. Clair Shores, MI 48080
Patricia Coristine & Joyce Collins
(810) 777-4555, (800) 662-6562
Fax: (401) 792-8058

Supplies
Supplier of **beneficial insects**: whitefly parasites, spider mite predators, aphid predators, thrip predators and nematodes. They also sell sticky traps, strips and insect barriers. No shipping to HI. Canadians can contact them at 1302 Highway 2, RR 3, Belle River, ON N0R 1A0. (1977)
📖 Catalog: Free, CAN, CC, SS:W
⊙ Shop: All year, daily, call ahead

B. L. Bibby Books
1225 Sardine Creek Road
Gold Hill, OR 97525-9730
George A. Bibby
(541) 855-1621

Books
Offers **used and out-of-print books** on plants and horticulture, gardening, flower arranging and other natural history subjects. Price of catalog is for five or six issues in one year, send long SASE for one list. (1963)
📖 Catalog: $3d, CAN/OV

Dorothy Biddle Service
HC 01, Box 900
Greeley, PA 18425-9799
Lynne Dodson
(717) 226-3239
Fax: (717) 226-0349
E-mail: dbsfrog@ptd.net

Books ∞ **Supplies** ∞ **Tools**
A broad selection of **supplies and equipment for flower arrangers** which would be useful to all who cut and bring flowers indoors. Books on arranging and drying flowers, tools, and some houseplant growing supplies. (1936)
📖 Catalog: $.50, R&W, CAN/OV, CC

Bio-Gard Agronomics
P.O. Box 4477
Falls Church, VA 22044-4477
Dr. Andrew J. Welebir
(703) 356-5690, (800) 673-8502
Fax: (703) 536-1094
E-mail: CALCIUM@aol.com
Web: www.biogard.com

Supplies
Offer their Calcium-25(R), a completely **organic foliar fertilizer**, which they say will increase yields 20% to 50%, and can be used on ornamental plants as well as food crops. (1987)
📖 Catalog: Free, R&W, CAN/OV

BioLogic Company
P.O. Box 177
Willow Hill, PA 17271-0177
Dr. Albert Pye
(717) 349-2789
Fax: (717) 349-2789
E-mail: PyeAlber@Epix.Net

Supplies
Sells Scanmask -- a strain of **beneficial, insect-eating nematodes** to control soil and boring pest insects such as black vine weevils, white grubs, cutworms, caterpillars and fly maggots; harmless to beneficial insects. Let them know if you are a home gardener or commercial grower. (1985)
📖 Catalog: Long SASE, CAN, CC

BioTherm Hydronic, Inc.
P.O. Box 750967
Petaluma, CA 94975-0957
Jim Rearden & Mike Muchow
(707) 794-9660, (800) 438-4328
Fax: (707) 794-9663
E-mail: biotherm@wco.com

Supplies
Manufactures and sells **heating systems for greenhouses**, mostly for warming benches by radiant heat. While most of their systems are for commercial growers and not inexpensive, they may have just what you need for your smaller greenhouse. (1989)
📖 Catalog: Free, R&W, CAN/OV, CC

Blue Planet, Inc.
305 Monmouth Avenue
Spring Lake, NJ 07762-1128
Frank Chester

Supplies
Manufactures the Composift **composting machine**, which tumbles and sifts compost, and which is powered by electricity, eliminating the effort of turning the drum. It will hold 33 cubic feet of raw materials. (1992)
📖 Catalog: Free, R&W, CAN, CC

Bodoh Quartz, Inc.
1222 4th Street
Key West, FL 33040
Ron Bodoh & Larry Henke
(305) 295-9002

Ornaments
A group of four artists who make **garden ornaments** out of recycled copper, brass and iron. They include whimsical sculptures, lanterns, bird houses, wind chimes, perfect crystal globes in several sizes, even some jewelry. Shown in color photographs. (1987)
📖 Catalog: $4d, R&W, CAN

Bookfinders General, Inc.
Box G, Madison Square Station
New York, NY 10159-1056
(212) 689-0772
Fax: (212) 481-0552
E-mail: bkfindgen@aol.com

Books ෨ Services
A free **book-finding service**: send your "wish list," and they will search for any book and send you a price quote when they find it. They have a limited number of books on hand, so call before ordering from the catalog to be sure the listed title is available. (1963)
📖 Catalog: $1, CAN/OV, $10m

BowBends
P.O. Box 900
Bolton, MA 01740-0900
Rogers Family
(508) 779-6464
Fax: (508) 779-2272

Ornaments
Offer **gazebos and garden structures** of classic design; the Belvedeary can be finished in several styles, even cut in half for a bay window. Also sell a domed temple, arbors, a pergola, changing structures, a Japanese tea house, bridges up to 40 feet, even a dog house. All very elegant. (1971)
📖 Catalog: $5($10 OV), R&W, CAN/OV

Bozeman Bio-Tech

See Planet Natural.

Brew & Grow

See Alternative Garden Supply, Inc.

Bridgeworks
432 N. Columbia Street
Covington, LA 70435
Paul Swain
(504) 893-7933
Fax: (504) 893-1249
E-mail: pdswain-bridgeworks@juno.com

Ornaments
Builders of **bridges** in several designs, including Monet's bridge at Giverny; you can have them customized to your length in even number lengths from 8 to 20 feet if the standard sizes won't fit your needs. Also make benches, but I haven't seen the designs. (1991)
📖 Catalog: Free, R&W, CAN/OV

Andy Brinkley Studio
P.O. Box 10282
4904 Highway 127 South
Hickory, NC 28603
Andy Brinkley
(704) 462-1137
Fax: (704) 462-4647

Ornaments
Offers a variety of **garden sculptures and fountains** with plant, animal and flower themes; most are made of brass, copper or bronze, some with verdigris finish. The animals are fanciful, and the flower and tree sculptures are very handsome; some can be used as light fixtures. (1976)
📖 Catalog: 3 FCS(3 IRC OV), R&W, CAN, CC
✪ Shop: All year, M-F, call ahead

Warren F. Broderick -- Books
P.O. Box 124
Lansingburgh, NY 12182-0124
Warren F. Broderick
(518) 235-4041(eves & weekends)

Books
Select stock of **used, rare, and out-of-print books** on garden design and history, plant monographs, general gardening books, garden art and architecture and botanical illustration. Catalog is mailed in the fall. (1977)
📖 Catalog: $2($4 OV), R&W, CAN/OV

Bronwood Worm Gardens
P.O. Box 69
Bronwood, GA 31726-0069
Jerry and Priscilla Seymour
(912) 995-5994

Supplies
Specialize in **bed-run redworms** in mixed sizes for composting and gardening; they also have gray nightcrawlers (Georgia wigglers). All shipments are by Air Mail or UPS, March through November, and include instructions for doing your own worm farming.
📖 Catalog: Long SASE, R&W, CAN, CC, $16m

Brooks Books
P.O. Box 21473
Concord, CA 94521-0473
Philip & Martha Nesty
(510) 672-4566
Fax: (510) 672-3338
E-mail: brooksbk@interloc.com

Books ∽ **Services**
Sells **horticultural and botanical books; new, used and out-of-print** and **rare**. Specializes in cacti, succulents, ornamental horticulture, floras and botanicals, plant monographs, fruit, Australian and South African plants, trees and shrubs. Offers a search service; buys book collections. (1986)
📖 Catalog: $1, R&W, CAN/OV, CC
✪ Shop: By appointment only

Builders Booksource
1817 Fourth Street
Berkeley, CA 94710
George & Sally Kiskaddon
(510) 845-6874, (800) 843-2028
Fax: (510) 845-7051
E-mail: booksite@earthlink.net
Web: www.buildersbooksite.com

Books
Very broad selection of **books on architecture and design, construction, interior design, landscaping and gardening** -- everything from start to finish; the store is a delight! They have a branch store at Ghirardelli Square in San Francisco, (415) 440-5773. Produce a yearly catalog and send irregular newsletters about new books.
📖 Catalog: Free, CAN/OV, CC
✪ Shop: All year, daily

Bulb Savers
P.O. Box 3024
Princeton, NJ 08543-3024
Alicia A. Magee
(609) 883-6250, (800) 472-3284

Supplies
Offers a **mesh bag with attached label** for planting and identifying bulbs when the time comes to find them again. They come in two depths, 8 inches and 16 inches, and expand to hold quite large bulbs or groups of small bulbs.
📖 Catalog: Free, R&W, CAN/OV, CC, $25m

Burford Brothers
P. O. Box 367
Monroe, VA 24574-0367
Thomas Burford
(804) 929-4950
Fax: (804) 929-4950

Books ∽ **Supplies** ∽ **Tools**
Long listed as a nursery selling a broad selection of fruit trees, Burford Brothers has stopped selling trees, but now sells **orchard supplies, grafting supplies, books on fruit production** and Felco pruning equipment. Tom also consults on fruit growing and designs and plants orchards for homes and historic sites.
📖 Catalog: Free, R&W

A. C. Burke & Co.
2554 Lincoln Blvd., Suite 1058
Marina Del Rey, CA 90291-5082
Andrew Burke
(310) 574-2770
Fax: (310) 574-2771
Web: www.acburke.com

Books ∽ **Supplies**
"Our goal is to bring user-friendly technology into the garden." They specialize in **videos, CD-Roms, software, books** and accessories for the garden; cover a range of subjects from vegetables to bonsai to wildlife in the garden. (1991)
📖 Catalog: Free($2 OV), CAN/OV, CC

Calendula Horticultural Books
160 S.W. Alfred Street
Chehalis, WA 98532
Heiko Miles
(360) 740-1784
E-mail: calendula@localaccess.com
Web: www.localaccess.com/calendula/hortbooks.htm

Books
Offers **rare, used and out-of-print books** on flowers and gardens, landscape architecture, flower arranging, pomology, floriculture and wildflowers. Ask for the horticultural catalog; most books are pre-1950. (1987)
📖 Catalog: 1 FCS($1 OV), R&W, CAN/OV

California Bonsai Service
P.O. Box 2037
1908 Marin Drive
Santa Rosa, CA 95405-2037
Ronald Kelley
(707) 525-9684

Books ∽ **Supplies** ∽ **Services**
Offers **bonsai tools, books, growing supplies** and more, including videos on how to do it and very nice display tables for your special bonsai. They'll even take care of your bonsai when you go on vacation. (1986)
📖 Catalog: $1($2 OV), CAN/OV
✪ Shop: All year, by appointment only

Capability's Books
2379 Highway 46
Deer Park, WI 54007-7506
Paulette Rickard
(715) 269-5346
Fax: (715) 269-5531
E-mail: lancelot@win.bright.net
Web: www.garden.com/Capabilitys

Books
A very broad selection of **horticultural and gardening books**, new or recently published in the US or England. They have nearly 1,000 books in 84 categories -- something for any special interest; they will accept credit card orders by Fax from overseas. They also sell videos and computer programs for gardeners. (1978)
📖 Catalog: Free, R&W, CAN/OV, CC
✪ Shop: All year, M-F

Cape Cod Worm Farm
30 Center Avenue
Buzzards Bay, MA 02532
Maggie L. Pipkins
(508) 759-5664
Fax: (508) 759-5664

Supplies
Sells **earthworms and worm castings**; an important ingredient in your garden soil.
📖 Catalog: Free, CAN/OV, SS:W, $19m

Carruth Studio, Inc.
1178 Farnsworth Road
211 Mechanic Street
Waterville, OH 43566
George & Deborah Carruth
(419) 878-5412, (800) 225-1178
Fax: (419) 878-3261

Ornaments
Offer cast concrete and terra cotta **wall plaques, bird feeders, birdbaths, statues, planters and garden accessories.** They say "Plant a smile in your garden." All have a charming, whimsical feeling, some are slyly medieval! Great gifts. No shipping to Taiwan, Korea or Mexico. (1975)
📖 Catalog: Free, R&W, CAN/OV, CC
✪ Shop: All year, M-Sa

Cart Warehouse
P.O. Box 4
Point Arena, CA 95468-0004
Peter Reimuller
(707) 882-2001, (888) 882-2110
Fax: (707) 882-2011

Supplies
Sells major brands of **garden carts** at a discount; brands include Fold-It, Garden Way, Homestead and Carry-It; prices include shipping. (1984)
📖 Catalog: Free

Cascade Greenhouse Supply

See Sunglo Solar Greenhouses.

Charley's Greenhouse Supply
1569 Memorial Highway
Mt. Vernon, WA 98273
Charles & Carol Yaw
(360) 428-2626, (800) 322-4707
Fax: (360) 428-0310
E-mail: cgh@charleysgreenhouse.com
Web: www.charleysgreenhouse.com

Books ∽ **Supplies** ∽ **Tools**
Broad selection of **growing supplies, tools, plant lights, drip** and **misting** systems, shade fabric, **books** and many other items. They also sell **greenhouses** and greenhouse materials and accessories, and have many hobby greenhouses on display on their property. (1975)
📖 Catalog: $2, CAN/OV, CC
✪ Shop: All year, M-Sa

Cieli
P.O. Box 151
La Honda, CA 94020-0151
Joyce Converse
(415) 369-2129
Fax: (415) 369-2082

Ornaments
I've fallen in love with these enchanting **garden fairies** that look as if they came from Edwardian children's books. They're made from recycled aluminum with a slightly luminous finish, and should bring good luck and perfect plants to any garden. Also make hares and dinosaurs. (1989)
📖 Catalog: $2d, R&W, CAN, $20m

Classic & Country Crafts

See Copper Craft Lighting, Inc.

Classic Garden Ornaments, Ltd. (R)
83 Longshadow Lane
Pomona, IL 62975
Charlotte Peters & Daniel Ward
(618) 893-4831
Fax: (618) 893-4833
E-mail: Lngshado@midwest.net

Ornaments
Makers of **garden ornaments** in hand cast reconstituted limestone: planters in a variety of styles, plaques, small statues, and supports for benches; they make the "Longshadow(R) Planters." Attractive, with substantial prices, but would make a striking focal point in a beloved garden. (1989)
📖 Catalog: $5($10 OV), R&W, CAN/OV, CC
✪ Shop: All year, by appointment only

Clothcrafters, Inc.
P.O. Box 176
Elkhart Lake, WI 53020-0176
John F. Wilson
(414) 876-2112, (800) 876-2009
Fax: (800) 876-2009
E-mail: catalog@clothcrafters.com
Web: www.clothcrafters.com

Supplies
Sell **clothing for gardeners**: gloves, kneepads and aprons. In addition, they sell Poly Ban row covers, mosquito netting, and various cloth wares made of cotton for the home and kitchen. (1936)
📖 Catalog: Free, CAN

Commodity Traders International
P.O. Box 6
502 Main Street
Trilla, IL 62469-0006
Charles & Connie Stodden
(217) 235-4322
Fax: (217) 235-3246

Tools
No longer a source of grain and corn seeds, they still offer seed handling equipment, including **seed cleaners**, which a lot of people have asked me about -- here they are!
📖 Catalog: Free

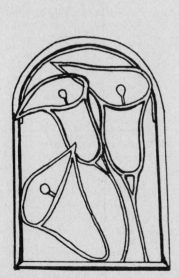

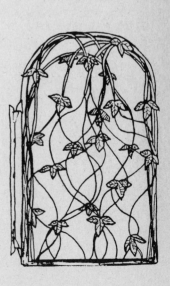

© Copper Gardens
Artist: David Burns

Computer/Management Services
1426 Medinah Court
Arnold, MD 21012
Charles W. Barbour
(410) 757-7429
E-mail: 75020.3275@compuserve.com

Services
Custom **computer programs** for orchid lovers and the nursery trade; both run on DOS or Windows computers. "Orchidata" is software for keeping track of an inventory of orchids; "Collector" makes an inventory of any type of collectible, including plants. Also sales and inventory programs for commercial nurseries. Web site: <www.netins.net/showcase/novacon/cyphaven/chorcmal.htm>
📖 Catalog: Free, CAN/OV, $60m

Cook's Consulting
RD 2, Box 13
Lowville, NY 13367
Peg Cook
(315) 376-3002
Fax: (315) 376-3002

Services
A **soil testing service** for agriculture that also serves home gardeners. They offer organic or chemical fertilizer and soil amendment recommendations depending on the preference of the customer. (1983)
📖 Catalog: Free, CAN

Coopersmith's England
P.O. Box 900
Inverness, CA 94937-0900
Paul Coopersmith
(415) 669-1914
Fax: (415) 669-1942

Services
Offer **garden tours** to England, Scotland, France, Italy and Spain; groups are small, pace is relaxed, with several nights at each country inn or stately home. Most tours seem to include a few historical sites and private gardens; offer a tour of literary England, as well.
📖 Catalog: Free

Copper Craft Lighting
5100-1B Clayton Road, Suite 291
Concord, CA 94521
Sue Siekierski, Pres.
(510) 672-4337
Fax: (510) 672-4337
E-mail: tedpski@hooked.net
Web: www.hooked.net/~tedpski

Ornaments
Makes very handsome **copper landscape lights** in several styles; these lights are on standards for use along paths or near parking areas, and will weather to an attractive patina over time. Somewhat Craftsman-period in style. (1989)
📖 Catalog: Free, R&W, CAN

Copper Gardens
P.O. Box 341
Rough & Ready, CA 95975-0341
David Burns
(916) 432-9598, (888) 431-1001
Fax: (916) 432-9599
E-mail: db@gv.net
Web: www.coppergardens.com

Ornaments
An artist in the California Mother Lode who makes beautiful **garden gates** made of copper and brass which will weather; he offers various styles fitted to your specifications, and he can also work with you on your own design ideas. (1995)
📖 Catalog: Free, R&W, CAN/OV, CC, $100m
○ Shop: M-Sa, by appointment only

Country Casual
17317 Germantown Road
Germantown, MD 21754-2999
Mrs. Bobbie Goldstein
(301) 540-0040
Fax: (301) 540-7364
E-mail: sales@countrycasual.com
Web: www.countrycasual.com

Furniture
Offer Lister and Verey British **teak benches and tables** in many styles and sizes, as well as their own Chippendale II designs; also several styles of garden swing, trellis work, wooden planting tubs and deck chairs. Suppliers have Friends of the Earth (UK) approval. They pay the freight on purchases. (1977)
📖 Catalog: $3, CAN, CC
○ Shop: March-Sept, daily; Oct-Feb, M-F; closed holidays

Country House Floral Supply
P.O. Box 853
Eastham, MA 02642-0853
Helga J. Frazzette
(508) 255-6664
Fax: (508) 240-2551

Ornaments ☙ Books ☙ Supplies ☙ Tools
Offers **flower arranging supplies,** a very broad selection, including many styles of vases, "frogs" (flower holders), bonsai stands, pruning tools and a number of books on flower arranging. (1974)
📖 Catalog: $1, CAN/OV, CC

Creative Enterprises, Inc.
P.O. Box 3452
Idaho Falls, ID 83403-3452
Donna & Lyle Hahn
(208) 523-0526
Fax: (208) 522-5096
E-mail: wweeder@sisna.com

Tools
Sell the Winged Weeder (R), a diamond-shaped **weeding tool** which skims along just under the surface cutting off weeds: it comes with a short or long handle, and with two sizes of head. (1988)
📖 Catalog: Free, R&W, CAN/OV, CC, $15m

Cropking, Inc.
5050 Greenwich Road
Seville, OH 44273
Dan J. Brentlinger
(330) 769-2002, (800) 321-5656
Fax: (330) 769-2616
E-mail: CropKing@CropKing.com
Web: www.cropking.com

Books ﷽ **Supplies**
Specialize in **greenhouses and supplies** and equipment for **hydroponic growers**. They have added a "gardening catalog" for home gardeners; they offer everything for indoor growing and propagation.They also sell **rockwool**, the latest word in growing media, as well as books and videos. (1981)
📖 Catalog: $3($15 OV), R&W, CAN/OV, CC, $25m
✪ Shop: All year, M-Sa

Dave & Sue's Aquarium & Greenhouse

See Stone Fish Studios.

Day-Dex Company
4725 N.W. 36th Avenue
Miami, FL 33142
J. Kim Motsinger

Supplies
Offer **galvanized steel tiered benches** in several styles and sizes for orchids and other indoor and patio plants; also sell **shade canopies** with 55% to 80% shade. In addition, they manufacture and sell Kinsman **carts**, dollies and flat barrows for moving heavy nursery loads.
📖 Catalog: Free, R&W, CAN/OV, $60m

Diamond Lights
628 Lindaro Street
San Rafael, CA 94901
Steve Stragnola
(415) 459-3994, (800) 331-3994
Fax: (415) 459-3994
E-mail: sales@DiamondLights.com
Web: DiamondLights.com

Supplies
Specialists in high intensity discharge (HID) **lighting for indoor gardening** as well as hydroponic gardening supplies, greenhouse controls and accessories, fertilizers, and indoor growing supplies. (1983)
📖 Catalog: Free, R&W, CAN/OV, CC
✪ Shop: All year, M-Sa

Digger's Product Development Company
P.O. Box 1551
Soquel, CA 95073-1551
Wayne & Lauri Morgan
(408) 462-6095
Fax: (408) 464-1825

Supplies
Ever notice that every letter to the editor about pocket gophers comes from Sebastopol, CA? This might be the answer -- prefabricated **wire gopher baskets**, which are shipped flat but pop open easily for planting. They come in three sizes, and Sebastipudlians can buy them by the case. (1988)
📖 Catalog: Free, R&W, CAN

Drip Rite Irrigation Products

See Strong Injectors.

DripWorks
380 Maple Street
Willits, CA 95490
E. Glassey, J. Jordan & L. Springer
(707) 459-6323, (800) 522-3747
Fax: (707) 459-9645
E-mail: dripwrks@pacific.net

Supplies
"We make it simple" say these **drip irrigation** specialists; they put out an informative catalog to help you design and install drip irrigation. Also sell pond liners for farm and irrigation ponds, and water storage tanks. (1992)
📖 Catalog: Free, R&W, CAN/OV, CC

Dyna-Gro Corporation
1065 Broadway
San Pablo, CA 94806
Susan P. Martin
(510) 233-0254, (800) 396-2476
Fax: (510) 233-0198
E-mail: dynagro@aol.com

Supplies
Offers a number of **fertilizers and growth stimulants** for many garden and greenhouse uses, including a product to raise or lower the pH of water, and a root growth stimulator for starting cuttings and transplanting. Also offer orchid and hydroponic growing media, testing instruments, and fertilizer injectors.
📖 Catalog: Free, R&W, CAN/OV, CC, $25m
✪ Shop: All year, M-F

Earlee, Inc.
P.O. Box 4480
2002 Highway 62
Jeffersonville, IN 47131-4480
Earl & Mary Stewart
(812) 282-9134
Fax: (812) 282-2640

Supplies
A broad selection of **organic products** for farmer and gardener; they manufacture Nature's Way growing supplies and sell many soil amendments, fertilizers, live animal traps, pest controls and bird repellents. They have a branch in New Albany, IN; call (812) 944-0751 for location and hours.
📖 Catalog: Free, R&W, CAN/OV, CC, $5m
✪ Shop: M-F, Sa am

Earthworks
P.O. Box 67
Hyattville, WY 82428-0067
Leonard Sherwin, Mgr.

Ornaments
Earthworks makes hand-cast **hypertufa troughs** for growing alpine and rock garden plants, herbs and small perennials or shrubs. They are available in rectangular or oval shapes and come in three colors. (1990)
📖 Catalog: Long SASE, R&W, CAN, $40m

Economy Label Sales Co., Inc.
515 Carswell Avenue
Holly Hill, FL 32117
Shawn Baer, Mgr.
(800) 874-4465
Fax: (904) 238-1410
E-mail: sales@elsco.com
Web: www.economylabel.com

Supplies
Various styles of **plastic, paper, and metal plant and garden labels**, label printers and custom labels to customer design, computer labels and software. New are "Sticky Pics," plastic self-adhesive pictures of popular nursery plants to stick on nursery signs. Minimum order for most items is 1,000 blank or printed of any one style, but you can get your friends or club to share an order.
📖 Catalog: Free, R&W, CAN/OV, CC

Erth-Rite

See Symo-Life, Inc.

Escort Lighting
201 Sweitzer Road
Sinking Spring, PA 19608
Michael Hartman
(610) 670-2517, (800) 856-7948
Fax: (610) 670-5170

Ornaments
Makes and sells **copper garden light fixtures** in several charming mushroom and toadstool designs, and they will make light fixtures and other garden ornaments such as birdbaths and bird houses to your designs. (1989)
📖 Catalog: Free, R&W, CAN/OV, CC

Evergreen Garden Plant Labels
P.O. Box 922
Cloverdale, CA 95425-0922
Gary Patterson

Supplies
Sell **metal plant label holders with metal name plates** for all types of plants, available 13 inches, 20 inches and 26 inches high; they will custom engrave plastic plant labels to fit. Also sell 30 inch **bloomstalk supports** for taller flowers, **tag holding stakes, and rose-pegging hooks**. (1970)
📖 Catalog: Long SASE, $15m

Expo Garden Tours
70 Great Oak
Redding, CT 06896
Michael Italiaander
(203) 938-0410, (800) 448-2685
Fax: (203) 938-0427
E-mail: gardentrav@aol.com
Web: trine.com/GardenNet/ExpoGardenTours/expotour.htm

Services
Travel agency which offers **garden tours** both internationally and in the US. The flyer I saw had tours to Costa Rica, the "Old South," Pacific Northwest, Holland and the Chelsea Flower Show. They'll also arrange custom tours for individuals and small groups. (1988)
📖 Catalog: Free

Fair Meadow Books
36 Rucum Road
Roxbury, CT 06783
Emily Collins & Laura Levine

Books
Offers a good selection of **used and out-of-print books**, especially in garden design, garden history, plant hunting, roses and other plant groups. (1993)
📖 Catalog: $3($6 OV), CAN/OV
❂ Shop: By appointment only

Barbara Farnsworth, Bookseller
P.O. Box 9
407 Route 128
West Cornwall, CT 06796-0009
Barbara Farnsworth
(860) 672-6571
Fax: (860) 672-3099
E-mail: bfbooks@snet.net

Books
A large general antiquarian and out-of-print bookstore in a tiny village in the country, with 40,000 books on all subjects; a specialty is **horticultural books**. Sounds great, I'm on my way! (1978)
📖 Catalog: $5($10 OV), R&W, CAN/OV, CC
❂ Shop: All year, Sa, or by appointment

Cliff Finch's Zoo
P.O. Box 54
16923 N. Friant Road
Friant, CA 93626-0054
Cliff & Joan Finch
(209) 822-2315
Fax: (209) 822-2315

Ornaments
Cliff's made **topiary frames** for the San Diego Zoo and Longwood Gardens, and his work has been featured in magazines. He offers a good selection of frames in animal shapes and other designs, and will do custom work. (1985)
📖 Catalog: Long SASE($1 OV), R&W, CAN/OV, CC, $4m
❂ Shop: All year, M-Sa, closed 12/25-1/2

Flora & Fauna Books
121 First Avenue South
Seattle, WA 98104
David Hutchinson
(206) 623-4727
Fax: (206) 623-2001

Books
A good selection of **new, used, rare and out-of-print books** in horticulture, botany, ornithology and natural history, and they welcome your "wish lists." Will also purchase used books and collections. (1983)
📖 Catalog: Free, CAN/OV, CC
❂ Shop: All year, M-Sa

Florapersonnel, Inc.
1740 Lake Markham Road
Sanford, FL 32771
Robert F. Zahra, Mgr.
Fax: (417) 320-8083
E-mail: HortSearch@aol.com
Web: www.florapersonnel.com

Services
A **horticultural employee seach and placement firm** which lists many types of jobs: managers of commercial operations, florists, landscape architects, estate managers, nursery supply and management, import and export -- you name it! A good way to find a job or a qualified worker. (1982)
📖 Catalog: Free

Florentine Craftsmen, Inc.
46-24 - 28th Street
Long Island City, NY 11101
Graham Brown
(718) 937-7632, (800) 876-3567
Fax: (718) 937-9858

Furniture ✺ Ornaments
Wide selection of fine **lead statuary, fountains, cast aluminum and cast iron furniture** in classic styles. Also sundials, bird baths, weathervanes, planters, cherubs and many animals of the most appealing sort; add an estate touch to your garden! (1928)
📖 Catalog: $5d($7 OV), R&W, CAN/OV, CC
❂ Shop: All year, M-Sa

Fortner Books
210 Winslow Way
Bainbridge Island, WA 98110
Nancy & Robert Fortner
(206) 842-6577, (800) 841-3932
Fax: (206) 780-5872
E-mail: fortnerbk@interloc.com

Books
Offer new, used, and out-of-print **garden books**, and will do book searches if there's something you're looking for and haven't been able to find.
📖 Catalog: $2d, CAN/OV, CC
❂ Shop: All year, daily

FrenchWyres
P.O. Box 131655
Tyler, TX 75713-1655
Paul & Terri Squyres
(903) 597-8322
Fax: (903) 597-9321

Ornaments
Make a variety of Victorian-style **wire plant stands and garden accessories**, including trellises, window boxes, cachepots, arbors and topiary frames. They will also do custom work. (1989)
📖 Catalog: $4, R&W, CAN/OV, CC

G. B. American, Inc.
P.O. Box 514
Rt. 3, Whitefield Road
Lancaster, NH 03584-0514
James Hampton
(603) 788-2825
Fax: (603) 788-4529

Supplies
Offers the "Aqua Spike," which turns a regular throwaway two liter plastic soda bottle into a **slow release watering reservoir** for plants. Formerly Jasco Distributing. (1990)
📖 Catalog: Free, CAN/OV, CC, $6m

The Garden Book Club
3000 Cindel Drive
Delran, NJ 08370-0001
Newbridge Communications
(609) 786-1000
Fax: (609) 786-3439

Books
Just like those other **book clubs** that have monthly selections and alternates. They've had the ineffable good taste to offer this book each time it comes out, so you know they're good pickers! They advertise good introductory offers in major gardening magazines -- watch for them.
📖 Catalog: Write for information, CAN/OV

Garden Concepts, Inc.
P.O. Box 241233
Memphis, TN 38124-1233
John B. Painter
(901) 756-1649
Fax: (901) 755-4564

Furniture ঙ Ornaments
A broad selection of upscale **ornaments and furnishings** for the garden -- pavilions, arbors, pergolas, bridges, gates, trellis-work, lighting systems, planters, plant stands, garden furniture in a variety of historical styles. Customers may submit designs for pricing and construction. (1985)
📖 Catalog: $10d($15 OV), R&W, CAN
✪ Shop: All year, M-F

Garden Room Books
792 Queen Street E.
Sault Ste. Marie, ON, Canada P6A 2B1
Michaela Keenan
(705) 256-6700, (888) 281-5501

Books
A small bookshop specializing in **garden books for northern climates**; they schedule talks by garden book authors and trips to local nurseries and gardens for their near-by customers. Send SASE for catalog in Canada, $1 to US/OV, $3 for catalog of out-of-print and antique books. (1993)
📖 Catalog: See notes, R&W, US/OV, CC
✪ Shop: February-December, Tu-Sa

Garden Street Books
P.O. Box 1811
Geelong, Victoria, Australia 3213
Elizabeth Kerr
61 (0) 35 229-1667
Fax: 61 (0) 35 223-3061
E-mail: gardenst@ozemail.com.au

Books
Elizabeth Kerr specializes in **new, used and antiquarian books on gardening** from all over the world. A good source of books on Australian plants and gardening. (1993
📖 Catalog: US$2, OV, CC
✪ Shop: By appointment only

Garden Trellises, Inc.
P.O. Box 105
LaFayette, NY 13084-0105
Gwyn Weaver & Marjorie Sheckler
(315) 498-9003
Web: www.GardenTrellises.com

Supplies
Offer steel **frames for vegetables**, which can be stacked in various combinations as you need them. They also sell **copper trellises and rose towers** in a variety of styles to be used free-standing or against walls.
📖 Catalog: Free, CC, $15m

Gardener's Kitchen
P.O. Box 322
Monument Beach, MA 02553-0322
Betty J. Rafferty
(508) 759-3208

Supplies
Offer canning lids, rings and press-on labels; they sell the #63 small canning lid which they say is still sought by many people. (1976)
📖 Catalog: Free, CAN/OV

Gardener's Supply Company
128 Intervale Road
Burlington, VT 05401-6100
Will Raap
(802) 660-3500, (800) 955-3370
Fax: (800) 551-6712
E-mail: info@gardeners.com
Web: www.gardeners.com

Ornaments ঙ Supplies ঙ Tools
Broad selection of **tools and equipment, organic fertilizers and pesticides, tillers and food preservation supplies**, most illustrated in a color catalog. They also sell greenhouses, composters, irrigation equipment, carts, sprayers, shredder/chippers, knee pads and much more.
📖 Catalog: Free, R&W, CC
✪ Shop: All year, daily

Gardens Alive!
5100 Schenley Place
776 Rudolph Way
Lawrenceburg, IN 47025
Niles Kinerk
(812) 537-8650
Fax: (812) 537-5108
E-mail: gardener@gardens-alive.com

Supplies
Natural insect and disease controls, supplies and equipment for organic gardening; all explained in an informative catalog. Offers organic insect controls, beneficial insects, fertilizers and drip irrigation systems. There are color pictures of insects and their damage in the catalog. (1984)
📖 Catalog: Free, R&W, CC
✪ Shop: All year, daily except holidays

Gardens for Growing People
P.O. Box 630
Point Reyes Station, CA 94956-0630
John & Ruth Lopez
(415) 663-9433
Fax: (415) 663-9433
E-mail: growpeople@nbn.com

Books ✀ Tools
Specializes in **children's gardening supplies** and backyard nature study. They offer books, tools, games and other garden items that will appeal to children. Also suggestions for garden projects, recommended periodicals and **resources for teachers**. (1991)
📖 Catalog: Free($1 CAN), R&W, CAN, CC

Gardenside, Ltd.
999 Andersen Drive
San Rafael, CA 94901
Eric Rulmont, Mgr.
(415) 455-4500
Fax: (415) 455-4505

Furniture
Offers **garden benches and furniture** made of teak in various classic designs, suitable for home or commercial use. (1992)
📖 Catalog: Free($5 OV), R&W, CAN/OV, CC
✪ Shop: All year, daily

V. L.T. Gardner Botanical Books
625 E. Victoria Street
Santa Barbara, CA 93103
Virginia L.T. Gardner
(805) 966-0246
Fax: (805) 966-9987
E-mail: vltgbooks@aol.com

Books
Offers **used, out-of-print, and antiquarian books** on horticulture, gardening, botany, landscape architecture and plants, and new books on gardens appropriate to southern California and other dry areas; no catalog at present; call or send a "wish list." Also does book searches. (1982)
📖 Catalog: See notes, R&W, CAN/OV
✪ Shop: By appointment only

Gateways
849 Hannah Branch Road
Burnsville, NC 28714
Richard Kennedy
Fax: (704) 675-5286

Ornaments
Offers garden **sculpture and ornaments** made of hand-cast stone; includes statues of St. Fiacre, the patron saint of gardens (with his shovel), St. Francis and Pan, as well as wall sculptures, side tables and candle holders. Designs by several local artists. (1989)
📖 Catalog: $1, R&W, CAN, CC

Genie House
P.O. Box 2478
56 N. Main Street (Medford)
Vincentown, NJ 08088-2478
Lloyd E. Williams, Jr.
(608) 859-0600, (800) 634-3643
Fax: (608) 859-0565

Ornaments
Hand-crafted brass, copper and tin reproduction **light fixtures** in classic styles for gardens and house exteriors; will also do custom work. (1967)
📖 Catalog: $5, R&W, CAN/OV, CC
✪ Shop: All year, M-Sa

Geostar Travel
1240 Century Court
Santa Rosa, CA 95403
Mansell Williams
(707) 579-2420, (800) 624-6633 (CA)
Fax: (707) 579-2704
E-mail: manselw@crl.com

Services
A travel agency which specializes in **horticultural, botanical and natural history tours** to England, Europe, Central and South America, Hawaii and Australia. The tours are led by experts; some are organized for various societies or special interest groups.
📖 Catalog: Free, R&W, CC
✪ Shop: All year, M-F

Gothic Arch Greenhouses
P.O. Box 1564
Mobile, AL 36633-1564
W. H. Sierke, Jr.
(334) 432-7529

Supplies
Redwood or red cedar **greenhouses** with fiberglass glazing in a pointed-arch style, either attached or free-standing. Also sells heating/cooling systems, shade cloth, benches and supplies. (1945)
📖 Catalog: $3, R&W, CAN/OV

The Green Spot, Ltd.
93 Priest Road
Nottingham, NH 03290-6204
Michael S. Cherim
(603) 942-8925
Fax: (603) 942-8932
E-mail: GrnSpt@internetMCI.com

Books ⁊ **Supplies**
Their thick "Green Methods" catalog gives masses of useful information on **beneficial insects** and how to use them, as well as other organic insect controls, and books on integrated pest management. Their motto is "Good Bugs Rule!" (1992)
📖 Catalog: $9($14 OV), R&W, CAN/OV, CC

Greenleaf Industries
2970 Lower River Road
Grants Pass, OR 97526
David James, Director
(541) 474-0571
Fax: (541) 474-2485

Ornaments
A sheltered workshop which has a year-round horticultural training program. For Christmas they make and sell 22-inch **Christmas wreaths**, which they'll ship in the US except to AK or HI; orders must be placed by December 5.
📖 Catalog: Free, CC, SS:11-12

Guano Company International, Inc.
3562 E. 80th Street
Cleveland, OH 44105-1522
(216) 641-1200
Fax: (216) 641-1310

Supplies
A source of **seabird guano** in several formulations for various uses, as well as "bat guano" and worm castings; literature gives good information on the benefits and use of each. They insist that only seabird droppings are guano, a word from the Inca civilization; they say "bat guano" is a misnomer.
📖 Catalog: Free, R&W, CAN

Happy Bird Corporation
P.O. Box 86
Weston, MA 02193-0086
Thomas Hollyday
(617) 899-7804
Fax: (617) 899-8447
E-mail: 76353.3666@compuserve.com
Web: petsforum.com/happybird/

Supplies
Offer **watering devices for birds and animals**. The bird baths are hanging, free standing or made to mount on a wall or stake. Also sell watering devices with reserve tanks for animals and small livestock, and a rain barrel for saving water for your garden.
📖 Catalog: Free, R&W, CAN/OV, CC

Harlane Company, Inc.
20 Stillhouse Road
Englishtown, NJ 07726
Frank A. Benardella
Fax: (908) 792-0959

Supplies ⁊ **Tools**
Sells **rose growing supplies**: garden markers with removable name plates, marking pens, Felco pruning shears, a rose pruning saw and goatskin gloves. They will custom-print rose nameplates. (1964)
📖 Catalog: Free, R&W, CAN

Harmony Farm Supply
P.O. Box 460
3244 Highway 116 North (Sebastopol)
Graton, CA 95444-0460
Kate Burroughs & David Henry
(707) 823-9125
Fax: (707) 823-1734
E-mail: info@harmonyfarm.com
Web: www.harmonyfarm.com

Books ⁊ **Supplies** ⁊ **Tools**
Only a mile or so from Tusker Press World Headquarters; I know it well! It's a real **emporium**, serving organic farmers/gardeners with a huge selection of drip and regular irrigation supplies, tools, organic pest controls, books, traps, fertilizers and soil amendments, grass and cover crop seed, beneficial insects and canning supplies. A very informative catalog. (1980)
📖 Catalog: $2d, R&W, CAN, CC
❂ Shop: All year, daily

Harper Horticultural Slide Library
354 Kirk Road
Decatur, GA 33030
Jimmy & Becky Stewart, Mgrs.
(404) 377-4940
Fax: (404) 377-0456

Services
Huge selection of **photographic slides of plants, gardens, landscaping and natural scenery**, available for sale for personal or lecture use only. Ms. Harper is a well-known photographer and garden writer, with several fine books. For photographs to be used in publications, fax Pamela Harper at (757) 890-9378. (1973)
📖 Catalog: $2, CAN/OV

Karen Harris
200 East Genesee Street
Fayetteville, NY 13066
Karen Harris

Ornaments
Offers **handmade hypertufa garden troughs**, carefully distressed to look like weathered stone and very well done, approximate size is 21"x11". (1991)
📖 Catalog: Long SASE, $60m

William R. Hecht, Gardening Books
P.O. Box 67
Scottsdale, AZ 85252-0067
(602) 948-2536

Books
A dealer in **used and out-of-print books**, some quite rare, in botany, gardening, horticulture, forestry and agriculture.
📖 Catalog: Free, CAN/OV

Heritage Garden Furnishings & Curios
1209 E. Island Highway, #6
Parksville, BC, Canada V9P 1R5
Karen Porter & Greger McLean
(250) 248-9598
Fax: (250) 248-9598

Furniture
Garden furniture made of Western red cedar, and available in kit form: they make gliders, lounges, Adirondack chairs, arbors, gates, swings and benches in rustic styles. Other items available at the shop. (1990)
📖 Catalog: Free, US/OV, CC, $10m
☉ Shop: Daily in summer, Tu-Sa in winter

Hollister's Hydroponics
P.O. Box 16601
Irvine, CA 92623
Steve & Jorgeen Hollister
(714) 551-3822
E-mail: hollihydro@earthlink.net
Web: home.earthlink.net/~hollihydro/

Books ∫ **Supplies**
Offer **hydroponic kits and supplies** and tell you how to create a system for your specific situation; they also sell books on hydroponics for those who want to plunge right in. (1975)
📖 Catalog: Free, CAN/OV, CC

Home Canning Supply & Specialties
P.O. Box 1158
1815 La Brea Street
Ramona, CA 92065-1158
Hugh & Myra Arrendale
(760) 788-0520, (800) 354-4070
Fax: (760) 789-4745

Books ∫ **Supplies**
A good selection of **home canning supplies and equipment**, also food dehydrators, books on canning, pectin and spices, and some baking supplies. I'm just delighted to think that people are canning food again; I've paid my dues peeling and cutting up fruit. (1991)
📖 Catalog: $1, CAN/OV, CC

Honingklip Book Sales
402 CPOA, 231 Main Road
Rondebosch, Cape Town, South Africa 7700
Walter Middelmann
27 (0) 21 689-1940
Fax: 27 (0) 21 689-1945

Books
Offer a broad selection of **books on southern African plants and gardens**; they also will search for used and out-of-print books. Prices given in US$ and may be paid in personal checks drawn on US, British or German banks.
📖 Catalog: Free, OV, US$20m

Hoop House
1358 Route 28
South Yarmount, MA 02664
Patti & Skip Pleau
(508) 760-5191
Fax: (508) 760-5244
E-mail: hoophouse@cms.net
Web: www.cms.net/hoophouse

Supplies
Offer inexpensive **greenhouse kits** which you can assemble in a weekend with the help of a friend. They come in two styles, and in lengths to fit your yard or your ambitions. Shipped by UPS. Formerly called Fox Hill Farm.
📖 Catalog: Free, R&W, CAN/OV, CC, $10m
☉ Shop: All year, M-F; July-August, daily

Hortulus
139 Marlborough Place
Toronto, ON, Canada M5R 3J5
Bruce Marshall
(416) 920-5057

Books
Sell a broad selection of **used, out-of-print and rare books** on gardening, landscape architecture, herbs, garden history, floral art and design, and specific plants; prices are in US dollars. (1976)
📖 Catalog: $3, US/OV
☉ Shop: By appointment only

Hurley Books
1752 Route 12
Westmoreland, NH 03467-4724
Henry Hurley
(603) 399-4342
Fax: (603) 399-8326
E-mail: hurleybk@interloc.com

Books
Historical or textual books on **agriculture and horticulture**, animal husbandry, cottage industries and rural miscellany. They also have older seed catalogs and 19th century horticultural periodicals; more than 2,000 titles.
📖 Catalog: $1($4 OV), CAN/OV, CC
☉ Shop: All year, M-Sa

Hydro-Farm West
1455 E. Francisco Blvd.
San Rafael, CA 94901
Tim Allega, Mgr.
(415) 459-6095
Fax: (415) 459-6096
E-mail: hydrofarm@aol.com
Web: www.hydrofarm.com

Books ℘ Supplies
Offering Hydrofarm **hydroponic systems**, as well as supplies, books and other equipment, and metal halide and high-pressure sodium **light systems**. Also carbon dioxide enrichment systems for home gardeners. They now have retail stores in Columbus, OH (614) 885-3369 and Bristol, PA (215) 781-1946 in addition to mail order; call for information and locations. (1977)
📖 Catalog: Free, R&W, CAN/OV, CC
✪ Shop: All year, M-Sa

Hydro-Gardens, Inc.
P.O. Box 25845
8765 Vollmer Road
Colorado Springs, CO 80936-5845
Mike Morton
(719) 495-2266, (800) 634-6362
Fax: (800) 634-6362
E-mail: hgi@usa.net
Web: www.hydro-gardens.com

Supplies
Greenhouse and hydroponic vegetable growing supplies of all kinds for the home grower or commercial operator, including their Chem-Gro Nutrient. Very broad selection, including beneficial insects and even cardboard boxes and labels to take the produce to market. (1972)
📖 Catalog: Free, R&W, CAN/OV, CC, $10m
✪ Shop: All year, M-F

IGS
P.O. Box 527
Dexter, MI 48130-0527
Tina Havro
(313) 426-9080
Fax: (313) 426-7803

Supplies
A good selection of **growing supplies for indoor and light gardening** and plant propagation: lighted plant stands, plant lights, capillary matting, meters, timers, pots, trays and more. Formerly Indoor Growing Supplies. (1973)
📖 Catalog: Free, CAN, CC

Idaho Wood
P.O. Box 488
Sandpoint, ID 83864-0488
Leon Lewis & Jerry Luther
(800) 635-1100
Fax: (218) 263-3102

Ornaments
Natural wood garden lights, mostly lights on standards for paths and gardens; they have a number of handsome styles made of either cedar or oak. Also sell handsome indoor and outdoor wall and ceiling fixtures in natural wood and wooden bathroom accessories. (1975)
📖 Catalog: Free, R&W, CAN/OV, CC

Indoor Gardening Supplies

See IGS.

© BowBends
Artist: Charlie Wilton

International Irrigation Systems
P.O. Box 360
Niagara Falls, NY 14304-0360
Robert L. Neff
(905) 688-4090
Fax: (905) 688-4093
E-mail: irrigro@computan.on.ca
Web: www.irrigro.com

Supplies
Irrigro(R) **drip irrigation systems** based on microporous tubing, for watering, either above or below ground, from a gravity flow tank or house faucet with low pressure. Water filters are not needed. Canadian buyers may request a catalog from Irrigro, P.O. Box 1133, St. Catharines, ON, Canada L2R 7A3.
📖 Catalog: Free(US$2 OV), R&W, CAN/OV, CC

Ironkneez

See MN Productions.

Myron Kimnach
5508 N. Astell Avenue
Azusa, CA 91702-5203
Myron Kimnach
(818) 334-7349
Fax: (818) 334-0658
E-mail: mkimnach@aol.com

Books
Specializes in **new, used and out-of-print books** on cacti and succulents -- quite a large selection, including back issues of journals. (1984)
📖 Catalog: Free, CAN/OV

Kinsman Company, Inc.
River Road
Old Firehouse, River Road
Point Pleasant, PA 18950-0357
Graham & Michele Kinsman
(215) 297-0890, (800) 733-4146
Fax: (215) 297-0450

Ornaments ∞ Supplies ∞ Tools
Importers of English **garden tools and equipment**, electric and handpowered shredders, compost bins, sieves, strawberry tubs and modular arbors. It's always fun to see what they've added. Offer capillary matting, cold frames, rain gutter guards, weathervanes, ornaments and much more. (1981)
📖 Catalog: Free, R&W, CC
✪ Shop: All year, daily

Kitchen Krafts
P.O. Box 442
Waukon, IA 52172-0442
Lynn and Dean Sorensen
(319) 535-8000, (800) 776-0575
Fax: (319) 535-8001
E-mail: 74363.1202@compuserve.com

Supplies
"Supplies for your summer kitchen." **Home canning supplies**, food dehydrators, bottles and caps for your home-made beer, books on canning, cake baking and decorating equipment. It reminds me of the zillions of jars of fruit and apple butter that we used to put up every summer. (1989)
📖 Catalog: Free($5 OV), CAN/OV, CC

Kunafin "The Insectary"
P.O. Box 190
Quemado, TX 78877-0190
Frank & Adele Junfin
(800) 832-1113
Fax: (210) 757-1468

Supplies
Specialists in biocontrol of insects and suppliers of **beneficial insects**: trichogramma wasps, fly parasites, Pymotes tritici and lacewings. They also supply Sitotroga cerella, a food source for beneficial insects. They consult with farmers about livestock operations (up to 10,000 head). (1959)
📖 Catalog: Free, R&W, CAN/OV, CC

The Lady Bug Company
P.O. Box 329
Berry Creek, CA 95916-0329
Julie Steele
(916) 589-5227

Supplies
Ladybugs, green lacewings, trichogramma, praying mantis egg cases, and Bio-Control Honeydew to attract **beneficial insects**. An informative leaflet explains the use of these biological insect controls. (1959)
📖 Catalog: Free, R&W, CAN
✪ Shop: All year, M,W,F, call ahead

Landscape Architecture Bookstore
4401 Connecticut Avenue NW
Washington, DC 20008
American Society of Landscape Architects
(301) 843-8567, (800) 787-2665
Fax: (301) 843-0159
E-mail: asla@tasco.com
Web: www.asla.org/asla/nonmembers/bookstore.html

Books
A good selection of professional **books** in the field of landscape architecture listed under categories such as "golf," "environment," "parks," "graphics" and more. Also books on plants and garden history. (1985)
📖 Catalog: Free, CAN/OV, CC

Landscape Books
P.O. Box 483
Exeter, NH 03833-0483
Jane W. Robie
(603) 964-9333
Fax: (603) 964-5739
E-mail: landscapeb@aol.com

Books ₡ **Services**
A very broad selection of **books on garden history, landscape architecture** and **city planning**: books are new, used, out-of-print and rare; all are well described as to contents and condition. Will do book searches, and assist with building collections and with garden history research. (1972)
📖 Catalog: $5, CAN/OV

Lee Valley Tools, Ltd.
12 East River Street
Ogdensburg, NY 13669
Leonard G. Lee
(613) 596-0350, (800) 871-8158
Fax: (800) 513-7885
Web: www.leevalley.com

Supplies ₡ **Tools**
Offers a good selection of imported **garden tools and growing supplies**, composting equipment, pruning tools, reel mowers and other useful items for home and garden. Also have a catalog of woodworking tools. (1978)
📖 Catalog: Free($5 OV), R&W, CAN/OV, CC
✣ Shop: All year, M-Sa

Lehman's
P.O. Box 41
One Lehman Circle
Kidron, OH 44636-0041
Lehman Family
(330) 857-5757
Fax: (330) 857-5785
E-mail: GetLehmans@aol.com
Web: www.lehmans.com

Supplies ₡ **Tools**
Lehman's is famous for its **"non-electric"** catalog, most of their local customers are Amish farmers. They offer **tools, oil lamps, canning supplies,** wood and gas-burning cook stoves and refrigerators, homesteading and farming equipment of all kinds, as well as old-fashioned farm tools. (1955)
📖 Catalog: $3($4 CAN, $8 OV), R&W, CAN/OV, CC
✣ Shop: All year, M-Sa

A. M. Leonard, Inc.
P.O. Box 816
Piqua, OH 45356-0816
Howard Kyle
(937) 773-2694, (800) 543-8955
Fax: (800) 433-0633
E-mail: info@amleo.com
Web: www.amleo.com

Supplies ₡ **Tools**
A very broad selection of **tools, supplies and equipment** for home and commercial gardeners -- almost everything you need for gardening and growing. They specialize in supplies for commercial operators, so some items come in large quantities. Most orders shipped UPS within 24 hours. (1885)
📖 Catalog: $1, R&W, CAN, CC

Linden House Gardening Books
148 Sylvan Avenue
Scarborough, ON, Canada M1M 1K4
Gerda Rowlands
(416) 261-0732
Fax: (416) 261-0615
Web: ICanGarden.com/Linden.htm

Books
A mail order bookshop, offering a very broad selection of **books on gardening**, including books for children, books on landscaping, horticulture and related crafts; accept only Visa credit cards. (1992)
📖 Catalog: Free($2 US), US, CC

Little's Good Gloves
P.O. Box 808
Johnstown, NY 12095-0808
Mark Dzierson
(518) 762-3312, (518) 736-5014
Fax: (518) 762-2980

Supplies
"We specialize in **garden gloves** that fit, especially for ladies." They make four styles, including gauntlets that shield the arm up to the elbow for working around roses or other thorny plants. I know they work very well! (1893)
📖 Catalog: Free($2 OV), R&W, CAN/OV, CC

Longshadow(R) Planters

See Classic Garden Ornaments, Ltd.

Lord & Burnham

See Under Glass Manufacturing Corporation.

Kenneth Lynch & Sons, Inc.
P.O. Box 488
84 Danbury Road
Wilton, CT 06897-0488
Timothy A. Lynch
(203) 762-8363
Fax: (203) 762-2999
E-mail: info@klynchandsons.com
Web: www.klynchandsons.com

Furniture ❧ Ornaments
A huge selection of **garden ornaments**: furniture, statues, planters and urns, gates, topiary frames, weathervanes, fountains and pools. Over 10,000 different items. I've always thought heaven would be like the Elysian Fields, now I think the fields must be peopled by gods and goddesses from the Lynch catalog! (1930)
📖 Catalog: $9.50($15 OV), CAN/OV, CC

McQuerry Orchid Books
5700 W. Salerno Road
Jacksonville, FL 32244-2354
Mary Noble McQuerry
(904) 387-5044
Fax: (904) 387-5044

Books
Specialize in **new, used, out-of-print and rare books on orchids** and also offer back issues of orchid magazines, old plant catalogs (orchids only) and antique orchid prints. They also publish and sell the "You Can Grow Orchids" series by Mary Noble. (1973)
📖 Catalog: Free, CAN/OV, CC
⊙ Shop: By appointment only

MN Productions
P.O. Box 577
Freeland, WA 98249-0577
Michael A. Nichols
(360) 331-7995
Fax: (360) 341-6208
E-mail: mnpro@whidbey.com

Supplies
Offers **gardening and "chore" sweat pants** called Iron-Kneez, with padded knees and a drawstring waist, made from a polyester/cotton blend. Also offers Iron-Kneez padded knee dungarees manufactured by OshKosh in two styles. Useful for gardeners, painters and carpenters, too. (1987)
📖 Catalog: Free, R&W, CAN/OV, CC

Marck Sales and Service
3119 Skyview Avenue
Pueblo, CO 81008-1447
Ronny Marck
(719) 543-6940
Fax: (719) 542-4660
E-mail: marck@usa.net
Web: execonn.com/brew

Supplies
Supply gardeners with **beer and wine making equipment and supplies** "to get more enjoyment from the fruits of their labors." They offer a good selection of what you'll need to make a little pilsner, elderberry wine, or even some cabernet sauvignon. (1978)
📖 Catalog: $2d($5 OV), R&W, CAN/OV, CC, $30m
⊙ Shop: All year, M-Sa

The Marugg Company
P.O. Box 1414
Tracy City, TN 37387-1414
John Baggenstoss
(615) 592-5042

Tools
The ultimate in weed whacking, a silent and efficient **Austrian scythe** with a metal or hickory snath (handle); you can order your scythe with a grass or bush blade. Marugg also offers sickles, and whetstones, anvils and hammers to sharpen your scythe.
📖 Catalog: Free, CAN/OV

Don Mattern
7117 Stoetz Lane
Sebastopol, CA 95472-9748
Don Mattern
(707) 874-1808
Fax: (707) 874-1808
E-mail: mattern@wco.com

Supplies
Offers the HERRmidifier, a **humidifier** with humidistat for greenhouse and orchid growers, available in 110 or 220 volts. It keeps track of the humidity and turns on and off as needed to keep it steady.
📖 Catalog: Free, CAN/OV

Emi Meade, Importer
16000 Fern Way
Guerneville, CA 95446-9322
Emi & Eugene Meade
(707) 869-3218, (800) 398-8418
Fax: (707) 869-3218
E-mail: jollys@sonic.net
Web: www.sonic.net/~jollys

Supplies
Offers two styles of Jollys, **waterproof garden clogs** from Europe in six colors; soft and comfortable, easy to rinse clean. The color goes all the way through, so they don't show wear easily. Also sells replacement insoles, and Atomocoll(R) for buffing rough skin, it really works! (1981)
📖 Catalog: Free(US$1 OV), R&W, CAN/OV, CC
⊙ Shop: Call ahead

Medina Agricultural Products Co.
P.O. Box 309
Hondo, TX 788610309
Stuart Franke
(210) 426-3011
Fax: (210) 426-2288
E-mail: medina@eden.com

Supplies
Sell the Medina **soil activator**, which they claim is like "yogurt for the soil," and Medina Plus, which contains micronutrients and growth hormones from seaweed extract for foliar feeding. They also offer HuMate humic acid to build soil, HastaGro fertilizers and other products. Informative flyer.
📖 Catalog: Free, R&W, CC

Moisture Mizer Products

See Multiple Concepts, Inc.

Morning Mist Worm Farm
P.O. Box 1155
Davis, CA 95617-1155
James & Karen Cain
(707) 448-6836
E-mail: mmcain@community.net

Supplies
Offer **redworms** for garden use or for "vermicomposting" in a tub or in your compost pile. They send a sheet of information on composting with redworms.
📖 Catalog: $.50 or 2FCS, R&W, SS:W

Multiple Concepts, Moisture Mizer Div.
P.O. Box 4248
Chattanooga, TN 37405-0248
Jim Crumley, Pres.
(423) 266-3967, (800) 278-9490
Fax: (423) 266-2200

Supplies
Sells Moisture Mizer **hydrogels** that slowly release water to potted and other plants. Available in several sizes; clubs could order larger sizes as a group and divide them among members.
📖 Catalog: Long SASE w/2 FCS(OV$1), R&W, CAN/OV, CC

The Natural Gardening Company
217 San Anselmo Avenue
San Anselmo, CA 94960
David Baldwin & Karin Kramer
(707) 456-5060
Fax: (707) 766-9747

Furniture ∞ **Supplies** ∞ **Tools**
Offer a nice selection of **imported garden tools**, supplies and a copper snail barrier which gives the little devils a mild shock -- they won't cross it. Also sell organic "gourmet" vegetable and herb seedlings, and drip irrigation systems to keep them growing, and much more. (1986)
📖 Catalog: Free, CAN/OV, CC
⊙ Shop: All year, daily

Natural Insect Control
R.R. #2
Stevensville, ON, Canada L05 1S0
Dave & Sandra Mitchell
(905) 382-2904
Fax: (905) 382-4418
E-mail: nic@niagara.com
Web: www.natural-insect-control.com

Supplies
Offers a broad range of **organic gardening supplies**: beneficial insects, lures for pests, live traps, bird houses and feeders, organic fertilizers, books on pest management, all in an informative catalog. (1989)
📖 Catalog: Free($2 OV), R&W, US/OV, CC
⊙ Shop: All year, M-F, call ahead

Nature's Control
P.O. Box 35
Medford, OR 97501-0035
Don Jackson
(541) 899-8318
Fax: (800) 698-6250
E-mail: bugsnc@teleport.com

Supplies
Predator mites, ladybugs, whitefly traps and parasites, mealybug predators and insecticidal soap for **natural pest control**; all especially useful for indoor or greenhouse growing. Stress helpful advice and fast service. Also sell **diatomaceous earth** and copper **Snail-Barr** against slugs and snails. No shipping to HI. (1980)
📖 Catalog: Free, R&W, CC

The Walt Nicke Company
P.O. Box 433
Topsfield, MA 01983-0433
Katrina Nicke
(508) 887-3388, (800) 822-4114
Fax: (508) 887-9853
Web: www.gardentalk.com

Books ∞ **Supplies** ∞ **Tools**
Garden tools, gadgets and supplies, many imported from Europe; a broad selection. One of my favorite tools is a heavy-duty steel trowel with a long handle which I bought from them many years ago. There's much here that's useful, decorative or just desirable for yourself or for gifts. The catalog is called "Gardentalk."
📖 Catalog: $1, CAN/OV, CC

Nitron Industries, Inc.
P.O. Box 1447
5703 Hewitt Road (Johnson)
Fayetteville, AR 72702-1447
Frank J. Finger
(501) 587-1777, (800) 835-0123
Fax: (501) 587-0177
E-mail: custserv@nitron.com
Web: www.nitron.com

Supplies
Offers a good selection of **organic growing supplies**: fertilizers, enzyme soil amendments including their own Nitron brand, and Wet Flex porous hose. Catalog gives good information on soil building, offers composting supplies, water purifiers, and a deodorizer for pet accidents called Sweet Pea. (1977)
📖 Catalog: Free, R&W, CAN/OV, CC
✪ Shop: All year, M-F, Sa am

Norway Company
E 9237 Highway O
Sauk City, WI 53583-9660
Brian Hanson
(608) 544-5000

Supplies
Sells two models of **garden cart** -- the Carryall, 42 inches wide, and the Carryette, 32 inches wide for access through doorways; sold complete or as kits for you to put together with your own plywood.
📖 Catalog: Free, R&W, CAN/OV, CC
✪ Shop: All year, M-F, by appointment only

OFE International
P.O. Box 164402
12100 S.W. 129th Court
Miami, FL 33116-4402
Carlos Cahiz, Mgr.
(305) 253-7080
Fax: (305) 251-8245

Supplies ✺ **Tools**
Offers **growing supplies for orchids and bromeliads**: clay orchid pots, wood and wire plant baskets, fertilizers, sprayers, watering accessories, growing media, plant labels, plant stands and books about orchids. (1980)
📖 Catalog: $3d($6 OV), R&W, CAN/OV, CC, $20m
✪ Shop: All year, daily

Ohio Earth Food, Inc.
5488 Swamp Street NE
Hartville, OH 44632
Larry & Cynthia Ringer
(330) 877-9356
Fax: (330) 877-4237

Supplies ✺ **Services**
Offer a broad selection of **natural soil conditioners and amendments**, including Erth-Rite and Maxicrop, insect controls and dormant oils; they also will do soil testing and make suggestions for which natural products to use. Farmers may request their quantity prices. (1972)
📖 Catalog: Free, R&W, CAN/OV, CC
✪ Shop: All year, M-Tu,Th-F; April-May, M-Sa am

Orchid Perfection
85 Upper Road
Sandwich, NH 03227
Derek Marshall
(603) 284-7000, (800) 497-3891
Fax: (603) 284-6237
E-mail: orchids@derekmarshall.com
Web: www.derekmarshall.com

Supplies
Offers special **orchid pots** in glazed stoneware and terra cotta; pots come in various sizes and shapes, some with cut-outs for air flow and all with feet to keep roots above the bench. Also some tipsy-looking tilted pots for growing phalaenopsis orchids. (1995)
📖 Catalog: Free, R&W, CAN/OV, CC

Organic Gardening Book Club
Customer Service
111 10th Street
Des Moines, IA 50300
Rodale Press, Inc.
(800) 754-2907

Services
Garden book club run by Rodale Press; they offer their own books as well as those of other publishers. Write or call for information.

The Original Bug Shirt(R) Company
P.O. Box 127
Trout Creek, ON, Canada P0H 2L0
Bob Meister & Sara Callaway
(705) 729-5620, (800) 998-9096
Fax: (705) 729-5625
E-mail: bugshirt@onlink.net
Web: www.gorp.com/bugshirt

Supplies
Offer a lightweight **bug-proof garment** which is both cool to wear and protects your arms and whole upper body from biting insects and ticks; it has long sleeves, a hood with a mesh face protector, and plenty of air vents. They have added **pants and gaiters** for complete protection.
📖 Catalog: Free, R&W, CAN/OV, CC

Mike Park Books
351, Sutton Common Road
Sutton, Surrey, England SM3 9H2
Mike Park & Ian Smith
44 (0) 181 641-7796
Fax: 44 (0) 181 641-3330

Books
A specialist in used, out-of-print and rare **books on gardening and horti-culture**, if you've been to the RHS shows in London, you've probably stopped at his booth. (1975)
📖 Catalog: $3(US Bills or 6 IRC), OV, CC
⭘ Shop: By appointment only

Paw Paw Everlast Label Co.
P.O. Box 93
Paw Paw, MI 49079-0093
Arthur & Dorothy Arens

Supplies
Manufacture and sell "Everlast" **metal plant and garden labels** with zinc nameplates. They offer styles to put in the ground and to hang on the plant; also sell special marking pencils and crayons to write on the labels. (1962)
📖 Catalog: Free, R&W, CAN/OV, $4m

Peaceful Valley Farm Supply
P.O. Box 2209
125 Spring Hill Drive
Grass Valley, CA 95945-2209
Eric & Patricia Boudier
(916) 272-4769
Fax: (916) 272-4794
Web: www.groworganic.com

Books ∾ **Supplies** ∾ **Tools**
Offers a very broad selection of **organic growing supplies**, as well as seeds of flowers and vegetables, seed potatoes and garlic, cover crop seed, and spring blooming bulbs. They will do soil testing by mail, offer row covers and beneficial insects, garden tools of every kind; in fact, a complete emporium in a very informative catalog. (1976)
📖 Catalog: $2d, R&W, CC, $20m
⭘ Shop: All year, M-Sa

PeCo, Inc.
P.O. Box 1197
100 Airport Road
Arden, NC 28704-1197
Peter Hall
(704) 684-1234, (800) 438-5823
Fax: (704) 684-0858

Supplies
Sell a completely self-contained **12-volt electric sprayer** which runs up to five hours on its rechargeable battery. It features a cart with big wheels to make it easy to move around and has a plug-in charger, an 8-foot hose and an opaque tank to keep track of fluid level; great for larger gardens. (1971)
📖 Catalog: Free, R&W, CAN/OV, CC, $15m
⭘ Shop: All year, M-F

Pine Garden Bonsai Company
20331 State Route 530 N.E.
Arlington, WA 98223
Kate Bowditch & Max Braverman
(360) 435-5995, (800) 746-3281
Fax: (360) 435-4865
E-mail: bonsai@tgi.net
Web: www.poppyware.com/pgb/

Supplies
Offer hand-made wheel-thrown ceramic **bonsai containers** (glazed or unglazed, in many styles), their own cast containers in the Japanese style, and bonsai tools. They also offer finished bonsai and pre-bonsai stock; ask for their plant list. No plants shipped to HI or PR. (1971)
📖 Catalog: Free, R&W, CC, $25m
⭘ Shop: All year, Th-Sa, by appointment only

Planet Natural
P.O. Box 3146
1612 Gold Avenue
Bozeman, MT 59772-3146
Wayne & Eric Vinje
(406) 587-5891, (800) 289-6656
Fax: (406) 587-0223
E-mail: ecostore@mcn.net
Web: www.planetnatural.com/

Supplies
"Producers and distributors of natural products for least-toxic, long-term protection from insect pests." Sell **pheromone traps, beneficial insects**, soaps, botanical extracts, fungicides and sprayers and much more; catalog is informative. Formerly Bozeman Bio-Tech. (1986)
📖 Catalog: Free, R&W, CAN/OV, CC
⭘ Shop: All year, M-F; April-October, M-Sa

Plastic Plumbing Products, Inc.
P.O. Box 186
17005 Manchester Road
Grover, MO 63040-0186
Robert Pisarkiewicz
(314) 458-2226
Fax: (314) 458-2760

Supplies
Sell supplies for **drip and mist irrigation** systems, and will develop custom-designed systems for customers in the Midwest. Also carry a large selection of drip and mist parts and fittings from several manufacturers. (1979)
📖 Catalog: $1, R&W, CAN

Pomona Book Exchange
P.O. Box 111
953 Highway 552
Rockton, ON, Canada L0R 1X0
Fred & Walda Janson
(519) 621-8897

Books ∞ **Supplies** ∞ **Services**
Offer **new, out-of-print and rare books** on plants, botany, gardening and horticulture, landscape design, fruit growing and related fields and will search for hard-to-find books. They recently compiled a bibliography of antique fruit literature. Also have a museum apple orchard and can supply propagation materials for several hundred varieties to local Canadian collectors! (1951)
📖 Catalog: Free, US/OV (books only)
✪ Shop: August-October, call ahead

Premiere Products
P.O. Box 944
Columbus, NE 68602-0944
Rodney & Georgia Behlen
(402) 564-4909, (800) 323-2799
Fax: (402) 564-3703

Supplies
Computemp **temperature monitor and alarm**: takes Fahrenheit or Celsius readings, both indoors and out; records high and low of the day; will monitor air, soil or water at up to nine locations; will sound an alarm at a pre-set temperature -- does everything but get up at midnight to fix things! They are offering a new Rain-O-Matic electronic rain gauge, too. Formerly Rodco Products Company. (1977)
📖 Catalog: Free, CAN/OV, CC

Larry W. Price Books
353 N.W. Maywood Drive
Portland, OR 97210-3333
(503) 221-1410

Books
Larry's a college professor who loves books; he specializes in **rare, old** and **antiquarian books** on natural history, botany and all types of plants and gardening. He insists that many of the books are useful, too! Tell him what interests you. (1985)
📖 Catalog: $2d, R&W, CAN/OV

V. L. Price Horticultural
506 Grove Avenue
Catawissa, PA 17820-1000
Viveca Price

Books ∞ **Supplies**
Offers **seed saving supplies**: paper, glassine and poly envelopes, as well as mesh bags for drying seed. Also sells guides to herb propagation, seed saving, and other home gardening subjects. (1987)
📖 Catalog: Long SASE(1 IRC), R&W, CAN/OV

Putterin Press
P.O. Box 667
Orinda, CA 94563-2224
Nancy Fisher
(510) 254-8481
Fax: (510) 254-4159

Supplies
Nancy has revised her wonderful **five-year garden diary** to be snazzier looking, but it is just as useful as before: spiral bound so that it lies flat to write in, with room for notes and weather records. I have nearly ten years of weather records at Lafalot in two of these diaries. It makes a wonderful housewarming or wedding gift.
📖 Catalog: Free, CAN/OV, $20m

Qualimetrics, Inc.

See Scientific Sales, Inc.

Quest Rare Books
774 Santa Ynez
Stanford, CA 94305
Gretl Meier
(415) 324-3119

Books
A specialist in **old and rare books** on gardening, landscape design and history and botany; she will also search for books worldwide and buy collections or single volumes. (1986)
📖 Catalog: $3, CAN/OV
✪ Shop: All year, by appointment only

Rainbow Gardens Bookshop

See Rainbow Gardens Nursery & Bookshop in Section A.

Raindrip, Inc.
2250 Agate Court
Simi Valley, CA 93065
Ruth Mehra, Mgr.
(805) 581-3344, (800) 367-3747
Fax: (805) 581-9999

Supplies
Sell Raindrip **drip irrigation systems and supplies**; informative booklet tells you how to get started and what you'll need. They have a multiplex dripper which will go on the sprinkler fittings of existing underground systems. They also sell a video cassette on how to do it. (1975)
📖 Catalog: Free, R&W, CAN/OV, CC, $10m

Bargyla Rateaver
9049 Covina Street
San Diego, CA 92126
Dr. Bargyla Rateaver
(619) 566-8994
E-mail: brateaver@aol.com

Supplies
A source for **organic growing supplies and pest controls**: sabadilla dust, ryania, BT, fish meal, compost starter, BX, nematode remedy, Maxicrop seaweed powder and more. Also sells some organic gardening literature, including their revised Organic Method Primer. (1973)
📖 Catalog: Long SASE($1 OV), CAN/OV, $5m

Recycled Plastics Marketing, Inc.
2829 152nd Avenue N.E.
Redmond, WA 98052
John Bissell
(800) 529-9110
Fax: (206) 867-3282
Web: www.rrpm.com

Supplies
Sells **recycled plastic garden equipment**: raised bed kits, planters, bird feeders, compost bins, a garden cart and a "worm barn" for worm composting.
📖 Catalog: Free, CAN/OV, CC

Reimuller's Cart Warehouse

See Cart Warehouse.

Resource Conservation Technology
2633 N. Calvert Street
Baltimore, MD 21218-4617
Lee Jaslow, Mgr.
(410) 366-1146, (800) 477-7724
Fax: (410) 366-1202

Supplies
Fabricates and sells **pond liners** of Butyl and EPDM synthetic rubbers; they come in several thicknesses; they also sell the pumps, fountain heads, and supplies you need to do the job and fix punctures. Catalog is full of how-to information. (1984)
📖 Catalog: Free($3 OV), R&W, CAN/OV, CC, $25m
✪ Shop: All year, M-F, call ahead

Rodco Products

See Premiere Products.

Roll'Erg Wheelbarrows
970 Golden Hills Road
Colorado Springs, CO 80919
Robert Pearce
(719) 598-5274, (800) 665-3949
Fax: (719) 590-1543

Tools
Offer the Roll'Erg Wheelbarrow(TM), an ergonomically designed **wheelbarrow** with two front wheels for stability, adjustable handles, and all-steel frame and handles for durability. They have conversion kits to make a hay or firewood carrier and a trailer for your garden tractor.
📖 Catalog: Free, R&W, CAN, CC

A. I. Root Company
623 W. Liberty Street
Medina, OH 44256
John Root
(330) 725-6677
Fax: (330) 725-5624
E-mail: bculture@aol.com
Web: www.airoot.com

Books ✻ **Supplies**
Everything for the home or commercial beekeeper and honey producer, even bee toys -- they've been in business since 1869 and have branches in three states. Also publish "Gleanings in Bee Culture," the monthly magazine of the beekeeping industry. (1869)
📖 Catalog: Free, R&W, CAN/OV, CC
✪ Shop: All year, daily

Rudon International Trading Company
P.O. Box 331104
Ft. Worth, TX 76163-1104
John D. Croslin
(817) 292-8485
Fax: (817) 292-0950
E-mail: Rudon@dfw.net

Tools
Sells the EZ-Digger, a traditional **hand tool from the Orient**; it is a combination of weeder, hand hoe and trowel that comes with a short or long handle. They've added a "disk hoe" for weeding and cultivating. (1988)
📖 Catalog: Free, R&W, CAN/OV

Ruesch International Financial Services
700 11th Street, N.W.
Washington, DC 20001-4507
(202) 408-1200, (800) 424-2923
Fax: (202) 408-1211

Services
Here's an answer to the problem of sending payments to societies or suppliers in foreign countries: you call and tell them how much you want to send and to "lock in" the exchange rate; they'll tell you the US dollar equivalent.Then send a personal or cashier's check for that amount plus $3 for a check, $15 for a wire transfer. There is no minimum amount necessary. They will also collect checks drawn on foreign banks for similar modest fees. They have offices in Washington, New York, Atlanta, Chicago, Boston, Los Angeles, as well as in London (01 71 734-2300) and Zurich (01 212-5300).

Samia Rose Topiary
P.O. Box 231208
1236 Urania Avenue
Encinitas, CA 92023-1208
Patricia Riley Hammer
(760) 436-0460 (800) 488-6742
Fax: (760) 436-6869
E-mail: samiarose@SRTopiary.com
Web: www.SRTopiary.com

Ornaments
Offers a variety of **topiary frames**, both frames alone or planted. If you live nearby, you can even rent topiaries for special events. They also sell **ivy plants**; most likely small leaved varieties suitable for topiary. Ms. Hammer is the author of "The New Topiary: Imaginative Techniques from Longwood Gardens." (1992)
📖 Catalog: Long SASE w/2 FCS, R&W, CAN/OV, CC
✪ Shop: All year, Tu-Sa

Savoy Books
P.O. Box 271
Lanesboro, MA 01237-0271
Robert Fraker
(413) 499-9968
Fax: (413) 499-7571
E-mail: frakerbook@vgernet.net

Books
Specializes in American, English and French **books on agriculture and horticulture**, mostly old and rare, for collectors. Also old nursery catalogs and other ephemera related to the history of gardening and agriculture. Material generally covers the 16th to 19th centuries. (1971)
📖 Catalog: Free, CAN/OV, CC
✪ Shop: By appointment only

Scanmask

See BioLogic.

Scientific Sales, Inc.
P.O. Box 6725
Lawrenceville, NJ 08548-6725
Thomas Tesauro
(609) 844-0055, (800) 788-5666
Fax: (609) 844-0466
E-mail: sciensales@aol.com
Web: www.scientificsales.com

Supplies
Offers a large selection of **weather instruments**; those of special interest to gardeners are a temperature-time indicator, growing degree-day totalizers, humidity indicators and recorders for greenhouses, wind speed indicators, soil thermometers and rain gauges. Even sells complete weather stations.
📖 Catalog: Free, R&W, CAN/OV, CC

© The Fragrant Path
  Artist: Christine Rasmussen

Sea Born/Lane, Inc.
1601 13th Avenue
Charles City, IA 50616
Warren K. Dunkle
(515) 228-2000, (800) 457-5013
Fax: (515) 228-4417

Supplies
Offers a variety of **seaweed fertilizers and other organic garden products**; the seaweed products are manufactured from Norwegian seaweed. Also offers fish meal, blood meal, bone meal, green sand, rock phosphates, some tools and technical crop data sheets, and a "sticker" to make foliar fertilizers stay where they're put. (1960)
📖 Catalog: Free, R&W, CAN/OV, CC

Season Extenders
P.O. Box 312
Stratford, CT 06497-0312
Bill Gavoli
(203) 375-0134
Fax: (203) 375-0135

Books ⁊ **Supplies**
Catalog offers **indoor and greenhouse growing supplies**, propagation equipment, fertilizers, some greenhouses and greenhouse accessories, lighted plant stands, row covers and plastic mulch, hydroponic supplies, books and more.
📖 Catalog: Free, CC

Silver Creek Supply, Inc.
RD 1, Box 70
Routes 11 and 25
Port Trevorten, PA 17864
James Harkins
(717) 374-8010
Fax: (717) 374-8071

Supplies ⁊ **Tools**
A supplier of **nursery supplies**: propagation supplies, pots and flats, plastic mulch, fertilizers, insect traps and controls, row covers, watering equipment, and even those neat wooden bushel baskets for fruit. They also sell vegetable seeds. (1976)
📖 Catalog: Free, R&W, CAN/OV, CC
☉ Shop: All year, M-Sa

Smith & Hawken
P.O. Box 6900
2 Arbor Lane
Florence, KY 41022-6900
CML Corporation
(800) 776-3336
Fax: (606) 727-1166
Web: www.vgmarketplace.com

Furniture ⁊ **Ornaments** ⁊ **Books** ⁊ **Tools**
Offer a very broad selection of **garden tools**, many imported from England or Japan, irrigation supplies, composting equipment, books, garden furniture, housewares and many items suitable for gifts. They now also have a number of retail stores. (1979)
📖 Catalog: Free, R&W, CC
☉ Shop: All year, daily

Snow Pond Farm Supply
R.R. 2, Box 1009
Belgrade, ME 04917-1009
Bill Getty
(207) 877-0870, (800) 768-9998
Fax: (207) 872-0929
E-mail: snowpond@mint.net
Web: www.mint.net/snowpond

Books ⁊ **Supplies** ⁊ **Tools**
Offers a good selection of **growing supplies**: beneficial insects, organic pest controls, hand tools, row covers, composting supplies, soil amendments, books on organic growing, and cedar seedling boxes and flats for those who hate plastic. They also sell **seed potatoes** and seed of cover crops. (1995)
📖 Catalog: Free, CAN/OV, CC
☉ Shop: Call ahead

Solarcone, Inc.
P.O. Box 67
Seward, IL 61077-0067
Lloyd & Dale Falconer
(815) 247-8454
Fax: (815) 247-8443
E-mail: LEF2226@aol.com
Web: members.aol.com/solarcone/solar.htm

Supplies
Distributors in the US of the Green Cone(TM) and the Green Keeper(TM), **composting containers**; the Green Cone breaks down kitchen waste, and produces small amounts of compost, the Green Keeper composts yard wastes. They sell direct to gardeners as well as to other suppliers. (1989)
📖 Catalog: Free, R&W, OV, CC, $9m

Spalding Laboratories
760 Printz Road
Arroyo Grande, CA 93420
Pat Spalding
(805) 489-5946, (800) 845-2847
Fax: (805) 489-0336
Web: www.spalding-labs.com

Supplies
Sells Fly Predators(R), **beneficial insects** for fly control, useful wherever flies are a problem -- around indoor plants, animals, farm buildings, greenhouses, compost piles, etc. Who doesn't have flies? (1976)
📖 Catalog: Free, R&W, CC, $10m

Spray-N-Grow, Inc.
P.O. Box 2137
Rockport, TX 78381-2137
The Muskopf Family
Fax: (512) 790-9313
E-mail: spraygro@shelley.dbstech.com
Web: www.spray-n-grow.com

Supplies
Offer Spray-N-Grow, a micronutrient **growth stimulant** which they say will make all plants grow better, and produce better and more fruit or flowers. Also sell Triple Action 20, a **fungicide** which controls bacteria, mold, germs, fungus, and mildew in home or garden. Also offer a fertilizer, wetting agent, and an animal repellent. (1982)
📖 Catalog: Free, R&W, CAN/OV, CC

Starcross Community
34500 Annapolis Road
Annapolis, CA 95412
Non-Profit Charity
(707) 886-1919
Fax: (707) 886-1921

Ornaments
Starcross is a small religious community near Tusker Press that cares for babies with AIDS; through their expertise they have helped orphanages in Eastern Europe to care for children with AIDS. A very worthy group, they sell **Christmas wreaths** and sun dried fruit to raise funds to support their work.
📖 Catalog: Free, CC

Steeling Nature
P.O. Box 96
New Castle, NH 03854
Walter Liff
(603) 431-7408
Fax: (603) 436-4390

Ornaments
Makes charming steel silhouette **sculptures**, mostly of animals and birds. There's one called "Feeding Time" of a little girl feeding cats that I'd kill for! Some are also available as bookends. (1993)
📖 Catalog: Long SASE w/2 FCS(2 IRC), R&W, CAN/OV, CC
✪ Shop: All year, daily, call ahead

Stillbrook Horticultural Supplies
P.O. Box 600
Bantam, CT 06750-0600
Bill Kennedy, Pres.
(800) 414-4468
Fax: (860) 567-5323

Supplies ∞ **Tools**
Offers a good selection of **hand tools**: Felco pruners and saws, trowels and weeders, plant labels, watering cans, plant stakes, fabric mulches and bird and deer netting, **bat and butterfly houses** and window boxes.
📖 Catalog: Free, CC

Stone Fish Studios
27887 Timber Road
Kelley, IA 50134
Dave & Sue Lowman
(515) 769-2446, (800) 528-2827
E-mail: lowman@netins.net

Books ∞ **Supplies** ∞ **Tools**
The name will fool you -- they sell **bonsai pots, books and tools**; a good selection of their own pots and imported pots as well. They also offer Artstone slabs and planting stones for bonsai and can make them to order from your sketch. Also sell plants for bonsai and finished bonsai. (1981)
📖 Catalog: $1, R&W, CAN/OV, CC
✪ Shop: All year, daily, call ahead

Stone Forest, Inc.
P.O. Box 2840
833 Dunlap Street
Santa Fe, NM 87504-2840
Michael Zimber
(505) 986-8883
Fax: (505) 982-2712

Ornaments
Offer hand-carved granite **garden ornaments**: lanterns, fountains and water basins, bridges, pedestals and lovely spheres, even some alpine troughs. The designs are Japanese in feeling, but not strictly traditional. (1989)
📖 Catalog: $3d($6 OV), R&W, CAN/OV, CC
✪ Shop: All year, M-Sa

Stony Point Ceramic Design
2080 Llano Road, #1B
Santa Rosa, CA 95407
Marni Turkel
(707) 579-5567, (800) 995-9553
Fax: (707) 579-1116
E-mail: mturkel@sonic.net

Supplies
Offers very attractive **ceramic pots** for flower arranging and as planters for orchids and houseplants. There are a number of designs, and you can ask to have a particular shape in the glaze of your choice. (1979)
📖 Catalog: $1d, R&W, CAN, CC
✪ Shop: All year, M-F, call ahead

Strong Injectors
3315 Monier Circle, Suite 2
Rancho Cordova, CA 95742
Tom Strong
(916) 635-7401
Fax: (916) 635-7402
E-mail: ADDIT123@aol.com
Web: www.jtr.com/DripIrr

Supplies
Offers several "Add-It" **fertilizer injectors**, which can be used in-line in your irrigation system, or with a hose; they can be used with any liquid fertilizer. Another catalog for Drip Rite Irrigation Products offers a complete line of drip irrigation supplies with lots of information. (1988)
📖 Catalog: Free, R&W, CAN/OV, CC
✪ Shop: All year, M-F

Stuewe and Sons, Inc.
2290 S.E. Kiger Island Drive
Corvallis, OR 97333
Eric & Shelly Stuewe
(541) 757-7798, (800) 553-5331
Fax: (541) 754-6617
E-mail: info@stuewe.com
Web: www.stuewe.com

Supplies
Stuewe is essentially a wholesale company, offering **forest seedling and deep nursery containers** and other tree propagation supplies, but anyone may buy from them; if you want less than a full case, they will charge you a modest repacking fee. Also offered are expanded polystyrene seedling blocks, "Cone-tainers," "Multi-pots," "Deepots," and "Treepots." (1981)
📖 Catalog: Free, CAN/OV, CC, $5m
☉ Shop: All year, M-F

Sturdi-Built Mfg. Co.
11304 S.W. Boones Ferry Road
Portland, OR 97219
Rick & Debby Warner
(503) 244-4100, (800) 722-4115

Supplies
Offers redwood **greenhouses** in a number of styles, both free-standing and lean-to, one model is round. Also sells accessories and equipment. They can be single or double-glazed and customized to fit your exact space. (1952)
📖 Catalog: Free, CAN, CC
☉ Shop: All year, M-F, or by appointment

Sumerset Arbors
P.O. Box 7243
Beaumont, TX 77726-7243
Sandra Fugitt
(800) 645-3391
Fax: (409) 892-0071

Ornaments
Offers beautiful **arbors** for the garden in several classical styles; available with gates, fencing or trellis. They even make a nice looking pergola. All are made from clear Western red cedar for durability. Prices are upscale for the larger structures.
📖 Catalog: Free($5 OV), R&W, CAN/OV

Sun Garden Specialties
P.O. Box 52382
Tulsa, OK 74152-0382
Tony Bishop
(800) 468-1638
Fax: (800) 468-1638

Ornaments
Offers custom made **ornaments for the Japanese garden**: signs and signposts in Japanese, a rustic Samurai seat, and sake barrel round signs in Japanese, all with your choice of text. (1990)
📖 Catalog: $2d($3 OV), R&W, CAN/OV, CC, $20m

Sundance Supply
1678 Shattuck Avenue, #173
Berkeley, CA 94709
Bob Daley
(800) 776-2534
E-mail: info@sundancesupply.com
Web: www.sundancesupply.com

Supplies
Offers design advice, parts and equipment for **greenhouses or sunrooms** that you build yourself. Sells double or triple-skin polycarbonate sheets, glazing parts, heaters, ventilators, and shading -- you buy the framing material locally. (1994)
📖 Catalog: $2, R&W, CAN, CC, $15m

Sunglo Solar Greenhouses
2626 15th Avenue W.
Seattle, WA 98119-2133
Joe Pappalardo
(206) 284-8900, (800) 647-0606
Fax: (206) 284-8945

Supplies
Manufacture and sell **greenhouses in kit form**, either freestanding or lean-to, with double or triple-wall construction; also offer greenhouse accessories in their Cascade Greenhouse Supply catalog.
📖 Catalog: Free, R&W, CAN, CC
☉ Shop: All year, M-Sa

Superior Growers Supply, Inc.
4870 Dawn Avenue
East Lansing, MI 48823
Jeff Gibson
(517) 332-2663, (800) 227-0027
Fax: (517) 332-6218
E-mail: SGSHydro@aol.com
Web: SGS-Hydroponic.com

**Books
 Supplies**
Offers **hydroponic growing supplies**: systems, rockwool, lights, propagation supplies, fans and temperature controls, organic and inorganic fertilizers, pest controls, books and magazines. People are always asking me where to find "Superthrive," and here it is!
📖 Catalog: Free, R&W, CAN/OV, CC

Symo-Life, Inc.
Route 1, Box 102
Gap, PA 17527
Floyd H. Ranck, Gen. Mgr.
(717) 442-4171

Supplies
Offers Erth-Rite **fertilizers and soil amendments** in several formulations for lawn and garden, roses, vegetables, trees, shrubs and bulbs; also greensand, bone meal, compost starter, diatomaceous earth, Maxicrop and other organic products. (1962)
📖 Catalog: Free, R&W, CAN/OV
☉ Shop: All year, M-F

TFS Injector Systems

See Strong Injectors.

Tec Laboratories, Inc.
P.O. Box 1958
Albany, OR 97321-1958
(541) 926-4577, (800) ITCHING
Fax: (541) 926-0218

Supplies
Tecnu **Poison Oak-n-Ivy Cleanser** really works! If you wash at once you can avoid the rash; it sits on my bathroom sink. They also make a sunscreen, a venom remover for insect bites and stings and a 10-hour insect repellent which repels ticks, and CalaGel, which makes poison oak rash disappear. Really! It worked for me! Call and they'll tell you where to buy them in your Zip Code.
📖 Catalog: Free, R&W, $5m

Terrace Software
P.O. Box 271
Medford, MA 02155-0002
Roberta Norin
(617) 396-0382
Fax: (617) 396-0382
E-mail: rln@metasoft.com

Services
Mum's the Word(TM) integrated **garden planning software** for the Macintosh; it combines object-oriented drawing tools with a horticultural database. Search for plants meeting your needs (or add your own plants), then "plant" it on your plan, automatically labeling the drawing.They also offer bel Terre Pro(TM), an advanced garden design program for the Mac. (1986)
📖 Catalog: Free, R&W, CAN/OV, CC

Texas Greenhouse Co., Inc.
2524 White Settlement Road
Ft. Worth, TX 76107
Kathy Carlile
(817) 335-5447, (800) 227-5447
Fax: (817) 334-0818
E-mail: tgci@why.net
Web: www.metroplexweb.com/tgci.htm

Supplies
Sells **greenhouses and lean-tos** with curved glass eaves, aluminum or redwood frames, and automatic venting in a variety of sizes; also a complete line of greenhouse equipment and accessories. (1948)
📖 Catalog: $4, CAN/OV, CC
⊙ Shop: All year, M-F

Timberleaf Soil Testing
39648 Old Spring Road
Murrieta, CA 92563
Bob & Valerie Russo
(909) 677-7510
Fax: (909) 677-7510
E-mail: bvrusso@alphainfo.com

Services
Small company does **soil testing** for the organic gardener and mini-farmer.
📖 Catalog: Free, CAN/OV

Topiary, Inc.
4520 Watrous Avenue
Tampa, FL 33629
Mia Hardcastle & Mary Beth Greiwe
Fax: (813) 282-9345
E-mail: mbgreiwe@topiaryinc.com
Web: topiaryinc.com

Ornaments
Painted galvanized wire **topiary frames** in many animal and other shapes, many available already planted. They also sell books, "The Complete Book of Topiary," and "The New Topiary" to help you get started. (1981)
📖 Catalog: Long SASE, R&W, CAN/OV, CC, $75m

Treesentials
P.O. Box 7097, Riverview Station
St. Paul, MN 55107-7097
Lawrence King & Joseph Lais
(800) 248-8239
Fax: (800) 809-5818

Supplies
Treesentials supplies **tree shelters** called "Supertubes"(TM); they offer seedling trees protection from animals and sunburn, provide good light and reduce moisture loss from transpiration. Also sell tree mats to suppress weeds, and a tree starting fertilizer. (1989)
📖 Catalog: Free, R&W, CAN/OV, CC, $5m

Tropical Plant Products, Inc.
P.O. Box 547754
1715 Silver Star Road
Orlando, FL 32854-7754
Kenneth & Janet Lewis
(407) 293-2451

Supplies
Sells **orchid growing supplies**: fertilizers, wire hanging baskets, coconut fiber, fir bark, moss, tree fern baskets, sphagnum moss and osmunda fiber, totems and plaques for mounting bromeliads, fertilizers and more. (1974)
📖 Catalog: Long SASE, R&W
⊙ Shop: All year, M-F, call ahead

Tumblebug
2029 N. 23rd Street
Boise, ID 83702
Henry Artis
(208) 368-7900, (800) 531-0102
Fax: (208) 343-2753
E-mail: TumbleBug@pcsedu.com
Web: webslingers.com/sites/TumbleBug/

Supplies
The Tumblebug(R) is a rolling **compost tumbler**, with angled sides so that it will stay where you put it -- you can roll it to where you want it, fill it, and then let your kids roll it around to make compost. (1991)
📖 Catalog: Free, R&W, CAN/OV, CC

Marni Turkel

See Stony Point Ceramic Design

Turner Greenhouses
P.O. Box 1260
Highway 117 South
Goldsboro, NC 27533-1260
Gary Smithwick
(919) 734-8345, (800) 672-4770
Fax: (919) 736-4550

Books ∾ Supplies
Galvanized steel-framed **greenhouses** in various sizes and configurations, available with fiberglass or polyethylene coverings, as well as a full line of equipment, accessories and books on propagation and gardening. (1939)
📖 Catalog: Free, R&W, CAN, CC, $10m
○ Shop: All year, M-F

Twinholly's
3633 NE 19th Avenue
Portland, OR 97212
Sandra H. Nigro
Fax: (503) 231-4609
E-mail: SandyN@kath.com

Supplies
Twinholly's has no catalog, but sells glassine **seed storage envelopes** useful for saving and sending seeds to gardening friends. They cost $4 for a package of 50 envelopes; each package contains three sizes. Available in bulk for growers, or presumably, to clubs for seed exchanges. (1991)
📖 Catalog: Long SASE, R&W, CAN/OV

U. S. Post Office
Every Town, USA

Services
You can purchase **international money orders** through your local post office: ask for an "Application for International Money Order." The post office will collect the money for payment and a fee, and a money order will be forwarded to the payee from St. Louis -- it will indicate who is sending the money.

Under Glass Mfg. Corp.
P.O. Box 798
Lake Katrine, NY 12449-0798
William D. Orange, Mgr.
(914) 336-5050
Fax: (914) 336-5097

Supplies
Manufacturers of **greenhouses and solariums**, they are the successors to Lord & Burnham and continue with their designs and features. They will put you in touch with a distributor if you live near one, or will sell to you direct if there's no distributor nearby. (1989)
📖 Catalog: $3, R&W, CAN/OV, CC

Unique Insect Control

See A-1 Unique Insect Control.

The Urban Farmer Store
2833 Vicente Street
San Francisco, CA 94116-2721
Tom Bressan
(415) 661-2201, (800) 753-3747
Fax: (415) 661-7826

Supplies
Specialize in **drip and automatic irrigation systems**; catalog is a good all-around introduction to the subject and offers all the necessary parts and equipment. Carry products of thirty manufacturers and kits of their own; also offer a wide selection of low voltage **outdoor lighting** systems, and water garden supplies and accessories.
📖 Catalog: Free, CC, $10m
○ Shop: All year, M-Sa

Valley Oak Tool Company
448 West 2nd Avenue
Chico, CA 95926-3816
David Grau
(916) 342-6188

Tools
Valley Oak makes a **wheel hoe**, an updated version designed to reduce back strain and be easy to use; a four-tine cultivator and furrow attachment are available. (1990)
📖 Catalog: Free, CAN/OV

Verilux, Inc.
P.O. Box 2937
9 Viaduct Road, Stamford, CT
Stamford, CT 06907-2937
Nicholas Harmon
(203) 921-2430, (800) 786-6850, X 11
Fax: (203) 921-2427
E-mail: Verilux@aol.com
Web: Ergolight.com

Supplies
Full spectrum Verilux Instant Sun **fluorescent plant lights** are balanced to promote normal, compact growth and blooming -- long-lasting and available in various sizes for home or commercial use. (1956)
- Catalog: Free, R&W, CAN/OV, CC, $35m
- Shop: All year, M-F, by appointment only

The Violet House
P.O. Box 1274
Gainesville, FL 32602-1274
Bill & Bebe Edwards
(352) 377-8465, (800) 377-8466
Fax: (352) 372-0102

Supplies
Offer **indoor growing supplies** -- plastic pots, wick-watering reservoirs, fertilizers, pesticides and potting materials for growing African violets and other houseplants. They also sell African violet seeds. (1975)
- Catalog: Free($1 OV), R&W, CAN/OV, CC
- Shop: All year, M-F, call ahead

West Coast Weather Vanes
417-C Ingalls Street
Santa Cruz, CA 95060
Lisbeth A. Jensen
(408) 425-5505, (800) 762-8736
Fax: (408) 425-5514
E-mail: wcwvane@ix.netcom.com
Web: WCWVanes@ix.netcom.com

Ornaments
Sell lovely hand-crafted **copper weathervanes** in a variety of designs. Some are available in several sizes to fit the situation in which they'll be used. Many are specific birds, dogs, and other animals or sea creatures. An investment, but a daily object of beauty and delight. (1988)
- Catalog: Free, CAN/OV, CC
- Shop: All year, M-F or by appointment

Wheeler Arts
66 Lake Park
Champaign, IL 61821-7132
Stephen Wheeler
(217) 359-6816
Fax: (217) 359-8716
E-mail: wheeler@aol.com
Web: users.aol.com/wheelers/

Services
For those caught up in the home-publishing frenzy, here is a source of nice **horticultural clip art** called "Quick Art," both printed or on either computer disk or CD-ROM. There is a nice variety of subjects, both horticultural and agricultural. (1973)
- Catalog: 3 FCS($2 OV), R&W, CAN/OV, CC

Wind & Weather
P.O. Box 2320
Watertower, Albion & Kasten Sts.
Mendocino, CA 95460-2320
Michael Rogers
(707) 964-1284, (800) 922-9463
Fax: (707) 964-1278

Ornaments ☙ **Books** ☙ **Supplies**
Everything you need to enjoy and record the weather: **weather instruments**, shelters for weather stations, weathervanes, wind chimes, sundials, whimsical garden ornaments, and books on weather -- even some for children. (1974)
- Catalog: Free($5 OV), CAN/OV, CC
- Shop: All year, daily

Windleaves
7560 Morningside Drive
Indianapolis, IN 46240
Bart Kister
(317) 251-1381

Ornaments
Manufacture and sell **windvanes** sculpted in the shapes of leaves -- several styles, such as tuliptree, dogwood, ginkgo and maple; they can be stuck in the ground in the garden or mounted on a roof; can inscribe special messages or reproduce other leaves on special order. (1983)
- Catalog: $1d, R&W, CAN/OV, $190m
- Shop: By appointment only

Winged Weeder

See Creative Enterprises.

Winterthur Museum & Gardens
Route 52
Winterthur, DE 19735
Nan Pritchard, Mgr.
(302) 888-4714, (800) 767-0500
Fax: (800) 676-3299

Furniture ✍ Ornaments
Catalog from the Winterthur Museum & Gardens offers beautiful reproductions of ornaments on display both in the gardens and in the house, as well as some special plants from the gardens. A good selection of **gifts and garden ornaments** for any garden or gardener -- many tempting items. Retail shops at Winterthur and at 207 King Street, Alexandria, VA.
📖 Catalog: Free, CAN/OV (ornaments only), CC
🔾 Shop: All year, daily

Wisconsin Wagon Co.
507 Laurel Avenue
Janesville, WI 53545
Albert and Lois Hough
(608) 754-0026

Supplies
Make wooden children's toys, including **wheelbarrows**, sleds and great Janesville wagons. They also make an awning-covered **patio cart**, and have added an adult-size wheelbarrow, probably because the little one is so cute that grown-ups had to have them, too. (1979)
📖 Catalog: Free, CAN/OV, CC
🔾 Shop: February-Christmas, M-F, call ahead

Wisconsin Woodworks
9707 Moen Valley Road
Black Earth, WI 53515
Jane & Jeff Heckman
(608) 767-2668
Fax: (608) 767-2668
E-mail: WiscWood@ITIS.com

Furniture
Sell rustic wooden **garden furniture**; some of their chairs and benches ride on rocking springs made by a farm equipment maker for durability and spring. They are made of red cedar or hard maple. (1989)
📖 Catalog: Free, R&W, CAN/OV, CC, $75m
🔾 Shop: All year, M-F

Womanswork
P.O. Box 543
York, ME 03909-0543
Nancy Bennett Phillips
(207) 363-0804, (800) 639-2709
Fax: (207) 363-0805
E-mail: wmnsgloves@aol.com

Supplies
Specialize in **gardening and work gloves** made to fit women's hands; they come in many styles and several weights, and in four sizes as well as long gauntlet gloves for working around roses. They also make a practical work-apron, sun visors, and a pair of heavy work boots for women. (1985)
📖 Catalog: Free, R&W, CAN/OV, CC

Wood Classics
20 Osprey Lane
Gardiner, NY 12525
Eric & Barbara Goodman
(914) 255-5599
Fax: (914) 255-7881

Furniture
Nicely crafted American-made **wooden outdoor (and indoor) furniture** in rustic and classic styles -- tables, chairs, lounges, porch swings and rockers, made of mahogany or teak; all available assembled or in kits. (1983)
📖 Catalog: $2, CAN/OV, CC
🔾 Shop: All year, M-Sa

Wood Violet Books
3814 Sunhill Drive
Madison, WI 53704
Debra S. Cravens
(608) 837-7207
Fax: (608) 825-3073
E-mail: wvbooks@aol.com

Books ✍ Services
New and used books, specializing in books on herbs and other garden subjects, including cookbooks for garden produce; they will search for hard-to-find books, and special order books you can't find. (1983)
📖 Catalog: $2, CAN/OV, CC
🔾 Shop: All year, by appointment only

Elisabeth Woodburn
P.O. Box 398
Hopewell, NJ 08525-0398
Bradford Lyon & Joanne Fuccello
(609) 466-0522

Books ✍ Services
Specialists in horticultural books, including **new, used, out-of-print and very rare books** for libraries and serious gardeners; separate catalogs for various categories are $2 each; let them know your interests. They do book searches and collection development, too. (1946)
📖 Catalog: See notes, CAN/OV
🔾 Shop: M-Sa, by appointment only

Gary W. Woolson, Bookseller
2514 Western Avenue
Newburgh, ME 04444-4753
Gary W. Woolson
(207) 234-4931

Books
Specializes in **used and out-of-print books** on plants and gardening; also carries used books in many other fields. (1967)
📖 Catalog: Free, R&W
🔾 Shop: By appointment or by chance

Worm's Way, Inc.
7850 North State Road 37
Bloomington, IN 47404-9477
Martin Heydt, Pres.
(812) 876-6450, (800) 274-9676
Fax: (800) 316-1264
E-mail: info@wormsway.com
Web: www.wormsway.com

Supplies
Supplier of a broad range of **hydroponic equipment, indoor growing supplies, pest controls** and even beer making supplies. They have retail stores in Indiana, Missouri, Massachusetts and Florida; call for locations. (1985)
📖 Catalog: Free, R&W, CAN/OV, CC
✪ Shop: All year, M-Sa

Yanzum -- Art for Gardens
P.O. Box 8573
1285 Peachtree Street N.E.
Atlanta, GA 31106-0573
Douglas Yaney
(404) 874-8063, (800) 388-4443
Fax: (404) 874-1600
E-mail: yanzum@mindspring.com

Ornaments
Offers a broad selection of **planters, statues, birdbaths** and **bird houses**, all very handsome, as well as many other garden ornaments, including works from local artists. Most are playful and amusing. (1989)
📖 Catalog: 2 FCS, CAN/OV, CC

Yonah Manufacturing Co.
P.O. Box 280
Airport Road
Cornelia, GA 30531-0280
Jim Bruce
(706) 778-8654, (800) 972-8057
Fax: (706) 776-2218

Supplies
Sell **shade cloth** providing from 30% to 92% shade, used for greenhouses, shade structures, patio covers, etc. Sold cut to your specifications with bindings and rust proof brass grommets. (1975)
📖 Catalog: Free, CAN/OV, CC
✪ Shop: All year, M-F, call ahead

© Topiary, Inc.
Artist: Mia Hardcastle

PROFESSIONAL SOCIETIES AND TRADE ASSOCIATIONS

Professional societies, trade associations and umbrella groups are listed alphabetically.

Except where indicated, membership in these organizations is limited to those in specific trades or professions. Umbrella groups, although not open to general membership, can put you in touch with local affiliates.

Trade associations are listed because they are often excellent sources of information not available elsewhere. Many have useful promotional publications available to anyone, others have an active public relations representative who will field your questions. Qualifications for membership do not include most people; contact the group for membership information.

Professional societies are listed to help you connect with or get information from groups in fields of professional interest; inquire about membership and dues.

Some of the organizations listed here are groups formed to promote some particular conservation goal and are open to all.

A table of the symbols and abbreviations used in this book
appears inside the front and back covers.

All America Selections
National Garden Bureau
1311 Butterfield Road, Suite 310
Downers Grove, IL 60515
(630) 963-0770

Introduce the "All-American Selections" each year -- a vegetable and an annual flower. They test new varieties of flowers and vegetables grown from seed. Send a long SASE for their list of trial gardens.

Alliance for Historic Landscape Preservation
Sharon Crawford
2252 Stanwood Drive
Santa Barbara, CA 93103
(805) 899-4922
AHLP Newsletter (2)

A professional organization dedicated to the preservation and conservation of historic landscapes in all their variety, from formal gardens and public parks to rural expanses, and the design of landscapes for historic buildings.
☐ E-mail: crawforddw@juno.com

American Association of Botanical Gardens & Arboreta
Andrea Mendel
786 Church Road
Wayne, PA 19087
(610) 688-1120
Fax: (610) 293-0149
The Public Garden (4)
AABGA Newsletter (12)

Professional association of botanical gardens, with regional meetings in various locations. Newsletter lists positions available in botanical gardens and they publish an annual Internship Directory. Focus is botanical garden management, curation of plant collections, education.
☐ Privileges: Conventions Library

American Association of Nurserymen
Beth Isom
1250 Eye Street NW, Suite 500
Washington, DC 20005
(202) 789-2900
Fax: (202) 789-1893
AAN Today (6)

Trade association providing services and information to nurserymen. Publish a directory of the nursery industry with a classified directory of goods and services; it includes many wholesale nurseries.
☐ E-mail: aanhq@aol.com
☐ Privileges: Conventions

American Community Gardening Association
100 North 20th Street
Philadelphia, PA 19103-1495
(215) 988-8785
Community Gardening Review (1)
ACGA Multilogue (6)

Umbrella association for the community gardening movement; write for information. You can call only on Tuesdays between 10-2 EST.
☐ Privileges: Conventions

American Horticultural Therapy Association
362A Christopher Ave.
Gaithersburg, MD 20879
(800) 634-1603
Journal of Therapeutic Horticulture (1)
People Plant Connection (11)

Professional association devoted to using horticulture to enhance the lives of special populations through therapy and vocational rehabilitation. They offer a free fact sheet describing the association, careers in horticultural therapy, and a resource list.
☐ Chapters: 10
☐ Privileges: Conventions

American Seed Trade Association
Dean Urmston, Executive V.P.
601 13th Street NW, Suite 570 South
Washington, DC 20005-1593
(202) 638-3128
Fax: (202) 638-3171

A trade group representing companies that sell seeds and related products.
☐ Web: amseed.com

American Society of Botanical Artists, Inc.
Michele Meyer
1290 Jackson St. #4
San Francisco, CA 94109-3224
(415) 440-6069
Fax: (516) 929-6215
The Botanical Artist (3)

A new group of botanical artists; they recommend "The Art of Botanical Illustration" by Wilfrid Blunt and William T. Stearn, and "Botanical Illustration in Watercolor" by Eleanor Wunderlich.
☐ E-mail: SFMCM@aol.com
☐ Web: Huntbot.andrew.cmu.edu/ASBA/ASBotArtists.html
☐ Privileges: Conventions Exhibits

American Society of Landscape Architects
Patricia Massey, Membership
636 Eye Street
Washington, DC 20001-3736
Fax: (202) 898-1185
Landscape Architecture (12)

An active professional association; write for information on membership.
☐ Web: www.asla.org/asla/
☐ Privileges: Conventions Library Books

Associated Landscape Contractors of America
Debra Atkins
150 Elden Street , Suite 270
Herndon, VA 20170
(703) 736-9666
Fax: (703) 736-9668
Landscape Contractors News (12)

Trade association devoted to exchange of business and technical information among its members; they have many educational programs and conferences.
☐ Web: alca.org

**Association for Living Historical Farms
& Agricultural Museums**
J. M. Sheridan
8774 Route 45 NW
North Bloomfield, OH 44450-9701
(216) 685-4410
Fax: (216) 685-4410
The Bulletin (6)

Group concerned with the preservation and interpretation of agricultural history and country life in earlier times. They share information on historic crops, fruits and garden plants.
☐ Web: www.mystic.org/alhfam
☐ Privileges: Conventions

Assn. of Professional Landscape Designers
Jack Lagershausen
11 S. La Salle St., Ste. 1400
Chicago, IL 60603
(312) 201-0101
Fax: (312) 201-0214
APLD News (3)

Formed to create professional guidelines and standards for landscape designers. They will send a list of landscape designers in your area on request.
☐ E-mail: 74733.1624@compuserve.com
☐ Privileges: Conventions

Association of Specialty Cut Flower Growers
Judy M. Laushman
M.P.O. Box 268
Oberlin, OH 44074-0268
(216) 774-2887
Fax: (216) 774-2435
Cut Flower Quarterly
Proceedings of National Conferences (1)

A group dedicated to growing cut flowers for market. They recommend "Specialty Cut Flowers" by Allan Armitage.
☐ Web: www.flora-source.com/ascfg
☐ Privileges: Conventions Books Exhibits Trips

Association of Zoological Horticulture
c/o Rob Halpern
Bronx Zoo
Bronx, NY 10460
Zoo Horticulture (4)

Group of horticulturists at zoos, promoting naturalistic landscaping and botanical collections which suit their animal exhibits.
☐ Privileges: Conventions

Bedding Plants Foundation, Inc.
Sue Goepp
P.O. Box 27241
Lansing, MI 48909-0517
(517) 694-8537
Fax: (517) 694-8560

The Foundation funds research for the greenhouse industry. They publish Final Research Reports of research funded by the BPFI. They recommend "Ball Culture Guide" and "Ball Redbook" for basic cultural guidelines on growing bedding plants.
☐ Privileges: Conventions Library Books Exhibits

Bedding Plants, International
John Greenslit, Director
P.O. Box 27517
Lansing, MI 48909-0517
(517) 694-7700
Fax: (517) 694-8560
PPGA News (12)

This group provides technical and business information for commercial growers and retailers. Formerly the Professional Plant Growers Association.
☐ Garden: Trial garden, 1980 N. College Rd., Mason, MI
☐ Privileges: Conventions Books Exhibits Trips Tours

California Urban Forests Council
Mel Johnson
1310 Clayton Street #12
San Francisco, CA 94114
(415) 431-6428
CUF-LINK (4)

A group that works to promote effective urban forestry, through planning, planting, management, research and education.
☐ E-mail: cufc@Pacbell.net
☐ Privileges: Conventions

Canadian Horticultural Therapy Association
Nancy Lee-Colibaba
c/o Royal Botanical Garden, Box 399
Hamilton, ON, Canada L8N 3H8
(905) 527-1158 X251
CHTA Newsletter (4)

Association provides support and training for people in recreational and occupational therapy programs. It publishes a looseleaf informational guide which is updated with pages that come with the newsletter.
☐ Privileges: Conventions

Canadian Plant Conservation Program
c/o Devonian Botanic Garden
University of Alberta
Edmonton, AB, Canada T6G 2EI

Write for information.

Center for Plant Conservation
Missouri Botanical Garden
P.O. Box 299
St. Louis, MO 63166-0299
(314) 577-9450
Fax: (314) 577-9465
Plant Conservation (2)

Coordinates the national collection of endangered plants, in cooperation with a consortium of 25 botanic gardens in the continental US and Hawaii.
☐ E-mail: cpc@mobot.org
☐ Web: www.mobot.org/cpc
☐ Garden: 25 gardens; write for list

The Council on Botanical & Horticultural Libraries, Inc.
John F. Reed
The New York Botanical Garden
Bronx, NY 10458-5126
(718) 817-8729
Fax: (718) 817-8956
Newsletter (4)

Association of libraries in the field of botany and horticulture. They recommend "Guide to Information Sources in the Botanical Sciences," 2nd ed., Englewood, CO, Libraries Unlimited, 1996.
☐ E-mail: jfreed@nybg.org
☐ Web: Huntbot.andrew.cmu.edu/CBHL
☐ Privileges: Conventions

Garden Centers of America
Clint Albin
1250 Eye Street Northwest, Suite 500
Washington, DC 20005
(202) 789-2900
GCA Newsletter (6)

The trade association of retail nurseries; has over 3,500 member firms.

The Garden Club of America
598 Madison Avenue
New York, NY 10022
(212) 753-8287
Fax: (212) 753-0134
GCA Bulletin (5)

Umbrella organization for 192 local garden clubs; it has programs for awards and scholarships, civic improvement and education to promote the love of gardening.
☐ Web: www.interport.net/~gca

The Garden Conservancy
Julie Kantor
P.O. Box 219
Cold Spring, NY 10516
(914) 265-2029
Fax: (914) 265-9620
Newsletter of the Garden Conservancy (3)

A group devoted to preserving private gardens of particular historical or horticultural interest. Membership open to all; members can purchase the directory of open gardens at a discount.
☐ E-mail: gardencons@aol.com
☐ Privileges: Trips Tours

Garden Writers Association of America
Robert C. LaGasse
10210 Leatherleaf Court
Manassas, VA 20111
(703) 257-1032
Fax: (703) 257-0213
Quill & Trowel (6)

Association of professional garden writers and broadcasters, and those involved in publicizing the horticultural industry.
☐ E-mail: AssnCntr@idsonline.com
☐ Privileges: Conventions Exhibits

The Gardeners of America
Men's Garden Clubs of America, Inc.
Carol Donovan, Exec. Sec.
P.O. Box 241; 5560 Merle Hay Road
Johnston, IA 50131-0241
(515) 278-0295
Fax: (515) 278-6245
The Gardener Magazine (6)
Newsletter (6)

Founded as the Men's Garden Club of America, this umbrella organization now welcomes women and has a broad program of service in local communities.
☐ Chapters: 128
☐ Garden: President's Perennial Park, Johnston, IA
☐ Privileges: Conventions Library Books Plants Exhibits

Great Northern Botanicals Association
P.O. Box 362
Helena, Montana 59624
GNBA Newsletter (4)

This is a regional association for growers of specialty crops.
☐ Privileges: Conventions

Herb Growing & Marketing Network
Maureen Rogers
P.O. Box 245
Silver Spring, PA 17575-0245
(717) 393-3295
Fax: (717) 393-9261
The Herbal Connection (6)
The Herbal Green Pages (1)

Group formed to unite those engaged in the production and marketing of herbs and to educate the public about herbs and herb-related products. "The Herbal Connection" is available by separate subscription; write for price.
☐ E-mail: herbworld@aol.com
☐ Web: www.herbnet.com
☐ Privileges: Conventions Tours

Historic Preservation Committee
American Society of Landscape Architects
636 Eye Street NW
Washington, D.C. 20001-3736
Fax: (202) 898-1185
Land and History (3-4)

This group is dedicated to the conservation and preservation of historic landscapes of all kinds.
☐ Privileges: Conventions

Horticultural Research Institute
1250 Eye Street Northwest, Suite 500
Washington, DC 20005
(202) 789-2900
Journal of Environmental Horticulture (4)

Trade association; this is the research arm of the American Association of Nurserymen.

International Plant Propagation Society
Dr. John A. Wott, Box 358010
Washington Park Arboretum
Seattle, WA 98195
(206) 543-8602
Fax: (206) 527-2796
Proceedings (1)

A professional group devoted to the art and science of plant propagation.
☐ E-mail: Jwott10623@aol.com
☐ Web: www.ipps.org/ipps
☐ Chapters: 8

International Society of Arboriculture
William P. Kruidenier
#6 Dunlap Ct. P.O. Box GG
Savoy, IL 61874
(217) 355-9411
Fax: (217) 355-9516
Journal of Arboriculture (6)
The Arborist News (6)

Dedicated to tree preservation and research.
❑ E-mail: isa@isa-arbor.com
❑ Web: www.ag.uiuc.edu/~isa

The Irrigation Association
Thomas Kimmell, Exec. Dir.
8260 Willow Oaks Corp. Dr. Suite 120
Fairfax, VA 22031
(703) 573-3551
Fax: (703) 573-1913
Irrigation Business and Technology (6)

Trade association to promote the use of modern irrigation equipment and water and soil conservation.
❑ Web: www.irrigation.org
❑ Privileges: Conventions Books

Landscape Ontario
Horticultural Trades Association
Toni DiGiovanni
7856 Fifth Line South, RR#4
Milton, ON, Canada L9T 2X8
(905) 875-1805
Fax: (905) 875-3942
Landscape Trades (9)
Horticulture Review (12)

Association for the horticultural trade in Ontario. Journals are available on subscription (each) for C$32 in Canada, C$42 in the US and overseas.
❑ E-mail: LO@mail.westonia.com
❑ Web: www.hort-trades.com
❑ Privileges: Conventions Exhibits Tours

The Lawn Institute
James Brooks
3020 Roswell Road, Suite 200
Marietta, GA 30062
(770) 977-5492
Fax: (770) 977-8205
Harvests Newsletter (4)

Non-profit trade association to enhance lawn grass research and education. Periodical is available on separate subscription.

Mailorder Gardening Association
P.O. Box 2129
Columbia, MD 21045
Fax: (410) 730-9619
Garden Catalog Guide (1)
Mail Order Gardening Reference Guide (1)

Trade association of mail-order nurseries. Sell an annual Garden Catalog Guide listing members; $2 ppd. (US$2.50 to Canada).
❑ Web: www.gardenscape.com/mgahomepage.htm
❑ Privileges: Conventions

Metro Hort Group, Inc.
Lisa Miller
P.O. Box 1113
New York, NY 10185
(212) 799-1276

An association of horticultural professionals in the New York City Area. They sponsor meetings, lectures, workshops, and field visits.
❑ Privileges: Exhibits Trips

National Arbor Day Foundation
100 Arbor Avenue
Nebraska City, NE 68410
(402) 474-5655
Fax: (402) 474-0820
Arbor Day (6)
Tree City USA Bulletin (6)

A national nonprofit educational organization dedicated to tree planting and conservation; offers special trees to its members. Membership open to all.
❑ Web: www.arborday.org
❑ Privileges: Plants Tours

National Council of State Garden Clubs, Inc.
401 Magnolia Avenue
St. Louis, MO 63110
The National Gardener (6)

Umbrella group for state garden clubs, which in themselves are umbrella organizations for 11,000 local garden clubs.

National Garden Bureau

See All America Selections.

National Wildflower Research Center
Membership Department
4801 La Crosse Avenue
Austin, TX 78739
(512) 292-4200
Fax: (512) 292-4627
Wildflower Newsletter (6)

National group to promote conservation and use of native plants in public and private landscapes. Membership open to all.
☐ E-mail: nwrc@onr.com
☐ Web: www.wildflower.org
☐ Garden: Display/research garden at the Center
☐ Privileges: Conventions Library Tours

Ontario Horticultural Association
Mrs. Bonnie Warner
RR #3
Englehart, ON, Canada POJ 1HO
(705) 544-2474
Fax: (705) 544-2474
Ontario Horticultural Assn. Newsletter (4)

Umbrella organization for horticultural societies in Ontario; publishes a schedule of agricultural fairs and exhibitions and helps local groups with suggestions for programs and useful resources.
☐ Privileges: Conventions

People-Plant Council
407 Saunders Hall
Blacksburg, VA 24061-0327
(540) 231-6254
Fax: (540) 231-3083
People-Plant Council News (4)

An umbrella group which encourages research into the sociological benefits that people derive from working with plants, through therapy, education and community efforts. They have published "Proceedings" from three Council symposia.
☐ E-mail: pdrelf@vt.edu
☐ Web: http://www.ext.vt.edu/hort/consumer/human
☐ Privileges: Books

Perennial Plant Association
Steven M. Still
3383 Schirtzinger Road
Hilliard, OH 43026
(614) 771-8431
Fax: (614) 876-5238
Perennial Plants (4)

Trade association; promotes the development of the perennial plant industry, holds symposia and conferences.
☐ Privileges: Conventions Books Tours

Soil & Water Conservation Society
Karen Howe
7515 N.E. Ankeny Road
Ankeny, IA 50021-9764
(515) 289-2331
Fax: (515) 289-1227
Journal of Soil & Water Conservation (6)

Purpose is to advance the science and art of good land use.
☐ Web: www.swcs.org
☐ Garden: Native grass meadow at headquarters, Ankeny, IA
☐ Privileges: Conventions Books

United Plant Savers
Membership Secretary
P. O. Box 420
East Barre, VT 05649
(802) 479-9825
Fax: (802) 476-3772
Newsletter (3)

A professional society, open to North American members, dedicated to preserving native medicinal plants. They recommend "Ecoherbalist Handbook" by Gregory Tilford.
☐ Garden: They have a "model farm" near Athens, Ohio
☐ Privileges: Conventions Seeds Plants

HORTICULTURAL SOCIETIES

Horticultural societies are listed alphabetically.

See the Index section for:

L. Society Index: an index of horticultural societies listed by plant and/or other special interests.

SOCIETIES

I have listed only societies that are of international, national or regional interest. There are also local garden clubs, regional chapters of national and state organizations and the "friends" groups at botanical gardens, all of which have activities and programs of interest. Ask at your favorite nursery, city recreation department, public or horticultural libraries, chamber of commerce or at the ornamental horticulture department of your local college to find out about local groups.

If you travel, consider the advantages of joining an international or foreign group a year or so before you go in order to find out about events and places you'd like to include in your plans.

I have to laugh now when I think how shy I was about daring to join the "experts." My experiences have been pure pleasure; I've learned a lot, volunteered time to useful projects, made many new friends — and I usually come home from meetings with a new plant. The gardener's greatest resource is other gardeners. The more you get into the network, the greater your pleasure will be!

WARNING!

Nothing seems to change more quickly than the membership secretaries, addresses and membership dues of societies. We no longer try to keep up with dues, and suggest that you write to the address listed and ask for information about the society so that you'll know how much to send and where to send it.

A table of the symbols and abbreviations used in this book appears inside the front and back covers.

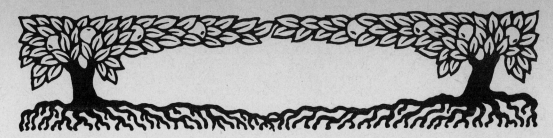

African Violet Society of America
Cindy Chatelain, Off. Mgr.
2375 North Street
Beaumont, TX 77702-1722
(409) 839-4725
Fax: (409) 839-4329
African Violet Magazine (6)

They recommend "Insect and Mite Pests of African Violets" by Charles Cole, "Growing to Show" by Pauline Bartholomew, and "The African Violet Society of America Handbook for Growers, Exhibitors and Judges."
☐ E-mail: avsa@avsa.org
☐ Web: avsa.org
☐ Privileges: Conventions Library Exhibits

African Violet Society of Canada
Mrs. Bonnie Scanlan
1573 Arbourdale Avenue
Victoria, BC, Canada V8N 5J1
Chatter (4)

Write for information.
☐ Chapters: 35
☐ Privileges: Conventions Library Seeds Exhibits Trips

Alabama Wildflower Society
George Wood
11120 Ben Clements Road
Northport, AL 35475
(205) 339-2541
Newsletter (2)

Write for information.
☐ E-mail: alawild1@aol.com
☐ Web: members.aol.com/alawild1/plant1.html
☐ Chapters: 8
☐ Privileges: Conventions Plants Exhibits Trips

Alaska Native Plant Society
Verna Pratt
P.O. Box 141613
Anchorage, AK 99514-1613
(907) 333-8212
Fax: (907) 333-4989
Borealis (8)

Society recommends reading Hulten's "Flora of Alaska" for a scientific study, or Pratt's "Field Guide to Alaskan Wildflowers" for a general introduction.
☐ E-mail: akkrafts@alaska.net
☐ Chapters: 2
☐ Privileges: Books Seeds Exhibits Trips

Aloe, Cactus & Succulent Society of Zimbabwe
Hon. Secretary
P.O. Box CY 300
Causeway, Zimbabwe
263 Harare 465-368
The INGENS Bulletin (2)
Excelsa (biennial)

Periodically holds major international conventions; also publishes the Excelsa Taxonomic Series.
☐ Privileges: Plants Exhibits Trips

Alpine Garden Society
The Secretary
AGS Centre, Avonbank
Pershore, Worcs., England WR10 3JP
44 (0) 1386 554-790
Fax: 44 (0) 1386 554-801
Quarterly Bulletin (4)
Newsletter (4)

Publishes a very interesting bulletin. This group has an excellent seed exchange and an extensive list of alpine and rock garden books for sale to members. They recommend their own two volume "Encyclopedia of Alpine Plants."
☐ E-mail: ags@alpinegardensoc.demon.co.uk
☐ Web: www.alpinegardensoc.demon.co.uk/
☐ Chapters: 61
☐ Garden: Display Garden at the Headquarters
☐ Privileges: Conventions Library Books Seeds Plants Exhibits Tours

American Bamboo Society
Membership Secretary
750 Krumkill Road
Albany, NY 12203-5957
(518) 458-7618
Fax: (518) 458-7625
Journal (1)
Newsletter (6)

The purpose of the society is to publish information about bamboo, and to introduce new species. Display gardens at Quail Botanical Gardens, Encinitas, CA; Coastal Gardens, Savannah, GA, and Fairchild Tropical Gardens, Coral Gables, FL.
☐ Web: www.bamboo.org/abs/
☐ Chapters: 9
☐ Garden: See notes
☐ Privileges: Conventions Books Seeds Plants Exhibits Trips Tours

American Begonia Society
John Ingles, Jr.
157 Monument Road
Rio Dell, CA 95562
(707) 764-5407
The Begonian (6)

There are a number of special interest round-robin letter "flights;" round robin members meet at conventions.
☐ Web: www.loop.com/-BEGONIA/Index.html
☐ Chapters: 51
☐ Garden: Dallas/Ft. Worth Botanical Gardens
☐ Privileges: Conventions Books Seeds Plants Exhibits Trips Tours

American Bonsai Society
Patricia DeGroot
P.O. Box 1136
Puyallup, WA 98371-1136
(206) 841-8992
Fax: (206) 841-8992
Bonsai Journal (4)

They publish and sell "Basic Bonsai Design," by David DeGroot. $15.50 postpaid.
☐ Web: www.paonline.com/abs
☐ Privileges: Conventions Books Tours

American Boxwood Society
Katherine Ward
134 Methodist Church Lane
W. Augusta, VA 24485
(540) 939-4646
The Boxwood Bulletin (4)

Has Boxwood Workshops twice a year, annual tour in Mid-Atlantic states. "The Boxwood Handbook" was published in late 1993; it's $15 postpaid. They also publish an excellent buyers guide for members.
☐ Garden: National Arboretum, Washington, DC
☐ Privileges: Conventions Books Plants

American Camellia Society
100 Massee Lane
Fort Valley, GA 31030
(912) 967-2358
Fax: (912) 967-2083
The Camellia Journal (4)
American Camellia Yearbook

Offers "Camellia Culture for Beginners" for $2.
☐ E-mail: acs@mail.peach.public.lib.ga.us
☐ Web: www.peach.public.lib.ga.us/ACS/acs.htm
☐ Garden: Historic Massee Lane Gardens, Ft. Valley, GA
☐ Privileges: Conventions Library Books Plants Exhibits

American Conifer Society
Maud Henne, Exec. Secy.
P.O. Box 360
Keswick, VA 22947-0360
(804) 984-3660
Fax: (804) 984-3660
American Conifer Society Bulletin (4)

Society of hobbyists, professionals, nurserymen, and educators. They will send you a free brochure introducing garden conifers with your membership application. They recommend "Conifers, The Illustrated Encyclopedia" edited by van Gelderen and van Hoey Smith, and "Manual of Cultivated Conifers" by Krussmann.
☐ E-mail: mbhchville@aol.com
☐ Chapters: 3
☐ Privileges: Conventions Books Seeds Plants

American Daffodil Society, Inc.
Naomi J. Liggett
4126 Winfield Road
Colombus, OH 43220-4606
(614) 451-4747
The Daffodil Journal (4)

They publish "Handbook for Growing, Exhibiting and Judging Daffodils," available for $7, and recommend "Daffodils for American Gardens," by Brent & Becky Heath.
☐ E-mail: NLiggett@compuserve.com
☐ Web: www.mc.edu/~adswww
☐ Chapters: 34
☐ Privileges: Conventions Library Books Plants Exhibits Tours

American Dahlia Society
Alan Fisher, Memb. Chair.
1 Rock Falls Court
Rockville, MD 20854
(202) 326-3516
Fax: (202) 326-3516
Bulletin (4)
Classification & Handbook of Dahlias (1)

They recommend their own "Guide to Growing and Caring for Dahlias," $3 postpaid and "Dahlias of Today" (see Puget Sound Dahlia Association).
- E-mail: afisher@ftc.gov
- Web: www.dahlia.com
- Chapters: 77
- Garden: Trial gardens throughout US
- Privileges: Conventions Books Seeds Plants Exhibits Trips

The American Dianthus Society
Rand B. Lee, Pres.
P.O. Box 22232
Santa Fe, NM 87502-2232
(505) 438-7038
The Gilliflower Times (4)

Group has "round robins" for special interests; they recommend "Border Pinks" by Richard Bird, and "Carnations and Pinks; the Complete Guide" by Sophie Hughes.
- E-mail: randbear@nets.com
- Web: www.nhn.uoknor.edu/% Ehoward/ads.html
- Garden: McDonald Northern Dianthus Garden, Grand Morais, MI
- Privileges: Seeds Plants

American Fern Society
David B. Lellinger
326 West Street N.W.
Vienna, VA 22180-4151
American Fern Journal (4)
Fiddlehead Forum (6)

The "American Fern Journal" is a strictly botanical publication. Spore exchange has fresh spore available by exchange or at nominal cost to memers. Membership and subscription information and an application are available at their web site.
- Web: www.visuallink.net/fern
- Privileges: Seeds

American Forests
Membership Director
P.O. Box 2000
Washington, D.C. 20013
(202) 667-3300
Fax: (202) 667-7751
American Forests (4)

This society, which was founded in 1875, is dedicated to balanced forest use. They sponsor tree planting and educational programs about the value of forests. They publish an interesting booklet, "Famous & Historic Trees."
- Web: www.amfor.org
- Privileges: Conventions Library Books Tours

American Fuchsia Society
Judy Salome
6979 Clark Road
Paradise, CA 95969-2210
(408) 257-0752
Bulletin (6)

Has a number of chapters on the Pacific Coast. Species fuchsia collection at the University of California Arboretum in Berkeley; collections at Lakeside Park in Oakland; Golden Gate Park, San Francisco; Mendocino Coast Botanical Garden near Ft. Bragg; and on the State Capitol grounds in Salem, Oregon.
- E-mail: sydnor@ix.netcom.com
- Web: members.aol.com/amfuchsias/fuchsias
- Chapters: 24
- Garden: Lakeside Park, Oakland; Golden Gate Park, SF
- Privileges: Conventions Library Books Plants Exhibits Trips

---

American Gloxinia & Gesneriad Society, Inc.
M.J. & D.B. Tyler
P.O. Box 1598
Port Angeles, WA 98362-0194
(360) 417-2172
The Gloxinian (4)

Seeds are sold at a nominal cost to members. Members can buy a copy of "How to Know and Grow Gesneriads." "Propagation of Gesneriads and Birds and Bees and Gesneriad Seeds" is available for $2. They recommend "The Miracle Houseplants" by V. & G. Elbert (out of print).
- E-mail: membership@aggs.org
- Web: www.aggs.org
- Chapters: 16
- Privileges: Conventions

American Gourd Society
Jean McClintock
7265 State Route 314
Mount Gilead, OH 43338-0274
(419) 362-6446
Fax: (419) 362-6446
The Gourd (4)

Annual meeting at Mt. Gilead Fairgrounds in July; annual show first full weekend in October, same location. Promotes the use of gourds for decorative and useful purposes; magazine shows beautifully decorated gourds. This group is about arts and crafts as much as plants.
- Chapters: 7
- Privileges: Conventions Books Seeds Plants Exhibits

American Hemerocallis Society
Elly Launius, Exec. Secy.
1454 Rebel Drive
Jackson, MS 39211-6334
(601) 366-4362
Daylily Journal (4)
Regional Newsletters

Has a slide library for members; publishes an extensive source list; has many round-robins on topics of special interest. Also sells "Daylilies: The Beginner's Handbook" for $6.
☐ Web: www.daylilies.org/daylilies.html
☐ Chapters: 15 US, 1 OV
☐ Garden: Many, see publications
☐ Privileges: Conventions Library Plants Exhibits Trips

American Hepatica Association
Paul Held
195 North Avenue
Westport, CT 06880
Newsletter (4)

Seed of many choice selections of hepatica are offered to members.
☐ E-mail: AmHepatica@aol.com
☐ Privileges: Seeds Plants

American Herb Association
Membership Secretary
P.O. Box 1673
Nevada City, CA 95959-1673
Fax: (916) 265-9552
AHA Newsletter (4)

Publishes a directory of sources as well as a directory of herb gardens and one of herb schools. Emphasis is on medicinal herbs and the healing arts. They recommend "Aromatherapy: A Complete Guide to the Healing Arts" by Keville and Green.
☐ Privileges: Books

American Hibiscus Society
Jeri Grantham, Exec. Secy.
P.O. Box 321540
Cocoa Beach, FL 32932-1540
Fax: (407) 783-2576
The Seed Pod (4)

Local chapters have shows, plant sales and exchange scions for grafting; they sell "The Hibiscus Handbook." Write for price.
☐ E-mail: seedpods@aol.com
☐ Web: www.trop-hibiscus.com
☐ Chapters: 22
☐ Privileges: Conventions Books Seeds Plants Exhibits

American Horticultural Society
Darlene Oliver, Membership
7931 East Boulevard Drive
Alexandria, VA 22308-1300
(800) 777-7931
Fax: (703) 768-8700
The American Gardener (8)

Has an extensive tour program, a gardener's information service for your plant problems, and plant labels and books for members at special prices.
☐ E-mail: GardenAHS@aol.com
☐ Web: www.emall.com
☐ Garden: River Farm, Alexandria, VA
☐ Privileges: Conventions Library Books Seeds Plants Exhibits Tours

American Hosta Society
Robyn Duback
7802 NE 63rd St.
Vancouver, WA 98662
Hosta Journal (2)

They have a list of display gardens throughout the country. Recommend "The Genus Hosta" by George Schmid. They also publish an excellent yearbook.
☐ E-mail: giboshiman@aol.com
☐ Garden: Minnesota Landscape Arboretum, Chanhassen MN
☐ Privileges: Conventions Exhibits

American Hydrangea Society
P.O. Box 11645
Atlanta, GA 30355
(404) 636-7886
Newsletter (3)

A new society; they recommend reading "Hydrangeas -- a Gardener's Guide" by Toni Lawson-Hall and Brian Rothera.
☐ Web: www.nwlink/.com/~dafox/
☐ Privileges: Trips

American Iris Society
Marilyn Harlow, Memb. Secy.
P.O. Box 8455
San Jose, CA 95155-8455
(408) 971-0444
Fax: (408) 971-6072
Bulletin of the American Iris Society (4)

Has many sections by types of iris; 24 regional affiliates and 127 chapters. A lively and active group. New members get a booklet on basic iris culture; many people recommend their publication "The World of Irises."
☐ E-mail: 103262.1512@compuserve.com
☐ Web: www/somedia.com/homes/ais
☐ Chapters: 24 regions
☐ Garden: Many test gardens, see literature
☐ Privileges: Conventions Books Plants Exhibits

American Ivy Society
Daphne Pfaff, Memb. Chair.
P.O. Box 2123
Naples, FL 34106-2123
(941) 261-0388
Fax: (941) 261-8984
The Ivy Journal (1)
Between the Vines (3)

Regional display gardens at Brookside Gardens, Wheaton, MD; Sugar Mill Botanic Gardens, Port Orange, FL; Chicago Botanic Gardens, Glencoe, IL; Mendocino Coast Botanical Garden, Fort Bragg, CA, and Lewis Ginter Botanical Garden, Richmond, VA. Publications list available from AIS. They recommend "The Ivy Book" by Suzanne Warner Pierot, and "The New Topiary" by Patricia Riley Hammer.
- ☐ E-mail: 103630.3722@compuserve.com
- ☐ Web: www.ivy.org
- ☐ Chapters: 5
- ☐ Garden: AHS Garden, River Farm, Mt. Vernon, VA
- ☐ Privileges: Conventions Books Exhibits Trips Tours

American Orchid Society
Membership Services
6000 S. Olive Avenue
West Palm Beach, FL 33405
(561) 585-8666
Fax: (561) 585-0654
Orchids (12)
Awards Quarterly

Publishes handbooks on various orchid subjects, including the "Handbook on Orchid Culture." Also publishes "Lindleyana;" see Section E. They recommend "The Illustrated Encyclopedia of Orchids" by Alec Pridgeon, "Home Orchid Growing" by Rebecca Northen, and "Orchid Growing Basics" by Dr. Gustav Schoser. They also publish "Growing Orchids," $12.50 in US, $14.50 overseas.
- ☐ E-mail: 71726.1741@compuserve.com
- ☐ Web: orchidweb.org
- ☐ Chapters: 519
- ☐ Privileges: Conventions Books Plants Exhibits Tours

American Penstemon Society
Ann W. Bartlett, Memb. Secy.
1569 S. Holland Court
Lakewood, CO 80232
(303) 986-8096
American Penstemon Society Bulletin (2)

Publishes a very good "Manual for Beginners," free to new members. One of their members, Bob Nold, is writing a book on penstemons, to be published by Timber Press.
- ☐ Privileges: Conventions Library Books Seeds Plants Trips

American Peony Society
Greta M. Kessenich
250 Interlachen Road
Hopkins, MN 55343
(612) 938-4706
Bulletin (4)

They publish an introductory booklet, "American Peony Handbook" for $5 postpaid, and "The Peonies" edited by John C. Wister for $22.50 postpaid.
- ☐ Privileges: Conventions Seeds

© Rocky Mountain Rare Plants
Artist: Rebecca Day-Skowron

The American Plant Collectors Society
Mary Anne Osborne
130 Abbott Run Valley Road
Cumberland, RI 02864
Fax: (401) 333-2731

Just getting underway, this society is a new attempt to gather together plant collectors. They hope eventually to publish a directory of gardens to visit and lists of collectors by genera, as well as offering tours and lectures.
☐ E-mail: brady69z@idt.net

American Primrose Society
Addaline W. Robinson
41809 SW Burgarsky Road
Gaston, OR 97119-9047
(503) 985-9596
Primroses (4)

Has slide programs and round-robins, an interesting journal and excellent seed exchanges. They recommend "Primulas" by John Richards and "The Genus Primula" by Joseph Halda.
☐ Chapters: 9
☐ Privileges: Books Seeds Plants Exhibits

American Rhododendron Society
Dee Daneri, Exec. Director
11 Pinecrest Drive
Fortuna, CA 95540
(707) 725-3043
Fax: (707) 725-1217
Journal, American Rhododendron Society (4)

A wide-spread group, with seventy chapters, so there must be one near you -- except in the desert Southwest, of course! They recommend "Azaleas" by Fred Galle, "Greer's Guide to Available Rhododendrons" Third Edition, by Harold Greer, and "Success with Rhododendrons and Azaleas" by H. E. Reiley.
☐ Web: www.rhodie.org/~ars
☐ Chapters: 70
☐ Privileges: Conventions Books Plants Exhibits Trips Tours

American Rose Society
Julia Cecil
P.O. Box 30,000
Shreveport, LA 71130-5405
(800) 637-6534
Fax: (318) 938-9405
The American Rose Magazine (11)
Annual and Handbook

One of the largest and most active societies in our country.
☐ E-mail: ars@ars-hq.org
☐ Web: www.ars.org
☐ Chapters: 382
☐ Garden: American Rose Center, Shreveport, LA
☐ Privileges: Conventions Library Books

American Sakurasoh Association
Paul Held
195 North Avenue
Westport, CT 06880
Newsletter (4)

Society devoted to a particular class of Asian primulas; members share seeds, plants, information. They recommend the only book on the subject "Sakurasoh" by E. Torii -- in Japanese.
☐ Privileges: Seeds Plants

American Willow Growers Network
Bonnie Gale
412 County Road 31
Norwich, NY 13815
(607) 336-9031
Newsletter (1)

A group sharing information and cuttings, and developing new uses for the willow; holds basket-making workshops.
☐ Garden: South New Berlin, NY, call for information
☐ Privileges: Plants

Aril Society International
Barbara Figge
6805 Kentucky Court N.E.
Albuquerque, NM 87110
(505) 881-3859
Yearbook (1)
Newsletter (3)

A society for aril iris lovers. They recommend "'The World of Irises," edited by Bee Warburton and "Iris" by F. Koehlein.
☐ E-mail: SWJordan@UNM.edu
☐ Web: www.rt66.com/~telp/asi.htm
☐ Privileges: Seeds Plants Exhibits

Arizona Native Plant Society
Membership Secretary
P.O. Box 41206
Tucson, AZ 85717
Plant Press (4)

Have informal seed exchanges among members.
☐ Chapters: 5
☐ Privileges: Conventions Seeds Exhibits Trips Tours

Arkansas Native Plant Society
Dr. Eric Sundell
Div. of Math & Science, Univ. of Arkasas
Monticello, AR 71656
(501) 460-1066
Fax: (501) 460-1316
Claytonia (2-4)

They recommend "'Wildflowers of Arkansas" and "Trees, Shrubs and Vines of Arkansas" by Carl Hunter, published by the Ozark Society Foundation.
☐ E-mail: Sundell@uamont.edu
☐ Privileges: Conventions Plants Trips

Australian Garden History Society
The Secretary
Royal Botanic Gardens, Birdwood Avenue
South Yarra, VIC, Australia 3141
61 (0) 3965 05043
Fax: 61 (0) 3965 05043
Australian Garden History (6)

Has a fine periodical and garden tours; planning a plant collection.
☐ Privileges: Conventions Books Exhibits Trips Tours

Australian Plants Society
Lyn Thompson
P.O. Box 38
Woodford, NSW, Australia 2778
61 (0) 29621-3437
Fax: 61 (0) 29676 7603
Australian Plants (4)
Native Plants Newsletter (4)

Help and information for those interested in Australian plants.
☐ Web: www.ozemail.com.au/~sgap/
☐ Chapters: 23
☐ Privileges: Library Books Seeds Plants Exhibits Trips

Azalea Society of America, Inc.
Membership Chairman
P.O. Box 34536
West Bethesda, MD 20827-0536
The Azalean (4)

Local societies have plant shows and sales. They have a slide library, and recommend "Azaleas" by Fred Galle.
☐ Chapters: 8
☐ Garden: Harding Garden at AHS River Farm, VA
☐ Privileges: Conventions Books Plants Exhibits Trips

Bio-Dynamic Farming & Gardening Association
Charles Beedy
P.O. Box 550
Kimberton, PA 19442
(610) 935-7797
Fax: (610) 983-3196
Bio-Dynamics (6)

Promotes the bio-dynamic method of farming and gardening. They recommend "Bio-Dynamic Farming Practice" by Sattler and Wistinghausen.
☐ Chapters: 29
☐ Privileges: Books

Bio-Integral Resource Center (BIRC)
Kathy Spalding
P.O. Box 7414
Berkeley, CA 94707
(510) 524-2567
Fax: (510) 524-1758
Common Sense Pest Control (4)
The IPM Practitioner (10)

Group devoted to the least toxic methods of pest management. Associate members receive the non-technical "Common Sense Pest Control." Professional members receive "The IPM Practitioner." Dual memberships available. They recommend "Common Sense Pest Control" by William & Helga Olkowski & Sheila Darr.
☐ E-mail: birc@IGC.apc.org
☐ Web: www.igc.apc.org/birc/
☐ Privileges: Library Books

Biological Urban Gardening Services
Membership Secretary
P.O. Box 76
Citrus Heights, CA 53211-0076
(916) 726-5377
BUGS Flyer (4)

Organization devoted to reducing the use of pesticides, particularly on landscape plants. "BUGS" offers a professional category of membership for $18 a year in the US, with additional services oriented toward horticultural professionals. They publish a number of pamphlets on natural pest control; write for prices.
☐ E-mail: bugs/rc@cwia.com

Bonsai Clubs International
Mary Turner, Business Mgr.
P.O. Box 1176
Brookfield, WI 53008-1176
(414) 860-8807
Fax: (414) 641-0757
Bonsai Magazine (6)

A large society, with many local chapters and activities.
- ☐ E-mail: BonsaiRMT@aol.com
- ☐ Web: www.bonsai-bci.com
- ☐ Privileges: Conventions Exhibits

Botanical Society of South Africa
Membership Secretary
BSA, Kirstenbosch
Claremont, Cape Town, South Africa 7735
27 (0) 21 797-2090
Fax: 27 (0) 21 797-2376
Veld & Flora (4)

In addition to Kirstenbosch, the society supports 7 other botanical gardens, promotes the conservation and cultivation of the indigenous flora of South Africa. Also publishes wildflower guides.
- ☐ E-mail: botsocsa@gem.co.za
- ☐ Chapters: 11
- ☐ Garden: Kirstenbosch Botanical Garden
- ☐ Privileges: Books Seeds Plants Exhibits Tours

British & European Geranium Society
Mrs. J. Hinchliffe
4, Higher Meadows, Clayton-le-Woods
Chorley, Lancs., England PR5 2RS
44 (0) 1772 453-383
The Geranium Gazette (4)

They recommend "Pelargoniums of South Africa," vols.1 & 2, by Van der Walt. Their "Pelargonium Primer" is free to new members.
- ☐ Chapters: 5
- ☐ Garden: Fibrex Nurseries, Pebworth, Warwickshire, England
- ☐ Privileges: Books Exhibits

The British Cactus & Succulent Society
Mr. P. A. Lewis
Firgrove, 1 Springwoods, Courtmoor
Fleet, Hants., England GU13 9SU
British Cactus and Succulent Journal (4)
Bradleya (1)

Members can send personal checks in US dollars for dues; no seed exchange, but seeds are sold to members. "Bradleya" is available on separate subscription.
- ☐ E-mail: bcss@mace.demon.co.uk
- ☐ Web: www.demon.co.uk/mace/bcss.html
- ☐ Chapters: 100
- ☐ Privileges: Conventions Books Exhibits Tours

The British Clematis Society
Mrs. Betty Risdon, Memb. Secy.
The Tropical Bird Gardens, Rode
Nr Bath, Somerset, England BA3 6QW
44 (0) 1373 830-326
Fax: 44 (0) 1373 831-288
The Clematis Journal (1)
The Clematis Supplement (1)

They recommend "Clematis" by Christopher Lloyd; "Clematis: Queen of Climbers" by Jim Fisk; "Making the Most of Clematis" by Raymond Evison; and "Clematis" by Barry Fretwell. They also publish a series of fact sheets on growing clematis.
- ☐ Garden: Rose Society Gardens, St. Albans
- ☐ Privileges: Conventions Books Seeds Plants Exhibits Trips Tours

---

British Columbia Fuchsia & Begonia Society
Lorna Herchenson
2402 Swinburne Avenue
North Vancouver, BC, Canada V7H 1L2
(604) 929-5382
The Eardrop (11)

They publish a basic guide, "How to Grow Fuchsias and Begonias" for $3 postpaid.
- ☐ E-mail: lherchenson@bc.sympatico.ca
- ☐ Web: www.hedgerows.com
- ☐ Privileges: Conventions Library Books Seeds Plants Exhibits Trips

---

British Fuchsia Society
Secretary
Little Brook Fuchsias, Ash Green Lane West
Ash Green, Nr. Aldershot, England GU12 6HL
44 (0) 1252 29731
Bulletin (2)
Yearbook

Publishes a number of leaflets on fuchsia culture; write for information.
- ☐ Privileges: Conventions Books Exhibits

British Iris Society
C.E.C. Bartlett
The Old Mill House, Shurton
Strogursy, Somerset, England TA5 1QG
The Iris Year Book

Three shows a year at the RHS Hall in London; conventions every five years or so.
- ☐ Chapters: 5
- ☐ Privileges: Conventions Library Books Seeds Plants Exhibits

British Pelargonium & Geranium Society
Les Hodgkiss, Secretary
75 Pelham Road
Bexleyheath, Kent, England DA7 4LY
44 (0) 1322 525-947
Pelargonium News (3)
Yearbook (1)

See also the Geraniaceae Group for those interested in species (hardy) geraniums.
☐ Garden: Fibrex Nurseries, Ltd., Nr. Stratford on Avon
☐ Privileges: Conventions Books Plants Exhibits

The British Pteridological Society
A. R. Busby
16 Kirby Corner Road, Canley
Coventry, West Midlands, England CV4 8GD
Pteridologist (1)
Fern Gazette (2)

Devoted to the growing, study and conservation of ferns and fern allies. They publish "Cultivation and Propagation of British Ferns" by J. W. Dyce (write for information on ordering). They also recommend "Ferns in Your Garden" by A. Kelly.
☐ Web: www.nhm.ac.uk/bps/
☐ Privileges: Books Seeds Plants

Bromeliad Society, Inc.
Carolyn Schoenau, Memb. Secy.
P.O. Box 12981
Gainesville, FL 32604-0981
(352) 372-6589
Fax: (352) 372-8823
Journal of the Bromeliad Society (6)

Local affiliates have exhibits and plant sales, libraries and field trips. Members are fairly serious hobbyists and professional botanists. They offer "Bromeliads, A Cultural Manual" for $3.00 and also recommend "Blooming Bromeliads" by Ursula and Ulrich Baensch, distributed by Book Division, Hagen, P.O. Box 9107, Mansfield MA 02048-9107.
☐ E-mail: BSI@nervm.nerdc.ufl,edu
☐ Web: BSI.ORG
☐ Chapters: 50
☐ Privileges: Conventions Books Plants Exhibits

Cactus & Succulent Society of America
Mindy Fusaro, Treasurer
P.O. Box 35034
Des Moines, IA 50315-0301
(515) 285-7760
Fax: (515) 285-1523
Cactus & Succulent Journal (6)
CSSA Newsletter (6)

An active society with many local branches and activities.
☐ E-mail: mpfusaro@aol.com
☐ Web: hpl.hp.com/bot/cssa/
☐ Chapters: 80
☐ Privileges: Conventions Library Books Seeds Plants Exhibits

---

California Garden & Landscape History Society
Membership Secretary
P.O. Box 1338
Sebastopol, CA 95473
Fax: (707) 829-2409
Eden (2-3)

This new society will hold two meetings a year, one in the north, and one in the south, including garden tours whenever possible. New members receive a reading list on California garden history.
☐ Privileges: Trips

California Horticultural Society
Mrs. Elsie Mueller
1847 - 34th Avenue
San Francisco, CA 94122-4109
(415) 566-5222
Pacific Horticulture (4)
Bulletin (11)

General interest in ornamental horticulture. The society is active in the greater San Francisco Bay area and Northern California. Send long SASE for information.
☐ Privileges: Seeds Plants Exhibits Trips Tours

California Native Grass Association
Mary Kate Sleeper
P.O. Box 72405
Davis, CA 95617
(916) 759-8458
Grasslands (4)

A group dedicated to the preservation of California's native perennial grasses, and restoration of grasslands. CNGA display gardens are at Davis, Winters, Lockeford, Moss Landing, Rio Vista, Santa Ana and Flores; write for addresses.
☐ E-mail: mksleeper@ucdavis.edu
☐ Web: www.mbay.net/~cnga
☐ Privileges: Conventions Exhibits Trips

California Native Plant Society
Membership Secy.
1722 J Street, #17
Sacramento, CA 95814
(916) 447-2677
Fax: (916) 447-2727
Fremontia (4)
Bulletin (4)

Some chapters have seed exchanges and plant sales. They sell a number of books and posters on the native plants of California.
☐ Web: www.calpoly.edu/~dchippin/cnps_main.html
☐ Chapters: 30
☐ Privileges: Library Books Seeds Plants Exhibits Trips

California Rare Fruit Growers, Inc.
Pamela Heffron
11261 Davenport Road
Los Alamitos, CA 90720
(562) 430-5366
Fax: (562) 430-5366
The Fruit Gardener (6)

For better understanding of growing subtropical fruits. They sell a set of 22 SRFG "Fruit Facts" for $13.50 ($19.50 OV), and recommend "Fruits of Warm Climates" by Julia Morton.
☐ E-mail: info@crfg.org
☐ Web: www.crfg.org/
☐ Chapters: 17
☐ Privileges: Conventions Books Plants Exhibits Trips Tours

The Calochortus Society
H.P. McDonald
P.O. Box 1128
Berkeley, CA 94701
Mariposa (4)

Members are interesting in seeing calochortus in the wild, photographing them and growing them; they receive a basic cultural guide when joining.
☐ Privileges: Seeds Plants

Canadian Begonia Society
Miree Lex
70 Enfield Avenue
Toronto, ON, Canada M8W 1T9

Write for information.

Canadian Chrysanthemum & Dahlia Society
Mrs. Karen Ojaste
17 Granard Boulevard
Scarborough, ON, Canada M1M 2E2
(416) 269-6960
Cuttings (12)
Yearbook

They offer basic cultural guides. Write for information.
☐ Privileges: Books Seeds Plants Exhibits Tours

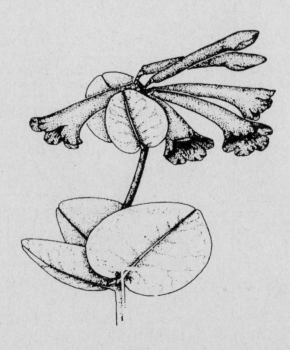

© The Bovees Nursery
Artist: Unknown

Canadian Geranium & Pelargonium Society
Kathleen Gammer, Memb. Secy.
303-2008 Fullerton Avenue
North Vancouver, BC, Canada V7P 3G7
Storksbill (4)

Write for information.
□ Privileges: Conventions Library Books Plants Exhibits

Canadian Gladiolus Society
Heidi Haines
189 Trudeau Drive
Bowmanville, ON, Canada L1C 1B9
Canadian Gladiolus Annual
Fall Bulletin (1)

Write for information.
□ Chapters: 10
□ Privileges: Conventions

Canadian Iris Society
Cathy Boyko
RR 9, 924 Bains Road
Dunville, ON, Canada N1A ZW8
(905) 774-8360
Canadian Iris Society Newsletter (4)

Iris shows and auctions, annual educational and awards program, regional activities. They publish cultural information on bearded and beardless iris.
□ Web: www.netcom.ca/~cris/cis.html
□ Privileges: Conventions Library Plants Exhibits

Canadian Orchid Congress
Janette Richardson
38 Straub Crescent
Regina, SK, Canada S4T 6S6
(306) 543-0560
COC Newsletter (6)

Umbrella group for orchid societies in Canada: they'll help you find a regional group to join. A group of enthusiastic greenhouse growers.
□ E-mail: ssaunder@fox.nstn.ns.ca
□ Web: www.ccn.cs.dal.ca/Recreation/OrchidsSNS/coc.html
□ Privileges: Conventions

Canadian Organic Growers
K. Lamarche
P.O. Box 6408, Station J
Ottawa, ON, Canada K2A 3Y6
(613) 256-1848
Fax: (613) 256-4453
COGnition (4)

Devoted to sustainable agriculture and an organically grown food supply; encourage farmers and gardeners alike. They recommend their own "Organic Resource Guide" and "Organic Field Crop Handbook."
□ Web: www.gks.com/cog/
□ Chapters: 10
□ Privileges: Conventions Library Books Plants Trips

Canadian Prairie Lily Society
M.E. Driver, Secy.
22 Red River Road
Saskatoon, SK, Canada S7K 1G3
(306) 242-5329
Newsletter (4)

Concerned with growing the native prairie lilies of Canada.
□ Garden: U. of Saskatchewan, Saskatoon, SK
□ Privileges: Conventions Library Plants Exhibits

Canadian Rose Society
Anne Graber, Secy.
10 Fairfax Crescent
Scarborough, ON, Canada M1L 1Z8
Fax: (416) 757-4796
Canadian Rosarian (3)
Canadian Rose Annual (1)

Promotes knowledge of rose-growing in northern climates; has a slide library and annual garden tour. List of demonstration gardens. They recommend "Roses for Canadian Gardens" by Robert Osborne, and "The Rose Expert" by D.G. Hessayon.
□ E-mail: crs@mirror.org
□ Web: www. mirror.org/groups/crs
□ Chapters: 32
□ Privileges: Library Plants Exhibits

The Canadian Wildflower Society
Business Secretary
Unit 12A, Box 228, 4981 Highway #7 East
Markham, ON, Canada L3R 1N1
(905) 294-9075
Fax: (416) 466-6428
Wildflower (4)

Society devoted exclusively to the wild flora of North America; interesting to beginners and experts alike; has a handsome magazine. They recommend the book "The Ontario Naturalized Garden."
□ Web: webcom/acorn-online.com/hedge/cws.html
□ Chapters: 5
□ Privileges: Conventions Seeds Plants Trips

Cascade Heather Society
Karla Lortz
E. 502 Haskell Hill Road
Shelton, WA 98584-8429
(360) 427-5318
Fax: (360) 427-5318
Newsletter (3)

A regional society. They publish a brochure on growing heathers and recommend "Handy Guide to Heathers" by David and Anne Small.
- ☐ E-mail: heaths@gte.net
- ☐ Privileges: Conventions Seeds Plants Exhibits

The Chile Institute
Box 30003, Dept. 3Q, NMSU
Las Cruces, NM 88003
(505) 646-3028
Fax: (505) 646-6041
Chile Institute Newsletter (4)

An organization dedicated to the study of chiles. They recommend "The Pepper Garden" by Dave De Witt and Paul W. Bosland, and "Capsicum: A Comprehensive Bibliography (Fourth Edition)" by Paul W. Bosland. They also sell a number of cultural pamphlets. The Chile Intitute is affiliated with the New Mexico State University chile breeding program.
- ☐ E-mail: hotchile@nmsu.edu
- ☐ Web: www.nmsu.edu/~hotchile/index.html

Clivia Club
The Treasurer
P.O. Box 74868, Lynnwood Ridge
Pretoria, South Africa 0040
27 (0) 12 991-0843
Fax: 27 (0) 12 991-1105
Clivia Club Newsletter (4)

A society devoted to improving and hybridizing various species of clivia.
- ☐ Chapters: 3
- ☐ Privileges: Conventions Seeds Plants Exhibits Trips

Coastal Georgia Herb Society
Membership Chairperson
P.O. Box 15201
Savannah, GA 31416
Coastal Georgia Herb Society Newsletter (4)

This is a regional group. Biblical Garden at St. Thomas Episcopal Church, Savannah, GA is another display garden.
- ☐ Garden: Discovery Herb Garden, Savannah, GA
- ☐ Privileges: Seeds Plants Trips

Colorado Native Plant Society
Myrna P. Steinkamp
P.O. Box 200
Fort Collins, CO 80522-0200
Aquilegia (4)

US members only. Pamphlet "The Prairie Garden" (1991) is available for $4. They recommend "Southwestern Landscaping with Native Plants" by J. Phillips.
- ☐ Chapters: 6
- ☐ Privileges: Conventions Trips

CORNS
Carl and Karen Barnes
Route 1, Box 32
Turpin, OK 73950
(405) 778-3615

This is for people who are dedicated to the preservation of the genetic diversity of open-pollinated corn varieties. For information send a long SASE. Overseas, send US$1. Mr. Barnes is writing a book on old corn varieties; those interested can visit his fields in growing season by appointment. He also has a seed museum, and sells seeds.
- ☐ Garden: Field testing at Turpin, OK
- ☐ Privileges: Seeds

Cottage Garden Society
Clive Lane
Hurstfield House, 244 Edleston Road
Crewe, Cheshire, England CW2 7EJ
44 (0) 2702 50776
Fax: 44 (0) 2702 50118
The Cottage Gardener (4)

Purpose is to keep alive the tradition of gardening in the cottage style and the use of old-fashioned plants. Arranges garden visits in the summer. They offer "A Cottage Garden Planner" for $6; they recommend "The Cottage Gardener's Companion," by Clive Lane.
- ☐ Privileges: Seeds Plants Exhibits Trips

The Cryptanthus Society
Secretary
18814 Cypress Mountain Drive
Spring, TX 77388
(281) 350-6809
Journal (4)

A cultural flyer is available free of charge.
- ☐ Chapters: 28
- ☐ Privileges: Conventions Books Seeds Plants Exhibits

The Cycad Society
William Tang
c/o Fairchild Trop. Gdn, 10901 Old Cutler Rd.
Miami, FL 33156
The Cycad Newsletter

They have a seed and pollen bank; their newsletter is "sporadic."
☐ Privileges: Seeds

The Cyclamen Society
Dr. D.V. Bent
Little Pilgrims, 2 Pilgrims Way East
Otford, Sevenoaks, Kent, England TN14 5QN
44 (0) 1959 522-322
The Cyclamen Society Journal (2)

Society works to preserve and conserve wild species, has an exchange of viable seed in late summer, offers growing advice from experts.
☐ E-mail: cyclamen@denny.demon.co.uk
☐ Privileges: Conventions Books Seeds Plants Exhibits

Cymbidium Society of America
Paula Butler
P.O. Box 2244
Orange, CA 92859
(714) 532-4719
Fax: (714) 532-3611
The Orchid Advocate (6)

Interested in cool-growing orchids, particularly cymbidiums.
☐ E-mail: cymbidium@earthlink.net
☐ Web: home.earthlink.net/~cymbidium/
☐ Chapters: 10
☐ Privileges: Conventions Plants Exhibits

The Daffodil Society (UK)
Mr. J. Pearson
"Hofflands", Bakers Green, Little Totham
Maloon, Essex, England CM9 8LT
44 (0) 1621 788-678
Daffodil Society Journal (1)
Newsletter (1)

They offer "Daffodil Society Cultural Guide & Show Handbook," and also recommend "Daffodils for Home, Garden and Show" by Don Barnes, and "Narcissus: A Guide to Wild Daffodils" published by the Alpine Garden Society.
☐ E-mail: 106255.1546@compuserve.com
☐ Garden: At Chobham, Surrey; write for address
☐ Privileges: Seeds Exhibits

The Delphinium Society
Mrs. Shirley E. Bassett
"Takakkaw," Ice House Wood
Oxted, Surrey, England RH8 9DW
Delphinium Year Book

Publishes a basic guide, "Simply Delphiniums" US$10 (IMO, air mail). No personal checks in US currency. They recommend "Delphiniums: a Complete Guide" by Colin Edwards.
☐ Garden: Delphinium Trial Ground, RHS Garden, Wisley, Surrey
☐ Privileges: Conventions Seeds Plants Exhibits

Desert Plant Society of Vancouver
Pat Campbell
6408 Marine Drive
West Vancouver, BC, Canada V7W 2S6
(604) 525-5315

This group is dedicated to growing succulent plants and cacti indoors and outdoors in British Columbia.
☐ Privileges: Seeds Plants Exhibits

Dwarf Iris Society of America
Lynda S. Miller
11974 E.191st Street
Noblesville, IN 46060
Dwarf Iris Society Newsletter (3)

A section of the American Iris Society, members receive a list of display gardens in various parts of the country.
☐ Privileges: Conventions Books

Elm Research Institute
John P. Hansel
Elm Street
Harrisville, NH 03450
(800) FOR-ELMS
Fax: (603) 827-3794
Elm Leaves (irreg.)

Distributes elms resistant to Dutch elm disease, primarily through Boy Scout Troops all over the country. Members receive a free elm tree.
☐ Privileges: Plants

Epiphyllum Society of America
Mrs. Patricia Ballard
5333 Thornburn Street
Los Angeles, CA 90045-2222
The Bulletin (6)

Society devoted to epiphyllum and epiphytic cactus hybrids and species, as well as epiphytic and tropical plants. Their recent "ESA Directory of Species and Hybrids" lists 10,000 hybrids and all known epiphytic cactus species. It's compiled by Myron Kimnach; US$28 plus shipping to non-members; $15 to members. Write and ask for shipping charges.
☐ Privileges: Plants Exhibits

Eucalyptus Improvement Association
P.O. Box 4460
Davis, CA 95617
(916) 753-4535
California Eucalyptus Grower (4)

A group dedicated to the genetic improvement of "eucalyptus as a crop," and improving growth and quality of the various species.
☐ Garden: Trial gardens throughout California
☐ Privileges: Conventions Seeds Plants Trips

Florida Native Plant Society
Betsy Bicknell
P.O. Box 6116
Spring Hill, FL 34606-0906
(813) 856-8202
The Palmetto (4)

Write to the society for a list of publications and information on local chapters' display gardens.
☐ E-mail: fnpsbetsy@aol.com
☐ Web: flmnh.ufl.edu/fnps/fnps.htm
☐ Chapters: 23
☐ Privileges: Conventions Books Seeds Plants Exhibits Trips Tours

---

The Flower & Herb Exchange
Membership Secretary
3076 North Winn Road
Decorah, IA 52101
(319) 382-5990
Fax: (319) 382-5872
Flower and Herb Exchange (1)

A group that is dedicated to the preservation and distribution of heirloom varieties of flowers and herbs. Members receive the annual seed exchange list, which has grown quite fat over just a few years. Free seed list now available to non-members.
☐ Garden: Heritage Farm, 3076 North Winn Rd, Decorah, IA
☐ Privileges: Seeds

Friends of ...

I have not listed the many "Friends" groups affiliated with botanical gardens, but encourage you to join such groups if you have them in your area: they offer many interesting activities, lectures, plant sales, and in many cases, the use of a botanical library. They do heroic work and deserve your support.

Friends of the Trees Society
Michael Pilarski
P.O. Box 4469
Bellingham, WA 98227
(360) 738-4972
Fax: (360) 671-9668
Newsletter (4)

A society whose "mission is to inspire, enable, educate and assist people to live in harmony with forests and trees."
☐ E-mail: tern@geocities.com
☐ Web: www:geocities.com/rainforest/4663
☐ Privileges: Books Tours

Garden History Society
Mrs. Anne Richards
5 The Knoll
Hereford, England HR1 1RU
44 (0) 1432 354-479
Garden History (2)
Newsletter (3)

Has excellent tours in Britain, Europe and elsewhere.
☐ Privileges: Conventions Books Seeds Plants Exhibits Trips Tours

---

Garden Research Exchange
Ken Allan
61 South Bartlett Street
Kingston, ON, Canada K7K 1X3
(613) 542-6547
Vegetable Garden Research Yearbook

A group of devoted vegetable gardeners doing research, something like the North American Fruit Explorers; they publish a yearbook with their results, available for C$12, US$12 outside of Canada. Write for more information.
☐ E-mail: allan@adan.kingston.net

Gardenia Society of America
Lyman Duncan
P.O. Box 879
Atwater, CA 95301
(209) 358-2231
Gardenia News & Notes (3)

Their newsletter contains basic cultural information.

Georgia Native Plant Society
Membership Chair
P.O. Box 422085
Atlanta, GA 30342-2085
(404) 256-2174
Fax: (404) 257-9424
Nativescapes (4)

They recommend "Wildflowers of the Southeastern United States" by Duncan and Foote, and "Manual of the Vascular Flora of the Carolinas" by Radford, Ahles, and Bell.
☐ E-mail: JFitts@compuserve.com
☐ Privileges: Conventions Books Plants Trips

Georgia Organic Growers Association
Norman Nichols
4505 Moon Station Lane
Acworth, GA 30101-3660
(770) 621-4642
GOGA Newsletter (4)

This group addresses the interests of backyard gardeners as well as market farmers.
☐ Privileges: Conventions Exhibits Trips Tours

The Geraniaceae Group
Penny Clifton
9 Waingate Bridge Cottages
Haverigg, Millom, Cumbria, England LA18 4NF
44 (0) 1229 770-377
The Geraniaceae Group News (4)
Member's Specialist Booklist (4)

Their booklist offers many titles on geraniums and pelargoniums.
☐ Privileges: Books Seeds Plants

Gesneriad Society International
Richard Dunn
11510 124th Terrace N.
Largo, FL 34648-2505
(813) 559-7772
Gesneriad Journal (6)

Membership dues include membership in Saintpaulia International. They have a slide library.
☐ Chapters: 20
☐ Privileges: Conventions Seeds Plants

© Arrowhead Alpines
Artist: Jane Cloutier

Great Plains Native Plant Society
Cindy Reed
P.O. Box 461
Hot Spring, SD 57747
Plains Plants (3-4)

They recommend "Jewels of the Plains" by Claude A. Barr.
☐ E-mail: cascade@gwtc.net
☐ Privileges: Conventions Books Seeds

Hardy Fern Foundation
Membership
P.O. Box 166
Medina, WA 98039-0166
Newsletter (4)

Purpose is to test ferns for ornamental value and hardiness. They have test gardens in different areas of the country. Members will receive list of test and display gardens and information on propagation and culture of ferns.
☐ E-mail: sueman@darkwing.uoregon
☐ Web: darkwing.uoregon.edu/~sueman
☐ Garden: Rhododendron Species Foundation, Federal Way, WA
☐ Privileges: Conventions Seeds Plants

Hardy Plant Society
Mrs. Pam Adams
Little Orchard, Great Comberton
Pershore, Worcs., England WR10 3DP
44 (0) 1386 710-317
Fax: 44 (0) 1386 710-117
The Hardy Plant (2)
Newsletter (3)

Offers seed exchanges, visits to members' gardens. See also Hardy Plant Society of Oregon, The Hardy Plant Society -- Mid-Atlantic Group. and the Willamette Valley Hardy Plant Group. There is a Correspondents' Group for people unable to join a local group -- ask when you write for information.
☐ Chapters: 30
☐ Garden: Pershore Horticultural College, Pershore, Worcs.
☐ Privileges: Conventions Books Seeds Plants Exhibits Trips Tours

Hardy Plant Society -- Mid-Atlantic Group
Pat Horwitz
801 Concord Road
Glen Mills, PA 19342
(610) 558-2857
The Newsletter (4)

Promotes interest in hardy plants, particularly perennials. They publish a number of pamphlets.
☐ Privileges: Conventions Library Seeds Plants Trips Tours

Hardy Plant Society of Oregon
Julie Maudlin, Memb. Secy.
2148 Summit Drive
Lake Oswego, OR 97034
(503) 635-2159
Fax: (503) 224-5734
HPSO Bulletin (2)
Newsletter (6)

Hold annual study weekends in various cities in the Northwest, highly recommended! Publish a guidebook to gardens open to their members in the Northwest; a very active and fun group.
☐ Privileges: Conventions Library Books Seeds Plants Exhibits Trips Tours

The Haworthia Society
Lois Burks
P.O. Box 1207
Benton, AR 72018-1207
(501) 794-3266
Haworthiad (4)

Overseas members should contact Stirling Baker, 15 Emmott Avenue, Barkingside, Ilford, Essex, England IG6 IAL. They recommend "Gasterias" by E. van Jaarsveld, "Haworthia & Astroloba" by John Pilbeam, "The New Haworthia Handbook" by M. B. Bayer, and "The Genus Haworthia" by Charles L. Scott.
☐ E-mail: 100733.1146@compuserve.com
☐ Garden: The Bates Collection, Leeds, West Yorkshire, England
☐ Privileges: Conventions Seeds Plants

The Heather Society
Mrs. A. Small
Denbeigh, All Saints Road, Creeting St. Mary
Ipswich, Suffolk, England 1P6 8PJ
44 (0) 1449 711-220
Fax: 44 (0) 1449 711-220
Bulletin (3)
Year Book

Has a slide library and a cultivar location service, and publishes basic cultural guides to growing heathers. There is a third display garden at Cherrybank Gardens, Perth, Scotland.
☐ E-mail: heathers@zetnet.co.uk
☐ Web: www.users.zetnet.co.uk/heather
☐ Garden: RHS Garden, Wisley; NHS Garden, Harlow Carr, Harrogate
☐ Privileges: Conventions Books Exhibits

The Hebe Society
Veronica Moss
Amble, Weir Quay, Bere Alston
Nr. Yelverton, Devon, England PL20 7BS
44 (0) 1822 840-728
Hebe News (4)

They recommend "Hebes and Parahebes" by Douglas Chalk, and "The Cultivation of New Zealand Trees and Shrubs" by Metcalf and Reed.
☐ Web: www.gwynfryn.demon.co.uk/hebesoc/index.htm
☐ Garden: The Duchy College of Agriculture, Rosewarne, Cornwall
☐ Privileges: Conventions Plants Exhibits

Heliconia Society International
c/o Fairchild Tropical Garden
10901 Old Cutler Road
Miami, FL 33156-4296
(305) 667-1651 X340
Fax: (305) 661-8953
HSI Bulletin (4)

Other collections at National Tropical Botanic Garden, Kauai, HI; Wilson Botanic Garden, Costa Rica; Jurona Bird Park, Singapore. They recommend "Heliconia - an Identification Guide," by Berry and Kress.
☐ Garden: Fairchild Tropical Garden, FL; Lyon Arboretum, HI
☐ Privileges: Conventions Tours

Herb Research Foundation
1007 Pearl Street, Suite 200
Boulder, CO 80302
(303) 449-2265
Fax: (303) 449-7849
HerbalGram (4)
Herb Research News (4)

Formed to stimulate and support research on both common and uncommon herbs, with an emphasis on medicinal herbs. Offers botanical literature searches. They recommend "Handbook for Herbal Healing; A Concise Guide to Herbal Products" by Christopher Hobbs.
☐ E-mail: info@herbs.org
☐ Web: www.herbs.org

Herb Society of America, Inc.
Membership Secretary
9019 Kirtland Chardon Road
Mentor, OH 44094
(216) 256-0514
Fax: (216) 256-0541
The Herbarist (1)
The Herb Society of America Newsletter (6)

Society is horticulturally oriented, and seeks to further use and knowledge of herbs. They recommend "The Herb Society of America Encyclopedia of Herbs and Their Uses" by Deni Bown, and publish a "Traveler's Guide to Herb Gardens," listing 480 gardens in the US and Canada (write for price).
☐ E-mail: herbsociet@aol.com
☐ Web: www.herb society.com
☐ Chapters: 34
☐ Garden: Herb Garden at The National Arboretum, Washington, DC
☐ Privileges: Conventions Library Books Seeds Plants Exhibits Trips Tours

---

Heritage Roses Group
Beverly Dobson
1034 Taylor Avenue
Alameda, CA 94501
(510) 522-3024
Heritage Rose Letter (4)

Local chapters have meetings and plant sales. Regional chapters have newsletters. They recommend "Random House Guide to Roses" by Phillips & Rix, the Sunset and Ortho paperback books on roses, and "The Combined Rose List" as a source guide ($18 from Peter Schneider, P.O. Box 677, Mantua, OH 44255) .
☐ Web: www.ostavizn.comm/hrg/hrghome.html
☐ Chapters: 15
☐ Privileges: Seeds Plants Exhibits Trips Tours

Historic Iris Preservation Society
Verona Wiekhorst
4855 Santiago Way
Colorado Springs, CO 80917
(719) 596-7724
Fax: (719) 596-7724
Roots Journal (2)

A section of the American Iris Society.
☐ E-mail: wiekhorst@aol.com
☐ Web: www.tricities/~mikelowe
☐ Garden: Members have display gardens
☐ Privileges: Conventions Plants

Hobby Greenhouse Association
HGA Membership
8 Glen Terrace
Bedford, MA 01730-2048
(617) 275-0377
Fax: (617) 275-5693
Hobby Greenhouse (4)
HGA News (4)

Publishes a "Directory of Manufacturers: Hobby Greenhouses, Solariums, Sunrooms and Window Greenhouses" which is available for $2.50. They recommend the "Greenhouse Gardener's Companion" by Shane Smith.
☐ E-mail: jhale@world.std.com
☐ Web: www.hortsoft.com/HGA.html
☐ Chapters: 6
☐ Privileges: Library Books Seeds

Holly Society of America, Inc.
Mrs. Linda R. Parsons
11318 West Murdock
Wichita, KS 67212-6609
Holly Society Journal (4)

Has holly auctions and cutting exchanges, informative pamphlets, local chapters and annual meetings near notable holly collections. They recommend "Hollies, The Genus Ilex" by Fred C. Galle.
☐ E-mail: hollysocam@aol.com
☐ Web: members.aol.com/hollysoca/page1.htm
☐ Chapters: 8
☐ Privileges: Conventions Books Plants Trips

Home Orchard Society
Chuck James
P.O. Box 230192
Tigard, OR 97281-0192
Fax: (503) 639-6250
Pome News (4)

Has scion and rootstock exchanges. For members in the Northwest; there are fruit exhibits and various other events. They recommend "Apples for the 21st Century" by Warren Manhart.
☐ Web: www.wvi.com/~dough/hos/hos1.html
☐ Chapters: 4
☐ Garden: HOS Arboretum, Clackamas Comm. Coll., Oregon City, OR
☐ Privileges: Library Plants Exhibits Trips

Horticultural Alliance of the Hamptons
Membership Chairman
P.O. Box 202
Bridgehampton, NY 11932
(516) 537-2223
Alliance Journal (2)

A rapidly growing and active local group.
☐ Privileges: Library Books Seeds Plants Exhibits Trips Tours

Horticultural Society of New York
Membership Secretary
128 W. 58th Street
New York, NY 10019-2103
(212) 757-0915
Fax: (212) 246-1207
HSNY Newsletter (4)

Producer of the New York Flower Show, held annually in March. They also have interesting day trips in the New York area, and an excellent library.
☐ Web: www.hsny.org
☐ Privileges: Conventions Library Books Plants Exhibits Trips Tours

The Hoya Society International
Christine M. Burton
P.O. Box 1043
Porterdale, GA 30270-1043
The Hoyan (4)

They offer plants and cuttings to members. They have begun publishing a series of folders, each devoted to a single species. A "Beginner's Issue" on hoya culture is sent to each new member.
☐ E-mail: hoya@mindspring.com
☐ Web: www.graylab.ac.uk/usr/hodgkiss/hoya1.html
☐ Privileges: Conventions Seeds Plants

Hydroponic Society of America
P.O. Box 3075
San Ramon, CA 94583
(510) 743-9605
Fax: (510) 743-9302
Soilless Grower (6)
Proceedings (1)

Members are interested in all aspects of hydroponics. They offer 70 publications on hydroponics.
☐ E-mail: hydrosocam@aol.com
☐ Chapters: 2
☐ Privileges: Conventions Books Tours

Idaho Native Plant Society
P.O. Box 9451
Boise, ID 83707
Sage Notes (4)

Write for information.
☐ Chapters: 5
☐ Privileges: Conventions Exhibits Trips

Indigenous Bulb Growers Association of South Africa
The Secretary/Treasurer
P.O. Box 12265
N 1 City, South Africa 7463
27 (21) 581 690
IBSA Bulletin (1)

Society devoted to the conservation of South African bulbous plants by means of cultivation and propagation. They recommend "Spring and Winter Flowering Bulbs of the Cape," by Barbara Jeppe; "Bulbous Plants of Southern Africa" by Niel du Plessis & Graham Duncan; and "Cape Bulbs" by Richard L. Doutt.
☐ Privileges: Conventions Books Plants Exhibits Trips Tours

Indoor Gardening Society of America , Inc.
Sharon Zentz
944 S. Munroe Road
Tallmadge, OH 44278
(330) 733-8414

Originally the Indoor Light Gardening Society of America. Chapters have plants sales and exhibits. Members grow plants under lights, on windowsills, and in greenhouses. They have an active round robin correspondence.
☐ Chapters: 15
☐ Privileges: Conventions Books Seeds Plants Exhibits Trips Tours

International Aroid Society
Don Burns, Membership Chairman
P.O. Box 43-1853
South Miami, FL 33143-1853
Aroideana (1)
IAS Newsletter (6)

Society devoted to members of the arum family (Aroidaceae); write for information.
☐ Web: aroid-l@mobo.org
☐ Privileges: Conventions Library Books Seeds Plants

International Asclepiad Society
L.B. Delderfield
2 Keymer Court
Burgess Hill, W. Sussex, England RH15 0AA
Asclepios (3)

Write for information; Americans should write to Sue Haffner, 3015 Timmy, Clovis, CA 93612.
☐ E-mail: ias@mace.demon.co.uk
☐ Web: www.demon.co.uk/mace/ias.html
☐ Privileges: Seeds

International Camellia Society
Mrs. Lew Fetterman
P.O. Box 306
Clinton, NC 28328
International Camellia Journal (1)
Mid-Year Newsletter (1)

Meets every other year in different host countries; dues may be paid in local currency through regional membership representatives. They publish the International Camellia Register, and are involved in scion exchanges with camellia growers all over the world.
☐ Web: ukh 3375.med-ph-uni-sh.de/camellia/home.html
☐ Privileges: Conventions

International Carnivorous Plant Society
Leo Song, Fullerton Arboretum
Calif. State University
Fullerton, CA 92634
Carnivorous Plant Newsletter (4)

Has a very interesting magazine with color photographs and articles on plant hunting. Their interests are botany, horticulture, tissue culture, conservation and ecology.
☐ E-mail: LeoSong@fullerton.edu
☐ Web: www.hpl.hp.com/bot/cp_home
☐ Chapters: 3
☐ Garden: Fullerton Arboretum
☐ Privileges: Seeds

International Geranium Society
Membership Secretary
P.O. Box 92734
Pasadena, CA 91109-2734
Geraniums Around the World (4)

This is a group for hobby growers who seek growing information on geraniums and pelargoniums.
☐ Chapters: 7
☐ Privileges: Conventions Seeds Plants Exhibits

International Golden Fossil Tree Society
Clayton A. Fawkes, Pres.
201 W. Graham Avenue
Lombard, IL 60148
(630) 627-5636
IGFTS Newsletter (4)

Society for lovers of ginkgo trees.

International Hoya Association
Ann Wayman
P.O. Box 5130
Central Point, OR 97502
(760) 758-4290
Fax: (760) 945-8934
Fraterna (4)

Recommend the "Hoya Handbook" by Ann Wayman.
☐ E-mail: rbgdns@aol.com
☐ Privileges: Books

International Lilac Society
David Gressley, Holden Arbor.
9500 Sperry Road
Kirtland, OH 44094-5172
(216) 946-4400
Fax: (216) 256-1655
Journal Of the ILS (4)

Publishes a booklet on lilac culture. They recommend "Lilacs: the Genus Syringa" by Father John Fiala.
☐ Privileges: Conventions Books Plants Exhibits

International Oak Society
Lisa Wright
P.O. Box 310
Pen Argyl, PA 18072-0310
(610) 588-1037
Fax: (610) 599-0968
IOS Journal (1)
Newsletter (2)

A society formed to increase the number of oak species in cultivation and to encourage the hybridization of oaks. They recommend "Oaks of North America" by Howard Miller and Samuel Lamb.
☐ Privileges: Conventions Seeds Trips

International Oleander Society
Elizabeth S. Head, Cor. Secy.
P.O. Box 3431
Galveston, TX 77552-0431
(409) 762-9334
Nerium News (4)

Publishes "Oleanders--Guide to Culture and Selected Varieties on Galveston Island," available for $10. They also recommend "The Handbook of Oleanders" by Richard & Mary Ellen Hegenberger.
☐ Garden: Moody Gardens, Galveston, TX
☐ Privileges: Conventions Seeds Plants Exhibits

International Ornamental Crabapple Society
David Allen, Exec. Director
9500 Sperry Road
Kirtland, OH 44094
Fax: (216) 256-1665
Malus (2)

They recommend "Flowering Crabapples, The Genus Malus" by Father John Fiala.
☐ E-mail: holden@holdenarb.org
☐ Privileges: Conventions

The International Palm Society
P.O. Box 1897
Lawrence, KS 66044-8897
Fax: (913) 843-1274
Principes (4)

Members in eighty countries. Chapters have plant sales.
☐ Web: www.compalms.org
☐ Chapters: 20
☐ Privileges: Conventions Books Plants

© Oregon Trail Daffodils
Artist: Lee Weber

The International Ribes Association
Jeanne Nickless
P.O. Box 428
Boonville, CA 95415
(707) 895-2811
Fax: (707) 895-2811
The Ribes Reporter (4)

This is a group for growers of edible gooseberries and currants, both commercial and hobbyists.
☐ E-mail: nickless@pacific.net

International Violet Association
Sandra Geyer
2285 Country Club Drive
Altadena, CA 91001-3201
(818) 797-1607
Sweet Times (4)

Group interested in preserving old varieties of violets.
☐ E-mail: 104357.2132@compuserve.com
☐ Web: ourworld@compuserve.com/homepages/abrice
☐ Garden: National Arboretum, Washington DC

International Water Lily Society
Charles Covington
1410 Johnson Ferry Rd., Ste.328-G12
Marietta, GA 30062
(770) 929-6601
Water Garden Journal (4)

Group has an annual symposium in various locations.
☐ Garden: Denver Bot. Garden, CO; Burnby Hall, Pocklington, UK
☐ Privileges: Conventions Library

Kansas Wildflower Society
Jane Freeman, Admin. Assist.
2045 Constant Avenue
Lawrence, KS 66047-3729
(913) 864-3453
Newsletter (4)

They publish a handbook, "Growing Native Wildflowers" and growing guides for specific native plants. Write for a publication list; regional members only.
☐ Privileges: Conventions Books Seeds Trips

Long Island Horticultural Society
Elisa Robinson
1087A Rt. 25A
Northport, NY 11768
(516) 757-6292
Newsletter (11)

Society has symposia for members, regular meetings, plant sales and exhibits.
☐ Privileges: Plants Exhibits Trips Tours

Los Angeles International Fern Society
Donald Wood
9914 Calmada Avenue
Whittier, CA 90605
(562) 698-7696
LAIFS Journal (6)

Has a spore store and book store. Also holds educational programs.
☐ Privileges: Library Books Plants Exhibits Trips

Louisiana Native Plant Society
216 Caroline Dorman Road
Saline, LA 71070
(318) 576-3379
Lousiana Native Plant Society News (4)

Write for information.
☐ Garden: Caroline Dormon Nature Preserve, Saline, LA
☐ Privileges: Conventions Seeds Plants Exhibits Trips

The Magnolia Society, Inc.
Roberta D. Hagen, Secy.
6616 81st Street
Cabin John, MD 20818
(301) 320-4296
Fax: (301) 320-4296
Magnolia, Journal of the MS (2)
Magnolia Magazine (2)

The society recommends "The World of Magnolias" by Dorothy Callaway, and "Magnolias" by J. M. Gardiner. Seeds offered to members at a nominal fee.
☐ E-mail: RHagen6902@aol.com
☐ Web: www.tallahassee.net/~magnolia
☐ Privileges: Conventions Books Seeds Plants Trips Tours

The Mammillaria Society
Dr. W.F. Maddams
26 Glenfield Road
Banstead, Surrey, England SM7 2DG
Jnl. of the Mammillaria Society (4)

Members in the US and Canada send checks to Steve Brack, Box 72, Belen, NM 87002.
☐ Web: http://www.demon.co.uk/mace/mann.html
☐ Privileges: Seeds Plants

The Maple Society
Alan Ball
4 Black Barn, High Street, Seal
Sevenoaks, Kent, England TN15 OAL
Newsletter (4)

Write for information on membership: found too late to contact.

Marshall Olbrich Plant Club
P.O. Box 1338
Sebastopol, CA 95473
(707) 829-9189
MOPC Newsletter (6)

A regional group that meets 6 times a year in the North San Francisco Bay area; has speakers on a wide variety of horticultural topics.
☐ E-mail: tusker@ap.net
☐ Privileges: Books Plants Trips

Maryland Native Plant Society
Membership Secretary
P.O. Box 4877
Silver Spring, MD 20914
Native News (4)

Write for information.
☐ Privileges: Conventions Library Seeds Exhibits Trips

Massachusetts Horticultural Society
Kathy Hart, Memb. Dir.
300 Massachusetts Avenue
Boston, MA 02115
(617) 536-9280
Fax: (617) 262-8780
Leaflet (4)

Has sponsored the New England Spring Flower Show in Boston for 127 years; members may join the New England Garden History Society.
☐ Web: www.masshort.org
☐ Privileges: Library Books Exhibits Trips

Master Gardeners International Corp. (MaGIC)
Mary Price, Exec. Director
P.O. Box 526
Falls Church, VA 22040-0526
(703) 241-3769
Fax: (703) 241-8625
Master Gardening Journal (4)

Umbrella group for people who have taken the Master Gardening Training. They publish a directory of Master Gardener programs in North America, prepare and distribute specialized publications, provide program support, and foster interest in the Master Gardener movement through media outreach.
☐ E-mail: mgic@capaccess.org
☐ Privileges: Conventions Books

Mediterranean Garden Society
Secretary
P.O. Box 14
Peania, Greece 19002
The Mediterranean Garden (4)

Write for information.

Mesemb Study Group
Suzanne Mace
Brenfield House, Bolney Road
Ansty, West Sussex, England RH17 5AW
44 (0) 1444 509-171
Fax: 44 (0) 1444 454-061
Mesemb Study Group Bulletin (4)

They recommend "The Genus Conophytum" by S. Hammer, published by Succulent Plant Publications in Pretoria, South Africa.
☐ E-mail: msg@mace.demon.co.uk
☐ Web: www.demon.co.uk/mace/msg.html
☐ Privileges: Conventions Books Seeds Plants Exhibits

Michigan Botanical Club
Dorothy & Beatrice Sibley
7951 Walnut Avenue
Newaygo, MI 49337
(616) 652-2036
The Botanist (4)
Arisaema (2)

A society dedicated to the conservation of wildflowers. They offer programs, field trips, and campouts to study wildflowers.
☐ Privileges: Conventions Books Exhibits Trips

Minnesota Native Plant Society
MNPS, 220 BioScience
1445 Gortner Avenue
St. Paul, MN 55108
Minnesota Plant Press (3)

Write for information.
☐ Privileges: Conventions Seeds Plants Trips

Minnesota State Horticultural Society
Membership Secretary
1755 Prior Avenue North
Falcon Heights, MN 55113-4449
(612) 643-3601
Fax: (612) 643-3638
Minnesota Horticulturist (9)

They have a list of display gardens in Minnesota. They also publish a series of books for Northern gardeners and offer seminars and classes. Of interest to all Northern gardeners.
☐ E-mail: rmenk@ix.netcom.com
☐ Web: www.gardenmn.org
☐ Chapters: 200
☐ Privileges: Conventions Library Books Exhibits Tours

Mississippi Native Plant Society
Miss. Museum of Nat. Science
111 North Jefferson Street
Jackson, MS 39202
(601) 354-7303
Newsletter (4)

Botanical Garden of the South being developed at Sessums, MS. They recommend "Wildflowers of Mississippi" by Steve Timme.
☐ Privileges: Conventions Books Seeds Plants Trips

Missouri Native Plant Society
Ms. Pat Grace
P.O. Box 20073
St. Louis, MO 63144
(314) 577-9522
Fax: (314) 577-9596
Missouriensis (2)
Petal Pusher (6)

They recommend "Flora of Missouri," by Julian Steyermark.
☐ E-mail: gyatskievych@lehmann.mobot.org
☐ Chapters: 7
☐ Privileges: Conventions Books Trips

Montana Native Plant Society
Membership Chair
P.O. Box 8783
Missoula, MT 59807-8783
Kelseya (4)

They recommend "Flora of the Pacific Northwest" by Hitchcock & Cronquist, and "Vascular Plants of Montana" by Robert Dorn.
☐ Chapters: 6
☐ Privileges: Conventions Books Plants Trips

National Auricula & Primula Society
Peter Ward
6 Lawson Close
Saltford, Somerset, England BS18 3LB
Yearbook

Write for membership information: the society has three regional groups.

National Chrysanthemum Society (UK)
Mrs. Y. Honnor
8 Amber Business Village, Amber Close
Tamworth, Stafs., England B77 4RP
44 (0) 1827 310-331
Fax: 44 (0) 1827 310-331
Autumn & Spring Bulletins
Yearbook

They offer a number of publications on growing and showing chrysanthemums. Write for a price list.
☐ Privileges: Books Exhibits

National Chrysanthemum Society, Inc. (USA)
Galen L. Goss
10107 Homar Pond Drive
Fairfax Station, VA 22039-1650
(703) 978-7981
The Chrysanthemum (4)

Society publishes and sells a number of cultural and exhibition handbooks.
☐ Chapters: 45
☐ Privileges: Conventions Books

National Dahlia Society (UK)
Membership Secretary
19 Sunnybank
Marlow, Bucks., England SL7 3BL
44 (0) 1628 473-500
Dahlia Annual
Winter Bulletin

Members may join through the American Dahlia Society; write for information.
☐ Privileges: Conventions Books Exhibits

National Fuchsia Society
Agnes Rietkerk
11507 E. 187th Street
Artesia, CA 90701
Fuchsia Fan (6)

Display gardens at the San Diego Wild Animal Park, CA and South Coast Botanical Gardens, Palos Verdes, CA. They publish a book on fuchsias, "A to Z" and also recommend "How to Grow Fuchsias" by Ken Pilkington.
☐ Chapters: 4
☐ Privileges: Library Books Plants Exhibits Trips

National Gardening Association
Susan Lefebure
180 Flynn Avenue
Burlington, VT 05401
(802) 863-1308
Fax: (802) 863-5962
National Gardening (6)
Growing Ideas (3)

Dedicated to teaching people to grow plants. Has a seed search service, a members' answer service, new books at a discount and an interesting magazine for home gardeners. This organization also develops educational curricula about plant growing for teachers.
☐ E-mail: NGA@Garden.org
☐ Web: www.Garden.org
☐ Privileges: Books Seeds

National Hot Pepper Association
Bob Payton
400 N.W. 20th Street
Ft. Lauderdale, FL 33311-3818
(954) 565-4972
Fax: (954) 566-2208
Newsletter (4)

An organization dedicated to growing and cooking with chiles. They recommend "Peppers, The Domesticated Capsicum," by Jean Andrews.
☐ Privileges: Conventions Seeds Plants

National Sweet Pea Society
J.R.F. Bishop
3 Chalk Farm Road, Stokenchurch
High Wycombe, Bucks., England HP14 3TB
Sweet Pea Bulletin (2)
Sweet Pea Annual

Members get a free copy of the booklet "How to Grow Sweet Peas." They recommend "The Complete Guide to Sweet Peas" by B.R. Jones, which they sell.
☐ Garden: Hotham Park, Bognor Regis, W. Sussex, England
☐ Privileges: Exhibits

Native Plant Society of British Columbia
Diane Gertzen
14275 - 96th Avenue
Surrey, BC, Canada V3V 7Z2
(604) 255-5719
Fax: (604) 258-0201
Newsletter (4)

A new society. They recommend "Gardening with Native Plants of the Pacific Northwest" by Arthur R. Kruckeberg.

Native Plant Society of New Jersey
Cook College, Cont. Ed.
P.O. Box 231
New Brunswick, NJ 08903-0231
(908) 671-6400
Fax: (908) 671-7365
NJNPS Newsletter (4)

They recommend "Native Species Planting Guide for New York City and Vicinity," published by the New York City Department of Parks and Recreation.
☐ Garden: Native Plant Garden, Cook College, New Brunswick
☐ Privileges: Conventions Seeds Plants Trips

Native Plant Society of New Mexico
Membership Chairperson
1105 Circle Drive
Las Cruces, NM 88005
Newsletter (6)

☐ Chapters: 6
☐ Privileges: Conventions Books Plants Trips

Native Plant Society of Oregon
Jan Dobak, Memb. Chair.
2584 NW Savier Street
Portland, OR 97210-2412
Bulletin (12)
Kalmiopsis (1)

They recommend "Flora of the Pacific Northwest" by Hitchcock and Cronquist.
☐ Web: www.teleport.com/nonprofit/npso
☐ Chapters: 12
☐ Privileges: Conventions Trips

Native Plant Society of Texas
Dana Tucker
P.O. Box 891
Georgetown, TX 78627
(512) 238-0695
Fax: (512) 238-0703
Texas Native Plant Society News (6)

They publish "Texas Natives: Ornamental Trees" ($3 postpaid) and "100 Texas Wildflowers" ($9.95 postpaid).
☐ E-mail: dtucker@io.com
☐ Chapters: 29
☐ Privileges: Conventions Library Books Seeds Plants Exhibits Trips

New England Garden History Society
Mass. Horticultural Society
300 Massachusetts Avenue
Boston, MA 02115
(617) 536-9280
Journal (1)

Members must also join the Massachusetts Horticulture Society.
☐ Web: www.masshort.org
☐ Privileges: Conventions Library Books Exhibits Tours

New England Wild Flower Society
Patty Laier
180 Hemenway Road
Framingham, MA 01701-2699
(508) 877-7630
Fax: (508) 877-3658
New England Wildflower (3)

Chapters in each state in New England. Many wildflower seeds offered each year through their "Seed Book & Catalog." They recommend their "Garden in the Woods Cultivation Guide." ($5; write for postage charges.)
☐ E-mail: newfs@newfs.org
☐ Web: www.newfs.org/~newfs/
☐ Chapters: 5
☐ Garden: Garden-in-the-Woods, Framingham, MA
☐ Privileges: Library Books Plants Trips Tours

© Bear Creek Nursery
Artist: Takao Butterfield

New Zealand Fuchsia Society, Inc.
Secretary
P.O. Box 11-082
Ellerslie, Auckland, New Zealand 5
New Zealand Fuchsia Society Newsletter (6)

There is also a garden at Regional Botanic Garden, Manurewa.
☐ Garden: Eden Garden, Omana Rd, Auckland
☐ Privileges: Library Trips Tours

Newfoundland Alpine & Rock Garden Club
Todd Boland
81 Stamp's Lane
St. John's, NF, Canada A1B 3H7

A chapter of the North American Rock Garden Society. They recommend the "Manual of Alpine Plants" and the "Encyclopedia of Alpines" available through The North American Rock Garden Society or the Alpine Garden Society.
☐ E-mail: tboland@nfld.com
☐ Garden: Memorial Univ. Bot. Garden, St. John's, NF
☐ Privileges: Seeds Plants Trips

North American Butterfly Association
Membership Secretary
4 Delaware Road
Morristown, NJ 07960
(201) 285-0936
Fax: (201) 285-0936
American Butterflies (4)

A society for North American members that promotes butterfly appreciation, as well as gardening to attract butterflies. They offer brochures on butterfly gardens and habitats with specific information for twelve regions of North America for $3.50.
☐ E-mail: naba@naba.org
☐ Web: www.naba.org
☐ Privileges: Conventions Trips

North American Fruit Explorers
Jill Vorbeck, Memb. Chair.
1716 Apples Road
Chapin, IL 62628
(217) 245-7589
Pomona (4)

Dedicated home fruit growers who are interested in finding and growing unsual fruits and nuts. Scion and budwood exchanges, computer programs for test groups, and an excellent library that circulates by mail.
☐ Privileges: Conventions Library

North American Gladiolus Council
Robert G. Martin
R.F.D. 1, Box 70
Belgrade, ME 04917
(207) 495-2244
Bulletin (4)

They recommend their own "How to Grow Glorious Gladious," $9.
☐ Chapters: 30
☐ Privileges: Conventions Exhibits

North American Heather Society
Karla Lortz
E. 502 Haskell Hill Road
Shelton, WA 98584
(360) 427-5318
Fax: (360) 427-5318
Heather News (4)

Their one-page membership brochure is very informative, listing display gardens, and giving a bloom time chart for heaths and heathers. Six regional chapters. They recommend "Hardy Heather Species" by Dorothy Metheny.
☐ E-mail: heaths@gte.net
☐ Chapters: 6
☐ Privileges: Conventions Library Plants Trips

North American Lily Society, Inc.
Executive Secretary
P.O. Box 272
Owatonna, MN 55060-0272
Lily Yearbook (1)
Quarterly Bulletin (4)

Introductory publication "Let's Grow Lilies" is available for $3.50 postpaid.
☐ E-mail: nals@ll.net
☐ Web: www.lilies.org
☐ Chapters: 22
☐ Privileges: Conventions Library Books Seeds Exhibits

North American Mycological Association
Executive Secretary
3556 Oakwood
Ann Arbor, MI 48104-5213
(313) 971-2552
The Mycophile (6)
McIlvainea (1)

A group for mushroom growers and enthusiasts.
☐ E-mail: kwcee@umich.edu
☐ Web: namyco.org
☐ Chapters: 60
☐ Privileges: Conventions

North American Rock Garden Society
Secretary
P.O. Box 67
Millwood, NY 10546-0067
(914) 762-2948
Rock Garden Quarterly (4)

A very active society, with many local chapters. Hold winter study weekends; one on the East Coast, one on the West Coast, and an annual spring meeting. Has an excellent bookstore for members. They recommend "Rock Gardening" by Lincoln Foster.
- E-mail: mommens@ibm.net
- Web: www.nargs.org
- Chapters: 32
- Privileges: Conventions Library Books Seeds Plants Trips

North American Sea Plant Society, Inc.
Pamela D. Jacobsen
P.O. Box 262
Feeding Hills, MA 01030-0262
Fax: (413) 789-2076
Maritima (4)

A new society formed to promote the study and enjoyment of plants indigenous to coastal areas throughout North America. They offer a "Resource Guide to Coastal Plants" for $5.00 postpaid.
- E-mail: 103242.2424@compuserve.com
- Privileges: Seeds Plants

The North American Truffling Society
Membership Chair
P.O. Box 296
Corvallis, OR 97339
NATS Current News (6)

A society devoted to the science and pleasure of truffles. "Something to do while walking in the woods." Many of their specimens are preserved in the Oregon State University herbarium.
- Privileges: Library Trips

North Carolina Wild Flower Preservation Society
Membership Chairperson
c/o UNC Botanical Garden
Chapel Hill, NC 27517
(919) 962-0522
Newsletter (2)

They recommend "Growing and Propagating Wildflowers" by Henry Phillips, UNC Press, 1984.
- Garden: North Carolina Botanical Garden, Chapel Hill, NC
- Privileges: Conventions Trips

Northeast Heather Society
Walter K. Wornick
P.O. Box 101, Highland View
Alstead, NH 03602-0101
(603) 835-6165
Heather Notes (4)

Display Gardens at Heritage Plantation, Sandwich, MA, the Osterville, MA gardens of the Cape Cod Horticultural Society, and the Heather Garden at the Berkshire Botanic Garden, Stockbridge, MA. They recommend the books "Heathers in Color" by Poudley and "The Heather Garden" by Fred J. Chappie.
- Garden: See notes
- Privileges: Conventions Books Plants Trips

Northern Horticultural Society
Harlow Carr Botanical Gardens
Crag Lane
Harrogate, No.Yorks, England HG3 1QB
44 (0) 1423 565-418
Fax: 44 (0) 1423 530-663
Northern Gardener (4)

Enthusiastic gardeners, devoted to hardy plants. The Study Centre at Harlow Carr includes a herbarium and a reference collection of botanical specimens. The magazine would be of interest to all in cold climates.
- Garden: Harlow Carr Gardens, Harrogate, No. Yorks
- Privileges: Conventions Library Books Seeds Plants Exhibits

---

Northern Nevada Native Plant Society
Memb. Chairman
P.O. Box 8965
Reno, NV 89507-8965
Mentzelia (irregular)
Occasional Papers

They suggest reading books in the Intermountain Flora Series, published by the New York Botanical Garden, Bronx, NY 10458-5126. Their interests are education, preservation, propagation, seed exchanges and field trips.
- Privileges: Library Books Seeds Trips

Northern Nut Growers Association
Kenneth Bauman
9870 S. Palmer Road
New Carlisle, OH 45344
(937) 878-2610
Nutshell (4)
Annual Report

Publish "Nut Tree Culture in North America," $17.50 in the US and Canada, US$18.50 overseas, postpaid.
- E-mail: kenbauman@sprintmail.com
- Chapters: 6
- Privileges: Conventions Library

Northwest Fuchsia Society
Donna Fellows
610 Fifth Street
Steilacoom, WA 98388-1802
(253) 588-4541
The Fuchsia Flash (10)

Local clubs have gardens in their areas.
- ☐ E-mail: DonaFellows@msn.com
- ☐ Chapters: 14
- ☐ Garden: Eight test gardens in Puget Sound area.
- ☐ Privileges: Conventions Library Books Plants Exhibits Trips Tours

Northwest Horticultural Society
Heidi Shifflette
Box 354115, Univ. of Washington
Seattle, WA 98195-4115
(206) 527-1794
Fax: (206) 685-2692
Pacific Horticulture (4)
Garden Notes (4)

A general interest group; horticulture, gardening, seed exchanges, garden design, garden tours and lectures.
- ☐ E-mail: 04170.1472@compuserve.com
- ☐ Privileges: Conventions Library Seeds Plants Exhibits Trips Tours

The Northwest Hosta Society
Jim Vahey
12045 SE Foster Place
Portland, OR 97266
(503) 761-4457

Group interested in propagating, raising, and growing for the love of hostas.

Northwest Perennial Alliance
Membership Secretary
P.O. Box 45574, University Station
Seattle, WA 98145
(206) 324-0179
Fax: (206) 324-8513
The Perennial Post (4)

This is a regional group. They have two borders at The Good Shepherd Center, Seattle, and their border at the Bellevue Botanical Garden near Seattle is justly world famous. They recommend "Perennials, A Modern Florilegium" by Graham Stuart Thomas.
- ☐ E-mail: mraitz@accessone.com
- ☐ Garden: Bellevue Botanical Garden, WA
- ☐ Privileges: Conventions Books Seeds Plants

Nova Scotia Wild Flora Society
c/o Nova Scotia Museum
1747 Summer Street
Halifax, NS, Canada B3H 3A6
NSWFS Newsletter

Write for information.

Ohio Native Plant Society
Executive Secretary
6 Louise Drive
Chagrin Falls, OH 44022
(216) 338-6622

This group assists with the gardens at the Holden Arboretum, and the Garden Center of Greater Cleveland. Chapters have local newsletters.
- ☐ E-mail: inky5@juno.com
- ☐ Chapters: 8
- ☐ Privileges: Conventions Seeds Plants Trips Tours

Oklahoma Native Plant Society
Clare Miller, Sec.
2435 S. Peoria
Tulsa, OK 74114
(918) 743-3149
Gaillardia (4)

They recommend "Roadside Flowers of the Southern Great Plains" by Freeman and Schofield.
- ☐ Chapters: 2
- ☐ Privileges: Conventions Library Seeds Plants Trips Tours

Pacific Northwest Lily Society
Madeleine Robertson
3948 Timber Trail NE
Silverado, OR 97381
(503) 873-4748
Bulletin (2)

They recommend "Lilies: A Guide for Growers and Collectors" by Ed McRae, soon to be published by Timber Press.
- ☐ Privileges: Conventions Library Plants Exhibits Trips

Passiflora Society International
Anna Zinno c/o Butterfly World
3600 W. Sample Road
Coconut Creek, FL 33073
(954) 977-4434
Fax: (954) 977-4501
Passiflora (4)

They recommend "Passion Flowers" by John Vanderplank.
- ☐ E-mail: rboender@aol.com
- ☐ Web: www.butterflyworld.com
- ☐ Privileges: Conventions Seeds

The Pennsylvania Horticultural Society
Elizabeth Gullan
100 N. 20th Street, 5th fl.
Philadelphia, PA 19103-1495
(215) 988-8778
Fax: (215) 988-8783
Green Scene (6)
PHS News (11)

Has a 14,000-volume horticultural library; offers workshops, lectures and other services. "Green Scene" is available on subscription for $9.75 a year.
- ☐ E-mail: janeteva@libertynet.org
- ☐ Web: www.libertynet.org/~phs
- ☐ Privileges: Library Books Exhibits Trips Tours

Pennsylvania Native Plant Society
George Beatty
P.O. Box 281
State College, PA 16802-0281
(814) 234-4779

They recommend "The Vascular Flora of Pennsylvania: Annotated Checklist and Atlas" by Rhodes and Klein.

Peperomia & Exotic Plant Society
Anita Baudean
100 Neil Avenue
New Orleans, LA 70131-4014
(504) 394-4146
The Gazette (3)

They have a number of round robins -- members exchange plants and seeds.
- ☐ Privileges: Seeds

Plant Amnesty
Cass Turnbull
906 N.W. 87th Street
Seattle, WA 98117
(206) 783-9813
Plant Amnesty Newsletter (4)

A liberation group dedicated to freeing trees and shrubs from the abuse and mutilation of poor pruning practices. Beginning to form branches out of the Seattle area; publications are interesting and witty. They recommend "The Complete Guide to Landscape Design, Renovation and Maintenance," by Plant Amnesty founder Cass Turnbull.
- ☐ Chapters: 2
- ☐ Privileges: Books Trips Tours

Puget Sound Dahlia Association
Roger L. Walker
P.O. Box 5602
Bellevue, WA 98006
PSDA Bulletin (11)
Dahlias of Today (1)

Their terrific annual, "Dahlias of Today," is available from Jean Knutson, 7335 4th Avenue SW, Seattle, WA 98126, in US for $6.50, CAN $7, OV $10. They also recommend their "Dahlias, a Monthly Guide" which they sell for US$4.75. Another display garden is located at Volunteer Park, Seattle, WA.
- ☐ Garden: Bellevue Botanical Garden, Bellevue, WA
- ☐ Privileges: Plants Exhibits

Rare Fruit Council International, Inc.
P.O. Box 561914
Miami, FL 33256
(305) 378-4457
Tropical Fruit News (12)
Membership Directory (1)

Has plant exchanges; publishes a cookbook. Germplasm currently located at a number of Florida locations. Meet the second Tuesday of each month at the Museum of Science, Miami.
- ☐ Privileges: Library Books Seeds Plants Exhibits Trips Tours

Rare Pit & Plant Council
Deborah Peterson
17 Circuit Avenue
Scituate, MA 02066
Fax: (617) 545-8557
The Pits (8)

Society meetings are strictly limited because members meet in each others' homes. However, their interesting newsletter, devoted to growing exotic fruit and ornamentals indoors, is available by subscription. They publish "Beyond the Avocado" and the "Joy of Pitting" and recommend "Fruits for Warm Climates" by Julia Morton.
- ☐ E-mail: debpits@aol.com
- ☐ Privileges: Seeds Exhibits

The Reblooming Iris Society
Charles Brown
3114 South FM 131
Denison, TX 75020-0724
(905) 463-4084
Reblooming Recorder (2)

A section of the American Iris Society; members are encouraged to join the AIS as well. They recommend "The World of Irises" from the AIS.
☐ E-mail: FPKT93A@prodigy.com
☐ Privileges: Conventions

Rhododendron Society of Canada
R.S. Dickhout
5200 Timothy Crescent
Niagara Falls, ON, Canada L2E 5G3
(905) 357-5981
Fax: (905) 375-0018
Journal-ARS (4)
Niagara Newsletter (4)

A chapter of the American Rhododendron Society for Canadian members only.
☐ Chapters: 3
☐ Privileges: Conventions Library Books Seeds Plants Exhibits

Rhododendron Species Foundation
Vickie O'Keefe
P.O. Box 3798
Federal Way, WA 98063-3798
(206) 838-4646
Fax: (206) 838-4686
RSF Newsletter (4)
Plant Distribution Catalog (1)

Offers classes, lectures and an independent study course by mail, has a rhododendron library, plant sales to members and pollen distribution for hybridizers. It has created a living collection of over 1,800 rhododendrons, and also displays the Weyerhauser Pacific Rim Bonsai Collection. They recommend "The Rhododendron Species" by H. H. Davidian, and the rhododendron books of Peter A. Cox, as well as "Azaleas" by Fred Galle.
☐ Garden: Rhododendron Species Foundation, Federal Way, WA
☐ Privileges: Conventions Library Books Plants Exhibits Trips Tours

Rose Hybridizers Association
Larry D. Peterson
21 S. Wheaton Road
Horseheads, NY 14845
(607) 562-8592
Newsletter (4)

Interest in breeding new roses: display garden at Gene Boerner Gardens, Hales Corner, WI. Data base available to members listing back issues, articles and authors. Publish a "Rose Hybridizers Handbook" for beginners, US$5 ppd.
☐ E-mail: petersld@servtech.com
☐ Garden: American Rose Ctr., Shreveport, LA; Hales Corners, WI
☐ Privileges: Conventions Library

The Royal Horticultural Society
Membership Secretary
P.O. Box 313, 80 Vincent Square
London, England SW1P 2PE
44 (0) 1718 344-333
Fax: 44 (0) 1716 306-060
The Garden (12)

Frequent plant and flower shows in London, including the Chelsea and Hampton Court Flower Shows. Also has a wonderful library at Vincent Square, and a fantastic bookshop at Wisley.
☐ E-mail: AW73@dial.pipex.com
☐ Garden: Wisley, Surrey; Rosemoor, Devon; Hyde Hall, Essex
☐ Privileges: Library Books Seeds Plants Exhibits

The Royal National Rose Society
The Secretary
Chiswell Green
St. Albans, Herts., England AL2 3NR
44 (0) 1727 850-461
Fax: 44 (0) 1727 850-360
The Rose (4)

Claims to be one of the oldest, largest and friendliest plant societies in the world.
☐ E-mail: mail@rhrs.org.uk
☐ Web: www.roses.co.uk
☐ Chapters: 5
☐ Garden: The Gardens of the Rose, St. Albans, UK
☐ Privileges: Conventions Library Books Exhibits Trips Tours

The Saintpaulia & Houseplant Society
The Secretary
33 Church Road, Newbury Park
Ilford, Essex, England IG2 7ET
44 (0) 1815 903-710
Quarterly Bulletin

They have eleven pamphlets on various plants; write for information. They recommend "African Violets -- the Complete Guide" by Joan Hill & Gwen Goodship.
☐ Chapters: 2
☐ Privileges: Library Books Plants Exhibits

Saintpaulia International

See Gesneriad Society International.

San Diego Horticultural Society
Don Walker
1781 Sunrise Drive
Vista, CA 92089
(760) 630-7307
Horticopia Newsletter (12)

A society devoted to the study of native and exotic subtropical plants which grow outdoors in Southern California. They are in the process of printing a book describing many unusual plants that flourish in USDA Zone 10.
☐ Privileges: Library Seeds Plants Exhibits Trips Tours

Saxifrage Society
Adrian Young, Secretary
c/o Devon House, 33 Church Road
Leatherhead, Surry, England KT22 8AT
44 (0) 1372 378-094
The Saxifrage Magazine (1)
Newsletter (3)

A society for the alpine gardener with an interest in saxifrages.
☐ Privileges: Plants Exhibits Trips

Scottish Rock Garden Club
Membership Secretary
P.O. Box 14063
Edinburgh, Scotland EH10 4YE
44 (0) 1833 650-068
Fax: 44 (0) 1833 650-068
The Rock Garden (2)

Has a very extensive seed exchange, and a good selection of books for sale to members. They recommend "Encyclopaedia of Alpines," edited by Kenneth Beckett.
☐ E-mail: fbcavdwell@bad.dundee.ac.uk
☐ Chapters: 17
☐ Privileges: Conventions Library Books Seeds Plants Exhibits Trips Tours

---

The Sedum Society
Ron Mills
173 Colchester Rd., West Bergholt
Colchester, Essex, England CO6 3JY
Sedum Society Newsletter (4)

Seed and cutting exchanges. They recommend "Sedums: The Cultivated Stonecrop" by Ray Stephenson.
☐ Garden: 55 Beverly Dr., Choppington, Northumberland, England
☐ Privileges: Seeds Plants

Seed Savers Exchange
3076 North Winn Road
Decorah, IA 52101
(319) 382-5990
Fax: (319) 382-5872
Seed Savers Summer Yearbook (1)
Seed Savers Harvest Yearbook (1)

Sells the "Garden Seed Inventory" ($24) and the "Fruit, Berry and Nut Inventory" ($22), add $4 each for shipping in US; these are excellent source books for heirloom varieties. It's hard to overestimate the broad influence that this group has had -- Kent Whealey won a MacArthur Genius Award for his wonderful work in saving heirloom varieties.
☐ Garden: Heritage Farm, 3076 N. Winn Road, Decorah, IA
☐ Privileges: Conventions Books Seeds Plants

Seeds of Diversity Canada
P.O. Box 36, Station Q
Toronto, ON, Canada M4T 2L7
(905) 623-0353
Seeds of Diversity Canada (3)
Seed Listing (1)

Formerly the Heritage Seed Program: Canadian group interested in saving heirloom and endangered varieties of food crops to guard against the loss of genetic diversity. They recommend their own "How to Save Your Own Vegetable Seeds," which they sell for $8 postpaid.
☐ Privileges: Seeds

The Sempervivum Society
The Secretary
11 Wingle Tye Road
Burgess Hill, W. Sussex, England RH15 9HR
44 (0) 1444 236-848
Newsletter (Irregular)

Sells a cultural guide, "Houseleeks -- An Introduction," for £2.50.
☐ Garden: Burgess Hill, West Sussex, England
☐ Privileges: Conventions Books Plants

Sino-Himalayan Plant Association
Chris Chadwell
81 Parlaunt Road
Slough, Berks., England SL3 8BE
44 (0) 1753 542-823
Fax: 44 (0) 1753 542-823
SHPA Newsletter (2)

Write for information, send 1 IRC. They recommend "Flowers of the Himalaya" by Polunin & Stainton.
☐ Garden: Kohli Memorial Botanic Garden, Slough, England
☐ Privileges: Seeds Plants Exhibits Trips

The Society for Japanese Irises
Robert Bauer
9823 E. Michigan
Galesburg, MI 49053
(616) 665-7500
Fax: (616) 665-7500
The Review (2)

A section of the American Iris Society. Private gardens are open to members to display well-grown plants and newer varieties. They recommend "The Japanese Iris" by Dr. Currier McEwen.
☐ E-mail: ensata@aol.com
☐ Privileges: Conventions Exhibits

Society for Louisiana Iris
Elaine L. Bourque
1812 Broussard Road, East
Lafayette, LA 70508
SLI Newsletter (4)

They recommend "The Louisiana Iris," published by Texas Gardener Press, P.O. Box 9005, Waco, TX 76714. Price postpaid is $31.70 ($34.01 in TX).
☐ Privileges: Conventions Exhibits

Society for Pacific Coast Native Iris
Adele S. Lawyer
4333 Oak Hill Road
Oakland, CA 94605
(510) 638-0658
Almanac: SPCNI (2)

A section of the American Iris Society. They sell several publications about Pacific Coast native iris.
☐ Privileges: Conventions Books Seeds Tours

Society for Siberian Irises
Howard L. Brookins
N75 W14257 North Point Drive
Menomonee Falls, WI 53051-4325
(414) 251-5292
Fax: (414) 251-8298
The Siberian Iris (2)

A section of the American Iris Society. There is a list of private display gardens available from the membership secretary. Recommend "Siberian Iris" by Dr. Currier McEwen.
☐ Privileges: Conventions Books

Society of Ontario Nut Growers
Ernie Grimo
RR 3, 979 Lakeshore Road
Niagara-on-the-Lake, ON, Canada LOS IJO
(905) YEH-NUTS
Fax: (905) YEH-NUTS
SONG News (2)

Encourage the planting of nut-bearing trees and promote research.
☐ Privileges: Seeds Exhibits

Southeastern Palm and Exotic Plant Society
William T. Roberds
2652 Woodbridge Drive
Decatur, GA 30033
(803) 849-8057
Fax: (803) 754-3996
Rapidophyllum (4)

Members are interested in growing palms and other subtropicals in the southeastern United States, north of Florida.
☐ E-mail: ambills@westvaco.com
☐ Privileges: Plants Trips

Southern California Botanists
Alan Romspert
Dept. of Biology, Fullerton State Univ.
Fullerton, CA 92634
(714) 449-7034
Fax: (714) 773-2428
Crossosoma (2)
Leaflets (5)

Devoted to the study, preservation and conservation of native plants and plant communities of California. Has an annual symposium and pot luck.
☐ E-mail: wpresch@fullerton.edu
☐ Privileges: Conventions Books Plants Trips

Southern California Camellia Society
Bobbie Belcher
7475 Brydon Road
La Verne, CA 91750
(909) 593-4894
Fax: (909) 593-6062
Camellia Review (4)

Publish "Camellia Nomenclature," listing over 3000 camellias registered since 1948; US$5 to members, US$15 to non-members. There is a supplement, which costs US$5 to all. People may join to the New Zealand Camellia Society or the Australian Camellia Research Society through this group.
☐ E-mail: mbb@gte.net
☐ Privileges: Conventions Seeds Exhibits Trips

Southern California Clematis Society
Edith Malek
P.O. Box 17085
Irvine, CA 92623-7085
(714) 224-9885
The Clematis Chronicle (6)

New group, the first American clematis society. They offer "Clematis Care and Fact Sheet" for $2.00 postpaid.
☐ E-mail: clematis@aol.com
☐ Web: www.clematis.org
☐ Garden: New collection at Descanso Garden, La Canada, CA
☐ Privileges: Plants Exhibits Trips Tours

Southern California Horticultural Society
Joan DeFato
P.O. Box 41080
Los Angeles, CA 90041-0080
(818) 567-1496
Pacific Horticulture (4)
Monthly Bulletin

Though this group's focus is horticulture in Southern California, all are welcome to join.
☐ Privileges: Plants Trips

Southern Fruit Fellowship
Retta Davis
2051 Evergreen Drive
Shreveport, LA 71118
Southern Fruit Fellowship (4)

Write for information: US members only.
☐ Privileges: Conventions

Southern Garden History Society
Kitty Walker, Membership Secy.
Old Salem, Inc., Drawer F, Salem Station
Winston-Salem, NC 27108
(910) 724-3125
Fax: (910) 721-7335
Magnolia (4)

Encourages research and preservation of materials on the history of gardens in the South. Their library is located in the Atlanta History Center, Atlanta, GA. They recommend "Landscapes and Gardens for Historic Buildings" by Rudy J. Favretti and Joy Putman Favretti.
☐ Privileges: Conventions Library

Species Iris Group of North America (SIGNA)
Colin Rigby
18341 Paulson Street S.W.
Rochester, WA 98679
SIGNA (2)

A section of the American Iris Society. Has an excellent seed exchange and an excellent periodical. They recommend reading "Iris" by Brian Mathew.
☐ Garden: List of display gardens available
☐ Privileges: Conventions Seeds Plants Exhibits

Species Lily Preservation Society
Julius Wadekamper
15980 Canby Avenue
Faribault, MN 55021
Specifically Lilium (2)

Members are interested in preserving lilies in the wild.
☐ Garden: Parkdale, OR
☐ Privileges: Conventions Seeds Plants Trips

Spuria Iris Society
Bobbie Shepard
3342 W. Orangewood
Phoenix, AZ 85051
(602) 841-1231
Fax: (602) 841-1231
Spuria Newsletter (2)

A section of the American Iris Society; they publish "The Spuria Irises, Introduction and Varietal Listing" every 5 years.
☐ Privileges: Conventions Books Exhibits

Succulent Society of South Africa
Mrs. A. Costa
Private Bag X10
Brooklyn, South Africa 0011
27 (0) 1298 3588
Fax: 27 (0) 1298 3588
Aloe (4)

A society devoted to the cultivation of succulents. Open to international members.
☐ Privileges: Conventions Seeds

Tennessee Native Plant Society
Kay Jones, President
P.O. Box 193
Hampshire, TN 38461-0193
(615) 285-2777
Newsletter (6)

Write for information.
☐ Privileges: Conventions Exhibits Trips Tours

The Terrarium Association
Robert C. Baur
P.O. Box 276
Newfane, VT 05345

Not really a society, but a source of information and literature on growing plants in terrariums; they sell modestly priced booklets on plants for terrariums, how to do it, etc. Write for publications brochure.

The Toronto Bonsai Society
Ena Davidson
190 McAllister Road
Downsview, ON, Canada M3H2NQ
(416) 635-6851
Fax: (416) 635-7750
Journal (10)

Write for information.
☐ E-mail: rgoebel@tor.hookup.net
☐ Web: www.hookup.net/~rgoebel
☐ Privileges: Library

The Toronto Cactus & Succulent Club
David Naylor
9091 Eighth Line Road, RR 2
Georgetown, ON, Canada L7G 4S5
(905) 877-6013
Cactus Factus (8)

This is a regional group. They recommend "The Cactus Handbook" by Erik Haustein; members get free "Care Sheets" for various genera.
☐ E-mail: david.naylor@projectx.com
☐ Privileges: Conventions Library Plants Exhibits

Toronto Gesneriad Society
Monte Watler
240 Burnhamthorpe Road
Etabicoke, ON, Canada M9B IZ5
(905) 233-6664

Write for information.

Tropical Flowering Tree Society
c/o Fairchild Tropical Garden
10901 Old Cutler Road
Miami, FL 33156
Bulletin (2)

Write for information.
☐ Privileges: Conventions Plants Exhibits Trips

Utah Native Plant Society
P.O. Box 520041
Salt Lake City, UT 84152-0041
Sego Lily (6)

They have an annual mushroom hunt.
☐ Chapters: 2
☐ Privileges: Trips

Victoria Orchid Society
P.O. Box 30038, Saanich Central Postal Outlet
Victoria, BC, Canada V8X 5E1
Bulletin (12)

Write for information.
☐ Privileges: Conventions Library Books Plants Exhibits Trips

---

Virginia Native Plant Society
Membership Chair
P.O. Box 844
Annadale, VA 22003
(703) 368-9803
Fax: (703) 368-0792
Bulletin (5)

Has a good book and gift sales list for members. Offers a list of sources free with a long SASE. They recommend "Wildflowers in your Garden" by Viki Ferreniea, "Growing and Propagating Wildflowers" by Harry Phillips, and "Handbook of Wildflower Cultivation" by Taylor & Hamblin.
☐ Chapters: 9
☐ Privileges: Conventions Books Plants Trips

Washington Native Plant Society
Catherine Hovanic
P.O. Box 28690
Seattle, WA 98118-8690
(206) 760-8022
Douglasia (4)

Has annual backpack trips and study weekends.
☐ E-mail: wnps@blarg.net
☐ Web: www.wnps.org
☐ Chapters: 11
☐ Privileges: Conventions Trips

West Virginia Native Plant Society
Corresponding Secretary
P.O. Box 2755
Elkins, WV 26241
Native Notes (4)

Society does not sell or exchange seeds.
☐ Privileges: Conventions Trips

Western Horticultural Society
Treasurer
P.O. Box 60507
Palo Alto, CA 94306
Pacific Horticulture (4)
Newsletter (8)

Have plant raffles at every meeting. This is a regional organization, active on the San Francisco peninsula.
☐ Privileges: Books Seeds Plants Exhibits Trips

Wild Ones -- Natural Landscapers
Membership Director
P.O. Box 23576
Milwaukee, WI 53223-0576
Wild Ones Journal (6)

An organization of gardeners dedicated to educating and sharing information on landscaping with native plants and promoting biodiversity. They have 11 chapters in the upper Midwest, and a new one in Portland, OR. They sell signs to members which read "This land is in harmony with nature," which may keep their neighbors from turning them in for growing "weeds." North American members only.
- [ ] Chapters: 12
- [ ] Privileges: Trips

Willamette Valley Hardy Plant Group
Diana Learner
3093 Solomon Loop
Eugene, OR 97405
(541) 342-6696
Newsletter (12)

Monthly meetings feature well-known speakers. They host the Hardy Plant Society of Oregon Study Weekend every four years.
- [ ] E-mail: dglearner@aol.com
- [ ] Web: www.egi.com/~egi/hardyplant
- [ ] Privileges: Plants Trips Tours

Worcester County Horticultural Society
Mary Elsner
Tower Hill Botanic Garden, 11 French Drive
Boylston, MA 01505-0598
(508) 869-6111
Fax: (508) 869-0314
Grow with Us (6)

Regional group maintains a display garden and sponsors the Worcester Spring Flower Show annually. Also listed in the nursery section as a source of scionwood of antique fruit varieties.
- [ ] E-mail: THBG@Towerhillbg.org
- [ ] Web: www.towerhillbg.org
- [ ] Garden: Tower Hill Botanic Garden, Boylston, MA
- [ ] Privileges: Conventions Library Books Plants Exhibits Trips Tours

World Federation of Rose Societies
Mrs. Jill Bennell
46 Alexandra Road, St. Albans
Hertfordshire, England AL1 3AZ
44 (0) 1727 833-648
World Rose News (2)

This is an umbrella group for national societies worldwide.
- [ ] Chapters: 27 countries
- [ ] Privileges: Conventions

World Pumpkin Confederation
Ray Waterman
14050 Rt. 62
Collins, NY 14034
(716) 532-5995
Fax: (716) 532-5690
Cucurbits (4-6)

Promotes the sport/hobby of growing giant pumpkins and other vegetables on a worldwide level.
- [ ] E-mail: 1gourd@aol.com
- [ ] Chapters: 22
- [ ] Garden: Giant Pumpkin Gardens at Collins, NY
- [ ] Privileges: Conventions Seeds Plants Exhibits Trips

Wyoming Native Plant Society
Secretary-Treasurer
1604 Grand Avenue
Laramie, WY 82070
Castilleja (4)

US members only. Annual meeting is usually a field trip.
- [ ] Privileges: Conventions Trips

Xerces Society
Membership Secretary
4828 SE Hawthorne Blvd.
Portland, OR 97215
(503) 232-6693
Fax: (503) 233-6794
Wings (2-3)

"The only conservation organization solely devoted to the protection of invertebrates -- insects, spiders, worms, snails, and creatures of the sea. They recommend "Butterfly Gardening: Creating Summer Magic in Your Garden" published by Sierra Club Books.
- [ ] E-mail: xerces@teleport.com
- [ ] Privileges: Conventions Books

$\boxed{\text{E}}$

MAGAZINES

Horticultural magazines and newsletters published in English and available by subscription from all over the world are listed alphabetically by title.

Since subscription rates are subject to change, I'd suggest that you write for information before sending payment for a subscription. We give subscription rates as of the time we are updating the book to give you an idea of the relative cost of each title.

The true gardener pulls the gardening magazines out of the mail and flops right down to read them first. They have an alarming way of multiplying — they must have invasive root systems. At any rate, they are very difficult to weed!

At the time of this revision, both *The Gardener's Index* and *Garden Literature* are unsure about their future publishing plans. Both are well worth your attention — write for information and subscribe!

A table of the symbols and abbreviations used in this book appears inside the front and back covers.

The Amateur's Digest
Cacti - Other Succulents - Caudex Plants
8591 Lochside Drive
Sidney, BC, Canada V8L 1M5
E-mail: amatrdigest@pinc.com
Web: vvv.com/~amdigest

A magazine written by its subscribers, those interested in cactus and succulent plants. Also publish a booklet on growing succulents & cacti from seeds and cuttings called "Succulents from Scratch." US$7 postpaid in the US and Canada, US$7.50 postpaid overseas.
- ☐ Price: US US$20 • CAN C$19 • OV US$22 (IMO)
- ☐ Issues/Year: 6
- ☐ Region: International

The American Cottage Gardener
131 E. Michigan Street
Marquette, MI 49855
Web: trine.com/GardenNet/ACG

A charming magazine, particularly good on old-fashioned plants. Very well written and a good read; a new favorite with me.
- ☐ Price: US $35 • CAN US$35 • OV US$40 (IMO)
- ☐ Issues/Year: 4
- ☐ Region: National

American Rose Rambler
P.O. Box 677
Mantua, OH 44255
E-mail: PeterSchneider@compuserve.com

A newsletter for passionate rose growers.
- ☐ Price: US $12 • CAN US$12 • OV US$17 (IMO,check)
- ☐ Issues/Year: 6

Arnoldia
125 Arborway
Jamaica Plain, MA 02130-3500
E-mail: Arnoldia@arnarb.harvard.edu
Web: arboretum.harvard.edu/

A fairly scholarly magazine, devoted to all aspects of plants.
- ☐ Price: US $20 • CAN US$25 • OV US$25 (IMO,CC)
- ☐ Issues/Year: 4
- ☐ Region: International

Australian Orchid Review
14 McGill Street
Lewisham, NSW, Australia 2049

An attractive magazine for orchid enthusiasts. Subscription can be paid with a US check or credit card. Back issues available for US$7.50 each; send self-addressed envelope for list.
- ☐ Price: US US$41 ($53 air)
- ☐ Issues/Year: 6
- ☐ Region: International

The Australian Gardener
P.O. Box 746
Darlinghurst, NSW, Australia 2010
E-mail: Mason@magna.com.au

An attractive magazine with features on many aspects of gardening in Australia and other areas with Mediterranean climates.
- ☐ Price: OV AU$75.00 (air mail)
- ☐ Issues/Year: 6
- ☐ Region: Australia

The Avant Gardener
P.O. Box 489
New York, NY 10028-0489

Summarizes new information on all phases of gardening. Lists new sources of garden materials, sometimes has special-interest issues.
- ☐ Price: US $20 • CAN US$24 • OV US$24 (IMO)
- ☐ Issues/Year: 12
- ☐ Region: National

Back in Thyme
P.O. Box 963
Toganoxie, KS 66086-0963
E-mail: BacknThyme@aol.com

A new newsletter "about heirloom flowers, herbs and prairie plants." Emphasis is on old time gardening and plants, includes recipes and book reviews.
- ☐ Price: US $20 • CAN US$24 • OV US$30 (IMO)
- ☐ Issues/Year: 6
- ☐ Region: National

Bonsai Today
P.O. Box 816
Sudbury, MA 01776
E-mail: jpalmer@stonelantern.com
Web: www.stonelantern.com

Beautifully illustrated bonsai magazine, full of how-to information and inspiration.
- ☐ Price: US $42 • CAN US$48 • OV US$52.50 surface (IMO,CC)
- ☐ Issues/Year: 6
- ☐ Region: International

John E. Bryan Gardening Newsletter
300 Valley Street, Suite 206
Sausalito, CA 94965

A gardening newsletter which focuses on northern California growing conditions, but contains a lot of general information and musings as well.
- ☐ Price: US $30 • CAN C$40 • OV US$30, £25
- ☐ Issues/Year: 12
- ☐ Region: Northern California

The Business of Herbs
439 Ponderosa Way
Jemez Springs, NM 87025-8025
E-mail: HerbBiz@aol.com

Newsletter for the small herb grower and seller, expanding into general articles of "more lasting significance" about herbs.
- ☐ Price: US $24 • CAN US$30 • OV US$36 (IMO)
- ☐ Issues/Year: 6
- ☐ Region: National

California Garden
Casa del Prado, Balboa Park
San Diego, CA 92101-1619

For gardeners in Mediterranean climates, particularly southern California; information on garden events in the San Diego area.
- ☐ Price: US $7 • CAN US$7 • OV US$13 (IMO)
- ☐ Issues/Year: 6
- ☐ Region: Southern California

Canadian Gardening
130 Spy Court
Markham, ON, Canada L3R 8N4
E-mail: letters@canadiangardening.com

A general interest magazine that covers all aspects of gardening in Canada, Zones 2-8. Might also be of interest in the upper Midwest.
- ☐ Price: US C$37.95 • CAN C$22.95 • OV C$67.95
- ☐ Issues/Year: 7
- ☐ Region: Canada

Canadian Horticultural History
P.O. Box 399
Hamilton, ON, Canada L8N 3H8

Journal features Canadian gardens, historical restorations, plant collectors, early nurseries, etc. Subscription is for 4 issues. Publication temporarily suspended in 1993, still very irregular in 1997; best to write for information.
- ☐ Price: US $22 • CAN C$20 • OV US$22
- ☐ Issues/Year: Irregular
- ☐ Region: Canada

Carolina Gardener
P.O. Box 4504
Greensboro, NC 27404
E-mail: hcovingt@nr.infi.net
Web: www.linksliving.com/HomeStyle/Carolina Gardener

For Southeastern gardeners; regional gardening suggestions and information on native plants and gardens to visit. Schedule of garden events.
- ☐ Price: US $16.95 + postage
- ☐ Issues/Year: 6
- ☐ Region: Southeastern US

Coastal Grower: Gardening in British Columbia
1075 Alston Street
Victoria, BC, Canada V9A 3S6
E-mail: grower@islandnet.com
Web: www.island net.com/~grower/homepage.html

Of interest to gardeners in British Columbia, and coastal Washington and Oregon. Formerly called The Island Grower.
- ☐ Price: US US$25 • CAN C$20 • OV C$40
- ☐ Issues/Year: 9
- ☐ Region: Northwestern Pacific Coast

Country Home: Country Gardens
1716 Locust Street
Des Moines, IA 50309-3023

A magazine aimed at the new and beginning gardener: information on plants, garden design and garden lifestyle.
- ☐ Price: US $16 • CAN US$20
- ☐ Issues/Year: 4
- ☐ Region: National

Country Living Gardener
P.O. Box 7335
Red Oak, IA 51591-2335
E-mail: gardeners@hearst.com
Web: www.homearts.com

A general interest magazine with many articles of interest to new gardeners.
- ☐ Price: US $19.97 • CAN $25.97
- ☐ Issues/Year: 6

The Country Shepherd Herb News
Route 1, Box 107
Comer, GA 30629
E-mail: mfzx30A@prodigy.com

Offers information for growing herbs in the Southeast; events, recipes, growing hints, sources, etc.
- Price: US $18
- Issues/Year: 6
- Region: Southeastern US

Desert Plants
2120 E. Allen Road
Tucson, AZ 85719
E-mail: mnorem@ag.arizona.edu
Web: ag/arizona.edu/BTA/btsa.html

Devoted to cultivated and wild desert plants; quite scholarly. Of interest in desert Southwest and other desert areas of the world.
- Price: US $15 • OV US$20 (IMO)
- Issues/Year: 2
- Region: International

East Coast Gardener
565 Windmill Road, Second Floor
Dartmouth, NS, Canada B3B 1B4
E-mail: ecg@klis.com

A new newsletter for the maritime provinces of Canada; also of interest to gardeners in the northeastern United States. Write for information.
- Issues/Year: 6

The English Garden
P.O. Box 345
Landisburg, PA 17040

A new English magazine that had only published one issue when we found out about it. They aim at the best of private gardens that are possible without hired gardeners, and include related gardening features; lots of glossy photographs. Canadians write to 3780 Peter Street, Windsor, ON N9C 4H2.
- Price: US $35.70 • CAN C$46 + GST
- Issues/Year: 6

European Gardens
34 River Court, Upper Ground
London, England SE1 9PE
E-mail: 100770.722@compuserve.com

An attractive magazine focused on preserving historic and estate gardens.
- Price: US US$43 • OV US$43 or £25 (IMO, check)
- Region: Europe and North America

Exotic Gardening
P.O. Box 241
San Jose, Costa Rica 1017

Monthly newsletter about growing tropical plants; both in gardens and particularly as houseplants.
- Price: US $24 • CAN C$24 (IMO) • OV US$24 (US check or IMO)
- Issues/Year: 12
- Region: International

Fine Gardening
63 South Main Street
Newtown, CT 06470-5506
E-mail: FG@Taunton.com
Web: www.taunton.com

One of the best general-interest gardening magazines, written by gardeners themselves. Many good color photographs and other illustrations.
- Price: US $32 • CAN C$39 • OV US$39 (IMO,CC)
- Issues/Year: 6
- Region: National

Florida Gardening
P.O. Box 500678
Malabar, FL 32950
E-mail: Flgarden@iu.net

A new general interest magazine devoted to the gardening conditions of Florida; editors formerly ran a seed company specializing in vegetables for the South, so they give good growing advice.
- Price: US $19
- Issues/Year: 6
- Region: Florida

Flower & Garden
P.O. Box 7503
Red Oak, IA 51591-0503
E-mail: kcpublishing@earthlink.net
Web: home.earthlink.net/~kcpublishing/

A general-interest gardening magazine, with articles on all phases of home gardening, regional reports and reports on new cultivars and products.
- Price: US $19.95 • CAN US$27.77 • OV US$25.95 (IMO,CC,check)
- Issues/Year: 6
- Region: National

The Four Seasons
Tilden Regional Park, Botanic Garden
Berkeley, CA 94708-2396

Magazine covering all aspects of California native plants, both technical and semipopular articles. For serious enthusiasts and botanists.
- Price: US $12
- Issues/Year: 1
- Region: California

Garden Design
P.O. Box 5429
Harlan, IA 51593-2929
E-mail: gardendesign@here.com

The emphasis has shifted from lavish domestic landscape architecture to somewhat more homey garden pursuits -- more information on plants, plant combinations, garden design ideas.
- ☐ Price: US $27.95 • CAN US$35 .95 • OV US$41.95 (CC)
- ☐ Issues/Year: 8
- ☐ Region: National

Garden Gate
2200 Grand Avenue
Des Moines, IA 50312
E-mail: gardengate@gardengatemag.com

Garden inspiration and advice for new and beginning gardeners.
- ☐ Price: US $24.95 • CAN US$29.95 • OV US$29.95
- ☐ Issues/Year: 6
- ☐ Region: National

Garden Literature - Sprout
398 Columbus Ave., Suite 181
Boston, MA 02116
E-mail: GardenLit@aol.com

A very thorough index to periodical articles and book reviews about a wide range of topics. Covers a baker's dozen of the leading gardening magazines in the US and Britain.
- ☐ Price: US $29.95 • OV US$34.95 (IMO,CC,check)
- ☐ Issues/Year: 2
- ☐ Region: International

Garden Paths
A Newsletter from Flowerplace Plant Farm
P.O. Box 4865
Meridian, MS 39304
E-mail: lgbarton@aol.com

A newsletter from the former proprietors of Flowerplace Plant Farm; chatty, full of interesting plant information and guest articles by plant loving friends.
- ☐ Price: US $15 • CAN US$25 • OV US$25 (IMO)
- ☐ Issues/Year: 4
- ☐ Region: Southeastern US

Garden Railways
21027 Crossroads Circle
Waukesha, WI 53187-1612
E-mail: gr@indra.com
Web: www.gardenrailways.com

Magazine for gardening railroaders -- or railroading gardeners! Emphasis is on railroading, but it's delightful.
- ☐ Price: US $21 • CAN $28 • OV US$28 (IMO)
- ☐ Issues/Year: 6
- ☐ Region: National

The Gardener's Gazette
P.O. Box 786
Georgetown, CT 06829
E-mail: GarGazette@aol.com
Web: www.cretech.co/GarGazette/

A regional newspaper that covers horticultural and environmental topics, with articles on nature and landscaping.
- ☐ Price: US $15
- ☐ Issues/Year: 6
- ☐ Region: New England

Gardener's Index
P.O. Box 27041
Kansas City, MO 64110-7041

A combined annual index to "American Horticulturist," "Fine Gardening," "Flower & Garden," "Horticulture," "National Gardening" and "Organic Gardening" -- very thorough and useful. Cumulative issues covering 1986-1990, and 1991, 1992, 1993, and 1994 are available. Write for prices.
- ☐ Issues/Year: 1
- ☐ Region: National

Gardenmart
P.O. Box 43502
Toronto, ON, Canada M4G 4G8
E-mail: gardenmart@compuserve.com
Web: cangarden.com

A new newsletter for Canadian gardeners, with articles on plants, schedule of events, gardening tips.
- ☐ Price: US $20 • CAN C$20 • OV C$20
- ☐ Issues/Year: 6
- ☐ Region: Canada

Gardens Illustrated
Fenner, Reed & Jackson, Box 754
Manhasset, NY 11030
E-mail: gardens@johnbrown.co.uk

A lavishly illustrated magazine with emphasis on British gardens and gardeners, but it is of interest to all keen gardeners. Credit cards may be used for payment. Outside the US and Canada, write to 186-142 Bramley Road, London W10.
- ☐ Price: US US$45 • CAN US$45 • OV £19.80 (IMO,CC)
- ☐ Issues/Year: 6
- ☐ Region: International

Gardens West
Box 2680 Stn Terminal
Vancouver, BC, Canada V6B 3W8
E-mail: gardenswest@mindlink.net

An attractive magazine with articles on plants and gardening, of interest to gardeners on the Pacific coast of Canada and the US. Includes a regional calendar of events.
☐ Price: US $27 • CAN C$22 • OV C$30 (IMO,CC)
☐ Issues/Year: 9
☐ Region: Pacific Northwest/Canada

The Gardener's Companion Newsletter
P.O. Box 420296
Palm Coast, FL 32142-0296
Web: www.almanac.com

A newsletter from the publisher of "The Old Farmer's Almanac," with short articles and a calendar of what to do in the garden each month.
☐ Price: US $30
☐ Issues/Year: 12
☐ Region: National

Green Prints
P.O. Box 1355
Fairview, NC 28730

A great favorite of mine, it is not a how-to magazine, but charming pieces short and long about how gardeners feel. Usually funny, sometimes sad, it's a great shot in the arm each time it comes.
☐ Price: US $17.97 • CAN US$21 • OV US$27 (IMO)
☐ Issues/Year: 4
☐ Region: National

The Growing Edge Magazine
P.O. Box 1027
Corvallis, OR 97339
E-mail: talexan@peak.org
Web: www.growingedge.com

"News and information for indoor and outdoor growers." This magazine is concerned primarily with hydroponic and greenhouse growing.
☐ Price: US $24.95 • CAN US$24.95 • OV US$45.95 (IMO,CC)
☐ Issues/Year: 6
☐ Region: International

Growing for Market
P.O. Box 3747
Lawrence, KS 66046

Aimed at the small market gardener selling at farm market; news and ideas.
☐ Price: US $27 • CAN US$30 • OV US$36 (IMO)
☐ Issues/Year: 12
☐ Region: US & Canada

Growing Native
P.O. Box 489
Berkeley, CA 94701

A newsletter of great interest in California; each issue features a particular type of native plant, and articles are frequently written by experts in native plants. Also carries interesting interviews of native plant "greats," and the wit and wisdom of long time gardeners.
☐ Price: US $30
☐ Issues/Year: 6
☐ Region: California, Western states

Hardy Enough
351 Pleasant Street, Suite 259
Northampton, MA 01060

A newsletter for adventurous gardeners who are trying to grow subtropical plants north of their usual hardiness range; particularly in USDA Zones 4-8.
☐ Price: US $30 • CAN US$33 • OV US$38 (IMO)
☐ Issues/Year: 6
☐ Region: USDA Zones 4-8

Harrowsmith: Canada's Magazine of Country Living
25 Sheppard Avenue W.
North York, ON, Canada M2N 6S7

Covers all phases of country living in the North.
☐ Issues/Year: 6
☐ Region: Canada

The Herb Companion
201 E. Fourth Street
Loveland, CO 80537
E-mail: HC@iwp.ccmail.compuserve.com

Very attractive general interest magazine on herbs: growing, history, cooking and crafts -- very well done.
☐ Price: US $24 • CAN US$31 • OV US$31 (IMO,CC)
☐ Issues/Year: 6
☐ Region: National

The Herb Quarterly
P.O. Box 689
San Anselmo, CA 94979
E-mail: HerbQuart@aol.com

Beautiful publication devoted to herbs: their culture, history, use and recipes. A regular feature is information on herb gardens to visit.
- ☐ Price: US $24 • CAN US$29 • OV US$31 (CC)
- ☐ Issues/Year: 4
- ☐ Region: International

The Herb, Spice and Medicinal Plant Digest
Dept. of Plant & Soil Science
U. of Mass., Amherst, MA 01003
E-mail: craker@pssci.umass.edu
Web: www-unix.oit.umass.edu/~herbdig

Quarterly for herb growers and those interested in uses of herbs; issues have surveys of recent literature, some technical material -- not for beginners. They publish "The International Directory of Specialists in Herbs, Spices, and Medicinal Plants." Write for information.
- ☐ Price: US $10 • CAN US$17 • OV US$17
- ☐ Issues/Year: 4
- ☐ Region: International

Herban Lifestyles
84 Carpenter Road
New Hartford, CT 06057-3003
E-mail: chrisu@esslink.com

Newsletter on "herban renewal," or ways to incorporate herbs into your lifestyle.
- ☐ Price: US $18 • CAN $24 • OV US$33
- ☐ Issues/Year: 4
- ☐ Region: International

Horticulture
P.O. Box 53880
Boulder, CO 80322-3880
E-mail: hortmag@aol.com

Probably the most widely known and appreciated American gardening magazine. Well-illustrated articles on all aspects of gardening, covering North America, with occasional articles on European gardens.
- ☐ Price: US $26 • CAN US$32 • OV US$32 (CC)
- ☐ Issues/Year: 10
- ☐ Region: National

HortIdeas
460 Black Lick Road
Gravel Switch, KY 40328
E-mail: rareideas@juno.com

A gardeners' "digest," the latest horticultural research, new sources of plants and supplies, book reviews. Always full of interest.
- ☐ Price: US $20 • CAN US$26 • OV US$35 (IMO,check)
- ☐ Issues/Year: 12
- ☐ Region: National

Hortus
Bryan's Ground Letchmore Lane
Stapleton, Herts, England LD8 2LP
E-mail: Hortus@bg.kc3ltd.co.uk
Web: www.kc3.co.uk/business/hortus

Quarterly devoted to writings by distinguished British gardeners, with a sprinkling of foreign writers; enough reading for several evenings.
- ☐ Price: US $65 (IMO,CC) • CAN $80 • OV £40
- ☐ Issues/Year: 4
- ☐ Region: International

In Good Tilth
11535 SW Durham Rd., Ste. C-1
Tigard, OR 97224
E-mail: oregontilth@compuserve.com

A newspaper for "farmers, gardeners, and consumers working for a sustainable agriculture."
- ☐ Price: US $25 • CAN $35 • OV US$35 (IMO)
- ☐ Issues/Year: 10
- ☐ Region: Pacific Northwest

International Bonsai
P.O. Box 23894
Rochester, NY 14692-3894
E-mail: intbonsai@aol.com
Web: wnv@internationalbonsai.com

Quarterly for the serious bonsai enthusiast. Add US$10 to the subscription price for overseas air mail. They also sell video tapes and have a bonsai arboretum; call (716) 334-2595 to arrange a visit.
- ☐ Price: US $26 • CAN US$35 • OV US$35
- ☐ Issues/Year: 4
- ☐ Region: International

Journal of Garden History
1900 Frost Road, Suite 101
Bristol, PA 19007-1598
E-mail: gah@tandfpa.com
Web: www.tandfdc.com

An international journal with a multi-disciplinary approach to garden history. Price to institutions is US$285 (£173) year.
- ☐ Price: US $119 • OV £70
- ☐ Issues/Year: 4
- ☐ Region: International

Kitchen Garden
63 S. Main Street , P.O. Box 5506
Newtown, CT 06470
E-mail: kg@Taunton.com
Web: www.taunton.com

A newish magazine devoted to growing, preserving and preparing food from the garden. Well illustrated with color photographs and diagrams.
☐ Price: US $24 • CAN US$30 • OV US$30
☐ Issues/Year: 6
☐ Region: National

Allen Lacy's homeground
Box 271
Linwood, NJ 08221

Allen Lacy was formerly a garden columnist at the Wall Street Journal, and then the New York Times. His newsletter is very interesting, aimed at the serious gardener and plant lover, and well worth reading and saving. It's somewhat aimed at the Mid-Atlantic and upper South of the US.
☐ Price: US $38 • CAN US$50 • OV US$50 (IMO)
☐ Issues/Year: 4
☐ Region: National

Lindleyana
6000 S. Olive Avenue
West Palm Beach, FL 33405
E-mail: 71726.1742@compuserve.com
Web: www.pathfinder.com/vg/gardens/AOS

The scientific journal of the American Orchid Society.
☐ Price: US $29 • CAN US$31 • OV US$31
☐ Issues/Year: 4
☐ Region: International

The Literate Gardener
Capilano Box 38044
Edmonton, AB, Canada T6A 3Y6

"Information for gardeners who love to read." Book reviews, coverage of special interests and suggested reading, with a bias toward Canadian gardening conditions and northern areas of the US.
☐ Price: US US$18 • CAN C$19.26 • OV C$30 (IMO)
☐ Issues/Year: 4
☐ Region: Canada/US

Living Off the Land, Subtropic Newsletter
P.O. Box 2131
Melbourne, FL 32902-2131
E-mail: vanatta@iu.net

A newsletter oriented toward growing edibles, particularly tropical fruits and crops; list of seeds "wanted" and "available" in each issue.
☐ Price: US $10 • CAN US$12 • OV US$12 (IMO)
☐ Issues/Year: 4
☐ Region: Subtropic climates

The Maine Organic Farmer & Gardener
P.O. Box 2176
Augusta, ME 04338

Tabloid periodical for organic gardeners and market farmers, lists gardens to visit, has a calendar of events.
☐ Price: US $12 • CAN US$18 • OV US$18 (IMO)
☐ Issues/Year: 4
☐ Region: New England

Mushroom Growers Newsletter
P.O. Box 5065
Klamath Falls, OR 97601-0017
E-mail: MycoWrld@cdsnet.net
Web: www.cdsnet.net/Business/mushroom/

A newsletter for small scale commercial and specialty mushroom growers, and hobbyists, too.
☐ Price: US $24 • OV US$45 (CC)
☐ Issues/Year: 12
☐ Region: International

Native Notes
985 Brushy Valley Road
Heiskell, TN 37754

A newsletter devoted to landscaping with native plants of the eastern US. Includes book reviews and a calendar of events.
☐ Price: US $15 • CAN US$15 • OV US$15 (IMO)
☐ Issues/Year: 4
☐ Region: Eastern US

The New Plantsman
P.O. Box 38
Ashford, Kent, England TN25 6PR

Fairly scholarly coverage of all types of plants in garden use; several well illustrated articles in each issue. Scope is international.
☐ Price: US US$45 (IMO,CC) • CAN C$45 (IMO,CC) • OV £29 (IMO,CC)
☐ Issues/Year: 4
☐ Region: International

New, rare and unusual PLANTS: a Journal for Plant Enthusiasts
2, Grange Close
Hartlepool, England TS26 0DU
E-mail: dirk@aquil.demon.co.uk
Web: www.netlink.co.uk/users/plants

A new journal for rabid plant lovers, with a decided British bent when it comes to cultivars and sources, giving details on newly selected or discovered plants. It's written in a cheerful, friendly manner for gardeners instead of botanists, many authors are dedicated readers with news to share. It costs £17 in Europe, £24 to Australia and New Zealand.
☐ Price: US $34 • CAN $44 • OV see notes
☐ Issues/Year: 4
☐ Region: International

Northland Berry News
595 Grand Avenue
St. Paul, MN 55102-2611

Of interest to all who grow more than a few raspberries, strawberries or blueberries, especially "pick-your-own" operations and market gardeners.
☐ Price: US $15 • CAN US$18 • OV US$25 (airmail)   (CC)
☐ Issues/Year: 4
☐ Region: Northern climates

Orchid Digest
P.O. Box 1216
Redlands, CA 92373-0402

A quarterly magazine for orchid enthusiasts; many color photographs.
☐ Price: US $20 • CAN US$22 • OV US$22.50
☐ Issues/Year: 4
☐ Region: International

The Orchid Review
P.O. Box 38
Ashford, Kent, England TN25 6PR

The orchid journal of the Royal Horticulture Society; international in scope.
☐ Price: US US$50 (IMO,CC) • CAN £34.95 (IMO,CC) • OV £24.95 (IMO,CC)
☐ Issues/Year: 6
☐ Region: International

Organic Gardening
P.O. Box 7304
Red Oak, IA 51591-2304

The "old standby" was upsized, updated and upscaled; but the homey touch has crept back in and it's even got a really "corny" editor.
☐ Price: US $19.96 • CAN C$24.96 • OV US$37
☐ Issues/Year: 8
☐ Region: National

Pacific Horticulture
P.O. Box 485
Berkeley, CA 94701-0485

Published by a consortium of Pacific Coast horticultural societies; a very interesting and beautiful magazine with worldwide readership.
☐ Price: US $20 • CAN US$23 (CC) • OV US$25 (CC,IMO)
☐ Issues/Year: 4
☐ Region: Pacific Coast

Paeonia Newsletter
46 Exeter Street
West Newton, MA 02165

A new newsletter for gardeners who enjoy growing peonies.
☐ Price: US $5 • CAN US$7 • OV US$7
☐ Issues/Year: 4
☐ Region: International

Plant Talk
P.O. Box 65226
Tuscon, AZ 85728-5226

The first international magazine on plant conservation. For overseas subscriptions, write to P.O. Box 500, Kingston upon Thames, Surrey, England, KTZ 5XB.
☐ Price: US US$25 • OV US$25 or £15
☐ Issues/Year: 4
☐ Region: Worldwide

Plants & Gardens News
1000 Washington Avenue
Brooklyn, NY 11225

Plants and Gardens News is a periodic newsletter of the Brooklyn Botanic Garden, but with your subscription, you also receive their wonderful quarterly 21st Century Gardening Series. This series has very fine single subject issues covering many topics, written by experts in the field.
☐ Price: US $35 • CAN US$40 • OV US$40 (IMO)
☐ Issues/Year: See notes
☐ Region: National

Rocky Mountain Gardener
P.O. Box 3484
Durango, CO 81302
E-mail: rmg@frontier.net

An attractive magazine that addresses the specific needs of experienced and/or passionate Rocky Mountain gardeners. They sell books on regional gardening.
- [ ] Price: US $15 • CAN $20 • OV US$25 (IMO)
- [ ] Issues/Year: 4
- [ ] Region: Rocky Mountain states

The Rose Garden
783 Oakglade Drive
Monrovia, CA 91016-1717

Focus on growing roses organically, companion plants for roses, beneficial insects, the environment, wildlife, monthly duties for rose growers.
- [ ] Price: US $15
- [ ] Issues/Year: 12
- [ ] Region: West Coast

Small Farm News
University of California
Davis, CA 95616-8699
E-mail: sfcenter@ucdavis.edu
Web: sfc.ucdavis.edu

A magazine aimed at the small farmer and market grower in California; free to California growers.
- [ ] Issues/Year: 6
- [ ] Region: California

Small Farm Today
3903 W. Ridge Trail Road
Clark, MO 65243-9525

A magazine for small farmers and market gardeners.
- [ ] Price: US $21 • CAN US$31 • OV US$31 (IMO,CC)
- [ ] Issues/Year: 6
- [ ] Region: National

The Southern California Gardener
P.O. Box 8072
Van Nuys, CA 91409
E-mail: scgardener@aol.com

An award-winning newsletter for gardeners from San Luis Obispo to San Diego; articles on plants, garden schedules, calendar of garden events, reviews of pertinent books.
- [ ] Price: US $20 • OV US$38
- [ ] Issues/Year: 6
- [ ] Region: Southern California

Southern Living
P.O. Box 830119
Birmingham, AL 35283-0119
Web: southernlivingpathfinder.com

Magazine has frequent articles on gardening in the South.
- [ ] Issues/Year: 12
- [ ] Region: Southeastern US

Neil Sperry's Gardens
P.O. Box 864
McKinney, TX 75070-0864
E-mail: Sperry@connect.net
Web: www.neilsperry.com

An attractive and well-illustrated magazine with articles on all aspects of gardening in Texas and on the Gulf coast.
- [ ] Price: US $22.50
- [ ] Issues/Year: 10
- [ ] Region: Texas, Gulf Coast

Sunset Magazine
P.O. Box 56653
Boulder, CO 80323-6653

A long published and much imitated "lifestyle" magazine, familiar to all in the 13 Western states; there are five regional editions, and each issue carries gardening features customized by region.
- [ ] Price: US $24 • CAN US$38 • OV US$38 (CC-US funds only)
- [ ] Issues/Year: 12
- [ ] Region: Western states

Temperate Bamboo Quarterly
TBQ, 30 Myers Rd.
Summertown, TN 38483-7323

A newsletter for beginning and experienced growers of bamboo; "a forum for sharing information and news among Bambuseros." International in scope.
- [ ] Price: US $24 • CAN US$32 • OV US$36 (IMO)
- [ ] Issues/Year: 4
- [ ] Region: International

Texas Gardener
P.O. Box 9005
Waco, TX 76714-9005
E-mail: suntex@calpha.com

"The magazine for Texas gardeners, by Texas gardeners."
- [ ] Price: US $16.95 • CAN US$22.95 • OV US$26.95
- [ ] Issues/Year: 6
- [ ] Region: Texas

The Tomato Club
P.O. Box 418
Bogota, NJ 07603
E-mail: tomatoclub@aol.com

Not a society, but a newsletter for "the tomato crowd." Concentrates on tomato growing: history, recipes, trivia and more.
☐ Price: US $15.95 • CAN US$18.95 (IMO) • OV US$22.95 (check)
☐ Issues/Year: 6
☐ Region: International

21st Century Gardening Series

See Plants & Gardens News (Brooklyn Botanical Garden)

The Vine Line
217 Argilla Road
Ipswich, MA 01938

The purpose of this new newsletter "is to educate gardeners in North America about growing clematis in our climate."
☐ Price: US $26 • CAN $32 • OV US$36
☐ Issues/Year: 4
☐ Region: North America

Virginia Gardening Guide
114 E. Main Street, Ste. 301
Charlottesville, VA 22902-5289
E-mail: cvggpub@aol.com

A general interest magazine for gardeners in Virginia and bordering states.
☐ Price: US $14
☐ Issues/Year: 6
☐ Region: Virginia

Water Gardening
49 Boone Village
Zionsville, IN 46077
E-mail: HNH20gar@aol.com
Web: watergardening.com

A beautiful new magazine, full of color illustrations and information about plants, construction, and water garden design.
☐ Price: US $30 • CAN US$40 • OV US$40 (IMO)
☐ Issues/Year: 10
☐ Region: International

The Weedpatch Gazette
P.O. Box 339
Richmond, IL 60071-4681
E-mail: weedpatch@rsq.org
Web: www.mbn.net/weedpatch

A newsletter devoted to gardening in the Chicago area; sources, calendar of events, news of local beautification and urban forestry projects. Very useful and well done.
☐ Price: US $22
☐ Issues/Year: 4
☐ Region: Chicago region, Midwest

$\boxed{\text{F}}$

LIBRARIES

Libraries with special horticultural collections are listed by state or province and then alphabetically by city.

Many public libraries have good collections of books on plants and gardening and will try to borrow books they don't have through interlibrary loan. Some cities, such as Philadelphia (the Library Company of Philadelphia) and San Francisco (the Mechanics Institute), have membership libraries with good horticultural collections. Some colleges and universities will allow alumni and local residents to use their libraries for an annual fee, or you can sign up for a horticultural course and get library privileges for a semester.

Many of the libraries listed, particularly those at botanical gardens, are supported by very active membership groups, horticultural societies or "friends" groups. It is well worth joining such a group to have the use of a good library, to say nothing of all the other interesting activities these groups offer.

A table of the symbols and abbreviations used in this book appears inside the front and back covers.

ALABAMA

Horace Hammond Memorial Library
Birmingham Botanical Gardens
2612 Lane Park Road
Birmingham, AL 35223
(205) 879-1227
Fax: (205) 879-3751
E-mail: bg*@athena.bhm.lib.al.us
Ida Burns

☐ Open: M-F 9-4
☐ Number of Books: 3,500
☐ Periodical Titles: 125
☐ Services: Loans to Public, Interlibrary Loans

ALASKA

Library
University of Alaska Museum Herbarium
907 Yukon Drive
Fairbanks, AK 99775-6960
(907) 474-7108

Generally open September to May. Call ahead to check.
☐ Open: M-F 9-4
☐ Number of Books: 400
☐ Periodical Titles: 5
☐ Services: Reference Only

ARIZONA

Richter Memorial Library
Desert Botanical Garden
1201 N. Galvin Parkway
Phoenix, AZ 85008
(602) 941-1225

Public may use books in the library with an admission fee or membership in the Garden. Phone advice on growing desert plants given weekdays from 10-11:30. Particularly strong collection on desert plants; also has a collection of garden catalogs.
☐ Open: M-F 8-5
☐ Number of Books: 10,000
☐ Periodical Titles: 100
☐ Services: Reference Only

Boyce Thompson Southwestern Arboretum Library
Boyce Thompson Southwestern Arboretum
37615 US Highway 60
Superior, AZ 85273
(602) 689-2723

Members and researchers may make an appointment to use the library; call or write for information.
☐ Open: Call for hours
☐ Number of Books: 3,000
☐ Periodical Titles: 40
☐ Services: Reference Only

BRITISH COLUMBIA, CANADA

Library
University of British Columbia Botanical Gdn.
6804 S.W. Marine Drive
Vancouver, BC, Canada V6T 1Z4
(604) 822-4372
Fax: (604) 822-2016
Judy Newton

Public may use books in the library.
☐ Open: M-F 10-4
☐ Number of Books: 1,700
☐ Periodical Titles: 200
☐ Services: Reference Only

VanDusen Gardens Library
Vancouver Botanical Gardens Association
5251 Oak Street
Vancouver, BC, Canada V6M 4H1
(604) 257-8668
Fax: (604) 266-4236
Barbara Fox

Open Tu-F and Su. Call for hours. Public may use books in the library.
☐ Open: See notes
☐ Number of Books: 3,800
☐ Periodical Titles: 50
☐ Services: Members Only

CALIFORNIA

Plant Science Library
The Arboretum of Los Angeles County
301 N. Baldwin Avenue
Arcadia, CA 91007-2697
(626) 821-3213
Fax: (626) 445-1217
E-mail: jdefato@co.la.ca.us
Joan DeFato

Public may use books in the library.
☐ Open: M-F 9-5 ; Sa 10-1
☐ Number of Books: 13,000
☐ Periodical Titles: 130
☐ Services: Interlibrary Loans

Rancho Santa Ana Botanic Garden Library
1500 N. College Avenue
Claremont, CA 91711-3157
(909) 625-8767 ext. 236
Fax: (909) 626-7670
E-mail: bbeck@rocky.claremont.edu
Web: wwwcgs.edy/inst/rsa
Beatrice M. Beck

The public may use books in the library. Collection strong in publications on drought-tolerant plants and water-saving concepts.
☐ Open: M-F 9-4
☐ Number of Books: 42,000
☐ Periodical Titles: 1,000
☐ Services: Reference Only

Quail Botanical Gardens Library
Quail Botanical Gardens Foundation
230 Quail Gardens Drive
Encinitas, CA 92024
(760) 436-3036
Fax: (760) 632-0917
Web: members.aol.com/quailbg/quail.html

The public may use books in the library.
☐ Open: Sa 11-3
☐ Number of Books: 1,536
☐ Periodical Titles: 7
☐ Services: Members Only

Fullerton Arboretum Library
Friends of the Fullerton Arboretum
1900 Associated Road
Fullerton, CA 92631
(714) 278-4795
Fax: (714) 278-7066
Celia Kutchner

Public may use books in the library. Located at the corner of Yorba Linda Boulevard and Associated Road.
☐ Number of Books: 2,500
☐ Periodical Titles: 25
☐ Services: Members Only

South Coast Plant Science Library
South Coast Botanic Garden
26300 Crenshaw Boulevard
Palos Verdes Penin., CA 90274
(310) 544-1948

This library is for members only.
☐ Open: M-F 9-4
☐ Number of Books: 600
☐ Periodical Titles: 10
☐ Services: Members Only, Reference Only

Library & Information Center
San Diego Floral Association
Room 105, Casa del Prado, Balboa Park
San Diego, CA 92101-1619
(619) 232-5762

Public may use books in the library.
☐ Open: M-F 10-3
☐ Number of Books: 3,500
☐ Services: Members Only

Helen Crocker Russell Library of Horticulture
Strybing Arboretum Society
Ninth Avenue at Lincoln Way
San Francisco, CA 94122-2384
(415) 661-1316, X 303
E-mail: bphcrl@ix.netcom.com
Web: www.mobot.org/aabga/member.pages/strybing
Barbara M. Pitschel, Brian K. Lym

The public may use books in the library.
☐ Open: Daily 10-4
☐ Number of Books: 18,000
☐ Periodical Titles: 450
☐ Services: Reference Only

(continued next page)

CALIFORNIA (continued)

Blaksley Library
Santa Barbara Botanic Garden
1212 Mission Canyon Road
Santa Barbara, CA 93105
(805) 682-4726
Fax: (805) 563-0352
E-mail: lhannah@sbbg.org
Web: www.sbbg.org
Laurie Hannah

Collection strong in California native plants. Public may use books in the library.
☐ Open: M-F 9-5
☐ Number of Books: 11,000
☐ Periodical Titles: 200
☐ Services: Reference Only

Wallace Sterling Library
Filoli Center & Friends of Filoli
Canada Road
Woodside, CA 94062
(415) 364-8300
Fax: (415) 366-7386
Web: www.filoli.org
Thomas Rogers

Collection in landscape architecture and garden design; members or researchers may call or write for an appointment.
☐ Open: Tu-Sa, call for appt.
☐ Number of Books: 1,600
☐ Periodical Titles: 20
☐ Services: Reference Only

COLORADO

Helen Fowler Library
Denver Botanic Gardens
909 York Street
Denver, CO 80206-3799
(303) 370-8014
Fax: (303) 370-8196
E-mail: dbglibry@ix.netcom.com
Susan C. Eubank

Public may use books in the library.
☐ Open: M-Su 9-5
☐ Number of Books: 25,000
☐ Periodical Titles: 500
☐ Services: Members Only, Interlibrary Loans

CONNECTICUT

Library
Garden Education Center of Greenwich
Bible Street
Cos Cob, CT 06807
(203) 869-9242
Fax: (203) 869-0619

The library is closed July and August.
☐ Open: M-F 9-4:00
☐ Number of Books: 1,000
☐ Periodical Titles: 50
☐ Services: Loans to Public

Bartlett Arboretum Library
Univ. of Connecticut at Stamford
151 Brookdale Road
Stamford, CT 06903-4199
(203) 322-6971

☐ Open: M-F 8:30-4
☐ Number of Books: 3,000
☐ Periodical Titles: 35
☐ Services: Loans to Public

DELAWARE

Delaware Center for Horticulture Library
Delaware Center for Horticulture
1810 N. DuPont Street
Wilmington, DE 19806-3308
(302) 658-1913
Fax: (302) 658-6267

Public may use books in the library.
☐ Open: M-F 10-3
☐ Number of Books: 2,000+
☐ Periodical Titles: 35
☐ Services: Members Only

DISTRICT OF COLUMBIA

Gerden Library
Dumbarton Oaks Garden
1703 - 32nd Street N.W.
Washington, DC 20007
(202) 342-3280
Fax: (202) 625-0432
Linda Lott

Open to researchers by appointment. Call or write for information.
☐ Open: M-F 9-5, call for appt.
☐ Number of Books: 14,000
☐ Periodical Titles: 42
☐ Services: Reference Only

(continued next page)

DISTRICT OF COLUMBIA (continued)

US National Arboretum Library
USDA, Agricultural Research Service
3501 New York Avenue N.E.
Washington, DC 20002
(202) 475-4815
Fax: (202) 245-4575
Web: www.ars-grin.gen/ars/beltsville/na/

Public may use books in the library.
- ☐ Open: By appointment
- ☐ Number of Books: 7,500
- ☐ Periodical Titles: 200
- ☐ Services: Members Only, Interlibrary Loans

Horticulture Branch Library
Smithsonian Institution
Arts & Industries Building, Room 2282
Washington, DC 20560
(202) 357-1544
Fax: (202) 786-2026
E-mail: libem061@sil.si.edu
Web: www.SiL.Si.EDU
Marca Woodhams

Library has 15,000 nursery and seed catalogs; focus is garden history and design. Also an excellent Botany Library in the Natural History Museum. Researchers may make an appointment to use the library.
- ☐ Open: M-F 10-4:30
- ☐ Number of Books: 6,000
- ☐ Periodical Titles: 300
- ☐ Services: Members Only, Interlibrary Loans

FLORIDA

Library
Rare Fruit & Vegetable Council
3245 College Avenue
Davie, FL 33314
(305) 941-0668
Frank Moretti

Collection on the use of food-producing plants for permaculture.
- ☐ Open: Open before meetings
- ☐ Number of Books: 500
- ☐ Periodical Titles: 3
- ☐ Services: Members Only

Montgomery Library
Fairchild Tropical Garden
10901 Old Cutler Road
Miami, FL 33156
E-mail: zonas@servax.fiu.edu

Members can borrow from the lending library portion of the collection.
- ☐ Open: By appointment
- ☐ Number of Books: 7,000
- ☐ Services: Reference Only

Research Library
Marie Selby Botanical Gardens
811 S. Palm Avenue
Sarasota, FL 34236
(813) 955-7553

Members may use the library for reference by appointment.
- ☐ Open: By appointment
- ☐ Number of Books: 5,000
- ☐ Services: Reference Only

GEORGIA

Cherokee Garden Library
(at the Atlanta History Center)
130 West Paces Ferry Road
Atlanta, GA 30305
(404) 814-4046
Anne Salter

Public may use books in the library.
- ☐ Open: M-F, call for hours
- ☐ Number of Books: 5,500
- ☐ Periodical Titles: 20
- ☐ Services: Reference Only

Fernbank Science Center Library
Fernbank Science Center
156 Heaton Park Drive N.E.
Atlanta, GA 30307
(404) 378-4311
Fax: (404) 370-1336
Web: www.fernbank.edu
Mary Larsen

Public may use books in the library.
- ☐ Open: M-Sa, call for hours
- ☐ Number of Books: 15,169
- ☐ Periodical Titles: 355
- ☐ Services: Reference Only

(continued next page)

GEORGIA (continued)

Sheffield Botanical Library
Atlanta Botanical Garden
P.O. Box 77246 Piedmont Park at the Prado
Atlanta, GA 30357
(404) 876-5859 ext. 225
Fax: (404) 876-7472
Lu Ann Schwarz or Miriam Boland

The public may use books in the library.
- ❏ Open: Tu-Su, 9-6
- ❏ Number of Books: 3,000
- ❏ Periodical Titles: 60
- ❏ Services: Reference Only

Library
American Camellia Society
One Massee Lane
Fort Valley, GA 31030
(912) 967-2358
Fax: (912) 967-2083
Web: www.peach.public.lib.ga.us/ACS/acs.htm

Public may use books in the library; books for reference only. Call or write for information.
- ❏ Open: M-F, 9-4
- ❏ Services: Reference Only

HAWAII

Waimea Arboretum Foundation Library
Waimea Arboretum Foundation
59-864 Kamehameha Highway
Haleiwa, HI 96712
(808) 638-8655

Call ahead.
- ❏ Open: 8-4, daily
- ❏ Number of Books: 500
- ❏ Periodical Titles: 50
- ❏ Services: Reference Only

Bishop Museum Library
Bernice Pauani Bishop Museum
1525 Bernice Street (P.O. Box 19000-A)
Honolulu, HI 96817-0916
(808) 848-4148
E-mail: library@bishop.hawaii.org
Web: www.bishop.hawaii.org
Duane Wenzel

Public may use books in the library. Library includes a horticultural collection.
- ❏ Open: Tu-F 1-4, Sa 9-12
- ❏ Number of Books: 100,000
- ❏ Periodical Titles: 1,100
- ❏ Services: Interlibrary Loans

University of Hawaii at Manoa Library
University of Hawaii
2550 The Mall
Honolulu, HI 96822
(808) 956-7205
Fax: (808) 956-5968
Web: nic2.hawaii.net/uhlibZ/welcome.htm
John R. Haak

Part of a large university library. The public may borrow from the library.
- ❏ Open: M-Su, call for hours

Research Library
National Tropical Botanical Garden
P.O. Box 340
Lawai, HI 96765
(808) 332-7324
Fax: (808) 332-9765
E-mail: rhanna@aloha.net
Richard Hanna

A strong collection on tropical plants. Public may use books in the library.
- ❏ Open: M-F 9-5
- ❏ Number of Books: 8,000
- ❏ Periodical Titles: 250
- ❏ Services: Loans to Public, Interlibrary Loans

ILLINOIS

Chicago Botanic Garden Library
Chicago Botanic Garden
1000 Lake-Cook Road
Glencoe, IL 60022
(847) 835-8200
Fax: (847) 835-4484
E-mail: cbglib@nslsilus.org
Web: www.chicago-botanic.org
Virginia Jusko and Nancy McCray

Public may use books in the library.
- ❏ Open: M-Sa 9-4
- ❏ Number of Books: 14,000
- ❏ Periodical Titles: 200
- ❏ Services: Members Only, Interlibrary Loans

(continued next page)

ILLINOIS (continued)

Sterling Morton Library
Morton Arboretum
4100 Illinois, Route 53
Lisle, IL 60532
(630) 719-2427
Fax: (630) 719-2433
E-mail: mstieber@mortonarb.org
Web: www.mortonarb.org
Michael T. Stieber or Rita Hassert

Public may use books in the library.
- ☐ Open: M-F 9-5, Sa 10-4
- ☐ Number of Books: 28,000
- ☐ Periodical Titles: 400
- ☐ Services: Members Only, Interlibrary Loans

INDIANA

Horticultural Science Library
Indianapolis Museum of Art
I.M.A. Horticultural Society
1200 W. 38th Street
Indianapolis, IN 46208
(317) 923-1331

Public may use books in the library.
- ☐ Open: W & Sa 1-4
- ☐ Services: Members Only

The Hayes Regional Arboretum Library
801 Elks Road
Richmond, IN 47374-2526
(317) 962-3745

- ☐ Open: Tu-Sa 1-5
- ☐ Number of Books: 1,000
- ☐ Services: Reference Only

IOWA

Library
Bickelhaupt Arboretum
340 S. 14th Street
Clinton, IA 52732
(319) 242-4771
F. K. Bickelhaupt

- ☐ Open: Daily, call for hours
- ☐ Number of Books: 800
- ☐ Periodical Titles: 20
- ☐ Services: Loans to Public

Gardeners of America
Men's Garden Clubs of America, Inc.
P.O. Box 241, 5560 Merle Hay Road
Johnston, IA 50131
(515) 278-0295

The library is open to members, and to researchers by appointment.
- ☐ Open: M-F 8:30-4:30
- ☐ Number of Books: 2,000
- ☐ Services: Members Only

KANSAS

Frank Good Library
Botanica, The Wichita Gardens
701 N. Amidon
Wichita, KS 67203
(316) 264-0448
Fax: (316) 264-0587
Web: www2.southwind.net/~scribe/Botanica
Amy Kaspar Woolf

Public may use books in the library.
- ☐ Open: M-F, call for hours
- ☐ Number of Books: 3,000
- ☐ Periodical Titles: 25
- ☐ Services: Members Only

MARYLAND

Cylburn Arboretum Association Library
Cylburn Arboretum Association
4915 Greenspring Avenue
Baltimore, MD 21209-4698
(410) 367-2217
Adelaide C. Rackemann

Public may use books in the library.
- ☐ Open: Th 1-3, and by appt.
- ☐ Number of Books: 1,500
- ☐ Periodical Titles: 3
- ☐ Services: Members Only

(continued next page)

MARYLAND (continued)

National Agricultural Library
US Department of Agriculture
10301 Baltimore Boulevard
Beltsville, MD 20705-2351
(301) 504-5204
Fax: (301) 504-5675
E-mail: agref@nal.usda.gov
Web: www.nal.usda.gov

Probably the largest of all the libraries -- the public may use it for reference only. There is a branch reading room in DC, at USDA South, Room 1052; for information call (202) 447-3434.
☐ Open: M-F 8-4:30
☐ Number of Books: 2 mil.
☐ Periodical Titles: 27000
☐ Services: Reference Only, Interlibrary Loans

Brookside Gardens Library
Maryland-National Capital Park & Plan. Comm.
1500 Glenallan Avenue
Wheaton, MD 20902
(301) 949-8231
Fax: (301) 949-0571

Public may use books in the library.
☐ Open: M-Su noon-5 p.m.
☐ Number of Books: 3,000
☐ Periodical Titles: 25
☐ Services: Reference Only

MASSACHUSETTS

The Library
The Massachusetts Horticultural Society
300 Massachusetts Avenue
Boston, MA 02115
(617) 536-9280
Fax: (617) 282-8780
Web: www.masshort.org

Public may use books in the library. The collection dates from the 15th century.
☐ Open: M-F 8:30-4:30, Sa 10-2
☐ Number of Books: 45,000
☐ Periodical Titles: 300
☐ Services: Members Only

Tower Hill Botanic Garden Library
Worcester County Horticultural Society
Tower Hill Botanic Garden, 11 French Dr.
Boylston, MA 01505-0589
(508) 869-6111
Web: www.towerhillbg.org
Jane Milligan

Public may use books in the library.
☐ Open: Call for days and hours
☐ Number of Books: 7,000
☐ Periodical Titles: 39
☐ Services: Members Only

The Botany Libraries
Harvard University Herbaria Building
22 Divinity Avenue
Cambridge, MA 02138
(617) 496-2366
Fax: (617) 495-8654
E-mail: warnemen@oeb.harvard.edu
Judith Warnement

Library of the Gray Herbarium, Arnold Arboretum, Economic Botany Library and Oakes Ames Orchid Library; available to serious users and researchers. Call or write for information.
☐ Open: M-F 9-5
☐ Number of Books: 250,000
☐ Periodical Titles: 1,500
☐ Services: Reference Only, Interlibrary Loans

Lawrence Newcomb Library
New England Wild Flower Society
180 Hemenway Road
Framingham, MA 01701-2699
(508) 877-7630 X3304
Fax: (508) 877-3658
E-mail: library@newfs.org
Web: www.newfs.org/~newfs
John Benson, Mary Walker

Public may use books in the library. Garden is closed Nov.1 to April 14, but library is open M-F 9-4:30.
☐ Open: M-F 9-5, see notes
☐ Number of Books: 3,000
☐ Periodical Titles: 100
☐ Services: Members Only

Berkshire Botanical Garden Library
Berkshire Botanical Garden
Stockbridge, MA 01262
(413) 298-3926
Dina Samfield

Public may use books in the library. Open Sa-Su, 10-4, May-October.
☐ Open: M-F 10-4
☐ Number of Books: 1,500
☐ Services: Members Only

MICHIGAN

Matthaei Botanical Gardens Library
The University of Michigan
1800 N. Dixboro Road
Ann Arbor, MI 48105
(313) 763-7061
Katherine R. French

Public may use books in the library.
- ☐ Open: M-F, call for hours
- ☐ Number of Books: 2,100
- ☐ Periodical Titles: 12
- ☐ Services: Reference Only

Kingman Museum of Natural History Library
Battle Creek Public Schools
175 Limit Street
Battle Creek, MI 49017
(616) 965-5117
Fax: (616) 962-5610
Kathy Ward

The public may use books in the library.
- ☐ Open: Call for days and hours
- ☐ Number of Books: 2000
- ☐ Periodical Titles: 30
- ☐ Services: Loans to Public

The Detroit Garden Center Library
The Detroit Garden Center
1460 E. Jefferson Avenue
Detroit, MI 48207
(313) 259-6363

Public may use books in the library.
- ☐ Open: Tu-Th 9:30-3:30
- ☐ Number of Books: 5,000
- ☐ Periodical Titles: 15
- ☐ Services: Members Only

Detroit Public Library
5201 Woodward Avenue
Detroit, MI 48202
(313) 833-1400 or 1450
E-mail: tgahman@cms.cc.wayne.edu
Web: www.detroit.lib.mi.vs

Has a collection on gardening, botany and agriculture.
- ☐ Open: Tu-Sa 9:30-5:30, W 1-9
- ☐ Number of Books: 5,500
- ☐ Periodical Titles: 61
- ☐ Services: Loans to Public, Interlibrary Loans

Library
Chippewa Nature Center
400 S. Badour Road, Route 9
Midland, MI 48640
(517) 631-0830

Public may use books in the library.
- ☐ Open: M-F 8-5, Sa 9-5, Su 1-5
- ☐ Number of Books: 2,500
- ☐ Periodical Titles: 86
- ☐ Services: Members Only

The Dow Gardens Library
The Dow Gardens
1018 W. Main Street
Midland, MI 48640
(517) 631-2677
Fax: (517) 631-0675
Elizabeth Chaussee

Public may use books in the library. Entrance to the library is through the Information Center, located at the corner of West Saint Andrews & Eastman Roads.
- ☐ Open: M-F 10-4
- ☐ Number of Books: 1,500
- ☐ Periodical Titles: 50
- ☐ Services: Reference Only

Fernwood Library
Fernwood Botanic Garden
13988 Rangeline Road
Niles, MI 49120-9042
(616) 683-8653
Eleanor Drew

Public may use books in the library.
- ☐ Open: M-F 9-5
- ☐ Number of Books: 3,500
- ☐ Periodical Titles: 49
- ☐ Services: Members Only

Hidden Lake Gardens Library
Michigan State University
Tipton, MI 49287
(517) 431-2060
Debbie Cheryl Rittenhouse

- ☐ Open: M-F 8-4:30, Sa-Su 10-6
- ☐ Number of Books: 3,500
- ☐ Periodical Titles: 8
- ☐ Services: Reference Only

MINNESOTA

Andersen Horticultural Library
Minnesota Landscape Arboretum, Univ. of Minn.
3675 Arboretum Drive
Chanhassen, MN 55317
(612) 443-2440
Fax: (612) 443-2521
E-mail: richard@arboretum.umn.edu
Web: www.arboretum.umn.edu
Richard T. Isaacson

Public may use books in the library.
☐ Open: M-F 8-4:30, Sa-Su 11-4:30
☐ Number of Books: 10,000
☐ Periodical Titles: 525
☐ Services: Reference Only

MISSOURI

Missouri Botanical Garden Library
Missouri Botanical Garden
2345 Tower Grove Avenue
St. Louis, MO 63110
(314) 577-5156
Fax: (314) 577-9590
E-mail: library@lehmann.mobot.org
Web: www.mobot.org/mobot/molib
Constance Wolf

The library is open to members and researchers by appointment. The collection is oriented towards botany.
☐ Open: M-F 8:30-5
☐ Number of Books: 120,000
☐ Periodical Titles: 2,000
☐ Services: Reference Only, Interlibrary Loans

NEW JERSEY

Elvin McDonald Horticultural Library
Monmouth County Park System
Deep Cut Gardens, 100 Red Hill Road
Middletown, NJ 07748
(732) 671-6050
Mae H. Fisher

Public may use books in the library.
☐ Open: Call for hours
☐ Number of Books: 3,100
☐ Periodical Titles: 24
☐ Services: Members Only

Julia Appleton Cross Horticultural Library
Frelinghuysen Arboretum/Morris Co. Park Comm.
53 East Hanover Avenue
Morris Township, NJ 07962-1295
(201) 326-7600

Public may use books in the library.
☐ Open: M-F 9-4:30
☐ Number of Books: 3,000
☐ Periodical Titles: 22
☐ Services: Members Only

NEW YORK

The New York Botanical Garden Library
The New York Botanical Garden
200th Street & Southern Boulevard
Bronx, NY 10458-5126
(718) 817-8604
Fax: (718) 817-8956
E-mail: libref@nybg.org
Web: www.nybg.org
John F. Reed, Susan Fraser

Public may use books in the library.
☐ Open: Tu-Th 12-6; F-Sa 12-5
☐ Number of Books: 117,400
☐ Periodical Titles: 2,200
☐ Services: Reference Only, Interlibrary Loans

Brooklyn Botanic Garden Library
Brooklyn Botanic Garden
1000 Washington Avenue
Brooklyn, NY 11225
(718) 941-4044 ext. 366
Brenda Weisman

Public may use books in the library.
☐ Open: Tu-F 9-4, see notes
☐ Number of Books: 15,000
☐ Periodical Titles: 2,800
☐ Services: Reference Only

(continued next page)

NEW YORK (continued)

Buffalo & Erie County
Botanical Garden Library
Buffalo & Erie Co. Bot. Garden Society
South Park & McKinley Parkway
Buffalo, NY 14128-0386
(716) 828-0370
Florence S. DaLuiso

Public may use books in the library.
☐ Open: M-F 9-4
☐ Number of Books: 450
☐ Periodical Titles: 9
☐ Services: Reference Only

George Landis Arboretum Library
P.O. Box 186, Lape Road
Esperance, NY 12066
(518) 875-6935
Fax: (518) 875-6394

Open by appointment to researchers.
☐ Number of Books: 8,000

Library
Liberty Hyde Bailey Hortorium
467 Mann Library, Cornell University
Ithaca, NY 14853-4301
(607) 255-7980
Fax: (607) 255-7979
E-mail: jidi@cornell.edu
Dr. Jerrold Davis

Collection in taxonomic botany. Similar collection in Mann Library.
☐ Open: M-F 9-4
☐ Number of Books: 10,000
☐ Periodical Titles: 350
☐ Services: Reference Only

Institute of Ecosystem Studies Library
The Cary Arboretum
P.O. Box AB
Millbrook, NY 12545
(914) 677-5343
Annette Frank

Public may use books in the library.
☐ Open: M-F 8:30-4:30

Garden Club of America Library
598 Madison Avenue
New York, NY 10022
(212) 753-8287
Paula Stewart

Members must pay a fee of $1 to borrow a book. Public may
use books in the library.
☐ Open: M-F 9-4:30, by appt.
☐ Number of Books: 3,000
☐ Services: Members Only

Horticultural Society of New York Library
Horticultural Society of New York
128 W. 58th Street
New York, NY 10019
(212) 757-0915
Fax: (212) 246-1207
E-mail: hsny@metgate.metro.org
Web: www.hsny.org
Katherine Powis

Public may use books in the library. Large collection of seed and
nursery catalogs.
☐ Open: M-F 10-6
☐ Number of Books: 6,000
☐ Periodical Titles: 120
☐ Services: Members Only, Interlibrary Loans

Garden Library
Planting Fields Arboretum
Planting Fields Road
Oyster Bay, NY 11771
(516) 922-9024
Fax: (516) 922-7603
Elizabeth Reilley

Public may use books in the library.
☐ Open: M & W 11-4, Sa 10-3
☐ Number of Books: 7,000
☐ Periodical Titles: 315
☐ Services: Members Only

Highland Botanical Park Library
Monroe County Parks Arboretum
180 Reservoir Avenue
Rochester, NY 14620
(716) 256-4967
Fax: (716) 256-4968
R. Hoepfl

Public may use books in the library.
☐ Open: By appointment
☐ Number of Books: 680
☐ Periodical Titles: 15
☐ Services: Reference Only

(continued next page)

NEW YORK (continued)

Rochester Civic Garden Center Library
Garden Center of Rochester
5 Castle Park
Rochester, NY 14620
(716) 473-5138
Fax: (716) 473-8136
E-mail: gardenc@rrlc.rochester.lib.ny.us
Regina Campbell

Public may use books in the library.
☐ Open: Tu-Th 9:30-3:30, Sa 10-12
☐ Number of Books: 3,500
☐ Periodical Titles: 30
☐ Services: Members Only

NORTH CAROLINA

Addie Williams Totten Library
North Carolina Botanical Garden -- UNC
Campus Box 3375, Totten Center
Chapel Hill, NC 27599-3375
(919) 962-0522
Fax: (919) 962-3531
E-mail: dotwilbu@email.unc.edu
Mary Ishaq

Public may use books in the library. Totten Center is located just off Highway 15-501/54 Bypass on Laurel Hill Road.
☐ Open: Call for days and hours
☐ Number of Books: 2,000
☐ Periodical Titles: 83
☐ Services: Reference Only

OHIO

Hoffman Horticultural Library
Civic Garden Center of Cincinnati
2715 Reading Road
Cincinnati, OH 45206
(513) 221-0981
Fax: (513) 221-0961
Carol M. Smith

Public may use books in the library.
☐ Open: M-Sa 9-4
☐ Number of Books: 2,000
☐ Services: Members Only

Lloyd Library
917 Plum Street
Cincinnati, OH 45202
(513) 721-3707
Fax: (513) 721-6575
E-mail: michael.flannery@uc.edu
Web: www.libraries.uc.edu/lloyd
Michael Flannery

Public may use books in the library.
☐ Open: M-Sa, call for hours
☐ Number of Books: 70,000
☐ Periodical Titles: 500
☐ Services: Reference Only

Eleanor Squire Library
Cleveland Botanical Garden
11030 East Boulevard
Cleveland, OH 44106
(216) 721-1600 ext. 22
Fax: (216) 721-2056
E-mail: cbg@en.com
Web: www.cleveland.com
Joanna C. Bristol

Public may use books in the library.
☐ Open: Tu-F 9-5, Sa 12-5, Su 1-5
☐ Number of Books: 16,000
☐ Periodical Titles: 250
☐ Services: Members Only

Cox Arboretum Library
Cox Arboretum/Five Rivers Metro Parks
6733 Springboro Pike
Dayton, OH 45449-3415
(937) 434-9005
Ruth McManis

Public may use books in the library.
☐ Open: M-F 8:30-4:30
☐ Number of Books: 2,500
☐ Periodical Titles: 20
☐ Services: Reference Only

(continued next page)

OHIO (continued)

The Herb Society of America Library
Herb Society of America
9019 Kirtland-Chardon Road
Kirtland, OH 44094
(216) 256-0514
Fax: (216) 256-0541
E-mail: Herbsociet@aol.com
Web: www.Herbsociety.com
Headquarters Office Secretary

Has slide lectures for rent on many aspects of herb history and culture.
The public may use materials in the library.
☐ Open: M-F 9-5
☐ Number of Books: 1,550
☐ Periodical Titles: 36
☐ Services: Members Only, Reference Only

Warren H. Corning Library
The Holden Arboretum
9500 Sperry Road
Kirtland, OH 44094-5172
(216) 256-1110 ext. 225
Fax: (216) 256-5836
E-mail: holdlib@pop.holdenarb.org
Web: www.holdenarb.org
Nadia Aufderheide

Public may use books in the library.
☐ Open: Tu-F 10-5
☐ Number of Books: 8,500
☐ Periodical Titles: 125
☐ Services: Reference Only

Kingwood Center Library
Kingwood Center
900 Park Avenue West
Mansfield, OH 44906
(419) 522-0211
Fax: (419) 522-0211
William W. Collins

Residents of Richland and five surrounding counties may borrow books.
☐ Open: Tu-Sa 9-5
☐ Number of Books: 8,500
☐ Periodical Titles: 100
☐ Services: Loans to Public, Interlibrary Loans

The Dawes Arboretum Library
The Dawes Arboretum
7770 Jacksontown Road S.E.
Newark, OH 43056-9380
(614) 323-2355

Members may use the library for reference; researchers should
make an appointment.
☐ Open: M-F 8-4:30
☐ Number of Books: 5,500
☐ Periodical Titles: 30

Library
Gardenview Horticultural Park
16711 Pearl Road
Strongsville, OH 44136
(216) 238-6653
Fax: (216) 238-6653
E-mail: 74724.3434@compuserve.com
Henry A. Ross

Library open to members only, by appointment.
☐ Open: See notes.
☐ Number of Books: 5,000
☐ Services: Members Only, Reference Only

Horticultural Library
Toledo Botanical Garden
5434 Bancroft Street
Toledo, OH 43615
(419) 936-2966
Fax: (419) 936-2987

☐ Open: By appointment only
☐ Number of Books: 1042
☐ Periodical Titles: 17
☐ Services: Reference Only

OKLAHOMA

Tulsa Garden Center Library
Tulsa Garden Center
2453 S. Peoria Avenue
Tulsa, OK 74114
(918) 746-5125
Fax: (918) 746-5128
Caroline Swinson

Public may use books in the library.
☐ Open: M-F 9-4
☐ Number of Books: 4,500
☐ Periodical Titles: 25
☐ Services: Members Only

ONTARIO, CANADA

Royal Botanical Gardens Library
Royal Botanical Gardens
P.O. Box 399
Hamilton, ON, Canada L8N 3H8
(905) 527-1158 ext. 246
Fax: (905) 577-0375
Linda Brownlee

Public may use books in the library. Address is 680 Plains Road West, Burlington, Ontario.
☐ Open: Tu-W 10-1, Su 1:30-4:30
☐ Number of Books: 12,000
☐ Periodical Titles: 600
☐ Services: Members Only, Interlibrary Loans

School of Horticulture Library
Niagara Parks Commission
Niagara Parkway North (P.O. Box 150)
Niagara Falls, ON, Canada L2E 6T2
(905) 356-7670
Fax: (905) 356-5488
Web: tourismniagara.com/npc.htm
Ruth Stoner

Public may use books in the library. Researchers may use the library at other times by appointment.
☐ Open: M-F 8-12
☐ Number of Books: 3,000
☐ Periodical Titles: 125
☐ Services: Members Only

Canadian Agriculture Library
Agriculture Canada
Ottawa, ON, Canada K1A OC5
(613) 996-1655
Fax: (613) 943-0953
Eva Gavora

Public may use books in the library.
☐ Open: M-F 8:15-4:30
☐ Number of Books: 800,000
☐ Services: Reference Only, Interlibrary Loans

Civic Garden Centre Library
The Civic Garden Centre
777 Lawrence Avenue East
Toronto, ON, Canada M3C 1P2
(416) 397-1340
Fax: (416) 397-1354
Roslyn Theodore

Public may use books in the library.
☐ Open: M-F 9:30-4, Sa-Su 12-4
☐ Number of Books: 9,000
☐ Periodical Titles: 75
☐ Services: Members Only, Interlibrary Loans

OREGON

Library
The Berry Botanic Garden
11505 S.W. Summerville Ave.
Portland, OR 97219-8309
(503) 636-4112
Fax: (503) 636-7496
E-mail: bbg@agora.rdrop.com
Web: www.berrybot.org
Janice Dodd

The public may use books in the library.
☐ Open: M-F 9-4:30
☐ Number of Books: 1,200
☐ Periodical Titles: 120
☐ Services: Members Only

PENNSYLVANIA

Joseph Krauskopf Memorial Library
Delaware Valley College
700 E. Butler Ave.
Doylestown, PA 18901
(215) 489-2953
Fax: (215) 230-2967
E-mail: Kupersmith@devalcol.edu
Peter Kupersmith

Public may use books in the library. The library is building a collection of current seed and nursery catalogs; specializes in science and agriculture.
☐ Open: Call for hours
☐ Number of Books: 50,300
☐ Periodical Titles: 662
☐ Services: Reference Only

Longwood Gardens Library
Longwood Gardens, Inc.
Kennett Square, PA 19348
(215) 388-6745 ext. 510
Enola J. N. Teeter

Library is open to researchers by appointment, and to students at the Garden.
☐ Open: M-F 8-4
☐ Number of Books: 20,000
☐ Periodical Titles: 280
☐ Services: Reference Only, Interlibrary Loans

(continued next page)

PENNSYLVANIA (continued)

The McLean Library
Pennsylvania Horticultural Society
100 North 20th Street
Philadelphia, PA 19106-2777
(215) 988-8779
Fax: (215) 988-8783
E-mail: janeteva@libertynet.org
Web: www.libertynet.org/~phs
Janet Evans

Public may use books in the library.
☐ Open: M-F 9-5
☐ Number of Books: 14,000
☐ Periodical Titles: 200
☐ Services: Members Only, Interlibrary Loans

Morris Arboretum Library
University of Pennsylvania
9414 Meadowbrook Avenue
Philadelphia, PA 19118
(215) 247-5777
Fax: (215) 248-4439
Joan Markham

Open to researchers and members of the soponsoring organization. Catalog
available through Univ. of Pennsylvania On-Line Catalog system.
☐ Open: M & W 9-1
☐ Number of Books: 3,000
☐ Periodical Titles: 60
☐ Services: Reference Only, Interlibrary Loans

Library
Carnegie Museum of Natural History
4400 Forbes Avenue
Pittsburgh, PA 15213-4080
(412) 622-3295
Fax: (412) 622-8837
E-mail: thompson@clpgh.org
Sue A. Thompson

Very large natural history collection; number of books cited are
just the botanical books.
☐ Open: M-F 8:30-12, 1-5
☐ Number of Books: 2,800
☐ Periodical Titles: 265
☐ Services: Reference Only, Interlibrary Loans

Hunt Botanical Library
Hunt Institute for Botanical Documentation
Carnegie Mellon University, Frew St.
Pittsburgh, PA 15213
(412) 268-2436
Fax: (412) 268-5677
E-mail: ct0u@andrew.cmu.edu
Web: huntbot.andrew.cmu.edu
Charlotte Tancin

Public may use books in the library; appointments are recommended.
☐ Open: M-F 1-5
☐ Number of Books: 24,000
☐ Periodical Titles: 650
☐ Services: Reference Only, Interlibrary Loans

Pittsburgh Civic Garden Center Library
Pittsburgh Civic Garden Center
1059 Shady Avenue
Pittsburgh, PA 15232
(412) 441-4442
Fax: (412) 665-2368
Jean Aiken

Public may use books in the library.
☐ Open: M-F 8:30-4:30, Sa 10-4
☐ Number of Books: 2,750
☐ Periodical Titles: 20
☐ Services: Members Only

Scott Arboretum Horticultural Library
Scott Arboretum
500 College Avenue
Swarthmore, PA 19081
(610) 328-8025
Education Intern

Public may use books in the library.
☐ Open: M-F 8:30-4:30
☐ Number of Books: 1,400
☐ Periodical Titles: 40
☐ Services: Members Only

QUEBEC, CANADA

Montreal Botanical Garden Library
Jardin Botanique de Montreal-Bibliotheque
4101 rue Sherbrooke est
Montreal, PQ, Canada H1X 2B2
(514) 872-1824
Fax: (514) 872-3765
Celine Arsenault

Public may use books in the library. The eMail address is
Celine_arseneault@ville.montreal.qc.ca
☐ Open: M-Sa 9-4:30
☐ Number of Books: 18,000
☐ Periodical Titles: 500
☐ Services: Members Only, Interlibrary Loans

TENNESSEE

Library
The Dixon Gallery & Gardens
4339 Park Avenue
Memphis, TN 38117-4698
(901) 761-5250
Fax: (901)682-0943
Diane Reed

Library is open to members only.
- ☐ Open: Tu-F 10-5
- ☐ Number of Books: 1,000
- ☐ Periodical Titles: 40
- ☐ Services: Reference Only

Sybil G. Malloy Memorial Library
Memphis Botanic Garden
750 Cherry Road
Memphis, TN 38117
(901) 685-1566
Ruth Cobb

From March-Oct. hours are M-Sa 9-6, Su 11-6. From Nov.-Feb. hours are M-Sa 9-4:30.
- ☐ Open: See notes
- ☐ Number of Books: 1,000
- ☐ Periodical Titles: 25
- ☐ Services: Reference Only

The Botanical Gardens Library
Cheekwood
1200 Forrest Park Drive
Nashville, TN 37205
(615) 353-2148
Fax: (615)353-2731
Web: www.cheekwood.org
Ida Galehouse

Public may use books in the library.
- ☐ Open: M-Sa 9-5, Su 1-5
- ☐ Number of Books: 4,500
- ☐ Periodical Titles: 125
- ☐ Services: Members Only

TEXAS

National Wildflower Research Center
Clearinghouse
4801 La Crosse Avenue
Austin, TX 78739
(512) 292-4200
Flo Oxley

Public may use books in the library.
- ☐ Open: M-F 9-4
- ☐ Number of Books: 1,500
- ☐ Periodical Titles: 60
- ☐ Services: Reference Only

W. J. Rogers Memorial Library
The Beaumont Council of Garden Clubs
P.O. Box 7962
Beaumont, TX 77726-7962
(409) 842-3135
Myra Clay

Public may use books in the library; it's located in Tyrrell Park. Collection related to plants which thrive on the Gulf Coast.
- ☐ Open: Daily, by appointment
- ☐ Number of Books: 2,500
- ☐ Periodical Titles: 7
- ☐ Services: Members Only

VIRGINIA

Harold B. Tukey Memorial Library
American Horticultural Society
7931 E. Boulevard Drive
Alexandria, VA 22308
(703) 768-5700
Alice Bagwill

Members may use the library for reference.
- ☐ Open: M-F 8:30-5
- ☐ Number of Books: 2,500
- ☐ Periodical Titles: 200
- ☐ Services: Reference Only

Blandy Experimental Farm Library
University of Virginia
P.O. Box 175
Boyce, VA 22620
(703) 837-1758

Library is open to researchers by appointment.
- ☐ Open: By appointment
- ☐ Number of Books: 1,200
- ☐ Periodical Titles: 20
- ☐ Services: Reference Only

Huette Horticultural Library
Norfolk Botanical Garden
Azalea Garden Road
Norfolk, VA 23518
(804) 441-5380
Lois Leach

Public may use books in the library.
- ☐ Open: M-Sa 10-4, Su 12-4
- ☐ Number of Books: 2,500
- ☐ Periodical Titles: 13
- ☐ Services: Members Only, Interlibrary Loans

WASHINGTON

Lawrence Pierce Library
Rhododendron Species Foundation
P.O. Box 3798
Federal Way, WA 98063
(206) 927-6960
Mrs. Richard B. Johnson

Public may use books in the library.
- ☐ Open: M-F 8-4:30
- ☐ Number of Books: 1,000
- ☐ Services: Reference Only

Elisabeth C. Miller Library
Center for Urban Horticulture, Univ. of Wash.
3501 NE 41st Street
Seattle, WA 98195-4115
(206) 543-0415
Fax: (206) 685-2692
E-mail: hortlib@u.washington.edu
Web: weber.u.washington.edu/~hortlib/

Public may use books in the library. Call for hours in July and August.
- ☐ Open: M-F 9-5; Sa 9-3
- ☐ Number of Books: 7,500
- ☐ Periodical Titles: 300
- ☐ Services: Reference Only

Walker Horticultural Library
Yakima Area Arboretum
1401 Arboretum Drive
Yakima, WA 98901
(509) 248-7337
Fax: (509) 248-8197
Rita Pilgrim

Public may use books in the library.
- ☐ Open: Tu-Sa 9-5
- ☐ Number of Books: 2,900
- ☐ Periodical Titles: 2
- ☐ Services: Members Only

WEST VIRGINIA

Wheeling Civic Garden Center Library
Wheeling Civic Garden Center, Inc.
Oglebay Park
Wheeling, WV 26003
(304) 242-0665
Phyllis Brown

Public may use books in the library.
- ☐ Open: M-F 10-5
- ☐ Number of Books: 1,200
- ☐ Periodical Titles: 7
- ☐ Services: Members Only

WISCONSIN

Reference Library
Boerner Botanical Gardens
5879 S. 92nd Street
Hales Corners, WI 53130
(414) 425-1131
Fax: (414) 425-8679
Web: www.uwm.edu/dept/biology/boerner

Open daily, call for appointment. Public may use books in the library.
- ☐ Open: See notes
- ☐ Number of Books: 2,000
- ☐ Services: Reference Only

Schumacher Library
Olbrich Botanical Garden
3330 Atwood Avenue
Madison, WI 53704-5808
(608) 246-5805

Public may borrow books from the library.
- ☐ Open: Call for hours
- ☐ Number of Books: 1,400
- ☐ Periodical Titles: 42
- ☐ Services: Loans to Public

BOOKS

Useful books on plants and gardening, for reference and daily use as well as for pleasure, are grouped into general categories by plant groups or plant uses. At the end of the list are "good reads," guidebooks of gardens to visit, and plant-finding source books.

The books listed in this section are all books I consider worthwhile. It is agony to pare down the list to roughly 230 books; I always leave it until last and approach the task with dread. The notes are my own opinions, except as noted, based on general garden and plant knowledge but no great expertise in any one field. There are many more fine books than I have room to mention here.

Most of the books are fairly recent and should be available in public libraries, bookstores, from secondhand bookshops or on remainder tables. However, I resent the idea that the newest books are always the best; it strikes me that the most quoted garden writer in America seems to be Louise Beebe Wilder, whose books are now more than fifty years old.

Books have been listed on merit without regard to price. Prices have not been given because books seem to go out of print so quickly. Check *Books in Print* at your local library for availability and price.

The most encouraging development is the recent surge of good American gardening and plant books and regional gardening guides. What we should admire in others is their love for and knowledge of plants; we should spend our limited book budgets on books written for our own unique gardening conditions and recommending the plants most available to us. When you pick up a book, carefully look to see where the author lives and gardens!! Many of the books originally published overseas are not very suitable for our gardening conditions, nor are many of the plants mentioned therein readily available here.

Mailorder sources of new, used and rare books are listed in the Garden Suppliers and Services section. Books on specific plants or areas of horticultural interest are often available from specialist nurseries and seed companies. In addition, many societies sell books to their members, often at special prices; some sell to non-members as well. This time we asked societies to recommend the best books in their area of interest, and many of them did so; see Section D for additional book suggestions.

You should ask horticultural book suppliers for books not commonly found in local bookstores; bookstores can also special-order such books if they are still in print. Addresses of publishers not listed in this section can be found in *Books in Print*, available in public libraries or larger bookstores; Internet bookstores frequently have *Books in Print* available through their Web Sites, but expect you to order through them. Society addresses not given are listed in the Horticultural Societies section of this book.

A table of the symbols and abbreviations used in this book
appears inside the front and back covers.

USEFUL REFERENCE BOOKS

Hortus Third. New York, Macmillan, 1976. A dictionary of plants cultivated in the US and Canada -- which means a very great many! It has been the standard North American reference, though it's becoming very dated, and should be in almost any library.

The New York Botanical Garden Illustrated Encyclopedia of Horticulture. Thomas Everett. New York, Garland, 1982. This 10-volume work is monumental; descriptions are more complete and easier to read than *Hortus Third*. Quite a bit of cultural information; most of the photographs are in black and white.

The New Royal Horticultural Society Dictionary of Gardening. Anthony Huxley, ed. New York, Stockton Press, 1992. This work, in 4 volumes, covers plants from anywhere in the world. It's very scientific in content and style, definitely *not* a curl-up-with book for the majority of home gardeners. Check your county library; consider the next book, and see the section on Books in Series.

The Index of Garden Plants. Mark Griffiths, ed. Portland, Timber Press, 1994. A distillation of information from the New RHS Dictionary of Gardening, it narrows its scope to cultivated garden plants in one fat volume. This sits next to my bed and gets a lot of use.

The Bernard E. Harkness Seedlist Handbook. Mabel G. Harkness. 2nd. ed. Portland, Timber Press, 1993. Originally written for people requesting unfamiliar seeds from seed exchange lists, it briefly describes a huge variety of plants by type, size, flower color and place of origin, and gives references to information about, and illustrations of, each plant in about 1,000 authoritative books and magazine articles.

Stearn's Dictionary of Plant Names for Gardeners. William T. Stearn. London, Cassell Publishers, Ltd., 1992. Covers over 6,000 plant names, giving the meanings and origins of botanical names.

Dictionary of Plant Names. Allen J. Coombes. Portland, Timber Press, 1985. Handy small book with information on pronunciation and derivation in concise entries. Still widely available.

Plant Names Simplified. A.T. Johnson & H.A. Smith. London, Hamlyn, 1972. Pocket-sized; gives pronunciation and derivation of plant names and very brief plant descriptions. Still widely available.

Botany for Gardeners: an Introduction and Guide. Brian Capon. Portland, Timber Press, 1990. A very well-illustrated guide through basic botany, or botany without tears! You'll pick up a lot of knowledge through osmosis. Available in paperback.

Healthy Harvest III: A Directory of Sustainable Agriculture & Horticultural Organizations. Davis, CA, Agaccess, 1998. Lists more than 1,000 organizations and sources, with subject and geographical indexes and a description of each. Includes apprenticeships and internships, consultants, courses, development organizations, marketing cooperatives, newsletters, volunteer programs and much more. An excellent reference. Contact Agaccess, in Section B.

Growing with Gardening: A Twelve-Month Guide for Therapy, Recreation, and Education. Bibby Moore. Chapel Hill, University of North Carolina Press, 1989. A week-by-week guide to horticultural projects for anyone using horticulture in teaching or therapy. Advice on how to develop and budget a program and how to find volunteers, lists of references and sources. A wonderful book.

* Books marked with an asterisk were honored by the American Horticultural Society on its list of 75 Great American Garden Books to mark its 75th Anniversary.

The Gardeners's Reading Guide: The Best Books for Gardeners. Jan Dean. New York, Facts on File, 1993. Organized by subject, here are about 3,000 books about gardens and gardening, each quite briefly annotated; helpful in finding information on recent books as well as older books you might find in a catalog of used and out-of-print books.

ILLUSTRATED BOOKS USEFUL FOR CHOOSING AND IDENTIFYING PLANTS

Dirr's Hardy Trees and Shrubs: an Illustrated Encyclopedia. Michael Dirr. Portland, Timber Press, 1997. Michael Dirr's *Manual of Woody Landscape Plants* is a favorite, but it will have to make room for this book. I've only seen it in galley prints, but it will be one of my favorite books forever! Great color photographs and brief descriptions of hardy trees and shrubs, written with wit and enthusiasm. *Dirrmania!*

Michael A. Dirr's Photo-Library of Woody Landscape Plants. PlantAmerica, 1996. Intended for landscapers, teachers and students, these four CD-Roms have 7,600 photographs of trees and shrubs, searchable by scientific, family or common name. You can build your own selection of favorites and put then on your hard disk, or you can set the program to show a picture every five seconds. If you have a color printer, you can even print out selected photographs. Available from Timber Press and Stipes Publishing. PlantAmerica, P.O. Box 589, Locust Valley, NY 11560 <www.plantamerica.com>.

Cultivated Plants of the World: Trees, Shrubs, Climbers. Don Ellison. 1994. Thousands of good color photographs of woody plants, primarily for Mediterranean, subtropical or tropical climates. Emphasis is on flowers and foliage, with few photographs of plant habits or plants in the landscape; very useful for identifying unfamiliar plants, especially from Australia and the tropics. Very brief plant descriptions. Flora Publications International Pty. Ltd., GPO Box 2927, Brisbane, Queensland, Australia 4001. Available in some horticultural bookstores.

Reader's Digest Encyclopedia of Garden Plants and Flowers. London, Reader's Digest Assn., 1975. My copy of this is nearly worn out. It has small color pictures of a great variety of plants, with good descriptions and some information on growing. Available new in England and here in used book stores.

The Complete Handbook of Garden Plants. Michael Wright. New York, Facts on File, 1984. A concise guide to popular garden trees, shrubs and flowers, with small color paintings of many to show scale.

*Exotica 4. Alfred B. Graf. East Rutherford, NJ, Roehrs, 1992. 2 v. A pictorial encyclopedia of exotic and tropical plants, including most plants that are grown indoors or in greenhouses.

Tropica. Alfred B. Graf. East Rutherford, NJ, Roehrs, 1992. 3rd ed. A color encyclopedia of tropical and subtropical plants of all kinds.

Rhododendron Portraits. D.M. Van Gelderen & J.R.P. van Hoey Smith. Portland, Timber Press, 1992. Excellent color photographs of over 1,100 species and hybrid rhododendrons, with name of the hybridizer, parentage, and size where applicable. Introduction gives all you need to understand the basic classification of rhododendrons, and a list of hybridizers past and present.

Hydrangeas: Species and Cultivars. V. 1, 1992. V. 2, 1994. Corinne Mallet. Wonderful for identification, showing a great number of species and cultivars in good color photographs, with plant descriptions of many (in English). Available from Capability's Books, or write to Editions Robert Mallet, Route de L'Eglise, 76119 Varengeville sur Mer, France.

The Illustrated Encyclopedia of Orchids: Over 1100 Species Illustrated and Identified. Alec Pridgeon, ed. Portland, Timber Press, 1992. A fascinating book, with orchids of every shape and color under the sun, brief descriptions of each species.

Cacti: the Illustrated Dictionary. Rod & Ken Preston-Mafham. Portland, Timber Press, 1994. Over a thousand color photographs of globe-shaped cacti, which are the most collected types. Photographs show form and flower, give size and place of origin. A good accompaniment to seedlists.

Cacti: Over 1,200 Species Illustrated and Identified. Clive Innis & Charles Glass. New York, Portland House, 1991. A very useful guide to cacti, with keys, good color photos, and cultivation symbols for growing guidelines. Though I don't grow any, I love cacti and find them irresistible in such a book.

Succulents: the Illustrated Dictionary. Maurizio Sajeva & Mariangela Costanzo. Portland, Timber Press, 1994. Contains 1,200 color photographs of species and varieties in 195 genera, and even tells you which are on the CITES list of protected plants. There is also a bibliography for further reading about the plants.

Poisonous Plants: A Color Field Guide. Lucia Woodward. New York, Hippocrene Books, 1985. Color photos, descriptions, symptoms, treatment and tables of season and types of danger.

Common Poisonous Plants and Mushrooms of North America. Nancy J. Turner & Adam F. Szczawinski. Portland, Timber Press, 1991. Pieris! Hydrangeas! Clematis! Yes, all poisonous. Good color photos, descriptions, discussions of toxicity and treatment. What *not* to plant if you have small children.

GARDENING ENCYCLOPEDIAS

*Sunset Western Garden Book. 40th Anniversary Edition. Menlo Park, CA, Sunset Books, 1995. An excellent guide to gardening anywhere in the western US. The West is divided into 24 climate zones, and the extensive plant encyclopedia indicates in which zones each plant will grow -- very useful for choosing plants. This very fine book turns up on lists of favorite books from people all over the country.

Sunset National Garden Book. Menlo Park, CA, Sunset Books, 1997. The long success of the previous book led to the development of specific climate zones for the lower 48 states and southern Canada, and the extensive plant encyclopedia describes plant adaptability to these newly created zones. People all over the country will soon start to refer to "Sunset zone X" just as we have for many years -- you'll find them more accurate than USDA Zones, as they take into account much more than the usual temperature highs and lows.

Taylor's Master Guide to Gardening. Frances Tenenbaum, ed. Boston, Houghton Mifflin, 1994. A very comprehensive guide to garden making and methods, with an extensive plant encyclopedia and lots of photographs for inspiration. It's absolutely huge and very heavy -- not for carrying into the garden.

*Wyman's Gardening Encyclopedia. New expanded 2nd ed. New York, Macmillan, 1986. An old favorite of mine, I can almost always find an answer here; I can't bear to discard it to make room for newer books. Watch for it in used book stores -- and pressure Macmillan to bring out a new edition!!

Reader's Digest Illustrated Guide to Gardening. Pleasantville, NY, Reader's Digest Assn., 1981. Still one of the best how-to gardening guides, with lots of illustrations and extensive sections on choosing appropriate plants. You'll know it's from Britain when you see all those short handled digging tools!

Start with the Soil. Grace Gershuny. Emmaus, PA, Rodale Press, 1993. A basic guide to improving your soil for organic gardening: how to judge your soil ("learn from your weeds"), testing it, and how to improve it and keep it fertilized for best garden results. Friendly and easy to understand.

The Pruning Book. Lee Reich. Newtown, CT, Taunton Press, 1997. Each chapter describes specific pruning techniques, then lists plants which should be pruned in that fashion. An index by common and botanical names, as well as by pruning styles, will take you just where you need to go for information; lots of photographs and diagrams.

Sunset Pruning Handbook. Menlo Park, CA, Sunset Books, 1983. Good clear advice, and an A to Z list of plants and specific instructions on how to prune them. Very good value, still readily available.

The Able Gardener: Overcoming Barriers of Age & Physical Limitations. Kathleen Yeomans. Pownal, VT, Garden Way, 1992. A general gardening book with suggestions for adapting methods to limitations, and sources of equipment for physically limited gardeners. Her best advice: "relax your standards, you don't have to have a perfect garden." We should all heed that.

Rodale's All New Encyclopedia of Organic Gardening: the Indispensable Resource for Every Gardener. Fern Bradley & Barbara Ellis, eds. Emmaus, PA, Rodale Press, 1992. Comprehensive guide to organic gardening, methods and crops, easy to read and use.

Organic Gardener's Composting. Steve Solomon. Portland, Van Patten Publishing, 1993. A basic "how-to'" guide to creating good compost and using it in your garden; includes methods useful to those with small lots or fussy neighbors.

Down-to-Earth Natural Lawn Care. Dick Raymond. Pownal, VT, Storey Publishing, 1993. By now I guess it's no surprise to you that I favor gardening without chemicals as much as possible, so this book appeals to me for its sensible approach.

The Greenhouse Gardener's Companion: Growing Food & Flowers in Your Greenhouse or Sunspace. Shane Smith. Golden, CO, Fulcrum Publishing, 1992. This thick paperback will really tell you just about all you need to know: how to arrange your greenhouse, selecting the best plants, propagating seeds and cuttings, growing plants on and dealing with pests and problems, and it makes it all sound like fun.

Drip Irrigation for Every Landscape and All Climates. Robert Kourik. 1992. A practical guide to planning and installing a drip system in ornamental gardens, orchards and vegetable gardens. Kourik has designed many systems and really knows his stuff. Metamorphic Press, P.O. Box 1841, Santa Rosa, CA 95402.

BOOKS FOR NEW GARDENERS

The Self-Taught Gardener: Lessons from a Country Garden. Sydney Eddison. New York, Viking, 1997. The best thing that could happen is to live next to Sydney; the next best is to curl up with her book. She's a self taught gardener, and she understands how scary it is to get started, and how hard it is to make the right choices the first time, or even the second or third time. Kindly advice and reassurance to calm you, and to help you start thinking about what you want to do.

The Garden Primer. Barbara Damrosch. New York, Workman, 1988. A fine basic gardening book, dealing with all aspects of gardening in a sensible and very easy-to-understand manner. Damrosch tells you how to adapt advice to your climate and introduces many useful plants. The perfect gift for a new gardener and useful as a reference to any gardener.

The Book of Outdoor Gardening. Smith & Hawkin. New York, Workman, 1996. This book deserves the "Duh!! Award for Titles," but it actually contains a lot of useful information and helpful illustrations; written by a number of recognized garden writers. Contains the basics, including an encyclopedia of plants.

Perfect Plants. Roger Phillips & Martin Rix. London, Macmillan, 1996. This is a double treat, a fine book for choosing garden plants, and a companion CD-Rom starring the irrepressible Roger, which lets you pick and sort plants by use, size, flower color, and growing conditions, and make your own custom list for your garden.

The Big Book of Garden Skills. Pownal, VT, Garden Way, 1993. A compendium of useful information on all types of gardening questions: soil, pest control, plants and planting, pruning, garden equipment. Basic training for beginners.

GARDEN PROBLEMS

Common-Sense Pest Control: Least-Toxic Solutions for your Home, Garden, Pets and Community. William Olkowski, Sheila Daar & Helga Olkowski. Newtown, CT, Taunton Press, 1991. This book appears daunting at first, but it is very useful, readable, and offers advice that most of us can quickly put into action. Highly recommended.

The Ortho Home Gardener's Problem Solver. San Ramon, CA, Ortho Books, 1993. Scaled down to about 400 pages, a more manageable size for using at home; it covers about 75% of the problems covered in the original *The Ortho Problem Solver*, which is huge. A color encyclopedia of plant diseases and pest problems, with color photographs of the problem, a discussion of the conditions that cause it and suggested solutions. Includes some cultural information and suggestions. Problems are entered by plant, making them fairly easy to locate. The big version is available for reference in most garden centers.

Rodale's Garden Insect, Disease & Weed Identification Guide. Miranda Smith & Anna Carr. Emmaus, PA, Rodale Press, 1988. Gives illustrations, descriptions, life cycles and organic prevention and controls of common garden pests, diseases and weeds.

Weeds of the United States and Their Control. Harri J. Lorenzi & Larry S. Jeffery. New York, AVI (Van Nostrand Reinhold), 1987. Color photos, maps, descriptions, habitat and suggested controls.

Rodale's Garden Problem Solver: Vegetables, Fruits, and Herbs. Jeff Ball. Emmaus, PA, Rodale Press, 1988. Problems are listed by plant host, so it's easy to find the problem and suggestions for an organic method of control. Also general suggestions for controlling insect and animal pests and diseases.

Preventing Deer Damage. 2nd ed., 1997. Small book full of suggestions on how to deal with deer in many different ways; some of them sound pretty noisy, but there are times when I feel I'd do anything! Robert G. Juhre, 1568 Pingston Creek Road, Kettle Falls, WA 99141-9771.

Dead Snails Leave No Trails: Natural Pest Control for Home and Garden. Loreen Nancarrow & Janet Hogan Taylor. Berkeley, Ten Speed Press, 1996. Discusses methods of ridding your garden and your house of many types of pest, and using beneficial insects and other creatures to help you. Includes recipes for harmless but effective repellents.

Pests of the Garden and Small Farm: a Grower's Guide to Using Less Pesticide. Mary Louise Flint. Oakland, CA, Division of Agriculture and Natural Resources, University of California, 1990. (Pub. #3332) An extremely useful and practical guide to pest control, with good photos of the pests and their damage and suggestions for control, using least toxic methods and beneficial insects. $25 postpaid: ANR Publications, 6701 San Pablo Ave., Oakland, CA 94619.

Pests of the West: Prevention and Control for Today's Garden and Small Farm. Whitney Cranshaw. Golden, CO, Fulcrum Publishing, 1992. A practical handbook covering most of the pest problems from the Rocky Mountains to the Sierras. Information on identification, bug life histories, biological and cultural controls.

BOOKS IN SERIES

A number of publishers issue books on basic gardening and plants, all of which offer good information and value. Some of these books are listed individually in this bibliography; all are worth consideration. Most cover single topics, have good color illustrations and contain the basic information that gardeners want at reasonable prices; many are readily available in bookstores.

The publishers include Ortho Books, Sunset Books, Fine Gardening (Taunton Press), Harrowsmith, Garden Way (Storey Communications), the Gardening for Dummies series (IDG Books) and the Taylor's Weekend Gardening Guides (Houghton Mifflin). See also the Brooklyn Botanic Garden 21st Century Gardening Series under Plant & Gardens in the Magazine Section.

Taylor Publishing Company has several regional "...Gardener's Book of Lists" which suggest plants, solutions for common garden problems, and advice from well known local experts. So far they have published editions for the South and the Pacific Northwest.

Slightly more expensive but also offering good value are the *Taylor's Guides* of Houghton Mifflin and the Time-Life gardening books. More specialized are the *Gardener's Guide to Growing* series from Timber Press, each covering a specific plant genus.

Most scholarly are the *Manuals* being excerpted from the *New Royal Horticultural Society Dictionary*; they allow you to buy the sections of greatest interest to you. So far I have seen *Bulbs, Climbers and Wall Plants, Grasses*, and *Orchids*. Planned are *Ferns*, and *Cacti and Succulents*. From Timber Press.

PROPAGATION

Seed Germination Theory and Practice. Norman C. Deno. This is the most talked about book on propagation in many years; it's quite technical, but with its first supplement it covers seed germination of over 3,500 species. The main volume is $20 anywhere in the world, the first supplement is $15, and there will be a second supplement in late 1997 (you can send well-wrapped US$ Notes from overseas). Write to Norman C. Deno, 139 Lenor Drive, State College, PA 16801.

Creative Propagation: a Grower's Guide. Peter Thompson. Portland, Timber Press, 1992. A fairly advanced guide to propagation, informative with tables of suggested methods for specific plants.

*Secrets of Plant Propagation. Lewis Hill. Pownal, VT, Storey Communications, 1985. Good overview of the subject, easy to understand.

The New Seed Starter's Handbook. Nancy Bubel. Emmaus, PA, Rodale Press, 1988. Good information on starting vegetables and some trees, shrubs and garden flowers from seed, with tips on seed saving.

Parks's Success with Seeds. Ann Reilly. Greenwood, SC. Park Seed Company, 1978. Brief information on habit, uses, germination and culture; very useful color photographs of the seedlings, so you'll know what not to weed. See Park Seed Company in Section A.

BOOKS ON PLANTS FOR SPECIFIC CONDITIONS & EFFECTS

Scented Flora of the World. Roy Genders. New York, St. Martin's, 1977. A very interesting and readable book on scented plants -- the author's nose is very lenient and coverage is broad. There are newer books, but this one's my favorite.

The Fragrant Garden: A Book About Sweet Scented Flowers and Leaves. Louise Beebe Wilder. New York, Dover, 1974. Here's a delightful chance to see why Mrs. Wilder is so often quoted by other garden writers.

The Evening Garden. Peter Loewer. New York, Macmillan, 1993. Peter points out that many people's lives are so busy that evening is the only time they can enjoy their gardens. Why not have a fragrant evening bower in which to sing and chat? A delightful read, with his usual striking illustrations.

The Garden in Autumn. Allen Lacy. New York, Atlantic Monthly Press, 1990. A fresh look at planting specifically for autumn bloom and extending the enjoyment of your garden as long as possible before the first frost. Very well done: it will tear holes in your already-decided garden plans, and have you scrambling for places to put plants which give their best display in the autumn.

Colour in the Winter Garden. Graham Stuart Thomas. Portland, Sagapress/Timber Press, 1994. Here he is again, but no one writes better about using plants in gardens! His suggestions for plants that give good value in winter assume you have at least a Zone 8 garden, or lower, but they're good suggestions.

The Natural Shade Garden. Ken Druse. New York, Clarkson Potter, 1992. An inspirational guide to creating a "natural" garden under trees or in other shady spots using interesting plants; lovely photos give you lots of ideas. Better start planting some trees if you have no shade.

*The Complete Shade Gardener. 2nd ed. George Schenk. Boston, Houghton Mifflin, 1991. Written by an experienced plantsman whose style and humor put him high on my list of "good reads."

Moss Gardening: Including Lichens, Liverworts, and Other Miniatures.George Schenk. Portland, Timber Press, 1997. Here's a neglected facet of gardening, one that the smooth-tongued George Schenk will bring to prominence with this little book. He writes with wit and in a conversational voice; if you have some shade you'll be tempted to look for a place to put a mossy glade, even a tiny one will please you.

The City and Town Gardener: a Handbook for Planting Small Spaces and Containers. Linda Yang. New York, Random House, 1995. Originally published as *The City Gardener's Handbook*, this book is full of practical advice and inspiration for working with small spaces to bring a garden touch to your city garden. Full of enthusiasm, humor and energy, she covers everything you need to know.

The Water Garden. Anthony Paul & Yvonne Rees. New York, Viking Penguin, 1986. Not as practical as the books below, but full of inspirational photos which will spark design ideas.

Sunset Water Gardens. Menlo Park, Sunset Books, 1997. How to design, build and plant small garden water features and ponds. Lots of design ideas, from trickles to pools and streams; information on plants and critters to stock your water garden.

The Natural Water Garden: Pools, Ponds, Marshes & Bogs for Backyards Everywhere. Brooklyn Botanic Garden, 21st Century Gardening Series #151, 1997. They have gotten an awful lot of information into this little book; basic design and construction, using natural features, and choosing plants for your region.

Perennial Ground Covers. Davis S. MacKenzie. Portland, Timber Press, 1997. The book for gardeners with a *lot* of ground to cover; it covers every type of plant from ground-hugging to those mounding up to several feet. It has detailed plant descriptions, good color photographs of many of the plants, and suggestions for use and maintenance.

Plants for Ground-Cover. Graham Stuart Thomas. Portland, Sagapress/Timber Press, 1990. As with all of Thomas' books, this is an interesting read, and it offers suggestions for many plants not usually thought of as ground covers.

Taylor's Guide to Ground Covers, Vines & Grasses. Boston, Houghton Mifflin, 1987. A good introduction to plants and grasses used for ground covers, as well as to vines for walls and trellises.

Reader's Digest Complete Container Garden. David Joyce. Pleasantville, NY, Reader's Digest, 1996. I haven't seen this new book yet, but I'm told it's the bee's knees. It lists about 1,000 plants for containers, listed by color and season of bloom, and tells you how to create good plant combinations.

Stonescaping: a Guide to Using Stone in your Garden. Jan Kowalczewski Whitner. Pownal, VT, Garden Way, 1992. A great little book on the use of stones in various styles of gardens, full of useful how-to information.

The Heirloom Garden: Selecting and Growing over 300 Old-Fashioned Ornamentals. Jo Ann Gardner. Pownal, VT, Storey Communications, 1992. A well researched study of old varieties, with dates of introduction and sources of plants, and a good bibliography of books on restoring historic gardens, preservation groups, and historic gardens to visit.

Planting Noah's Garden: Further Adventures in Backyard Ecology. Sara Stein. Boston, Houghton Mifflin, 1997. Sara Stein started a revolution when she told people that they could have low maintenance wildlife refuges in their yards, and they could be beautiful, too. Now she tells you how to do it in practical terms.

Forest Gardening: Cultivating an Edible Landscape. Robert Hart. White River Junction, VT, Chelsea Green Publishing, 1996. Not a book about ornamental woodland landscaping, but a manifesto on backyard permiculture -- how to grow a wide range of fruits, nuts and vegetables in a mixed garden that's also welcoming to wildlife.

Butterfly Gardening: Creating Summer Magic in your Garden. Xerces Society and Smithsonian Institution. San Francisco, Sierra Club Books, 1990. There's a lot of interest in butterfly gardening, and this book will help you understand the life cycles of butterflies, and how to choose plants that they find attractive. A new edition is in the works.

Songbirds in your Garden. 5th ed. John K. Terres. Chapel Hill, Algonquin Books, 1994. There is no logical place to put this book, but I think all gardeners are also birdwatchers. Good advice on attracting birds, providing housing, feeding and enjoying. Mostly Eastern birds, but the principles apply everywhere. Algonquin Books of Chapel Hill, P.O. Box 2225, Chapel Hill, NC 27515-2225.

REGIONAL GARDENING BOOKS

The Best of the Hardiest. John J. Sabuco. 3rd ed., 1991. Essential to the cold-climate gardener; covers many types of plants, source lists. Plantsman's Press, P.O. Box 1, Flossmore, IL 60422.

Cold Climate Gardening: How to Extend your Growing Season by at Least 30 Days. Lewis Hill. Pownal, VT, Storey Communications, 1987. A guide to "defensive" gardening for cold climates, written with humor and good hard-won advice.

Gardening: Plains & Upper Midwest. Roger Vick. Golden, CO, Fulcrum Publishing, 1991. Written by a Canadian from Alberta, this is a good basic guide to gardening in very cold climates and covers everything from ornamentals to vegetables, and from insect pests to monthly chores. Well done, and fun to read.

Successful Southern Gardening: A Practical Guide for Year-Round Beauty. Sandra F. Ladendorf. Chapel Hill, University of North Carolina Press, 1989. A fine modern guide to gardening in the hot and humid climate of the South. She offers good practical advice, lists recommended plants and suggests further reading and sources. Her lengthy credits are testimony to the joy of gardening friends.

*A Southern Garden: A Handbook for the Middle South. Elizabeth Lawrence. Rev. ed. Chapel Hill, University of North Carolina Press, 1984. I've only recently discovered Lawrence, a regional writer who gives great pleasure with her information.

Neil Sperry's Complete Guide to Texas Gardening. 2nd ed. Dallas, Taylor Publishing, 1991. From the flowery cowboy boots on the cover to the last page, it covers everything: it's comprehensive, anticipates every question and recommends suitable plants and landscaping solutions -- all in a friendly manner.

Perennial Garden Color for Texas and the South. William C. Welch. Dallas, Taylor Publishing, 1989. A very fine book for gardeners in difficult garden climates of the South, with good suggestions for plant selection, culture and garden design.

The Southern Heirloom Garden. William C. Welch & Greg Grant. Dallas, Taylor Publishing, 1995. Carries the previous book into the realm of historic garden restoration. If you're lucky enough to live in an old house in the South, this wonderful book's a must! It discusses many styles and traditions, shown with many good color photographs of gardens and plants.

*The Undaunted Gardener: Planting for Weather-Resilient Beauty. Lauren Springer. Golden, CO, Fulcrum Publishing, 1994. A godsend for those who live in hot, dry, windy climates -- particularly the intermountain West. Her plant suggestions and combinations are masterful -- you've run out of excuses for not being able to garden because conditions are too harsh!

Landscape Plants for Western Regions. Bob Perry. Claremont, CA, Land Design Publishing, 1992. An update of Perry's excellent *Trees and Shrubs for Dry California Landscapes*, it discusses drought tolerant plants especially for southern California, and various uses including erosion and fire control. Includes a plant encyclopedia, descriptions of various habitats, and discussions of various plant families.

The Low-Water Flower Garden. Eric Johnson & Scott Millard. Tucson, Ironwood Press, 1993. All through the nurseries section we talk about the "dry garden," and this book pretty well defines what we mean: plants which will grow in hot climates with only occasional watering. Many plants suggested, lots of color photographs of plant combinations and suggestions for using plants to best advantage.

Waterwise Gardening: Beautiful Gardens with Less Water. Menlo Park, CA, Lane Publishing Co., 1989. Landscaping ideas, irrigation systems and plant selection for gardens that use less water. Before long this won't apply just to western gardeners.

Growing California Native Plants. Marjorie G. Schmidt. Berkeley, University of California Press, 1980. The definitive book on growing California natives, which are different in most respects from the wildflowers and native plants of the rest of the country.

Pat Welsh's Southern California Gardening: a Month-by-Month Guide. Pat Welsh. San Francisco, Chronicle Books, 1992. A very practical guide, full of interesting seasonal tidbits and suggestions, offering a lifeline to gardeners unfamiliar with the many microclimates of Southern California.

Gardens of the Sun. Trevor Nottle. Portland, Timber Press, 1996. Gardening in Mediterranean climates, and of particular interest to gardeners in California with its wet winter-dry summer climate. Many plant suggestions for creating lovely gardens without lots of water.

Plants for Dry Climates: How to Select, Grow and Enjoy. Mary Rose Duffield & Warren D. Jones. Los Angeles, Price Stern Sloan, 1981. Good information on selecting plants for very dry conditions, especially for the Southwestern deserts. You might find this one in a used book store.

Gardening in Dry Climates. Scott Millard. San Ramon, CA, Ortho Books, 1989. We're all learning to get along with less water; this book offers good advice on garden strategy and plant selection for dry climates.

Growing Desert Plants from Windowsill to Garden. Theodore B. Hodoba. 1995. Ted is the proprietor of Desert Moon Nursery and teaches a university course on landscaping and maintaining desert plants. He gives great advice on using what grows in the desert in natural planting schemes; perfect for desert gardeners transplanted from different regions. Red Crane Books, 2008 Rosina, Ste B, Santa Fe, NM 87503

The Subtropical Garden. Jacqueline Walker & Gil Hanly. Portland, Timber Press, 1996. Lavish ideas from two New Zealanders; would be of interest to gardeners in Florida and along the Gulf coast.

Gardening in the Tropics. R.E. Holttum & Ivan Enoch. 1993. Distributed by Timber Press, Portland. Published in Singapore, this book will be of interest to Hawaiians and those few Floridians who qualify, as well as gardeners anywhere in the world who garden in tropical conditions. Some general cultural suggestions and good information on plant selection; many good color pictures.

TREES AND SHRUBS

*****North American Landscape Trees.** Arthur Lee Jacobson. Berkeley, Ten Speed Press, 1996. A fantastic encyclopedia of trees, it describes zillions, including selections which have been available in this country for a hundred years or more, with good notes on many species and cultivars, some line drawings and color photographs. 700+ pages of pure delight and honest opinions for any tree lover, useful for selecting new trees as well as identifying trees planted many years ago in older gardens. AHS Best Garden Book 1996. American Horticulture Society Book Award for 1996.

*****Flowering Plants in the Landscape.** Mildred E. Mathias, ed. Berkeley, University of California Press, 1982. Excellent color photographs of trees, shrubs and vines for subtropical climates, with hardiness indicated.

*****Manual of Woody Landscape Plants: Their Identification, Ornamental Characteristics, Culture, Propagation and Uses.** 5th ed.Michael A. Dirr. Champaign, IL, Stipes Pub. Co., 1997. Full of excellent information (it's really a college text), but also wittily written and not afraid to express opinions of plants. For years it's sat next to my bed, and I've checked his write-up on every tree or shrub I've lusted after.

Shrubs. Roger Phillips & Martyn Rix. New York, Random House, 1989. Like their other wonderful photographic books, this will help you identify and choose among over 1,900 shrubs; the authors are British, and so are many of the cultivars shown. Even the late J. C. Raulston liked it and could find only two errors.

Trees & Shrubs Hardy in the British Isles. W. J. Bean. 8th ed. rev. London, John Murray, 1976-1988. The British standard for looking up trees and shrubs; it lists woody plants hardy enough to grow in Britain. Plant descriptions are exhaustive, few illustrations. Check a horticultural library.

Manual of Cultivated Broad-Leaved Trees & Shrubs. Gerd Krüssmann. Portland, Timber Press, 1985-1986. Wonderful multi-volume set giving great detail; a challenge to "Bean," and usually more fun to read.

*****Plants that Merit Attention: V. 1, Trees.** Janet Poor, ed. Portland, Timber Press, 1984. Suggests the use of many beautiful trees not well known or widely used in the past; good photographs of most trees mentioned.

Plants that Merit Attention: V. 2, Shrubs. Janet Poor., ed. Portland, Timber Press, 1996. At last, the companion volume to *Trees.* Written in the same wonderfully informative style, suggesting many unusual shrubs, and well illustrated with color photographs of flower and plant habit.

Manual of Cultivated Conifers. Gerd Krüssmann. Portland, Timber Press, 1985. An excellent reference for information on conifers; a perfect companion to the next book.

Conifers. D.M. Van Gelderen & J.R.P. van Hoey Smith. 2nd ed. Portland, Timber Press, 1996. Expanded into two volumes with many more color photographs showing trees in gardens and in their natural habitats. Many cultivars illustrated; it's an excellent companion to Krüssmann's book on conifers.

Dwarf & Unusual Conifers Coming of Age: A Guide to Mature Garden Conifers. Sandra McLean Cutler. What happens to dwarf conifers after a few years? Some creep away, some bolt to larger than expected sizes. Cutler has studied several famous dwarf conifer collections, and shows both the charm of the plants and their growth at ten or more years. Barton-Bradley Crossroads Publishing Co., P.O. Box 802, North Olmstead, OH 44070-0802.

The Hillier Manual of Trees and Shrubs. 6th ed. Newton Abbot, Devon, David & Charles, 1991. This manual is the outgrowth of the plant catalogs of Hillier's Nursery, which once offered the widest selection of trees and shrubs in the world. It describes over 9,000 plants in 650 genera, with brief descriptions and comments on garden habits; very useful indeed. This new edition is much thicker, but if you have the 5th edition, keep it too; it seems somehow slightly more readable.

Ornamental Shrubs, Climbers and Bamboos. Graham Stuart Thomas. Portland, Timber Press, 1992. Organized along the lines of his incomparable book on perennials, and as before, his comments are well worth studying, though it's not quite as personal a read as his perennials book.

Hedges, Screens and Espaliers. Susan Chamberlin. Los Angeles, Price Stern Sloan, 1982. Well-illustrated guide to choosing and caring for hedges, screens and espaliered shrubs and fruit trees.

Complete Garden Guide to the Native Shrubs of California. Glenn Keator. San Francisco, Chronicle Books, 1994. California native shrubs are admired all over the world, and now more and more Westerners are using them for low water gardening. This will give them all the help they need to choose good plants and grow them well. His *Complete Garden Guide to the Native Perennials of California* was also published by Chronicle Books.

*Azaleas. Fred Galle. Portland, Timber Press, 1987. According to azalea lovers, this is the bible: it is a monumental work and won't be improved on for many years.

Success with Rhododendrons and Azaleas. H. Edward Reiley. Portland, Timber Press, 1992. A fine how-to guide to the practical aspects of growing these plants, including lists of "good doers" for various climates and regions. Covers everthing from pests to propagation, from hybridizing to showing.

Bamboos. Christine Recht & Max Wetterwald. Portland, Timber Press, 1992. A transplanted German book on growing bamboo, with emphasis on adaptability to gardens. Descriptions and color photographs of many species.

The Color Dictionary of Camellias. Stirling Macoboy. Topsfield, MA. Merrimack Publishing Circle, 1983. Good color photographs of many cultivars, good introductory treatment.

Hardy Heather Species and Some Related Plants. Dorothy M. Metheny. Written by a lifelong heather gardener, this book describes plants suitable to the Temperate Zone very well, and illustrates many with botanical drawings. She also gives references to other published sources of information. Write to the American Heather Society for information.

Hydrangeas: a Gardeners Guide. Toni Lawson-Hall & Brian Rothera. Portland, Timber Press, 1995. Hydrangeas are growing in popularity, and in my large yard they are a godsend -- big and long blooming! This book offers lots of cultural information, and information on many species and cultivars.

*Japanese Maples. J.D. Vertrees. Portland, Timber Press, 1987. Certainly the definitive book on Japanese maples -- at least in English. Well illustrated with color photographs, and excellent plant descriptions and information on culture. A beautiful book in itself, updated from the 1978 edition.

Maples of the World. D.M. van Gelderen, P.C. de Jong & H.J. Oterdoom. Portland, Timber Press, 1994. An excellent treatment of the whole genus Acer, with many line drawings and color photographs: buy it while you're young and treasure it your whole life!

The World of Magnolias. Dorothy J. Callaway. Portland, Timber Press, 1994. Written by a magnolia scholar and a budding nurserywoman, this is a fine treatment of a class of beloved garden trees. Good information on both species and cultivars, and good color photographs; this will be the standard book on magnolias for some time to come.

Palms Throughout the World. David L. Jones. Washington, DC, Smithsonian Institution Press, 1995. A very thorough treatment of the family, including culture and propagation, and an encyclopedia of palms with many color photographs.

Willows: the Genus Salix. Christopher Newsholme. Portland, Timber Press, 1992. Get rid of the idea that willows are common; here's a terrific guide to willows that will open your eyes to the possibilities, from creepers to stately trees. Makes me wish for a few acres of bottom land.

ALPINE & ROCK GARDEN PLANTS

*Rock Gardening: A Guide to Growing Alpines & Other Wildflowers in the American Garden. H. Lincoln Foster. Portland, Timber Press, 1982. Remains the standard; it has recently been reissued.

Bulbs for the Rock Garden. Jack Elliott. Portland, Timber Press, 1995. Written by a former president of the Alpine Garden Society, this book's a primer on how to use the smaller bulbs; you don't have to have a rock garden to enjoy them!

Rock Garden Plants of North America. North American Rock Garden Society. Portland, Timber Press, 1996. This is an anthology of articles from 50 years of the society's *Bulletin*, divided by regions and written by many contributors. Catnip to plant trekkers all over North America, and visitors from abroad.

BULBS

All About Bulbs. Rev. ed. San Ramon, CA, Ortho Books, 1986. Color guide to growing bulbs; good cultural advice, broad coverage of Dutch and species bulbs.

The Random House Book of Bulbs: A Photographic Guide to Over 800 Hardy Bulbs. Martin Rix & Roger Phillips. New York, Random House, 1989. Good for identification of both plants and bulbs; mostly species bulbs.

The Little Bulbs. Elizabeth Lawrence. Durham, NC, Duke University Press, 1986. A "good read" that contains good information on species bulbs, especially narcissus.

Growing Bulbs: The Complete Practical Guide. Brian Mathew. Portland, Timber Press, 1997. I liked this book very much; it gives all of the principles of growing bulbs, and how to adapt their growth to your climate, instead of being biased to any specific region. Includes information on propagation, pests and diseases, and an encyclopedia of bulbous plants.

Daffodils for American Gardens. Brent & Becky Heath. Washington, DC, Elliott & Clark, 1995. The Heaths were for many years the proprietors of The Daffodil Mart, and their expertise and love of daffodils fill this book. They'll teach you what you need to know, and show you many blooms in color so you can choose your favorites.

Modern Miniature Daffodils: Species and Hybrids. James S. Wells. Portland, Timber Press, 1989. These charming little bulbs may not be everybody's cup of tea (but would fit into one), but I absolutely fell in love with them when I opened this book and so will you; they make 'King Alfred' look like Hulk Hogan.

Cape Bulbs. Richard L. Doutt. Portland, Timber Press, 1994. For those lucky enough to live in the right climate (Mediterranean), there are bulbs which love the dry summer-wet winter pattern, and they are abso lutely gorgeous. Dr. Doutt was the proprietor of Bio-Quest International and a long time grower and collector of South African bulbs; his long study and expertise will make it easier to grow these lovelies.

FERNS

Ferns to Know and Grow. F. Gordon Foster. 3rd ed. Portland, Timber Press, 1993. A practical guide to choosing and growing ferns in the home garden. Considered a classic; reprinted with updated nomenclature.

Encyclopedia of Ferns. David L. Jones. Portland, Timber Press, 1987. Growing, propagation, disease control, good descriptions and color and black and white photos.

FLOWER ARRANGING

The Flower Arranger's Garden. Rosemary Verey. Boston, Little, Brown, 1989. The inspiration in this book comes from the arrangements themselves, which use a variety of unusual plants and containers to create delightful results.

Fresh Cuts: Arrangements with Flowers, Leaves, Buds & Branches. Elizabeth von Gal & John H. Hall. New York, Artisan, 1997. The trend in flower arranging is definitely away from big, formal set pieces to smaller and more intimate looks at individual beauties; offers many ideas for charming floral decorations.

*Flowers Rediscovered: Mädderlake. Rev. Ed. Tom Pritchard & Billy Jarecki. New York, Artisan, 1994. Another book that will change your ideas about putting a few flowers in a vase; it's the flowers that count, they seem to declare independence and demand their due attention in these lovely photographs.

Cutting Gardens. Anne Halpin & Betty Mackey. New York, Simon & Schuster, 1993. All you need to know to choose good flowers to grow for flower arranging, including propagation, garden layout, and conditioning flowers to last well in arrangements.

HERBS

Gardening with Herbs. Emelie Tolley & Chris Mead. New York, Clarkson Potter, 1995. A visual feast of ideas for herb gardens, showing lovely examples from the US, Britain and Europe in many styles, with lots of advice from the gardeners themselves.

Rodale's Illustrated Encyclopedia of Herbs. C. Kowalchik & William H. Hylton, eds. Emmaus, PA, Rodale Press, 1987. Color photos and drawings; history, uses and cultivation, index of botanical names and medicinal uses, bibliography of books and newsletters.

Herb Garden Design. Faith Swanson & Virginia Rady. Hanover, NH, University Press of New England, 1984. Full of plans and suggestions for planting herb gardens of all kinds and styles.

*Landscaping with Herbs. James Adams. Portland, Timber Press, 1987. Good advice on choosing and using herbs as garden plants; well written and interesting. I find the diagrams confusing, but the photographs are good. Recipes scattered throughout.

Growing and Using Herbs Successfully. Betty Jacobs. Pownal, VT, Garden Way, 1981. An herb maven tells me that this is the best and most informative introduction to herbs and herb growing; it must be, it's on the thirteenth or fourteenth printing. It has growing and propagating information, recipes, even information on starting an herb business.

The Complete Book of Herbs: a Practical Guide to Growing and Using Herbs. Lesley Bremness. New York, Viking, 1988. Another book recommended by my maven for general herbal information -- lots of color photos.

All About Herbs. San Ramon, CA, Ortho Books, 1990. Good introduction to herb growing; lots of color pictures and useful information.

Using Herbs in the Landscape: How to Design and Grow Gardens of Herbal Annuals, Perennials, Shrubs and Trees. Debra Kirkpatrick. Harrisburg, PA, Stackpole, 1992. I can't add much to that title!

HOUSE & GREENHOUSE PLANTS

The Savage Garden. Peter D'Amato. Berkeley, Ten Speed Press, 1997. Peter fell in love with carnivorous plants as a child, and now has a huge collection and runs a carnivorous plant nursery. He tells you how to grow them successfully, and shows many of the plants in photographs.

The Essence of Paradise: Fragrant Plants for Indoor Gardens. Tovah Martin. Boston, Little, Brown, 1991. A lovely book, beautifully illustrated, guiding enthusiasts through a year of fragrant indoor plants. Tovah writes with great charm, gentle humor and a sense of history.

Growing Beautiful Houseplants: an Illustrated Guide to the Selection and Care of more than 1,000 Varieties. Rob Herwig. New York, Facts on File, 1992. A lavishly illustrated and very informative guide to growing houseplants; it should answer all your needs.

Fuchsias for Greenhouse and Garden. David Clark. Portland, Timber Press, 1992. There are very few places in this country where one can grow fuchsias outdoors, but they make lovely greenhouse plants, and this little book contains a lot of information about growing them, and descriptions of many cultivars.

Reader's Digest Success with Houseplants. New York, Random House, 1979. Very good information on plants and their cultural requirements, with nice color paintings throughout. Still available.

The Houseplant Survival Guide. Pat Regel. Newtown, CT, Taunton Press, 1997. This book will come in handy when you're wringing your hands and thinking about throwing your plant away. It goes through all of the conditions necessary to growing houseplants: potting, repotting, feeding and watering. Discusses pests and diseases, how to choose good plants, and how to go on vacation and leave plants safe.

*Foliage Plants for Decorating Indoors. Virginie & George Elbert. Portland, Timber Press, 1989. Of interest to both indoor plant professionals and hobbyists, this book is packed with essential information and includes an excellent indoor plant encyclopedia; it will be a standard for years to come.

Blooming Bromeliads. Ulrich & Ursula Baensch. A lavishly illustrated guide to bromeliads, with brief plant descriptions and cultural symbols for each. Tropic Beauty Publishers, P.O. Box N 1105, Nassau, Bahamas.

Taylor's Guide to Orchids. Judy White. Boston, Houghton Mifflin, 1996. This introduction to growing orchids is so user-friendly that I found myself at an orchid nursery almost at once. The author takes a lot of the mystery and terror out of growing these lovely plants in a home environment; forget the greenhouse and get started now!

Orchids as House Plants Rebecca Northen. Rev. ed. New York, Dover, 1976. And *Home Orchid Growing*, 4th ed., published in 1990. Northen's books are highly recommended by several orchid nurseries for their easy to understand information. She takes a sensible approach to growing orchids, which many people assume are very difficult to handle.

PERENNIALS

Perennials. 2 v. Roger Phillips & Martyn Rix. New York, Random House, 1991. Wonderful color photos of thousands of perennial plants, many are species plants growing in the wild and not at all common to gardens, with good descriptions and some cultural notes. It's arranged by season of bloom and general plant families instead of alphabetically by botanical name, which makes you refer to the index for every plant you want to look up. Still, well worth using!

Hardy Herbaceous Perennials. 2 v. Leo Jelitto & Wilhelm Schacht. Portland, Timber Press, 1990. This is a very fine work, updated from an earlier German edition; the plant descriptions are very good, there are some cultural notes and many black and white and color photographs. More scientific in tone than Phillips

& Rix, this does not have color photographs of every plant, but it's arranged in encyclopedic alphabetical order, making it easier to use.

Perennials for American Gardens. Ruth Rogers Clausen & Nicolas H. Ekstrom. New York, Random House, 1989. A very fine encyclopedia of perennial plants, including many that are too little known, with good general cultural information and many color photographs. It has an extensive bibliography.

Herbaceous Perennial Plants: A Treatise on Their Identification, Culture and Garden Attributes. Allan M. Armitage. 2nd ed. Champaign, IL, Stipes Publishing, 1997. This excellent book should be on every perennial gardener's shelf -- it's beautifully written, has special features such as keys to species for quick identification, information on propagation and references to further reading on many plants. Line drawings, some color photographs. Deserves to be much better known!

Perennial Garden Plants or the Modern Florilegium. Graham Stuart Thomas. 2nd ed. London, Dent, 1982. Written by one of the great English plantsmen, this is a "good read," with sound advice on plant selection. See also his excellent *The Art of Planting* (Boston, Godine, 1984).

Perennials: How to Select, Grow & Enjoy. Pamela Harper & Frederick McGourty. Los Angeles, Price Stern Sloan, 1985. An excellent joint effort by two experts, with situation and growing well covered; beautiful color photographs.

The Smaller Perennials: An Illustrated Guide to Over 3000 plants, Ideal for the Small Garden. Jack Elliott. Portland, Timber Press, 1997. This book arrived just as I said "no more books," but it's too nice not to mention. He discusses many perennials growing up to two and a half feet, and great for small spaces.

Color Echoes: Harmonizing Color in the Garden. Pamela Harper. New York, Macmillan, 1994. Pam's eye for color combinations has been honed by years of peering into a view finder. This book is smashing!

The Green Tapestry: Choosing and Growing the Best Perennial Plants for your Garden. Beth Chatto. New York, Simon & Schuster, 1989. This is the sort of book I love, showing how plants look in combination. This book is full of inspiring ideas and color photographs. What an eye she has!

Designing with Perennials. Pamela J. Harper. New York, Macmillan, 1991. Pam Harper has two advantages over many garden writers; she really knows her plants, and since she takes her own photos, she's able to illustrate her concepts perfectly. Her text is thoughtful and practical; she's distilled a lifetime of growing experience and plant love into this terrific book.

The American Mixed Border: Gardens for all Seasons. Ann Lovejoy. New York, Macmillan, 1993. I make no secret of my admiration for Ann Lovejoy; she's up there with the very best of garden writers, both for her original ideas and her lively writing style. This is a book to read for inspiration, new thinking, and fresh perspectives on the joys of garden making. The photos are nearly perfect; a good bedside book.

INDIVIDUAL PERENNIALS

Clematis. Barry Fretwell. Deer Park, WI, Capability's Books, 1989. Clematis has been underused in American gardens and our choice of plants has been limited, but the rash of books on clematis will soon change all that. This one has good descriptions and many good color photographs. See Section B for address.

Making the Most of Clematis. 2nd ed. Raymond J. Evison. Wisbech (UK), Floraprint, 1991. Written by one of England's clematis experts, it contains practical information on growing, pruning techniques, propagation, training on walls and through other plants, and descriptions of many species and cultivars.

Daylilies: the Perfect Perennial. Lewis & Nancy Hill. Pownal, VT, Garden Way, 1991. Nothing's perfect, but even I, the imperfect gardener, have had good luck with daylilies, and I found this book able to answer most of my questions, even what to do with all the seeds I collected.

The Encyclopedia of Ornamental Grasses. John Greenlee. Emmaus, PA, Rodale Press, 1992. If you've ever heard John Greenlee sing the praises of ornamental grasses, you'd know that he'd do a great job spreading the faith. He describes over 250 grasses, gives a good picture and lots of cultural information. You'll start looking around for a place to put some ornamental grasses!

The Gardener's Guide to Growing Hellebores. Graham Rice & Elizabeth Strangman. Portland, Timber Press, 1993. One of my favorite new books this year -- if hellebores don't become the rage of the 90's, there's just no good sense left! The photos will convert you to these lovely flowers of late winter and early spring; lots of good advice on growing them.

The Genus Hosta. W. George Schmid. Portland, Timber Press, 1992. The absolutely final word on hostas: descriptions of species, nomenclature, an alphabetical listing of all known cultivars, history of cultivation of hostas, critical analysis of previous writings. Hosta fanatics, and there are many of them, will keep this book next to their beds for the next decade. Some color pictures.

The World of Irises. Wichita, KS, American Iris Society, 1978. A very thorough treatment of a very popular group of plants; it should make all of the confusing categories clear.

Iris. Fritz Köhlein. Portland, Timber Press, 1987. Iris are a huge and, to me, very confusing group of plants. This book by an eminent German plantsman makes it all easier to understand, and is friendly and packed with information; there are many good color photos. You'll fall in love!

Peonies. Allan Rogers. Portland, Timber Press, 1995. Allan has loved peonies since he got one for his eighth birthday, and his book imparts all his love and experience to new converts. It covers everything, including many plant descriptions and color photographs to lure you in.

Poppies: the Poppy Family in the Wild and in Cultivation. Christopher Grey-Wilson. Portland, Timber Press, 1993. At last, a poppy book, and a very nice one! Covers all members of the poppy family with good plant descriptions and some information on cultivation: color photos and a number of good line drawings.

The Genus Primula in Cultivation and the Wild. Josef Halda. Denver, Tethys Books, 1992. Primulas described by section, with information on distribution, habitat and cultivation. Each is illustrated by a very charming and accurate line drawing by Halda's wife Jarmila; useful to the amateur gardener who will find illustrations of each species useful when checking seed exchange lists. (Tethys Books, 2735 S. Pennsylvania, Englewood, CO, 80110)

Primula. John Richards. Portland, Timber Press, 1993. More technical than the book above, but readable to the amateur. Illustrated with lovely color paintings and some color photos, but not every species is shown; it will especially interest growers and hybridizers.

A Book of Salvias: Sages for Every Garden. Betsy Clebsch. Portland, Timber Press, 1997. In the San Francisco area we all know Betsy, and have been waiting for her book. Now we can point to it with pride -- she had written a very readable book full of information; written with years of growing experience and study, and travel to seach for new species and cultivars. Bravo, Betsy, it was worth all the hard work.

ROSES

All About Roses. Rex Wolf & James McNair. San Ramon, CA, Ortho Books, 1983. A good introductory treatment of rose growing, with color photographs of many roses; information on pruning, propagating and treating problems.

The Organic Rose Garden. Liz Druitt. Dallas, Taylor Publishing, 1996. A book to dispel the popular conception of roses as plants which need constant spraying with powerful and dangerous chemicals. She gives advice on designing and planting your rose garden, fertilizing and pruning, propagation, and a list of roses that take to organic methods -- there are plenty to choose from.

Roses. Roger Phillips & Martyn Rix. New York, Random House, 1988. If I only had a dollar for every time I've looked longingly through this book! It is an absolute must for lovers of roses, with good coverage of the very popular old roses. The treatment of the modern hybrids is biased toward English varieties.

The Graham Stuart Thomas Rose Book. Portland, Timber Press, 1994. A combination of Thomas' three classic rose books, *The Old Shrub Roses, Shrubs Roses of Today,* and *Climbing Roses Old and New,* revised and illustrated with many color photographs. Very readable as are all his books.

Antique Roses for the South. William C. Welch. Dallas, Taylor Publishing, 1990. There are lots of rose books, but few as much fun to read as this one. A very personal discussion of old roses which have thrived for years in difficult conditions: how to grow them, propagate them, arrange them, and enjoy them.

Rosa Rugosa. Suzanne Verrier. Deer Park, WI, Capability's Books, 1991. Guaranteed to make rugosa roses much more popular, as they really deserve to be. Candid descriptions of over eighty cultivars and hybrids, photos of many, and a list of sources. A second book gave *Rosa Gallica* the same treatment, available from the same source. See Section B for the address.

VEGETABLE & FRUIT GROWING

Field and Garden Vegetables of America. Fearing Burr. Chillicothe, IL, American Botanist, 1988. Originally published in 1863, this book describes nearly 1,100 vegetable varieties in cultivation at that time; it is an invaluable source of information to those interested in identifying and preserving heirloom vegetables. Beautifully reprinted, fun to read! (See Section B.)

High-Yield Gardening: How to Get More From Your Garden Space and More From Your Garden Season. Marjorie B. Hunt & Brenda Bortz. Emmaus, PA, Rodale Press, 1986. A very practical guide, with sources and reading lists.

Gardening: The Complete Guide to Growing America's Favorite Fruits and Vegetables. National Gardening Assn. Reading, MA, Addison-Wesley, 1986. A beautiful and basic introduction to the food garden.

Seed to Seed: Seed Saving Techniques for the Vegetable Gardener. Suzanne Ashworth. 1991. Offers both general seed saving techniques and variety-by-variety instructions, with information on seed viability, storage, and germination testing. Available from the Seed Savers Exchange, see Section D.

How to Grow More Vegetables than You Ever Thought Possible on Less Land than You Can Imagine. John Jeavons. 5th ed. Berkeley, Ten Speed Press, 1995. Good book on the bio-dynamic or French intensive method of organic growing by a disciple of Alan Chadwick.

The New Organic Grower: a Master's Manual of Tools and Techniques for the Home and Market Gardener. Eliot Coleman. Chelsea, VT, Chelsea Green, 1989. Extremely practical -- the title says it all. Coleman has also written *The New Organic Grower's Four-Season Harvest,* about extending the harvest throughout the year. (Chelsea Green, 1992)

Growing Vegetables West of the Cascades. Steve Solomon. Seattle, Sasquatch Books, 1989. Essential to the Northwestern vegetable gardener; everything from start to finish.

Citrus -- How to Select, Grow, and Enjoy. Richard Ray and Lance Walheim. Los Angeles, Price Stern Sloan, 1980. An informative and well-illustrated book on growing all sorts of citrus, including unusual kinds.

All About Citrus & Subtropical Fruits. San Ramon, CA, Ortho, 1985. A book that covers citrus and other fruit for warmer climates.

A Guide to Tropical and Subtropical Vegetables. Nick Acrivos. Melbourne, FL, Brevard Rare Fruit Council, 1988. An excellent guide to vegetables for hot climates, including many favorites of the Orient, Africa, Central and South America. Available for $6 ppd. from *Florida Gardening,* P.O. Box 500678, Malabar, FL 32950.

A Guide to Tropical Fruit Trees and Vines. Nick Acrivos. Melbourne, FL, Brevard Rare Fruit Council, 1987. A companion to the book above, describing many tropical fruits. Same source and price as book above.

The Backyard Orchardist: a Complete Guide to Growing Fruit Trees in the Home Garden. Stella Otto. 1993. A terrific guide to growing fruit and helpful to anyone starting a small orchard. Lots of practical advice, suggestions for treating diseases and insects, and a troubleshooting guide. $18.95 postpaid from Ottographics, 8082 Maple City Rd., Maple City, MI 49664 (add 6% sales tax in Michigan). Her similar *The Backyard Berry Book* is available for $19.95 postpaid (plus sales tax in Michigan).

Uncommon Fruits Worthy of Attention: a Gardener's Guide. Lee Reich. Reading, MA, Addison-Wesley Publishing Company, 1991. Here are good cultivar descriptions, growing and harvesting suggestions and propagation information on many off-beat fruits: pawpaws, kiwis, medlar, jujubes, persimmons and other fruiting trees and berries suitable for growing in most of the US and southern Canada.

Fruits & Berries for the Home Garden. Lewis Hill. Pownal, VT, Storey Communications, 1992. Practical advice on growing all sorts of fruits, including pruning and controlling diseases and insects; even recipes.

The Harvest Gardener: Growing for Maximum Yield, Prime Flavor, and Garden-Fresh Storage. Susan McClure. Pownal, VT, Garden Way, 1993. If growing and preserving your own food is your goal, this book will give you growing and harvesting suggestions, recipes for using fresh produce, and instructions for pickling, freezing, drying and root cellaring your harvest.

The Kitchen Garden. Sylvia Thompson. New York, Bantam Books, 1997. Written by a gardener who grows good things to eat, it's full of advice on specific vegetables and herbs for flavor and for use in cooking and preserving. Her companion volume, *The Kitchen Garden Cookbook* is full of wonderful sounding recipes to put into immediate use. Both available in paperback.

Edible Flowers: From Garden to Palate. Cathy Wilkinson Barash. Golden, CO, Fulcrum Publishing, 1993. I've never taken to the idea of eating flowers, but this book will have me doing it this summer. Kathy will tell you what to grow, and gives many appealing recipes; the color pictures of how to serve them up are irresistible.

Cooking from the Garden: Creative Gardening & Contemporary Cuisine. Rosalind Creasy. San Francisco, Sierra Club Books, 1988. This is a super book, combining gardening with producing wonderful meals from your garden; a bonus is that a number of the people listed in *Gardening by Mail* are featured.

WILDFLOWERS

*Growing and Propagating Wildflowers. Harry R. Phillips. Chapel Hill, University of North Carolina Press, 1985. Advice on growing wildflowers, including seed collecting and germination methods, cultivation and use in a garden setting.

*The Wildflower Meadow Book: A Gardener's Guide. Laura C. Martin. Chester, CT, Globe Pequot, 1986. There's more to planting a meadow than sprinkling wildflower seeds and hoping -- here's practical step-by-step information on how to do it successfully.

A Garden of Wildflowers: 101 Native Species and How to Grow Them. Henry W. Art. Pownal, VT, Storey Communications, 1986. National in scope; maps, culture and propagation, list of sources and botanical gardens with native plant collections. See also his *The Wildflower Gardener's Guide* from the same publisher; specifically for the Northeast, Great Lakes and Mid-Atlantic regions.

A Gardener's Encyclopedia of Wild Flowers. C. Colston Burrell. Emmaus, PA, Rodale Press, 1997. They call it "An organic guide to choosing and growing over 150 beautiful wildflowers," and it does that, but the plants described are not native to the western third of the country, few will thrive in the West.

Wildflowers in Your Garden: A Gardener's Guide. Viki Ferreniea. New York, Random House, 1993. A guide to natural landscaping with native shrubs, wildflowers and ferns in sun, shade, bogs and rock gardens; most of her planting suggestions are best suited to areas with regular summer rain.

LANDSCAPE HISTORY AND DESIGN

The Principles of Gardening. Hugh Johnson. New York, Simon & Schuster, 1984. This is one of my very favorite books. An all-round discussion of gardening in all aspects, it will open your eyes to the look of a garden and everything that goes into making one. Wine is all very well, but I wish he'd write more gardening books. It's been updated, but not improved -- look for the first edition.

The Education of a Gardener. Russell Page. New York, Random House, 1985. Again, not a how-to book but a thoughtful discussion of making gardens by a master. It will repay reading many times over; my copy is heavily marked up so I can find points that struck my fancy.

The Gardens of Russell Page. Marina Schinz & Gabrielle van Zuylen. New York, Stewart, Tabori & Chang, 1991. Wonderful photos combined with descriptions and personal recollections by a friend and client of Page; it's a fine book to study and observe, and to accompany his own *The Education of a Gardener*.

The Quest for Paradise: A History of the World's Gardens. Ronald King. New York, W.H. Smith, 1979. This is still one of the best one-volume introductions to garden history that I have found, covering major gardens the world over, with good color illustrations. Look for it in used book stores.

*Decorating Eden: a Comprehensive Sourcebook of Classic Garden Details. Elizabeth Wilkinson & Marjorie Henderson. San Francisco, Chronicle Books, 1992. Formerly published as *The House of Boughs*, this is a very interesting compendium of garden ornaments of many periods and garden styles -- well worth studying, especially for creating period gardens, full of ideas to trigger your creativity.

The Oxford Companion to Gardens. Geoffrey & Susan Jellicoe, Patrick Goode, Michael Lancaster. New York, Oxford University Press, 1986. An encyclopedic reference to garden history, design and ornament; European in emphasis.

*Gardens are for People. Thomas Church. 2nd ed. New York, McGraw-Hill, 1983. A treatise on creating gardens by a celebrated California landscape architect, illustrated primarily with photographs of gardens he designed.

Natural Landscaping: Gardening with Nature to Create a Backyard Paradise. Sally Roth. Emmaus, PA, Rodale Press, 1997. Lots of ideas and inspiration for letting go of perfection in favor of a relaxed and more natural garden. It will make you and the local wildlife happy at the same time.

Sunset Western Landscaping. Menlo Park, CA, Sunset Books, 1997. While all of the gardens and garden details shown have a distinctly Western flavor, there's much to learn from these gardens, almost all of which are fairly small and personal in character. There's every style from cottage to formal, every climate from desert to rainforest, it's hard to imagine a gardener who couldn't find a number of good ideas and plant combinations here.

Northwest Garden Style: Ideas, Designs, and Methods for the Creative Gardener. Jan Kowalczewski Whitner. Seattle, Sasquatch Books, 1996. Sure, we'd all live there if we could, but here are many wonderful design ideas and details which would work anywhere with the plants that you *can* grow.

The Four-Season Landscape: Easy-Care Plants and Plans for Year-Round Color. Susan A. Roth. Emmaus, PA, Rodale Press, 1994. Very useful for stretching out your garden enjoyment by providing something of interest in every season. It's full of practical advice and good suggestions.

Designing and Maintaining Your Edible Landscape Naturally. Robert Kourik. Santa Rosa, CA, Metamorphic Press, 1986. Everything there is to know about growing vegetables and fruit to make your food garden attractive as well as productive. (P.O. Box 1841, Santa Rosa, CA 95402.)

GOOD READS

The Collector's Garden: Designing with Extraordinary Plants. Ken Druse. New York, Clarkson Potter, 1996. A window onto the "gardening underground," the people whose gardens everyone in the know wants to see. It's great fun to read about the gardeners and their passions, and to see wonderful pictures of their gardens; a book full of inspiration.

*The Essential Earthman: Henry Mitchell on Gardening. New York, Farrar, Straus & Giroux, 1983. This book is so full of plant love and humor that you'll want to start over again when you finish. Then look for

One Man's Garden (Boston, Houghton Mifflin, 1992) another collection of Henry Mitchell's columns from the Washington Post, and they're every bit as funny! Sadly, there won't be more columns to collect.

*Onward and Upward in the Garden. Katharine S. White. New York, Farrar, Straus & Giroux, 1979. A book full of vinegary opinions; and good reading, but if you don't live in New England, you'll get no sympathy from her!

V. Sackville-West's Garden Book. New York, Macmillan, 1979. Excerpts from Vita Sackville-West's garden books and columns, organized by the months of the year. Her love of plants and ideas for plantings bubble out of the pages. A visit to Sissinghurst Castle proves that she knew her stuff.

The Illustrated Garden Book: A New Anthology. Robin Lane Fox, ed. New York, Atheneum, 1986. Mostly new excerpts from the *London Observer* garden columns of Vita Sackville-West. Nice illustrations, pictures of Sissinghurst Castle in all seasons.

*Home Ground: A Gardener's Miscellany. Allen Lacy. New York, Farrar, Straus & Giroux, 1985. A collection of essays by one of our very best garden writers. See also his *Further Afield: A Gardener's Excursions* (New York, Farrar, Straus & Giroux, 1986).

*The Opinionated Gardener: Random Offshoots From an Alpine Garden. Geoffrey B. Charlesworth. Boston, Godine, 1988. Very amusing essays on gardening, not just of alpines, by a man who admits that he loves to weed; he can also write with the best of them. A newer book, *The Gardener Obsessed* (Boston, Godine, 1994) follows the same pattern: the chapter "What is a Garden?" is must reading!

The 3,000 Mile Garden. Leslie Land & Roger Phillips. New York, Viking, 1996. A lively correspondence between an American artist and an irrepressible English photographer covering everything from mushroom hunting to cooking to gardening to life itself. If "good reads" means fun reading, this book fills the bill; these friends will feel like your friends when you finish.

Thyme on my Hands. Eric Grissell. Portland, Timber Press, 1987. The trials and travails of a garden maker, amusingly written and well worth his trouble if the photo on the cover is any proof. Well-developed appreciation of the garden cat. He had enough thyme on his hands to write *A Journal in Thyme*, published by Timber Press in 1994. What next? Keeping thyme? Thyme's up? Hot thymes!

The Gardener's Year. Karel Capek. Madison, University of Wisconsin, 1984. Proof that gardening knows no boundaries, this little book written in Prague in the 1930s will make you laugh out loud -- his wry observations are timeless.

The Year in Bloom: Gardening for all Seasons in the Pacific Northwest. Ann Lovejoy. Seattle, Sasquatch Books, 1987. Ann Lovejoy's writing has deservedly carried her to the peaks, but this funny little book is what got her started, and it's a charmer.

The Gardener's Bed-Book. Richardson Wright. New York, PAJ Publications, 1988. I picked up a copy of this years ago and loved it! Humorous short essays make it perfect for the bedside table.

The Leaf Men and the Brave Good Bugs. William Joyce. New York, Harper Collins, 1996. I've never listed a book for children, but I fell in love with this imaginative tale of courage, selfless cooperation and facing down bullies, and can't wait to read it with some of my little grand nieces and nephews. Bravo!!

Through the Garden Gate. Elizabeth Lawrence, edited by Bill Neal. Chapel Hill, University of North Carolina Press, 1990. A collection of newspaper columns which covers the seasons for a year. You'll fall in love with her modest, quiet observations.

*The Wild Gardener: on Flowers and Foliage for the Natural Border. Peter Loewer. Harrisburg, PA, Stackpole Books, 1991. I'm listing this book here because I enjoyed reading it so much; it's a real charmer and full of interesting plant history and lore.

A Passion for Daylilies: the Flowers and the People. Sydney Eddison. New York, HarperCollins, 1992. This book might be listed elsewhere, it's a delightful ramble through a world of plants and plant people, in this case daylilies, but it could be about any group of plant fanatics.

Red Oaks & Black Birches: the Science and Lore of Trees. Rebecca Rupp. Pownal, VT, Garden Way, 1990. Sure, it's about trees, but it's a terrific read, and so full of interest and history that you'll wallow in it. Her book about vegetables, *Blue Corn and Square Tomatoes* is equally interesting (Garden Way, 1987).

The Greek Plant World in Myth, Art and Literature. Hellmut Baumann. Translated and augmented by William T. Stearn & Eldwyth Ruth Stearn. Portland, Timber Press, 1993. From earliest times, Greece has been a center of botanical interest: this is a fascinating account of historical botanical lore.

GUIDES TO GARDENS

Luckily gardens don't move around much, because there are not many recent guidebooks. It's best to call ahead to check open days and hours, which might have changed.

Handbook on American Gardens: A Traveler's Guide. Brooklyn, NY, Brooklyn Botanic Garden, 1986. Gives good concise coverage of gardens in the United States. BBG Handbook #111.

The Traveler's Guide to American Gardens. Mary Helen Ray & Robert P. Nicholls, eds. Chapel Hill, University of North Carolina Press, 1988. A state-by-state guide to gardens of interest; each is briefly described, those of special merit are starred.

Gardens of North America and Hawaii: A Traveler's Guide. Irene & Walter Jacob. Portland, Timber Press, 1986. Very useful; small enough to take with you on a trip; rates the gardens.

The Garden Conservancy Open Days Directory. Cold Spring, NY, annual. The 1997 edition lists private gardens in 17 states. These gardens are open to benefit the Garden Conservancy -- last year 28,000 people visited, and they expect to add more gardens every year. Usually a cluster of gardens are open on the same day to make it easier to tour. The Garden Conservancy, P.O. Box 219, Cold Spring, NY 10516.

Complete Guide to North American Gardens. 2 v. William Milligan. Boston, Little, Brown, 1991. Not complete, these two volumes cover the Northeast (from Canada to Pennsylvania) and the West Coast, with good garden descriptions.

Travelers' Guide to Herb Gardens: over 500 Gardens in the United States and Canada Featuring Herbs. 4th ed. Compiled by The Herb Society of America. Mentor, OH, 1998. Brief descriptions of gardens, open days and hours, and maps of each state and province give location of a variety of public and private herb gardens. Write or call for price: see Section D.

Herb Gardens in America: a Visitor's Guide. Karen S.C. Morris & Lyle E. Craker. 1991. A directory of herb gardens divided into two main sections, one giving detailed descriptions of major gardens, the other giving brief descriptions of "all known herbs gardens open to the public." $10.75 postpaid, $11.75 overseas. HSMP Press, 176 Heatherstone Road, Amherst, MA 01002 .

The Garden Tourist: a Guide to Garden Tours, Garden Days and Special Events. Lois G. Rosenfeld, ed., annual. This is a neat idea, a schedule of special events, flower shows, plant society conventions and such, listed regionally so that you can find out what's going on near you, or where you plan to visit. Includes major events overseas as well. Garden Tourist Press, 300 W. 72nd St., Ste. 12B, New York, NY 10023.

Garden Touring in the Pacific Northwest: a Guide to Gardens and Specialty Nurseries in Oregon, Washington, and British Columbia. Jan Kowalczewski Whitner. Seattle, Alaska Northwest Books, 1993. Essential to the gardener traveling in the Northwest, this book gives good descriptions of the gardens and nurseries there, and an idea of how many there are! Buy a copy as you cross into the territory, or to study before you travel.

Beautiful Gardens: Guide to over 80 Botanical Gardens, Arboretums and More in Southern California and the Southwest. Eric A. Johnson & Scott Millard. Tucson, Ironwood Press, 1991. Complete information for visiting public gardens in Arizona, Nevada and New Mexico as well as southern California.

Collins Book of British Gardens: A Guide to 200 Gardens in England, Scotland & Wales. George Plumptre. London, Collins, 1985. Organized by region, then by county; black and white photos, regional maps, a page or two on each garden.

The Gardener's Guide to Britain. Patrick Taylor. Portland, Timber Press, annual. This book has it right, it lists nurseries, so that you can visit some of the terrific plant collections as well as the famous gardens. All guides to British gardens should have an index by county as well as by garden name; as it is, you have to buy two guides to plan your trip. This one is indexed only by garden name, with regional maps.

The Good Gardens Guide. Graham Rose & Peter King. London, Barrie & Jenkins, annual. Lists over 1,000 gardens open to the public in Great Britain and Ireland, with lots of information for visitors (teas, dogs on lead, and much more) and descriptions of the gardens. There are many good guides to gardens in Great Britain, but this one and the one above are comprehensive, light enough to carry, and paperback, so you'll feel free to take them with you.

The Gardens of Europe. Penelope Hobhouse & Patrick Taylor, eds. New York, Random House, 1990. Too heavy to carry with you on a trip, this book makes good study before you go to Europe. It covers 700 gardens in Britain, Europe, and the former Eastern Bloc countries. Essentials for visiting are given, as are special features of the gardens; some of the gardens are private and you must write ahead for an appointment.

PLANT-FINDING SOURCEBOOKS

One would think that through the magic of computers, it would be easy to compile directories of sources by botanical name. *Au contraire!* Such magic takes endless hours of inputting and checking; sources come and go, catalogs change every year; people spending endless hours at the computer turn to stone as their tempers grow very short! These people are heros! Listed below are some fine efforts.

*Andersen Horticultural Library's Source List of Plants and Seeds. 4th ed. 1996. This excellent plant finder completely indexes over 450 retail and wholesale catalogs from all over the country; lists over 59,000 plants by botanical name. Updated every few years. $34.95 ppd. Minnesota Landscape Arboretum, Box 39, Chanhassen, MN 55317.

The RHS Plant Finder: 70,000 Plants and Where to Buy Them. London, Royal Horticultural Society, annual. Created by Chris Philip and now produced by The Royal Horticultural Society of Great Britain, this fat book has become the envy of the horticultural world. The book indicates which British nurseries ship overseas. It also has one of the best bibliographies of books on specific plants that you'll find anywhere. Available from many horticultural book suppliers, and in some large bookstores.

The Plant Finder Reference Library. A new endeavor of Chris Philip, this CD-ROM includes the RHS Plant Finder, Plant Finders for Europe, even some nursery sources from Gardening by Mail, and several other useful databases, including a directory of 2,000 horticultural World Wide Web sites. For information, write to The Plant Finder, Freepost, Lewes BN7 2ZZ, England.

The Seed Search...Over 33,000 seeds and where to buy them. Karen Platt. First published in 1997, this is somewhat like the *Plant Finder*, listing seeds offered by seed companies and seed exchanges all over the world; a great effort! You must send £15 sterling. Write to Karen Platt at 35 Longfield Road, Crookes, Sheffield, S10 1WQ, England. Web site: <www.seedsearch.demon.co.uk>

The Canadian Plant Sourcebook. Ottawa, Anne & Peter Ashley. 1996-97. A very fine plant finder listing sources of 21,000 hardy plants in Canada; it tells you which nurseries ship to the US. US$18 ppd. to the US, C$18 ppd. in Canada. Anne & Peter Ashley, 93 Fentiman Avenue, Ottawa, ON, Canada K1S 0T7.

Northwest Gardener's Resource Directory. Stephanie Feeney. Biennial. Thank God Stephanie hasn't yet decided to cover the whole country! She does cover western Oregon, Washington and British Columbia and tells you about *everything!* Lists nurseries, courses, plant sales, garden services, societies, gardens to visit, Web Sites, and much more. If you visit or live in Feeneyland, you must have it! $25.45 postpaid, (WA add 7.8% tax), C$32.45 to Canada. Cedarcroft Press, 59 Strawberry Point, Bellingham, WA 98226.

Where on Earth: a Guide to Specialty Nurseries and Other Resources for California Gardeners. 3rd ed. Barbara Stevens & Nancy Conner. Berkeley, Heyday Books, 1997. Californians should keep this little guide in their cars so that every trip includes a nursery or a garden tour; includes listings for the whole state; always call ahead if you're driving very far. Heyday Books, P.O. Box 9145, Berkeley, CA 94709.

The Combined Rose List. Mantua, OH, Beverly Dobson & Peter Schneider, annual. This is a tour de force: 1997 edition lists 10,113 species and hybrid rose cultivars in commerce, offered by 226 rose nurseries in the US, Canada and overseas. They are listed by botanical or cultivar name, with brief information on year of introduction, breeder, color of flower and where you can get it. Write to Peter Schneider, P.O. Box 677, Mantua, OH 44255.

Sources of Propagated Native Plants and Wildflowers. 1995. A list of nurseries selling plants which they have propagated from stock plants, not collected in the wild. $4.50 ppd. New England Wildflower Society, 180 Hemenway Road, Framingham, MA 01701-2699.

Northwind Farm's Herb Gardener's Resource Guide. 4th ed. 1996. Nearly a thousand sources of herbs, herb supplies and products, herb gardens and more. Available from Northwind Publications, 439 Ponderosa Way, Jemez Springs, NM 87025-8025. $12.98 ppd. in US, US$13.98 to Canada, US$15.95 overseas.

Hortus West. Dale Shank, ed. A directory of commercial sources of Western native plants and seeds. Lists over 160 nurseries in the West, many of which sell retail as well as wholesale; each issue also has interesting articles. Issued twice a year: $12 a year in the US, US$15 outside the US. Hortus West, P.O. Box 2870, Wilsonville, OR 97070-9957.

*Garden Seed Inventory. Kent Whealy, ed. 4th ed. Decorah, IA, Seed Savers Publications, 1995. Lists every nonhybrid vegetable variety available from seed companies in the US and Canada, with descriptions and sources for each. One of those wonderful original ideas, laboriously and lovingly compiled and extremely useful to the whole world of horticulture. Bravo! $28 ppd., US$33 ppd. to Canada. (See Seed Savers Exchange, Section D)

Fruit, Berry and Nut Inventory. Kent Whealy, ed. Decorah, IA, Seed Saver Publications, 1993. Like their *Garden Seed Inventory;* this book lists fruit and nut varieties, with plant descriptions and sources. $26 ppd., US$31 to Canada.

Cornucopia. Rev. ed. Stephen Facciola. A staggering effort, this directory tells you where to find seeds and plants of hundreds and hundreds of edibles -- everything from baby vegetables to rare tropical fruits, including many varieties of each type. There will be a new edition late in 1997, and the database will also be available on computer disk. Write to Kampong Publications, 1870 Sunrise Drive, Vista, CA 92084.

Well, dear gardening friends, another marathon has been run and finished! I finally get to go outside and enjoy my own garden, my family and friends and my pets. As always, I'm afraid that tomorrow I'll remember something I forgot to tell you, another wonderful book will arrive, a catalog offering plants so new and rare that no one's ever heard of them will come shouting out of my mail box! This very morning, as the book was finished, I got some beautifully engraved permanent garden markers from Lark Label, 2800 Edgewater Drive, Greenwood, AR 72936-6042. I couldn't *not* tell you about them. That done, here's wishing you all of the joy that plants and plant friends bring to our lives, and all of the excitement of finding new things to try. It's time to say good night and creep out the door. Have lots of fun until we meet again!

© Tripple Brook Farm
Artist: Betty Stull Schaffer

INDEXES

H. Plant Sources Index: an index of plant and seed sources by plant specialties. Two-letter geographical codes are included to help you find the closest source or a source in a similar climate.

J. Geographical Index: an index of plant and seed sources by location. U.S. and Canadian sources are listed by state or province. Overseas sources are listed by country. Within each primary location, cities or post offices are listed alphabetically.

K. Product Sources Index: an index of suppliers and services listed by specialty.

L. Society Index: an index of horticultural societies listed by plant and/or other special interests.

NOTES ON INDEXING

Each plant source or supplier is indexed; we have increased our indexing so that we can give you sources of more specific plant groups and products. When a source didn't indicate which specialties it preferred, we have chosen for them from a study of its catalog. The companies vary from small to large, and their specialties from narrow to very broad.

For those with few specialties, the indexing is very specific, but as offerings become greater, the indexing usually becomes broader. A small nursery that offers only ivy is listed under "Ivy," but a large nursery that includes ivy as one of its many offerings may be listed under "Ivy" and "Ground Covers." Similarly, "Sundials" is a specific category, versus the more general "Garden Ornaments."

You should check both the specific category and the general category to be sure you find all possible sources. Where specific plants are indexed — for instance, Crabapples — it is because we have found a better-than-usual selection offered by that source.

The notes on catalogs in the alphabetical listings include some specialties that we were unable to index because of space considerations. To jog your memory, you could jot the company name into the index next to the appropriate category. Always read this book with a color "highlighter" in hand so that you can mark the items of greatest interest to you!

A table of the symbols and abbreviations used in this book
appears inside the front and back covers.

Page	Source

ABUTILONS
A 13	Buena Creek Gardens, CA
A 42	Glasshouse Works, OH
A 46	Harborcrest Gardens, BC
A 59	Kartuz Greenhouses, CA
A 67	Logee's Greenhouses, CT
A 68	L.J. McCreary & Co. Perennial Seeds, TX
A 106	Southern Perennials & Herbs, MS
A 116	Trans Pacific Nursery, OR
A 118	Valhalla Nursery, CA

ACACIAS
A 7	B & T World Seeds, Fr
A 7	The Banana Tree, PA
A 14	Bushland Flora, Au
A 20	Chiltern Seeds, En
A 21	Colvos Creek Nursery, WA
A 27	Deep Diversity, NM
A 28	Desert Citizens, CO
A 28	Desert Moon Nursery, NM
A 32	Ellison Horticultural Pty., Ltd., Au
A 38	Forestfarm, OR
A 40	Fruit Spirit Botanical Gardens, Au
A 53	J. L. Hudson, Seedsman, CA
A 58	Joe's Nursery, CA
A 62	Kumar International, In
A 65	Legendary Ethnobotanical Resources, FL
A 78	Nindethana-Seed Service, Au
A 83	D. Orriell -- Seed Exporters, Au
A 86	Phoenix Seed, Au
A 92	Rainforest Seed Company, Co
A 104	Silverhill Seeds, So

ACERS
See Maples

ACHIMENES
A 9	Belisle's Violet House, WI
A 41	Gardenimport, Inc., ON
A 46	Harborcrest Gardens, BC
A 59	Karleen's Achimenes, GA
A 64	Lauray of Salisbury, CT
A 68	McKinney's Glassehouse, KS
A 84	Pat's Pets, MO
A 114	Tiki Nursery, NC

ADENIUMS
A 46	Grigsby Cactus Gardens, CA
A 67	Living Stones Nursery, AZ
A 111	Sunrise Nursery, TX

AECHMEAS
A 7	B & T World Seeds, Fr
A 9	Bird Rock Tropicals, CA

AECHMEAS (continued)
A 71	Michael's Bromeliads, FL
A 117	Tropiflora, FL

AESCHYNANTHUS
A 9	Belisle's Violet House, WI
A 51	Hill 'n dale, CA
A 64	Lauray of Salisbury, CT
A 68	Lyndon Lyon Greenhouses, Inc., NY
A 68	McKinney's Glassehouse, KS
A 84	Pat's Pets, MO
A 114	Tiki Nursery, NC

AESCULUS
See Horse Chestnuts

AFRICAN VIOLET LEAVES
A 9	Belisle's Violet House, WI
A 10	Bluebird Greenhouse, NC
A 71	Mighty Minis, CA
A 84	Pat's Pets, MO
A 97	Rozell Rose Nursery & Violet Boutique, TX
A 114	Tiki Nursery, NC
A 116	Travis' Violets, GA
A 119	Violets By Appointment, NY
A 120	Violets, Etc., Inc., FL
A 123	Wildman's African Violets, NY

AFRICAN VIOLETS
A 9	Belisle's Violet House, WI
A 10	Bluebird Greenhouse, NC
A 46	Harborcrest Gardens, BC
A 68	Lyndon Lyon Greenhouses, Inc., NY
A 68	McKinney's Glassehouse, KS
A 71	Mighty Minis, CA
A 84	Pat's Pets, MO
A 94	Rob's Mini-o-lets, NY
A 97	Rozell Rose Nursery & Violet Boutique, TX
A 114	Tiki Nursery, NC
A 114	Tinari Greenhouses, PA
A 116	Travis' Violets, GA
B 33	The Violet House, FL
A 120	Volkmann Bros. Greenhouses, TX

AGAPANTHUS
A 4	Amaryllis, Inc., LA
A 30	Dunford Farms, WA
A 32	Ellison Horticultural Pty., Ltd., Au
A 42	Glasshouse Works, OH
A 43	Russell Graham, Purveyor of Plants, OR
A 68	L.J. McCreary & Co. Perennial Seeds, TX
A 88	Plant Delights Nursery, NC
A 106	Southern Perennials & Herbs, MS
A 118	Valhalla Nursery, CA

Page	Source

AGASTACHES
- A 3 Alplains, CO
- A 16 Canyon Creek Nursery, CA
- A 31 Edgewood Farm & Nursery, VA
- A 37 Flowery Branch Seed Company, GA
- A 43 Goodwin Creek Gardens, OR
- A 49 The Herb Garden, NC
- A 50 High Country Gardens, NM
- A 55 Ion Exchange, IA
- A 68 L.J. McCreary & Co. Perennial Seeds, TX
- A 74 Mountain Valley Growers, Inc., CA
- A 84 Passionflower Herb & Perennial Nursery, VA
- A 90 Prairie Moon Nursery, MN
- A 94 Richters Herbs, ON
- A 95 Rocky Mountain Rare Plants, CO
- A 98 Sandy Mush Herb Nursery, NC
- A 101 Seedhunt, CA
- A 105 Sleepy Hollow Herb Farm, KY
- A 107 Southwestern Native Seeds, AZ
- A 114 The Thyme Garden, OR
- A 121 Weiss Brothers Nursery, CA
- A 121 Well-Sweep Herb Farm, NJ
- A 125 Woodside Gardens, WA

AGAVES
- A 1 Abbey Gardens, CA
- A 7 B & T World Seeds, Fr
- A 28 Desert Citizens, CO
- A 28 Desert Moon Nursery, NM
- A 46 Grigsby Cactus Gardens, CA
- A 58 Joe's Nursery, CA
- A 62 Gerhard Koehres Cactus & Succulent Nursery, Ge
- A 67 Living Stones Nursery, AZ
- A 67 Loehman's Cacti & Succulents, CA
- A 71 Mesa Garden, NM
- A 72 Miles' to Go, AZ
- A 76 Nature's Curiosity Shop, CA
- A 76 Neon Palm Nursery, CA
- A 88 Plant Delights Nursery, NC
- A 92 Rare Plant Research, OR
- A 97 Doug & Vivi Rowland, En
- A 110 Succulenta, CA
- A 111 Sunrise Nursery, TX
- A 117 Tropic to Tropic Plants, BC
- A 126 Yucca Do Nursery, TX

AJUGAS
- A 18 Carroll Gardens, MD
- A 20 Coastal Gardens & Nursery, SC
- A 41 Garden Place, OH
- A 90 Powell's Gardens, NC
- A 91 Prentiss Court Ground Covers, SC

ALLIUMS
- A 4 Jacques Amand, Bulb Specialists, MD
- A 6 Arrowhead Alpines, MI
- A 6 Avon Bulbs, En
- A 7 B & T World Seeds, Fr
- A 18 Cascade Bulb & Seed, OR
- A 20 Chiltern Seeds, En
- A 20 Paul Christian -- Rare Plants, Wa
- A 26 The Daffodil Mart, CT
- A 34 Far West Bulb Farm, CA

ALLIUMS (continued)
- A 35 Field House Alpines, En
- A 39 Frosty Hollow Ecological Restoration, WA
- A 41 Gardens North, ON
- A 43 Russell Graham, Purveyor of Plants, OR
- A 52 Honeywood Lilies, SK
- A 68 McClure & Zimmerman, WI
- A 70 Mary's Plant Farm & Landscaping, OH
- A 73 Monocot Nursery, En
- A 74 Charles H. Mueller Co., PA
- A 78 North Green Seeds, En
- A 89 Potterton & Martin, En
- A 94 Robinett Bulb Farm, CA
- A 99 John Scheepers, Inc., CT
- A 100 The Seed Guild, Sc
- A 114 A Thousand Alliums, WA
- A 118 Van Engelen, Inc., CT

ALOES
- A 1 Abbey Gardens, CA
- A 7 B & T World Seeds, Fr
- A 28 Desert Theatre, CA
- A 31 Ecoscape, CA
- A 46 Grigsby Cactus Gardens, CA
- A 58 Joe's Nursery, CA
- A 59 K & L Cactus & Succulent Nursery, CA
- A 62 Gerhard Koehres Cactus & Succulent Nursery, Ge
- A 67 Living Stones Nursery, AZ
- A 71 Mesa Garden, NM
- A 76 Nature's Curiosity Shop, CA
- A 76 Neon Palm Nursery, CA
- A 79 Northridge Gardens, CA
- A 92 Rare Plant Research, OR
- A 97 Doug & Vivi Rowland, En
- A 104 Silverhill Seeds, So
- A 106 South Bay Growers, FL
- A 107 Southwestern Exposure, AZ
- A 110 Succulenta, CA
- A 111 Sunrise Nursery, TX
- A 126 Roy Young, Seeds, En

ALPINE PLANTS
See also specific plants
- A 3 Alpine Gardens, WI
- A 3 Alplains, CO
- A 6 Arrowhead Alpines, MI
- A 11 Bluestone Perennials, OH
- A 15 C K S, Cz
- A 20 Chehalis Rare Plant Nursery, MO
- A 27 Daystar, ME
- A 31 Edge of the Rockies, CO
- A 33 Euroseeds, Cz
- A 33 Evergreen Gardenworks, CA
- A 39 Frosty Hollow Ecological Restoration, WA
- A 44 Great Basin Natives, UT
- A 50 High Altitude Gardens, ID
- A 50 High Country Gardens, NM
- A 54 W. E. Th. Ingwersen, Ltd., En
- A 57 Jelitto Perennial Seeds, USA Office, KY
- A 60 Kelly's Color, CA
- A 74 Mt. Tahoma Nursery, WA
- A 75 NZ Alpine Seeds, Ne
- A 76 Nature's Garden, OR

Page	Source	Page	Source

Page	Source		Page	Source

AQUILEGIAS (continued)

A 102   Select Seeds -- Antique Flowers, CT
A 114   Thompson & Morgan, NJ

ARCTOSTAPHYLOS
See Manzanitas

ARISAEMAS

A 3   Alplains, CO
A 4   Jacques Amand, Bulb Specialists, MD
A 5   Appalachian Wildflower Nursery, PA
A 16   Camellia Forest Nursery, NC
A 20   Paul Christian -- Rare Plants, Wa
A 21   Collector's Nursery, WA
A 24   Cricklewood Nursery, WA
A 38   Fraser's Thimble Farm, BC
A 49   Heronswood Nursery, WA
A 58   Junglemania, CA
A 88   Plant Delights Nursery, NC
A 92   Rainforest Gardens, BC
A 93   Red's Rhodies, OR
A 93   Reflective Gardens, WA
A 97   Roslyn Nursery, NY
A 102   Seneca Hill Perennials, NY

ARISTOLOCHIAS

A 23   Coombland Gardens & Nursery, En
A 67   Logee's Greenhouses, CT
A 75   NWN Nursery, FL
A 118   Valhalla Nursery, CA

AROIDS

A 5   Appalachian Wildflower Nursery, PA
A 6   Arrowhead Alpines, MI
A 19   Chadwell Himalayan Seed, En
A 20   Paul Christian -- Rare Plants, Wa
A 21   Collector's Nursery, WA
A 31   Eastern Plant Specialties, ME
A 31   Eco-Gardens, GA
A 38   Fraser's Thimble Farm, BC
A 42   Glasshouse Works, OH
A 43   Russell Graham, Purveyor of Plants, OR
A 53   Jerry Horne Rare Plants, FL
A 58   Junglemania, CA
A 69   Ann Mann's Orchids, FL
A 70   Meadow View Farms, OR
A 73   Monocot Nursery, En
A 88   Plant Delights Nursery, NC
A 93   Reflective Gardens, WA
A 97   Roslyn Nursery, NY
A 102   Seneca Hill Perennials, NY
A 105   Siskiyou Rare Plant Nursery, OR
A 106   Southern Exposure, TX
A 107   Southern Shade, FL
A 116   Trennoll Nursery, OH
A 117   Underwood Shade Nursery, MA
A 121   We-Du Nurseries, NC
A 125   Woodlanders, Inc., SC

ARTEMISIAS

A 16   Canyon Creek Nursery, CA
A 18   Carroll Gardens, MD
A 22   Companion Plants, OH

ARTEMISIAS (continued)

A 31   Edgewood Farm & Nursery, VA
A 37   Flowery Branch Seed Company, GA
A 37   Foothill Cottage Gardens, CA
A 43   Goodwin Creek Gardens, OR
A 44   Great Basin Natives, UT
A 49   The Herb Garden, NC
A 49   Heronswood Nursery, WA
A 50   High Country Gardens, NM
A 58   Joy Creek Nursery, OR
A 65   Lewis Mountain Herbs & Everlastings, OH
A 70   Mary's Plant Farm & Landscaping, OH
A 71   Milaeger's Gardens, WI
A 74   Mountain Valley Growers, Inc., CA
A 81   Olympic Coast Garden, WA
A 90   Powell's Gardens, NC
A 94   Richters Herbs, ON
A 95   Robyn's Nest Nursery, WA
A 96   Rose Hill Herbs and Perennials, VA
A 98   Sandy Mush Herb Nursery, NC
A 105   Sleepy Hollow Herb Farm, KY
A 106   Southern Perennials & Herbs, MS
A 111   Sunnybrook Farms Nursery, OH
A 112   Surry Gardens, ME
A 113   Theatrum Botanicum, CA
A 121   Weiss Brothers Nursery, CA
A 121   Well-Sweep Herb Farm, NJ
A 125   Wrenwood of Berkeley Springs, WV

ASCLEPIAS

A 11   Bluestem Prairie Nursery, IL
A 20   Chiltern Seeds, En
A 37   Flowery Branch Seed Company, GA
A 38   Forestfarm, OR
A 38   The Fragrant Path, NE
A 43   Goodwin Creek Gardens, OR
A 55   Ion Exchange, IA
A 57   Jelitto Perennial Seeds, USA Office, KY
A 58   Joe's Nursery, CA
A 63   Landscape Alternatives, Inc., MN
A 64   Las Pilitas Nursery, CA
A 75   NWN Nursery, FL
A 75   Native American Seed, TX
A 87   Pine Ridge Gardens, AR
A 90   Prairie Moon Nursery, MN
A 91   Prairie Nursery, WI
A 92   Randy's Nursery & Greenhouses, GA
A 104   Silverhill Seeds, So
A 121   We-Du Nurseries, NC
A 122   Western Native Seed, CO

ASHES

A 5   Arborvillage Nursery, MO
A 38   Forestfarm, OR
A 100   F. W. Schumacher Co., Inc., MA
A 103   Sheffield's Seed Co., Inc., NY
A 105   Smith Nursery Co., IA

ASIMINA
See Pawpaws

ASPARAGUS

A 2   Allen Plant Company, MD

Page	Source

AZALEAS, SPECIES (continued)
A 94	The Rhododendron Species Foundation, WA
A 100	F. W. Schumacher Co., Inc., MA
A 116	Transplant Nursery, GA
A 125	Woodlanders, Inc., SC

BAMBOO
A 7	A Bamboo Shoot Nursery, CA
A 7	Bamboo Sourcery, CA
A 10	Kurt Bluemel, Inc., MD
A 14	Burt Associates Bamboo, MA
A 33	Exotica Rare Fruit Nursery, CA
A 42	Glasshouse Works, OH
A 62	Kumar International, In
A 66	Linton & Linton Bamboo, GA
A 73	Miniature Plant Kingdom, CA
A 93	Steve Ray's Bamboo Gardens, AL
A 115	Tradewinds Bamboo Nursery, OR
A 118	Valhalla Nursery, CA

BAMBOO, HARDY
A 7	A Bamboo Shoot Nursery, CA
A 7	Bamboo Sourcery, CA
A 10	Kurt Bluemel, Inc., MD
A 14	Burt Associates Bamboo, MA
A 20	Cloud Mountain Nursery, WA
A 21	Colvos Creek Nursery, WA
A 42	Glasshouse Works, OH
A 45	Greer Gardens, OR
A 57	Japonica Water Gardens, OR
A 66	Linton & Linton Bamboo, GA
A 75	NWN Nursery, FL
A 76	Neon Palm Nursery, CA
A 78	Northern Groves, OR
A 79	Northwoods Nursery, OR
A 82	Oregon Exotics Rare Fruit Nursery, OR
A 88	The Plant Farm, BC
A 92	Raintree Nursery, WA
A 93	Steve Ray's Bamboo Gardens, AL
A 115	Tradewinds Bamboo Nursery, OR
A 117	Tripple Brook Farm, MA
A 117	Tropic to Tropic Plants, BC
A 118	Valhalla Nursery, CA

BANANAS
A 3	Aloha Tropicals, CA
A 7	The Banana Tree, PA
A 33	Exotica Rare Fruit Nursery, CA
A 40	Fruit Spirit Botanical Gardens, Au
A 40	Garden of Delights, FL
A 42	Going Bananas, FL
A 59	Just Fruits, FL
A 76	Neon Palm Nursery, CA
A 83	Pacific Tree Farms, CA
A 89	The Plumeria People, TX
A 92	Rainforest Seed Company, Co
A 110	Stokes Tropicals, LA
A 117	Tropic to Tropic Plants, BC
A 118	Valhalla Nursery, CA

BANKSIAS
A 7	B & T World Seeds, Fr
A 14	Bushland Flora, Au

BANKSIAS (continued)
A 20	Chiltern Seeds, En
A 32	Ellison Horticultural Pty., Ltd., Au
A 40	Fruit Spirit Botanical Gardens, Au
A 62	Gerhard Koehres Cactus & Succulent Nursery, Ge
A 78	Nindethana Seed Service, Au
A 83	D. Orriell -- Seed Exporters, Au
A 116	Trans Pacific Nursery, OR

BASILS
A 13	Brown's Edgewood Gardens, FL
A 22	Companion Plants, OH
A 31	Edgewood Farm & Nursery, VA
A 37	Flowery Branch Seed Company, GA
A 42	Good Scents, ID
A 49	The Herb Garden, NC
A 49	Herbs-Liscious, IA
A 53	Horus Botanicals, Ethnobotanical Seeds, AR
A 56	It's About Thyme, TX
A 58	Johnny's Selected Seeds, ME
A 84	Passionflower Herb & Perennial Nursery, VA
A 93	Rasland Farm, NC
A 94	Richters Herbs, ON
A 94	River View Herbs, NS
A 96	Rose Hill Herbs and Perennials, VA
A 103	Shepherd's Garden Seeds, CT
A 110	Story House Herb Farm, KY
A 114	The Thyme Garden, OR
A 114	Tinmouth Channel Farm, VT
A 121	Well-Sweep Herb Farm, NJ
A 125	Wrenwood of Berkeley Springs, WV

BEANS
A 9	Berton Seeds Company, Ltd., ON
A 33	Evergreen Y. H. Enterprises, CA
A 34	Fern Hill Farm, NJ
A 40	Garden City Seeds, MT
A 48	Heirloom Seed Project, PA
A 48	Heirloom Seeds, PA
A 50	High Altitude Gardens, ID
A 53	Horus Botanicals, Ethnobotanical Seeds, AR
A 76	Native Seeds/SEARCH, AZ
A 90	Prairie Grown Garden Seeds, SK
A 98	Salt Spring Seeds, BC
A 101	Seeds Blum, ID
A 101	Seeds of Change, NM
A 101	Seeds West Garden Seeds, NM
A 119	Vermont Bean Seed Co., VT
A 123	Willhite Seed Co., TX

BEE PLANTS
A 102	Select Seeds -- Antique Flowers, CT

BEECHES
A 5	Arborvillage Nursery, MO
A 14	Burnt Ridge Nursery, WA
A 21	Coenosium Gardens, WA
A 29	Dilworth Nursery, PA
A 34	Fairweather Gardens, NJ
A 38	Forestfarm, OR
A 42	Girard Nurseries, OH
A 45	Greer Gardens, OR
A 70	Mary's Plant Farm & Landscaping, OH

Page	Source	Page	Source

Page	Source

Page	Source

Page	Source

CAMPANULAS (continued)
A 90	Powell's Gardens, NC
A 92	Rainforest Gardens, BC
A 97	Roslyn Nursery, NY
A 100	The Seed Guild, Sc
A 102	Select Seeds -- Antique Flowers, CT
A 102	Seneca Hill Perennials, NY
A 102	Shady Oaks Nursery, MN
A 105	Siskiyou Rare Plant Nursery, OR
A 112	Surry Gardens, ME
A 114	Thompson & Morgan, NJ
A 121	Well-Sweep Herb Farm, NJ
A 125	Woodside Gardens, WA
A 125	Wrightman Alpines, ON

CANNAS
A 3	Aloha Tropicals, CA
A 25	Crystal Palace Perennials, Ltd., IN
A 30	Dutch Gardens, NJ
A 42	Glasshouse Works, OH
A 44	Green & Hagstrom, Inc., TN
A 57	Japonica Water Gardens, OR
A 58	Junglemania, CA
A 60	Kelly's Plant World, CA
A 76	Nature's Curiosity Shop, CA
A 81	Old House Gardens, MI
A 84	Paradise Water Gardens, MA
A 84	Park Seed Company, SC
A 88	Pinetree Garden Seeds, ME
A 88	Plant Delights Nursery, NC
A 89	The Plumeria People, TX
A 90	Powell's Gardens, NC
A 105	Slocum Water Gardens, FL
A 117	Tropic to Tropic Plants, BC
A 118	Valhalla Nursery, CA
A 118	Van Bourgondien Bros., NY

CANTALOUPES
A 14	D. V. Burrell Seed Growers Co., CO
A 97	Roswell Seed Company, NM
A 119	Vermont Bean Seed Co., VT
A 123	Willhite Seed Co., TX

CARAMBOLA
A 118	Valley Vista Kiwi, CA

CARNATIONS
See Dianthus

CARNIVOROUS PLANTS
See also specific plants
A 10	Black Copper Kits, NJ
A 16	California Carnivores, CA
A 42	Glasshouse Works, OH
A 54	Indigo Marsh, SC
A 57	Japonica Water Gardens, OR
A 62	Gerhard Koehres Cactus & Succulent Nursery, Ge
A 65	Lee's Botanical Garden, FL
A 82	Orgel's Orchids, FL
A 86	Peter Pauls Nurseries, NY
A 88	Plant Delights Nursery, NC
A 92	Randy's Nursery & Greenhouses, GA
A 97	Doug & Vivi Rowland, En

CARNIVOROUS PLANTS (continued)
A 104	Silverhill Seeds, So
A 105	Slocum Water Gardens, FL
A 117	Tropic to Tropic Plants, BC
A 122	Wild Earth Native Plant Nursery, NJ
A 126	Roy Young, Seeds, En

CARPINUS
See Hornbeams

CAUDICIFORMS
A 1	Abbey Gardens, CA
A 7	The Banana Tree, PA
A 46	Grigsby Cactus Gardens, CA
A 53	Jerry Horne Rare Plants, FL
A 58	Joe's Nursery, CA
A 59	K & L Cactus & Succulent Nursery, CA
A 67	Living Stones Nursery, AZ
A 72	Miles' to Go, AZ
A 79	Northridge Gardens, CA
A 92	Rare Plant Research, OR
A 110	Succulenta, CA
A 111	Sunrise Nursery, TX
A 125	Guy Wrinkle Exotic Plants, CA

CEANOTHUS
A 16	Callahan Seeds, OR
A 21	Colvos Creek Nursery, WA
A 29	Digging Dog Nursery, CA
A 38	Forestfarm, OR
A 64	Las Pilitas Nursery, CA
A 79	Northplan/Mountain Seed, ID
A 85	Theodore Payne Foundation, CA

CERCIS
See Redbuds

CESTRUMS
A 13	Buena Creek Gardens, CA
A 46	Harborcrest Gardens, BC
A 59	Kartuz Greenhouses, CA
A 67	Logee's Greenhouses, CT
A 106	Southern Perennials & Herbs, MS
A 113	Theatrum Botanicum, CA

CHERIMOYAS
A 40	Fruit Spirit Botanical Gardens, Au
A 40	Garden of Delights, FL
A 65	Legendary Ethnobotanical Resources, FL
A 82	Oregon Exotics Rare Fruit Nursery, OR
A 83	Pacific Tree Farms, CA
A 118	Valley Vista Kiwi, CA

CHERRIES
A 1	Adams County Nursery, Inc., PA
A 20	Cloud Mountain Nursery, WA
A 45	Greenmantle Nursery, CA
A 55	Inner Coast Nursery, BC
A 58	Johnson Nursery, Inc., GA
A 92	Raintree Nursery, WA
A 97	St. Lawrence Nurseries, NY
A 105	Sonoma Antique Apple Nursery, CA

Page	Source

Page	Source

COLCHICUMS (continued)
A 68   McClure & Zimmerman, WI
A 73   Monocot Nursery, En
A 89   Potterton & Martin, En
A 105 Siskiyou Rare Plant Nursery, OR

COLEUS
A 6   Avant Gardens, MA
A 21   Color Farm Growers, FL
A 42   Glasshouse Works, OH
A 49   Heronswood Nursery, WA
A 114 Thompson & Morgan, NJ

COLUMBINES
See Aquilegias

COLUMNEAS
A 9   Belisle's Violet House, WI
A 64   Lauray of Salisbury, CT
A 68   Lyndon Lyon Greenhouses, Inc., NY
A 68   McKinney's Glassehouse, KS
A 80   Oak Hill Gardens, IL
A 84   Pat's Pets, MO
A 114 Tiki Nursery, NC

CONIFERS
See also specific plants
A 5   Appalachian Gardens, PA
A 5   Arborvillage Nursery, MO
A 8   Beaver Creek Nursery, TN
A 16   Callahan Seeds, OR
A 19   Cascade Forestry Nursery, IA
A 20   Chiltern Seeds, En
A 21   Coenosium Gardens, WA
A 21   Colvos Creek Nursery, WA
A 27   Deep Diversity, NM
A 31   Eastern Plant Specialties, ME
A 32   Ellison Horticultural Pty., Ltd., Au
A 33   Evergreen Gardenworks, CA
A 34   Fairweather Gardens, NJ
A 34   Fantastic Plants, TN
A 38   Forest Seeds of California, CA
A 38   Forestfarm, OR
A 38   Fraser's Thimble Farm, BC
A 42   Girard Nurseries, OH
A 45   Greer Gardens, OR
A 49   Heronswood Nursery, WA
A 59   Kasch Nursery, OR
A 62   Kumar International, In
A 74   Musser Forests Inc., PA
A 76   Neon Palm Nursery, CA
A 79   Northplan/Mountain Seed, ID
A 83   D. Orriell -- Seed Exporters, Au
A 83   Owen Farms, TN
A 83   Pacific Tree Farms, CA
A 88   Plants of the Southwest, NM
A 89   Porterhowse Farms, OR
A 97   Roslyn Nursery, NY
A 98   Sandy Mush Herb Nursery, NC
A 100 F. W. Schumacher Co., Inc., MA
A 103 Sheffield's Seed Co., Inc., NY
A 104 Sierra Seed Supply, CA
A 122 Western Native Seed, CO

CONIFERS (continued)
A 123 Wildwood Farm, CA
A 124 Windrose Ltd., PA

CONIFERS, AUSTRALIAN
A 83   D. Orriell -- Seed Exporters, Au

CONIFERS, DWARF
A 6   Arrowhead Alpines, MI
A 8   Beaver Creek Nursery, TN
A 13   Broken Arrow Nursery, CT
A 16   Camellia Forest Nursery, NC
A 20   Cloud Mountain Nursery, WA
A 21   Coenosium Gardens, WA
A 21   Collector's Nursery, WA
A 23   Corn Hill Nursery, NB
A 25   The Cummins Garden, NJ
A 27   Daystar, ME
A 29   Dilworth Nursery, PA
A 31   Eastern Plant Specialties, ME
A 33   Evergreen Gardenworks, CA
A 34   Fairweather Gardens, NJ
A 34   Fantastic Plants, TN
A 38   Forestfarm, OR
A 42   Girard Nurseries, OH
A 42   Glasshouse Works, OH
A 45   Greer Gardens, OR
A 49   Heronswood Nursery, WA
A 58   Joy Creek Nursery, OR
A 59   Kasch Nursery, OR
A 70   Matsu-Momiji Nursery, WV
A 70   Meehan's Miniatures, MD
A 73   Miniature Plant Kingdom, CA
A 88   Plant Delights Nursery, NC
A 89   Porterhowse Farms, OR
A 90   Powell's Gardens, NC
A 97   Roslyn Nursery, NY
A 103 Shepherd Hill Farm, NY
A 105 Siskiyou Rare Plant Nursery, OR
A 108 Squaw Mountain Gardens, OR
A 120 Wavecrest Nursery & Landscaping Co., MI
A 123 Wildwood Farm, CA

CONIFERS, SEEDLING
A 17   Carino Nurseries, PA
A 21   Cold Stream Farm, MI
A 36   Flickingers' Nursery, PA
A 42   Girard Nurseries, OH
A 70   Mellinger's, Inc., OH
A 74   Musser Forests Inc., PA
A 89   Plants of the Wild, WA
A 105 Smith Nursery Co., IA

CONOPHYTUMS
A 67   Living Stones Nursery, AZ
A 71   Mesa Garden, NM

CORAL BELLS
See Heucheras

CORN
A 14   D. V. Burrell Seed Growers Co., CO
A 30   E & R Seed, IN

Page	Source		Page	Source

CORN (continued)

A 66	Liberty Seed Company, OH
A 73	Morgan County Wholesale, MO
A 77	Nichols Garden Nursery, Inc., OR
A 104	Siegers Seed Co., MI
A 110	Stokes Seed, Inc., NY
A 123	Willhite Seed Co., TX

CORN, HEIRLOOM

A 1	Abundant Life Seed Foundation, WA
A 27	Deep Diversity, NM
A 48	Heirloom Seed Project, PA
A 53	Horus Botanicals, Ethnobotanical Seeds, AR
A 66	Liberty Seed Company, OH
A 76	Native Seeds/SEARCH, AZ
A 88	Plants of the Southwest, NM
A 93	Redwood City Seed Co., CA
A 101	Seeds Blum, ID
A 101	Seeds of Change, NM
A 101	Seeds West Garden Seeds, NM
A 104	R. H. Shumway Seedsman, SC
A 106	Southern Exposure Seed Exchange(R), VA

CORNUS

See Dogwoods

CORYDALIS

A 6	Arrowhead Alpines, MI
A 6	Avant Gardens, MA
A 6	Avon Bulbs, En
A 20	Paul Christian -- Rare Plants, Wa
A 21	Collector's Nursery, WA
A 38	Forestfarm, OR
A 38	Fraser's Thimble Farm, BC
A 41	Gardenimport, Inc., ON
A 45	Greer Gardens, OR
A 49	Heronswood Nursery, WA
A 54	W. E. Th. Ingwersen, Ltd., En
A 56	Jackson & Perkins Co., OR
A 57	Jelitto Perennial Seeds, USA Office, KY
A 64	Laurie's Landscape, IL
A 74	Mt. Tahoma Nursery, WA
A 88	Plant Delights Nursery, NC
A 88	Plant World Seeds, En
A 89	Potterton & Martin, En
A 90	Powell's Gardens, NC
A 91	The Primrose Path, PA
A 97	Roslyn Nursery, NY
A 105	Siskiyou Rare Plant Nursery, OR
A 117	Underwood Shade Nursery, MA
A 121	Wayside Gardens, SC
A 122	White Flower Farm, CT
A 125	Woodside Gardens, WA

CORYPHANTHAS

A 71	Mesa Garden, NM
A 88	Plantasia Cactus Gardens, ID
A 103	Shein's Cactus, CA

COTINUS

A 5	Arborvillage Nursery, MO
A 43	Gossler Farms Nursery, OR
A 45	Greer Gardens, OR

COTINUS (continued)

A 49	Heronswood Nursery, WA
A 77	New Gardens, NJ
A 105	Smith Nursery Co., IA
A 124	Windrose Ltd., PA

COVER CROPS

A 12	Bountiful Gardens, CA
A 26	William Dam Seeds, ON
A 30	E & R Seed, IN
A 34	Fedco Seeds & Moose Tubers, ME
A 35	Filaree Farm, WA
A 40	Garden City Seeds, MT
A 58	Johnny's Selected Seeds, ME
A 62	Kumar International, In
A 64	Ledden Brothers, NJ
A 70	Mellinger's, Inc., OH
A 73	Morgan County Wholesale, MO
A 86	Phoenix Seed, Au
A 96	Ronniger's Seed Potatoes, WA
A 101	Seeds of Change, NM
A 104	R. H. Shumway Seedsman, SC
B 28	Snow Pond Farm Supply, ME
A 109	Stock Seed Farms, Inc., NE
A 113	Territorial Seed Company, OR

CRABAPPLES

A 5	Arborvillage Nursery, MO
A 8	Bay Laurel Nursery, CA
A 18	Carroll Gardens, MD
A 33	Evergreen Gardenworks, CA
A 34	Fairweather Gardens, NJ
A 38	Forestfarm, OR
A 42	Girard Nurseries, OH
A 45	Greer Gardens, OR
A 69	Martin & Kraus, ON
A 70	Mary's Plant Farm & Landscaping, OH
A 73	Miniature Plant Kingdom, CA
A 79	Northwind Nursery & Orchards, MN
A 100	F. W. Schumacher Co., Inc., MA
A 105	Smith Nursery Co., IA

CRANBERRIES

A 20	Cloud Mountain Nursery, WA
A 28	DeGrandchamp's Farms, MI
A 32	Edible Landscaping, VA
A 47	Hartmann's Plantation, Inc., MI
A 72	J. E. Miller Nurseries, Inc., NY
A 79	Northwoods Nursery, OR
A 97	St. Lawrence Nurseries, NY

CRAPE MYRTLES

A 5	Appalachian Gardens, PA
A 7	Barber Nursery, TX
A 8	Beaver Creek Nursery, TN
A 18	Carroll Gardens, MD
A 20	Coastal Gardens & Nursery, SC
A 34	Fairweather Gardens, NJ
A 38	Forestfarm, OR
A 45	Greer Gardens, OR
A 83	Owen Farms, TN
A 97	Roslyn Nursery, NY
A 116	Transplant Nursery, GA

Page	Source

CRAPE MYRTLES (continued)
A 124 Windrose Ltd., PA

CRASSULAS
A 1 Abbey Gardens, CA
A 64 Lauray of Salisbury, CT
A 71 Mesa Garden, NM
A 76 Nature's Curiosity Shop, CA

CRINUMS
A 20 Paul Christian -- Rare Plants, Wa
A 54 Indigo Marsh, SC
A 60 Kelly's Plant World, CA
A 76 Nature's Curiosity Shop, CA
A 81 Old House Gardens, MI
A 87 Pine Heights Nursery, Au
A 89 The Plumeria People, TX
A 97 Rust-En-Vrede Nursery, So
A 116 Trans Pacific Nursery, OR
A 118 Valhalla Nursery, CA

CROCOSMIA
A 6 Avon Bulbs, En
A 25 The Crownsville Nursery, MD
A 29 Digging Dog Nursery, CA
A 34 Fairweather Gardens, NJ
A 43 Gossler Farms Nursery, OR
A 45 Greer Gardens, OR
A 54 Indigo Marsh, SC
A 58 Joy Creek Nursery, OR
A 68 McClure & Zimmerman, WI
A 87 Pine Heights Nursery, Au
A 92 Randy's Nursery & Greenhouses, GA
A 106 Southern Perennials & Herbs, MS
A 125 Woodside Gardens, WA

CROCUS
A 4 Jacques Amand, Bulb Specialists, MD
A 12 Breck's, IL
A 15 C K S, Cz
A 20 Paul Christian -- Rare Plants, Wa
A 26 The Daffodil Mart, CT
A 30 Dutch Gardens, NJ
A 39 French's Bulb Importer, VT
A 41 Gardenimport, Inc., ON
A 68 McClure & Zimmerman, WI
A 73 Monocot Nursery, En
A 74 Charles H. Mueller Co., PA
A 81 Old House Gardens, MI
A 89 Potterton & Martin, En
A 99 John Scheepers, Inc., CT
A 99 Schipper & Co., CT
A 118 Van Bourgondien Bros., NY
A 118 Van Dyck's Flower Farms, Inc., NY
A 118 Van Engelen, Inc., CT

CROWN VETCH
A 61 Kester's Wild Game Food Nurseries, WI
A 74 Musser Forests Inc., PA

CRYPTANTHUS
A 71 Michael's Bromeliads, FL
A 106 Southern Exposure, TX

CUPHEAS
A 13 Buena Creek Gardens, CA
A 42 Glasshouse Works, OH
A 67 Logee's Greenhouses, CT
A 106 Southern Perennials & Herbs, MS
A 118 Valhalla Nursery, CA

CURRANTS
A 8 Bear Creek Nursery, WA
A 19 Chehalem Creek Nursery, OR
A 20 Cloud Mountain Nursery, WA
A 47 Hartmann's Plantation, Inc., MI
A 50 Hidden Springs Nursery -- Edible Landscaping, TN
A 79 Northwoods Nursery, OR
A 85 Pense Nursery, AR
A 89 Plumtree Nursery, NY
A 92 Raintree Nursery, WA
A 97 St. Lawrence Nurseries, NY
A 107 Southmeadow Fruit Gardens, MI
A 122 Whitman Farms, OR

CYCADS
See also specific plants
A 7 The Banana Tree, PA
A 25 Cycad Gardens, CA
A 32 Ellison Horticultural Pty., Ltd., Au
A 53 Jerry Horne Rare Plants, FL
A 58 Joe's Nursery, CA
A 59 Kapoho Palms, HI
A 62 Gerhard Koehres Cactus & Succulent Nursery, Ge
A 67 Living Stones Nursery, AZ
A 76 Neon Palm Nursery, CA
A 83 D. Orriell -- Seed Exporters, Au
A 97 Doug & Vivi Rowland, En
A 107 Southern Shade, FL
A 117 Tropiflora, FL
A 125 Guy Wrinkle Exotic Plants, CA

CYCLAMEN, HARDY
A 4 Jacques Amand, Bulb Specialists, MD
A 5 Jim & Jenny Archibald, Wa
A 6 Arrowhead Alpines, MI
A 6 Ashwood Nurseries, En
A 6 Avon Bulbs, En
A 15 CTDA, En
A 20 Chiltern Seeds, En
A 20 Paul Christian -- Rare Plants, Wa
A 30 Dunford Farms, WA
A 38 Fraser's Thimble Farm, BC
A 43 Russell Graham, Purveyor of Plants, OR
A 46 Hansen Nursery, OR
A 73 Monocot Nursery, En
A 77 Nicholls Gardens, VA
A 78 North Green Seeds, En
A 89 Potterton & Martin, En
A 101 Seeds of Distinction, ON
A 114 Tile Barn Nursery, En

CYPRIPEDIUMS
A 6 Arrowhead Alpines, MI
A 38 Fraser's Thimble Farm, BC
A 41 Gardens of the Blue Ridge, NC
A 82 Orchid Gardens, MN

Page	Source

Page	Source	Page	Source

DAYLILIES (continued)

A 65	Lee Gardens, IL
A 68	McClure & Zimmerman, WI
A 69	McMillen's Iris Garden, ON
A 69	Maple Tree Garden, NE
A 71	Mid-America Garden, OK
A 72	Miller's Manor Gardens, IN
A 75	Nancy's Daylilies & Perennials, PA
A 77	Nicholls Gardens, VA
A 78	North Pine Iris Gardens, NE
A 78	Northern Grown Perennials, WI
A 80	Oakes Daylilies, TN
A 80	Olallie Daylily Gardens, VT
A 81	Olympic Coast Garden, WA
A 84	Parkland Perennials, AB
A 87	Pinecliffe Daylily Gardens, IN
A 90	Powell's Gardens, NC
A 95	Rollingwood Garden, FL
A 99	Schmid Nursery & Garden, MI
A 100	R. Seawright Daylilies & Hostas, MA
A 106	Soules Garden, IN
A 106	Southern Perennials & Herbs, MS
A 109	Stark Gardens, IA
A 111	Sunnyridge Gardens, TN
A 112	Swann's Daylily Garden, GA
A 113	Terra Nova Gardening, MN
A 116	Tranquil Lake Nursery, MA
A 118	Valente Gardens, ME
A 118	Van Bourgondien Bros., NY
A 119	Andre Viette Farm & Nursery, VA
A 120	Walnut Hill Gardens, IA
A 122	Gilbert H. Wild & Son, Inc., MO
A 125	York Hill Farm, MA

DELPHINIUMS

A 2	Aimers Seeds, ON
A 18	Carroll Gardens, MD
A 28	Digger's Club, Au
A 29	Donaroma's Nursery, MA
A 41	Gardens North, ON
A 43	Graceful Gardens, NY
A 47	Hauser's Superior View Farm, WI
A 57	Jelitto Perennial Seeds, USA Office, KY
A 64	Le Jardin du Gourmet, VT
A 68	L.J. McCreary & Co. Perennial Seeds, TX
A 71	Milaeger's Gardens, WI
A 100	The Seed Guild, Sc
A 112	Surry Gardens, ME
A 114	Thompson & Morgan, NJ
A 121	Weiss Brothers Nursery, CA
A 122	White Flower Farm, CT

DESERT PLANTS

See also specific plants

A 6	Aztekakti, TX
A 28	Desert Citizens, CO
A 28	Desert Moon Nursery, NM
A 52	Homan Brothers Seed, AZ
A 55	Intermountain Cactus, UT
A 59	K & L Cactus & Succulent Nursery, CA
A 64	Las Pilitas Nursery, CA
A 67	Loehman's Cacti & Succulents, CA
A 71	Midwest Cactus, MO

DESERT PLANTS (continued)

A 76	Native Seeds/SEARCH, AZ
A 85	Theodore Payne Foundation, CA
A 97	Doug & Vivi Rowland, En
A 107	Southwestern Exposure, AZ
A 107	Southwestern Native Seeds, AZ
A 125	Guy Wrinkle Exotic Plants, CA

DIANTHUS

A 2	Aimers Seeds, ON
A 5	Appalachian Wildflower Nursery, PA
A 6	Arrowhead Alpines, MI
A 7	B & T World Seeds, Fr
A 11	Bluestone Perennials, OH
A 15	Busse Gardens, MN
A 16	Canyon Creek Nursery, CA
A 18	Carroll Gardens, MD
A 23	Coombland Gardens & Nursery, En
A 29	Donaroma's Nursery, MA
A 31	Edgewood Farm & Nursery, VA
A 33	Euroseeds, Cz
A 33	Evergreen Gardenworks, CA
A 37	Flower Scent Gardens, OH
A 37	Foothill Cottage Gardens, CA
A 38	The Fragrant Path, NE
A 41	Garden Place, OH
A 43	Goodwin Creek Gardens, OR
A 50	High Country Gardens, NM
A 50	Highfield Garden, WA
A 53	Hortico, Inc., ON
A 57	Jelitto Perennial Seeds, USA Office, KY
A 58	Joy Creek Nursery, OR
A 70	Meadow View Farms, OR
A 73	Miniature Plant Kingdom, CA
A 89	Porterhowse Farms, OR
A 90	Powell's Gardens, NC
A 92	Rainforest Gardens, BC
A 95	Rocky Mountain Rare Plants, CO
A 98	Sandy Mush Herb Nursery, NC
A 100	The Seed Guild, Sc
A 102	Select Seeds -- Antique Flowers, CT
A 104	Silverhill Seeds, So
A 105	Siskiyou Rare Plant Nursery, OR
A 106	Southern Perennials & Herbs, MS
A 111	Sunnyslope Gardens, CA
A 112	Surry Gardens, ME
A 116	Trennoll Nursery, OH
A 121	Well-Sweep Herb Farm, NJ
A 125	Woodside Gardens, WA
A 125	Wrenwood of Berkeley Springs, WV
A 125	Wrightman Alpines, ON

DIGITALIS

A 6	Arrowhead Alpines, MI
A 18	Carroll Gardens, MD
A 20	Chiltern Seeds, En
A 37	Flowery Branch Seed Company, GA
A 41	Gardens North, ON
A 47	Hauser's Superior View Farm, WI
A 53	J. L. Hudson, Seedsman, CA
A 58	Joy Creek Nursery, OR
A 88	Plant World Seeds, En
A 114	Thompson & Morgan, NJ

Page	Source

DYE PLANTS
A 22	Companion Plants, OH
A 37	Flowery Branch Seed Company, GA
A 43	Goodwin Creek Gardens, OR
A 49	The Herb Garden, NC
A 53	J. L. Hudson, Seedsman, CA
A 74	Mountain Valley Growers, Inc., CA
A 76	Native Seeds/SEARCH, AZ
A 86	Perennial Pleasures Nursery, VT
A 93	Rasland Farm, NC
A 94	Richters Herbs, ON
A 98	Sandy Mush Herb Nursery, NC
A 114	The Thyme Garden, OR

EARTH-STARS
See Cryptanthus

ECHEVERIAS
A 1	Abbey Gardens, CA
A 59	K & L Cactus & Succulent Nursery, CA
A 64	Lauray of Salisbury, CT
A 108	Squaw Mountain Gardens, OR

ECHINACEAS
A 11	Bluestem Prairie Nursery, IL
A 31	Edgewood Farm & Nursery, VA
A 32	Elixir Farm Botanicals, LLC, MO
A 41	Gardens North, ON
A 42	Good Scents, ID
A 55	Ion Exchange, IA
A 57	Jelitto Perennial Seeds, USA Office, KY
A 75	Native Gardens, TN
A 77	Niche Gardens, NC
A 86	Perennial Pleasures Nursery, VT
A 87	Pine Ridge Gardens, AR
A 90	Powell's Gardens, NC
A 90	Prairie Moon Nursery, MN
A 91	Prairie Nursery, WI
A 91	Prairie Ridge Nursery/CRM Ecosystems, Inc., WI
A 93	Redwood City Seed Co., CA
A 94	Richters Herbs, ON
A 101	Seeds of Change, NM
A 111	Sunlight Gardens, TN
A 114	The Thyme Garden, OR
A 122	Western Native Seed, CO
A 125	Woodlanders, Inc., SC

ECHINOCEREUS
A 3	Alplains, CO
A 6	Aztekakti, TX
A 28	Desert Moon Nursery, NM
A 55	Intermountain Cactus, UT
A 71	Mesa Garden, NM
A 97	Doug & Vivi Rowland, En
A 111	Sunrise Nursery, TX
A 126	Roy Young, Seeds, En

ELDERBERRIES
A 2	Agroforestry Research Trust, En
A 5	Arborvillage Nursery, MO
A 32	Edible Landscaping, VA
A 38	Forestfarm, OR
A 43	Gossler Farms Nursery, OR

ELDERBERRIES (continued)
A 49	Heronswood Nursery, WA
A 82	Oregon Exotics Rare Fruit Nursery, OR
A 85	Pense Nursery, AR

ELMS
A 5	Arborvillage Nursery, MO
A 38	Forestfarm, OR
A 70	Meehan's Miniatures, MD
A 73	Miniature Plant Kingdom, CA
A 98	Sandy Mush Herb Nursery, NC
A 105	Siskiyou Rare Plant Nursery, OR

EPHEDRAS
A 3	Alplains, CO
A 44	Great Basin Natives, UT
A 88	Plant Delights Nursery, NC
A 101	Seedhunt, CA

EPIMEDIUMS
A 4	Ambergate Gardens, MN
A 15	Busse Gardens, MN
A 18	Carroll Gardens, MD
A 19	Cattail Meadows, Ltd., OH
A 21	Collector's Nursery, WA
A 29	Digging Dog Nursery, CA
A 31	Eco-Gardens, GA
A 34	Fairweather Gardens, NJ
A 35	Fieldstone Gardens, Inc., ME
A 38	Forestfarm, OR
A 41	Garden Vision, MA
A 41	Gardenimport, Inc., ON
A 43	Russell Graham, Purveyor of Plants, OR
A 45	Greer Gardens, OR
A 49	Heronswood Nursery, WA
A 50	Highfield Garden, WA
A 52	Homestead Division of Sunnybrook Farms, OH
A 56	Ivy Garth Perennials, OH
A 58	Joy Creek Nursery, OR
A 65	Lee Gardens, IL
A 70	Meadow View Farms, OR
A 74	Mt. Tahoma Nursery, WA
A 76	Naylor Creek Nursery, WA
A 90	Powell's Gardens, NC
A 91	The Primrose Path, PA
A 92	Rainforest Gardens, BC
A 93	Reflective Gardens, WA
A 95	Robyn's Nest Nursery, WA
A 97	Roslyn Nursery, NY
A 102	Shady Oaks Nursery, MN
A 105	Siskiyou Rare Plant Nursery, OR
A 105	Sleepy Hollow Herb Farm, KY
A 116	Trennoll Nursery, OH
A 119	Andre Viette Farm & Nursery, VA
A 121	We-Du Nurseries, NC
A 125	Woodlanders, Inc., SC

EPIPHYLLUMS
A 28	Desert Theatre, CA
A 33	Epi World, CA
A 42	Golden Lake Greenhouses, CA
A 43	Gray/Davis Epiphyllums, CA
A 46	Harborcrest Gardens, BC

Page	Source

Page	Source

EUONYMUS (continued)

A 62	Klehm Nursery, IL
A 85	Peekskill Nurseries, NY
A 89	Porterhowse Farms, OR
A 97	Roslyn Nursery, NY
A 103	Sheffield's Seed Co., Inc., NY
A 124	Windrose Ltd., PA

EUPHORBIAS, BORDER

A 6	Arrowhead Alpines, MI
A 16	Canyon Creek Nursery, CA
A 18	Carroll Gardens, MD
A 20	Chiltern Seeds, En
A 29	Digging Dog Nursery, CA
A 38	Forestfarm, OR
A 43	Gossler Farms Nursery, OR
A 45	Greer Gardens, OR
A 49	Heronswood Nursery, WA
A 50	Highfield Garden, WA
A 57	Jelitto Perennial Seeds, USA Office, KY
A 58	Joy Creek Nursery, OR
A 70	Meadow View Farms, OR
A 88	The Plant Farm, BC
A 88	Plant World Seeds, En
A 92	Rainforest Gardens, BC
A 125	Woodside Gardens, WA

EUPHORBIAS, SUCCULENT

A 1	Abbey Gardens, CA
A 20	Chiltern Seeds, En
A 28	Desert Theatre, CA
A 42	Glasshouse Works, OH
A 46	Grigsby Cactus Gardens, CA
A 58	Joe's Nursery, CA
A 59	K & L Cactus & Succulent Nursery, CA
A 62	Gerhard Koehres Cactus & Succulent Nursery, Ge
A 67	Living Stones Nursery, AZ
A 67	Loehman's Cacti & Succulents, CA
A 79	Northridge Gardens, CA
A 92	Rare Plant Research, OR
A 106	South Bay Growers, FL
A 110	Succulenta, CA
A 111	Sunrise Nursery, TX
A 125	Guy Wrinkle Exotic Plants, CA

EVERLASTING FLOWERS

A 2	Aimers Seeds, ON
A 22	Companion Plants, OH
A 25	Dacha Barinka, BC
A 26	William Dam Seeds, ON
A 34	Fedco Seeds & Moose Tubers, ME
A 37	Flowery Branch Seed Company, GA
A 40	Garden City Seeds, MT
A 43	Goodwin Creek Gardens, OR
A 49	The Herb Garden, NC
A 53	J. L. Hudson, Seedsman, CA
A 56	It's About Thyme, TX
A 58	Johnny's Selected Seeds, ME
A 65	Lewis Mountain Herbs & Everlastings, OH
A 74	Mountain Valley Growers, Inc., CA
A 83	D. Orriell -- Seed Exporters, Au
A 88	Pinetree Garden Seeds, ME
A 91	Prairie Oak Seeds, MO

EVERLASTING FLOWERS (continued)

A 94	Richters Herbs, ON
A 96	Rose Hill Herbs and Perennials, VA
A 98	Sandy Mush Herb Nursery, NC
A 101	Seeds Blum, ID
A 101	Seeds West Garden Seeds, NM
A 103	Shepherd's Garden Seeds, CT
A 104	Silverhill Seeds, So
A 105	Sleepy Hollow Herb Farm, KY
A 106	South Cove Nursery, NS
A 110	Stokes Seed, Inc., NY
A 114	Thompson & Morgan, NJ
A 114	The Thyme Garden, OR
A 119	Vesey's Seeds, Ltd., PE
A 121	Well-Sweep Herb Farm, NJ

FAGUS
See Beeches

FERNS

A 10	Kurt Bluemel, Inc., MD
A 37	Foliage Gardens, WA
A 42	Glasshouse Works, OH
A 53	Jerry Horne Rare Plants, FL
A 65	Lee's Botanical Garden, FL
A 67	Logee's Greenhouses, CT
A 76	Neon Palm Nursery, CA
A 84	Palm Hammock Orchid Estate, FL

FERNS, HARDY

A 6	Arrowhead Alpines, MI
A 10	Kurt Bluemel, Inc., MD
A 15	Busse Gardens, MN
A 18	Carroll Gardens, MD
A 20	Coastal Gardens & Nursery, SC
A 21	Collector's Nursery, WA
A 25	The Crownsville Nursery, MD
A 27	Daystar, ME
A 31	Eastern Plant Specialties, ME
A 31	Eco-Gardens, GA
A 34	Fancy Fronds, WA
A 34	Fantastic Plants, TN
A 37	Foliage Gardens, WA
A 38	Forestfarm, OR
A 38	Fraser's Thimble Farm, BC
A 41	Gardens of the Blue Ridge, NC
A 43	Russell Graham, Purveyor of Plants, OR
A 45	Greer Gardens, OR
A 52	Homestead Division of Sunnybrook Farms, OH
A 52	Homestead Farms, MO
A 53	Hortico, Inc., ON
A 65	Lee Gardens, IL
A 70	Mary's Plant Farm & Landscaping, OH
A 71	Milaeger's Gardens, WI
A 75	Native Gardens, TN
A 76	Nature's Garden, OR
A 76	Nature's Nook, MS
A 80	Oakridge Nurseries, NH
A 82	Orchid Gardens, MN
A 83	Owen Farms, TN
A 88	Plant Delights Nursery, NC
A 88	The Plant Farm, BC
A 90	Powell's Gardens, NC

Page	Source

FRANKLINIA (continued)
A 111 Sunlight Gardens, TN
A 120 Wavecrest Nursery & Landscaping Co., MI
A 125 Woodlanders, Inc., SC

FRAXINUS
See Ashes

FREESIAS
A 30 Jim Duggan Flower Nursery, CA
A 39 French's Bulb Importer, VT
A 68 McClure & Zimmerman, WI
A 87 Pine Heights Nursery, Au
A 97 Rust-En-Vrede Nursery, So
A 99 John Scheepers, Inc., CT
A 110 Sunburst Bulbs C.C., So

FRITILLARIAS
A 4 Jacques Amand, Bulb Specialists, MD
A 5 Jim & Jenny Archibald, Wa
A 6 Avon Bulbs, En
A 15 C K S, Cz
A 20 Paul Christian -- Rare Plants, Wa
A 23 Coombland Gardens & Nursery, En
A 26 The Daffodil Mart, CT
A 33 Euroseeds, Cz
A 39 French's Bulb Importer, VT
A 41 Gardenimport, Inc., ON
A 68 McClure & Zimmerman, WI
A 74 Charles H. Mueller Co., PA
A 78 North Green Seeds, En
A 89 Potterton & Martin, En
A 94 Robinett Bulb Farm, CA
A 99 John Scheepers, Inc., CT
A 118 Van Engelen, Inc., CT

FRUIT TREES
See also specific fruits
A 1 Adams County Nursery, Inc., PA
A 4 Ames' Orchard & Nursery, AR
A 8 Bay Laurel Nursery, CA
A 8 Bear Creek Nursery, WA
A 14 W. Atlee Burpee & Company, PA
A 16 Campberry Farms, ON
A 23 Corn Hill Nursery, NB
A 30 Earth's Rising Trees, OR
A 34 Fedco Seeds & Moose Tubers, ME
A 35 Henry Field Seed & Nursery Co., IA
A 45 Greer Gardens, OR
A 46 Gurney's Seed & Nursery Co., SD
A 47 Hartmann's Plantation, Inc., MI
A 55 Inner Coast Nursery, BC
A 58 J. W. Jung Seed Co., WI
A 59 Just Fruits, FL
A 64 Lawson's Nursery, GA
A 69 Martin & Kraus, ON
A 70 Mellinger's, Inc., OH
A 72 J. E. Miller Nurseries, Inc., NY
A 79 Northwind Nursery & Orchards, MN
A 79 Northwoods Nursery, OR
A 83 Pacific Tree Farms, CA
A 92 Raintree Nursery, WA
A 95 Rocky Meadow Orchard & Nursery, IN

FRUIT TREES (continued)
A 97 St. Lawrence Nurseries, NY
A 109 Stark Bro's Nurseries & Orchards Co., MO
A 113 T & T Seeds, Ltd., MB

FRUIT TREES, ANTIQUE
A 4 Ames' Orchard & Nursery, AR
A 45 Greenmantle Nursery, CA
A 55 Inner Coast Nursery, BC
A 64 Lawson's Nursery, GA
A 65 Henry Leuthardt Nurseries, Inc., NY
A 79 Northwind Nursery & Orchards, MN
A 95 Rocky Meadow Orchard & Nursery, IN
A 107 Southmeadow Fruit Gardens, MI

FRUIT TREES, DWARF
A 1 Adams County Nursery, Inc., PA
A 8 Bay Laurel Nursery, CA
A 38 Four Winds Growers, CA
A 65 Henry Leuthardt Nurseries, Inc., NY
A 95 Rocky Meadow Orchard & Nursery, IN
A 107 Southmeadow Fruit Gardens, MI

FRUIT TREES, ESPALIERED
A 65 Henry Leuthardt Nurseries, Inc., NY

FRUIT TREES, LOW-CHILL
A 8 Bay Laurel Nursery, CA

FRUIT, NEW VARIETIES
See also specific fruits
A 1 Adams County Nursery, Inc., PA
A 4 Ames' Orchard & Nursery, AR
A 8 Bay Laurel Nursery, CA
A 14 Burnt Ridge Nursery, WA
A 25 Cummins Nursery, NY
A 45 Greenmantle Nursery, CA
A 92 Raintree Nursery, WA
A 95 Rocky Meadow Orchard & Nursery, IN
A 104 Sherwood's Greenhouses, LA

FRUIT, TROPICAL
See also specific fruits
A 7 B & T World Seeds, Fr
A 7 The Banana Tree, PA
A 12 The Borneo Collection, Au
A 32 Ellison Horticultural Pty., Ltd., Au
A 33 Exotica Rare Fruit Nursery, CA
A 40 Fruit Spirit Botanical Gardens, Au
A 40 Garden of Delights, FL
A 65 Legendary Ethnobotanical Resources, FL
A 83 Pacific Tree Farms, CA
A 92 Rainforest Seed Company, Co
A 92 Raintree Nursery, WA
A 111 Sunny Land Seeds (Semillas Solanas), CO
A 118 Valley Vista Kiwi, CA

FRUITS, UNCOMMON
A 7 The Banana Tree, PA
A 8 Bear Creek Nursery, WA
A 12 The Borneo Collection, Au
A 14 Burnt Ridge Nursery, WA
A 32 Edible Landscaping, VA

Page	Source

Page	Source

HAWORTHIAS (continued)
A 79	Northridge Gardens, CA
A 92	Rainbow Gardens Nursery & Bookshop, CA
A 103	Shein's Cactus, CA
A 106	South Bay Growers, FL
A 107	Southwestern Exposure, AZ
A 110	Succulenta, CA
A 111	Sunrise Nursery, TX

HAZELNUTS
A 14	Burnt Ridge Nursery, WA
A 19	Cascade Forestry Nursery, IA
A 46	Grimo Nut Nursery, ON
A 80	Oikos Tree Crops, MI
A 105	Smith Nursery Co., IA

HEATHERS
See also specific plants
A 6	Arrowhead Alpines, MI
A 18	Carroll Gardens, MD
A 27	Daystar, ME
A 31	Eastern Plant Specialties, ME
A 33	Ericaceae, CT
A 48	The Heather Garden, ME
A 48	Heather Heaven, CA
A 48	Heaths & Heathers, WA
A 83	D. Orriell -- Seed Exporters, Au
A 88	The Plant Farm, BC
A 95	Rock Spray Nursery, MA
A 122	White Flower Farm, CT

HEBES
A 21	Colvos Creek Nursery, WA
A 29	Digging Dog Nursery, CA
A 38	Forestfarm, OR
A 49	Heronswood Nursery, WA
A 58	Joy Creek Nursery, OR
A 89	Porterhowse Farms, OR
A 105	Siskiyou Rare Plant Nursery, OR

HEDYCHIUMS
A 3	Aloha Tropicals, CA
A 20	Coastal Gardens & Nursery, SC
A 54	Indigo Marsh, SC
A 58	Junglemania, CA
A 88	Plant Delights Nursery, NC
A 89	The Plumeria People, TX
A 106	Southern Perennials & Herbs, MS
A 107	Southern Shade, FL
A 110	Stokes Tropicals, LA
A 117	Tropic to Tropic Plants, BC
A 118	Valhalla Nursery, CA

HELIANTHUS, SPECIES
A 16	Canyon Creek Nursery, CA
A 18	Carroll Gardens, MD
A 37	Flowery Branch Seed Company, GA
A 55	Ion Exchange, IA
A 57	Jelitto Perennial Seeds, USA Office, KY
A 75	Native Gardens, TN
A 87	Pine Ridge Gardens, AR
A 90	Powell's Gardens, NC
A 90	Prairie Moon Nursery, MN

HELIANTHUS, SPECIES (continued)
A 91	Prairie Nursery, WI
A 91	Prairie Seed Source, WI
A 106	Southern Perennials & Herbs, MS
A 111	Sunlight Gardens, TN
A 121	We-Du Nurseries, NC

HELICONIAS
A 3	Aloha Tropicals, CA
A 7	The Banana Tree, PA
A 87	Pine Heights Nursery, Au
A 89	The Plumeria People, TX
A 107	Southern Shade, FL
A 110	Stokes Tropicals, LA

HELLEBORES
A 2	Aimers Seeds, ON
A 5	Appalachian Wildflower Nursery, PA
A 6	Arrowhead Alpines, MI
A 6	Ashwood Nurseries, En
A 6	Avon Bulbs, En
A 10	Kurt Bluemel, Inc., MD
A 15	CTDA, En
A 16	Camellia Forest Nursery, NC
A 18	Carroll Gardens, MD
A 20	Chiltern Seeds, En
A 24	Cricklewood Nursery, WA
A 29	Digging Dog Nursery, CA
A 31	Eco-Gardens, GA
A 34	Fairweather Gardens, NJ
A 43	Gossler Farms Nursery, OR
A 43	Russell Graham, Purveyor of Plants, OR
A 45	Greer Gardens, OR
A 49	Heronswood Nursery, WA
A 54	W. E. Th. Ingwersen, Ltd., En
A 56	Jackson & Perkins Co., OR
A 57	Jelitto Perennial Seeds, USA Office, KY
A 62	Klehm Nursery, IL
A 68	L.J. McCreary & Co. Perennial Seeds, TX
A 70	Mary's Plant Farm & Landscaping, OH
A 70	Meadow View Farms, OR
A 71	Milaeger's Gardens, WI
A 78	North Green Seeds, En
A 86	Phedar Nursery, En
A 88	Plant Delights Nursery, NC
A 88	Plant World Seeds, En
A 90	Poyntzfield Herb Nursery, Sc
A 92	Rainforest Gardens, BC
A 92	Randy's Nursery & Greenhouses, GA
A 93	Reflective Gardens, WA
A 97	Roslyn Nursery, NY
A 98	Sandy Mush Herb Nursery, NC
A 101	Seeds of Distinction, ON
A 105	Siskiyou Rare Plant Nursery, OR
A 114	Thompson & Morgan, NJ
A 117	Underwood Shade Nursery, MA
A 122	White Flower Farm, CT

HERBS
See also specific plants
A 1	Abundant Life Seed Foundation, WA
A 3	Allen, Sterling & Lothrop, ME
A 9	Berton Seeds Company, Ltd., ON

Page	Source

Page	Source		Page	Source

Page	Source	Page	Source

IRIS, SIBERIAN (continued)

Page	Source
A 55	Iris Country, OR
A 55	The Iris Gallery, CA
A 57	Joe Pye Weed's Garden, MA
A 62	Klehm Nursery, IL
A 69	McMillen's Iris Garden, ON
A 69	Maple Tree Garden, NE
A 71	Mid-America Garden, OK
A 72	Miller's Manor Gardens, IN
A 77	Nicholls Gardens, VA
A 78	North Pine Iris Gardens, NE
A 80	Olallie Daylily Gardens, VT
A 81	Olympic Coast Garden, WA
A 84	Parkland Perennials, AB
A 88	The Plant Farm, BC
A 90	Powell's Gardens, NC
A 93	Reath's Nursery, MI
A 94	Riverdale Gardens, MN
A 111	Sunnyridge Gardens, TN
A 113	Terra Nova Gardening, MN
A 116	Tranquil Lake Nursery, MA
A 119	Andre Viette Farm & Nursery, VA
A 120	Walnut Hill Gardens, IA
A 125	York Hill Farm, MA

IRIS, SPECIES

Page	Source
A 1	Adamgrove, MO
A 2	Aitken's Salmon Creek Garden, WA
A 4	Amberway Gardens, MO
A 5	Appalachian Wildflower Nursery, PA
A 5	Jim & Jenny Archibald, Wa
A 6	Arrowhead Alpines, MI
A 6	Avon Bulbs, En
A 7	B & T World Seeds, Fr
A 11	Bois d'Arc Gardens, LA
A 15	C K S, Cz
A 17	Cape Iris Gardens, MO
A 19	Chadwell Himalayan Seed, En
A 20	Paul Christian -- Rare Plants, Wa
A 21	Collector's Nursery, WA
A 22	The Conservancy, AB
A 23	Coombland Gardens & Nursery, En
A 30	Draycott Gardens, MD
A 31	Eco-Gardens, GA
A 31	Edgewood Farm & Nursery, VA
A 32	Ensata Gardens, MI
A 38	Forestfarm, OR
A 38	Fraser's Thimble Farm, BC
A 41	Gardens North, ON
A 41	Gardens of the Blue Ridge, NC
A 43	Russell Graham, Purveyor of Plants, OR
A 46	Hansen Nursery, OR
A 49	Heronswood Nursery, WA
A 51	Holly Lane Iris Gardens, MN
A 55	The Iris Gallery, CA
A 57	Jelitto Perennial Seeds, USA Office, KY
A 57	Joe Pye Weed's Garden, MA
A 68	McAllister's Iris Gardens, NM
A 73	Monocot Nursery, En
A 76	Nature's Garden, OR
A 77	Niche Gardens, NC
A 77	Nicholls Gardens, VA
A 78	North Green Seeds, En

IRIS, SPECIES (continued)

Page	Source
A 78	North Pine Iris Gardens, NE
A 81	Olympic Coast Garden, WA
A 83	Pacific Rim Native Plants, BC
A 87	Pine Ridge Gardens, AR
A 89	Potterton & Martin, En
A 93	Reflective Gardens, WA
A 94	Riverdale Gardens, MN
A 95	Robyn's Nest Nursery, WA
A 100	The Seed Guild, Sc
A 105	Siskiyou Rare Plant Nursery, OR
A 106	Southern Perennials & Herbs, MS
A 113	Terra Nova Gardening, MN
A 116	Trennoll Nursery, OH
A 118	Van Engelen, Inc., CT
A 120	Walnut Hill Gardens, IA
A 121	We-Du Nurseries, NC
A 125	Woodlanders, Inc., SC
A 125	York Hill Farm, MA

IRIS, SPURIA

Page	Source
A 1	Adamgrove, MO
A 2	Aitken's Salmon Creek Garden, WA
A 8	Bay View Gardens, CA
A 17	Cape Iris Gardens, MO
A 20	Chehalem Gardens, OR
A 55	Iris Country, OR
A 55	The Iris Gallery, CA
A 103	Shepard Iris Garden, AZ

IRIS, TALL BEARDED

Page	Source
A 1	Adamgrove, MO
A 2	Agua Viva Seed Ranch, NM
A 2	Aitken's Salmon Creek Garden, WA
A 4	Amberway Gardens, MO
A 4	Anderson Iris Gardens, MN
A 8	Bay View Gardens, CA
A 10	Bluebird Haven Iris Garden, CA
A 17	Cape Iris Gardens, MO
A 21	Comanche Acres Iris Gardens, MO
A 23	Cooley's Gardens, OR
A 34	Ferncliff Gardens, BC
A 41	Gardenimport, Inc., ON
A 51	Holland Gardens, WA
A 51	Holly Lane Iris Gardens, MN
A 55	Iris & Plus, PQ
A 55	Iris Acres, IN
A 55	Iris Country, OR
A 55	The Iris Gallery, CA
A 57	Jasperson's Hersey Nursery, WI
A 60	Keith Keppel, OR
A 67	Long's Gardens, CO
A 69	McMillen's Iris Garden, ON
A 69	Maple Tree Garden, NE
A 69	Mary's Garden, TX
A 70	Maryott's Gardens, CA
A 71	Mid-America Garden, OK
A 72	Miller's Manor Gardens, IN
A 77	Nicholls Gardens, VA
A 78	North Pine Iris Gardens, NE
A 100	Schreiner's Gardens, OR
A 106	Sourdough Iris Gardens, MT
A 108	Spruce Gardens, NE

Page	Source	Page	Source

LABIATES, (MINT FAMILY) (continued)
A 107 Southwestern Native Seeds, AZ
A 121 Well-Sweep Herb Farm, NJ

LAGERSTROEMIAS
See Crape Myrtles

LANTANAS
A 75 NWN Nursery, FL
A 76 Nature's Nook, MS
A 122 White Flower Farm, CT

LATHYRUS, SPECIES
A 20 Chiltern Seeds, En
A 44 Peter Grayson - Sweet Peas, En
A 78 North Green Seeds, En
A 101 Seeds of Distinction, ON

LAVENDERS
A 16 Canyon Creek Nursery, CA
A 18 Carroll Gardens, MD
A 22 Companion Plants, OH
A 29 Digging Dog Nursery, CA
A 31 Edgewood Farm & Nursery, VA
A 42 Good Scents, ID
A 43 Goodwin Creek Gardens, OR
A 49 The Herb Garden, NC
A 50 High Country Gardens, NM
A 58 Joy Creek Nursery, OR
A 67 Logee's Greenhouses, CT
A 70 Meadow View Farms, OR
A 74 Mountain Valley Growers, Inc., CA
A 77 Nichols Garden Nursery, Inc., OR
A 93 Rasland Farm, NC
A 94 Richters Herbs, ON
A 94 River View Herbs, NS
A 98 Sandy Mush Herb Nursery, NC
A 103 Shepherd's Garden Seeds, CT
A 105 Sleepy Hollow Herb Farm, KY
A 111 Sunnybrook Farms Nursery, OH
A 113 Theatrum Botanicum, CA
A 114 The Thyme Garden, OR
A 121 Weiss Brothers Nursery, CA
A 121 Well-Sweep Herb Farm, NJ
A 125 Woodside Gardens, WA

LEPTOSPERMUMS
A 32 Ellison Horticultural Pty., Ltd., Au
A 78 Nindethana Seed Service, Au
A 83 D. Orriell -- Seed Exporters, Au

LEUCODENDRONS
A 7 B & T World Seeds, Fr
A 34 Feathers Wild Flower Seeds, So
A 83 D. Orriell -- Seed Exporters, Au
A 104 Silverhill Seeds, So

LEUCOSPERMUMS
A 34 Feathers Wild Flower Seeds, So
A 104 Silverhill Seeds, So

LEWISIAS
A 6 Arrowhead Alpines, MI

LEWISIAS (continued)
A 6 Ashwood Nurseries, En
A 35 Field House Alpines, En
A 38 Fraser's Thimble Farm, BC
A 54 W. E. Th. Ingwersen, Ltd., En
A 57 Jelitto Perennial Seeds, USA Office, KY
A 60 Kelly's Color, CA
A 71 Mesa Garden, NM
A 74 Mt. Tahoma Nursery, WA
A 83 Pacific Rim Native Plants, BC
A 89 Porterhowse Farms, OR
A 92 Rare Plant Research, OR
A 105 Siskiyou Rare Plant Nursery, OR
A 107 Southwestern Native Seeds, AZ
A 112 Surry Gardens, ME

LIGULARIAS
A 18 Carroll Gardens, MD
A 38 Fraser's Thimble Farm, BC
A 49 Heronswood Nursery, WA
A 102 Shady Oaks Nursery, MN

LILACS
A 5 Appalachian Gardens, PA
A 5 Arborvillage Nursery, MO
A 8 Bay Laurel Nursery, CA
A 13 Broken Arrow Nursery, CT
A 18 Carroll Gardens, MD
A 21 Colvos Creek Nursery, WA
A 23 Corn Hill Nursery, NB
A 38 Forestfarm, OR
A 38 Fox Hill Nursery, ME
A 45 Greer Gardens, OR
A 47 Heard Gardens, Ltd., IA
A 69 Martin & Kraus, ON
A 70 Mary's Plant Farm & Landscaping, OH
A 102 Select Plus International Nursery, PQ
A 105 Smith Nursery Co., IA
A 121 Wayside Gardens, SC
A 122 White Flower Farm, CT

LILIES, HYBRID
A 4 Jacques Amand, Bulb Specialists, MD
A 4 Ambergate Gardens, MN
A 6 B & D Lilies, WA
A 12 Borbeleta Gardens, MN
A 14 The Bulb Crate, IL
A 18 Carroll Gardens, MD
A 18 Cascade Bulb & Seed, OR
A 30 Dutch Gardens, NJ
A 35 Fieldstone Gardens, Inc., ME
A 41 Gardenimport, Inc., ON
A 42 Goodness Grows, GA
A 44 Green Mountain Transplants, VT
A 47 Hartle-Gilman Gardens, MN
A 52 Honeywood Lilies, SK
A 56 Jackson & Perkins Co., OR
A 66 The Lily Nook, MB
A 66 The Lily Pad, WA
A 68 McClure & Zimmerman, WI
A 71 Mid-America Garden, OK
A 74 Charles H. Mueller Co., PA
A 84 Parkland Perennials, AB

Page	Source

LILIES, HYBRID (continued)

A 99	John Scheepers, Inc., CT
A 118	Van Bourgondien Bros., NY
A 118	Van Dyck's Flower Farms, Inc., NY
A 118	Van Engelen, Inc., CT
A 120	The Waushara Gardens, WI
A 122	White Flower Farm, CT

LILIES, MARTAGON

A 4	Ambergate Gardens, MN
A 15	C K S, Cz
A 18	Cascade Bulb & Seed, OR
A 66	The Lily Nook, MB
A 68	McClure & Zimmerman, WI
A 84	Parkland Perennials, AB
A 100	The Seed Guild, Sc
A 104	John Shipton (Bulbs), Wa
A 122	White Flower Farm, CT

LILIES, SPECIES

A 5	Jim & Jenny Archibald, Wa
A 6	Avon Bulbs, En
A 6	B & D Lilies, WA
A 18	Cascade Bulb & Seed, OR
A 20	Paul Christian -- Rare Plants, Wa
A 34	Far West Bulb Farm, CA
A 43	Russell Graham, Purveyor of Plants, OR
A 53	J. L. Hudson, Seedsman, CA
A 64	Las Pilitas Nursery, CA
A 66	The Lily Nook, MB
A 68	L.J. McCreary & Co. Perennial Seeds, TX
A 78	North Green Seeds, En
A 94	Robinett Bulb Farm, CA
A 101	Seeds of Distinction, ON

LILY TURF
See Liriope

LIMA BEANS

A 34	Fern Hill Farm, NJ

LINDENS

A 2	Agroforestry Research Trust, En
A 5	Arborvillage Nursery, MO
A 38	Forestfarm, OR
A 103	Sheffield's Seed Co., Inc., NY

LINGONBERRIES

A 28	DeGrandchamp's Farms, MI
A 50	Hidden Springs Nursery -- Edible Landscaping, TN
A 82	Oregon Exotics Rare Fruit Nursery, OR
A 92	Raintree Nursery, WA
A 97	St. Lawrence Nurseries, NY

LIRIOPE

A 34	Fantastic Plants, TN
A 75	NWN Nursery, FL
A 91	Prentiss Court Ground Covers, SC

LITHOPS

A 1	Abbey Gardens, CA
A 23	Coombland Gardens & Nursery, En
A 28	Desert Theatre, CA

LITHOPS (continued)

A 62	Gerhard Koehres Cactus & Succulent Nursery, Ge
A 67	Living Stones Nursery, AZ
A 71	Mesa Garden, NM
A 97	Doug & Vivi Rowland, En
A 111	Sunrise Nursery, TX
A 126	Roy Young, Seeds, En

LIVING STONES
See Lithops

LOBELIAS, PERENNIAL

A 25	Crystal Palace Perennials, Ltd., IN
A 49	Heronswood Nursery, WA
A 57	Jelitto Perennial Seeds, USA Office, KY
A 58	Joy Creek Nursery, OR
A 71	Milaeger's Gardens, WI
A 88	Plant Delights Nursery, NC
A 92	Randy's Nursery & Greenhouses, GA
A 97	Roslyn Nursery, NY
A 98	Sandy Mush Herb Nursery, NC
A 125	Woodside Gardens, WA

LOBIVIAS

A 71	Mesa Garden, NM
A 103	Shein's Cactus, CA

LOTUS

A 25	Crystal Palace Perennials, Ltd., IN
A 44	Green & Hagstrom, Inc., TN
A 57	Japonica Water Gardens, OR
A 61	Kester's Wild Game Food Nurseries, WI
A 66	Lilypons Water Gardens, MD
A 70	Maryland Aquatic Nurseries, MD
A 73	Moore Water Gardens, ON
A 85	Patio Garden Ponds, OK
A 87	Picov Greenhouses, ON
A 100	Scottsdale Fishponds, AZ
A 105	Slocum Water Gardens, FL
A 109	Stigall Water Gardens, MO
A 116	William Tricker, Inc., OH
A 120	Waterford Gardens, NJ
A 124	Windy Oaks Aquatics, WI

LUPINES

A 29	Donaroma's Nursery, MA
A 39	Frosty Hollow Ecological Restoration, WA
A 43	Graceful Gardens, NY
A 47	Hauser's Superior View Farm, WI
A 54	Indigo Marsh, SC
A 57	Jelitto Perennial Seeds, USA Office, KY
A 63	Larner Seeds, CA
A 64	Le Jardin du Gourmet, VT
A 71	Milaeger's Gardens, WI
A 85	Theodore Payne Foundation, CA
A 103	Sherry's Perennials, ON

LYCHEE

A 118	Valley Vista Kiwi, CA

MACADAMIA NUTS

A 23	Coopers Nut House, CA
A 40	Fruit Spirit Botanical Gardens, Au

Page	Source		Page	Source

MULLEINS
See Verbascums

MUSHROOM SPAWN
A 35   Field & Forest Products, Inc., WI
A 37   Florida Mycology Research Center, FL
A 40   Fun Guy Farm, ON
A 40   Fungi Perfecti, WA
A 43   Gourmet Mushrooms, CA
A 47   Hardscrabble Enterprises, WV
A 74   Mushroompeople, TN
A 75   Mycelium Fruits, NC
A 79   Northwest Mycological Consultants, OR
A 79   Northwoods Nursery, OR
A 82   Oregon Exotics Rare Fruit Nursery, OR
A 113   Territorial Seed Company, OR
A 121   Western Biologicals, Ltd., BC

MUSHROOMS, KOMBUCHA
A 37   Florida Mycology Research Center, FL
A 40   Fun Guy Farm, ON
A 94   Richters Herbs, ON

MUSHROOMS, MOREL
A 35   Field & Forest Products, Inc., WI
A 37   Florida Mycology Research Center, FL
A 40   Fungi Perfecti, WA
A 43   Gourmet Mushrooms, CA
A 74   Mushroompeople, TN
A 79   Northwest Mycological Consultants, OR
A 121   Western Biologicals, Ltd., BC

MUSHROOMS, OYSTER
A 35   Field & Forest Products, Inc., WI
A 37   Florida Mycology Research Center, FL
A 40   Fun Guy Farm, ON
A 40   Fungi Perfecti, WA
A 43   Gourmet Mushrooms, CA
A 74   Mushroompeople, TN
A 75   Mycelium Fruits, NC
A 79   Northwest Mycological Consultants, OR
A 121   Western Biologicals, Ltd., BC

MUSHROOMS, SHIITAKE
A 35   Field & Forest Products, Inc., WI
A 37   Florida Mycology Research Center, FL
A 40   Fun Guy Farm, ON
A 40   Fungi Perfecti, WA
A 43   Gourmet Mushrooms, CA
A 47   Hardscrabble Enterprises, WV
A 74   Mushroompeople, TN
A 75   Mycelium Fruits, NC
A 79   Northwest Mycological Consultants, OR
A 121   Western Biologicals, Ltd., BC

NATIVE PLANTS, AUSTRALIAN
A 7   B & T World Seeds, Fr
A 13   Buena Creek Gardens, CA
A 14   Bushland Flora, Au
A 16   Callahan Seeds, OR
A 20   Chiltern Seeds, En
A 25   Cycad Gardens, CA
A 32   Ellison Horticultural Pty., Ltd., Au

NATIVE PLANTS, AUSTRALIAN (continued)
A 40   Fruit Spirit Botanical Gardens, Au
A 53   J. L. Hudson, Seedsman, CA
A 78   Nindethana Seed Service, Au
A 83   D. Orriell -- Seed Exporters, Au
A 86   Phoenix Seed, Au
A 116   Trans Pacific Nursery, OR

NATIVE PLANTS, CALIFORNIAN
A 5   Jim & Jenny Archibald, Wa
A 7   B & T World Seeds, Fr
A 16   Callahan Seeds, OR
A 21   Colvos Creek Nursery, WA
A 38   Forest Seeds of California, CA
A 38   Fraser's Thimble Farm, BC
A 39   Freshwater Farms, CA
A 53   J. L. Hudson, Seedsman, CA
A 60   Kelly's Color, CA
A 63   Larner Seeds, CA
A 64   Las Pilitas Nursery, CA
A 76   Neglected Bulbs, CA
A 85   Theodore Payne Foundation, CA
A 93   Redwood City Seed Co., CA
A 94   Robinett Bulb Farm, CA
A 104   Sierra Seed Supply, CA
A 107   Southwestern Native Seeds, AZ

NATIVE PLANTS, CANADIAN
A 22   The Conservancy, AB
A 90   Prairie Grown Garden Seeds, SK

NATIVE PLANTS, CENTRAL AMERICAN
A 6   Aztekakti, TX
A 9   Bird Rock Tropicals, CA
A 19   Chadwell Himalayan Seed, En
A 25   Cycad Gardens, CA
A 27   Deep Diversity, NM
A 53   J. L. Hudson, Seedsman, CA
A 65   Legendary Ethnobotanical Resources, FL
A 67   Loehman's Cacti & Succulents, CA
A 92   Rainforest Seed Company, Co
A 92   Rare Plant Research, OR
A 97   Doug & Vivi Rowland, En
A 107   Southwestern Native Seeds, AZ
A 111   Sunny Land Seeds (Semillas Solanas), CO
A 116   Trans Pacific Nursery, OR
A 125   Guy Wrinkle Exotic Plants, CA
A 126   Yucca Do Nursery, TX

NATIVE PLANTS, EASTERN EUROPEAN
A 5   Jim & Jenny Archibald, Wa
A 33   Euroseeds, Cz

NATIVE PLANTS, GREAT BASIN
A 3   Alplains, CO
A 5   Jim & Jenny Archibald, Wa
A 44   Great Basin Natives, UT
A 55   Intermountain Cactus, UT
A 79   Northplan/Mountain Seed, ID
A 88   Plantasia Cactus Gardens, ID
A 95   Rocky Mountain Rare Plants, CO
A 100   Seca Scape of Utah, UT
A 122   Western Native Seed, CO

Page	Source

Page	Source

NATIVE PLANTS, SOUTH AFRICAN (continued)
A 125 Guy Wrinkle Exotic Plants, CA

NATIVE PLANTS, SOUTH AMERICAN
A 5 Jim & Jenny Archibald, Wa
A 6 Aztekakti, TX
A 7 B & T World Seeds, Fr
A 16 Callahan Seeds, OR
A 22 The Conservancy, AB
A 65 Legendary Ethnobotanical Resources, FL
A 67 Loehman's Cacti & Succulents, CA
A 82 Oregon Exotics Rare Fruit Nursery, OR
A 92 Rare Plant Research, OR
A 97 Doug & Vivi Rowland, En
A 116 Trans Pacific Nursery, OR

NATIVE PLANTS, SOUTHEASTERN U.S.
A 1 Stacy Adams Nursery, GA
A 5 Appalachian Gardens, PA
A 7 B & T World Seeds, Fr
A 7 Barber Nursery, TX
A 20 Coastal Gardens & Nursery, SC
A 31 Eco-Gardens, GA
A 32 Elk Mountain Nursery, NC
A 41 Gardens of the Blue Ridge, NC
A 42 Goodness Grows, GA
A 57 The Thomas Jefferson Center, VA
A 63 Lamtree Farm, NC
A 64 Lazy K Nursery, Inc., GA
A 69 Mail-Order Natives, FL
A 75 NWN Nursery, FL
A 75 Native Gardens, TN
A 76 Nature's Nook, MS
A 77 Niche Gardens, NC
A 87 Pine Ridge Gardens, AR
A 88 Plant Delights Nursery, NC
A 92 Randy's Nursery & Greenhouses, GA
A 104 Shooting Star Nursery, KY
A 111 Sunlight Gardens, TN
A 121 We-Du Nurseries, NC
A 125 Woodlanders, Inc., SC
A 126 Yucca Do Nursery, TX

NATIVE PLANTS, SOUTHWESTERN U.S.
A 6 Aztekakti, TX
A 7 B & T World Seeds, Fr
A 16 Callahan Seeds, OR
A 28 Desert Citizens, CO
A 28 Desert Moon Nursery, NM
A 38 Forest Seeds of California, CA
A 50 High Country Gardens, NM
A 52 Homan Brothers Seed, AZ
A 63 Larner Seeds, CA
A 67 Loehman's Cacti & Succulents, CA
A 71 Mesa Garden, NM
A 76 Native Seeds/SEARCH, AZ
A 88 Plants of the Southwest, NM
A 107 Southwestern Native Seeds, AZ
A 111 Sunny Land Seeds (Semillas Solanas), CO
A 123 Wild Seed, AZ
A 126 Yucca Do Nursery, TX

NEOREGELIAS
A 9 Bird Rock Tropicals, CA
A 42 Golden Lake Greenhouses, CA
A 71 Michael's Bromeliads, FL
A 87 Pineapple Place, FL

NEPENTHES
A 16 California Carnivores, CA
A 42 Glasshouse Works, OH
A 65 Lee's Botanical Garden, FL
A 82 Orgel's Orchids, FL
A 86 Peter Pauls Nurseries, NY

NERINES
A 30 Jim Duggan Flower Nursery, CA

NOTOCACTUS
A 6 Aztekakti, TX
A 28 Desert Theatre, CA
A 71 Mesa Garden, NM
A 97 Doug & Vivi Rowland, En

NUT TREES, HARDY
See also specific plants
A 8 Bay Laurel Nursery, CA
A 8 Bear Creek Nursery, WA
A 14 Burnt Ridge Nursery, WA
A 16 Campberry Farms, ON
A 19 Cascade Forestry Nursery, IA
A 20 Cloud Mountain Nursery, WA
A 21 Cold Stream Farm, MI
A 25 Dacha Barinka, BC
A 32 Edible Landscaping, VA
A 35 Henry Field Seed & Nursery Co., IA
A 46 Grimo Nut Nursery, ON
A 55 Inner Coast Nursery, BC
A 70 Mellinger's, Inc., OH
A 72 J. E. Miller Nurseries, Inc., NY
A 78 Nolin River Nut Tree Nursery, KY
A 79 Northwind Nursery & Orchards, MN
A 79 Northwoods Nursery, OR
A 80 Oikos Tree Crops, MI
A 82 Oregon Exotics Rare Fruit Nursery, OR
A 92 Raintree Nursery, WA
A 97 St. Lawrence Nurseries, NY
A 105 Smith Nursery Co., IA
A 115 Toll Gate Gardens & Nursery, MI

NUT TREES, LOW-CHILL
See also specific nuts
A 20 Chestnut Hill Nursery, FL
A 23 Coopers Nut House, CA
A 33 Exotica Rare Fruit Nursery, CA
A 40 Garden of Delights, FL

OAKS
A 1 Stacy Adams Nursery, GA
A 5 Arborvillage Nursery, MO
A 7 Barber Nursery, TX
A 14 Burnt Ridge Nursery, WA
A 16 Callahan Seeds, OR
A 19 Cascade Forestry Nursery, IA
A 21 Coenosium Gardens, WA

Page	Source

ORCHIDS, EPIDENDRUMS (continued)

A 81	Orchid Art, NY
A 84	Palm Hammock Orchid Estate, FL
A 98	Santa Barbara Orchid Estate, CA
A 112	Sunswept Laboratories, CA

ORCHIDS, FRAGRANT

A 56	J & L Orchids, CT

ORCHIDS, HYBRIDS
See also specific genera

A 2	Aitken's Salmon Creek Garden, WA
A 18	Carter & Holmes, Inc., SC
A 40	G & B Orchid Laboratory, Inc., CA
A 45	Green Plant Research, HI
A 52	Hoosier Orchid Company, IN
A 54	Huronview Nurseries & Garden Centre, ON
A 56	J & L Orchids, CT
A 56	J. E. M. Orchids, FL
A 60	Kensington Orchids, MD
A 61	Klehm Growers, IL
A 65	Lenette Greenhouses, NC
A 69	Ann Mann's Orchids, FL
A 80	Oak Hill Gardens, IL
A 82	Orchid Thoroughbreds, PA
A 83	Owens Orchids, NC
A 85	Penn Valley Orchids, PA
A 98	Santa Barbara Orchid Estate, CA
A 112	Sunswept Laboratories, CA

ORCHIDS, LAELIAS

A 52	Hoosier Orchid Company, IN
A 54	Huronview Nurseries & Garden Centre, ON
A 68	MCM Orchids, IL
A 80	Oak Hill Gardens, IL
A 81	Orchid Art, NY
A 98	Santa Barbara Orchid Estate, CA
A 112	Sunswept Laboratories, CA

ORCHIDS, MASDEVALLIAS

A 52	Hoosier Orchid Company, IN
A 54	Huronview Nurseries & Garden Centre, ON
A 56	J & L Orchids, CT
A 68	MCM Orchids, IL
A 98	Santa Barbara Orchid Estate, CA

ORCHIDS, MILTONIAS

A 40	G & B Orchid Laboratory, Inc., CA
A 65	Lenette Greenhouses, NC

ORCHIDS, MINIATURE

A 18	Carter & Holmes, Inc., SC
A 52	Hoosier Orchid Company, IN
A 56	J & L Orchids, CT
A 61	Klehm Growers, IL
A 65	Lenette Greenhouses, NC
A 82	Orchid Thoroughbreds, PA
A 83	Owens Orchids, NC
A 112	Sunswept Laboratories, CA

ORCHIDS, NATIVE SPECIES (U.S.)

A 6	Arrowhead Alpines, MI
A 31	Eastern Plant Specialties, ME

ORCHIDS, NATIVE SPECIES (U.S.) (continued)

A 41	Gardens of the Blue Ridge, NC
A 65	Lee's Botanical Garden, FL
A 80	Oakridge Nurseries, NH
A 82	Orchid Gardens, MN
A 97	Roslyn Nursery, NY
A 107	Spangle Creek Labs, WA

ORCHIDS, ODONTOGLOSSUMS

A 52	Hoosier Orchid Company, IN
A 68	MCM Orchids, IL
A 81	Orchid Art, NY

ORCHIDS, ONCIDIUMS

A 40	G & B Orchid Laboratory, Inc., CA
A 56	J & L Orchids, CT
A 60	Kensington Orchids, MD
A 65	Lenette Greenhouses, NC
A 98	Santa Barbara Orchid Estate, CA
A 112	Sunswept Laboratories, CA

ORCHIDS, PAPHIOPEDILUMS

A 18	Carter & Holmes, Inc., SC
A 56	J. E. M. Orchids, FL
A 60	Kensington Orchids, MD
A 61	Klehm Growers, IL
A 65	Lenette Greenhouses, NC
A 68	MCM Orchids, IL
A 82	Orchid Thoroughbreds, PA
A 85	Penn Valley Orchids, PA
A 112	Sunswept Laboratories, CA

ORCHIDS, PHALAENOPSIS

A 18	Carter & Holmes, Inc., SC
A 40	G & B Orchid Laboratory, Inc., CA
A 54	Huronview Nurseries & Garden Centre, ON
A 60	Kensington Orchids, MD
A 61	Klehm Growers, IL
A 65	Lenette Greenhouses, NC
A 67	Logee's Greenhouses, CT
A 68	MCM Orchids, IL
A 80	Oak Hill Gardens, IL
A 81	Orchid Art, NY
A 83	Owens Orchids, NC
A 98	Santa Barbara Orchid Estate, CA
A 112	Sunswept Laboratories, CA

ORCHIDS, PLEIONE
See Pleiones

ORCHIDS, SPECIES
See also specific genera

A 18	Carter & Holmes, Inc., SC
A 45	Green Plant Research, HI
A 52	Hoosier Orchid Company, IN
A 54	Huronview Nurseries & Garden Centre, ON
A 56	J & L Orchids, CT
A 56	J. E. M. Orchids, FL
A 60	Kensington Orchids, MD
A 61	Klehm Growers, IL
A 64	Lauray of Salisbury, CT
A 68	MCM Orchids, IL
A 69	Ann Mann's Orchids, FL

Page	Source		Page	Source

ORCHIDS, SPECIES (continued)

Page	Source
A 80	Oak Hill Gardens, IL
A 81	Orchid Art, NY
A 82	Orchid Thoroughbreds, PA
A 82	Orgel's Orchids, FL
A 83	Owens Orchids, NC
A 85	Penn Valley Orchids, PA
A 93	Red's Rhodies, OR
A 98	Santa Barbara Orchid Estate, CA
A 104	Silverhill Seeds, So
A 107	Spangle Creek Labs, WA
A 108	Springwood Pleiones, En
A 112	Sunswept Laboratories, CA
A 117	Tropic to Tropic Plants, BC
A 117	Tropiflora, FL
A 125	Guy Wrinkle Exotic Plants, CA

ORCHIDS, TERRESTRIAL

Page	Source
A 4	Jacques Amand, Bulb Specialists, MD
A 6	Arrowhead Alpines, MI
A 6	Avon Bulbs, En
A 15	C K S, Cz
A 20	Paul Christian -- Rare Plants, Wa
A 31	Eastern Plant Specialties, ME
A 38	Fraser's Thimble Farm, BC
A 41	Gardens of the Blue Ridge, NC
A 45	Greer Gardens, OR
A 65	Lee's Botanical Garden, FL
A 68	MCM Orchids, IL
A 80	Oakridge Nurseries, NH
A 81	Orchid Art, NY
A 82	Orchid Gardens, MN
A 88	Plant Delights Nursery, NC
A 89	Potterton & Martin, En
A 90	Powell's Gardens, NC
A 92	Rainforest Gardens, BC
A 93	Red's Rhodies, OR
A 97	Roslyn Nursery, NY
A 98	Santa Barbara Orchid Estate, CA
A 104	John Shipton (Bulbs), Wa
A 104	Silverhill Seeds, So
A 105	Siskiyou Rare Plant Nursery, OR
A 107	Spangle Creek Labs, WA
A 108	Springwood Pleiones, En
A 121	We-Du Nurseries, NC
A 123	Wildginger Woodlands, NY

ORCHIDS, VANDAS

Page	Source
A 40	G & B Orchid Laboratory, Inc., CA
A 56	J. E. M. Orchids, FL
A 60	Kensington Orchids, MD
A 61	Klehm Growers, IL
A 65	Lenette Greenhouses, NC
A 68	MCM Orchids, IL

OREGANOS, ORNAMENTAL

Page	Source
A 16	Canyon Creek Nursery, CA
A 22	Companion Plants, OH
A 31	Edgewood Farm & Nursery, VA
A 43	Goodwin Creek Gardens, OR
A 49	Heronswood Nursery, WA
A 58	Joy Creek Nursery, OR
A 74	Mountain Valley Growers, Inc., CA

OREGANOS, ORNAMENTAL (continued)

Page	Source
A 94	Richters Herbs, ON
A 98	Sandy Mush Herb Nursery, NC
A 105	Siskiyou Rare Plant Nursery, OR
A 113	Theatrum Botanicum, CA
A 114	The Thyme Garden, OR
A 121	Well-Sweep Herb Farm, NJ
A 125	Woodside Gardens, WA
A 125	Wrenwood of Berkeley Springs, WV

OXALIS

Page	Source
A 30	Jim Duggan Flower Nursery, CA
A 42	Glasshouse Works, OH
A 67	Logee's Greenhouses, CT
A 68	McKinney's Glassehouse, KS
A 73	Monocot Nursery, En
A 89	Potterton & Martin, En
A 105	Siskiyou Rare Plant Nursery, OR

PACHYPODIUMS

Page	Source
A 42	Glasshouse Works, OH
A 46	Grigsby Cactus Gardens, CA
A 62	Gerhard Koehres Cactus & Succulent Nursery, Ge
A 67	Living Stones Nursery, AZ
A 67	Loehman's Cacti & Succulents, CA
A 79	Northridge Gardens, CA
A 92	Rare Plant Research, OR
A 111	Sunrise Nursery, TX
A 125	Guy Wrinkle Exotic Plants, CA

PACHYSANDRA

Page	Source
A 85	Peekskill Nurseries, NY
A 91	Prentiss Court Ground Covers, SC
A 102	Shady Oaks Nursery, MN

PALMS

Page	Source
A 7	B & T World Seeds, Fr
A 7	Barber Nursery, TX
A 20	Chiltern Seeds, En
A 21	Colvos Creek Nursery, WA
A 32	Ellison Horticultural Pty., Ltd., Au
A 33	Exotica Rare Fruit Nursery, CA
A 40	Fruit Spirit Botanical Gardens, Au
A 44	The Green Escape, FL
A 58	Joe's Nursery, CA
A 59	Kapoho Palms, HI
A 62	Gerhard Koehres Cactus & Succulent Nursery, Ge
A 75	NWN Nursery, FL
A 76	Neon Palm Nursery, CA
A 83	D. Orriell -- Seed Exporters, Au
A 83	Pacific Tree Farms, CA
A 84	Palms for Tropical Landscaping, FL
A 88	Plant Delights Nursery, NC
A 117	Tropic to Tropic Plants, BC
A 118	Valhalla Nursery, CA
A 125	Woodlanders, Inc., SC

PALMS, RHAPIS

Page	Source
A 40	Garden of Delights, FL
A 44	The Green Escape, FL
A 59	Kapoho Palms, HI
A 84	Palms for Tropical Landscaping, FL

Page	Source

PALMS, TROPICAL
A 7	B & T World Seeds, Fr
A 7	The Banana Tree, PA
A 33	Exotica Rare Fruit Nursery, CA
A 40	Garden of Delights, FL
A 44	The Green Escape, FL
A 53	Jerry Horne Rare Plants, FL
A 59	Kapoho Palms, HI
A 83	D. Orriell -- Seed Exporters, Au
A 84	Palms for Tropical Landscaping, FL
A 92	Rainforest Seed Company, Co
A 107	Southern Shade, FL

PAPAYAS
A 7	The Banana Tree, PA
A 92	Rainforest Seed Company, Co

PARODIAS
A 62	Gerhard Koehres Cactus & Succulent Nursery, Ge
A 71	Mesa Garden, NM
A 103	Shein's Cactus, CA
A 126	Roy Young, Seeds, En

PASSION FLOWERS
A 7	B & T World Seeds, Fr
A 20	Chiltern Seeds, En
A 23	Coombland Gardens & Nursery, En
A 32	Ellison Horticultural Pty., Ltd., Au
A 40	Fruit Spirit Botanical Gardens, Au
A 42	Glasshouse Works, OH
A 59	Kartuz Greenhouses, CA
A 67	Logee's Greenhouses, CT
A 75	National Collection of Passiflora, En
A 84	Passionflower Herb & Perennial Nursery, VA
A 89	The Plumeria People, TX
A 111	Sunny Land Seeds (Semillas Solanas), CO
A 113	Theatrum Botanicum, CA
A 114	Thompson & Morgan, NJ
A 117	Tripple Brook Farm, MA
A 118	Valhalla Nursery, CA
A 122	Wild Ridge, CA

PAWPAWS
A 7	Barber Nursery, TX
A 14	Burnt Ridge Nursery, WA
A 32	Edible Landscaping, VA
A 46	Grimo Nut Nursery, ON
A 47	Hartmann's Plantation, Inc., MI
A 50	Hidden Springs Nursery -- Edible Landscaping, TN
A 59	Just Fruits, FL
A 69	Mail-Order Natives, FL
A 78	Nolin River Nut Tree Nursery, KY
A 79	Northwoods Nursery, OR
A 80	Oikos Tree Crops, MI
A 92	Raintree Nursery, WA
A 104	Sherwood's Greenhouses, LA
A 112	Sweetbay Farm, GA
A 115	Toll Gate Gardens & Nursery, MI

PEACHES
A 1	Adams County Nursery, Inc., PA
A 8	Bay Laurel Nursery, CA
A 30	Earth's Rising Trees, OR

PEACHES (continued)
A 55	Inner Coast Nursery, BC
A 58	Johnson Nursery, Inc., GA
A 105	Sonoma Antique Apple Nursery, CA
A 107	Southmeadow Fruit Gardens, MI
A 109	Stark Bro's Nurseries & Orchards Co., MO

PEARS
A 1	Adams County Nursery, Inc., PA
A 4	Ames' Orchard & Nursery, AR
A 8	Bay Laurel Nursery, CA
A 20	Cloud Mountain Nursery, WA
A 25	Cummins Nursery, NY
A 30	Earth's Rising Trees, OR
A 35	The Fig Tree Nursery, FL
A 45	Greenmantle Nursery, CA
A 55	Inner Coast Nursery, BC
A 58	Johnson Nursery, Inc., GA
A 64	Lawson's Nursery, GA
A 79	Northwind Nursery & Orchards, MN
A 92	Raintree Nursery, WA
A 95	Rocky Meadow Orchard & Nursery, IN
A 97	St. Lawrence Nurseries, NY
A 109	Stark Bro's Nurseries & Orchards Co., MO

PEARS, ANTIQUE
A 55	Inner Coast Nursery, BC
A 105	Sonoma Antique Apple Nursery, CA
A 107	Southmeadow Fruit Gardens, MI

PEARS, ASIAN
A 1	Adams County Nursery, Inc., PA
A 4	Ames' Orchard & Nursery, AR
A 8	Bay Laurel Nursery, CA
A 8	Bear Creek Nursery, WA
A 14	Burnt Ridge Nursery, WA
A 20	Cloud Mountain Nursery, WA
A 30	Earth's Rising Trees, OR
A 58	Johnson Nursery, Inc., GA
A 72	J. E. Miller Nurseries, Inc., NY
A 79	Northwoods Nursery, OR
A 82	Oregon Exotics Rare Fruit Nursery, OR
A 92	Raintree Nursery, WA
A 95	Rocky Meadow Orchard & Nursery, IN
A 105	Sonoma Antique Apple Nursery, CA

PECANS
A 46	Grimo Nut Nursery, ON
A 78	Nolin River Nut Tree Nursery, KY
A 80	Oikos Tree Crops, MI
A 109	Stark Bro's Nurseries & Orchards Co., MO

PELARGONIUMS
A 26	Davidson-Wilson Greenhouses, IN
A 27	Deerwood Geraniums, WV
A 42	Geraniaceae, CA
A 61	Killdeer Farms, WA
A 67	Logee's Greenhouses, CT

PELARGONIUMS, SPECIES
A 17	Cape Flora, So
A 27	Deerwood Geraniums, WV
A 42	Geraniaceae, CA

Page	Source

Page	Source

PERENNIALS, SHADE (continued)

Page	Source
A 76	Nature's Garden, OR
A 76	Naylor Creek Nursery, WA
A 77	Niche Gardens, NC
A 88	Plant Delights Nursery, NC
A 88	The Plant Farm, BC
A 88	Plant World Seeds, En
A 90	Powell's Gardens, NC
A 91	The Primrose Path, PA
A 92	Rainforest Gardens, BC
A 93	Reflective Gardens, WA
A 95	Robyn's Nest Nursery, WA
A 97	Roslyn Nursery, NY
A 101	Seeds of Distinction, ON
A 102	Seneca Hill Perennials, NY
A 102	Shady Oaks Nursery, MN
A 113	Terra Nova Gardening, MN
A 114	Thompson & Morgan, NJ
A 117	Underwood Shade Nursery, MA
A 121	We-Du Nurseries, NC
A 122	White Flower Farm, CT
A 125	Woodside Gardens, WA

PERSIMMONS

Page	Source
A 7	Barber Nursery, TX
A 8	Bay Laurel Nursery, CA
A 14	Burnt Ridge Nursery, WA
A 20	Chestnut Hill Nursery, FL
A 32	Edible Landscaping, VA
A 40	Fruit Spirit Botanical Gardens, Au
A 46	Grimo Nut Nursery, ON
A 50	Hidden Springs Nursery -- Edible Landscaping, TN
A 58	Johnson Nursery, Inc., GA
A 59	Just Fruits, FL
A 78	Nolin River Nut Tree Nursery, KY
A 79	Northwoods Nursery, OR
A 82	Oregon Exotics Rare Fruit Nursery, OR
A 92	Raintree Nursery, WA

PHILADELPHUS

Page	Source
A 5	Arborvillage Nursery, MO
A 18	Carroll Gardens, MD
A 37	Flower Scent Gardens, OH
A 38	Forestfarm, OR
A 43	Gossler Farms Nursery, OR
A 49	Heronswood Nursery, WA

PHILODENDRONS

Page	Source
A 106	Southern Exposure, TX

PHLOX

Page	Source
A 5	Appalachian Wildflower Nursery, PA
A 6	Arrowhead Alpines, MI
A 11	Bluestone Perennials, OH
A 15	Busse Gardens, MN
A 18	Carroll Gardens, MD
A 20	Coastal Gardens & Nursery, SC
A 25	The Crownsville Nursery, MD
A 29	Donaroma's Nursery, MA
A 31	Eco-Gardens, GA
A 35	Fieldstone Gardens, Inc., ME
A 38	Forestfarm, OR
A 40	Garden Perennials, NE

PHLOX (continued)

Page	Source
A 41	Garden Place, OH
A 41	Gardens of the Blue Ridge, NC
A 42	Goodness Grows, GA
A 53	Hortico, Inc., ON
A 54	Indigo Marsh, SC
A 62	Klehm Nursery, IL
A 65	Lee Gardens, IL
A 68	Lower Marlboro Nursery, MD
A 71	Milaeger's Gardens, WI
A 75	Native Gardens, TN
A 76	Nature's Nook, MS
A 77	Niche Gardens, NC
A 86	Perennial Pleasures Nursery, VT
A 90	Powell's Gardens, NC
A 91	The Primrose Path, PA
A 97	Roslyn Nursery, NY
A 98	Sandy Mush Herb Nursery, NC
A 105	Siskiyou Rare Plant Nursery, OR
A 106	Southern Perennials & Herbs, MS
A 111	Sunlight Gardens, TN
A 116	Trennoll Nursery, OH
A 117	Tripple Brook Farm, MA
A 118	Van Bourgondien Bros., NY
A 119	Andre Viette Farm & Nursery, VA
A 121	Wayside Gardens, SC
A 121	We-Du Nurseries, NC
A 121	Weiss Brothers Nursery, CA
A 125	Woodside Gardens, WA

PHORMIUMS

Page	Source
A 43	Gossler Farms Nursery, OR
A 76	Neon Palm Nursery, CA
A 88	The Plant Farm, BC

PIERIS

Page	Source
A 13	Broken Arrow Nursery, CT
A 31	Eastern Plant Specialties, ME
A 43	Gossler Farms Nursery, OR
A 45	Greer Gardens, OR
A 60	Kelleygreen Nursery, OR
A 97	Roslyn Nursery, NY
A 105	Siskiyou Rare Plant Nursery, OR

PIMELEAS

Page	Source
A 78	Nindethana Seed Service, Au
A 83	D. Orriell -- Seed Exporters, Au

PINES

Page	Source
A 16	Callahan Seeds, OR
A 17	Carino Nurseries, PA
A 21	Colvos Creek Nursery, WA
A 38	Forest Seeds of California, CA
A 38	Forestfarm, OR
A 59	Kasch Nursery, OR
A 83	Pacific Tree Farms, CA
A 103	Sheffield's Seed Co., Inc., NY
A 124	Windrose Ltd., PA

PISTACHIOS

Page	Source
A 100	F. W. Schumacher Co., Inc., MA

Page	Source	Page	Source

Page	Source		Page	Source

Page	Source		Page	Source

RUDBECKIAS (continued)
A 18   Carroll Gardens, MD
A 20   Coastal Gardens & Nursery, SC
A 25   The Crownsville Nursery, MD
A 29   Donaroma's Nursery, MA
A 29   Doyle Farm Nursery, PA
A 41   Gardens North, ON
A 42   Goodness Grows, GA
A 47   Hauser's Superior View Farm, WI
A 57   Jelitto Perennial Seeds, USA Office, KY
A 71   Milaeger's Gardens, WI
A 76   Nature's Nook, MS
A 77   Niche Gardens, NC
A 92   Randy's Nursery & Greenhouses, GA
A 104   Shooting Star Nursery, KY
A 121   We-Du Nurseries, NC

RUELLIAS
A 20   Coastal Gardens & Nursery, SC
A 67   Logee's Greenhouses, CT
A 106   Southern Perennials & Herbs, MS

SALIX
See Willows

SALVIAS
A 3   Alplains, CO
A 6   Arrowhead Alpines, MI
A 6   Avant Gardens, MA
A 13   Buena Creek Gardens, CA
A 16   Canyon Creek Nursery, CA
A 22   Companion Plants, OH
A 29   Digging Dog Nursery, CA
A 31   Edgewood Farm & Nursery, VA
A 37   Flowery Branch Seed Company, GA
A 43   Goodwin Creek Gardens, OR
A 49   Herbs-Liscious, IA
A 49   Heronswood Nursery, WA
A 58   Joy Creek Nursery, OR
A 64   Las Pilitas Nursery, CA
A 74   Mountain Valley Growers, Inc., CA
A 83   Owen Farms, TN
A 84   Passionflower Herb & Perennial Nursery, VA
A 87   Pine Ridge Gardens, AR
A 88   Plant Delights Nursery, NC
A 89   Pleasant View Nursery, En
A 90   Powell's Gardens, NC
A 93   Rasland Farm, NC
A 94   Richters Herbs, ON
A 94   River View Herbs, NS
A 98   Sandy Mush Herb Nursery, NC
A 101   Seedhunt, CA
A 105   Sleepy Hollow Herb Farm, KY
A 106   Southern Perennials & Herbs, MS
A 107   Southwestern Native Seeds, AZ
A 113   Theatrum Botanicum, CA
A 114   The Thyme Garden, OR
A 121   Well-Sweep Herb Farm, NJ
A 125   Woodside Gardens, WA
A 125   Wrenwood of Berkeley Springs, WV
A 126   Yucca Do Nursery, TX

SANSEVIERIAS
A 1   Abbey Gardens, CA
A 42   Glasshouse Works, OH
A 46   Grigsby Cactus Gardens, CA
A 58   Joe's Nursery, CA
A 67   Loehman's Cacti & Succulents, CA
A 106   Southern Exposure, TX
A 110   Succulenta, CA

SARRACENIAS
A 16   California Carnivores, CA
A 57   Japonica Water Gardens, OR
A 65   Lee's Botanical Garden, FL
A 82   Orgel's Orchids, FL
A 86   Peter Pauls Nurseries, NY
A 88   Plant Delights Nursery, NC
A 92   Randy's Nursery & Greenhouses, GA

SASKATOONS
A 8   Bear Creek Nursery, WA
A 47   Hartmann's Plantation, Inc., MI
A 80   Oikos Tree Crops, MI
A 82   Oregon Exotics Rare Fruit Nursery, OR

SAXIFRAGES
A 6   Arrowhead Alpines, MI
A 15   C K S, Cz
A 57   Jelitto Perennial Seeds, USA Office, KY
A 74   Mt. Tahoma Nursery, WA
A 89   Porterhowse Farms, OR
A 95   Rocky Mountain Rare Plants, CO
A 105   Siskiyou Rare Plant Nursery, OR
A 108   Squaw Mountain Gardens, OR
A 125   Wrightman Alpines, ON

SCIONWOOD, FRUIT TREES
A 8   Bear Creek Nursery, WA
A 10   Bluebird Orchard & Nursery, MI
A 48   Heirloom Seed Project, PA
A 79   Northwind Nursery & Orchards, MN
B 25   Pomona Book Exchange, ON
A 95   Rocky Meadow Orchard & Nursery, IN
A 105   Sonoma Antique Apple Nursery, CA
A 125   Worcester County Horticultural Society, MA

SCIONWOOD, GRAPES
A 95   Lon J. Rombough, OR
A 105   Sonoma Grapevines, CA

SCUTELLARIA
A 3   Alplains, CO
A 88   Plant World Seeds, En
A 106   Southern Perennials & Herbs, MS
A 121   We-Du Nurseries, NC

SEDUMS
A 3   Alpine Gardens, WI
A 11   Bluestone Perennials, OH
A 35   Fieldstone Gardens, Inc., ME
A 39   Frosty Hollow Ecological Restoration, WA
A 41   Garden Place, OH
A 58   Joy Creek Nursery, OR
A 60   Kelly's Color, CA

Page	Source		Page	Source

Page	Source

SHRUBS, DWARF (continued)
A 78   Nindethana Seed Service, Au
A 83   Owen Farms, TN
A 105   Siskiyou Rare Plant Nursery, OR
A 120   Wavecrest Nursery & Landscaping Co., MI

SHRUBS, FLOWERING
See also specific plants
A 5   Appalachian Gardens, PA
A 5   Arborvillage Nursery, MO
A 8   Bay Laurel Nursery, CA
A 8   Beaver Creek Nursery, TN
A 11   Bluestone Perennials, OH
A 12   The Bovees Nursery, OR
A 13   Broken Arrow Nursery, CT
A 14   W. Atlee Burpee & Company, PA
A 16   Camellia Forest Nursery, NC
A 18   Carroll Gardens, MD
A 20   Chiltern Seeds, En
A 20   Cloud Mountain Nursery, WA
A 21   Collector's Nursery, WA
A 21   Colvos Creek Nursery, WA
A 23   Corn Hill Nursery, NB
A 25   The Crownsville Nursery, MD
A 27   Daystar, ME
A 29   Digging Dog Nursery, CA
A 34   Fairweather Gardens, NJ
A 34   Fantastic Plants, TN
A 35   Henry Field Seed & Nursery Co., IA
A 38   Forestfarm, OR
A 38   The Fragrant Path, NE
A 41   Gardens of the Blue Ridge, NC
A 42   Girard Nurseries, OH
A 42   Goodness Grows, GA
A 43   Gossler Farms Nursery, OR
A 45   Greer Gardens, OR
A 49   Heronswood Nursery, WA
A 58   J. W. Jung Seed Co., WI
A 63   Lamtree Farm, NC
A 69   Martin & Kraus, ON
A 70   Mellinger's, Inc., OH
A 72   J. E. Miller Nurseries, Inc., NY
A 77   Niche Gardens, NC
A 79   Northwoods Nursery, OR
A 89   The Plumeria People, TX
A 90   Powell's Gardens, NC
A 97   Roslyn Nursery, NY
A 100   F. W. Schumacher Co., Inc., MA
A 100   The Seed Guild, Sc
A 103   Sheffield's Seed Co., Inc., NY
A 104   Silverhill Seeds, So
A 105   Smith Nursery Co., IA
A 107   Spring Hill Nurseries Co., IL
A 109   Starhill Forest Arboretum, IL
A 109   Stark Bro's Nurseries & Orchards Co., MO
A 117   Tripple Brook Farm, MA
A 120   Wavecrest Nursery & Landscaping Co., MI
A 121   Wayside Gardens, SC
A 121   We-Du Nurseries, NC
A 122   White Flower Farm, CT
A 124   Windrose Ltd., PA
B 34   Winterthur Museum & Gardens, DE
A 125   Woodlanders, Inc., SC

SHRUBS, FLOWERING (continued)
A 126   Yucca Do Nursery, TX

SHRUBS, FOLIAGE
See also specific plants
A 5   Arborvillage Nursery, MO
A 8   Beaver Creek Nursery, TN
A 43   Gossler Farms Nursery, OR
A 49   Heronswood Nursery, WA
A 83   Owen Farms, TN
A 100   F. W. Schumacher Co., Inc., MA
A 109   Starhill Forest Arboretum, IL
A 124   Windrose Ltd., PA

SHRUBS, HARDY
A 2   Agroforestry Research Trust, En
A 7   B & T World Seeds, Fr
A 22   The Conservancy, AB
A 23   Corn Hill Nursery, NB

SHRUBS, SMALL GARDEN
A 21   Collector's Nursery, WA
A 25   The Cummins Garden, NJ
A 38   Forestfarm, OR
A 43   Gossler Farms Nursery, OR
A 45   Greer Gardens, OR
A 79   Northwoods Nursery, OR
A 120   Wavecrest Nursery & Landscaping Co., MI
A 125   Woodlanders, Inc., SC

SINNINGIAS
A 9   Belisle's Violet House, WI
A 58   Just Enough Sinningias, FL
A 59   Karleen's Achimenes, GA
A 59   Kartuz Greenhouses, CA
A 64   Lauray of Salisbury, CT
A 68   Lyndon Lyon Greenhouses, Inc., NY
A 68   McKinney's Glasshouse, KS
A 84   Pat's Pets, MO
A 97   Rozell Rose Nursery & Violet Boutique, TX
A 114   Tiki Nursery, NC
B 33   The Violet House, FL

SORBUS
A 2   Agroforestry Research Trust, En
A 5   Arborvillage Nursery, MO
A 21   Colvos Creek Nursery, WA
A 31   Eastern Plant Specialties, ME
A 38   Forestfarm, OR
A 49   Heronswood Nursery, WA
A 78   North Green Seeds, En
A 100   The Seed Guild, Sc
A 103   Sheffield's Seed Co., Inc., NY

SPIREAS
A 5   Arborvillage Nursery, MO
A 34   Fairweather Gardens, NJ
A 34   Fantastic Plants, TN
A 45   Greer Gardens, OR
A 70   Mary's Plant Farm & Landscaping, OH

SPRUCES
A 38   Forest Seeds of California, CA

Page	Source

Page	Source

SUNFLOWERS (continued)
A 113 Territorial Seed Company, OR
A 114 Thompson & Morgan, NJ

SWEET PEAS
A 2 Aimers Seeds, ON
A 11 Robert Bolton & Son, En
A 12 S & N Brackley, En
A 20 Chiltern Seeds, En
A 41 Gardenimport, Inc., ON
A 44 Peter Grayson - Sweet Peas, En
A 101 Seeds-by-Size, En
A 102 Select Seeds -- Antique Flowers, CT
A 113 Terra Edibles, ON
A 114 Thompson & Morgan, NJ

SWEET POTATO PLANTS
A 39 Fred's Plant Farm, TN
A 53 Horus Botanicals, Ethnobotanical Seeds, AR
A 87 Piedmont Plant Company, GA
A 98 Sand Hill Preservation Center, IA
A 109 Steele Plant Company, TN
A 119 Vermont Bean Seed Co., VT

SYRINGAS
See Lilacs

TERRARIUM PLANTS
A 16 California Carnivores, CA
A 42 Glasshouse Works, OH
A 58 Just Enough Sinningias, FL
A 59 Kartuz Greenhouses, CA
A 65 Lee's Botanical Garden, FL
A 68 McKinney's Glassehouse, KS

THYMES
A 22 Companion Plants, OH
A 25 Dabney Herbs, KY
A 31 Edgewood Farm & Nursery, VA
A 42 Good Scents, ID
A 43 Goodwin Creek Gardens, OR
A 49 The Herb Garden, NC
A 49 Herbs-Liscious, IA
A 50 High Country Gardens, NM
A 58 Joy Creek Nursery, OR
A 65 Lewis Mountain Herbs & Everlastings, OH
A 67 Logee's Greenhouses, CT
A 70 Meadow View Farms, OR
A 74 Mountain Valley Growers, Inc., CA
A 93 Rasland Farm, NC
A 94 Richters Herbs, ON
A 94 River View Herbs, NS
A 96 Rose Hill Herbs and Perennials, VA
A 98 Sandy Mush Herb Nursery, NC
A 105 Siskiyou Rare Plant Nursery, OR
A 105 Sleepy Hollow Herb Farm, KY
A 106 Southern Perennials & Herbs, MS
A 110 Story House Herb Farm, KY
A 111 Sunnybrook Farms Nursery, OH
A 113 Theatrum Botanicum, CA
A 114 The Thyme Garden, OR
A 114 Tinmouth Channel Farm, VT
A 116 Trennoll Nursery, OH

THYMES (continued)
A 121 Weiss Brothers Nursery, CA
A 121 Well-Sweep Herb Farm, NJ
A 125 Woodside Gardens, WA
A 125 Wrenwood of Berkeley Springs, WV

TILLANDSIAS
A 1 Abbey Gardens, CA
A 9 Bird Rock Tropicals, CA
A 42 Golden Lake Greenhouses, CA
A 51 Holladay Jungle, CA
A 62 Gerhard Koehres Cactus & Succulent Nursery, Ge
A 71 Michael's Bromeliads, FL
A 87 Pineapple Place, FL
A 113 Teas Nursery Co., Inc., TX
A 117 Tropiflora, FL
A 125 Guy Wrinkle Exotic Plants, CA

TOAD LILIES
See Tricyrtis

TOBACCO, SMOKING
A 53 Horus Botanicals, Ethnobotanical Seeds, AR
A 53 J. L. Hudson, Seedsman, CA
A 76 Native Seeds/SEARCH, AZ
A 93 Redwood City Seed Co., CA

TOMATOES, HEIRLOOM
A 1 Abundant Life Seed Foundation, WA
A 27 Deep Diversity, NM
A 28 Digger's Club, Au
A 29 Down on the Farm Seeds, OH
A 38 Fox Hollow Seed Company, PA
A 47 Harris Seeds, NY
A 48 Heirloom Seed Project, PA
A 48 Heirloom Seeds, PA
A 50 High Altitude Gardens, ID
A 53 Horus Botanicals, Ethnobotanical Seeds, AR
A 58 Johnny's Selected Seeds, ME
A 73 Morgan County Wholesale, MO
A 76 Native Seeds/SEARCH, AZ
A 77 Nichols Garden Nursery, Inc., OR
A 98 Sand Hill Preservation Center, IA
A 98 Santa Barbara Heirloom Nursery, Inc., CA
A 101 Seeds Blum, ID
A 101 Seeds of Change, NM
A 101 Seeds West Garden Seeds, NM
A 106 Southern Exposure Seed Exchange(R), VA
A 113 Terra Edibles, ON
A 113 Territorial Seed Company, OR
A 115 Tomato Growers Supply Company, FL
A 115 Totally Tomatoes, GA

TOMATOES, HYBRID
A 14 D. V. Burrell Seed Growers Co., CO
A 22 The Cook's Garden, VT
A 47 Harris Seeds, NY
A 58 Johnny's Selected Seeds, ME
A 58 J. W. Jung Seed Co., WI
A 61 Kilgore Seed Company, FL
A 73 Morgan County Wholesale, MO
A 77 Nichols Garden Nursery, Inc., OR
A 86 Peters Seed & Research, OR

Page	Source

VEGETABLES - WIDE ASSORTMENT (continued)

A 101 Seeds West Garden Seeds, NM
A 101 Seeds-by-Size, En
A 103 Shepherd's Garden Seeds, CT
A 104 R. H. Shumway Seedsman, SC
A 104 Siegers Seed Co., MI
B 28 Silver Creek Supply, Inc., PA
A 110 Stokes Seed, Inc., NY
A 113 T & T Seeds, Ltd., MB
A 114 Thompson & Morgan, NJ
A 119 Vermont Bean Seed Co., VT
A 119 Vesey's Seeds, Ltd., PE
A 123 Willhite Seed Co., TX

VEGETABLES, EUROPEAN
See also specific vegetables

A 1 Abundant Life Seed Foundation, WA
A 2 Aimers Seeds, ON
A 9 Berton Seeds Company, Ltd., ON
A 12 Bountiful Gardens, CA
A 22 The Cook's Garden, VT
A 26 William Dam Seeds, ON
A 38 Fox Hollow Seed Company, PA
A 41 Gardenimport, Inc., ON
A 43 The Gourmet Gardener, KS
A 48 Heirloom Seeds, PA
A 50 High Altitude Gardens, ID
A 64 Le Jardin du Gourmet, VT
A 77 Nichols Garden Nursery, Inc., OR
A 88 Pinetree Garden Seeds, ME
A 93 Redwood City Seed Co., CA
A 103 Shepherd's Garden Seeds, CT
A 113 Territorial Seed Company, OR

VEGETABLES, GIANT

A 83 P & P Seed Company, NY
A 94 W. Robinson & Sons, Ltd., En
A 113 T & T Seeds, Ltd., MB
A 114 Thompson & Morgan, NJ

VEGETABLES, HEIRLOOM
See also specific vegetables

A 1 Abundant Life Seed Foundation, WA
A 12 Bountiful Gardens, CA
A 14 W. Atlee Burpee & Company, PA
A 15 Butterbrooke Farm Seed, CT
A 22 The Cook's Garden, VT
A 27 Deep Diversity, NM
A 28 Digger's Club, Au
A 29 Down on the Farm Seeds, OH
A 34 Fern Hill Farm, NJ
A 38 Fox Hollow Seed Company, PA
A 43 The Gourmet Gardener, KS
A 45 greenseeds(TM) from Underwood Gardens, IL
A 48 Heirloom Seed Project, PA
A 48 Heirloom Seeds, PA
A 50 High Altitude Gardens, ID
A 50 High Mowing Organic Seed Farm, VT
A 53 Horus Botanicals, Ethnobotanical Seeds, AR
A 53 J. L. Hudson, Seedsman, CA
A 56 Island Seed Company, BC
A 58 Johnny's Selected Seeds, ME
A 63 D. Landreth Seed Company, MD

VEGETABLES, HEIRLOOM (continued)

A 76 Native Seeds/SEARCH, AZ
A 88 Pinetree Garden Seeds, ME
A 88 Plants of the Southwest, NM
A 90 Prairie Grown Garden Seeds, SK
A 93 Redwood City Seed Co., CA
A 96 Ronniger's Seed Potatoes, WA
A 98 Salt Spring Seeds, BC
A 98 Sand Hill Preservation Center, IA
A 98 Santa Barbara Heirloom Nursery, Inc., CA
A 101 Seeds Blum, ID
A 101 Seeds of Change, NM
A 101 Seeds West Garden Seeds, NM
A 103 Shepherd's Garden Seeds, CT
A 104 R. H. Shumway Seedsman, SC
A 106 Southern Exposure Seed Exchange(R), VA
A 113 Terra Edibles, ON

VEGETABLES, HYBRID
See also specific vegetables

A 14 W. Atlee Burpee & Company, PA
A 22 The Cook's Garden, VT
A 26 William Dam Seeds, ON
A 44 Green Mountain Transplants, VT
A 47 Harris Seeds, NY
A 61 Kilgore Seed Company, FL
A 84 Park Seed Company, SC
A 87 Piedmont Plant Company, GA
A 94 W. Robinson & Sons, Ltd., En
A 102 Seymour's Selected Seeds, VA
A 104 Siegers Seed Co., MI

VEGETABLES, LATIN AMERICAN

A 53 J. L. Hudson, Seedsman, CA
A 82 Oregon Exotics Rare Fruit Nursery, OR
A 88 Pinetree Garden Seeds, ME
A 98 Santa Barbara Heirloom Nursery, Inc., CA
A 101 Seeds of Change, NM

VEGETABLES, NATIVE AMERICAN

A 1 Abundant Life Seed Foundation, WA
A 27 Deep Diversity, NM
A 40 Garden City Seeds, MT
A 53 Horus Botanicals, Ethnobotanical Seeds, AR
A 76 Native Seeds/SEARCH, AZ
A 77 Nichols Garden Nursery, Inc., OR
A 88 Pinetree Garden Seeds, ME
A 88 Plants of the Southwest, NM
A 93 Redwood City Seed Co., CA
A 101 Seeds of Change, NM
A 101 Seeds West Garden Seeds, NM

VEGETABLES, OPEN-POLLINATED
See also specific vegetables

A 1 Abundant Life Seed Foundation, WA
A 12 Bountiful Gardens, CA
A 15 Butterbrooke Farm Seed, CT
A 29 Down on the Farm Seeds, OH
A 30 E & R Seed, IN
A 40 Garden City Seeds, MT
A 45 greenseeds(TM) from Underwood Gardens, IL
A 47 Harris Seeds, NY
A 48 Heirloom Seed Project, PA

Page	Source

WALNUTS (continued)
A 100   F. W. Schumacher Co., Inc., MA
A 109   Stark Bro's Nurseries & Orchards Co., MO

WATER LILIES
A 20   Coastal Gardens & Nursery, SC
A 25   Crystal Palace Perennials, Ltd., IN
A 36   A Fleur D'Eau, PQ
A 44   Green & Hagstrom, Inc., TN
A 57   Japonica Water Gardens, OR
A 66   Lilypons Water Gardens, MD
A 70   Maryland Aquatic Nurseries, MD
A 73   Moore Water Gardens, ON
A 84   Paradise Water Gardens, MA
A 85   Patio Garden Ponds, OK
A 87   Picov Greenhouses, ON
A 99   S. Scherer & Sons, NY
A 100   Scottsdale Fishponds, AZ
A 105   Slocum Water Gardens, FL
A 109   Stigall Water Gardens, MO
A 116   William Tricker, Inc., OH
A 118   Van Ness Water Gardens, CA
A 120   Waterford Gardens, NJ
A 124   Windy Oaks Aquatics, WI

WATERMELONS
A 14   D. V. Burrell Seed Growers Co., CO
A 61   Kilgore Seed Company, FL
A 66   Liberty Seed Company, OH
A 97   Roswell Seed Company, NM
A 98   Sand Hill Preservation Center, IA
A 98   Santa Barbara Heirloom Nursery, Inc., CA
A 101   Seeds of Change, NM
A 104   Siegers Seed Co., MI
A 106   Southern Exposure Seed Exchange(R), VA
A 123   Willhite Seed Co., TX

WATERMELONS, GIANT
A 83   P & P Seed Company, NY
A 123   Willhite Seed Co., TX

WETLAND PLANTS
A 20   Coastal Gardens & Nursery, SC
A 39   Freshwater Farms, CA
A 55   Ion Exchange, IA
A 61   Kester's Wild Game Food Nurseries, WI
A 90   Prairie Moon Nursery, MN
A 91   Prairie Ridge Nursery/CRM Ecosystems, Inc., WI
A 91   Prairie Seed Source, WI
A 104   Shooting Star Nursery, KY

WILD RICE
A 61   Kester's Wild Game Food Nurseries, WI
A 99   S. Scherer & Sons, NY

WILDFLOWERS, ALASKAN
A 7   B & T World Seeds, Fr

WILDFLOWERS, AUSTRALIAN
A 7   B & T World Seeds, Fr
A 14   Bushland Flora, Au
A 32   Ellison Horticultural Pty., Ltd., Au
A 78   Nindethana Seed Service, Au

WILDFLOWERS, AUSTRALIAN (continued)
A 83   D. Orriell -- Seed Exporters, Au

WILDFLOWERS, CALIFORNIAN
A 2   Albright Seed Company, CA
A 17   Carmel Valley Seed Company, CA
A 30   Jim Duggan Flower Nursery, CA
A 38   Fraser's Thimble Farm, BC
A 39   Freshwater Farms, CA
A 63   Larner Seeds, CA
A 64   Las Pilitas Nursery, CA
A 73   Moon Mountain Wildflowers, CA
A 85   Theodore Payne Foundation, CA
A 94   Robinett Bulb Farm, CA
A 104   Sierra Seed Supply, CA
A 107   Southwestern Native Seeds, AZ

WILDFLOWERS, ENGLISH
A 104   John Shipton (Bulbs), Wa

WILDFLOWERS, GREAT BASIN
A 44   Great Basin Natives, UT
A 124   Wind River Seed, WY

WILDFLOWERS, JAPAN
A 7   B & T World Seeds, Fr

WILDFLOWERS, MANY REGIONS
A 2   Albright Seed Company, CA
A 17   Carmel Valley Seed Company, CA
A 20   Chiltern Seeds, En
A 29   Donaroma's Nursery, MA
A 31   Earthly Goods, Ltd., IN
A 33   Euroseeds, Cz
A 53   J. L. Hudson, Seedsman, CA
A 73   Moon Mountain Wildflowers, CA
A 104   Shooting Star Nursery, KY
A 119   Vermont Wildflower Farm, VT

WILDFLOWERS, MIDWESTERN U.S.
A 11   Bluestem Prairie Nursery, IL
A 19   Cattail Meadows, Ltd., OH
A 22   Companion Plants, OH
A 51   Holland Wildflower Farm, AR
A 55   Ion Exchange, IA
A 63   Landscape Alternatives, Inc., MN
A 82   Orchid Gardens, MN
A 87   Pine Ridge Gardens, AR
A 90   Prairie Moon Nursery, MN
A 91   Prairie Nursery, WI
A 91   Prairie Ridge Nursery/CRM Ecosystems, Inc., WI
A 91   Prairie Seed Source, WI
A 109   Stock Seed Farms, Inc., NE
A 123   Wildflowers from Nature's Way, IA

WILDFLOWERS, NEW ZEALAND
A 75   NZ Alpine Seeds, Ne
A 107   Southern Seeds, Ne

WILDFLOWERS, NORTH AMERICAN
A 6   Arrowhead Alpines, MI
A 7   B & T World Seeds, Fr
A 20   Chiltern Seeds, En

Page	Source

WILLOWS (continued)
A 38	Forestfarm, OR
A 42	Glasshouse Works, OH
A 49	Heronswood Nursery, WA
A 57	Japonica Water Gardens, OR
A 97	Roslyn Nursery, NY
A 98	Sandy Mush Herb Nursery, NC
A 105	Smith Nursery Co., IA

WINDBREAK PLANTS
A 8	Bear Creek Nursery, WA
A 19	Cascade Forestry Nursery, IA
A 21	Cold Stream Farm, MI
A 35	Henry Field Seed & Nursery Co., IA
A 36	Flickingers' Nursery, PA
A 70	Mellinger's, Inc., OH
A 74	Musser Forests Inc., PA
A 79	Northwoods Nursery, OR
A 113	T & T Seeds, Ltd., MB

WISTERIA
A 18	Carroll Gardens, MD
A 20	Coastal Gardens & Nursery, SC
A 21	Collector's Nursery, WA
A 38	Forestfarm, OR
A 45	Greer Gardens, OR
A 75	NWN Nursery, FL
A 121	Wayside Gardens, SC
A 125	Woodlanders, Inc., SC

WITCH HAZELS
A 18	Carroll Gardens, MD
A 29	Dilworth Nursery, PA
A 32	Elk Mountain Nursery, NC
A 34	Fairweather Gardens, NJ
A 34	Fantastic Plants, TN
A 38	Forestfarm, OR
A 42	Girard Nurseries, OH
A 43	Gossler Farms Nursery, OR
A 45	Greer Gardens, OR
A 70	Mary's Plant Farm & Landscaping, OH
A 97	Roslyn Nursery, NY
A 125	Woodlanders, Inc., SC

WOODLAND PLANTS
See also Shade Plants
A 5	Appalachian Wildflower Nursery, PA
A 12	The Bovees Nursery, OR
A 13	Broken Arrow Nursery, CT
A 16	Canyon Creek Nursery, CA
A 31	Eco-Gardens, GA
A 32	Elk Mountain Nursery, NC
A 34	Fancy Fronds, WA
A 37	Foliage Gardens, WA
A 38	Fraser's Thimble Farm, BC
A 39	Frosty Hollow Ecological Restoration, WA
A 41	Gardens of the Blue Ridge, NC
A 43	Gossler Farms Nursery, OR
A 43	Russell Graham, Purveyor of Plants, OR
A 51	Holland Wildflower Farm, AR
A 62	Kumar International, In
A 63	Landscape Alternatives, Inc., MN
A 68	Lower Marlboro Nursery, MD

WOODLAND PLANTS (continued)
A 76	Nature's Garden, OR
A 77	Niche Gardens, NC
A 80	Oakridge Nurseries, NH
A 82	Orchid Gardens, MN
A 90	Prairie Moon Nursery, MN
A 91	Prairie Nursery, WI
A 91	Prairie Ridge Nursery/CRM Ecosystems, Inc., WI
A 91	The Primrose Path, PA
A 92	Rainforest Gardens, BC
A 102	Shady Oaks Nursery, MN
A 104	Shooting Star Nursery, KY
A 105	Siskiyou Rare Plant Nursery, OR
A 111	Sunlight Gardens, TN
A 114	Thompson & Morgan, NJ
A 121	We-Du Nurseries, NC
A 122	White Flower Farm, CT
A 123	Wildginger Woodlands, NY

WORMWOODS
See Artemisias

XANTHORRHOEAS
A 32	Ellison Horticultural Pty., Ltd., Au
A 62	Gerhard Koehres Cactus & Succulent Nursery, Ge
A 76	Neon Palm Nursery, CA
A 78	Nindethana Seed Service, Au
A 83	D. Orriell -- Seed Exporters, Au
A 97	Doug & Vivi Rowland, En

YAM PLANTS
| A 109 | Steele Plant Company, TN |

YEWS
A 29	Dilworth Nursery, PA
A 42	Girard Nurseries, OH
A 74	Musser Forests Inc., PA
A 89	Porterhowse Farms, OR
A 97	Roslyn Nursery, NY
A 100	F. W. Schumacher Co., Inc., MA

YUCCAS
A 3	Alplains, CO
A 6	Aztekakti, TX
A 18	Carroll Gardens, MD
A 21	Colvos Creek Nursery, WA
A 28	Desert Citizens, CO
A 28	Desert Moon Nursery, NM
A 58	Joe's Nursery, CA
A 62	Klehm Nursery, IL
A 62	Gerhard Koehres Cactus & Succulent Nursery, Ge
A 64	Las Pilitas Nursery, CA
A 71	Mesa Garden, NM
A 71	Midwest Cactus, MO
A 76	Neon Palm Nursery, CA
A 85	Theodore Payne Foundation, CA
A 88	Plant Delights Nursery, NC
A 93	Reflective Gardens, WA
A 97	Doug & Vivi Rowland, En
A 107	Southwestern Exposure, AZ
A 107	Southwestern Native Seeds, AZ
A 111	Sunrise Nursery, TX
A 126	Yucca Do Nursery, TX

Page	Source		Page	Source

City	Source	City	Source
ALABAMA		**BRITISH COLUMBIA, CANADA (continued)**	
Newville	Kirkland Daylilies	Sardis	Pacific Rim Native Plants
Springville	Steve Ray's Bamboo Gardens	South Delta	Tropic to Tropic Plants
		Victoria	Harborcrest Gardens
ALBERTA, CANADA		Victoria	Island Seed Company
Sherwood Park	The Conservancy	Victoria	The Butchart Gardens
Spruce Grove	Parkland Perennials		
		CALIFORNIA	
ARIZONA		Albion	Digging Dog Nursery
Apache Junction	Southwestern Exposure	Altadena	Nuccio's Nurseries
Cortaro	Miles' to Go	Anaheim	Evergreen Y. H. Enterprises
Glendale	Homan Brothers Seed	Atascadero	Bay Laurel Nursery
Parks	Strong's Alpine Succulents	Atascadero	Mohns Nursery
Phoenix	Shepard Iris Garden	Berkeley	Neglected Bulbs
Scottsdale	Scottsdale Fishponds	Bolinas	Larner Seeds
Tempe	Wild Seed	Boyes Hot Springs	Marca Dickie Nursery
Tucson	Living Stones Nursery	Branscomb	Ros-Equus
Tucson	Native Seeds/SEARCH	Camarillo	Albright Seed Company
Tucson	Southwestern Native Seeds	Cameron Park	Roses, Wine & Evergreens
		Carlsbad	Bird Rock Tropicals
ARKANSAS		Carmel Valley	Carmel Valley Seed Company
Benton	Burk's Nursery	Carpinteria	Moon Mountain Wildflowers
Elkins	Holland Wildflower Farm	Cathey's Valley	Superstition Iris Gardens
Fayetteville	Ames' Orchard & Nursery	Chico	Covered Bridge Gardens
London	Pine Ridge Gardens	Chula Vista	Pacific Tree Farms
Mountainburg	Pense Nursery	Chula Vista	Tiny Petals Nursery
Pettigrew	Highlander Nursery	Chula Vista	Valhalla Nursery
Salem	Horus Botanicals, Ethnobotanical Seeds	Clements	King's Mums
		Cupertino	Epi World
AUSTRALIA		Davis	Flowers & Greens
Albany, WA	Nindethana Seed Service	Encinitas	Jim Duggan Flower Nursery
Dorroughby, NSW	Fruit Spirit Botanical Gardens	Etna	Kelly's Color
Dromana, VIC	Digger's Club	Eureka	Freshwater Farms
El Arish, North QLD	The Borneo Collection	Fallbrook	Coopers Nut House
Everton Hills, QLD	Pine Heights Nursery	Forestville	California Carnivores
Nowra, NSW	Ellison Horticultural Pty., Ltd.	Fort Bragg	The Iris Gallery
Perth, WA	D. Orriell -- Seed Exporters	Fortuna	Heather Heaven
Snug, Tasmania	Phoenix Seed	Fountain Valley	Valley Vista Kiwi
Yanchep, WA	Bushland Flora	Freedom	Seedhunt
		Fremont	Four Winds Growers
BRITISH COLUMBIA, CANADA		Fremont	Regan Nursery
Abbotsford	Mar-Low Epi House	Fresno	Hill 'n dale
Aldergrove	Western Biologicals, Ltd.	Fresno	Holladay Jungle
Chilliwack	Dacha Barinka	Ft. Bragg	Heritage Roses of Tanglewood Farms
Christina Lake	Bluestem Nursery	Garberville	Greenmantle Nursery
Cortes Island	Inner Coast Nursery	Garberville	Nancy Wilson Narcissus
Grand Forks	Hardy Roses for the North	Grass Valley	Foothill Cottage Gardens
Langley	Erikson's Daylily Gardens	Grass Valley	Weiss Brothers Nursery
Maple Ridge	Rainforest Gardens	Graton	Gourmet Mushrooms
Mission	Ferncliff Gardens	Greenville	Sierra Seed Supply
Salt Spring Island	Florabunda Seeds	Healdsburg	Petite Vines
Salt Spring Island	Fraser's Thimble Farm	Healdsburg	Sonoma Antique Apple Nursery
Salt Spring Island	Salt Spring Seeds	Ione	K & L Cactus & Succulent Nursery
Salt Spring Island	The Plant Farm	Kentfield	Geraniaceae

City	Source	City	Source
CALIFORNIA (continued)		**CALIFORNIA (continued)**	
Kenwood	Wildwood Farm	Vista	New Leaf Nurseries
La Habra	Abbey Gardens	Vista	Rainbow Gardens Nursery
La Honda	J. L. Hudson, Seedsman	Watsonville	Desert Theatre
Laytonville	Mountain Maples	Willits	Bountiful Gardens
Los Angeles	Cycad Gardens		
Los Angeles	Succulenta	**COLORADO**	
Marina	Shein's Cactus	Bayfield	Edge of the Rockies
Mendocino	Mendocino Heirloom Roses	Boulder	Long's Gardens
Modesto	Woodland Iris Gardens	Franktown	Rocky Mountain Rare Plants
Moorpark	Golden Lake Greenhouses	Glenwood Springs	Campanula Connoisseur
Navarro	Theatrum Botanicum	Kiowa	Alplains
North Hollywood	Guy Wrinkle Exotic Plants	Kiowa	Desert Citizens
Northridge	KSA Jojoba	Paradox	Sunny Land Seeds (Semillas Solanas)
Northridge	Northridge Gardens	Rocky Ford	D. V. Burrell Seed Growers Co.
Ojai	Kusa Seed Research Foundation	Salida	Western Native Seed
Oregon House	Far West Bulb Farm		
Oroville	Canyon Creek Nursery	**CONNECTICUT**	
Paramount	Loehman's Cacti & Succulents	Bantam	John Scheepers, Inc.
Paso Robles	Arena Rose Company	Bantam	Van Engelen, Inc.
Petaluma	Garden Valley Ranch Nursery	Danielson	Logee's Greenhouses
Petaluma	Petaluma Rose Company	Deep River	Ericaceae
Placerville	Forest Seeds of California	Easton	J & L Orchids
Plymouth	Amador Flower Farm	Gaylordsville	Bloomingfields Farm
Porterville	Sutton's Green Thumber	Greenwich	Schipper & Co.
Potter Valley	A Bamboo Shoot Nursery	Hamden	Broken Arrow Nursery
Prunedale	Wild Ridge	Lebanon	Chappell Nursery
Redwood City	Redwood City Seed Co.	Litchfield	White Flower Farm
Sacramento	Mighty Minis	Oxford	Butterbrooke Farm Seed
Salinas	The Rose Ranch	Salisbury	Lauray of Salisbury
San Gabriel	Sunnyslope Gardens	Stamford	Shanti Bithi Nursery
San Jose	Kitazawa Seed Co.	Thomaston	Cricket Hill Garden
San Jose	Maryott's Gardens	Torrington	Shepherd's Garden Seeds
San Marcos	Buena Creek Gardens	Torrington	The Daffodil Mart
San Marcos	Cordon Bleu Farms	Union	Select Seeds -- Antique Flowers
Sanger	Kelly's Plant World		
Santa Barbara	Santa Barbara Heirloom Nursery, Inc.	**COSTA RICA**	
Santa Barbara	Santa Barbara Orchid Estate	San Jose	Rainforest Seed Company
Santa Cruz	Antonelli Brothers Begonia Gardens		
Santa Cruz	Bay View Gardens	**CZECH REPUBLIC**	
Santa Cruz	Ecoscape	Novy Jicin	Euroseeds
Santa Cruz	Junglemania	Ostrava-Poruba	C K S
Santa Margarita	Las Pilitas Nursery		
Santa Rosa	Neon Palm Nursery	**ENGLAND**	
Santa Rosa	Sonoma Grapevines	Aylesbury, Bucks.	S & N Brackley
Santee	Gray/Davis Epiphyllums	Bedford	Doug & Vivi Rowland
Sebastopol	Bamboo Sourcery	Benenden, Kent	Tile Barn Nursery
Sebastopol	Miniature Plant Kingdom	Bingley, W. Yorkshire	Craven's Nursery
Sebastopol	Robinett Bulb Farm	Chesterfield, Derbyshire	Peter Grayson - Sweet Peas
Sebastopol	Vintage Gardens	Clevedon, Avon	Monocot Nursery
Somerset	Bluebird Haven Iris Garden	Clevedon, No. Somerset	National Collection of Passiflora
Squaw Valley	Mountain Valley Growers, Inc.	East Grinstead, W. Sussex	W. E. Th. Ingwersen, Ltd.
Stockton	Stockton Iris Gardens	Halstead, Essex	Robert Bolton & Son
Studio City	Sunswept Laboratories	Hemel Hempstead, Herts.	Seeds-by-Size
Sun Valley	Theodore Payne Foundation	King's Lynn, Norfolk	Roy Young, Seeds
Ukiah	Evergreen Gardenworks	Kingswinford, W.Mid.	Ashwood Nurseries
Upland	Van Ness Water Gardens	Leeds, West Yorkshire	Springwood Pleiones
Visalia	Sequoia Nursery -- Moore Miniature Roses	London	CTDA
Vista	Aloha Tropicals	Newton Abbot, Devon	Plant World Seeds
Vista	Exotica Rare Fruit Nursery	Newton Abbot, Devon	Pleasant View Nursery
Vista	G & B Orchid Laboratory, Inc.	Norwich, Norfolk	North Green Seeds
Vista	Grigsby Cactus Gardens	Nottingham	Field House Alpines
Vista	Joe's Nursery	Nr. Caistor, Lincs.	Potterton & Martin
Vista	Kartuz Greenhouses	Nr. Preston, Lancs.	W. Robinson & Sons, Ltd.
Vista	Nature's Curiosity Shop	Slough, Berks.	Chadwell Himalayan Seed

City	Source	City	Source
ENGLAND (continued)		**GEORGIA (continued)**	
South Petherton, Somerset	Avon Bulbs	Lexington.	Goodness Grows
Stockport	Phedar Nursery	Ochlocknee	Travis' Violets
Totnes, Devon	Agroforestry Research Trust	Palmetto	Wilkerson Mill Gardens
Ulverston, Cumbria	Chiltern Seeds	Pine Mountain	Lazy K Nursery, Inc.
West Sussex	Coombland Gardens & Nursery	Savannah	Linton & Linton Bamboo
		Valdosta	Karleen's Achimenes
FLORIDA		Warner Robins	Swann's Daylily Garden
Alachua	Chestnut Hill Nursery	West Point	Stacy Adams Nursery
Alachua	Daylily Discounters		
Auburndale	Color Farm Growers	**GERMANY**	
Chipley	NWN Nursery	Erzhausen/Darmstadt	Gerhard Koehres Cactus & Succulents
Clearwater	Violets, Etc., Inc.		
Crawfordville	Just Fruits	**HAWAII**	
Davie	Garden of Delights	Honolulu	Hoyas by Michael Miyashiro
Delray Beach	J. E. M. Orchids	Kaaawa	Green Plant Research
Enterprise	Floyd Cove Nursery	Pahoa	Kapoho Palms
Eustis	Rollingwood Garden		
Fort Lauderdale	The Pepper Gal	**IDAHO**	
Fort Myers	Tomato Growers Supply Company	Boise	Seeds Blum
Gulf Hammock	The Fig Tree Nursery	Hailey	High Altitude Gardens
Homestead	Florida Colors Nursery	Meridian	Good Scents
Homestead	Going Bananas	Moscow	Northplan/Mountain Seed
LaBelle	Lee's Botanical Garden	Twin Falls	Plantasia Cactus Gardens
Lee	Mail-Order Natives		
Lithia	South Bay Growers	**ILLINOIS**	
Longwood	Big Tree Daylily Garden	Bensenville	greenseeds(TM) from Underwood Gardens
Longwood	Pineapple Place	Champaign	Klehm Nursery
Melbourne	Southern Shade	Chapin	Applesource
Miami	Jerry Horne Rare Plants	Downers Grove	Laurie's Landscape
Miami	Legendary Ethnobotanical Resources	Dundee	Oak Hill Gardens
Miami	Orgel's Orchids	Hampshire	Klehm Growers
Miami	Palm Hammock Orchid Estate	Hillsboro	Bluestem Prairie Nursery
Miami	Palms for Tropical Landscaping	Peoria	Breck's
New Port Richey	Sunshine State Tropicals	Peoria	Spring Hill Nurseries Co.
Orlando	Brown's Edgewood Gardens	Petersburg	Starhill Forest Arboretum
Orlando	Just Enough Sinningias	Riverwoods	The Bulb Crate
Palm Harbor	The Green Escape	Tremont	Lee Gardens
Pensacola	Florida Mycology Research Center	Wheaton	MCM Orchids
Pompano Beach	Winn Soldani's Fancy Hibiscus(R)		
Sanford	Daylily World	**INDIA**	
Sanford	Kilgore Seed Company	Etawah (U.P.)	Kumar International
Sarasota	Tropiflora		
Sebring	Caladium World	**INDIANA**	
Sebring	Rainbow Acres	Crawfordsville	Davidson-Wilson Greenhouses
St. Petersburg	Michael's Bromeliads	Floyds Knob	Pinecliffe Daylily Gardens
Weirsdale	Ivies of the World	Indianapolis	Hoosier Orchid Company
Windermere	Ann Mann's Orchids	Indianapolis	Soules Garden
Winter Haven	Slocum Water Gardens	Monroe	E & R Seed
Winter Springs	Lady Bug Beautiful Gardens	New Albany	Earthly Goods, Ltd.
		New Salisbury	Rocky Meadow Orchard & Nursery
FRANCE		Noblesville	Miller's Manor Gardens
Paguignan, Olonzac	B & T World Seeds	St. John	Crystal Palace Perennials, Ltd.
Plouzelambre	Barnhaven Primroses	Valparaiso	Coburg Planting Fields
		Winamac	Iris Acres
GEORGIA			
Albany	Piedmont Plant Company	**IOWA**	
Augusta	Totally Tomatoes	Atalissa	Walnut Hill Gardens
Ball Ground	Lawson's Nursery	Calamus	Sand Hill Preservation Center
Coolidge	Sweetbay Farm	Cascade	Cascade Forestry Nursery
Decatur	Eco-Gardens	Charles City	Smith Nursery Co.
Ellijay	Johnson Nursery, Inc.	Harpers Ferry	Ion Exchange
Flowery Branch	Flowery Branch Seed Company	Johnston	Heard Gardens, Ltd.
Lavonia	Transplant Nursery	Marshalltown	Herbs-Liscious
Lawrenceville	Randy's Nursery & Greenhouses	Norwalk	Stark Gardens

City	Source	City	Source

IOWA (continued)

Shenandoah	Henry Field Seed & Nursery Co.
Woodburn	Wildflowers from Nature's Way

KANSAS

Burlington	Huff's Garden Mums
Overland Park	The Gourmet Gardener
Wichita	McKinney's Glassehouse

KENTUCKY

Frankfort	Shooting Star Nursery
Fulton	Ferry-Morse Seeds
Lancaster	Sleepy Hollow Herb Farm
Louisville	Dabney Herbs
Louisville	Jelitto Perennial Seeds, USA Office
Murray	Story House Herb Farm
Upton	Nolin River Nut Tree Nursery

LOUISIANA

Baton Rouge	Amaryllis, Inc.
New Iberia	Stokes Tropicals
Schriever	Bois d'Arc Gardens
Shreveport	Donovan's Roses
Sibley	Sherwood's Greenhouses

MAINE

Albion	Johnny's Selected Seeds
Falmouth	Allen, Sterling & Lothrop
Freeport	Fox Hill Nursery
Freeport	The Heather Garden
Georgetown	Eastern Plant Specialties
New Gloucester	Pinetree Garden Seeds
No. Berwick	Valente Gardens
Scarborough	Royall River Roses
Surry	Surry Gardens
Vassalboro	Fieldstone Gardens, Inc.
Waldoboro	The Roseraie at Bayfields
Waterville	Fedco Seeds & Moose Tubers
West Gardiner	Daystar

MANITOBA, CANADA

Neepawa	The Lily Nook
Winnipeg	T & T Seeds, Ltd.

MARYLAND

Baldwin	Kurt Bluemel, Inc.
Baltimore	D. Landreth Seed Company
Boonsboro	Meehan's Miniatures
Brookville	Heritage Rosarium
Buckeystown	Lilypons Water Gardens
Crownsville	Bridgewood Gardens
Crownsville	The Crownsville Nursery
Dunkirk	Lower Marlboro Nursery
Frederick	Dan's Garden Shop
Fruitland	Allen Plant Company
Jarrettsville	Maryland Aquatic Nurseries
Kensington	Kensington Orchids
Potomac	Jacques Amand, Bulb Specialists
Salisbury	Brittingham Plant Farms
Upperco	Draycott Gardens
Westminster	Carroll Gardens

MASSACHUSETTS

Agawam	Pleasant Valley Glads & Dahlias
Boylston	Worcester County Horticultural Society

MASSACHUSETTS (continued)

Carlisle	Joe Pye Weed's Garden
Carlisle	R. Seawright Daylilies & Hostas
Dartmouth	Avant Gardens
Edgartown	Donaroma's Nursery
Falmouth	Cape Cod Vireyas
Georgetown	York Hill Farm
Hubbardston	Garden Vision
Ipswich	Completely Clematis
North Attleboro	Underwood Shade Nursery
Rehoboth	Tranquil Lake Nursery
Rowley	Nor'East Miniature Roses
Sandwich	F. W. Schumacher Co., Inc.
South Deerfield	Nourse Farms, Inc.
Southampton	Tripple Brook Farm
Truro	Rock Spray Nursery
Westford	Burt Associates Bamboo
Whitman	Paradise Water Gardens

MICHIGAN

Albion	Balash Gardens
Ann Arbor	Old House Gardens
Baroda	Southmeadow Fruit Gardens
Bellevue	Toll Gate Gardens & Nursery
Fennville	Wavecrest Nursery & Landscaping Co.
Fowlerville	Arrowhead Alpines
Free Soil	Cold Stream Farm
Galesburg	Ensata Gardens
Grand Junction	Hartmann's Plantation, Inc.
Grand Rapids	Bluebird Orchard & Nursery
Hartford	Krohne Plant Farms
Hopkins	Englearth Gardens
Jackson	Schmid Nursery & Garden
Kalamazoo	Oikos Tree Crops
Niles	Oakwood Daffodils
South Haven	DeGrandchamp's Farms
Vulcan	Reath's Nursery
Zeeland	Siegers Seed Co.

MINNESOTA

Andover	Orchid Gardens
Chaska	Ambergate Gardens
Cokato	Busse Gardens
Edina	Savory's Gardens, Inc.
Faribault	Borbeleta Gardens
Forest Lake	Anderson Iris Gardens
Hastings	Sam Kedem Greenhouse & Nursery
Minneapolis	Sevald Nursery
Minneapolis	Terra Nova Gardening
Oakdale	Griffin Gardens
Osseo	Holly Lane Iris Gardens
Owatonna	Hartle-Gilman Gardens
Princeton	Northwind Nursery & Orchards
Rockford	Riverdale Gardens
Roseville	Landscape Alternatives, Inc.
St. Paul	The New Peony Farm
Waseca	Shady Oaks Nursery
White Bear Lake	Cascade Daffodils
Winona	Prairie Moon Nursery

MISSISSIPPI

Meridian	Nature's Nook
Tylertown	Southern Perennials & Herbs

City	Source	City	Source
MISSOURI		**NEW MEXICO (continued)**	
Barnett	Morgan County Wholesale	Veguita	Desert Moon Nursery
Brixey	Elixir Farm Botanicals, LLC		
California	Adamgrove	**NEW YORK**	
Cape Girardeau	Cape Iris Gardens	Babylon	Van Bourgondien Bros.
Gower	Comanche Acres Iris Gardens	Boonville	Bluebird Nursery
Hillsboro	Pat's Pets	Brightwaters	Van Dyck's Flower Farms, Inc.
Holt	Arborvillage Nursery	Buffalo	Stokes Seed, Inc.
Kansas City	Stigall Water Gardens	Canandaigua	J. E. Miller Nurseries, Inc.
Lebanon	Chehalis Rare Plant Nursery	Canandaigua	Peter Pauls Nurseries
Louisiana	Stark Bro's Nurseries & Orchards Co.	Collins	P & P Seed Company
Maryville	Prairie Oak Seeds	Dix Hills	Roslyn Nursery
New Melle	Midwest Cactus	Dolgeville	Lyndon Lyon Greenhouses, Inc.
Owensville	Homestead Farms	Dunkirk	Cooks Nursery/Eagle Bay Hosta Garden
Sarcoxie	Gilbert H. Wild & Son, Inc.	East Moriches	Henry Leuthardt Nurseries, Inc.
St. Louis	Amberway Gardens	East Rochester	Crosman Seed Corp.
		Geneva	Cummins Nursery
MONTANA		Hewlett	Orchid Art
Bozeman	Sourdough Iris Gardens	Locke	Sheffield's Seed Co., Inc.
Hamilton	Garden City Seeds	Mecklenburg	Graceful Gardens
Kalispell	Alpen Gardens	Naples	Rob's Mini-o-lets
Kalispell	Homestead Gardens	New Paltz	Plumtree Nursery
		North Collins	Concord Nurseries, Inc.
NEBRASKA		Northport	S. Scherer & Sons
Ft. Calhoun	The Fragrant Path	Oswego	Seneca Hill Perennials
Murdock	Stock Seed Farms, Inc.	Potsdam	St. Lawrence Nurseries
Norfolk	North Pine Iris Gardens	Putnam Valley	Shepherd Hill Farm
Omaha	DeGiorgi Seed Company	Queensbury	Northland Gardens
Ponca	Maple Tree Garden	Rochester	Harris Seeds
Wayne	Garden Perennials	Shrub Oak	Peekskill Nurseries
Wisner	Spruce Gardens	Smithtown	Bonsai Boy of New York
		South Salem	Carlson's Gardens
NEW BRUNSWICK, CANADA		Syracuse	Wildman's African Violets
Petitcodiac	Corn Hill Nursery	Webster	Wildginger Woodlands
		West Sayville	Violets By Appointment
NEW HAMPSHIRE			
East Kingston	Oakridge Nurseries	**NEW ZEALAND**	
Nashua	Lowe's Roses	Canterbury	Southern Seeds
Walpole	Boulder Wall Gardens	Dunedin	NZ Alpine Seeds
NEW JERSEY		**NORTH CAROLINA**	
Adelphia	Dutch Gardens	Apex	Bluebird Greenhouse
Clarksboro	Fern Hill Farm	Asheville	Elk Mountain Nursery
Freehold	Wild Earth Native Plant Nursery	Bailey	Finch Blueberry Nursery
Glassboro	Summerville's Gladiolus World-Wide	Chapel Hill	Camellia Forest Nursery
Greenwich	Fairweather Gardens	Chapel Hill	Green Hill Farm
Greenwich	New Gardens	Chapel Hill	Niche Gardens
Jackson	Thompson & Morgan	Dunn	Jernigan Gardens
Marlboro	The Cummins Garden	Fairview	Tiki Nursery
Pittsgrove	Jersey Asparagus Farms	Godwin	Rasland Farm
Pompton Lakes	Black Copper Kits	Iron Station	Mycelium Fruits
Port Murray	Well-Sweep Herb Farm	Kannapolis	Lenette Greenhouses
Saddle River	Waterford Gardens	Kill Devil Hills	Chris Weeks Peppers
Sewell	Ledden Brothers	Leicester	Sandy Mush Herb Nursery
		Marion	We-Du Nurseries
NEW MEXICO		Pilot Mountain	The Herb Garden
Albuquerque	Seeds West Garden Seeds	Pineola	Gardens of the Blue Ridge
Belen	Mesa Garden	Pisgah Forest	Owens Orchids
Fairacres	McAllister's Iris Gardens	Princeton	Powell's Gardens
Roswell	Roswell Seed Company	Raleigh	Plant Delights Nursery
Santa Fe	Deep Diversity	Rocky Point	Lewis Strawberry Nursery
Santa Fe	High Country Gardens	Warrensville	Lamtree Farm
Santa Fe	Plants of the Southwest		
Santa Fe	Seeds of Change	**NORTHERN IRELAND**	
Taos	Agua Viva Seed Ranch	Ballymena, Co. Antrim	Carncairn Daffodils, Ltd.

City	Source	City	Source
NOVA SCOTIA, CANADA		**OREGON (continued)**	
Maitland, Hants Co.	River View Herbs	Canby	Northwoods Nursery
Yarmouth	South Cove Nursery	Canby	Oregon Trail Groundcovers
		Canby	Swan Island Dahlias
OHIO		Central Point	Callahan Seeds
Alliance	Adrian's Flowers of Fashion Nursery	Corbett	Bonnie Brae Gardens
Athens	Companion Plants	Corbett	Oregon Trail Daffodils
Bedford	Bedford Dahlias	Corvallis	Northern Groves
Brecksville	Kuk's Forest Nursery	Corvallis	Northwest Mycological Consultants
Chesterland	Homestead Div. of Sunnybrook Farms	Cottage Grove	Territorial Seed Company
Chesterland	Sunnybrook Farms Nursery	Drain	Kelleygreen Nursery
Cygnet	Rocky Ford Gourd	Eagle Point	Vicki's Exotic Plants
Doylestown	Flower Scent Gardens	Estacada	Squaw Mountain Gardens
Gates Mills	Crintonic Gardens	Eugene	Delta Farm & Nursery
Gates Mills	Ivy Garth Perennials	Eugene	Greer Gardens
Geneva	Girard Nurseries	Gold Beach	Tradewinds Bamboo Nursery
Geneva	Holly Ridge Nursery	Grants Pass	Oregon Exotics Rare Fruit Nursery
Hamilton	Mary's Plant Farm & Landscaping	Gresham	Kasch Nursery
Hiram	Down on the Farm Seeds	Hubbard	Grant Mitsch Novelty Daffodils
Independence	William Tricker, Inc.	McMinnville	Trans Pacific Nursery
Madison	Bluestone Perennials	Medford	Jackson & Perkins Co.
Manchester	Lewis Mountain Herbs & Everlastings	Medford	Meadow View Farms
Mentor	Garden Place	Medford	Siskiyou Rare Plant Nursery
New Philadelphia	Liberty Seed Company	Monroe	Earth's Rising Trees
North Lima	Mellinger's, Inc.	Myrtle Creek	Peters Seed & Research
Solon	Cattail Meadows, Ltd.	Newberg	Chehalem Gardens
Stewart	Glasshouse Works	North Bend	Hansen Nursery
Trenton	Trennoll Nursery	Philomath	Freshops
		Philomath	Wild Garden Seed
OKLAHOMA		Portland	Hobbs and Hopkins Ltd.
Moore	Patio Garden Ponds	Portland	Rare Plant Research
Oklahoma City	Mid-America Garden	Portland	The Bovees Nursery
		Roseburg	Garden Valley Dahlias
ONTARIO, CANADA		Salem	Keith Keppel
Ajax	Picov Greenhouses	Salem	Russell Graham, Purveyor of Plants
Aurora	Aimers Seeds	Salem	Schreiner's Gardens
Bright's Grove	Huronview Nurseries & Garden Centre	Salem	Whitman Farms
Carlisle	Martin & Kraus	Sandy	A Sandy Rhododendron
Cedar Springs	Sherry's Perennials	Sandy	Porterhowse Farms
Dundas	William Dam Seeds	Scappoose	Joy Creek Nursery
Goodwood	Fun Guy Farm	Scio	Nature's Garden
Goodwood	Richters Herbs	Scotts Mills	Cascade Bulb & Seed
Kerwood	Wrightman Alpines	Scotts Mills	Ingraham's Cottage Roses
Niagara-on-the-Lake	Campberry Farms	Sherwood	Brothers Herbs & Peonies
Niagara-on-the-Lake	Grimo Nut Nursery	Sherwood	Caprice Farm Nursery
North Gower	Gardens North	Sherwood	Red's Rhodies
Norwich	McMillen's Iris Garden	Silverton	Cooley's Gardens
Pickering	Pickering Nurseries, Inc.	Springfield	Gossler Farms Nursery
Port Stanley	Moore Water Gardens	Springfield	Japonica Water Gardens
Stirling	Terra Edibles	St. Paul	Heirloom Old Garden Roses
Thornhill	Gardenimport, Inc.	Tangent	Chehalem Creek Nursery
Toronto (Etob)	Seeds of Distinction	Tillamook	West Coast Japanese Maples
Trout Creek	Becker's Seed Potatoes	Turner	Frey's Dahlias
Uxbridge	Loon Designs	Williams	Forestfarm
Virgil	Carl Pallek & Son Nurseries	Williams	Goodwin Creek Gardens
Waterdown	Hortico, Inc.	Williams	Horizon Herbs
Weston	Berton Seeds Company, Ltd.	Wilsonville	Edmunds' Roses
		Wilsonville	Justice Miniature Roses
OREGON		Woodburn	Wooden Shoe Bulb Company
Albany	Nichols Garden Nursery, Inc.		
Alsea	The Thyme Garden	**PENNSYLVANIA**	
Aurora	Hydrangeas Plus	Aspers	Adams County Nursery, Inc.
Aurora	Lon J. Rombough	Delta	Doyle Farm Nursery
Beaverton	Oregon Miniature Roses	Dillsburg	Orchid Thoroughbreds
Brooks	Iris Country	Easton	The Banana Tree

City	Source	City	Source

PENNSYLVANIA (continued)

City	Source
Gettysburg	Friendship Gardens
Huntingdon Valley	Tinari Greenhouses
Indiana	Carino Nurseries
Indiana	Musser Forests Inc.
Kittanning	Fox Hollow Seed Company
Lancaster	Heirloom Seed Project
Lionville	Hedera etc.
Loretto	Hickory Hill Gardens
New Alexandria	Nancy's Daylilies & Perennials
New Hope	Charles H. Mueller Co.
Norristown	Pepper Joe's
North East	Mums by Paschke
Oxford	Dilworth Nursery
Pen Argyl	Windrose Ltd.
Port Matilda	Limerock Ornamental Grasses
Reedsville	Appalachian Wildflower Nursery
Sagamore	Flickingers' Nursery
Scottdale	The Primrose Path
Warminster	W. Atlee Burpee & Company
Waynesboro	Appalachian Gardens
West Elizabeth	Heirloom Seeds
Wynnewood	Penn Valley Orchids

PRINCE EDWARD ISLAND, CANADA

City	Source
York	Vesey's Seeds, Ltd.

QUEBEC, CANADA

City	Source
Mascouche	Select Plus International Nursery
Stanbridge-East	A Fleur D'Eau
Sutton	Iris & Plus

SASKATCHEWAN, CANADA

City	Source
Cochin	Prairie Grown Garden Seeds
Parkside	Honeywood Lilies
Prairie River	Saskaberia Nursery
Saskatoon	Early's Farm & Garden Centre, Inc.

SCOTLAND

City	Source
Carnwath, Lanark	The Seed Guild
Ross & Cromarty	Poyntzfield Herb Nursery

SOUTH AFRICA

City	Source
Brackenfell	Rust-En-Vrede Nursery
Constantia, Western Cape	Feathers Wild Flower Seeds
Howard Place	Sunburst Bulbs C.C.
Kenilworth, Cape Town	Silverhill Seeds
Port Elizabeth	Cape Flora
Stutterheim, Eastern Cape	The Croft Wild Bulb Nursery

SOUTH CAROLINA

City	Source
Aiken	Woodlanders, Inc.
Cross Hill	The Mini-Rose Garden
Florence	Indigo Marsh
Graniteville	R. H. Shumway Seedsman
Greenville	Prentiss Court Ground Covers
Greenwood	Park Seed Company
Hodges	Wayside Gardens
Myrtle Beach	Coastal Gardens & Nursery
Newberry	Carter & Holmes, Inc.

SOUTH DAKOTA

City	Source
Yankton	Gurney's Seed & Nursery Co.

TENNESSEE

City	Source
Andersonville	Sunlight Gardens
Bartlett	Fantastic Plants
Cookeville	Hidden Springs Nursery
Corryton	Oakes Daylilies
Gleason	Steele Plant Company
Greenback	Native Gardens
Knoxville	Beaver Creek Nursery
Knoxville	Sunnyridge Gardens
Martin	Fred's Plant Farm
Nashville	Green & Hagstrom, Inc.
Ripley	Owen Farms
Summertown	Mushroompeople

TEXAS

City	Source
Adkins	Bonsai Farm
Austin	It's About Thyme
Beaumont	Southern Exposure
Bellaire	Teas Nursery Co., Inc.
Brenham	Antique Rose Emporium
Burleson	Artistic Plants
Carrizo Springs	Dixondale Farms
Dallas	Volkmann Bros. Greenhouses
El Paso	Aztekakti
Grangerland	L.J. McCreary & Co. Perennial Seeds
Hempstead	Yucca Do Nursery
Hico	Mary's Garden
Houston	Air Expose
Junction	Native American Seed
Leander	Sunrise Nursery
Leander	The Plumeria People
Poolville	Willhite Seed Co.
San Antonio	Kay's Greenhouses
Tyler	Rozell Rose Nursery & Violet Boutique
Tyler	Tate Rose Nursery
Willis	Barber Nursery

UTAH

City	Source
Holden	Great Basin Natives
Jensen	High Country Roses
Kaysville	Intermountain Cactus
Salt Lake City	Seca Scape of Utah

VERMONT

City	Source
Charlotte	Vermont Wildflower Farm
Derby Line	High Mowing Organic Seed Farm
East Hardwick	Perennial Pleasures Nursery
East Montpelier	Green Mountain Transplants
Fair Haven	Vermont Bean Seed Co.
Londonderry	The Cook's Garden
Pittsfield	French's Bulb Importer
South Newfane	Olallie Daylily Gardens
St. Johnsbury Center	Le Jardin du Gourmet
Tinmouth	Tinmouth Channel Farm

VIRGINIA

City	Source
Afton	Edible Landscaping
Amherst	Rose Hill Herbs and Perennials
Charlottesville	The Thomas Jefferson Center
Christiansburg	Passionflower Herb & Perennial Nursery
Earlysville	Southern Exposure Seed Exchange(R)
Fishersville	Andre Viette Farm & Nursery
Gainesville	Nicholls Gardens
Gloucester	Orchard Lane Growers
Stanardsville	Edgewood Farm & Nursery

City	Source	City	Source

VIRGINIA (continued)

City	Source
Sussex	Seymour's Selected Seeds,
Washington	Eastwoods Nurseries

WALES

City	Source
Llandysul, Dyfed	Jim & Jenny Archibald
Whitland, Dyfed	John Shipton (Bulbs)
Wrexham, Clwyd	Paul Christian -- Rare Plants

WASHINGTON

City	Source
Arlington	Hammond's Acres of Rhodys
Battle Ground	Collector's Nursery
Bellevue	Foliage Gardens
Blaine	Brown's Kalmia Nursery
Centralia	Cedar Valley Nursery
Chimacum	Naylor Creek Nursery
Chimacum	Woodside Gardens
Eatonville	Coenosium Gardens
Everson	Cloud Mountain Nursery
Federal Way	The Rhododendron Species Foundation
Gold Bar	Fancy Fronds
Graham	Holland Gardens
Graham	Mt. Tahoma Nursery
Kingston	Heronswood Nursery
Langley	Frosty Hollow Ecological Restoration
Longview	Watershed Garden Works
Morton	Raintree Nursery
Northport	Bear Creek Nursery
Oakville	Dan's Dahlias
Okanogan	Filaree Farm
Olympia	F. W. Byles Nursery
Olympia	Fungi Perfecti
Olympia	The Lily Pad
Onalaska	Burnt Ridge Nursery
Orting	Ronniger's Seed Potatoes
Port Townsend	Abundant Life Seed Foundation
Port Townsend	B & D Lilies
Poulsbo	Reflective Gardens
Ridgefield	Killdeer Farms
Seattle	A Thousand Alliums
Seattle	Sea-Tac Dahlia Gardens
Sequim	Olympic Coast Garden
Shelton	Heaths & Heathers
Snohomish	A & D Nursery
Snohomish	Cricklewood Nursery
Spangle	Spangle Creek Labs
Spokane	Tower Perennial Gardens, Inc.
Sumner	Dunford Farms
Tacoma	Connell's Dahlias
Tekoa	Plants of the Wild
Vancouver	Aitken's Salmon Creek Garden
Vancouver	Robyn's Nest Nursery
Vashon Island	Colvos Creek Nursery
Woodland	Highfield Garden

WEST VIRGINIA

City	Source
Berkeley Springs	Wrenwood of Berkeley Springs
Buckhannon	Deerwood Geraniums
Franklin	Hardscrabble Enterprises
Hurricane	Matsu-Momiji Nursery

WISCONSIN

City	Source
Bayfield	Hauser's Superior View Farm
Eagle	Windy Oaks Aquatics
Ferryville	Northern Grown Perennials

WISCONSIN (continued)

City	Source
Friesland	McClure & Zimmerman
Mt. Horeb	Prairie Ridge Nursery
North Lake	Prairie Seed Source
Ojibwa	Belisle's Violet House
Omro	Kester's Wild Game Food Nurseries
Peshtigo	Field & Forest Products, Inc.
Plainfield	The Waushara Gardens
Racine	Milaeger's Gardens
Randolph	J. W. Jung Seed Co.
Spring Valley	Spring Valley Roses
Stitzer	Alpine Gardens
Wausau	Hsu's Ginseng Enterprises, Inc.
Westfield	Prairie Nursery
Wilson	Jasperson's Hersey Nursery

WYOMING

City	Source
Manderson	Wind River Seed

© Van Engelen Inc.
Artist: Bobbi Angell

Page	Source

Page	Source

Page	Source

BOOKS, RARE & ANTIQUARIAN (continued)

B 20	Landscape Books, NH
B 21	McQuerry Orchid Books, FL
B 24	Mike Park Books, En
B 25	Pomona Book Exchange, ON
B 25	Larry W. Price Books, OR
B 25	Quest Rare Books, CA
B 27	Savoy Books, MA
B 34	Wood Violet Books, WI
B 34	Elisabeth Woodburn, NJ

BOOKS, REGIONAL GARDENING

B 8	Capability's Books, WI
B 13	Fortner Books, WA
B 14	Garden Room Books, ON
B 15	V. L.T. Gardner Botanical Books, CA
A 50	High Country Gardens, NM
A 76	Native Seeds/SEARCH, AZ
A 88	Plants of the Southwest, NM

BOOKS, ROSES

A 4	Antique Rose Emporium, TX
B 4	Bell's Book Store, CA
B 7	Brooks Books, CA
B 8	Capability's Books, WI
B 13	Fair Meadow Books, CT
A 47	Hardy Roses for the North, BC
A 48	Heirloom Old Garden Roses, OR
A 50	High Country Roses, UT
B 20	Linden House Gardening Books, ON
A 93	Regan Nursery, CA
A 108	Spring Valley Roses, WI

BOOKS, SEED SAVING

A 28	Digger's Club, Au
A 76	Native Seeds/SEARCH, AZ
A 106	Southern Exposure Seed Exchange(R), VA

BOOKS, SHADE GARDENING

A 102	Shady Oaks Nursery, MN

BOOKS, SOUTH AFRICAN BULBS

A 97	Rust-En-Vrede Nursery, So

BOOKS, SOUTH AFRICAN PLANTS

B 7	Brooks Books, CA
B 17	Honingklip Book Sales, So

BOOKS, TREES & SHRUBS

A 42	Glasshouse Works, OH
A 112	Sweetbay Farm, GA

BOOKS, TROPICAL PLANTS

B 3	Arborist Supply House, Inc., FL
A 42	Glasshouse Works, OH
A 83	Pacific Tree Farms, CA
A 110	Stokes Tropicals, LA

BOOKS, USED AND OUT-OF-PRINT
See also specific subjects

B 2	The American Botanist, Booksellers, IL
B 4	Carol Barnett, Books, OR
B 4	Bell's Book Store, CA

BOOKS, USED AND OUT-OF-PRINT (continued)

B 5	B. L. Bibby Books, OR
B 6	Bookfinders General, Inc., NY
B 7	Warren F. Broderick — Books, NY
B 7	Brooks Books, CA
B 8	Calendula Horticultural Books, WA
B 13	Fair Meadow Books, CT
B 13	Barbara Farnsworth, Bookseller, CT
B 13	Flora & Fauna Books, WA
B 13	Fortner Books, WA
B 14	Garden Room Books, ON
B 14	Garden Street Books, Au
B 15	V. L. T. Gardner Botanical Books, CA
B 17	William R. Hecht, Gardening Books, AZ
B 17	Honingklip Book Sales, So
B 17	Hortulus, ON
B 17	Hurley Books, NH
B 19	Myron Kimnach, CA
B 20	Landscape Books, NH
B 21	McQuerry Orchid Books, FL
B 24	Mike Park Books, En
B 25	Pomona Book Exchange, ON
B 25	Larry W. Price Books, OR
B 25	Quest Rare Books, CA
A 92	Rainbow Gardens Nursery & Bookshop, CA
B 27	Savoy Books, MA
B 34	Wood Violet Books, WI
B 34	Elisabeth Woodburn, NJ
B 34	Gary W. Woolson, Bookseller, ME

BOOKS, VEGETABLE & FRUIT GROWING

B 1	AgAccess, CA
A 12	Bountiful Gardens, CA
A 22	The Cook's Garden, VT
A 64	Lawson's Nursery, GA
B 20	Linden House Gardening Books, ON
A 79	Northwind Nursery & Orchards, MN
B 25	Pomona Book Exchange, ON
A 93	Redwood City Seed Co., CA
A 96	Ronniger's Seed Potatoes, WA
A 97	St. Lawrence Nurseries, NY
A 105	Sonoma Antique Apple Nursery, CA

BOOKS, WATER GARDENING

A 25	Crystal Palace Perennials, Ltd., IN
A 44	Green & Hagstrom, Inc., TN
A 66	Lilypons Water Gardens, MD
A 73	Moore Water Gardens, ON
A 84	Paradise Water Gardens, MA
A 85	Patio Garden Ponds, OK
A 87	Picov Greenhouses, ON
A 105	Slocum Water Gardens, FL
A 116	William Tricker, Inc., OH
A 118	Van Ness Water Gardens, CA
A 120	Waterford Gardens, NJ

BOOKS, WEATHER

B 2	American Weather Enterprises, PA
B 33	Wind & Weather, CA

BOOKS, WILDFLOWERS

A 63	Larner Seeds, CA
A 85	Theodore Payne Foundation, CA

Page	Source

GROWING SUPPLIES, INDOOR (continued)
B 18 Hydro-Farm West, CA
B 18 IGS, MI
A 68 McKinney's Glassehouse, KS
A 80 Oak Hill Gardens, IL
A 92 Rainbow Gardens Nursery & Bookshop, CA
B 28 Season Extenders, CT
B 30 Sunglo Solar Greenhouses, WA
A 113 Teas Nursery Co., Inc., TX
B 31 Tropical Plant Products, Inc., FL
B 33 The Violet House, FL
B 35 Worm's Way, Inc., IN

GROWTH STIMULANTS
B 5 Bio-Gard Agronomics, VA
B 12 Dyna-Gro Corporation, CA
B 22 Medina Agricultural Products Co., TX
B 26 Bargyla Rateaver, CA
B 28 Sea Born/Lane, Inc., IA
B 29 Spray-N-Grow, Inc., TX

GUANO, BAT
B 11 Diamond Lights, CA
B 16 Guano Company International, Inc., OH
B 23 Nitron Industries, Inc., AR
B 35 Worm's Way, Inc., IN

GUANO, SEABIRD
B 16 Guano Company International, Inc., OH

HAMMOCKS
B 20 Lee Valley Tools, Ltd., NY

HANGING BASKETS
A 5 Antonelli Brothers Begonia Gardens, CA
B 19 Kinsman Company, Inc., PA
B 23 OFE International, FL
B 31 Tropical Plant Products, Inc., FL
B 34 Winterthur Museum & Gardens, DE

HASTA GRO (R)
B 22 Medina Agricultural Products Co., TX

HERBICIDES, AQUATIC
B 3 Aquacide Company, MN

HISTORICAL REPRODUCTIONS, ORNAMENTAL
See also specific type
B 6 BowBends, MA
B 9 Classic Garden Ornaments, Ltd. (R), IL
B 10 Copper Craft Lighting, CA
B 10 Copper Gardens, CA
B 13 Florentine Craftsmen, Inc., NY
B 13 FrenchWyres, TX
B 14 Garden Concepts, Inc., TN
B 15 Genie House, NJ
B 21 Kenneth Lynch & Sons, Inc., CT

HORTICULTURAL CLIP ART
B 33 Wheeler Arts, IL

HORTICULTURAL TOURS
B 10 Coopersmith's England, CA

HORTICULTURAL TOURS (continued)
B 12 Expo Garden Tours, CT
B 15 Geostar Travel, CA

HU MATE (R)
B 22 Medina Agricultural Products Co., TX

HUMIDIFIERS
B 8 Charley's Greenhouse Supply, WA
A 69 Ann Mann's Orchids, FL
B 21 Don Mattern, CA
B 30 Sturdi-Built Mfg. Co., OR
B 32 Turner Greenhouses, NC

HUSKY-FIBER (R)
A 69 Ann Mann's Orchids, FL

HYDROFARM (R) SYSTEMS
B 18 Hydro-Farm West, CA

HYDROGELS
B 22 Multiple Concepts, Moisture Mizer Div., TN

HYDROPONIC SUPPLIES
B 2 Alternative Garden Supply, Inc., IL
B 11 Cropking, Inc., OH
B 11 Diamond Lights, CA
B 17 Hollister's Hydroponics, CA
B 18 Hydro-Farm West, CA
B 18 Hydro-Gardens, Inc., CO
B 28 Sea Born/Lane, Inc., IA
B 30 Superior Growers Supply, Inc., MI
B 35 Worm's Way, Inc., IN

HYDROPONIC SYSTEMS
B 2 Alternative Garden Supply, Inc., IL
B 11 Cropking, Inc., OH
B 11 Diamond Lights, CA
B 17 Hollister's Hydroponics, CA
B 18 Hydro-Farm West, CA
B 18 Hydro-Gardens, Inc., CO
B 35 Worm's Way, Inc., IN

INSECT CONTROLS, ORGANIC
See also Pest Controls, Organic
B 1 A-1 Unique Insect Control, CA
B 5 Better Yield Insects, MI
B 6 BioLogic Company, PA
A 12 Bountiful Gardens, CA
B 8 Charley's Greenhouse Supply, WA
A 30 E & R Seed, IN
B 12 Earlee, Inc., IN
B 15 Gardens Alive!, IN
B 16 The Green Spot, Ltd., NH
A 58 Johnny's Selected Seeds, ME
B 19 Kunafin "The Insectary", TX
B 19 The Lady Bug Company, CA
B 22 The Natural Gardening Company, CA
B 22 Natural Insect Control, ON
B 22 Nature's Control, OR
B 23 Nitron Industries, Inc., AR
B 23 OFE International, FL
B 23 Ohio Earth Food, Inc., OH

Page	Source

Page	Source

© Robyn's Nest Nursery
Artist: Mari Eggebraaten

Page   Society

Page   Society

GARDEN CONSERVATION
C 4   The Garden Conservancy

GARDEN HISTORY
C 1   Alliance for Historic Landscape Preservation
C 2   Association for Living Historical Farms
D 7   Australian Garden History Society
D 9   California Garden & Landscape History Society
C 4   The Garden Conservancy
D 14   Garden History Society
C 4   Historic Preservation Committee
D 25   New England Garden History Society
D 33   Southern Garden History Society

GARDEN WRITING
C 4   Garden Writers Association of America

GARDENIAS
D 15   Gardenia Society of America

GARDENING, PUBLICITY
C 4   Garden Writers Association of America

GASTERIAS
D 16   The Haworthia Society

GENERAL INTEREST
C 1   All America Selections
D 4   American Horticultural Society
D 9   California Horticultural Society
D 14   Friends of ...
D 18   Horticultural Alliance of the Hamptons
D 18   Horticultural Society of New York
D 21   Long Island Horticultural Society
D 22   Marshall Olbrich Plant Club
D 22   Massachusetts Horticultural Society
D 23   Minnesota State Horticultural Society
D 27   Northern Horticultural Society
D 28   Northwest Horticultural Society
D 29   The Pennsylvania Horticultural Society
D 30   The Royal Horticultural Society
D 31   San Diego Horticultural Society
D 33   Southern California Horticultural Society
D 35   Western Horticultural Society
D 36   Worcester County Horticultural Society

GERANIUMS
D 8   British & European Geranium Society
D 9   British Pelargonium & Geranium Society
D 11   Canadian Geranium & Pelargonium Society
D 15   The Geraniaceae Group
D 19   International Geranium Society

GERANIUMS, HARDY
D 9   British Pelargonium & Geranium Society
D 15   The Geraniaceae Group

GESNERIADS
D 1   African Violet Society of America
D 3   American Gloxinia & Gesneriad Society, Inc.
D 15   Gesneriad Society International
D 34   Toronto Gesneriad Society

GINKGOES
D 19   International Golden Fossil Tree Society

GLADIOLUS
D 11   Canadian Gladiolus Society
D 26   North American Gladiolus Council

GLOXINIAS
D 3   American Gloxinia & Gesneriad Society, Inc.

GOOSEBERRIES
D 21   The International Ribes Association

GOURDS
D 3   American Gourd Society

GRASSES
D 9   California Native Grass Association
D 36   Wild Ones -- Natural Landscapers

GREENHOUSE GARDENING
D 17   Hobby Greenhouse Association

HARDY PLANTS
D 16   Hardy Plant Society
D 16   Hardy Plant Society -- Mid-Atlantic Group
D 16   Hardy Plant Society of Oregon
D 23   Minnesota State Horticultural Society
D 27   Northern Horticultural Society
D 28   Northwest Perennial Alliance
D 36   Willamette Valley Hardy Plant Group

HAWORTHIAS
D 16   The Haworthia Society

HEATHERS
D 12   Cascade Heather Society
D 16   The Heather Society
D 26   North American Heather Society
D 27   Northeast Heather Society

HEATHS
D 27   Northeast Heather Society

HEBES
D 17   The Hebe Society

HEIRLOOM FLOWERS
D 12   Cottage Garden Society
D 14   The Flower & Herb Exchange
D 17   Historic Iris Preservation Society
D 21   International Violet Association

HEIRLOOM VEGETABLES
D 12   CORNS
D 31   Seed Savers Exchange
D 31   Seeds of Diversity Canada

HELICONIAS
D 17   Heliconia Society International

HEPATICAS
D 4   American Hepatica Association

Practical Matters

This section contains some practical forms which I hope you will find useful. All can be removed or photocopied for your use. As a matter of "good formsmanship" and to be sure you get what you request, carefully print or type your name and address.

❀ **Catalog and Information Request:** use this form to request catalogs or to ask companies if they can supply specific items on your "wish list." You can also use it to ask for membership or subscription information from societies and magazines.

The best use of this form is to photocopy it once, print or type in your name and address, and then photocopy it again as many times as you like. You can then check off the appropriate boxes for each specific request. If you don't use this form, please mention that you found them in *Gardening by Mail*.

❀ **Reader Feedback and Update Order Form:** I'm eager to hear your opinions of and suggestions for *Gardening by Mail.* Please let us know what you like and don't like, any improvements you'd like to see, and how you use the book — readers have suggested many improvements.

Please list sources and organizations that you think we should list on a separate sheet. Before you recommend a source, please check to see if they sell by mail order; Weston Nurseries and Western Hills Nursery do not!

For the 5th edition of Gardening by Mail, we will be preparing only one Update each year.

❀ **Listing Request and Update of Current Listing:** if you feel your company, society, publication or library should be listed in the next edition of Gardening by Mail, please let us know by filling in and sending us this form as soon as possible. The information requested on the form is the minimum we need to know about you. Companies and organizations already listed in this edition may use this form to update their listing; all information will be verified before the publication of the next edition. We include address changes in our periodic updates.

❀ **Mailing Labels:** Tusker Press will rent mailing labels for the various listings in this book for one time use. Inquire about our rental agreement and charges; we ask to see your mailing piece or whatever you are mailing to protect the recipients from unnecessary junk mail.

Readers are reminded that photocopying, scanning or storing the information in this book into a computer for any personal or business use is against copyright law.

I found you in the 5th edition of
Gardening by Mail: A Source Book
by Barbara J. Barton
Published by Houghton Mifflin Company
Boston & New York, 1997

Catalog and Information Request Form

Date: _____

To: _____

☐ Please send me your free catalog.

☐ I enclose a long self-addressed envelope with $_____ postage or _____ International Reply Coupons.

☐ Please send me your catalog, for which I enclose $_____

☐ You did not provide the price of your catalog; please send me one or advise me of the cost.

☐ Please send me information on joining your society.

☐ I'd like to subscribe to your periodical; please tell me your current rates.

☐ Please let me know if you have _____

_____

☐ Other information I need: _____

_____

- -

My name and address are:

Name:_____

Mailing Address:_____

City and State:_____

Country: _____ Postal Code: _____

Daytime Phone: _____ Evening Phone: _____

eMail Address: _____

Reader Feedback & Update Order Form

DATE: _____

What I like about *Gardening by Mail*

_____
_____
_____
_____
_____

What I don't like about *Gardening by Mail*

_____
_____
_____
_____
_____

Suggestions for improvements in the next edition

_____
_____
_____
_____

Please list your recommendations for new plant and product sources, societies, magazines, etc. on a separate sheet of paper.

By identifying your special interests, the following information will help us improve the contents of the book.

I am a	☐ home gardener	☐ professional/commercial horticulturist	☐ both
	☐ new gardener	☐ experienced gardener	☐ very experienced gardener
I have a	☐ small garden	☐ medium-sized garden	☐ large garden (acre or more)
I grow	☐ lawn	☐ flowers	☐ vegetables
	☐ fruit	☐ ornamental shrubs	☐ trees
	☐ greenhouse plants	☐ indoor plants	☐ special interests (list below)

_____
_____

Please send this form to:

Please continue on back. ➞

Tusker Press, Reader Feedback
P.O. Box 1338, Sebastopol, CA 95473

I use *Gardening by Mail* for:

☐ mail orders
☐ finding local sources
☐ visiting display gardens
☐ reference when traveling
☐ finding plants by climate zone
☐ finding products/services
☐ finding gardening books
☐ finding magazines
☐ Other uses: _____

_____

☐ finding societies
☐ finding libraries
☐ making professional contacts
☐ buying plants/products for resale
☐ selling plants/products for retailers
☐ compiling a mailing list for prospects
☐ finding unusual plants or products for customers

Name: _____

Mailing Address: _____

City and State: _____

Country: _____ Postal Code: _____

Daytime Phone: _____ Evening Phone: _____

eMail Address: _____

Order for Updates to *Gardening by Mail*

Over the years that we have been collecting information about horticultural sources, we have learned one sobering lesson: things change — and rapidly. As fast as we gather information, our listees are changing their names, addresses and ownership, going out of business or ceasing to fill mail orders. We try to keep current and we're constantly on the lookout for changes, but it's like trying to catch sand in a hairnet.

In addition, we are continually finding new and exciting sources of plants and supplies, new societies, libraries, magazines and books which we'd like to share with our readers.

Tusker Press issues periodic updates to *Gardening by Mail* which include any name and address changes that **we know about** for the listings in the book. Updates are cumulative, so order **only** the most recent or future issues.

To order updates, send **U.S. $2.00 for each update desired ($3 overseas)** to Tusker Press and check the updates you wish.

☐ October 1998   ☐ October 1999   ☐ October 2000

Total enclosed: $_____

Please put your name and address on this form and let us know if you move.

Request for Listing in
Gardening by Mail
or Update of Current Listing

If you would like to be listed in the next edition of *Gardening by Mail*, please return this form as soon as possible.

Current listees: Please use this form to notify us of any changes. **Mailing address changes are included in our updates.**

To be listed in *Gardening by Mail:*

Seed companies, nurseries, other plant suppliers, and garden suppliers must sell direct by mail order to buyers in the U.S. and/or Canada and **must enclose their most recent catalog with this request.**

Plant and horticultural societies must welcome members from the U.S. and/or Canada and **must include a current issue of their periodical with this request.**

Libraries must allow members of their sponsoring organizations and/or the public to use their facilities for reference.

Questionnaires will be sent when a new edition is planned. Those listed in the current edition will automatically receive one but must meet the same conditions AND return the completed questionnaire and their catalog or literature to be listed again.

Questionnaires vary by type of company or organization. Please specify your **primary** category:

DATE: _____

☐ Seed company   ☐ Plant or horticultural society

☐ Nursery   ☐ Horticultural library

☐ Garden suppliers   ☐ Gardening/horticultural magazine or newsletter

☐ Trade, professional or umbrella organization

- -

Please type or print — if we can't read it, we can't use it.

☐ Request for listing   ☐ Current listing update (provide current listing name, and new name, if changed.

Name of Business or Organization: _____

Proprietor/Manager: _____

Mailing Address: _____

City and State: _____

Country: _____ Postal Code: _____

Phone: _____ Fax: _____

eMail: _____

World Wide Web Site: http://_____

Please send this form to:

Please continue on
back. ➞

Tusker Press, Database Department
P.O. Box 1338, Sebastopol, CA 95473

GBM5

☐ We have added Tusker Press to our mailing list.

☐ Name of the individual who will promptly complete and return your future questionnaires.

_____

The following information is the **minimum** Tusker Press needs to know now:

The price of our catalog is $_____ ☐ Long SASE ☐ Free

☐ Minimum retail mail order is $ _____

☐ We accept credit cards. Minimum retail mail order is $ _____

☐ We sell wholesale AS WELL AS retail by mail order.

☐ We ship to ☐ USA ☐ Canada ☐ overseas.

☐ We ship live/perishable materials in the months _____

☐ We sell MAIL ORDER ONLY (no nursery or shop/sales location).

☐ We also sell at this sales address: _____

☐ We have a display garden or many plants/products on display at sales location.

The most important plants/products that we sell are:

_____

_____

_____

_____

_____

Comments/other information:

_____

_____

_____

_____

_____

_____

_____

Final selection of those listed is at the discretion of the author.

Changes and Corrections

The following are all of the changes we know of as of February, 1998. Please let us know if you know of others; we depend on Readers for obscure information! Our mail and eMail addresses are on the back of the title page; the Gardening by Mail World Wide Web address shown on that page is now inoperative.

Changes are listed by Section and Page Number to make them easier to write into your book.

A	7	Barber Nursery	14292 Rogers Road	
A	26	The Daffodil Mart	30 Irene Street	Torrington, CT 06790
A	28	Desert Citizens	P.O. Box 409	Kiowa, OK 74553
A	38	Fox Hollow Seed Co.	P.O. Box 148	McGrann, PA 16236
A	110	Succulenta	Out of business	
A	110	Summerville's Gladiolus	1330 Ellis Mill Road	Glassboro, NJ 08028
A	113	Terra Edibles	P.O. Box 164	Foxboro, ON KOK2B0
A	114	Tinmouth Channel Farm, now Ladybug Herbs of Vermont		
			RR 1, Box 3380	Wolcott, VT 05680
A	125	York Hill Farm, now Greywood Farm		
			73 Prospect Street	Topsfield, MA 01983-1715
A	126	Yucca Do	Route 3, Box 104	Hempstead, TX 77445
B	4	The Basket Case	Same	West Trenton, NJ 08628-7848
B	8	Capability's Books	Out of business	
B	14	Garden Room Books	503 Queen Street East	Sault Ste. Marie, ON P6A 2A2
B	29	Strong Injectors	4235 Pacific St., Suite H	Rocklin, CA 95677
B	30	Sundance Supply	HC 1, Box 116	Olga, WA 98279
C	1	AABGA	351 Longwood Road	Kennett Square, PA 19348
E	4	Garden Paths	Will cease publication 12/98	
E	6	Herban Lifestyles	Ceased publication	
E	7	The Literate Gardener	Ceased publication	

Note: To our horror, we inadvertantly dropped the <u>**Louisiana Nursery**</u>, a very fine nursery! Please make a note at the bottom of page **A 67** to refer you to this page, and you should note their specialties in the plant index.

Louisiana Nursery
5853 Highway 182
Opelousas, LA 70570
Ken Durio
(318) 948-3696
Fax: (318) 942-6404
E-mail: DEDurio@aol.com

Plants
Offers a huge selection of magnolias, daylilies, Louisiana iris, crinums, clivias and bamboos and grasses , hydrangeas, and fruiting trees, shrubs and vines. Plants are briefly described. Catalogs: Magnolias $6 ($15 OV), Daylilies $4, Crinums & rare bulbs $5, Fruiting Trees $4, Bamboos & Grasses $4, Hydrangeas $4, Clivia species & cultivars $3. All but the Magnolia catalog are $12.50 Overseas. You can request the catalog order form by fax or eMail. Magnolia catalog contains some of all the other plants.
📖 Catalog: See Notes, CAN/OV, CC, $40m, bn/cn
✪ Nursery: M-Sa, call ahead
❀ Garden: M-Sa, call ahead

Please note that there will be only three Updates sold for this edition: there will be none published after October 2000.